THE AMERICAN ENEMY

THE AMERICAN ENEMY

THE HISTORY OF FRENCH ANTI-AMERICANISM

PHILIPPE ROGER
Translated by Sharon Bowman

The University of Chicago Press
Chicago and London

The University of Chicago Press, Chicago 60637
The University of Chicago Press, Ltd., London
© 2005 by The University of Chicago
All rights reserved. Published 2005
Paperback edition 2006
Printed in the United States of America
14 13 12 11 10 09 08 07 06   5 4 3 2

ISBN (cloth): 0-226-72368-2
ISBN-13: 978-0-226-72369-3 (paper)
ISBN-10: 0-226-72369-0 (paper)

Originally published as *L'Ennemi Américain: Généalogie de l'antiaméricanisme français,*
© Éditions du Seuil, Septembre 2002.

The University of Chicago Press gratefully acknowledges a subvention from the government of France, through the French Ministry of Culture, Centre National du Livre, in support of translating this volume.

Library of Congress Cataloging-in-Publication Data

Roger, Philippe, 1949–
    [Ennemi américain. English]
    The American enemy : a story of French anti-Americanism / Philippe Roger ;
    translated by Sharon Bowman.
        p.   cm.
    Translation of: L'ennemi américain.
    Includes bibliographical references and index.
    ISBN 0-226-72368-2 (cloth : alk. paper)
    1. United States—Relations—France.   2. France—Relations—United States.
    3. Anti-Americanism—France.   I. Title.
    E183.8.F8R6513   2005
    303.48′273044—dc22

                                                    2004020975

♾ The paper used in this publication meets the minimum requirements of the American National Standard for Information Sciences—Permanence of Paper for Printed Library Materials, ANSI Z39.48-1992.

Washington had pronounced this beautiful and true idea:
"The nation which indulges toward another an habitual
hatred or an habitual fondness is in some degree a slave.
It is a slave to its animosity or to its affection."
—Alexis de Tocqueville,
Democracy in America

Contents

Introduction

Great Britain, Germany, Spain, and Italy have all been at war with the United States at one time or another. France has not. Yet as Michel Winock noted not long after the World Trade Center attacks, France is the country where "anti-Americanism has been, and remains, the most strident."[1] This extreme paradox is part of the historical and cultural riddle of French anti-Americanism. Why are the French so anti-American? The question is all the more pertinent because it goes beyond any real or imagined relationship between France and the United States.

The recent crisis in French-American relations, serious as it was (and remains), is just the last, spectacular installment of a long and bizarre story: a century-old war of words. French anti-Americanism is not a recent fever we could use polls to chart, correlating the fluctuations with any given episode of Franco-American relations. Analyzing it as a short-term reaction to specific events or situations has never been a good way of understanding it. In the mid-1980s, pollsters and political analysts proclaimed that anti-American sentiment was in recession and would soon be extinct in France: to hear them talk, French anti-Americanism was on its last legs. Its stereotypes were outmoded, and the general public was warned against falling prey to the other extreme, a triumphant "Americanomania." Even the intellectuals, we were told, had found their "road to Damascus"; a "conversion of the intelligentsia" was described in lavish detail.[2]

Of course the word "conversion" would not have been so out of place if the miracle had really happened. But whether it was real or only imagined, the "clearing up" didn't last.[3] By the turn of the third millennium, the clocks had been reset. Farmers stormed McDonald's. The French government briefly took Coke off the market for public health reasons. "Lite high school" and the Americanization of higher education were publicly reviled. Accusations of "arrogance" and "unilateralism" became the daily bread of the French media again. And in the thick of the Kosovo intervention, the same French citizens who globally approved what NATO was doing in the former Yugoslavia responded to a CSA-*Libération* poll with more anti-American opinions than ever.[4] France had gotten its wits back, and the intelligentsia, annoyed that a passing lull could ever have been taken for desertion, had retaken its position on the front line. With precious few exceptions, the French intelligentsia's reaction to the events of September 11, 2001, refuted any suspicion of a conversion. Only days after the attacks, the op-ed pages of major French newspapers were filled with the usual America-bashing contributions, which greatly outnumbered the declarations of sympathy or solidarity—with unexpected consequences. Exhibited in such tragic circumstances, the French intelligentsia's rampant anti-American bias backfired for the first time ever, unleashing a yearlong public debate in France on the previously taboo notion of *antiaméricanisme*. Such was the paradoxical effect of 9/11 in France: it confirmed how deeply rooted anti-Americanism was and, almost simultaneously, paved the way for the first national discussion of the phenomenon. At long last, the French were looking at anti-Americanism without blinking; and what they saw involved France's identity much more than America's.

French anti-Americanism is a historical construct with deep roots in French culture. If you try to understand it by reading anything into its seasonal varieties, it is bound to slip through your fingers. Developed over and shaped by the long haul, it forces the investigator to plunge into the long haul. It did not start with the Vietnam War or with the cold war—or even in the 1930s, which was its peak. Nearly all the ingredients were there more than a century ago: its narrative structures had largely been formed, its argumentation polished up, and its rhetoric broken in as early as the 1890s. And even more surprisingly, it was already consensual. In a time of strident divisions, it was (already) the most commonly shared idea in France. From then on, it was neither exclusively right wing nor left wing. It brought together spiritualists and secularists, nationalists and internationalists. Favored by the extremes, as might be expected of any "anti" stance, it also permeated the more moderate segments of the population.

Everyone knows how the Statue of Liberty was finished before its pedestal. The statue of the American Enemy raised by the French, however, is a work in progress: each successive generation tinkers at it, tightening its bolts. But its pedestal is well established. And its foundations—the Enlightenment's strange hostility to the New World, which I will examine in the prologue—are over two hundred years old.

The present work stems from the firm belief that it is impossible to unravel the riddle of French anti-Americanism without taking a deep dive into the past. As we have noted and will see in detail, this strange cultural object is just not subject to circumstance. Passing trends have no important or lasting effect on it. Happenstance might have had a role in the early days of its development; we will see this in the case of the Civil War and the Spanish-American War of 1898. Quickly, though, the thick layering of discourses and representations amassed by French anti-Americanism allowed it to absorb exterior shocks without deviating from its flight path. France's anti-American discourse is not solipsistic, but it is largely self-referential and autarchic—two characteristics inseparable from its Sartrian "bad faith." How many incendiary rants and hyperbolic indictments of the United States are backed up and fueled by the reassuring and inadmissible thought that "nothing is really at stake here"? Clearly, that is just one more illusion or self-deception—and not the least dangerous, considering how, to give one example, such thinking helped hone France's diplomatic, economic, and moral isolation in the 1930s; or, more recently, how otherwise perfectly legitimate political and diplomatic differences could easily evolve into an all-out confrontation, by triggering anti-Americanism again and again and setting off the infernal machine of a nearly Pavlovian hostility.

Where does all this come from? Semiotics generally has a hard time defining the exact critical moment when "it takes," as Barthes put it; when a discourse takes on a certain *consistency;* when it can run on its own obtuseness. In France, anti-Americanism attracts a strong adherence by being a *narrative,* and this adherence need not necessarily be linked to any *felt* animosity—whence the honest protestation of those who, after spouting typical anti-American clichés, deny any ill-will toward the Americans. A discourse of this kind works through repetition. Its strength is in its stubbornness. Its peaks can of course be charted (by opinion polls, for instance), but its most important element is elsewhere: in a long, drawn-out stratification of images, legends, jokes, anecdotes, beliefs, and affects. Shedding light on all of these elements takes more than just opinion polls (which, rather than plumbing the depths, offer a snapshot of a given moment): you have to root around, dig up old deposits, excavate the matter, clear out the veins, and follow the seams.

"I'm not anti-American. I don't even know what the word means," declared Sartre in 1946.[5] His logic would have delighted Lewis Carroll—not to mention the Mad Hatter. The same logic still is running the show in current attempts to obstruct the concept of anti-Americanism. In fact, since Sartre's day, the hard line has only gotten harder. Anti-Americanism was an incomprehensible word for him—or comprehensible just long enough to absolve himself of it. *Antiaméricanisme* has been regularly described in France as "one word too many," whose use is "not innocent" and which needs to be eradicated, a machination contrived by "rabid 'philo-Americans,'"[6] a semantic plot concocted by the Yankee fifth column. As the French essayist Serge Halimi discovered and exposed in *Le Monde diplomatique* in May 2000, individuals with ulterior motives are hiding behind this empty word, and their mission is to "intimidate the last rebels against a social order whose laboratory is the United States." Anti-Americanism? Never heard of it. Except as a fabrication, pure and simple. Since Sartre's day, this denial has been the obligatory preamble to any use of anti-American rhetoric. Halimi's article is only a typical example of a widespread rhetorical device: everything in it works by mirror image, from the accusation of intimidation, introduced to justify censorship of the undesirable word, to the imputation that the opponent uses a "tightly screwed-together binary logic" (this masks the Manichean political views of the accusation itself). The semantic objection is there only to set the polemical machine in motion.

Now for a more methodological objection. Even if we admit that anti-Americanism exists and that its manifestations can be pinpointed, does that give us the right to turn it into an analytical category? Given that "anti-Americanism" is part of the French "logosphere" and might even determine a certain number of attitudes and behaviors, does that mean we can raise it to the level of a concept? Doesn't that—wrongly—lend credence to the idea that America has an "essence" to which anti-Americans would thus be opposed? We cannot address this objection without quickly examining the link it presupposes between "Americanism" and "anti-Americanism."

At the end of the nineteenth century, Americanism meant, in the United States, a set of values judged to be constituent parts of a national identity, as well as the attitude of those who adopted them and attempted to conform their personal identity to this national ideal. The expression, popularized by Theodore Roosevelt at the turn of the twentieth century, was inseparable from notions like being "100 percent American"—as opposed to "hyphenated American." Its intent is clear. Its content, however, is vague, as Marie-France Toinet notes, quoting Theodore Roosevelt: "Americanism signifies the virtues of courage, honor, justice, truth, sincerity, and strength—the virtues that made America."[7] Glorified and reinforced in the 1920s by a boom in prosperity, Americanism began to expand beyond the realm of innate virtues to encompass a certain number of traits characteristic of American "civilization," not of the American man: efficiency, productivity, access to material goods. Americanism's credo, though it kept its nationalist and even chauvinistic overtones, was thus coupled with another self-defining tautology: *the American way of life,* which was the material facet of the word "Americanism." The key element here is that, since it came out of the need to affirm an uneasy national cohesion through the emotional and intellectual adherence of each citizen to an "idea of America" as broad as it was vague, "Americanism" never attained the status of a political or ideological doctrine.

A narcissistic self-portrait and a slogan for internal use, "Americanism" would seem to be hard to export: yet America's power overflow pushed the term all the way across the ocean to Europe. The French discovered it in the full upswing of a new (polemic) interest in the United States in the late 1920s. But their attempts to give it ideological or political substance bumped up against resistant matter: "Americanism" means above all pride in being American; apart from that, it is a catch-all. So, logically enough, the French took the word over and gave it a meaning, most often negative, that reflected their own view of the United States. David Strauss, in his book on French anti-Americanism in the 1920s, rightly notes that in French, *américanisme* means "the cultural values and institutions which were *believed* by Frenchmen to be an integral part of American civilization."[8] Only Sartre, just after the war, would attempt to translate "Americanism" culturally: not by giving it a meaning it does not have, but by analyzing it as the psychological key to the way Americans are socialized.[9] But his was a very personal attempt, and it had no effect on the fate of a term decidedly destined for invective in France.[10] Régis Debray neatly summed up the semantic situation of the word in a book written in 1992. After giving a long catalog of its negative connotations, Debray concludes: "Americanism seems to mean a blackened America, stripped of everything positive it has."[11] At the end of its ambiguous career, *américanisme* has wound up denoting nothing more than a repertoire of anti-American clichés about America.

Now we can come back and respond to the initial objection about essentializing America. The mistake there was imagining that anti-Americanism was derived from the notion of "Americanism." In fact, the false antonym has nothing to do with it, either historically or logically. As Sartre could have put it, in France, anti-Americanism's existence always preceded any essence of America.

☆ ☆ ☆

One last scruple: our investigation covers two centuries. It might seem problematic, then, that the word *anti-Americanism* is so much more recent. Can we trace the genealogy of a nameless notion?

First we have to clear up the chronology. The word made a late entrance into the French dictionaries (1968 for the *Petit Robert*). But as we all know, dictionaries always lag behind usage. The first use of the term "anti-Americanism" catalogued by lexicographers dates back to 1948; by the early 1950s, it was a part of ordinary political language.[12] And it would not be going out on a limb to suggest that the term spread as a counterpoint to "anti-Sovietism." Its entry into the French lexicon seems to have been a direct consequence of the cold war.

As for the epistemological root of the question, we can look to one of the pioneers of semantics applied to cultural history, Reinhart Koselleck, for help with that one. Koselleck warns against falling prey to a "new nominalism," which would have us believe that the emergence of a notion or a category of thought is dependent on the creation of the term designating it. "It is not necessary for persistence and change in the meanings of words to correspond with persistence and change in the structures they specify," writes Koselleck; "words which persist are in themselves insufficient indicators of stable contents and, . . . vice versa, contents undergoing long-term change might be expressed in a number of very different ways."[13] The invitation is clear and the voice authoritative. It would be reductive to use lexicographical indications to limit the field of investigation on concepts or behaviors. There is indisputably in France, as of the late nineteenth century, an as-yet-unnamed anti-Americanism. (A name for it would probably have taken some form of "Yankism" or "Yankeeism" at the time.)[14] The lesson we can draw from dictionaries is elsewhere: they usefully remind us that "anti-Americanism" is the only noun in French with the prefix "anti-" based on the name of a country. That this strange word finally emerged and became common coinage (and now seems to be impossible to get rid of) is in itself a sign of exceptional treatment, if not favoritism.

☆ ☆ ☆

A genealogy of French anti-Americanism—what exactly does that mean? First, that anti-Americanism will be considered here as a long war of words (and images) that France has been waging against the United States, and whose argumentative logic it is our task to untangle. We will therefore keep to the *disagreeable* side of Franco-American relations, where the punches are thrown and the low blows dealt. We will hang out dirty laundry that has never seen the end of the wash. We'll also follow the anti-American discourse into its weakest patches, where it runs in little rivulets, far from the torrential roar of invective. That is, we will track it back to the place where it *flows from the source.*

I open Claudel's *Journal* and find the following passage, written in 1933 in Washington, D.C.: "Al[exander] Hamilton in *The Federalist* notes that in his day they already attributed a degenerative influence to the American climate. 'In this country, even the dogs no longer bark.'" And Claudel adds, in parentheses: "Moreover, it is perfectly true."[15] Except that it is perfectly false. First of all, American dogs do bark. Second, Hamilton does not "note"; he decries as absurd the degenerative hypothesis: "Men admired as profound philosophers have, in direct terms, attributed to [Europe's] inhabitants a physical superiority and have gravely asserted that all animals, and with them the human species, degenerate in America—that even dogs cease to bark after having breathed awhile in our atmosphere." It is not Hamilton speaking against the dogs, but a Dutch-born naturalist writing in French, Cornelius De Pauw, whom he footnotes.[16] From the Enlightenment naturalist to the French poet-ambassador, despite a century and a half of proof to the contrary, as well as Hamilton's own words, the chain has held, shackling America to the legend of the mute dog. For more recent examples, we only need to open a newspaper or turn on the radio on any given day. This one was heard on a French public radio station in 2000. The day I finished this book, I found myself listening to a Toulouse bistro owner. He was strongly criticizing a new law reducing to nearly Scandinavian levels the authorized blood-alcohol content for anyone behind the wheel. Though he conceded that drinking too much *pastis* could be bad for you, the *cafetier* insisted on the well-known fact that Coca-Cola, a so-called soft drink, was in reality much harder on your stomach and more detrimental for your health than alcoholic beverages: "Try leaving a twenty-centime coin in a glass of Coke. . ." The legend of the dissolving coin is less antique than the tale of the mute dog; it only dates back to the Coke war of 1949—still, more than half a century. (It will proba-bly take as long for the anecdote to switch over to the euro.) The bistro owner and the ambassador, each in his own way, *forge the chain* I call anti-Ameri-canism. Whether they personally are anti-American or not is unimportant.

Anti-Americanism is not "felt," as I said before. For that reason and a few others (starting with the semantic nature of its appearance in particular his-torical contexts), it cannot simply be included among the "French passions" analyzed by the British historian Theodore Zeldin. It is worth stressing, apro-pos of passions, that French anti-Americanism, although deeply rooted, is in no way a gut reaction: there is nothing personal, so to speak, in French America-bashing; offensive anti-American clichés are usually proffered as so many innocently obvious statements and with no (personal) offense meant to any American in particular. Many Americans have had the same experi-ence of dining with French people who, completely oblivious to their Amer-ican guest, kept trashing the United States and, when reminded of the guest's nationality, hastened to add with perfect sincerity: "Oh! We didn't mean you."

However, despite its linguistic nature, anti-Americanism is not a myth, in Barthes's sense of the word, because it is not a "second language" in which the connotative meaning is insidiously "naturalized." Anti-Americanism lacks this structural sneakiness.

Is it an ideology? The sheer number of existing definitions for the word "ideology" makes that a tricky question to answer. One of the most com-prehensive definitions describes ideology as "a polemical discursive forma-tion by which a passion attempts to attain a certain value through the exer-cise of power in a given society."[17] The first part of this definition fits anti-Americanism perfectly, but not the second: the link between anti-Americanism and the politics of power seems more complex than that, given that on the one hand anti-Americanism is often coupled with the most mutu-ally ideologically hostile political discourses and, on the other, that it is often used outside of any political agenda or objective we can pinpoint.

So, what is it?

We will just say: *anti-Americanism is a discourse.* After all, a discourse—as its etymology indicates (*dis-correre*) and as the use of the word up to the Renaissance attests—is a way of "running here and there." Anti-American-ism is an unbridled discourse, not only because it is rife with irrationality and bubbling with humors, but also because it takes an essayistic form, rather than that of a dissertation or a demonstration. (It does not follow "orders" either; there is no anti-American conspiracy.) Its logic is one of accumulation, accretion—"I'll take that one" or "give me a little more of that"—in short, it is a mad dash that deliberately ignores the Aristotelian principle of non-contradiction. (Anti-Americanism has never been ashamed to utter two mutually exclusive grievances at the same time.) But even with all its leaps and bounds, it is never "gratuitous," and still less absurd. Only the complexity of its crisscrossing strategies gives it the false appearance of a bunch of individual whims. The whims are there, make no doubt about it; they flesh out the words and bulk up the sentences. But the anti-American discourse grounds them.

The word "discourse" brings Foucault's name into the picture. This would be the early or the late Foucault, as opposed to the 1970s Foucault, who spoke of discourse as emanating from certain practices, or as a way of relaying domination. The anti-American discourse is *en situation,* but it remains autonomous and "acratic"—as Barthes said of discourses with no link to power. This does not, however, mean it is placeless or detached: the intelligentsia massively produces it; it is their emanation.

Which also indicates all that this book is not.

Though the United States is omnipresent here, this is not a book about the United States. Or a polemic history of Franco-American relations seen through mud-colored glasses. Or an ethnological exploration of the intercultural misunderstandings "of daily life."[18] It is not (only) a thematic catalogue of the anti-American motifs circulating in contemporary France, either. Or a list of the "crossed images" the two countries send back and forth to each other and which would need to be inventoried to give a "balanced" assessment. French anti-Americanism has mostly been approached up to now as one of the aspects of an ambivalent, ambiguous, contradictory relationship— a flip side of the coin that is nonetheless recognized as the much more visible side. Our approach will be fundamentally different. Far from purporting to attain an impossible exhaustiveness or an illusory weighing of the "pros" and "cons," we will look at anti-Americanism as a historical stratification that it is possible and even *preferable* to isolate in order to analyze it. In the following pages, positive representations of America, those (brief) moments of shared euphoria between the French and the Americans, will only come into the picture insofar as they elucidate a given inflection or strain of the anti-American discourse. Many kinder, gentler readers of America will thus be relegated to the sidelines of our investigation or treated obliquely (for the distortions they were subject to, or for the anti-American counterattacks they provoked). Their discreet presence indicates a fundamental choice of approach, not a sneaky attempt to muffle the voice of French Americanophiles.

The following chapters aim to be the genealogy of this anti-Americanism understood as a "discourse"—a genealogy in which history and semiology will have to silence their vain quarrels: history by accepting that a false "narrative" can be a true fact;[19] semiology by taking on the impurity Barthes incited it to accept in *Lesson*—in finally becoming "a work that collects language's impurities, linguistics' refuse, the message's immediate corruption: nothing less than desires, fears, scowls, intimidations."[20]

After over twenty months of French-American diplomatic tensions and inflammatory mutual accusations, a last caveat may be in order: this book owes nothing to a crisis it deliberately leaves out, but can perhaps shed light on—from the past.

On the morning of September 11, 2001, I was in New York City working on one of the last chapters of this book when I saw the first of the hijacked planes fly vertically over my building on Third Street. Less than a minute later, it crashed into the north tower of the World Trade Center. That the chapter I was writing was "Metropolis, Cosmopolis," which deals with French hatred of the American city, struck me afterward as a tragic irony.

A witness to the catastrophe and a longtime resident of New York (where I had spent seven years of my life), I had a hard time relating to the very "distant" French perception of the event, when I got home a month later, and I was especially struck by the general eagerness to *relativiser* what seemed to me anything but relative and to see as unreal ("It was like a movie . . .") what had been a shocking reality.

My memory of that morning is not so much visual as auditory: the unbelievable sound that, twice, as each tower crumbled, rose up from the city—a kind of gigantic bellow, the cry simultaneously leaping from 500,000 mouths (or a million, or more), a roar rising from the streets, squares, balconies, and roofs, the antique, formidable *planctus* of an entire city engulfed in horror. The images repeated ad nauseam of the towers falling can lose all meaning—if they ever had one. This inconceivable cry, so different from the din of the stadium or the clamor of a riot, will always—for me—cover over the clatter of "intelligent" commentaries.

French anti-Americanism has of course no direct connection with the aggression committed that day. But in all fairness, those who have been urging the Americans, since 9/11, to "get the message," "learn from the lesson," and, finally, take responsibility for the wound inflicted upon them would be better off doing their own homework and asking themselves to what extent systematic anti-Americanism, French and otherwise, has had a hand in the global process of demonization that facilitates slippage from a war of words to a war of the worlds.

Prologue

The Enlightenment versus America

French anti-Americanism not only has a history, but also a pre-history—one that has been overlooked, forgotten, and buried under the successive layers of a collective depiction. This prehistory occurred in the second half of the eighteenth century. It preceded the United States' emergence as an independent nation and represents the first layer of a long drawn-out sedimentation. The whole continent was vilified on strange charges imputed by the Europeans—what Antonello Gerbi once dubbed "the dispute of the New World"[1]—but it was the newborn United States that would inherit the dispute, and Jefferson himself who would take up the gauntlet.

The "dispute" started around 1750 and went full swing in the 1770s and 1780s. It was then that it evolved into a Franco-American debate. Frenchmen and Americans had been allies on the battlefields of the American Revolution, but now they were locking scholarly horns over humidity levels in Virginia, the nitrate levels in Pennsylvania's soil, the wheat yield, and colonists' birthrate. The dispute was really more of a trial, scientifically brought against the New World by the scholars and philosophers of the Old World. The stakes were anything but low. On the agenda were such weighty matters as deciding whether the land could keep its promises or if Nature had "gotten an entire hemisphere wrong";[2] revising the overly naive or respectful images that had been proliferating at the hands of America's apologists, especially over the course of the previous half century; and offering proof that this was in fact a disappointing continent. All in all, it was a crusade against the budding imposture of America worship—part scientific debate, part image war. Scholars, philosophers, and "men of letters" were all strikingly persistent and unexpectedly vehement in pursuing their new objective. And so our prologue could also be called the "age of disconcerting denigration."

The first surprise is the origin of these debates. Unexpectedly, or, in any event, contrary to the eighteenth-century stereotype linking the New World with new ideas, anti-Americanism was born and prospered in philosophical circles. Not only was it contemporary with the Enlightenment at its brightest, it was forged and disseminated by men who were unquestionably associated with the program and progress of the "philosophical spirit." Emanating from a Parisian epicenter, the dispute quickly spread throughout Europe and reached the United States at the end of the century. Its initiators were not marginal figures, social isolates, or temperamental misanthropes harboring some specific grudge against America. They were men such as Buffon, Voltaire, and Raynal. Others who are now less illustrious but were not without a certain reputation in their day, such as Cornelius De Pauw, followed suit. Together, they sought to alert blinkered or hoodwinked Europeans to the New World's flaws. "If it was philosophy's efforts that led to America's discovery,"[3] as Voltaire wrote in his *Essai sur les moeurs* two and a half centuries after Columbus, it was once more through philosophy's efforts that America would be rediscovered or, better put, revisited—somewhere between disappointment and repulsion.

A second characteristic: the anti-Americanism of the time presented itself as resolutely scientific and, more specifically, "naturalist." Only later, in a second logical and chronological stage, would it take a political and moralistic turn. It was not until 1780 that the American controversy's center of gravity shifted into the realm of political philosophy—though that did not temper earlier naturalist accusations. Quite the contrary: naturalist accusations would be revived in reaction to American pamphleteers bent on doing their own justice to the "French calumnies." The Americans—with Jefferson first in line—were as anxious to prove that their country was of a naturally sound constitution as they were to defend its political institutions.

Right up through its later politicized permutations, anti-Americanism sought validation in the natural sciences: from geology to zoology, from botany to anthropology. Buffon was an instrumental figure, both initiating the trend and lending it his authority. All of America's later detractors would write from the standpoint of a "natural history from which we can only ever distance ourselves with great reluctance," as Cornelius De Pauw wrote.[4] Buffon's system provided the ammunition as well as the base camp, and in a pinch, even supplied the trenches. "When attacking a book written about a science," De Pauw continued, "arguments drawn from this science, and not another, must be used."[5] With this solid scientific footing, De Pauw, like Buffon, firmly confronted America's defenders. The natural sciences were "modern," taking a logical rather than descriptive tack, or, as with Buffon, using description itself as a means of demonstration. The naturalists, none of whom ever crossed the Atlantic, did not feel the need to describe America's environment in detail in order to dismiss it as a whole. Zoology and botany were used not to establish a colorful inventory of "indigenous productions," but rather to sum up the natural characteristics of America itself. The most striking of these—the most astonishing to us now—was the "smallness" of America's productions. As though in reaction to the many dazzling features found in earlier accounts of the New World, America's natural elements were reduced to a short list of qualities: cold (even in the tropics, it was said, the earth was cold just a few inches below the surface), wet, salty. Likewise, an astonishing jumble of new and unusual fauna was reduced to a few numbers. Weight? Height? Distinguishing features? The New World's animals were there, first and foremost, to be *measured* by the philosophers. Weighed and judged, they were used as evidence of a meager land.

Third characteristic: the scientific critique of the new continent's shortcomings was made at the expense of any diversity in the images presented. The dispute attacked the New World as a whole, which in and of itself was a novelty. Until then, descriptions of America, from the first discovery narratives to more recent accounts by missionaries such as Lafitau and Charlevoix, had juxtaposed distinctly different portraits. From the kingdom of the Incas to the nomadic lands of the north, America was an immense patchwork of climates, physical types, and customs. The "West Indies" were rife with violent contrasts and hard to generalize about. To observers—even those who believed the natives all had the same origins—the inhabitants seemed as diverse as their different ways of life. Endlessly strange places, scattered populations, myriad customs: such was the European vision of post-Columbian America. A considerable change was thus instigated by imposing taxonomies

that, though they did not entirely refrain from evoking picturesque particularities—we will come back to the most detrimental of these—stressed the
continent's homogeneous nature. A unified picture of America emerged,
both continental (from Patagonia to Labrador) and insular (the Antilles and
the Caribbean being the most salient examples). Though it had once been a
place riddled with mysteries and rife with contrasts, the New World became,
for the uses of the attack waged against it, a continuum where likeness won
out over contrast, uniformity over difference. The "English colonies"—the
future United States—had trouble struggling their way out of this massive
composite. Around 1750 they were still completely swallowed up in it.
Durand Echeverria notes that of the two hundred authors cited as authorities
on America in the *Encyclopédie,* only eight spoke of the English colonies
"specifically."[6]

The fourth and final characteristic: for the men of the Enlightenment,
anti-Americanism was also anticolonialism. Depreciating the country and
denigrating its inhabitants were ways of saving those they could by dis-
paraging colonization. "We should leave the savages to vegetate in peace,"
De Pauw pleaded, "and pity them if their misfortunes surpass our own, and
if we cannot contribute to their happiness, we should not increase their misery."[7] America, disdained by Mother Nature, had been devastated by the conquest. It was a vast graveyard of men, languages, and customs, the wreckage
of a successful extermination. Its detractors were not at all unaware of the
tragic dimensions of America's fate; on the contrary, De Pauw and Raynal (or
Diderot writing under Raynal's name) can be counted among those who
most stridently denounced Europe's crimes. But their hatred for the wrong-
doers did not lead them to idealize the victims. The New World's destroyed
civilizations filled them with a regret that lacked empathy. For Cornelius De
Pauw—as for his sovereign, Frederick II, who was hostile to any demographic outpouring to America's advantage—and for the authors of the *Histoire des deux Indes* recopying Montesquieu, the most important thing was to
pull European compatriots back from the shores and discourage "crossings."
It was a twofold philosophical crusade; the aim was both to spare the natives
and, at the same time, prevent Europe from being drained. But the argument
was dressed up to look like a law of nature: "the law of climates is such that
each living and vegetable species grows and dies in its native land."[8]

It was a watershed moment, then. The magical kaleidoscope bequeathed
by the first explorers, the mobile vignettes painted by subsequent travelers,
and the ethnological tables minutely compiled by missionaries gave way to a
massive tableau of the continent as a whole. Globes were still white with
unknown lands, yet a compact image of America was already being imposed.

These *terrae incognitae,* once populated by singular creatures sprung from cartographers' flights of fancy—as though while awaiting discovery they needed to be filled with the stuff of dreams—were now nothing but "unexplored" lands, suspended spaces: temporary gaps in a world where all the pieces fit together under the naturalist's and philosopher's gaze.

Early anti-Americanism repainted the New World as a single world. But not only was this new coat of paint uniform, its palette was gloomy. Instead of the colorful tiles of a mosaic, a drab fresco appeared: America in shades of gray.

Diluvian America

America's new detractors rose up to express their disappointment, proclaim their disgust, or cast anathema against an entire continent—its fauna, its flora, and its natives and colonists willy-nilly. But what exactly did they have to reproach the New World with? What bee had gotten into these Enlightenment men's bonnets? Or rather, what terrible tarantula, like the ones they so generously sprinkled throughout the continent in their zoological accounts? Their first complaint against the "New" World was precisely that—it was far too new. The stereotype of America's youthfulness began here, with the naturalists. And for them it was not a compliment.

Here, we have to go back to the flood. The age of the world was one of the great debates of the eighteenth century, and had heavy religious and philosophical implications. The concept of the flood, criticized by freethinkers, had been rehabilitated; the tale of Noah was once more afloat, so to speak, and was espoused by the most unexpected allies: geologists and the first "religious historians." Nicolas-Antoine Boulanger was both of these. As a civil engineer, he mapped the roads in Touraine and, using Réaumur's techniques, notoriously discovered seashells—later called fossils—in the marl beds, proving that the region known as the "Garden of France" had once been a sunken garden. A chemist and comparative mythologist, Boulanger was one of those atheists who said no to the Bible and yes to the flood. No to the Bible's chronology and the Ark's providential journey, yes to the material reality of a universal flood, whose physical traces (seashells) were corroborated by cultural and religious traces. If every single religion included accounts of the earth's inundation, it was, in Boulanger's estimation, because of a real superstitious dread lingering in all men. Rehabilitating the flood narrative reoriented inquiries as to the age of humanity. Now the question was whether humanity predated the flood and had survived it, albeit considerably diminished—which was Boulanger's theory—or, on the contrary, humanity had begun some time after the flood and come into being with the progressive ebb of the universal immersion, as Benoît de Maillet argued in his *Telliamed* (1748). In the latter system, the ages of different populations corresponded to the lands they inhabited: in lands that had emerged from the waters long ago, there were old civilizations; in more recently dried-off lands, there were new populations, still wet behind the ears. America would become an object of scrutiny in light of these different hypotheses.

The reigning consensus was indeed that of the youthfulness of the American peoples. Naturalists and philosophers agreed: these populations displayed physiological and intellectual immaturity, and their institutions were embryonic or inexistent. Such was the anthropological "evidence" that geology was called on to explain. It did so willingly and in many different ways.

First possibility: the American continent had been formed more recently than the Old World.[9] Its population, believed to be indigenous, was therefore more recent as well. Second possibility: the earth was the same age everywhere, but America had been "overtaken" at a later point in time than the other continents; it thus presented a relative youth in relation to the other continents, as calculated according to a series of "floods" staggered over several eras—with the same results for its population's immaturity. Third possibility (adopted by De Pauw): floods occurred simultaneously on the different continents, but the chances of survival were uneven. The American populations were unable to find subsistence on the "summits of their mountains, which are all the more sterile, all the more arid, because they are so high," and which "could not produce enough nourishing plants to sustain the refugee families with their flocks." In this last scenario, the Americans *had been* as old as the rest of humanity, but they did not survive a catastrophe the Tartars (for instance) had been better able to weather because their mountains were "convexities."[10] Since the antediluvian Americans were not lucky enough to have flat mountains, America's current inhabitants were new, postdiluvian peoples. The three scenarios were based on incompatible systems, but what is important is that they reached the same conclusion: rationalizing the juvenile developmental stage of America's human population.

But there was more. The American flood, either because it had been a recent event or for some other reason yet to be elucidated, had not entirely gone away. This gave the continent its most overarching and disastrous quality: it was *wet*. A new America emerged, an America that had almost been forgotten since the days of the first explorers' accounts.[11] It was a gloomy vastness, less hostile than repulsive, less frightening than simply disheartening. This was an America where colors were washed out and contours blurred. Sharp lines melted into hazy horizons. Oceans, land, and lagoons merged and were muddled. Tangled vegetation crept and twisted into inextricable clumps. Even the animals seemed shifty, with their ambiguous physiognomies. Dogs no longer barked; tigers were cowardly. Men were deficient. Buffon described vast solitudes, wandered over rather than peopled by "so-called nations,"[12] silhouettes roving in the darkness of the forests. Water, mist, fog, and wind held empire in the naturalists' America. Especially water, which encircled the coasts and colonized the land. Just past the coastline, America stretched out in a giant marsh. A boundless swamp of a continent, a "fetid and boggy terrain,"[13] an unending backwater over which towered, far in the distance to the west, pitiless peaks—rock barriers as hostile to life as the briny element in which their colossal base was sunk. Echoing Buffon, De Pauw wrote: "The land, either bristling with mountainous peaks or covered with forests and swamps, looked much like a vast and sterile desert."[14]

The wary Europeans who rediscovered America from their studies in Paris or Berlin believed that the continent was saddled with an immense geological and geographical flaw, and only its discoverers' folly or treachery could ever have made them portray it as rich in marvels. A new New World flowed from their pens and took shape. But the shape they gave it was formless, and the world itself, hardly viable. America's "manifest destiny" for Buffon, Raynal, or De Pauw was stagnation. It is hard to imagine more intensely contrasting depictions than the ones coming from either side of the Atlantic: just as the New England colonies were solidifying their aspirations for a *vita nuova,* the most listened-to voices in Europe were consigning America to sterility and death.

Things could have stopped there, with the diluvian conclusion that America was eternally scarred by its abysmal start. But naturalists and philosophers did not see it that way. In any case, it would be a shame to interrupt them—they're just getting started.

Buffon Shrinks America

So, America was a rudimentary continent that had just barely emerged from the flood. Neither its crumbling peaks nor its stagnant plains did mankind any favors. Even now—circa 1770—it was sparsely inhabited, if at all, and by youngsters still wet behind the ears, who had most likely come from far off—maybe even Asia? Or were they the result of some local, spontaneous generation? An unanswerable and therefore superfluous quandary. What's the use, Voltaire inquired mockingly, of asking "every day how it came about that men could be found on that continent and who led them there," if "one does not marvel that there are flies in America"?[15] In either case, they had gotten there hopelessly *late*. And their tardiness would be their undoing; their sketchy history would be overrun by Others—sprung from the waves wearing boots and helmets and riding on strange sheep.

But the worst was yet to come. Under natural historians' scrutiny, the New World not only seemed disenchanted; it was a lesser world, atrophied and shrunken, a world where living things vegetated, men withered away, and species got smaller. That was natural history's astounding revelation. That was the strange vision, or bizarre conviction, that took hold of the best minds of the second half of the eighteenth century.

One man played a major role here: Buffon. He was the one who proclaimed that America and its productions were physically inferior. He had a scholar's authority and a genius's prestige. He was given a respect bordering on veneration. Painters depicted him in a one-on-one discussion with Mother Nature anxiously revealing all her secrets to him. A cult sprang up around him, no less fervent than the ones devoted to Voltaire or Rousseau. Travelers set out for Montbard just to catch a glimpse of the great man. It was not easy to contradict someone with a reputation like his. Jefferson, when he refuted Buffon in 1784, took pains (in the English version as well as the French one) to pepper his text with flattering remarks and praise for the "celebrated Zoologist." "It is one of those cases," Jefferson explained, "where the [public's] judgment has been seduced by a glowing pen." He himself was unfortunately obliged to contradict Buffon, but not without "every tribute of honor and esteem."[16] The Virginian tendered a velvet hand; he knew he would not ingratiate himself to the French by scratching "Nature's confidant." Well aware of the danger in being iconoclastic, he instead chose to soften the sharp angles of his attack and take a few exegetical liberties, writing to the Marquis de Chastellux that "as to the degeneracy of the man of Europe transplanted to America, it is no part of Monsieur de Buffon's system."[17] It was clearly a better idea to have Buffon on your side than against you! Jefferson played the part of the good apostle; but in private, when he jotted down commentaries in the margins of his own copy of Buffon's works, he was less flattering to the "celebrated zoologist": "No writer, equally with M. de Buffon, proves the power of eloquence, and uncertainty of theories."[18] But the fact that Buffon's part in constructing a naturalist base for anti-Americanism had been decisive was not lost on Jefferson, who spent a long chapter of his *Notes on the State of Virginia* refuting him.

America's Sickly Animals

What earth-shattering information about the American continent did Buffon reveal? Something that sounds strange to us now, given that the most common image of America is one of sheer size and even disproportionate measure: on the new continent, everything was small, much smaller than in the Old World. The species were slighter. The animals, timid. Even human beings were more modest in size—except for the famous Patagonian giants, whose existence was moreover rather doubtful. Over the course of several successive studies—*Variétés dans l'espèce humaine* (Varieties in the Human Species, 1749), *Animaux de l'ancien continent, Animaux du nouveau monde, Animaux communs aux deux continents* (Animals of the Old Continent, Animals of the New World, Animals Common to Both Continents, 1761), *De la dégénération des animaux* (On the Degeneration of Animals, 1766)—Buffon hammered in the same fact: on this huge new continent, living things were atrophied. The fundamental lesson he repeated from chapter to chapter and from treatise to treatise was simple: "we have said that in general all the animals in the New World were much smaller than those of the ancient continent."[19] But what exactly does that mean?

It means that, for example, the tapir was markedly less impressive than the elephant, rhinoceros, or hippopotamus. That llamas were smaller than camels. That vicuñas were like miniature sheep. And to the impartial observer, the peccary seemed to be a shrunken pig. Not that Buffon confirmed the same hereditary relationship in each case. The peccary unquestionably belonged to the same "family" as its counterpart, the pig. The tapir, on the other hand, was not part of the hippopotamus family, the rhinoceros family, or the elephant family. And in a third possible case, the llama and the vicuña both had ambiguous ties to their Old World counterparts. Buffon informed his readers that they "appear to have more distinctive signs" than the tapir "of their former kinship" with their Old World siblings, the camel and the sheep, respectively. But the relationship immediately broke down and became a simple proximity—a proximity whose exact nature was as ambiguous as the word Buffon used to describe it: *voisinage* (being neighbors). "They are neighbors and are not relatives,"[20] he wrote. So the vicuña could be the sheep's neighbor but not its (American) cousin? The idea is not strikingly clear. Buffon replaced a proposed, then immediately refuted, relationship with a notion as hazy as it was paradoxical, considering that these were animals whose habitats lay thousands of miles apart.

His system warrants closer examination, especially given the considerable influence it had on representations of America up to the end of the eighteenth century. His reasoning is clearest in the extreme example of the tapir. The tapir, far from being related to the rhinoceros, hippopotamus, or elephant, was not even their "neighbor." It did not share important features with them. It only resembled them in a few secondary morphological or environmental ways—one of which was the moderately distinctive trait that "like the hippopotamus, it often stands in the water." The three animals to which the tapir was likened only had "slight relations" with it, as Buffon wrote. So slight that we might ask why they were being correlated in the first place.

What justified these comparisons, in Buffon's opinion, was the relative situation occupied by the animals observed in the broader context of their hemisphere's fauna. It was because the tapir was "on its continent the first in size" that it was equated with the rhinoceros, hippopotamus, or elephant, though it was barely, Buffon admitted, "the size of a donkey." Buffon's method is disconcerting: rather than relying on an observation of common features, which could have been shown to be numerous enough to justify comparing the two continents, it seems to give morphological appraisal short shrift. However, it is not as impressionistic as any given portrait, such as the llama's, might lead us to believe ("The llama has, like the camel, high legs, a very long neck, a light head, a cleft upper lip; it also resembles it in its gentle nature, etc."). The method was founded on the explicitly acknowledged use of analogy.

Analogy has a bad reputation, scientifically speaking. Buffon, however, took the risky step of rehabilitating it, both as an accurate, coherent view of living things and as a more refined investigative tool that could be used to complement or rectify simple observation. On a theoretical level, the idea of using analogy did seem to him to go hand in hand with the notion of human and animal species' fundamental unity—even in the apparently separate place known as the New World. The unity hypothesis was essential to Buffon's way of thinking. It was part of his naturalist's and philosopher's credo. He extended it without hesitation to the Americans: "As for their first origins, I do not doubt—even independent of theological reasons—that it is the same as our own."[21] Natural history was thus confronted with the task of identification, or, rather, recognition. The lineage from the Old World to the New had to be reestablished, whenever possible; or, failing that, relationships hidden beneath apparent differences uncovered. The unity of the planet's living things implied a universal correspondence from one world to the other. The American fauna and that of the old continent, if put side by side, could and should divulge their points of correspondence.

The method was simple. The first thing to do was draw up tables of all the animals on each continent. Juxtaposing the two tables would then help pinpoint parents, cousins, or "neighbors." Since naturalists, like nature, abhor a vacuum, the animals in the New World were kindly asked to fill all the slots at their disposition, with analogous respect to their already indexed siblings. This led Buffon to write—still comparing the tapir to the hippopotamus, rhinoceros, and elephant—that the tapir "alone represents all three in these small ways," which included, for instance, their "muscular and protruding upper lip" or their tendency to wallow in the mud. "Represent" is the key word here. On the one hand, it reminds us how important representing animals was to the naturalist: rhetorical and physical description was the backbone of natural history. But in a passage like the one just quoted, "represent" is used in another sense: it refers to the correspondences between the two continents and discreetly legitimates the analogical method. The hippopotamus's representation by the tapir, in this second sense, was inextricably linked to the system's own preconception: that the New World animal, however dissimilar it might be in appearance and even in reality, *took the place* of one or several animals from the Old World. It was their transatlantic *representative*. This was comparative natural history on a macrocosmic scale; it did not compare specific animals so much as it superposed two organized wholes in which all the animals of each continent were indexed. Buffon was proposing not portrait galleries, but conversion charts.

Transplantation and Degeneration

All the protagonists in the American dispute would draw on another text by Buffon, *Dégénération des animaux,* published in 1766, which attempted to theoretically justify the combined use of "analogy" and "experiments." There were cases, Buffon more or less argued, where observation alone was insufficient. In those, one had to "resort to the most attentive inspection, and even to experiments and analogy."[22] What cases was he talking about? Ones in which animals had been transplanted or forced into exile, "constrained to abandon their native land" by "revolutions of the globe or man's force." A displaced animal was a deformed animal.

Buffon's tactic shows through the page here and confirms the strong link between the analogical method and the American problem in his work. The analogical method, a kind of fine tuning applied to morphology, was the naturalist's secret weapon for revealing the true "nature" of transplanted and thus "degenerated" animals. The New World's ambiguous beasts forced the naturalist to redouble his efforts: the geometrical precision of his universal tables would go unheeded without the persuasive force of his analogical flair. *We have to pay attention,* Buffon was saying, *close attention! If we do not look very closely, if we do not go beyond appearances, if we just toss a heedless glance, we will not see anything, we will not recognize them, because their tribulations under horrendous climates have made these animals unrecognizable.* Whence his use of the twenty-question method. Is it like a sheep? Then it must be a vicuña. . . Confronted with America, Buffonian zoology turned into a series of morphological riddles, or a game of hidden pictures, where only the vigilant observer would find the missing clues.

Buffon's animals were malleable, unstable, shaped by their climate and diet, of course, but also by all the vicissitudes of their habitat, which had marked them with its "stigmata." The same was true for humans. Buffon, as we know, believed that black people's skin color was a function of the climate they lived in, and he imagined in vivo experiments to determine "how much time would be needed" for blacks "transported" to Denmark "to re-establish man's nature"—that is, for their skin to get back its original whiteness. . . Humans, animals, and plants all lived under the law of "alteration," the key word in Buffonian interpretation. We find it in the very first sentence of *Dégénération des animaux:* "Once man began to change skies, when he spread out from climate to climate, his nature underwent alterations." The change in humans' skin color was an alteration; the change in size and shape of America's animals was an alteration. Alteration and degeneration, not change or mutation: the Old World was still the reference point and, at least implicitly, the source.

But what stayed with Buffon's readers, and would particularly appeal to America's detractors, was less the method than the "results." Buffon's works offered illustrations—better yet, *measurements*—of the disparity between the species, and always to the new continent's detriment. They offered a demonstration, bestiary included, of Nature's widespread "degeneration" in America. There were of course a few methodological snags in Buffon's tables: a hint of circularity,[23] a dollop of prejudice. No matter; the eloquent Buffon, as Jefferson would say, won people over, and America came out lastingly diminished, with its long procession of stunted animals. His affirmation of a "degeneration of animals in America" gave the concept of America's inferiority scientific credentials. It was a valuable endorsement, and one that provided anti-Americanism with an unhoped-for legitimacy. The idea that living things atrophied on the American continent needed this kind of clout in order to counteract two and a half centuries of favorable, enthusiastic, or simply credulous accounts.

American Degeneration

Buffon's analysis was pivotal: all naturalist anti-Americanism can be traced back to it. It not only gave an account of America's general deficiency—exploited with fiendish panache by De Pauw in the first pages of his *Recherches philosophiques sur les Américains*—it also framed America's future, using the rhetorical model of decline. Right from the start, the comparative gaze was slanted. Its mission was to uncover and record indications of the American world's "alteration." Not only was the pitiful "smallness" of American species brought to light; the whole process of their degeneration was, as well: their "sizable diminishment in size," as Buffon put it in a strange and revealing expression that betrays the preconceptions of the comparative gaze. From now on, it was one or the other: either the animals in the New World were decidedly too estranged (neither neighbors nor "allies") from those of the Old World, in which case their indigenous nature would be recognized and their smallness in comparison to their distant "correspondents" played up; or else an animal (such as the peccary) could be linked to a "source" present on the old continent (the pig "type"), and so "it has degenerated to the point of forming a distinct and different species from the one it originally belonged to."[24] The analysis, in both cases, shamed America, which had either given birth to mediocre species or had atrophied species that had thrived elsewhere.

What America's detractors found in Buffon's writings was thus the conjunction of a "climate" theory reformulated as strident physiological determinism, coupled with a set of "observations" that led to the conclusion of a lesser development or degeneration of all living things in America. According to Montesquieu, climate influenced all bodies and fashioned behaviors, which in turn created dispositions toward certain mores and favored different political institutions. For Buffon, climate was a more direct and absolute dictator. It brutalized humans and animals right into their morphology. It brought on transformations even in the distinguishing features of different races. It was what had "varnished [man] in black . . . under torrid zones" and "weathered and shrunk [him] by the glacial cold" near the pole.[25] It was what would restore the Negro's or Lapp's "original traits, . . . primitive size, and . . . natural color"[26] once they returned to more clement climes. And once again, it was what created even more "prompt and sizable" changes in animals, "because they cleave[d] to the earth much more closely than man"[27] and suffered its caprices without any of the protective measures human culture had invented. If a climate's effects had been able to "shrink" human beings, they could clearly shrivel the peccary a little. . .

The concept of *alteration* was useful in rounding out Buffon's explanatory system. Alteration affected all life forms, and, since Buffon linked it to the climate and nourishing earth, it was considered an unavoidable consequence of species' (including humans') spatial relocation from one climate to another, from one land to another. *De la dégénération des animaux* begins not with the animal kingdom, but with man and his malleability. "Once man began to change skies, when he spread out from climate to climate, his nature underwent alterations: these were slight, in the temperate zones, which we suppose neighbored on his place of origin; but they increased as he moved farther away from it."[28] Then it was not only animals that "degenerated." Human nature was "altered," too, even if man's resources (habitation, clothing, etc.) made the alteration slower and less mechanical. It was not a negligible advantage for Buffon's anti-American descendants that "alteration" was an extremely ill-defined concept. Cornelius De Pauw got it right away. If by chance a peccary was more corpulent than expected, it was because "alteration" had taken a different path, changing the animal's shape, for example: "the pigs that atrophy in Pensilvania [sic] change shape in other places without losing any of their size."[29] A peccary that had not grown smaller was considered an exception that proved the rule, and its "degeneration" could be found in some haphazard change other than a "diminishment of its largeness."

Blaming migration as a cause of alteration and degeneration was a way of radicalizing—and popularizing—the political, naturalist theory of transplanted Europeans' physiological and intellectual collapse. Buffon was thus the source of a surge of scientific denigration of America that for the next twenty years would continue using natural history to justify itself. However much Cornelius De Pauw might scoff at the old master—"such an ingenious naturalist—sometimes more ingenious than nature itself"[30]—however much he might niggle about the age of humanity in America or some other hypothesis he judged too tenuous, his *Recherches philosophiques sur les Américains* owed its force to Buffon's breakthrough.

Poisonous America

The New World was too new. Its climate was hostile and ruled by the cold, the wet, or both. It was a sterile land, or at least scantily fruitful. Often barren, always underpopulated; a place where all of nature's kingdoms emerged "altered"—man being no exception: man's humanity itself was problematic. In America, people did not live, they "vegetated." Those were the kinds of scholarly words used by the earliest anti-Americans. And their words blossomed into portraits. America had no shortage of amateur Hieronymus Boschs keen on filling it with Acephaluses, Antipodes, and sheep trees. It found its El Greco in Las Casas, who painted a martyred continent's torments in stark colors. Lafitau, Charlevoix, the Jesuits, and the Franciscans cloaked the savages in royal purple and lit the canvas from above, like an Annunciation. Then, in 1768, America found its Goya: Cornelius De Pauw.

De Pauw was born in Holland. He lived at the court of Frederick II and wrote in French. He was not even thirty when he published his *Recherches philosophiques sur les Américains*. Fame came to him overnight among the European intelligentsia: his book was talked about, discussed, considered important enough to bother refuting. In Berlin, De Pauw weathered attacks from the French Benedictine monk Antoine-Joseph Pernety. It was a comprehensive attack, followed by a *Defense* from De Pauw and a counterattack by Pernety. The skirmish kept tongues wagging in the city, court, and academy for two years.

We might be tempted to call it just a local quibble, a struggle for influence among the denizens of Frederick II's philosophical zoo. Yet the influence of the *Recherches* went beyond the small, inbred world of Berlin politics. Raynal was putting together the first draft of the *Histoire des deux Indes* at the time; it is full of traces of De Pauw's work. And if Pernety, Frederick II's librarian, had personal reasons to resist what he saw as a young rival and rising star, the same could not be said of Delisle de Sales, for instance, who added a discussion of De Pauw's book into his *Système de la nature*, though the American debate was not really relevant to his topic. It was as though around 1770 no one could discuss cause and effect without crossing swords with De Pauw.

De Pauw was hyperactively negative. He cast the whole edifice of respectful or enthusiastic accounts of America into the mud. He castigated sham specialists, dubious missionaries, and shoddy writers left and right. Practically every traveler was suspect: "A general rule can be established that for every hundred travelers, sixty are lying for no reason, as though out of imbecility; thirty are lying out of self-interest or, if you will, guile; and finally, ten are telling the truth and are men."[31] And the facts coming from those ten still needed to be picked through. . . De Pauw hit hard and did not let up. He trampled the noble-savage tradition still dear to so many philosophers—and which had even started to appear in sentimental novels and plays.[32] He painted a strikingly dark picture. Goya at his bleakest is not even an accurate point of comparison; De Pauw's America conjures up images of the morbid currents of lava and blood found in Mexican muralism. Not Rivera, whose works are too full of life even amid the bloodshed; more like Orozco's hideously charred spectrum—though De Pauw's atrocities were even more irrevocable. Death had not come to America in battle dress, with the European invaders; it emanated from the very earth, putrid and infectious. Not that De Pauw neglected to denounce Europe's crimes, with a detailed description of the conquest at its most gruesome; he did this vehemently. But for him, the evil went deeper. The massacre's instigators were

loathsome and should be denounced, but America was accursed and he stigmatized it.

"I shall place at the start of this work several striking and decisive observations," wrote De Pauw. Striking indeed. In Buffon's honor, the first shots
were fired at the fauna. "America's climate at the time of its discovery was
very contrary for most quadruped animals, which were a sixth smaller than
their analogs on the old continent." A second round came right on the heels
of the first and blasted human bipeds: "This climate was especially pernicious to men, who were astonishingly idiotic, enervated, and vitiated in all
the parts of their organism." The third was aimed at nature as a whole: "a
vast and sterile desert." De Pauw did not spare his efforts—or his readers.
With three vigorous brushstrokes, he painted the background onto which the
inexorable Spaniards would proceed. And what Spaniards they were! No
Cortez or Pizarro came marching forth from the pages of De Pauw's book.
There were no destroyers of empires, conquerors of continents, or even mass
torturers; just a bunch of anonymous riffraff. The Spanish were starving
"fortune hunters"—so starving they ended up eating each other. "From time
to time, the Spaniards were forced to eat Americans and even Spaniards, for
lack of other food." The French, too, for that matter: "The first French
colonists sent into this unfortunate world ended up devouring each other."
The English had a little more luck (or self-restraint): they escaped this living
hell and went back home, but got there in a state of starvation so severe that
"in London, they were taken for specters"!

And this is only page 3—there are 769 more in the original edition.
How's that for a preamble? With this extraordinary primal scene, De Pauw
was killing two birds with one stone: he proved that this was a wretched, des-
olate country where no one could survive, and he hinted at the terrible
"revolution" that America provoked in its invaders, who were transformed
into cannibals as surely as Circe's visitors had been turned into swine.
Three birds with one stone, actually. Because this unbelievable opening
could also be read as an allegory of the fate of colonizing countries: Europeans devouring each other symbolized the draining of their vital energy into
the human abyss known as America. Even now, De Pauw affirmed, several
colonies were "absolutely unable to feed themselves with their own productions." Instead of nourishing humans, America devoured them. De Pauw
was in agreement with a whole century of philosophers on that point, from
Montesquieu to Diderot. Right from the start, he proclaimed that the fate of
America's indigenous populations and colonizers would converge in misery.
He enlarged the traditional snapshot of the historical evils inflicted on America into a fresco of eternal and natural misfortune, a land into which the

Europeans had intruded for the natives' greater misery as well as their own. De Pauw was a painter of disaster rather than battle and was less interested in the conquest and its butchery than in the deep-reaching putrefaction of a morbid continent that would be its illusory conquerors' grave.

Now he could get to the point: the land and its climate. Now he could follow the lethal logic that went from salt to sap, brine to poison. From now on he would speak scientifically.

First off, salt. It was everywhere. It rose from the ubiquitous swamps and endless marshes into the atmosphere and fell back down on the vegetation in a deadly sedimentation. America's waters, "corrupted, harmful, and even mortal," waters subject to "fermentation," sat under the sun and gave off a miasma of salt that "then crystallize[d] on each leaf dipped into this brine."[33] According to De Pauw, plant life in America was not so much plant *life* as plant *preserves,* a gigantic heap of sauerkraut. A thick salt fog suffocated the vegetation, which stopped being "tender and herbaceous," as in Europe, and survived only in the "ligneous" form "of underbrush." Because, to make matters worse, on top of the salt there was also "earth niter," which dried out the continent's feeble productions from the inside. It was a researched and undeniable fact, De Pauw added: when the colonists in New France went to scrub their laundry with ashes, as was done back in Paris, they were "astonished to find that this washing powder instantly shredded the cloth to tatters and then reduced it to parenchyma, which was attributed—rightly so—to the violence of the acrid, copious salt the ashes contained."[34] This unpalatable chemistry experiment echoes earlier accounts of America's wonders. De Pauw's stroke of genius was to master the rhetoric and parody the clichés while turning them against America. He kept the verve and the astonishment, but there was nothing enchanting about his remarks. Get your head out of the clouds! Enough fun and games! All the *lusus naturae,* the strange marvels that had enchanted curious Europeans for two centuries, were rewritten by De Pauw as a long series of unhappy surprises, like the rotten tricks played on human beings by a flippant or frankly sadistic Mother Nature. De Pauw did not describe the devouring laundry detergent with its party-trick overtones in order to amuse. His goal was to fill the reader with fear and disgust for a place that was fecund only in traps.

An "evil stepmother" like the one Sade would later describe, Nature had filled America with snares and treacherous turns. And along with the nitrate, she had even equipped it with saltpeter, which the Spanish would use to replenish their depleted powder stocks and subjugate the Mexicans—who were thus betrayed by their own soil. This vitiated land was also a vicious land. And the fact that it had rearmed its invaders was the least of its evils. It had been slaughtering men since the dawn of time. It sought to depopulate the continent with its anemic sap—and did not do a bad job of it. (De Pauw, like his forerunners, emphasized the human emptiness of America's lands.) America was not only repulsive and sterile, it was poisonous. Its "fetid and swampy terrain" made "more venomous trees vegetate than grow in all parts of the rest of the known universe."[35] A champion of malevolence, the vegetation secreted death out of every pore. Curare, which—as reported by innumerable travelers—the savages daubed on the points of their arrows, had a symbolic value for De Pauw. Poison is mentioned on the first page of his essay and is the main topic of the last chapter on "the use of poison arrows"; it literally bookends the *Recherches.* An overabundance of vegetable toxins confirmed nature's *criminality* in America. But the terrible curare was nothing next to the horrors of manioc. For even the few plants that could be used to nourish human beings were poisonous, too. De Pauw, stressing the "causticity" of the starches that were the mainstay of the American diet, constructed the striking paradox of humanity surviving by eating poison— *alimentum in veneno.* "The Americans' principal food," he wrote, evoking the era of the first contacts, "was a poisonous plant that only skill could render comestible." The "skill" was simply cooking it, but by using the term, De Pauw suggested that there was somehow a secret struggle going on between a barbaric nature and men reduced to a state of desperation. Death lurked between the raw and the cooked. Yucca and manioc in their natural state made for a fatal pittance: "I am speaking of so many species of *Jucas* and *Manihots,* which are almost all mortal when eaten raw, as they come from the bowels of the earth. It was nevertheless this *Manihot* which, for the Indians, took the place of rye and wheat, which they did not know of." America was stupefying—it pretended to nourish its offspring in order to kill them! As De Pauw wrote: "One must admit that the history of the old continent offers no comparable example, and whatever the sum of misfortunes may have been, there has never been an entire population constrained to draw its primary fodder from a venomous vegetable."

So it came as no surprise that this many-poisoned land had also poisoned Europe—not with manioc or yucca, but by flooding it with the "venomous germs" of venereal disease. De Pauw obviously considered "risible" any hypothesis that situated the origin of syphilis elsewhere than in America (such as Africa, for example): that "the venereal plague was born in America" was a proven point and "irrefutable."[36] The contrary would have been implausible. He did not go so far as to give the statement a specific source. But he framed his comments on syphilis with two "naturalist" remarks, as though better to moor the disease to American soil. Because even if in all truthfulness he could not really say where the malady had originated, De Pauw did not neglect to affirm that it was aggravated and sometimes reawakened by consuming excessive amounts of iguana. There was thus a suspicious symbiosis between a malady quite wrongly called "from Naples," given that it came from the New World, and the "American lizard," the ingestion of which was "deadly for those affected." Moreover, this burrowing malady, which went to the very roots of the reproductive system, could be argued to have the same cause as the Americans' "weakness." Americans were all "deprived of the living, physical force that results from the tension and resistance of the muscles and nerves."[37] De Pauw seemed to believe this; once again, it was the flood, the "atmosphere's great humidity," the "incredible quantity of stagnant waters stretched out over its surface" that had "vitiated and depraved its inhabitants' temperament."[38]

In the horrible place known as America, humanity was born losing and lame. The Americans' recent history had been disastrous, but from the dawn of time, America's natural history had been a tale of woe, an irreparable misdeal. "Struck with putrefaction," "deluged with lizards, snakes, serpents, reptiles, and monstrous insects,"[39] unhealthy and malevolent, America was not the patriarchs' Canaan that feverish missionaries had described:[40] it was an Egypt beset by more plagues than men could withstand.

The "Americans' Moronic Spirit"

The first victim of the "unfortunate world" was man—starting, of course, with the savage, whose complete dereliction was proclaimed by De Pauw, before Joseph de Maistre and for other reasons.

"On the Americans' Moronic Spirit": the title, which is the heading of the fourth part of the *Recherches,* sets the tone for a chapter the author himself considered decisive. As a direct consequence of the handicaps forced on him by nature's abominable cruelty, the American was both feeble and feebleminded. "A stupid imbecility is the fundamental disposition of all Americans," De Pauw warned, judging them "deprived of both intelligence and perfectibility."[41] But instead of looking for the reason for this in some extraordinary "prevarication," some mind-boggling sin committed by their forefathers—as the author of the *St. Petersburg Dialogues,* De Maistre, later would—De Pauw found the reason more naturally to be poor blood circulation, which led to a "weakness of the understanding."[42] The Indians' ideas were "poorly imprinted" because of the "coarse and viscous humors" that characterized their temperament. Their fundamental disposition was one of insentience. "In them, insentience is a vice of their altered constitution: they are unpardonably lazy, invent nothing, undertake nothing, and do not stretch the sphere of their conception beyond what they see: pusillanimous, cowardly, enervated, with no nobility of mind; discouragement and the absolute lack of that which constitutes a reasonable animal make them useless to themselves and to society." De Pauw was "tempted to refuse a soul" to these beings who "vegetate rather than live."[43]

Since the days of Buffon's first remarks in 1749, observations about America had gotten worse and worse. *Variétés dans l'espèce humaine* insisted first and foremost on the fundamental imperfectability of the indigenous Americans. De Pauw depicted beings somewhere between humanity and nonhumanity, physiologically undermined by the "secret vice" nature had inflicted on them. Physical and mental weakness were the main results, but there were other defects, as well: probable impotence; men's confirmed lack of desire for women ("alienation for the fair sex"); even hardiness under torture, the major topos of the savages' nobility, was transformed into supplementary proof of atrophied sensibilities: it was not so much the sublime heroism of their resolve at the torture stake as a simple defect of their "fibers."

Was the inhabitant of this "unfortunate world" really a man, or was he a monster? The dismal and limited savage was a forerunner of natural history's later fixation on *abnormality*. The American man was neither virile nor hirsute; his breasts often lactated; he fled women in order to engage in his predilection for "antiphysical" acts.[44] This predilection was so notorious that De Pauw did not need to insist; Diderot had written about it at length. The *Histoire des deux Indes* had confirmed it: "They have few children, because they have no taste for women: and it is a national vice, with which the elders ceaselessly reproach the young men." Those were pointless lectures, De Pauw laughed; they "could not master their temperament, no more than where the contrary is preached." And what about women? Wanton and lascivious, the women furiously threw themselves at their invaders, who probably would not otherwise have managed to subjugate such immense lands. The women's libido was inversely proportional to the men's, yet this did not imply that they were feminine. It simply confirmed the inversion of gender roles. Moreover, the American male was hard to distinguish from the female: it was "difficult to distinguish between the sexes by their faces."[45] And whereas milk came readily in men, "in several regions, the American women do not experience any flow at any time."[46] American men and women faced off like Sodomites and Tribades.

But love was not the only monstrous thing in America. Anomaly roamed the hills and populated the forests. There were "blafards" in abundance; also called "kackerlackes," blafards were strange albinos long surmised to be the result of some kind of simian crossbreeding, but which De Pauw, like Buffon, believed to be a simple "accidental variety." Their proliferation was just one more symptom of America's "degeneration." Caused by a deficiency "in their parents' spermatic liquor," they were "absolutely deprived of the power of generation, or [did] not engender children that resemble them."[47] It is not surprising that they cropped up so frequently in naturalist writings on America. And no less symbolic than the blafard was the hermaphrodite, which epitomized America's sexual disorder. A fallen monster, as well, the Floridian hermaphrodite lacked the androgyne's completeness; the hermaphrodite was a man "less perfect than those who only have one sexual organ." Lafitau had denied their existence and affirmed that they were simply men dressed and treated like women. De Pauw objected that the "unheard-of custom of disguising men and tyrannizing them is . . . as surprising in the moral order as the quantity of hermaphrodites in the physical order."[48] Why shouldn't there be a real race of hermaphrodites, after all, in a land where nature seemed to delight in breaking all the rules?

The "Creole" Question

Such was the portrait of the American degenerate—or monster—as it was tirelessly reproduced between 1750 and 1770. Did this only apply to the savages? Not at all, replied Buffon, De Pauw, and Raynal. It applied to all the "inhabitants" of the "unfortunate world." Opinions, it is true, were more discordant on this point, and pronouncements more hesitant. But the main argument was clear: there was every reason to believe and conclude that the horrible effects of nature in all its brutality had not spared transplanted Europeans any more than it had the chickens, which were sterile, and the dogs, which had become mute. The *Défense des* Recherches philosophiques sur les Américains, written in response to Dom Pernety, gave De Pauw the chance to add a few more brushstrokes to an already bleak canvas and, above all, to extend unambiguously to the Creole—that is, any European born in America—the law of deformation and degeneration established by Buffon. It was a decisive development. From then on, in the anti-American discourse inspired by natural history, the Indian and the Creole shared the same fate. "In northern America," wrote De Pauw, this time backing up his statements using the Swedish naturalist Peter Kalm's recently translated *Histoire Naturelle & Politique de la Pensilvanie,* "Europeans are perceptibly degenerating, and their constitution is altered with each successive generation."[49] The "degeneration of Europeans settled in America" was an indubitable fact. And just as chickens brought across the Atlantic often went thirty years without laying an egg, for four or five generations, by the same principle, Creoles could be expected to suffer the same "tepidness in love" and near-sterility as the natives.[50] Here De Pauw forcefully confirmed the hypothesis he had put forth in the *Recherches:* "All the animals led from the Old World to the New have suffered, without a single exception, a perceptible alteration, either in their form or in their instinct"; it could only be the same for humans; "and through reiterating observations on this subject," comparing the Creoles who had been living there for some time with newly arrived Europeans, "one became convinced that the degeneration one had believed possible was real."[51] The "one" here clearly implies Buffon, whose authority De Pauw uses again and again, all the while lamenting his tentativeness; Buffon would finally denounce the way his disrespectful disciple had distorted his works.

It would not be true, however, to say that De Pauw stretched Buffon's ideas all that far from the shape they had taken in 1766. *Dégénération des animaux* justified, at least hypothetically (precisely as De Pauw says), extending the climate theory of animals' degeneration to humans. Over the course of these texts, the defect natural history saw as marking living things in America became more and more pronounced: the native inhabitants' "degeneration" was considered a proven fact, and that of the European colonists seemed at least probable. And at the same time—in the 1770s—descriptions started to reach beyond the field of natural history, in both its scholarly and its popularized versions. Explanatory schemas crossed over into the general public and took hold. It was an alarming trend for the colonists, who witnessed the clinical analysis of America's inferiority and the hypothesis of their own unavoidable decrepitude winning out as scientific realities in such widely read works as the *Histoire des deux Indes.*

The main topic of the *Histoire des deux Indes* was not America's natural history but "European establishments" throughout the world. It was presented as an "economic, philosophical, and political" work. Written by several different authors and published under the Abbé Raynal's name, modified with each successive printing, it offered shifting, sometimes contradictory glimpses of its subject. Its presentation of America owed a great deal to Buffon's explanatory schemas and faithfully transcribed his alteration-degeneration theory, but it was also influenced by De Pauw's mephitic painting, especially since De Pauw's anticolonialism fell in line with Raynal's own. The influence is particularly apparent in the first edition (1770), which presents the hypothesis of man's degeneration. Raynal was even more heavy-handed about it than De Pauw. Concerning "free men" in "English America," he wrote in the first edition: this class of men "has visibly degenerated. None of the Creoles is as robust in his work, as strong in war, as the Europeans." Yet these offspring of transplanted Europeans had been born in America and were "accustomed to the climate from the cradle." With this remark, Raynal suggested that their deficiency could not simply be explained as trouble adapting. Worse, he added, "under this foreign sky, the mind has become as enervated as the body." And Raynal concluded by stressing the absence of any "man of genius" in colonial America: "it should amaze us that America has not yet produced a good poet, a skillful mathematician, a man of genius in any art, or any science." The reason for this was a "facility" in all areas and a precocity much like the climate's; both quickly ran out of steam: "precocious and mature before us, they fall well behind when we come to completion [that is—when we reach maturity]."[52] The Anglo-Americans were feeble-bodied and feeble-minded; precocious and lively in their youth, they were incapable of prolonged reflection. Their intellectual inferiority was no less certain than their physical weakness was "visible."

The representatives of the insurgent colonies would have paid dearly to have a page like that one ripped out of the *Histoire des deux Indes*. At least they managed to have it rewritten.

French Prejudice's "Augean Stables"

Benjamin Franklin arrived in Paris in December 1776 to represent the rebel colonies. Eighteen months had gone by since the first military skirmish between the American militia and the British army, in Lexington on April 19, 1775. These had been trying months for the insurgents.

Franklin, with his bonnet and overcoat, was wildly popular in the city and at court; everyone was crazy about the strange fellow, who was often taken for a Quaker. Diplomatically, though, he sensed things were not ripe. The king, Louis XVI, would commit himself only to a sure thing and with the approval of Vergennes, who had become all-powerful since Turgot had stepped down. Patience was in order: *le bonhomme Richard* cultivated his popularity and bided his time. A year went by. Finally, in Saratoga on October 17, 1777, an English army of ten thousand men, exhausted and cut off from their provisions, surrendered to the insurgents. The shock wave was considerable. It reached London on the night of December 2–3. Despite ministerial efforts to minimize the affair, everyone could sense that this was a turning point in the war. The news was no less resounding in Paris. It was now or never—*aut nunc aut nunquam*—Vergennes decided. On December 6, Louis XVI had Franklin informed of his decision to recognize the colonies' independence and draw up a treaty with the insurgents for future trade, friendship and alliance. Vergennes and Franklin signed it on February 6, 1778.

Yet the "dispute" continued, despite the alliance. The fact that "extremely polite society"—to use Crébillon's expression—was crazy about George Washington did not stop the naturalists from sticking to their theories and "political writers" such as the Abbé de Mably from joining the debate and criticizing the American Constitution. The situation was paradoxical, intellectually speaking: the insurgents were a new high-society fad—rhymed couplets and hairdos were dedicated to them—which made for a strange contrast with the universally negative image of America now firmly anchored in cultivated people's minds. Buffon's prestige and De Pauw's impressive success (the *Recherches* would go into its eleventh printing in 1799, and his response to Pernety, its ninth) were the principal reasons for this. De Pauw, the all-out detractor, was even asked to write the article "Americans" for the *Encyclopédie*'s supplement in 1776—a pretty symbolic year. To make matters worse, in 1777 the English naturalist William Robertson produced an inspired compendium of Buffon's ideas—one that was caustic toward America, a place where nature was "less prolific" and "less vigorous in her productions" than in Europe, where the fauna was "inactive and timid," and even man, far from having a kind of savage energy, was "a pensive melancholy animal."[53] Through Robertson, the Buffonian virus made new progress in Europe, particularly in Germany, where the anemic-America theory was approved by Humboldt.

Neither Franklin nor Jefferson, his successor in Paris in 1785, took the endlessly rehashed stories of sterile chickens and cowardly tigers lightly. We might imagine that they could have been more legitimately concerned with the political criticism the Franco-American alliance had encountered, from, among others, Linguet, a lawyer and brilliant, paradoxical polemicist, who predicted that if the colonies won their independence the result would be a crop of small-scale, localized tyrants, and that in the long run a kind of "rogue state" would emerge, using all kinds of military tactics to take over global trade. They might also have worried about the severe institutional criticism developed by the Abbé de Mably in his *Observations sur le gouvernement et les lois des États-Unis d'Amérique* (Observations on the Government and Laws of the United States of America, 1784). There was indeed a concerted rejoinder from the Americans—but it did not address political or institutional criticism, a fact that speaks volumes. Linguet was ignored. Mably was left to Mazzei, an American citizen originally from Florence whose refutation, published in Paris, was not a success; Jefferson himself took care of selling off the leftover copies.

Jefferson's informal brain trust considered the decisive arena to be the field of natural history, with the calamitous images of America it had produced. That was where the main effort went, and the Americans profited from a sudden uncertainty among enemy ranks in the face of recent events: could the soldiers of Valley Forge, Long Island, and Saratoga still be depicted as degenerates? The theorists of America as a "lesser world" had also started tearing into each other. De Pauw had annoyed Buffon with his ironic description of America as both young and decrepit: "It is not easy to conceive how any beings could be, just after their creation, in a state of decrepitude and old age." If the Americans had degenerated—a point everyone agreed on—then America's youth was "untenable."[54] Buffon's answer in 1779 in *Époques de la nature* was concise but fairly confusing. He suddenly distinguished between northern America (which was clearly on its way up) and southern America, where "nature, far from having degenerated through great age, was on the contrary born late, and has never existed with the same force, the same active power as in northern lands." But Buffon's argument ended on a different note. He went back to generalizing about America as a whole and maintained the hypothesis of a "principle" of lesser activity, of Nature as "less active" than in Europe. Neither Buffon nor his fellows naturalists were quite ready to surrender. . .

Things were not much better with the Abbé Raynal and his torrential *Histoire des deux Indes*. The stakes were high, given the work's popularity in France and Europe. How could you get around the abbé? It seems that Franklin first decided on an object lesson. According to Jefferson, he invited an equal number of Americans and Frenchmen to his dinner table in Passy—including Raynal as guest of honor. Franklin got the abbé started on America's "smallness," then suddenly stopped the conversation and asked his guests, who were grouped by nationality, to stand up. All the Americans were taller than the tallest Frenchman. Raynal, who was himself very short ("a mere shrimp"), apparently took the joke gracefully, but refused to accept the argument. There was no way he would defer to the crudest empiricism when the greatest minds in Europe all agreed that in America nature was anemic. However, the 1780 and 1781 editions of the *Histoire des deux Indes* show the distinct effect, if not of this particular episode, then at least of Franklin's salutary influence. Several passages were rewritten to put America in a more favorable light. The most spectacular change dealt with something the Americans in Paris were particularly touchy about: the "degeneration of the Creoles"—that is, their own degeneration. The lengthy argument developed in the 1770 edition on the American continent's inability to produce geniuses was still there, but this time as an example of a prejudice that should be suppressed! "To dissipate this unjust prejudice," the text now read, "it took a Franklin to teach the physicians of our astonished continent to master lightning, etc."[55] The lightning rod had been invented in 1753, so the authors of the *Histoire des deux Indes* could conceivably have recognized Franklin's genius sooner—but better late than never.

The match was far from over, though. Even after its change of heart, the *Histoire des deux Indes* continued to blow hot ("the glory and good fortune of changing [the Americans] must be the work of English America") and cold ("which is what it has not yet done"). Remorse and rewrites still left whole swaths of prejudice intact. Devoid of self-criticism, sparing with revisions, the *Histoire des deux Indes* perpetuated the stereotype of North America as a harsh place for humanity and so bereft of resources that nothing, not even independence, could pull it out of its congenital anemia. "America lacks everything,"[56] De Pauw had pronounced. Raynal would not be as categorical in 1780. He was forced to admit that "the country will more or less attain self-sufficiency." But that was it; no progress was in sight. In these lands, which "are very rapidly degenerating," Raynal noted, "if ten million men ever find assured subsistence there, it will be a lot."[57] In the conclusive chapter, "Quelle idée il faut se former des treize provinces confédérées" (What Idea One Should Have of the Thirteen Confederated Provinces), he insisted once again on the poor quality of the land and its rapid depletion. In the south, the plantations were only producing a third of the tobacco they had been "formerly." Toward the north (Maryland, New York, and New Jersey), an acre that had once produced sixty bushels of wheat "only rarely now produces twenty," given the way "the ground has rapidly deteriorated there." Raynal's United States still looked a lot like the "unfortunate world" described by De Pauw: a few "lands that are almost generally bad or of mediocre quality"; further on, "swamps"; and "when the country rises, there is nothing but rebellious sands or frightful rocks, interspersed every now and then with pastures of a bulrush nature." Reading these lines written in the heady days of the Franco-American alliance by declared supporters of the insurgents gives a good idea of how deeply rooted the naturalist prejudice against America was—and helps us understand why Jefferson himself entered the fray.

Like Franklin, Jefferson wanted to get to the root of the evil and "scientifically" rehabilitate America in French opinion, which had been fed calamitous images of the New World for the past thirty years. The most urgent task, and one that was more profoundly political than any political or institutional controversy, was to dismantle and destroy the mass of prejudices, which John Adams, in a letter written in 1785, interestingly compared to the "Augean stables."[58] Jefferson's political apology of the United States consisted in demonstrating the country's physical and economic viability. Let others refute the criticism or reservations that were being shot off from various quarters against America's institutions. The emergency, the first priority for Jefferson, was to rectify the disastrous image of America as *deteriorating*. In order for American political innovation to acquire any credibility, the negative mythology that had held sway since Buffon's day had to be uprooted.

In his *Notes on the State of Virginia,* Jefferson responded to all the New World's critics—but with a subtle sense of their hierarchies and a perfect intuition of the best way to win over his anticipated readers—a Parisian intelligentsia raised on philosophy. He treated De Pauw (who was not even French) with contempt. He stridently but quickly chided Raynal, to whom he attributed the theory of white men's degeneration in America, and reproached him with having thoughtlessly affirmed, before repenting, that America had not produced any men of genius. It had already produced three: Washington, Franklin, and David Rittenhouse, which for three million inhabitants matched the European average.[59]

But above all, he refuted Buffon point by point, going so far as to fill several pages with his own tables listing the animals of each continent and giving their comparative weights. Weigh and judge, Jefferson told his French readers. First, judge: is it really fair to face America off against the rest of the world? Would it not in fact be more reasonable to oppose one part of the world to another and, since this is a European debate, compare America to Europe alone? Then weigh the animals, and see if your bear (153.7 pounds) holds its own against ours (410 pounds).[60] Most important, look at the discrepancy at the top of the lists: far larger than the bear, which is now your largest animal, we have the bison (1,800 pounds) and perhaps even a giant animal of which skeletons have been found and which the Delaware Indians assure us still exists in the northwest—a mastodon called the *mammoth.*

But even excluding this perhaps extinct champion of American immensity, the cross-examination sufficiently proved that Count Buffon had lacked prudence, if not discernment. His triple "opinion"—first, that animals found in both the Old and New Worlds were smaller in the latter; second, that those that were found only in the New World were small in size; third, that those that had been domesticated in both worlds had degenerated in America—was entirely invalidated by the comparative method (the very one he advised) if it was scrupulously applied. As for Monsieur de Buffon's considerations on the climate and the cold and damp nature of America in general, Jefferson practically forgave him for that. He simply noted that the humidity measured in Philadelphia seemed to be inferior to that of Paris or London; moreover, he voiced reservations—still respectfully—about the scientific prejudice underlying Monsieur de Buffon's opinions, which seemed to consider humidity intrinsically adverse to living things... No, decidedly, Jefferson concluded, there was no good reason for the "celebrated Zoologist" to write (he quoted him verbatim) that "la nature vivante est beaucoup moins agissante, beaucoup moins forte"[61] in America than in the Old World.

This was how a founding father, a reader of Montesquieu and the English constitutionalists and an architect of the New World's political landscape, took the stand for enlightened opinion; this was how he pleaded in America's favor, from a wanderer's, meteorologist's, and botanist's standpoint; this was how—completely deadpan—he surprisingly and amusingly compared precipitation figures, exhibited different types of plant life, and weighed and measured the slandered bestiary of the American homeland. Revitalizing "American nature" was no longer just a matter of natural history, but of history itself. It was as though America's political and diplomatic fate—the solidification of a foundling republic—also (chiefly?) depended on uprooting the extraordinarily detrimental prejudices about the new continent that had grown out of the philosophers' sciences.

From here on in, the battle would take place on the representational front. Such was the unspoken conclusion that dictated Jefferson's strategy. If he pursued the adversary into his own territory—that of natural history, where Buffon and his followers were hiding out—it was so he could calmly take over. It was up to the Americans to *speak* America. The land would not be as marshy as it was in Monsieur de Buffon's writings, it would be less "venomous" than De Pauw imagined it to be, and it would not be quite so "deteriorated" as the Abbé Raynal described it. Jefferson countered figures with figures, theories with observations, descriptions with specimens, disagreeable hypotheses with flattering possibilities (such as the existence of the giant mammoth)—a rhetoric of denigration with a poetics of glorification. The European gentlemen said the American tiger was cowardly? No matter: Jefferson threw a wondrous "megalonyx" at them. All's fair in image war...

Jefferson spared no effort in tugging intellectual France back to a more positive view of America. Nor money. Buffon was curious to see an elk; Jefferson sent him a moose from Vermont. The trophy and its shipping cost a breathtaking sixty guineas; but the truth, like the unsullied honor of the New World's great ruminants, was priceless. Despite Jefferson's financial sacrifices (he also procured a magnificent cougar skin), Monsieur de Buffon died in 1788 without keeping his promise to fully rehabilitate America's nature and humans. As for Raynal, whom the Revolution had at first coddled as the last remaining "patriotic" philosopher, he was brutally shoved off his pedestal when he dared to criticize the disorderly conduct of his revolution-

ary countrymen in 1791. De Pauw lived until 1799, but he turned his interest exclusively to the Greeks and Egyptians and, taking his own advice, "left
America in peace." The "dispute of the New World" was not over, but France
now had other things to quibble with America about than the size of the elk
or the megalonyx's fearlessness.

Michelet described 1790 as the French Revolution's finest hour and the
Fête de la Fédération as its euphoric pinnacle. It was doubtless also in 1790
that the celebration of America reached its apex in France, with the three
days of mourning decreed after Franklin's death. Though a touching event, it
was an isolated tribute. The Revolution became more radical and France was
soon cut off from any reference to America, except purely declamatory ones.
Advocates of the American model and the men who symbolized the Franco-
American alliance left the public sphere or lost their lives. Diplomatic relations grew tense between the federal government and revolutionary France,
whose militant minister in Washington, Genet, made increasingly belligerent declarations and attempted to form French commandos on American
soil in order to attack the British in the Antilles. The Terror, which impris-
oned Paine, alienated the French Revolution from the sympathies of an
American government careful to avoid any Jacobin contamination, as well as
a major part of American public opinion, which was shocked by the executions. Robespierre's fall did not bring about any great change. The United
States negotiated and signed a secret treaty with Great Britain (Jay's Treaty).
When Paris found out about this treacherous agreement, the dismayed
authorities of the Directory launched a violent press campaign against the
United States. French privateers started attacking American ships. Twenty
years after the "trade, friendship, and alliance" treaty, France and the United
States were in a state of belligerence. American historians call this the
"Undeclared War"; and it is true, it was a war in all but name. It makes for a
strange epilogue to a century of enlightenment in which, even before the
birth of the American nation had taken place, the French anti-American
image war had begun. To clean these Augean stables would be a labor more
Sisyphean than Herculean.

PART I

THE IRRESISTIBLE RISE OF THE YANKEE

What a commercial smell! as Joseph de Maistre said . . .
  Baudelaire

. . . and over there, no opera.
  Stendhal

 1

The Age of Contempt

The empire died a second death at Waterloo. "We saw the sons of the North again, and Ukrainian mares gnawed at the bark of the trees in our gardens once more."[1] The restored peace was a refuge for downtrodden France. Soon, though, a whole generation would complain of feeling suffocated in what had suddenly become a smaller world. You needed a passport to go from Paris to Pontoise. You also needed one (it cost ten francs) to go to America—or more precisely, to leave France. Back then, you could go to America without papers, a passport, or a visa.

But America was far, far away. Physically, it took a month of sailing in optimal conditions to get there—and up to eight weeks if the weather was bad. In 1817, Monsignor Dubourg, the unfortunate bishop of New Orleans, spent sixty-five days traveling from Bordeaux to Annapolis. (Though it is true that in 1795, fortune had not exactly smiled on Volney, who spent eighty-nine days crossing the sea. . .) Information circulated at the same snail's pace: it took over two months to receive an official dispatch, which of course did not facilitate diplomatic work. The French minister in Washington, Roux, found out about the Revolution of 1830 forty days after the fact. But in the 1830s, clippers came into use, and a drastic improvement appeared in the form of the Cunard line's steamers, which could make the crossing in fifteen days. The steamers started operating in 1840, but only to and from England; the first regular French line would not be established until 1864. The chronological gap is more telling than any number of statistics.

So, there was a great "distance." There was also what René Rémond has called the "remove" (*l'éloignement*):[2] the distance was not only geographical, it was also psychological. The Anglo-American war, with its blockade and counterblockade, had complicated transatlantic exchange. More important, the disappointments of the revolutionary period had cooled France's enthusiasm even before the Louisiana Purchase cut its umbilical cord with continental America. Immigration remained at a very low level even during peacetime and could not compensate for the loss of colonial ties.

A few Bonapartists emigrated in 1815–16, followed by a handful of utopians, mostly after 1848. These were modest exoduses: the disciples of Cabet and his *Icarie* were the most numerous, and they barely numbered five hundred. In any event, America as tabula rasa did not really appeal to social innovators. Significant in this respect was the Saint-Simonian movement's[3] change of heart in the early 1830s: even though Saint-Simon himself had been Lafayette's brother in arms and a member of the Order of Cincinnatus, and had always portrayed America as an example to meditate on, his spiritual inheritors voiced increasing criticism and discouraged the Saint-Simonian hive from swarming over to the New World.[4] And as for emigration by the impoverished, it was a trickle rather than a flood. All in all, René Rémond gives the average number of departures for America as 4,204 persons a year between 1820 and 1850. Not really enough to create strong ties between the motherland and the new country.

"Social disgrace," Rémond adds, played a part in this wave of emigration. It marked the image of the emigrant: he was often an outcast. This can also be seen in the literature of the time. In Balzac's novels, it is always good-for-nothings—such as Philippe Bridau, the unworthy brother of the gentle and gifted Joseph in *La Rabouilleuse*—who go off to America and come back hardened criminals. You really had to be a sordid (and secondary) character in the French novel of the first half of the nineteenth century to cross the sea. America is good enough for Philippe Bridau, but it seems worse than suicide for Vautrin (in Balzac's *Splendeurs et misères des courtisanes*). Stendhal's Fabrizio del Dongo does not even give it a thought; he is too happy in prison, close to the adorable Clelia Conti; Count Mosca considers it as a possibility for him but immediately rejects the idea: "In America, in the Republic, one must waste a whole day in paying serious court to the to the shopkeepers in the streets, and must become as stupid as they are; and over there, no opera."[5]

It seemed extraordinary to the French (and even more so to literary Parisians) that people could go live *over there* without being forced to by the most stark necessity or blatant disgrace. "If I stay here for a year, I will die," Talleyrand wrote to Madame de Staël.[6] The fact that America could wrench such a heartfelt cry from the most rakish of political expatriates must have made an impression on his illustrious correspondent. Talleyrand's despair was not disingenuous. It was fairly common in the small but turbulent French colony in Pennsylvania: there was a general sense of withering away, pining for Paris, loss of any sense of *existence*. Whether it was hell on earth or an eternal limbo, the United States engulfed exiles so completely that if by chance one reappeared, it was as though he had come back from the dead. This is how Renan described Lakanal's reappearance after being forced into exile in 1816 for his role in the Convention and on charges of regicide. His return after twenty-two years in America and reinstatement at the Institute in 1837 made for a scene right out of Balzac's *Colonel Chabert*: his colleagues at the Institute, aghast, received the minister of public instruction "like a phantom"—a ghost of the Convention transformed into an American zombie.

For the whole first half of the century, relations stagnated between France and the United States. Repeated friction over tax barriers and navigation rights soured what were already dismal relations. A serious crisis arose in 1834–35 concerning indemnities the United States had demanded; it was quickly stifled but left a bad aftertaste.[7] If calm prevailed on the whole, it was an apathetic calm. And one of the consequences of this general lack of interest was a "stability of images"—they were out of date with respect to American realities. America presented "the savage look of an almost universal forest that appears at the shores of the ocean and continues thicker and thicker into the land," Volney, obviously more used to the deserts of the Middle East, wrote in 1803.[8] In a volume published in 1816, the landscape had not budged an inch: "The territory of the United States is nothing but a kind of immense forest that starts at the ocean."[9] It would not change any time soon. René Rémond points out that until the 1840s, books whose information dated back to the days before the French Revolution were reproduced unchanged. In some cases, the "time lapse between events and news about them" was as long as a half century, and "it would be an illusion to believe it shrank after 1830."[10]

It was a gloomy time, but less sterile for anti-American imagery than we might think. Because even though descriptions and details were repeated without much modification, the same was not true of commentaries on or judgments of the United States. So we should correct the idea of a "stability of images"; the images were the same, but there was a change of perspective, a new angle on things. Little by little, "naturalist" attacks on the continent lost their bite or were worked into theodicies in which history took the place of natural history. And the debate over the institutional model lost its sense of urgency: even though France's republican fringe paid perfunctory homage to the land of "real republicanism," it never really managed to get enthusiastic about Andrew Jackson, a swaggerer who served two terms,[11] or to accept slavery's embarrassing continuation.

In the relative void left by this disaffection, a new discourse rose up against America: an *aesthetic* anti-Americanism, which would be the primitive base of the *cultural* anti-Americanism of the twentieth century. Following in the naturalists' and politicians' footsteps, artists, aesthetes, and hedonists started giving America the once-over. The new detractors, however, could not care less about Buffon's comparative tables, his trembling tigers, or his mute dogs. Nor were they interested in the political and legal debates over America's institutions that had gotten their elders so heated up: the fact that postcolonial America was a "democracy" was considered a given (a conviction that would not be as commonplace two generations later)—but it was a democracy they intended to judge by its literary, philosophical, and artistic output, as well as by the effect it had had on social mores, "manners," and behavior. The judgment was severe. It was not nature's "degeneration" in America that troubled them; in their view, America's artistic sterility was the only tragedy. They gave little thought to the risk of instability or anarchy threatening the Federal Republic: they railed against the leveling effect of a democracy obsessed with the "useful," hostile to talent, stifling to genius. They were not all of the school of "art for art's sake"; far from it. But Stendhal, though a political rebel and visceral opponent of the old world of priests and kings, created protagonists who regarded the United States just like Balzac the legitimist's. And when Beyle, behind the thin mask of his characters, attacked America for being a land of shopkeepers, he used the same words as Joseph de Maistre, a defender of the throne, the altar, and the executioner. Baudelaire, bringing the crusade to a head, simply compiled a thirty-year build-up of grievances against the American philistines to make his conclusion, then added a prophetic finishing touch: America's dependence on tools and machines.

By the end of a half-hearted half century, on the eve of the Civil War, France's image of the United States, despite its apparent stability, had been profoundly transformed by the muffled sabotage carried out, all hatred aside, by theocrats and liberals, mystics and rationalists, henchmen and saboteurs of the establishment.

Forget Rousseau, Ditch America

The great shift to an aesthetic satire of American democracy was foreshadowed at the tail end of the eighteenth century by a revisionist trend that was both anti-American and anti-Rousseauist. Here we have to take a quick look back to the years of the Directory, when Franco-American relations fell into a state of extreme disrepair and yet at the same time numerous books about the United States were published, mostly owing to political expatriates' return to France—for example, Ferdinand Bayard's *Voyage dans l'intérieur des États-Unis* (1797) and La Rochefoucauld-Liancourt's eight-volume *Voyages dans les États-Unis d'Amérique* (1799). In the hostile climate created by Jay's Treaty, between England and America, the reserved and sometimes hostile reports written by Frenchmen who had been to America out of sympathy for the country took on a certain weight. Even in works that were not fundamentally negative in their presentation of the republic across the sea, readers noticed (and the press commented on) the disappointments and doubts.

As an emigrant literature, the new mass of documents was marked by the disorder and frustration of individuals who had been brutally uprooted from their world of Parisian salons and plunged into a profoundly foreign universe. "All the Frenchmen I have seen up to now," noted one of the most even-handed of the bunch, not long after his arrival in Philadelphia, "like America little and still less the Americans, whom they depict as vain, greedy, grasping, and engaged in cheating in all of their business dealings."[12] The lack of manners (or bad manners), the inanity of the conversation, and the lack of interest in intellectual speculation on the part of their American hosts all made a bad impression on the French—and one they communicated to their contemporaries. Rudimentary social mores, an indifference to intellectual pursuits, and an utter incomprehension of art would be the first things these accounts noted in describing America. The disdainful attitude of the romantics for the philistine American has often been interpreted as a somewhat servile imitation of British contempt emanating from such writers as Frances Trollope and Major Hall. But though they did have a certain influence—we will discuss Mrs. Trollope's in a moment—there was still a very French first wave of unflattering reports, which were adopted all the more confidently by the reading public because of a preexisting bitterness, along with the fact that the authors' former sympathy for America lent their criticism even greater credibility.

Even before the French Revolution, Brissot, an enthusiastic admirer of the United States (where he had spent nine months), had been the first to propose that a consequence of American egalitarianism was the entire nation's tendency to orient its efforts toward the utilitarian "arts." But a Rousseauist faith led the future head of the Gironde to reach a more favorable conclusion about the Americans: surely it was better to have sturdy bridges, comfortable houses, and well-lit streets than the showy monuments Europe was so vain and proud about, he argued.[13] So-called accomplishments could be sacrificed for a more general and more widespread prosperity.

The travelers of the 1790s all made the same observation. They recognized the rapid material progress that was being made by the former English colonies, but their conclusions were very different from Brissot's. It was probably a matter of personality—and pedigree; there was a good share of the Constitutant Assembly's[14] social elite among the émigrés. But culture, literature, and the arts had also become more legitimate pursuits since the days of their persecution in France under the flag of equality. The tide had turned. Indeed, the Rousseauist reference that had legitimated Brissot's enthusiasm for America had been compromised by its popularity among radical militants. Since Thermidor, "revolutionary vandalism" had been in the hot seat, and the chosen enemy of artists and men of letters was no longer the pre-1789 "despotic" minister or censor, but rather the "terrorist of prey" who quoted Rousseau along with Marat.

With the widespread defection from pre-Revolutionary and Revolutionary Rousseauism went also a disaffection for the ideological belief in humanity's general progress, handed down to the same generation by the Enlightenment and particularly Condorcet. Accounts by French exiles seriously shook up this formerly solid conviction. Not that they were not generally conscious of America's economic development and often awed by how quickly it was taking place. Several who had fought in the American Revolution had a point of comparison and could easily measure the great strides made. But they all stressed the fact that material progress, instead of going hand in hand with similar progress in the arts and letters—not to mention the more impalpable realms of taste and wit—seemed on the contrary to be detrimental to cultural development. That was La Rochefoucauld-Liancourt's opinion, and would be Volney's in his 1803 *Tableau du climat et du sol des États-Unis d'Amérique*. The misgivings were considerable, and the American lesson, bitter. Everyone had expected the experiment of "young" America to confirm humanity's general and continuous progress. But there was nothing like that to be found, and the remarks of French observers produced "a contradictory and confusing picture of simultaneous progress and retrogression"[15] that was confusing for them, as well.

So, after giving up on the idea of man as fundamentally good, did the idea of progress as one and indivisible have to be shelved, too? Would every material advancement come with the trade-off of intellectual regression? On the not-so-distant horizon of these agonizing reconsiderations would loom Baudelaire, with his radical anti-Rousseauism, his aversion to progress, and his devastating vision of "Americanization."

Meanwhile, the writings of the little group that had chosen America as its port in the revolutionary storm would undermine the positive myth forged during the decade leading up to the Revolution by advocates and activists such as Brissot. Fits of bad humor punctuate their accounts, along with tirades about the boredom they suffered and the vulgar or vacuous nature of American life—all of which have a far more than anecdotal importance. In a climate where primitivism and progress had both fallen out of fashion, these men's disgust for their refuge, their satire of daily existence, and their damning assessment of intellectual life captivated French readers and created a new cliché: an America in which, despite all possible political good intentions, a normally constituted Frenchman— that is, someone interested in art, letters, and pleasure—could never be happy.

Hell and Damnation: From Talleyrand to Joseph de Maistre

Talleyrand's case is interesting. He was the most famous of dissatisfied expatriates. The eminent part he played in the Constitutant Assembly and the functions he would take on, after his return, as indispensable head of French diplomacy under the Directory, Consulate, Empire, and Restoration gave his aversion a particular weight. Even during the interregnum of his American exile, his wide-ranging connections and reputation as a peerless mind made his opinions resonate and his humors trickle down throughout Europe.

Talleyrand had hardly set foot onto American soil in 1794 when he took a sudden dislike to the country for which he had fled the radicalizing Revolution. He poured out caustic remarks at dinners in Philadelphia and the émigré meetings that gathered in Moreau de Saint-Méry's bookstore and printshop. His voluminous correspondence gave him the chance to communicate his disgust to numerous friends and acquaintances back in Europe. We have seen how he complained to Madame de Staël about America being a place where

everything annoyed him. His frustration at finding himself both far from public affairs and unsuccessful in financial dealings he had thought would be
lucrative were what lay behind a bitterness that was mostly aimed at the mediocrity of American life. Talleyrand was bored to death in hidebound Philadelphia for lack of entertainment and intrigues, banquets and banter. He was also
so wasted by the anemic environment that, according to La Rochefoucauld-
Liancourt, he ended up making "dutiful little witticisms no one appreciates."[16]
Spiteful toward the Americans, he found them, in turn, generally hostile to the
French. Liancourt noted that it was "impossible to have a worse opinion of
them in all regards, or to speak worse of them" than Talleyrand.[17]

The explanation Talleyrand found for this personality clash transformed
his personal aversion into a political issue: he discovered the Englishman
hiding inside the American. While many of his compatriots and companions
in exile were still, despite their disappointment, steeped in the fact that the
French and Americans had recently been brothers in arms and fought
together against the English, Talleyrand discovered with surprise and alarm
that the Americans were much more British than people in France were
ready to believe, and that even with all the resentment toward England that
had built up during the American Revolution, "America is nonetheless
utterly English."[18] The Anglo-American rapprochement was logical and
inevitable, considering the strength of old ties, the weight of current interests, and the advantage of a common language. In those Anglophobic times,
this was a disturbing observation. Its popularity would grow in France, and
in 1803 Volney would add a scientific justification to the mix.

America? "Thirty-two religions and only one dish to eat," was how the
former bishop of Autun summed it up. The witticism delighted Stendhal. It
brilliantly reflected the hedonistic side of what was still a very ancien-régime
satire of the United States. Many Frenchmen who were less nostalgic than
Charles-Maurice de Talleyrand-Périgord would enthusiastically subscribe to
this kind of mockery. The teeming "sects" and lack of culinary options (roast
beef with potatoes being lord and master of the dinner table) would be the
French traveler's two major complaints up to the end of the nineteenth century. The strong suit of Talleyrand's anti-Americanism was that it belittled
Philadelphia *amusingly*. The first step was to ridicule an America that had
been idealized to the point of cliché, after which the more serious shots of
criticism could be fired. The future Prince de Bénévent's "witticisms,"
whether witty or less so, shook the foundations of France's former idol.
Their success foreshadowed the country's abandonment of the solemn
myth it had forged of Washington's America as neo-Roman, agrarian, and
virtuous.

For Talleyrand himself, mockery was only a preamble. His showy disdain for America's graceless rusticity paved the way for "philosophical" criticism that aimed at being more profound. This was already taking shape in the *Mémoire sur les relations commerciales des États-Unis avec l'Angleterre* (Paper on the United States' Commercial Relations with England), which Talleyrand read before the Institute on Germinal 5, year VII.[19] The *Mémoire* might seem slight, compared to La Rochefoucauld-Liancourt's and Volney's voluminous tomes, but its immediate impact was significant. Talleyrand had been minister of the exterior under the Directory and retained the post under the Consulate. This was a critical time: fear of an Anglo-American alliance that would threaten the French Antilles was pushing France to regularize its relations with the United States; accordingly, the "scientific" paper Talleyrand presented before the Institute took on important political overtones. But the most revealing passage of the *Mémoire* was undoubtedly an anti-Rousseauist argument slipped into the economic and geopolitical exposé. Talleyrand drew up an unflattering anthropological table of the Americans he had observed. Putting aside the frivolous tone of his personal recriminations about the lack of urbanity in America's cities, he attempted to debunk the rustic American, the frontiersman, the farmer idealized by John Crèvecoeur's *Letters*.

In so doing, he blackened the image of America much more deeply: he took on the whole topos of egalitarian innocence and happy frugality spun around the young United States and Washington-Cincinnatus. So the merchants in Boston were now as unpleasant as the ones in Europe, fine. And maybe the Quakers were no longer what they had once been, if it came to that.[20] But it was frankly disturbing that the country-dwelling forest pioneer had sunk so far that he was now barely clinging to the lowest rung of the human ladder. Talleyrand had met these real Americans. He had even gone out to their distant settlements, into a wilderness Rousseauist fools had depicted as full of virtue and vitality. Balderdash, Talleyrand replied. Deep in the woods, you only find apathetic rubes living in shoddy cabins. And as far as proud farmers go, in these solitary lands, you only come across perverted peasants and indolent woodcutters who "look a lot like the indigenous savages they have replaced." This was the fin-de-siècle Creole's final incarnation: as the Anglo-Saxon colonist, lost on the frontier of savagery. Far from regenerating or at least energizing his native characteristics, he had become a pale echo of De Pauw's savage, inert and idiotic. "Poor and dispassionate," the phlegmatic brute was as lacking in morals as he was in intelligence: "his vices are worsened by his ignorance." And as for the so-called harmonies of unspoiled nature intoned by Bernardin de Saint-Pierre and Chateaubriand, the Europeans were free to believe or fantasize about them: these Americans-turned-savages did not have the slightest inkling of all that. They were blind to the grandiose spectacle surrounding them; they lacked all sensitivity, just as their city brothers lacked taste; and the only thing that interested them was the "number of chops needed to fell a tree." The new savages would have been accountants if they had not already been woodcutters. Talleyrand suggested that one could not live on the edge of the civilized world with impunity. Savagery overcame the unwary souls who got too close to it. Rural Americans were thus caught in the trap of a strange torpor, an "indolence" that rapidly dehumanized them. The journey into the American heartland took on a radically different meaning. Rather than being a source of replenishment or a rediscovery of humanity's robust childhood, wandering through America was a Conradesque trip into the heart of darkness: one had "the impression of traveling backward through the progress of the human spirit." The journey into the heart of America was progress thrown in reverse, a dismal dive into the abyss of primitivism. "One sinks lower and lower," Talleyrand said, losing "day by day one of the inventions our proliferating desires have made into necessities." Entering the wilderness did not mean "sloughing off the old man," but, rather, giving up and accepting a painful retraction toward absolute zero, the flatlining of the human spirit.

Volney's theory, which denounced "the extravagant mistake of writers who call a *new* and *virgin people* an assemblage of inhabitants from old Europe: Germans, Dutch, and especially Englishmen from the three kingdoms,"[21] only superficially contradicts Talleyrand's views. Despite the fact that he was still using a vocabulary stocked with the very constructs he repudiated, Talleyrand was not really describing a "youthful" world; he was describing a process of deculturation, mapping out a regression, stigmatizing a gradual decline: humanity's slow shipwreck on the shores of savagery. Volney's America, ripped from its mythical youthfulness, and Talleyrand's, where "the source" was only the last step in a topographical regression, were profoundly alike in countering the idea of America as "new." Deriding "savagery" and associating the Americans with the old inhabitants of Europe were two different tactics that went in the same direction: they both pointed to a disenchantment with America, which had ceased to be seen as a window on the state of nature and the site of a tough but invigorating confrontation between savagery and civilization.

Ostensibly, Volney's *Tableau du climat et du sol des États-Unis* is geographically precise and neutral. But its preface betrays a very different disposition. And since it appears at the beginning of a scientific work, the anti-American message is all the more striking—and its lesson all the more enduring in that the *Tableau* would be widely read for the next half century. It is time, Volney stressed for his readers in 1803, for the French to gain a more accurate idea of the United States "by rectifying a few prejudices established in a time of enthusiasm."[22] Yet already, back in the heady days of the Franco-American love affair, Raynal had exhorted the French to "resist the torrents of opinion and enthusiasm."[23] For lack of time, Volney would not draw out his reflections on the United States' political and social state; science came first! There was too much to be said, too many wrong opinions to right: it would have to wait for another time.

Of course, this was all just a rhetorical pose. Along the way, Volney would produce an energetic summary of his impressions of America. Like the other emigrants, he bulked up his testimony with the weight of personal experience. He increased his credibility by stressing his original plan to stay in the United States over the long haul: contrary to many others (such as Monsieur de Talleyrand), he had been in no rush, he wrote, to get back to France once the danger was over. It was the Americans' animosity, starting in the spring of 1798, that had forced him to leave. He had fled the Terror only to find "real *terrorism*"[24] against the French in America. It is a loaded word. This American-style terrorism had opened his eyes, sharpened his gaze. "I will say it regretfully: my research has not led me to find in the Anglo-Americans the fraternal and benevolent dispositions that several writers seem to believe we enjoy." Volney, like Talleyrand before him, had made precisely the opposite discovery. The Americans had remained eminently British; "toward us, they have conserved a marked tinge of the national prejudices of their original metropolis." Our brief time as brothers in arms did not change a whole lot, Volney added, unwittingly producing a future theme: these prejudices had been but "feebly altered by our alliance during the insurrection, [and] very powerfully revived of late by invectives"—an allusion to the France-bashing campaigns unleashed during the Undeclared War. American politicians railed against the French, while teachers forced "prizes for defamatory developments and dissertations against the French" on their students—for instance, the *collège de Princetown* had put Francophobic subjects on its entrance examinations two years in a row, in 1797 and 1798.[25]

But it was vital that the "rectification" get to the heart of the matter. Above and beyond the crisis of 1798, and independent of the alarm caused by England and America's consanguinity, Volney wanted to demonstrate that the United States had betrayed the political promise of its inception and was already a traitor to its own ideals. Right when Joseph de Maistre was dismissing the United States as a defective and thus unfeasible entity, Volney, using a completely different method and writing for a completely different audience, put forth the notion that America had turned its back on the principles, sound in and of themselves, that had presided over its foundation: that it had "retrograded." Between the end of the Revolutionary War and the creation of the federal government, Volney affirmed, ideals and behaviors had profoundly degenerated: there had been "an alteration of good faith and primal simplicity."[26] Probity, pure morals, a sense of justice between the nation's citizens: "in almost all of these matters, the nation has regressed from the principles of its formation." De Maistre wanted nothing from this republic other than its disappearance, which he believed, moreover, would be a natural consequence of its basic unsuitability; Volney, perhaps more seriously, described a society that was visibly degenerating. Whatever the Americans might say, whatever their last remaining "supporters" purported, over the course of the previous fifteen years "there [had] reigned, in the United States—proportionally to its population, the amount of business, and multiplicity of combinations—no more financial thrift, good faith in transactions, decency in public morality, moderation in party spirit, or care in education and instruction than in most of the nations of old Europe."[27]

Maybe it was better after all, Volney concluded, to have postponed his political description of the United States, because "its results might have appeared bizarre." Especially, he added, if it meant discussing America in terms of a Frenchman's potential "happiness," because in that case, "I would not have encouraged many of our Frenchmen to follow my example"[28]—the example of expatriation, which he would not embody for very long.

Joseph de Maistre and America as Anathema

Disqualifying America was a trend throughout Europe, but it took a different shape in each country. In Germany, Herder produced an anthropological and theological version of the naturalist theory of the "unfortunate continent": America did not fit into providence's grand scheme, and the savage was nothing but a "dead branch" on the tree of humanity. Hegel construed the same exclusion, but with a different logic: America was purely natural and physical and therefore out of bounds, in his opinion. Absent from the gravitational field of universal history, excluded from the Europe-Asia-Africa triad, America was confined to the limbo of a congenital "impotence."[29] This was an "error to the second degree," comments Antonello Gerbi: Hegel backed up a specious argument with inaccurate data (taken from the anti-American natural historians of the previous century). And it hardly seems open to question that Hegel had principally gone sifting through the dubious docket put together by the naturalists of the Enlightenment to find justification for an exclusion he had decided on a priori.

The most vehement repudiation of America in the first years of the nineteenth century drew on Herder's lessons. It was given a new direction by a writer often annexed to France, like his country: the Savoyard Joseph de Maistre. An expatriate who vociferously refused to be called an *émigré,* De Maistre left Savoie after it was taken over during the Revolution, moving first to Bern, then St. Petersburg, in the service of the king of Sardinia. An impassioned spokesman for "reactionary thought" (as Cioran would say), a radical antidemocrat and paradoxical theocrat, the author of *Considerations on France* and *St. Petersburg Dialogues* considered the United States of America's very existence a regrettable aberration, but fortunately a temporary one. He anathematized all the subspecies of the *Homo americanus:* the American European was a lost soul, and the savage, a reprobate. This was not his most original conclusion. The combined strategic defense of the Native Americans and the colonists adopted by Jefferson and his friends in the 1780s had provoked an ironic reaction in Volney, who found their adulation of the savages strange, "as if, through some bizarre fiction, they had set themselves up as the representatives and avengers of the natives, their predecessors."[30] Turn-of-the-century anti-Americans rebutted this apologetic solidarity with a negatively symmetrical composite. But with De Maistre, the double condemnation took a distinctive shape: as an utter anti-Rousseauist, he stamped America-bashing, which had been completely secular until then, with the seal of Catholic dogma. For him, stigmatizing the savage on theological grounds and politically disqualifying the American republic were part and parcel of the same fight against the Enlightenment. The idealized savage was a creature born of Rousseau's sophistry, and American democracy was no more than a philosophical fetish. From *Considerations on France* in 1797 to the *St. Petersburg Dialogues* in 1809 (published posthumously in 1821), De Maistre combined antinaturalist and antimodern criticism of America, a tactic Baudelaire would directly and openly continue.

De Maistre pretty much dismissed the United States as early as 1797 in *Considerations on France.* A scathing counterrevolutionary attack, *Considerations* aimed to show that the French republic was not feasible; America was thus a conspicuous thorn in the critic's side. De Maistre brings up the subject fairly late in the game: "At the most one could mention America, but I have replied in advance to this by saying that the time has not yet come to cite it." A footnote refers back to the fourth chapter: "Can the French Republic Last?" There, however, America goes unnamed, and De Maistre merely repeats dogma borrowed from the Enlightenment (and the hated Rousseau) on the impossibility of great republics: "So-called *Fortune* [has been] tirelessly throwing the die for over four thousand years. Has LARGE REPUBLIC ever been rolled? No. Therefore, that *number* is not on the die."[31] The explicit conclusion: republican France was a pipe dream. The implicit conclusion ("I have replied in advance"): the United States did not exist. De Maistre then gets caught up in the game and makes a strange wager about the city of Washington: "One could bet a thousand to one that the city will not be built, that it will not be called *Washington,* or that the Congress will not meet there."[32] No luck for the senator: De Maistre would lose his prudently versatile gamble three times over.

Confronted with America, this vigorously logical thinker got caught up in unbridled wishful thinking: "All those things that are really new in their government, all those things that are the result of popular deliberation, are the most fragile parts of the system; one could scarcely combine more symptoms of weakness and decay." And even more heedless wishes: "Not only do I doubt the stability of the American government, but the particular establishments of English America inspire no confidence in me."[33] They would make do without it. . .

After dooming the United States to failure, the only thing left to do was sentence the savage to death. The *Homo democraticus* does not come out smelling like a rose in De Maistre's world, but the "noble savage" invented by overgenerous missionaries or ill-intentioned philosophers had no worse enemy. Rousseau's most serious mistake as "one of the most dangerous sophists of his century" was that he "constantly mistook the savage for the primitive man, although the savage is and can only be the descendant of a man detached from the great tree of civilization by some transgression."[34] "Absolutely no precisions on the nature of this transgression," Cioran would note.[35] Clearly that is not of great importance. What is important is the caricature. In an inversion of the primitivist topos as radical as it was impudent, Joseph de Maistre made the savage out to be the very model of the "degraded" being. The savage's person, language, and customs did not reflect any real origins; they were nothing but "debris," "ruins." The savage was tossed back into time immemorial and shackled with an original sin as monumental as it was mysterious. He was a guilty version of Herder's "dead branch"—as punishment for some monstrous crime, he had been cut from the tree and left on a faraway continent to become the atrophied being the Europeans had discovered. In describing the savage, De Maistre took on the same tone De Pauw had used to depict the Indians (indeed, he would openly acknowledge De Pauw's influence in his *On the Sovereignty of the People*)[36] or Talleyrand's in describing the frontiersmen. "It is this final degree of base stupidity that Rousseau and his like call the *state of nature*."[37] Philosophy had whitewashed this "appalling state" into a bucolic golden age in order "to prop up its vain and culpable declamations against the social order."[38] The savage was hideous and idiotic, with a "curse . . . written not only on his soul but even on the exterior form of his body." The "formidable hand" of providence had come down on "these condemned races" [*races dévouées*], De Maistre added: the savage was a *devotus,* a sacrificial creature: "He is visibly condemned; he has been stricken in the deepest layers of his moral being."[39] The most indispensable qualities for survival—foresight and perfectibility— had been erased from his consciousness. With every passing century, this pseudo-primitive moved further and further away from man's true, divine origin, as inexorably as, for Talleyrand, humanity lost a little of itself with every step into the wilderness.

Joseph de Maistre's was of course an anti-Rousseauist and antiphilosophical crusade, but it was also indisputably an anti-American one, using theology to reformulate the Enlightenment's naturalist "malediction." The new America irritated him as a paragon of detestable modernity; savage America exasperated him as the most shameless of philosophical lies.

Now, the early nineteenth century was a turning point for French representations of America. It was a moment that would be retrospectively associated with Chateaubriand, in whose poetic prose the savage's sublime nature and America's grandeur still intertwined. With the same generosity that De Maistre criticized in the missionaries smitten with their biblical Indians, Chateaubriand's exalted vision of America came between the cold gaze of the anti-Rousseauists and their designated victim, the sacrificial savage. Chateaubriand was thus repeating in the realm of fiction the charitable, albeit ambivalent gesture of protection extended to the Indians both by missionaries and humanitarian "advocates." But all the trees along the Meschacebée, "from the maple to the tulip tree and from the tulip tree to the hollyhock,"[40] could not hide the forest of warning signs of a disenchantment with America. Long before the Europeans became aware of what was clearly a much more rapid extinction than the one Raynal had foreseen, the Indian was brutally expelled from humanity by Joseph de Maistre and from history by Herder. But wasn't he also expelled, with a poetic flourish, by Chateaubriand himself? Wasn't the dead Natchez child painted by Delacroix (and now at the Metropolitan Museum in New York) the very allegory of the Indians' demise? And, in the end, were Chateaubriand's magnificent stylistic embellishments pronouncing anything other than a funeral rite? The first Indian page Chateaubriand ever wrote—the famous night described in a footnote of the *Essai sur les révolutions* in 1797—was already a testament to an extinct race. Charlevoix and Lafitau dressed up the Indians in Old Testament garb; Chateaubriand embalmed them in Christ's mercy. His romantic savages would bring tears to readers' eyes (which probably had Joseph de Maistre cursing him), but their epic or sublime profiles were nevertheless vanishing outlines, faces fading away to nothingness in the harsh, too-bright glare of Chateaubriand's words—like the frescoes that vanish as they appear at the end of *Fellini Roma*.

"The description of *savage* America would naturally lead to the picture of *civilized* America," Chateaubriand wrote in his preface to *The Natchez* in 1826, "but to me this picture would appear misplaced in a work of the imagination."[41] So he transported "civilized America" into his *Voyages*: "History will thus form a sequel to history, and the different subjects will not be intermingled." It would be hard to better express the split between the Indian myth and American history. For Chateaubriand, too, the Indian was no longer a part of history. True, he had gone above and beyond it into the sublime and epic status of a lost race, but still, he was excluded. Joseph de Maistre could stigmatize in Chateaubriand's writings "mistakes of charity" in the Indians' favor, as in Las Casas, Charlevoix, or Lafitau. But in the end, Chateaubriand did not make the "extravagant mistake" Volney had condemned; he believed neither that America was young nor that the savage would survive.

From Mrs. Trollope to Arrigo Beyle

Whether they were epic savages, monumental reprobates, or unnecessary extras in the progress of the intellect, the Indians faded out into the horizon of myth or tumbled into one of history's black holes. By rising above and beyond or simply falling by the wayside, the Indians were evicted from European writings in the early nineteenth century; they were herded into "imaginative" works and, later, penned into the wildlife preserve of children's literature. The rich image of America was markedly impoverished by their disappearance. Where the smoke of Indian camps had once risen, factory smoke would soon billow, but for the time being, villages with pompous names—Rome, Paris, Syracuse—would make travelers snicker. Weedy little towns took on airs of great capitals. Cities without monuments amassed clumps of buildings without distinction. The habitat lacked elegance, the clothing lacked refinement, and manners were simply lacking. . . Forgetting their recent enthrallment with Franklin, French travelers quickly grew tired of so much austerity: the pseudo-Quaker outfit had worked wonders at Louis XVI's court, but running into it every day on the streets of Philadelphia discouraged Voltairian Frenchmen for whom "one day, boredom was born of uniformity." Soon all the showy simplicity would be judged hypocritical.

To be fair, the French were not the only ones criticizing the plodding American lifestyle. When "revenants'" accounts started to wane, the French looked to their British neighbors. For a twenty-year period, from 1815 to 1835, the English became Europe's purveyors of ill-will against their former colonies. France was just entering a new period of Anglomania, the second in forty years. Whether it was horses or novels or cleaners, England set the tone. Guizot gave well-attended lectures on English history in 1828 and 1829, and Parisians went to London to get their fill of jockeys, medieval adventures, and redingotes. Who could be better suited to criticize the Americans than the English?

British writers, travelers, and memoirists did not hold back. The War of 1812 revived an ill-suppressed rancor. Several retired military officers, such as Captain Hall and Major Hamilton, embarked on new campaigns, pen in hand, against America's mediocrity. The new skirmish only heightened Yankee patriotism, to which the British responded with a volley of devastating books. The first success in this vein would go to Basil Hall, with *Travels in America in the Years 1827 and 1828* (1829). Copycats would follow, such as Thomas Hamilton, author of *Men and Manners in America* (1833). Each of these books was an unabashed success, but among the stiff competition, the trophy—first British, then European—would unquestionably go to Frances Trollope for *Domestic Manners of the Americans,* published in 1832.

Frances Trollope's itinerary was far from ordinary. Born in 1779 in Bristol, the daughter of an eccentric pastor and inventor with a fondness for Petrarch and drink, in 1809 she married a lawyer whose hopes for an inheritance were dashed and whose agricultural business turned into a disaster. In 1827, she resolved to accept an invitation from her good friend Fanny Wright, a militant abolitionist and feminist who had founded a utopian pedagogical community in Tennessee for the purpose of sheltering and schooling the children of runaway slaves. Setting out from England with one of her sons and two young daughters (leaving the future novelist Anthony Trollope at home), Frances Trollope discovered on her arrival that the school was nothing but a few roofless log cabins in a malaria-infested forest. Keeping her chin up in the face of adversity, she reached Cincinnati, where she opened a strange "bazaar," part fashion boutique, part art gallery and proto–cultural center. The building, which she had decorated herself, did not go unnoticed. Thomas Hamilton saw a "Greco-Moorish-Gothic-Chinese" inspiration.[42] Miss Martineau described it as "Gothic-Greco-Turco-Egyptian" and defined it less charitably as "the great deformity of the city."[43] After the business went bankrupt and Mrs. Trollope left in 1831, her bazaar was turned into a dance school, then the headquarters of a scholarly association, and last—and most lastingly—a well-known brothel.

Luckless in her American undertakings, Mrs. Trollope sailed back to Great Britain in August 1831. She had left it a Whig, feminist, and reformer. She returned disgusted with America, egalitarianism, uncultivated social climbers, insolent servants, shady religious sects, and greedy shopkeepers. At fifty-five, having returned to the flock and reconciled with Britannia, this energetic woman drew from her American mishaps the stuff of literary triumph: with four English editions and four American ones in the first year, followed by rapid French, Spanish, German, and Dutch translations, *Domestic Manners of the Americans* afforded her short-lived material comfort (by 1834, she and her husband were once more fleeing their creditors) and a notoriety that would last longer than her royalties.

Chateaubriand enjoyed it. Stendhal reveled in it. Reading *Domestic Manners* tends to leave you wondering why. Its portrait of America circa 1830 (Mrs. Trollope does not breathe a word about her personal misadventures) is often long-winded. And the moral of the story is succinct: "I do not like them. I do not like their principles. I do not like their manners. I do not like their opinions."[44] Fanny Trollope had a flair for bad-mouthing, but little humor and no inventiveness. Her complaints all derive from a few well-known charges: the average American's lack of culture; the innate mercantilism, vulgar manners, and unrefined amusements; the country's ugliness in general and particularly its cities'; the population's ineptitude for *délassement* (she uses the French term); and the social separation of the two sexes, with men and women less than eager to rub shoulders beyond the bare minimum. None of it is groundbreaking, and Mrs. Trollope herself does not make any claims of being original, but rather exhaustive, when she recapitulates the shortcomings that have been "so often mentioned."[45]

But that was probably the key to her success: compiling prejudices that had been forming since the Revolutionary War, she lent the authority of things seen and experienced to a set of negative characteristics that had already been largely accepted by the cultivated European public. As a daughter of the Enlightenment, she had not forgotten her natural history or the lessons proffered by Buffon and repeated by Robertson. Her story opens with a vision of unspeakable desolation: miry waters, sterile land, "congeries of leaves that have been rotting since the flood."[46] She is describing the Mississippi and its delta. Mrs. Trollope invoked Dante, but she was also rewriting Cornelius De Pauw. French readers were not disoriented. There were other reasons for the particular zeal she aroused in France. This Francophilic

Englishwoman, who sprinkled her tale with gallicisms, did not hesitate to approvingly quote a witticism Talleyrand had made to Napoleon, for example. She especially valued the exchange of ideas and defended the art of conversation as it was practiced in the French salons of the Enlightenment, considering it a harmonious balance of politeness and conviction, rhetorical elegance and intellectual audacity. The Americans, who had "no charm, no grace in their conversation,"[47] were the perfect counterexample of this. This somewhat eccentric neoconservative gave the American Republic's ideological enemies cause for joy without ruffling the literary Left, especially since she was still faithful to her youth on two important points: anticlericalism and abolitionism. But then, even without her personal trajectory—which, when all is said and done, was that of a more settled but still bohemian leftist—Fanny Trollope would not have had much trouble appealing to French readers who agreed with her even before they opened her book.

"I Should Get Bored in America"

Stendhal's case speaks volumes. In 1834, he annotated Mrs. Trollope's book with relish. He also quickly requested her next book, on the Belgians. Every detail of *Domestic Manners of the Americans* pleased and amused him. He was of course delighted to come across Talleyrand, who, when asked by Napoleon what the Americans were like, briskly replied, "Sire, ce sont de fiers cochons et des cochons fiers." Fanny Trollope approved of the definition;[48] Stendhal applauded, noting "Good" in the margin.[49]

But to be honest, she was preaching to the converted. *The Red and the Black* had been published in 1830, two years before the English version of *Domestic Manners*. In the first chapter, "A Small Town," Stendhal immortalized Verrières. It opens with the unforgettable rapid-fire X-ray of "one of the prettiest [towns] in the Franche-Comté," which becomes the symbol of suffocating provinciality. But perhaps less remembered is the chapter's strange conclusion. "In actual fact, [the] wise folk keep everyone there in the grip of the most irksome *despotism*. This dirty word sums up why it is that life in a small town is unbearable to anyone who has dwelt in the great republic of Paris." Paris versus Verrières, period? No, Paris versus America. Stendhal concludes, "Public opinion—and you can just imagine what it's like!—exercises a tyranny that is every bit as *mindless* in small towns of France as it is in the United States of America."[50] America is stupidity's universal benchmark, tyranny's yardstick. America equals one, two, three, a thousand Verrières. . .

In all his later novels, Stendhal would simply restate a rhetorical question he had already resolved on the third page of *The Red and the Black*. In *The*

Charterhouse of Parma, as we have seen, Count Mosca, worried for Fabrizio, dismisses the possibility of America. Fabrizio himself dreams only of Clelia and does not think of America at all. But the thought had occurred to him, a few years earlier, on coming back from Waterloo. What would he do with his life? Unconvinced of his vocation as a prelate, "Fabrizio at first utterly rejected the notion of entering the priesthood; he spoke of going to New York, of becoming a citizen, a soldier in the Republic of America." In this first deliberation, the Duchess is the one voicing the standard remarks about life in America: "What a mistake you're making! There will be no war for you to wage, and you'll fall back into café life, only without elegance, without music, without love affairs. . . . Believe me, for you as for me, an American life would be a sad business." And Stendhal continues: "She explained to him the cult of the god dollar, and the respect that must be paid to merchants and artisans in the street, who by their votes determine everything."[51] *Lucien Leuwen,* a novel that is much more French and more rooted in contemporary history than *The Charterhouse of Parma,* repeats the terms of a dilemma more than a few politically "imprudent" young men had been confronted with in France—starting with Auguste Hervieu, a painter and conspirator who had been taken in by the Trollopes and joined them on their American expedition. The affable Lucien Leuwen, expelled from Polytechnique for republicanism, full of sympathy for conspiring noncoms using Roman pseudonyms in their subversive tracts, wonders the same thing: "It would be more worth while if we all took ship for America . . . would I go on board with them?" Once again, the reflection does not turn to America's advantage. "Over this question Lucien brooded for a long time as he walked with a troubled air. 'No,' he said at last . . . 'What's the good of deceiving oneself? . . . I should get bored in America, among men who are perfectly just and reasonable, if you like, but vulgar, and with no thought of anything but dollars.'" The confession is also a profession of faith. Stendhal is announcing his creed, an aesthetic and hedonistic anti-Americanism *à la française:* "I can't live with people incapable of subtle ideas, however virtuous they are; I'd a hundred times rather the elegant ways of a corrupt court. Washington would bore me to death; I prefer to find myself in the same drawing-room as M. de Talleyrand. No, the feeling of esteem is not all in all for me; I need the pleasures offered by an ancient civilization."

The monologue is a first in the French novel: anti-Americanism is presented as an existential prejudice capable of winning out over the subject's convictions. The cultural has already triumphed over the political. Stendhal stresses this very deliberately: "All right, you ass, then support the corrupt governments produced by this ancient civilization." But it is no use reprimanding (himself), and the sincere Lucien, like his clearheaded author, brings his speech to a crescendo: starting with Talleyrand, he goes on to prefigure Baudelaire.

> I am horrified by the tedious common sense of an American. But stories of the life of young General Bonaparte, victor at the bridge of Arcole, carry me off my feet; for me they're Homer, Tasso, and a hundred times better than that. American morality seems to me horribly vulgar, and when I read the works of their famous men I feel only one desire, never to come across them in the world. That model country seems to me the triumph of stupid, egotistic mediocrity—, and, on pain of death, one has to pay court to it.[52]

Courting mediocrity, "paying serious court to the shopkeepers in the street," respecting "merchants and artisans in the street"—Lucien, Mosca, and the Duchess all speak with one voice: Stendhal the ventriloquist's.

Almost a century later, André Maurois would have his Princeton students read *The Charterhouse of Parma*. "They came to class dissatisfied." It is too long. Too strange. " 'And besides,' said Plug, 'that Stendhal is anti-American. There's a really mean dig at the 'god dollar.' . . . In 1830, was it already 'in' to say bad things about America?'"[53] Young Plug's intuition was not wrong; circa 1830, it really was "in" in Europe to sneer at America. Mrs. Trollope's success did not exhaust the possibilities. In 1842, Charles Dickens set out for the United States and came back with some caustic *American Notations*. But it would take a novel, *Martin Chuzzlewit,* to empty out his anti-American bag. Dickens's accusations are both more moralizing and more social in nature; they would probably not have amused Stendhal as much as Monsieur de Talleyrand's barbs—but there is no way of knowing; when Dickens's novel started appearing in print in 1843, Stendhal had just died. All that remained were Stendhal's novelistic fabrications, which, in book after book, dressed up British anti-Americanism in French garb, giving Talleyrand more weight than Washington and opera a certain priority over democracy.

Tocqueville & Co.: "A Sugar-Coated America"

"I believe there is no country, on the face of the earth, where there is less freedom of opinion on any subject in reference to which there is a broad difference of opinion, than in this"—America, of course. A rough draft from Tocqueville? No, a letter by Dickens.[54] The novelist wrote these lines to John Forster after he came back from his American trip in 1842. As for Tocqueville, in 1835 he wrote in the first volume of *Democracy in America:*

"I know no country in which, speaking generally, there is less independence of mind and true freedom of discussion than in America. . . . In America the majority has enclosed thought within a formidable fence. A writer is free inside that area, but woe to the man who goes beyond it."[55] Tocqueville and Dickens agree: there was nothing more problematic in America than having unorthodox opinions. Baudelaire would soon repeat it, in one of his articles on Poe: nothing was harder over there than exercising the two rights of man all the Declarations had left out—the right to contradict oneself and the right to take one's leave.[56] These lines by Tocqueville and the chapter they are from, "The Omnipotence of the Majority," would become, in France, the most readily cited from *Democracy in America* for over a century. In this respect, we can speak of an anti-American use of Tocqueville; it is this use and not Tocqueville himself we will discuss here. We will need to take some distance from his works—as well as some chronological liberties—and evoke the rarely ingenuous "revival" of the *Democracy* by anti-Americans of the next two generations. It will be a glance back at Tocqueville, downstream.

A play that caused a flap in Paris in 1873, Victorien Sardou's *L'Oncle Sam,* depicted a young Frenchman striking out for the United States with *Democracy in America* under his arm. Fortunately Madame Bellamy, an experienced compatriot, warns him against such dangerous reading: "It is a sugar-coated America—beware!"[57]

"The majority in the United States," Tocqueville had written, "takes over the business of supplying the individual with a quantity of ready-made opinions."[58] It is as though the *doxa,* which he unmasked across the Atlantic, had avenged itself in France: after his death in 1859, Tocqueville became a prisoner to his caricature. For several decades, he was presented as a man with only one thing to say (which was judged untrue: that the United States was essentially democratic); and as a militant with a single cause (promoting the idea of democracy by systematically praising America). He would be simultaneously and contradictorily portrayed as an abstract dogmatist and a patent lobbyist, as well as a pontificating prophet constantly proved wrong by events. The American Civil War did not help his reputation. Tocqueville had dismissed as very improbable any desire for secession by one or several states. And even if, against all odds, such a thing should occur, he had guaranteed that no armed conflict would result and that the Union would come to terms with these defections.[59] This double "mistake" would be put to his discredit all the more because his book had nothing to offer either camp during or after the war. Supporters of the Southerners could hardly be proud of the very negative portrait Tocqueville had painted of the South, which he depicted as unable to compete with the Puritan and democratic North. And

as for those in favor of the Union, for whom the slavery issue was fundamental, they were irritated by Tocqueville's position: after affirming his abolitionist principles, he still concluded that upholding the status quo for as
long as possible was the South's only chance for survival.

Writing off *Democracy in America* in three words—"sugar-coated America"—Victorien Sardou pretty much summed up the reductive impression of
Tocqueville held by his 1873 Parisian audience, which had not needed
Madame Bellamy's advice in order to stop reading him. Nowadays, Tocqueville's book strikes us as uncommonly high-minded and intellectually isolated, but the image its detractors gave of it up to the end of the nineteenth
century was very different. Whenever it was mentioned (it was almost never
quoted), it was most often lumped together with works by Gustave de Beaumont, Tocqueville's traveling companion, and Michel Chevalier or Philarète
Chasles.[60] These books were not very similar, yet they were criticized for
being dictated by the same apologist bias. Their authors were presented as a
little club, a clique. Critics said: look how they scratch each other's backs!
Look how Monsieur de Tocqueville gives his pal De Beaumont such good
press.[61] Look how Philarète Chasles, fifteen years later, defers to Tocqueville's
and Chevalier's authority on the very first page of his *Études sur la littérature
et les moeurs des Anglo-Américains au XIXe siècle* (1851).[62] For the early anti-
Americans of the 1880s, this warranted throwing them into the same basket.

If these so-called henchmen of America and democracy played a part in
the birth of French anti-Americanism, it was despite themselves, by being
misused. The anti-American discourse that took off in the 1880s exploited
them in two overlapping, and often overlapped, ways. First, by artificially
conflating the works and making this corpus out to be an American lobby, it
justified itself as a counterattack. A secret plan was decried in Tocqueville
and Chasles—one that preached imitating America, though this was not in
fact to be found in either work. In Tocqueville, descriptions were not at all
prescriptive, and Chasles explicitly warned his readers against the temptation to copy America and its institutions: "are the decrepit children of our
jaded world right in imitating, despite their past, an American autonomy of
which they do not even have the seeds? Will they succeed in the attempt? We
might well be doubtful."[63] Paying such remarks no heed, their detractors
gained an argumentative legitimacy from this supposed conspiracy.

A second use of Tocqueville and his "group" appeared at the end of the
century: a certain number of "con" propositions were singled out in the
works of reputedly "pro" authors in order to bulk up the docket of anti-
American accusations. *Democracy in America* was revisited—but this time as
an abandoned monument where each visitor took the stone he wanted for his

own little hovel. The fragmentary hijacking of the work was facilitated by its state of neglect. It was "a celebrated book, about which everybody speaks and which scarcely anybody reads now-a-days,"[64] observed the author of *American Life* in 1892. Current Tocqueville specialists say he was right. During its author's lifetime, *Democracy*'s exposure was a glass-half-full, glass-half-empty situation. Published in two volumes in 1835 and 1840, the book had a first printing of 500 copies and "never went beyond 10,000 copies in its author's lifetime. It therefore had few readers," writes Françoise Mélonio in her introduction to the first *Democracy*, "but what readers they were!" She goes on to cite Royer-Collard, Guizot, Chateaubriand, Vigny, and Lamartine.[65] So it was only relatively unsuccessful? Successful but limited to a specific circle? Assessment of the book's initial reception varies. But it is undeniable that an eclipse followed. Even as Parisians were applauding *L'Oncle Sam,* and the Third Republic, for better or for worse, was settling in, Tocqueville was heading into "long-lasting neglect."[66]

The only people who did not completely forget about him were the anti-American polemicists. Few of them quoted him, as we have noted, and no one bothered to refute him. But his name was ritually pronounced and then immediately cast aside. Late-nineteenth-century anti-Americans never tired of repeating the theme of "a sugar-coated America." Their fundamental charge was the same as Sardou's: Tocqueville had sugar-coated the United States, selling the French his democratic America like a fraudulent delicacy. Early anti-Americans were remarkably unanimous on this point, and we will see their opinion reappear later on in very different political families: Frédéric Gaillardet would give his book the title *L'Aristocratie en Amérique* as an invitation to his readers to "turn Tocqueville inside out," and the Baron de Mandat-Grancey would apologize for being somewhat related to the viscount, but pride himself on not sharing any of Tocqueville's detestable democratic opinions. Paul de Rousiers, a representative sent by the Musée Social, would denounce Tocqueville's mistake in "giv[ing] French people the idea that affairs in the United States are entirely managed by the democracy," saying he was not "excusable for forming such an opinion."[67] This Tocqueville-as-straw-man was often mirrored, in preambles and prefaces, by a Tocqueville-as-foil. The former was synonymous with fraud, the second with failure: he had not discovered America's secrets; they remained to be exposed. In short, his book needed to be rewritten. This was Paul Bourget's strategy in 1895. He only mentioned Tocqueville in order to stress his inadequacy: "The book that sums up such a society remains to be written."[68] At last Bourget was here. . .

Disdained and speedily dismissed by the majority of anti-American polemicists up to the end of the nineteenth century, Tocqueville paradoxically came back into favor at the turn of the century, as though by a new turn of the wheel of fate. The discovery was made that it was not impossible to use him, despite himself, for the right cause, and that weapons against America could be culled from the *Democracy*. One book in particular was a turning point in its double use of Tocqueville: Émile Boutmy's *Éléments d'une psychologie politique du peuple américain* (Elements of a Political Psychology of the American People). The writings compiled in this volume by the founder of the École Libre des Sciences Politiques date from 1890 to 1892; he updated and supplemented them in 1901. Right from the start, Boutmy seems to lament the discredit Tocqueville has fallen into. In so doing, he confirms the anti-Tocquevillian atmosphere holding sway in those years: "People willingly imply that *Democracy in America* is now a dated, outmoded book, which politicians no longer look into to learn something." Readers looked to less "abstract" authors, such as Bryce, the author of *American Commonwealth*, whom Boutmy tells us has "dethroned" Tocqueville.[69]

An introduction like that seems to suggest Tocqueville will be categorically rehabilitated. But such is not the case. Purporting to reopen the case and, we might think, overturn the ruling, Boutmy condemns the convict. Tocqueville, in Boutmy's opinion, was less a political observer or a social analyst than an "impatient moralist." A pathetic guide to the action, he was grievously wrong "in several of his predictions," such as the lasting dissolution of the different political parties and the Federal Union: "Tocqueville convinced himself that the Union, without ending legally and actually, would soon be no more than a shadow and a name. These were two utter mistakes: the Union was finally consolidated, the theory of states' rights was abandoned, and the two parties have remained the framework for all political activity." A bad analyst and unlucky prophet, Tocqueville had the additional shortcoming of using outdated methodology unworthy of the irrefutable science now known as "political psychology": "the political deductions Tocqueville so complacently makes hardly touch on universal man, a personage we do not encounter. As for a racial or national psychology, something especially important for a politician to master, he does no better than offer particular facts to help tease one out, through corrections and shades of meaning, from the mediocre base of abstract psychology." In the end, Boutmy comes back to Mr. Bryce and recommends reading him instead of "militant observers" such as Monsieur de La Boulaye, Monsieur Claudio Jannet . . . and Monsieur de Tocqueville. Not only is the Englishman scientifically superior to them, but his works, moreover, "contain, for whosoever looks closely, elements for the most sizable case ever brought against a people."[70] Between the "abstract" Frenchman, with his blameworthy leniency, and the

Englishman, whose severity was backed by science, there was no need to weigh the pros and cons.

So, was it curtains for Tocqueville? Yes, but not completely. After throwing out his appeal, Boutmy saw no problem with calling him back as a witness. For the prosecution, of course. It was a discreet entrance, a modest reappearance, but nevertheless it ushered in the new role *Democracy in America* would play: lending the anti-American discourse, by choice cullings, its unassailable authority. Since Boutmy was eager to persuade his readers that the United States was an "unbearable environment" and that no Frenchman in his right mind could survive there, he tugged at Tocqueville's sleeve and courted his approval. You think I am exaggerating, Boutmy seemed to be telling his readers; lend Tocqueville your ears: "This democracy has spiritualized violence."[71] We can listen to him, then—but only when he is against the United States.

"Anyone who supposes that I intend to write a panegyric is strangely mistaken," Tocqueville wrote in his 1835 introduction.[72] His early-twentieth-century opponents did not just take his word for it; they looked for concrete proof. From then on they would use several passages—and always the same ones—to develop arguments that were all the more precious because they came from the enemy's mouth. Tocqueville's subtlety, his exhaustive twists and turns—and also, admittedly, his contradictions—lightened these scavengers' workload. They compiled a little anthology of salvageable ideas: in the United States, there was no legislative continuity; the government had no administrative stability; it was not money-wise, as was believed in Europe; the House of Representatives was an incredibly vulgar assembly; America's immorality was the immorality of social climbers and more dangerous than the immorality of the "great" under a monarchy; the inhabitants had "a sort of prejudice" against everything intellectual; there was an "absence of great writers in America so far" because "literary genius cannot exist without freedom of the spirit"; the country was nothing but turmoil and commotion; society appeared "agitated and monotonous"; the Americans were "restless in the midst of their prosperity," "serious and almost sad even in their pleasures."[73] All those things *could* effectively be found in *Democracy in America,* and many others as well, like the reproach Mrs. Trollope made against the Americans of being unable to accept criticism.[74]

All these excerpts and highlights, plucked out of the Tocquevillian garden, would be haphazardly replanted into anti-American flower beds, with the central bouquet being the famous page on "the power exercised by the majority in America over thought" in chapter 7 of the first *Democracy.* "Formerly tyranny used the clumsy weapons of chains and hangmen; nowadays even despotism, though it seemed to have nothing more to learn, has been perfected by civilization."[75] This is already far from Verrières and the petty despotism of provincial America criticized by Stendhal; it is, however, much closer to modern fears of despotism, which no longer needs to "clumsily str[i]ke at the body" but instead exerts its control directly in people's minds.

Baudelaire: America as Belgian Apocalypse

In what was not yet a chorus but still a series of anti-American arias, we have to pinpoint Baudelaire's singularly vibrant voice—the Baudelaire of the Poe articles, of course, but also and especially the Baudelaire responsible for a startling page of *Fusées* predicting the future of an "Americanized" world.

Mrs. Trollope, hounded by debt and bent on capitalizing on the success of her American book, took on Belgium. If Baudelaire had deigned to comment on her, he could only have approved of her way of thinking. After all, what could be more *Belgian* than America? Twin deceptions, brother monstrosities: *young* Belgium and *young* America. The same utilitarianism, the same sentimentality, the same democratic depravity, the same hatred for genius—and, of course, the same "commercial smell."[76] Baudelaire's view lumped the two countries together in combined revulsion. Denouncing them both was an essential part of his final projects and goals. "It is time to tell the truth about *Belgium,* and about *America,* the other Eldorado of the French rabble," he wrote to Édouard Dentu in 1866, two years before his death.[77] In his famous book on Belgium, which only exists as a series of drafts, America is right there on the first page of the outline: "How we sang the glory and fortune of the United States of America, twenty years ago! Similar idiocy regarding Belgium."[78] Looking over the fragments of his *Belgique déshabillée* (or *Pauvre Belgique*) (Belgium Unclothed, or Poor Belgium), one often gets the sense that Baudelaire is settling two scores with one stroke of the pen. "A general and absolute horror of the mind," "Spirit of obedience and CONFORMITY," "Associative spirit. By associating, individuals dispense with thinking individually," "Lack of commercial integrity (anecdotes)," "Everyone is a salesman, even the rich," "*Hatred for beauty,* to offset the *hatred for the mind,*" "Professional studies. Hatred for poetry. Education to produce engineers or bankers": Baudelaire was throwing stones at Belgium, but behind it was America.

This also means that Baudelaire's America was not just the country responsible for Poe's martyrdom. "Martyrdom," moreover, was not a metaphor for Baudelaire; when he made his vow of daily prayer, he would designate Poe one of his three intercessors.[79] Baudelaire's devotion to Poe, which

Asselineau called a "possession," was truly passionate. It went far beyond the admiration he felt for the man who "by himself . . . represent[ed] the romantic movement on the other side of the Atlantic."[80] It was a radiant emotion the poet extended to the rare beings he deemed worthy of redemption, such as Mrs. Clemm, whom he made out to be a figure of charity. Since he had no reliable information on his idol, Baudelaire had at first used American chronicles to construct a fanciful Poe, a Southern dandy who was aristocratic by birth as well as genius. When he discovered that it was all wrong and that Poe had not had the privileged existence he had imagined, Baudelaire felt an even greater tenderness for the "poor Eddie" who was so different from the "Edgar Poe created by [his] imagination": "the ironic antithesis fills me with an inescapable compassion."[81]

A passionate champion of the poet and the man, Baudelaire was no less passionately angry at America, the evil stepmother that had ignored the former and murdered the latter: "Edgar Poe and his country were not on the same level."[82] Poe's life and death were grounds for a general accusation against his country. "The various documents which I have just read have convinced me that for Poe the United States was a vast cage, a great counting-house, and that throughout his life he made grim efforts to escape the influence of that antipathetic atmosphere."[83] Persecution was frankly unavoidable. "Dazzling a young and unformed country by his mind, shocking men who considered themselves his equals by his manners, Poe was fated to become a most unhappy writer."[84] He was both precise and imaginative, "an antithesis come to life."[85] This was enough to arouse hatred in the foot-soldiers of the useful and the sentimental. As an American, Poe had been in greater danger than anyone else: he was on the front lines. That was because "for a long time there has been a utilitarian movement in the United States which seeks to carry poetry along with it, like everything else."[86] They had even tried to make him write "a book for the whole family"! "Ask Edgar Poe to write a book for the whole family! It is true then that human stupidity will always be the same, in all climates, and that critics will always wish to fasten heavy vegetables on rare, exotic plants."[87]

The same in all climates: that means that America was not the only country at fault. "Moreover, Society does not like these mad wretches"—society itself, regardless of nationality. There had been no shortage of rabble in France ready to spit on Nerval, French society's suicide.[88] We are all Belgians in this respect, all Americans, all democrats, Baudelaire was saying. And while it is true that Poe was "stifled . . . by the American atmosphere,"[89] we should recognize—and spread the word—that this "greedy world, hungry for material things," with its hazardously "rising tide of democracy" was our own, your own—hypocrite reader. The Americans were too democratic not to hate their great men, and they were fated to smother Poe. But America was only democracy's geographical name. And what was democracy? For Stendhal it was still a place where you courted shopkeepers. Baudelaire, though, had "*heard it said* that there exists in the United States a tyranny much more cruel and inexorable than that of a monarchy, namely public opinion."[90] Of course, this was a horrible blasphemy that brought the "slaver of indignant patriotism" to Americans' lips. But wrongly so. This kind of despotism no longer had a homeland: it was the future of the world—that is, its end.

"The world is about to end"—these words open the longest of the "sky-rockets" Baudelaire would begin writing in 1855.[91] And it would end *Americanized*. America is thus on the threshold and at the (unfinished) closing of Baudelaire's last project. On the threshold because Baudelaire once more placed his undertaking under the tutelary invocation of Poe, in whose works he found two titles he hesitated between: "Sky-Rockets" and "Suggestions."[92] At the closing, because fragment 22, which contains the sinister evocation of Americanized humanity, would be the last. The prophetic rage of the first pages gives way to a funereal resignation, as though it were already too late: "Nevertheless, I will let these pages stand—since I wish to record my days of anger." On the manuscript, Baudelaire added a last word to this final sentence (to replace "anger"?): the word "sorrow." The last sky-rocket was slow-burning. The American night won out over the poet's lapidary writing and prophetic energy. Baudelaire's America was not the world's youth but rather man's "old age"—"corresponding to the period which we are about to enter and whose beginning is marked by the supremacy of America and of industry."[93] America was tolling the bell of sterile decline—the opposite of fruitful decadence.

André Guyaux, in his edition of *Fusées,* calls the fragment "a meteor packed with the world's last fires."[94] The striking prophecy in which Baudelaire, a century before Baudrillard, describes the already-present advent of a world of nonevents, is worth quoting *in extenso:* "a tumult in which there is nothing new, whether of enlightenment or of suffering." The American end of the world is a state of dull and dreary stasis, an apocalypse without a revelation, a simple cessation of spiritual activity, a moral lassitude, the total "degradation of the human heart." But it is also the dissolution of all family ties, a nosedive into the waters of egotistical calculation, a universal prostitution to Pluto. Society thrown out of joint, religion annihilated, a daily bill of fare of unspeakable horror, Leviathans of wickedness. "Need I describe how the last vestiges of statesmanship will struggle painfully in the clutches of universal bestiality, how the governors will be forced—in maintaining themselves and erecting a phantom of order—to resort to measures which would make our men of today shudder, hardened as they are?"

This page (which Baudelaire most likely wrote in 1861) would be made public only in 1887, twenty years after the poet's death. Among the readers immediately captivated by "the violence and truthfulness of this voice from the other side," were Bloy, Claudel, and Proust. One of the first was Nietzsche, who read and annotated a volume of Baudelaire's posthumous works in early 1888. He found in it "invaluable *Psychologicis* of decadence."[95] But fragment 22 also foreshadows a whole body of literature on decline with close ties, as we will see later on, to the specter of Americanization—ties that Baudelaire, in these searing pages, was the first to establish. If decadence could be joyous and even "vigorous" (as Bourget put it), Europe's decline was not. It had nothing epic about it, and the end of this "vile world" would be as bland as progress, as cold as a machine, as inexorable as America. It was not even death; more like non-life. "I appeal to every thinking man to show me what remains of Life."

The vision of a future with nothing before it, a godless heaven, humanity wallowing "in the clutches of universal bestiality," the end of history and the enthronement of immutable tyrannies—that all this, that the entire landscape after the downfall should be called America, makes the last fragment of *Fusées* a premonitory text and Baudelaire, who felt like a "ridiculous prophet," the torch-bearer of resistance to Americanization, understood as humanity's clinical death. If the world becomes American, Baudelaire asked, "What, under Heaven, has this world henceforth to do?"

If Baudelaire created the word *Americanize*, a verb with an illustrious future, it was not through a slip of the pen or some accidental impulse. The neologism logically and inevitably arose from a series of his writings that gave it life and force. Between its first use in 1855 and the one Baudelaire made of it in fragment 22, the word had already taken on a full load of meanings—and threats. It appeared for the first time in an article on the 1855 World's Fair that Baudelaire published in *Le Pays*, in the course of a tirade against "the idea of 'progress,'" a "very fashionable error," a "grotesque idea, which has flowered upon the rotten soil of modern fatuity." The progressive man was the average Frenchman, who read newspapers and confused "the material and the spiritual orders"; he was the modern simpleton brainwashed by material philosophy: "The poor man has become so Americanized by zoöcratic and industrial philosophers that he has lost all notion of the differences which characterize the phenomena of the physical and the moral world—of the natural and the supernatural."[96] This 1855 vision is pretty pitiful, with "decadence" taking the form of a "driveling slumber of decrepitude." The same vision, now tragic and suddenly terrible, would be amplified by the "end of the world" fragment in *Fusées*. "So far will machinery have Americanized us, so far will Progress have atrophied in us all that is spiritual, that no dream of the Utopians, however bloody, sacrilegious or unnatural, will be comparable to the result."

From one text to the other, from 1855 to 1861 (if that is in fact when the fragment was written), the *Americanized* man had changed. He was no longer an average Homais, a taproom regular poring over "*his* newspaper"; it is me, you, Baudelaire, it is the "we" of dying humanity. "The time is near," the prophet insists. And the end of the world would be an American night where, behind the ruins of the "spiritual," were as-yet unspeakable horrors.

2

The Divided States of America

Sunday, June 19, 1864. It is shaping up to be a beautiful day on the shores of the English Channel. Cherbourg, a village more accustomed to naval uniforms than crinoline petticoats, has been overrun by Parisians since Saturday morning. It is as if the high society of the Second Empire, having graced Biarritz and Deauville with its fashionable presence, had suddenly decided to flock to an austere military port on the Cotentin peninsula. Good news, of course, for the Western Railroad—a brand-new weekend railway package, set at sixteen francs round-trip from the Gare Saint-Lazare (twelve francs in third class), has become an instant success.

But the Sunday morning train back to Paris is nearly empty when it pulls out of the station. As it happens, the June sun, the whims of fashion, and the enticing ticket price are not why this elegant invasion has engulfed Cherbourg on such a gorgeous Sunday morning. Vacation is not what these fine people have in mind, and it is not the sea air they are here to breathe. What they are after is a whiff of blood. A show more exciting than the Epson Derby and more bracing than the premier of *Tannhaüser* is about to start. It is time to watch a battle.

June 19, the American Civil War is on tour in the Cotentin. Now playing: *Yankee ironclad takes on Confederate cruiser! North against South! The USS* Kearsarge *to fight the CSS* Alabama! So as not to miss a second of it, the onlookers—Parisians and locals, soldiers and civilians—are elbowing each other out of the way; pushing onto terraces, docks and piers; rushing out to the steep Roule overlook; heading all the way to Querqueville, where the best view of the sea is to be had, in an enormous jumble of carriages, coaches, hackneys and carts. A handful of privileged spectators, among them the novelist Octave Feuillet and his wife, have ringside seats: they are watching from Port Admiral Augustin Dupouy's boat. Well before ten o'clock, everyone is in place. The fighting can begin.

☆ ☆ ☆

In 1864, the *Alabama* was already the stuff of legend. Under Raphael Semmes's command, it had spent two years terrorizing the North's commercial fleet, making light work of the Union cruisers sent out to destroy it. A wooden cargo-passenger ship, unarmored and rigged with three masts to economize on coal, the *Alabama* was built for speed and handling. Time after time, it escaped its pursuers—except the ones it sank, like the armored gunboat USS *Hatteras*. The damage it inflicted on the Union was so considerable that after the war, the United States would levy hefty fines on Great Britain for having allowed the ship to be built on British soil.[1]

The *Alabama*'s fate was entwined in the tangled pro-South politics of England and France, which were more ostensibly than authentically neutral. Secretly built in Liverpool at the instigation of James D. Bulloch, who had been sent by the Confederate Congress, the elegant ship first known as the *Enrica* set out to sea before the Union's protests could force the British government to call it back. Warned of that risk by the numerous Southern allies in the British government, the ship left Liverpool on July 29, 1862, ostensibly for a pleasure cruise, complete with music and champagne. It turned out to be a one-way trip—the invited guests aboard were brought back to shore in a towboat. In the Azores, just outside neutral Portugal's territorial waters, the ship was given its real name and its cannons and powder; this is also where it took on its commanding officer, Semmes, the most famous of all the blockade runners. The Confederate flag was hoisted. The cruiser's career started there and spanned from the Antilles to the China Sea, much to the detriment of Northern commerce.

Twenty-three months and sixty-two prizes later, the *Alabama* sailed into the English Channel, on its way back from the cape. The ship was in disrepair; the furnaces needed to be fixed. Semmes, himself exhausted, had decided to call in at Cherbourg. As soon as the ship had docked, the *Alabama* declared its damage and asked permission to stay for repairs.

The situation was not without precedent. Other Southern ships had dropped anchor in French ports. This does not mean it was any less embarrassing. The cruiser's exploits had made it the Union government's bête noire, in addition to which the documents detailing France's neutrality stipulated that in no case could a "belligerent make use of a French port to increase its gun power, or order—as alleged repairs—procedures that heighten its military potential." For a cruiser whose speed is its strength, that law, taken literally, could be stretched to include furnace repair. . . To win time—since the same law limited calls by belligerents to seventy-two hours—a commission was appointed. Its task was to examine the ship's condition and report back to the port authorities, and more important, the political ones. The matter was too serious to be settled in Cherbourg.

But events moved quickly. Three days later, on June 14, the Northern cruiser *Kearsarge* sailed up to the edge of the harbor. The challenge was clear. Raphael Semmes chose to accept, despite his vessel's weaknesses. That same day, he asked for a full load of coal, effectively eliminating his previous request to put in for repairs, as the port admiral did not neglect to inform him. On June 15, he sent a note to his opponent (and former classmate) Winslow, offering a fight.

The next Sunday, at 10 A.M., the *Alabama* drew out of the port at Cherbourg, accompanied to the edge of French waters by the battleship *La Couronne*. It headed straight for the *Kearsarge,* which in turn led it farther out to sea, in accordance with the instructions its captain had received. Then it was set for battle. The *Alabama* fired.

Was Semmes unaware that the enemy ship had armored siding, camouflaged by its wooden sheathing? Whatever the case may be, the *Kearsarge,* with equal firepower, was in perfect condition and manned by a well-rested, well-prepared crew. It was an uneven fight. The *Alabama* was dealt its death blow and sank within minutes. Semmes, however, was not struck down in battle, nor did he fall into enemy hands: a rich pro-Confederate Englishman took him aboard his steam yacht, the *Deerhound,* and sailed him off to Southampton.

At noon, under a decidedly summery sun, Captain John Winslow strode triumphantly, pistols in his belt, over the docks of Cherbourg, which for a week had harbored the last Confederate cruiser. The Parisian audience, somewhat disappointed, disbanded into the city while they waited for the next train.

Manet as History Painter

The military importance of the event is not what makes the June 19 battle worth retelling—though this importance is far from insignificant, given that the destruction of the *Alabama* marked the end of a fruitful streak of blockade running and dashed the South's last hopes of breaking the Union blockade, which had held up since the start of the war. What makes it important is the *image* it gave its contemporaries, both literally and figuratively. The June 25 issue of *L'Illustration* featured detailed coverage of the event and was illustrated with an engraving by Lebreton: in the foreground, the *Alabama* is hit by the fatal blast; the ship is tilted and looks as though it is about to fall over on its side, toward the viewer; the Confederate flag floating over the deck fills the center of the engraving; from the *Kearsarge,* in the background on the left, black furnace smoke and white cannon smoke rise up; on the far right in the background, you can just make out the shadow of the *Deerhound;* and several other skiffs can be seen around the warships. The horizon is not sea but land: the French coast frames the scene, as though the duel were taking place in an amphitheater or an arena. By contrast, the most frequent American image shows two ships facing off, stems pointed as though they were about to harpoon each other. It is an unseen battle, out at sea and far from European eyes.

The contrast between the American depiction and the French dramatization of the scene is even more striking in the real masterpiece inspired by the June 19 duel: *The Battle of the* Kearsarge *and the* Alabama, an oil painting by Manet from the same year, 1864.[2] The seascape has often been described as Manet's first "documentary" painting. But the boldness of its antirealistic composition, along with an intentionally artistic treatment, make it more than a simple journalistic artifact, and in its hermeneutic underpinnings it is closer in spirit to classical historical painting.

First of all, its composition is similar to that of the *Illustration* engraving—so much so that the engraving has been considered a direct influence.[3] The Confederate ship, majestic and expiring beneath its valiant rigging, takes up the center of the frame. The Union vessel in the background is a formidable presence, though it is almost completely hidden by the *Alabama*'s shadow and the thick smoke of battle. On opposite sides, in the background on the right and in the foreground on the left—helpful and futile—are the English and French: Englishman John Lancaster's *Deerhound* and a local boat flying a pilots' flag, where the strident white of truces and capitulations dominates. The sea, intensely green and almost vertical, seems to be casting off the scene, throwing it in the viewer's face.

In all probability, Manet did not witness the June 19 duel. He does not "give" us the scene Rondin, a photographer, might have—Rondin set up his camera in a bell tower, but the photograph he took has been lost. Manet shows us both the spectacle and the spectators (French sailors leaning out of their skiff); he translates the reality of the Civil War as well as the French view of the war. What his strange seascape shows is a tangle of spontaneous or concerted sympathies for the South, France's wait-and-see policy, its indecision, and also a certain impotent voyeurism.

In Manet's hands, the sinking of the *Alabama* outside of Cherbourg becomes a moment of truth—a bolt from the blue of the kind that, historically speaking, is sparked by a singular event because of its very singularity. Bureaucrats, politicians, soldiers, writers, journalists, and socialites—the battle's spectators were all watching the shipwreck of imperial France's diplomatic strategy. Along with the *Alabama*, France's secret wish for a lasting division of the United States was sunk. Manet painted this, too. It is not out of "coquetry" that he made the ships smaller and set them back on the horizon, as Barbey d'Aurevilly wrote at the time (Barbey admired and defended the painting without reading into its political charade.)[4] Manet's choice had better motives. Beyond a simple battle, what the painter wanted to show was France's reaction to that battle and, more generally, to the American Civil War. Manet is saying, *Here's how you're reacting to the war— you're looking at it through the wrong end of the telescope. Your perspective's wrong. In fact, you have no perspective at all. You don't know how to frame an America that's come violently back into focus.* (The humorist Cham, attacking Manet's painting as did so many others, suggested the following caption, which was perhaps truer than he realized: "The *Kearsarge* and the *Alabama*, finding Manet's sea unrealistic, sail off to fight on the edge of the frame.")[5] Manet's painting is allegorical. It is—though not *only*—what Barbey called "a very simple and very powerful sensation of nature and landscape"; it is not documentary or anecdotal. Even the people who scoffed at it knew this: Manet's painting shows a mindset; it represents a representation. "We can see from the fish's facial expressions what they think about the battle going on over their heads," commented another humorist.[6] Blame the fish, if you want—what Manet is actually showing us is imperial France's facial expression.

Manet, or political truth in painting? The sheer number and ferocity of the painting's critics is proof that no one wanted to hear the truth about imperial France's blind voyeurism in the face of the Civil War.[7] The diplomatic dithering and public ambivalence of the time also suggest that Manet's intuition was profoundly right and that France, which had been brutally forced out of a long period of indifference, was having trouble coming to terms with a war it did not completely grasp.

A Most Exciting War

The Civil War was America's big comeback onto the French ideological scene. From 1860 to 1865, it garnered a passionate interest in the press and public opinion, one that seems disproportionate to what was really at stake for France in the conflict. The historian W. Reed West finds the intellectual mobilization surprising, given that "things of great importance were taking place in Europe, and developments in Italy, Russia and Germany might well have absorbed the thoughts of intelligent Frenchmen."[8] France's focus on the American war seems to him to be a distraction of those intelligent citizens' attention, a serious error in judgment, and a bad investment of public interest, which was diverted from such important issues as Prussia's growing power. In fact, the Cherbourg onlookers of 1864 prefigured the Sadowa gawkers of 1866[9] and hinted at the 1870 catastrophe.[10]

There really was nothing in the American conflict that affected France's vital interests. Its negative effects on certain sectors of the economy (the textile industry deprived of cotton, a sharp drop in silk and wine exports) could be felt as early as 1861, but their scope was modest. As for the long-term consequences of the war, they were not important enough to unsettle the global balance of power or threaten France's position—and that would have been the case no matter who won. West is right in stressing that what was happening in Europe at the time was serious in a very different way. The long march toward Italian unity was entering its final phase—the reintegration of Rome and Venetia—and becoming a sticky diplomatic situation for France, which had protected papal possessions in Rome since 1849. While French imperial diplomacy was stuck in that rut, Bismarck defeated Denmark and had his conquest of Schleswig and Lauenbourg ratified in Gastein in August 1865, a forerunner of the following year's victorious blitzkrieg against Austria. Prussia's inexorable rise to power, France's growing isolation: *there* was a situation that "might well have absorbed the thoughts of intelligent Frenchmen." And as for their compassion, it too could have found other objects closer to home in Europe, starting with the Polish insurrection of 1863, which was brutally suppressed by Russia.

During these years, though, France had good reasons for its unexpectedly passionate interest in the fratricidal battles taking place across the sea. Along with the intrinsic importance of the war as a potential laboratory for distilling a new continent or a testing ground for modern warfare, there were two significant domestic issues at stake, for both the imperial government and its opponents.

Within the government, the enthusiasm stirred up by the war was far from a mere whim, as the final, disastrous outcome of Napoleon III's Mexican and American policies might lead us to believe. What ended up a miscalculation started out as an exciting speculation. French diplomacy was aiming for the breakup of the American federation—a breakup that could only be advantageous for France. A dream was born: that of a long and inexpiable North American war, a deadlock with no winner that would bleed the country dry. Though it was lamented by a few woeful humanists and a handful of disconsolate republicans, the Civil War seemed more like a windfall to the more calculating "realists"—or those who proclaimed they were. This is why in French the war was given a name that sounded almost like a promise: not "American Civil War" but the "War of Secession." Those feelings could never be admitted in public, though. For things to work out right, silence, caution, and patience were in order. America's split would be a dream come true for the stock exchange, the chancellery, and the chamber of commerce. When dissent began to stir in France, it came from other quarters—from an opposition that jumped at the chance to exist at all.

America in the Public Eye

In the well-controlled press of the Second Empire, the opposition did not often have its choice of battleground or of which opinion wars it wanted to wage. Government control of the press was in fact a personal obsession of the emperor's. It was so notorious that Sainte-Beuve used it as an excuse to switch from writing for the *Constitutionnel* (semiofficial) to the *Moniteur* (officially official), explaining, "Since the government controls all the newspapers these days, it's wiser to write for the government itself."[11] The November 24, 1860, order that ushered in the "liberal empire" did nothing to end an administrative supervision of the newspapers. The flood of warnings and suspensions continued—not to mention the fines and prison sentences levied by the courts. It was extremely problematic and risky for even the bravest of papers to editorialize about late-breaking or urgent crises in which imperial diplomacy was actively (if not effectually) at work.

The American situation, on the other hand, was discussed in all its contradictions and from every angle, precisely because it was more marginal and less touchy, and also because the sudden start of the war took France's imperial regime off guard. Clearly, when the first shots were fired in late 1860, there was no official party line. Two right-thinking newspapers,

Le Constitutionnel and *Le Pays,* backed the North on an essential point: its refusal to send runaway slaves seeking refuge in abolitionist states back to their Southern masters. In addition to this point of contention on the part of the slave states, which was presented as unreasonable, there was also the "detestable institution" of slavery, which the press, including the "semioffi- cial" papers, considered too outdated to be defended. *Le Constitutionnel* said it would lament any compromise that would save the Union "with slavery constitutionally recognized over all the land." If such were to be the case, added the editorialist, "the nineteenth century, which has always favored progress, will have had one more letdown." The newspaper's "wishes" on December 26, 1860, were "both for the salvation of the great American republic and the gradual diminishment of slavery."[12] In November, *Le Pays* had suggested early on that "a fine cause to defend and help triumph [was] that of the abolition of slavery," while wondering exactly what might be the best way to do this.[13] As early as December, however, *Le Pays* changed its angle and started a quarrel with *Le Constitutionnel,* which had shown too much admiration for America. Over three successive issues, Granier de Cas- sagnac offered a long historical summing-up: "Admire the Americans as much as you like, and take them for republicans, if it suits you; but do not deceive your readers, who have faith in your erudition, by telling them that the founders of the American republic had put into the Constitution exactly the opposite of what is really there."[14] Those who favored the North, naive champions of a sham republic, were no less blind about the North's so-called generosity. "It is sectarianism, a taste for controversy, and philosophical prin- ciples that have the North denouncing slavery, not some love for the slave or a sense of equality."[15] And the final argument, used regularly by partisans of the South right up to the end of the war: slavery was already headed toward extinction, and in no case did its immediate abolition justify a civil war.

Once the emperor's pro-South leanings had become general knowledge, though, the governmental press, for better or for worse, went back to the drawing board and crossed out anything in its analyses that could seem to favor the North. But the opposition, led by the *Journal des débats,* had had time to set up camp. Forced to respond, the official and semiofficial press, as of the first months of 1861, entered a war of words that would last as long as the real war. Analysis and commentary of the American war gave Orleanist, liberal, and republican opposition an excuse to strike out against the empire. Considering the emperor's tortuous and transparent maneuvers in favor of the South, it was a good chance for the opposition to make itself heard, be it by openly championing the North, as did the *Revue des deux mondes,* or by advocating a "real" neutrality and condemning the helping hand discreetly offered to the Confederates by a government that was won over to their cause but fearful. It was the American war that helped a silenced opposition speak out once more.

The opposition did so without shouting. This was in part because of the strict rules governing the press and reflects an understandable caution on the part of the opposition. But it also reveals a more unexpected side to the situation: the analyses of the American war in the pro-North and pro-South papers were extremely similar. There was a profound divergence in the sympathies of each side, and the outcomes they wanted to see were diametrically opposed. But there was fundamental agreement on three crucial points: that secession was legally legitimate; that slavery as an institution was morally and politically illegitimate; and that a clear-cut victory by one of the two sides was impossible. The consensus was widespread on these points throughout the conflict; it was almost unanimous at the start of the war, and as the fighting dragged on, even those who started to doubt had to adapt their arguments to public opinion, which, on the whole, thought that way.

Out of the three consensual propositions listed above, the first favored the South, the second the North, and the third either one, depending on the current tide of the war. Which means that in order to integrate them into French public opinion, each of the two sides had to devise an apologetic or critical strategy sometimes fairly removed from the official line of the side it favored. Pleas for and defenses of the Union or the Confederacy thus had considerable autonomy from their American originals. French editorialists had to take liberties with the reality of America's positions, not only in order to cater to French concerns, but also so they could fit their demonstrations into the framework of their audience's expectations. As with any constraint, this one gave strength and shape to the new representations of America that were being generated by the Civil War. The war did more than simply put America back in the spotlight of current events. It also created a *vision* of America, which had been left fallow for several decades; suddenly there was a bumper crop of ideas, stories, and judgments.

By grafting hostility (the accusations voiced by each camp against the American side backed by the other camp) onto consensus (the acceptance by both camps of a certain number of "truths" about America, and the war as a foundation for the discussion), the French reinterpreted the tragedy of the Civil War from day to day for five years running, and without realizing it laid the groundwork for a much later anti-Americanism. But the matter deserves closer attention.

Sterile Sympathy

The government's sympathies quickly became apparent. The emperor wanted to help tip the scales for the South, the Confederacy. This inclination was never publicly acknowledged, but it was an open secret. Napoleon III, as usual, divulged it in private conversations and had it distilled by select editorialists. Hostile to the North but unprepared to recognize the Confederacy de jure, ready to turn a blind eye to certain slips in neutrality (such as the fact that ships intended for the South were being built in France) but not to acknowledge them when leaks made things public, the empire settled into a holding pattern, broken up by vague gestures of intervention or "mediation." At the same time, profiting from the outbreak of the Civil War, Napoleon III launched a Mexican venture with the grandiose aim of creating a Catholic and Latin empire he conceived as an "insuperable wall to United States encroachment."[16]

On the diplomatic front, the imperial government's erratic behavior would lead it to total failure. The only serious opportunity for breaking with the Union, a joint venture with England, fell through. This was the *Trent* affair, named after an English steamer stopped on the high seas on November 8, 1861, by a Union battleship, the *San Jacinto*, using "visiting rights." On board the *Trent* were two Southern diplomats, James M. Mason from Virginia and John Slidell from Louisiana, recognized as Confederate commissioners in Great Britain and France, respectively. The two men were taken captive by Captain Wilkes in a manifest violation of the rights of neutral nations—a point underscored in France by the Thouvenel Note, which was approved of even by the North's supporters. While the semiofficial press openly called for France and Great Britain to enter the war against the Union and its "despotism," Captain Wilkes was given a hero's welcome on reaching Union soil. Faced with an international outcry, Lincoln had the two southern commissioners released. There had been considerable alarm. The incident, which Lincoln's wise retraction brought to a close, would not be forgotten in France: years later, as we will see, it would flow from the pens of French anti-Americans, who would criticize the deposed emperor for this missed opportunity. In the fall of 1862, belated or disingenuous French proposals for mediation were ignored or refused.[17] Mistrust reappeared between France and Great Britain—aggravated on the English side by the presence of French troops in Maximilian's Mexico, a possible beachhead for French interference in the former Spanish colonies.

The South was defeated, having gotten nothing from France but a few words of encouragement. As for the North, it nurtured a lasting resentment over the attitude Paris had adopted. One of the victors' first actions in 1865 was refusing to recognize Maximilian of Habsburg, whom France had put on the throne of Mexico—effectively sealing the fate of both an illusory empire and its unfortunate monarch.

"Inexorable Fatality"

During the *Trent* affair, "one could have counted on his fingers about all the people in Europe not Americans who still retained any hope or expectation of the perpetuity of our Union," wrote John Bigelow, a consul who was then the Union chargé d'affaires in Paris. "Our political friends among the French people," Bigelow added, meaning the small circle of his contacts, who were very left-leaning, such as Pagès or Reclus, were "thoroughly demoralized." Generally speaking, "they took for granted that we would fight until we were satisfied that there was no use of fighting any longer, and then we would agree to some terms of separation."[18] The feeling was unanimous in late 1861 and remained widespread after the *Trent* affair, right up to the very end of the war. In another passage, Bigelow attributed this "almost universal impression" to the underhanded work of Southern commissioners, who "had for three or four years been insidiously propagating that two republics at least would be found at the close of the war occupying the territory which had before been occupied by the United States alone."[19] It was hard, however, to consider such a widespread and seemingly unshakable French conviction a simple consequence of psychological warfare by Confederate agents, who had only needed to water particularly fertile soil.

If the South, in its French-directed arguments, stressed the notion that the country could only, unavoidably split, it was in order to go with the grain of the emperor's obsessions and flatter the "intelligent classes," which they considered their surest allies in Europe. A split, as we have noted, was French diplomacy's barely secret dream. A long war, followed by the fracture of the United States, made inevitable by all the accumulated hatred and suffering, was the preferred scenario. The empire's dithering can be explained in part by this "vision." On the one hand, the South was not after victory but rather its own autonomy; on the other, the North could not possibly overcome the South and still less take lasting control of it. This logic led to the conclusion that it was not so much a matter of helping the South to victory as it was of keeping the North from decisively winning. The decay caused by such a bitter war would naturally, without outside help, lead to the Union's decomposition, which was in the French nation's best interests. In short, the logic was that "good things come to those who wait." France would wait until

the belligerents' rage blew over—although this might include discreetly en-
couraging Great Britain to make a pro-South intervention it balked at undertaking itself.

Sympathy for the South fed on economic realities and was colored by
complicated emotions, as we will see; but it began and ended with the
South's war goal of division, which coincided with imperial France's diplomatic expectations. Whatever the case may have been, and whatever the outcome of the war, the federation's breakup seemed to be the unavoidable way
out of a no-win situation. Most commentators, despite Tocqueville, implicitly
accepted the idea that such an enormous nation, held together only by the
loose ties of federalism, would one day succumb to the centrifugal forces that
were inevitably perturbing it. The United States at its 1860 size could not last:
this opinion was held from one end of the French political spectrum to the
other, but on different grounds—monarchists and imperialists judging the
government too democratic to be viable, while many liberals continued to
doubt (like the whole eighteenth century had) that republicanism could be
suitable to large empires.

The strange certainty of watching a war that could not have a winner
undercut partisan rifts. The Union's defenders agreed with their adversaries
on this point; no one in France believed one side could crush the other.
Judged highly improbable in 1861, it seemed every bit as unlikely and even
"impossible" in 1863. This was Eugène Chatard's opinion in a reputedly progressive newspaper like La Presse. "The reunion of the separated states by use
of force becomes more impossible with each passing day," he wrote on June
24, 1863. "The fight is no more than a work of destruction inspired by savage obstinacy." And he concluded, "The only thing left to do is draw the borders."[20] Even the Battle of Gettysburg, which the North had indisputably
won, was interpreted as further proof that the conflict would never have a
military resolution, rather than as a warning sign of the South's downfall.[21]
The North had lost four times on Southern soil, the South had just lost for
the second time on Northern soil: this was proof that the fight was too even.
The journalists keeping score all predicted a stalemate. Moreover, even if the
North took advantage on the field *in fine*, the possibility that it could or would
want to militarily occupy the South was ruled out. For the pro-North *Revue
des deux mondes*, the South, if invaded, would become the New World's
"Ireland at its worst, a Hungary, a Poland," an eternal thorn in its conqueror's side, a subjugated but never pacified territory. "In order to hold on
to a plague like that, the American Union would be obligated to abandon its
institutions and enslave itself, for how could a federal republic govern by
force such a large territory and so many millions of men so hostile to its

domination?"[22] If the North won, the Union would be beaten, and the American Prometheus would find itself shackled to a devouring conquest.

No one in France, moreover, seemed to want that decisive outcome, that extreme situation—not even the liberals and democrats in favor of the North, who feared that too great a success would go to its champion's head and were even worried that a win by the North would favor the emergence of a victory-crowned strongman who would threaten American liberties. A governmental newspaper, Le Pays, did not beat around the bush: it predicted as early as January 1861 that the North, if it won the war, would inevitably become a dictatorship. "The United States [would] no longer be a confederation of equals in a union of sovereign states, but truly a confederation of unequals in a union of masters and subjects," and this impossible federation would lead straight to despotism: "the dictatorship of a conquering section over a conquered section would not bring back the former harmony; it would directly lead to an empire, the absolute rule of one side."[23] Though they did not go quite as far down this path, the liberal newspapers were also worried about the Union's slide into authoritarianism, as evidenced by the 1863 arrest and trial in a military court in Cincinnati of Clement Vallandigham, a Democratic congressman from Ohio who was a strident opponent of Lincoln's policies. His prison sentence, commuted by Lincoln to deportation, was widely commented on in France. "Civil liberties are completely disappearing amid this show of military power," wrote La Presse, which compared Vallandigham to its founder and editor-in-chief, Girardin: "It is a repetition of the episode of Mr. Émile de Girardin's arrest on General Cavaignac's orders."[24] The sanctions taken against a publicly elected official shocked and embarrassed many pro-North Frenchmen. They also complicated the Northern consul Bigelow's task of "explaining" his country; one of his (American) associates did not mince words, writing to him that "there was great stupidity in arresting Vallandigham and in suppressing the Chicago Times."[25]

The Vallandigham affair validated the alarmist analyses advanced by the French press since the start of the war. It confirmed (some people's) fears and (others') suspicions of a radical transformation in the North's political government. Didn't the logic of war create the risk that constitutional liberties and rights would be brushed aside? Hadn't Lincoln's September 1862 decree, which handed over to martial law any person attempting to obstruct the draft, already legalized the slide into military dictatorship? By 1861 the very passionate sympathizers with the North's cause who wrote for the Journal des débats were worried by the "situation's extreme dangers" and wanted the government in Washington "to open its eyes to its policies' serious drawbacks," characterized by "a series of despotic actions that were profoundly

antipathetic to the spirit of the American peoples; . . . revolutionary measures that were contrary to the spirit of the constitution and that went against
the country's principles."[26] The "Union's dismemberment," which the same
editorialist judged probable,[27] was perhaps not the worst evil looming over
America.

Whether they were inspired by hostility or solicitude, the French scenarios all looked alike. Total war implied control of the press, preventive arrests,
and the hindrance of individuals' free movement. All of these measures,
deplorable in and of themselves, could lead to unrest, which, in turn, would
push the North to adopt exceptional laws. In France, the government press
took pleasure in embarrassing the pro-North press, which had trouble hiding its apprehension: it feared "revolutionary measures"—the very ones
Marx and Engels, writing from London, criticized Lincoln for not taking[28]—
which could lead to the setting up of a popular military general as a dictator
over the ruins of America's liberties.

France was strangely unanimous in its view of the war as one without a
loser or a winner, though not only, or even mainly, because it had analyzed
the balance of power. The stance betrayed, on one side, the desire for a perpetual separation of the United States, and on the other, a wish to save the
essential, that is, the democratic form, even if it meant a smaller Union.
More neutral observers judged the country's dissolution logical and more
than probable; engaged observers saw advantages for the side they championed, whichever that might be. It was in good faith that the French set
about cutting and recutting the map of the United States; the press got lost
in scholarly suppositions about the country's dismantlement, and every
neighborhood Talleyrand used his imagination to line up new nations like
dominoes.

The Divided States of North America; how many divisions would there
be? How many sections would this oversized worm be cut into? At least two,
that was a given. In France, supporters of the North restricted themselves to
hoping that the Confederate section would be the smaller of the two. The
Journal des débats, as we have seen, considered the secession a fait accompli
in early 1861; it would continue long afterward to consider it probable that
a—hopefully minimal—number of states would not come back into the
Union. A handful of more gluttonous observers leaned toward an American
cake cut into three pieces. This three-way scenario seemed to have the imperial chancellery's favor. The postwar United States would fracture into a
North, which would inevitably renew ties with its British family; a South,
which would become France's natural ally; and a West, which, having used
the war as an excuse to break away from the others, could establish privileged

relations with France, because of some vague and ill-defined affinities. But then again, why stop there? At its most euphoric, the government press got bold enough to count up to five! *La Patrie*'s Oscar de Watteville gave this forecast in March 1861: "A separation into republics of the North, Center, South, West, and Pacific is the tendency developing in the Republic currently derisorily known as the United States."[29] "Hindering this development, this explosion, is a dream to be left to Mr. Lincoln," mockingly added *La Patrie*, which was not fond of dreaming and firmly believed in the reality of its desires.

With the South's collapse, a military occupation, and the rapid reconstruction of the federal system, not only did indecisive French diplomacy's fleeting dream vanish; a collective mirage dissipated as well.

The South's Right, the North's "Pretext"

What surprised the French was the conflict's violence and durability more than the secession itself. Most observers considered the latter logical and in keeping with the terms of America's original *covenant*. Supporters of the South insisted that the right to secede that the Confederates had made use of was inherent in the United States' Constitution. Detractors avoided legal grounds as unfavorable and attempted to steer the debate into the realm of abolitionist principles. It was a waste of their energy, though, because the South's supporters professed to be every bit as abolitionist as they were.

This was perhaps the most disconcerting aspect of the French attitude toward the Civil War: a majority sympathetic to the South coexisted with a massive condemnation of slavery. It was a contradiction that would have to be skirted, at least rhetorically, by reformulating the problem. In order to reconcile pro-South sentiment and abolitionism, wasn't the best idea deciding that slavery was not really the main reason for the war? So in France, with the help of pro-South propaganda, which was very attentive to this point, the war was carefully separated from the slavery question, and slavery was presented as a mere pretext for the North's aggression.

If the interventionist hypothesis scared off many Frenchmen, the majority undeniably felt sympathy for the South, particularly at the top of the social ladder. It was the "elite" who were, with a few intellectual exceptions, the most pro-South. Slidell, the Confederate commissioner in Paris, was pleased to inform his minister, Benjamin, that "the sentiment of the intelligent classes is nearly unanimous in our favor."[30] This sympathy was deepened by the reality of economic interests and commercial ties; it was encouraged by zealous Catholic circles, bolstered by the inveterate myth of shared roots (it was believed and often repeated that half of the South's inhabitants had

French blood),[31] and relayed by regional and Parisian papers largely won over to the Confederate cause—the Southern propaganda agent Hotze estimated that three-quarters of the Parisian newspapers were favorable to his government and only counted two, all in all, that were openly hostile.

But, as contradictory as it may seem, opposition to slavery was still more unanimous, a fact that Southern diplomats and agents were the first to recognize, marvel at, and worry about. De Leon, in his confidential dispatches, saw this as an enormous handicap to his work. He considered the problem even more serious than in Great Britain, though abolitionist groups were strong and effective there. "Almost incredible as it may appear," De Leon wrote to the same Benjamin, "the Slavery Question is more of a stumbling-block to our recognition in France than in England, for it is really and truly a matter of sentiment with the French people, who ever have been more swayed by such consideration than their cooler and more calculating neighbors on the other side of the channel."[32] The French, De Leon insisted in the same dispatch, had a "sentimental repugnance" toward slavery.

Whether this disposition was "sentimental" or not, the observation seems accurate. In France, the South's staunchest supporters unequivocally diverged with Confederate doctrine on the legitimacy of their "peculiar institution"—a euphemism the Southerners held dear, and that fell on deaf ears in France. Nothing seemed able to shake a French conviction that was a mix of Enlightenment and Christian humanism and was dominated by the certainty that slavery was not only morally unjustifiable but historically outdated.

But it was precisely the widely held belief that slavery was incompatible with the modern world that would give the South its best chance with the French. Slavery was more than morally objectionable, it was historically doomed; that much was clear for all to see. Even the Southerners knew it. There was no way for them to ignore it. The French press repeated it over and over: in good faith, you could not suspect the South of wanting to eternally prolong a clearly outdated institution. How much of this was naiveté on the part of the South's French apologists? How much was duplicity? It does not matter. While Hotze, who replaced De Leon in France, dreamed of rallying to the Confederate flag men of science with "correct views of the place assigned by providence to different branches of the human family,"[33] the pro-South French press found better answers to its readers' hopelessly "sentimental" "repugnance" for slavery.

Le Constitutionnel gave an example of this type of pro-South justification that is all the more remarkable because the newspaper had at first strongly favored the North. In May 1861, negotiating a tricky turn, it affirmed as self-evident—"we know only too well"—that the immediate goal of this "war of no ideas" was not "to exterminate slavery." Repeating a motif that was popular in the pro-South press, the paper added that "the Negroes do not have many friends among those who will defend Washington," which was being threatened by Confederate troops at the time.[34] The press as a whole struck the same chord. "And above all it was insisted that slavery counted for nothing in the causes of the struggle."[35] One year later the same *Constitutionnel*, decidedly cured of its former naiveté, recognized "the truth" in "these recent words from Mr. Gladstone: the North is fighting for supremacy, the South is fighting for its independence." And then it moralized on the South's behalf: "it is a fact often overlooked, moreover, that more than six million souls would be subjugated," on the pretext of liberating four million blacks.[36] This accusation would show up again, post factum, in the writings of anti-American essayists of the 1880s. A shift can be sensed even in liberal circles like that of the *Revue contemporaine*, which reckoned, in the summer of 1862, that the tide of the war had turned, and opposed a South that knew or "felt" that slavery was doomed to a North that was cynically using the fact as a weapon:

> The North is no longer waging war against slavery; it uses abolitionism here and there as a weapon, as a way of undermining its enemy. The South is no longer fighting for slavery; it is perfectly aware that the war, whatever its outcome, has given slave owners' prosperity the deathblow; it even suspects that the only way of prolonging slavery's existence even a little and galvanizing a dying institution would be to put it back under the federal government's protection.[37]

France, which had witnessed two emancipation proclamations in the course of its own history, had trouble understanding Lincoln's dithering: his "preliminary emancipation proclamation" in 1862, which did not decree pure and simple abolition, met with consternation from supporters of the North in France. *La Presse* noted that "half-measures will satisfy no one."[38] As for *Le Constitutionnel*, it was indignant and triumphal over what it saw as Lincoln's hypocrisy: "Far from banishing slavery, [Lincoln] is promising to uphold it; he has made it the bonus incentive for any state willing to come back into the Union before January 1." Having witnessed this incredibly unprincipled stance, "who could still dare to say that the North is fighting for the suppression of slavery?"[39]

Unanimity against slavery coupled with a predominant sympathy for the South would lead to a paradoxical but not illogical situation: the conviction that the Civil War had in no way been a high-principled, liberating crusade, but rather a pitiless attempt by the North to politically and economically subjugate the South would become lastingly rooted in French public opinion. The South was doubtlessly wrong in being so slow to eliminate its "peculiar institution," but weren't the Northerners a hundred times more blameworthy for having cynically exploited the slavery question in order to demolish the South?

A "Purely Industrial" War?

As it was commented on in France in the vast majority of publications, the war the North was waging was anything but a righteous war. It could not be called righteous either technically—given that the Confederacy was in fact the "wronged" party—or morally—because the abolition of slavery was a false pretense, just one of the weapons in the North's arsenal. So what was the heart of the matter?

The Confederacy had an answer, which it gave its spokesmen the job of spreading throughout Europe: the war was economic in nature. The North wanted to shore up its industrial and financial hegemony using prohibitive, protectionist tariffs that the South did not accept and might modify if emancipated. It was this ironclad law and not some antislavery idealism that made compromise impossible; the North was much less interested in freeing the slaves than in making sure its manufactured goods could circulate freely throughout the continent and that it could continue to tax its rivals at exorbitant rates, even if the South's agricultural economy was damaged by inevitable retaliatory measures from Europe. The South added that though the war had started for economic reasons, as it dragged on it was starting to look more and more like a war of attrition. From its ports to its plantations, the Confederate territory's means of production were being systematically destroyed by the North, and if emancipation became a reality, the damage would be redoubled by a severe loss of "human capital."

This was the central argument of a pro-South pamphlet by Edwin De Leon: *La Vérité sur les États Confédérés d'Amérique* (The Truth about the Confederate States of America). Skilled at shaping his arguments to fit French prejudices, the Southern agent steered clear of defending the notorious "peculiar institution" of slavery, contenting himself with denouncing the hypocrisy of Unionists who waved the flag of emancipation while de facto apartheid made blacks' freedom in the North "a dead letter."[40] De Leon's Yankees were utterly indifferent to the blacks' fate and had only used the slavery question as an excuse for their aggression. In the growing tension between the North and the South in the years leading up to the war, "the slavery question was not even an issue, though the North skillfully used this excuse to put

Europe off the scent."[41] Tensions, De Leon insisted, were of an entirely different nature; they were very real conflicts of completely material interest: "The real roots of the present difficulties can be traced back to purely industrial concerns; the North is industrial, while the South is agricultural."[42] There were thus economic roots, along with a structural hostility. Between the South and the North, the degree of separation was not unlike the one between France and England. "France and England have never been more divided in their interests, feelings, habits, and experiences than the two sections, North and South, of the American republic have been these last twenty years."[43] Using the word "section" was a strange and cunning choice; De Leon was insinuating that the war would simply formalize the separation of two entities that were already economically and historically "sectioned off."

The explanation was easily admitted in France. Even before De Leon's pamphlet came out, the semiofficial press—with *Le Pays* first in line—had advanced the notion that the war had started for economic reasons. The conflict's "real causes" were very different from the ones invoked by the North: "Slavery has nothing to do with it: it is an economic question compounded by an agricultural one."[44] As time went on and the South was increasingly ravaged by the war, French opinion became progressively more troubled by what it saw as a concerted policy aimed at annihilating the South's infrastructures and wealth. Some twenty years later, these impressions had taken on the weight of certainties, and the Civil War's economic motives would become the cliché of every French analysis of the war. Impenitent monarchists and repentant republicans would come to agree with Marxist theorists and endorse the hypothesis Edwin De Leon had stated as early as 1862: "the spirit presiding over this war and the goal it is headed for" was "a takeover of the South's property" by the North.[45]

But for the time being, while the war was still being waged, such tangible logic was challenged in French opinion by a differently angled and more directly mobilizing approach. Backing the hypothesis of an economic war in order to annihilate the Union's moral pretenses was all well and good, but for the South's most fervent supporters, it was not enough. If the American conflict was only a fight between the two "sections" of the former United States over big money, why should the French get involved at all? The advantageous consequences of a Confederate win—lowered customs duties, for example—did not justify what would be costly and risky direct hostilities. Here, pro-South propaganda came up against two problems.

The first problem was that in order to win France's sympathy, the South had to be portrayed as the victim, yet the Confederacy also had to appear indomitable and durable. The South would play David to the North's Goliath, but though there was pleasure in backing the little guy against the big guy, the little guy had to be able to hold his ground. De Leon did what he could to rhetorically reconcile these two requirements. First, he presented the North's pretenses as utterly preposterous—"the South's submission will seem like just a dream to any man who cares to reflect seriously"[46]—but his introduction struck a different, more melodramatic note when he portrayed the "confiscation measures taken by the North's Congress" as "giving twelve million inhabitants the death sentence."[47]

The second problem was that after stripping the Civil War of all emotional, moral, and ideological weight by presenting it as a simple conflict of interest, it imperatively needed to be instilled with historical meaning so that the French, rather than simply turning their backs on it, would feel implicated in its outcome.

A new "explanation" would get this idea across, and though this new explanation was on a completely different plane than the economic one, the two could be used simultaneously. This explanation made the Civil War out to be an ethnic and cultural confrontation between the Anglo-Saxons and the Latins. The scenario was innovative and appealing to the South's French defenders, who were for the most part conservatives or reactionaries. It allowed them to transcend (after having exploited) an economic viewpoint that had gone too far in playing up their political adversaries' materialism, and, above all, it repatriated a foreign war into the field of French concerns: the conflict was no longer an intra-American Civil War, but the first episode of an interethnic world war.

Pan-Latinism versus the "Anglo-American Race"

This is how the new argument would be put together. The importance of material interests in the duel was only too clear, but even though it was obvious, France should not turn a blind eye to a more hidden and secret dimension of the conflict—one war can hide another. The so-called War of Emancipation masked a gigantic attempt to subjugate the South; the crusade in favor of the blacks covered over a punitive expedition against the Latin race, and the very men purporting to be racial liberators were in fact bent on absolute racial domination. In short, the French were asked to look behind the smokescreen of appearances and disingenuous declarations and discover this truth: the Civil War was a struggle to the death led by the Anglo-Saxon race in order to establish its supremacy over the entire American continent.

Making the Civil War an episode of a new, global antagonism for world supremacy thus became, quite logically, a key feature in the pro-Confederacy

French stance. The strategy was merely hinted at by the Southern propagandists. De Leon, for instance, compared the Confederate States of America to Italy, which had proved itself worthy of "being recognized by the nations of Europe" by "fighting for its independence and Constitution."[48] (He made sure not to add "and its unification" . . .) But it was the South's French advocates who would systematically exploit the perceived "parallels," with the double objective of embarrassing the North's supporters and pulling indifferent or undecided Frenchmen into the debate.

This discursive strategy most notably produced an analogy between America and Russia that was hammered in by the official press. In the 1860s, three-quarters of a century before productivist competition between the two systems had begun, the analogy was far from obvious. But the Union itself, anxious to break out of its diplomatic isolation, provided its adversaries with plausible evidence of an uncanny complicity: in 1863, a spectacular official visit by the czarist navy to Union ports strengthened accusations of a collusion between Alexander II's autocracy and Lincoln's war government. Southern commissioners in Europe were aware of how shocking—especially to the French—was this apparently cordial agreement between Poland's oppressors and the defenders of the blacks. De Leon did not conceal his joy: "The mutual endearments which have passed between the Lincoln and Russian despotisms have greatly edified and surprised the European world and have embarrassed not a little the democratic friends of 'The Model Republic' who are rabid partisans of Poland. To cover their chagrin, they have revived the old cry of slavery, the real 'bête noire' of the French imagination."[49] At the same time, the governmental daily *La Patrie* offered its readers a new "key" to the American conflict: the Union was the dissident states' oppressor, just as czarist Russia oppressed nations seeking freedom. And far from being a purely rhetorical gesture written by a satirist or a fanatic, the article "Russia and the United States of America" published by *La Patrie* had been examined and approved by Napoleon III himself, according to Delamarre, the paper's owner. This was the year Poland's insurrection had been cruelly suppressed, and it was obviously opportune to impose on the French public an image of the South's martyrdom, similar to that of the Poles, at the hands of a brutal and unscrupulous power. Though it was a rhetorical maneuver with limited objectives (undermining the French republican camp), comparing the American North with Russia had a real future before it—even if the pamphleteers of the 1930s were in no rush to recognize their rhetorical debt to the Second Empire.

In the pro-South arsenal, however, the parallel between the Russians and the Yankees was little more than a tactical tool. The long-term strategic weapon, one that extended the American battlefield to the entire "civilized world," was the idea of a confrontation between the Anglo-Saxon "race" and the Latin peoples. This idea was something the emperor held dear; we have seen how it guided his grand scheme in Mexico for containing the United States' pressure. It was also a very appealing idea for many Frenchmen, who were quick to react to the threat presented by an "Anglo-Saxon"-dominated United States that could eventually ally itself with a consistently troublesome Great Britain. In this analysis, the Civil War changed in scope and meaning. It was no longer a relatively localized internal clash, but rather the first stage of global hostilities. The fight between the North and the South reflected a much larger ethnic and cultural split; the Yankees' relentless aggressiveness indicated a thirst for domination that conquering the South could not quench.

This interpretation of the war was not completely absent from the South's way of presenting its case to the French. Edwin De Leon could sense that it would be useful and added a few racial considerations to his exposé on the war's economic roots. "To these [economic] causes must be added," he wrote, "the difference in race and aptitude that exists between the two peoples." And he gave a quick summing-up of the ethnic and cultural divide between the North and the South: "As statistics show, the North was populated by races of Anglo-Saxon extraction, and the South chiefly by the Latin race. General Butler, a descendent of the Puritans who wages war even on women, is now the North's distinguished proconsul in New Orleans, where the inhabitants' French language and customs reveal their roots."[50] It was a clever way of getting the French interested in the cause of near-compatriots mistreated by a Puritan roughneck. But De Leon's aim was a little off when he depicted the North's armies as a bunch of immigrants: "It must be admitted that the majority of soldiers in the army whose mission is to 'restore the Union' is made up of German and Irish emigrants."[51] He forgot that the Irish were part of the mythic Celto-Latin tribe that was the reference point, as we will see, of the most anti-North French discourse. This was because when it came to America's white population, the Southern agent's logic was one of castes, cultures, and religions, not races. For him the Yankees were more "Puritan" than English; the "German emigrants" not so much German as emigrants, that is "reds," as he explained further on: "The North has also drawn all the starved and disgruntled revolutionaries in Germany, all the red republicans . . . to shore up its army's numbers."[52] The ethnic split was neither decisive nor absolute. In De Leon's opinion, there were of course good Anglo-Americans, too, starting with the "Anglo-Saxon element found in the South," which he contrasted with Puritan stock by tracing it back to "the royal nobility banished by Cromwell."[53] Between whites, social, religious, and political characteristics were more important than ethnic ones. The South would have to try harder if it wanted to be "pan-Latin"!

French interventionists had an opposite view of the hierarchy of these arguments. The economic line of reasoning was not a great enough mobilizing force, so it was replaced with an assertion of racial competition on a global scale. In their opinion, the course of current (and future) events was ruled by a much more imperious logic than that of calculated interests: there was a logic of blood and "civilization." Next to forces inexorably pulling the Union and Great Britain together, despite friction at the start of the war, France's meager ties with the North American world did not carry much weight. The wilted memories of Lafayette and Rochambeau would be quickly forgotten, if they had not already been. "Racial affinities" and "ancestral traditions" would take over:[54] these realities, which were even more real than economic interests, linked France and the South. And a fortiori, they intertwined the Yankees' fate with that of the British.

The North's victory would be the triumph of the Yankee—called by ancestral voices to rejoin the Englishman in a common front against the Latins, and thus against the French, the Latin world's lords and protectors. The North was not an idea, principle, or type of government. It was a people antagonistic to the South's: "Already different from the start, because one had mainly been recruited among the French and Spanish, while the other was principally composed of Englishmen, Dutch, Germans, and Swedes; separated by considerable distances, living in other latitudes, performing different occupations, . . . the two peoples have always considered themselves rivals."[55] If the North won out, the "Anglo-American race" would be consolidated and ready to take on other conquests.

Pervasive in a scattered form in the government press, the theme of a clash between races and civilizations can be found, fully developed, in a pamphlet from 1863 titled *Du Panlatinisme* and subtitled "Necessity of an Alliance between France and the Southern Confederacy."[56] In thirty pages the pamphlet manages to regroup many of the anti-Yankee traits that would constitute the armature of late-nineteenth-century anti-Americanism.

From its first lines, the scope was widened, and the Civil War no longer seemed so American. For in order to understand and interpret it correctly, the situation had to be seen from a wider angle: "Three forces, or elements of civilization, are spreading over the world and aim at sharing the future among them. They can be identified as: Russo-Slavism, Anglo-Saxonism, and Gallo-Latinism."[57] The first of the three forces might seem the most threatening to the superficial observer. But that was not really the case. Of course, "Russian domination, a benefit for ignorant and savage peoples, or ones corrupted by the vices of decrepit civilizations, would be a calamity for Europe," but Russo-Slavism had the right to spread into Asia, and "as long as Europe remains what it is today, that is, strong and disciplined, the czars' cannons will knock at its door in vain":[58] the European populations would be preserved by their "vitality."

Quite different was Anglo-Saxonism, the second "civilization lever," which, for its part, had "two populations in its service, the English and the Americans, an aristocracy and a democracy." In any case, it was a remarkable race, both by its double propensity to "count on no one but itself" and "make the greatest possible profit from its personal activity": "self-reliance" and "help yourself," in the vernacular, as the author put it. It was an efficient and industrious race, and its success should inspire rather than discourage the French, because there was no reason to believe "that the Anglo-Saxon race is naturally superior to the others," "as the English and Americans are prepared to."

There was, however, a considerable difference between Great Britain and the colonies it had been forced to part with, thanks to a French policy that "had not lacked in foresight or cunning," that is, military aid to the insurgents. Great Britain was both "Tyre and Carthage"—a double parallel first used in the eighteenth century. It needed a free world to further its trade and commerce and, as an old and wise power, "it [did] not give in to the vagaries of presumption." It preferred, "through commerce, to teach European civilization to the innumerable peoples of Asia, Africa, and Oceania." In short, France could reach an understanding with Britain. The same was not true of "the descendents of her sons"! If Great Britain represented the good side of the Anglo-Saxon "civilization lever," North America embodied its aggressive propensity to destroy other civilizations. Relentless rather than tenacious, not so much strong as simply violent, the Americans were the sorcerer's apprentices of their race. A steamroller running over the world, they were "suppressing the forests of northern America," flattening the continent, "improvising cities," and "creating populations." They also destroyed them, and with the same energy: "In this enormous theater, the Anglo-Saxon element has wiped out or is headed toward wiping out all the others: the Dutch on the banks of the Hudson, the Swedes in Delaware, the French in Missouri, Michigan, Arkansas, Texas, Louisiana, Indiana, Wisconsin, and Alabama, the Spaniards in Florida, California, and New Mexico; it is on its way to absorbing all the varieties of the white race. As for the red and black races, it has largely destroyed the former or violently cast all of that race's remnants to the extreme frontiers of its sphere of action; and the latter, in the

North, has been pushed away with a cold, hard caste pride that considers even living as neighbors sullying; while in the South [the Anglo-Saxon element] has been juxtaposed with it in the more sociable conditions of master and slave."[59]

This was the context and the real perspective in which the French should understand the Civil War.

It should first of all be considered—not surprisingly—a godsend or at least a reprieve for Europe. "Barely three years ago, it was calculated that the territory over which the Anglo-American race seemed destined to spread was equal to three-quarters of Europe," and plausible projection had calculated that its population would reach the "figure of one hundred fifty and a half million" in 125 years.[60] "People wondered who would stop the American population's expansion. Who? It is probably the Americans who have taken this task upon themselves, at least for now." It would be harder to more clearly state the great hopes France had for the Civil War as a check America had put on itself. The topos of an inevitable dismantlement cropped up once more: "The Union has been dealt a blow from which it is impossible that it will rise again as it was before, whatever the outcome of the struggle we are witnessing."

But this optimism was short-lived. In the end, who knew what the fanatical North was capable of? Who could say what extremes its rage would lead it to? Bluntly observing that a conquered but not broken South would be an ideal beachhead and "a support base for any foreign power at war with the United States," the author of *Du Panlatinisme* drew a conclusion that was inexorable for the North: the war must become a war "of extermination"; it already was, since the North "has seriously undertaken to extirpate by death and proscription a population of eight million souls." The impassible Northerners would stop at nothing: "history teaches [them] that this enormous immolation is not impossible; without looking for examples in the Old World, where there is clearly no shortage of them, the North has one among its neighbors and even in its own past: . . . did the New England Puritans not manage to wipe out even the last traces of the red race?"

This was, of course, not the first time France had denounced the Indians' extermination. But it was apparently the first time the extermination was used as an example of a kind of genocidal vocation on the part of the "Anglo-Americans"; it was also the first time the New England Puritan, recently rehabilitated by Tocqueville as the source and origin of democratic American liberties, had been identified as a pure and simple murderer. Once, he had massacred the redskins; now he was massacring another race that had tried to resist his domination: the whites of the South. "The Confederates have no illusions about the fate that awaits them if they are beaten: they know how far the fanaticism of the North's sectarians can go, a fanaticism of which we clearly do not have a precise idea in France, and which is, strictly speaking, the ambitious, furious monomania of a people which truly believes it is the chosen one of the God of armies, the exterminating God of the Amalecites and the Moabites."[61] The argument fell in line with De Leon's anti-Puritan remarks, which described the "ancient Puritan doctrine" as it had been up-dated by the warmongers of the North: "1st, that the earth and all it encloses belongs to the saints; 2nd, that we ourselves are the saints."[62]

This was also the first appearance of a French domino theory that would become commonplace in the 1880s and 1890s: the North American ogre was proceeding bite by bite. The South was a real mouthful, a hearty main dish. But even after gobbling it up, the ogre would not be satisfied. The land feast would continue. Other populations were clearly marked for the slaughter; their "absorption" had only been "postponed" by the Southerners' heroic defense.[63] After the South, Latin America would be next. All the Latins knew it, felt it, their "instinct of self-preservation" screamed it: the "Anglo-Saxon nationality" was the enemy! Currently the South's enemy, soon the enemy of Latin America, which "inevitably, sooner or later" would be "invaded" if it did not put up its guard by "regenerating [itself]" and appealing to France for protection.[64]

The Civil War looked very different from these ethno-strategic heights. Doubtless the blacks' emancipation was only a "pretext" for the North,[65] but even if it was more than that—an "occasional cause"—it was Frenchmen's job to put it in perspective and not "allow the generous impulses of their hearts to lead their judgment astray." Abolishing a system that had already been largely "modified and tempered" and would peter out on its own was not such a big deal! The real issue was serious and decisive in a different way. The fate of the world was being played out on the battlefields of Maryland and Virginia: "When one considers Europe's future, what is at stake for this part of the world in an already overly protracted struggle is something very different than slavery and the Negroes' emancipation. Will the Americans of the North establish over the entire transatlantic continent a domination like the one the Romans had weighing down upon the world?"[66] Conclusion: Napoleon III's Mexican policy was a "great policy," but it was "incomplete" and hardly "guaranteed" if it did not go hand in hand with a military alliance with the Confederacy.

We should not be misled by these closing "audacities": the pamphlet was as close as can be to France's official position, and, moreover, it used the same rhetorical particularities and characteristic tics as the government press, particularly in denouncing the "pact between the Yankees and

Poland's aggressors."[67] Making the confrontation of three great races-*cum*-civilizations out to be the key to Europe's future, the author was simply rationalizing a way of thinking that was already that of France's leadership and a large part of the "intelligent classes," to use Slidell's terminology. It is significant that Morny, who met with John Bigelow in January 1865 just after he replaced Dayton as Union ambassador, chose to bring up the topic of a "Latin race" in order to deny using it as the main thrust of his policy. Faced with this denial-tinged disclosure, Bigelow used the clever tactic of replying in the very terms that Morny purported to frown on, stressing that "there are more of the latin [*sic*] race in New York City than in all the Southern States, and more Catholics in the State of New York than in the whole Confederacy."[68] It was an elegant way of saying that he was not fooled by Morny's ostensible distance from an ethno-strategic "theory" that was effectively central to the empire's political logic.

Mercier's pamphlet offers a concentrate of all this theorizing: *Du Panlatinisme* is like the distillation of a war-long mass of propaganda that was a mix of fact and fantasy. In this digest of pro-South leanings were all the ingredients that would soon be used to brew the anti-American potion.

The pamphlet's most striking and, at the same time, most novel aspect was the way it ethnicized the political and used "scientific" references as justification (the pamphlet contains several pages discussing the dangers of "mongrelism" for the South and explicitly refers to the budding field of American racial anthropology, which used the term to designate a "mix of the white, black, and red races"),[69] but it was really driven by an obsession with France's decline. *Du Panlatinisme* thus offers a particularly early example of the French fixation on dispossession and decadence in the face of the new "great peoples"—America and Russia, both so arrogant and sure of themselves.[70] Resisting what would soon be called *yankeesme* did not hinge on history's misleading lessons or political philosophy's hazy speculations: it was and should be a vital jolt, a physiological reaction against the "spirit of conquest" of Anglo-Saxon America, which believed that its "manifest destiny" was to conquer the entire hemisphere all the way to Cape Horn—until something better came along?[71]

The Saga of North against South

Is *Du Panlatinisme* a "representative" work? No, if that means it expressed the average French opinion of the American war. Yes, if you admit that it uses the same logic—pushed to its extreme consequences—as the one governing the empire's political decisions (or indecisiveness) throughout the war; it is

also the one that seeped, for better or for worse, into many politically independent commentaries. It was, moreover, its lasting echoes and not its
immediate impact that made its arguments an important part of future
French anti-Americanism. The pro-South leanings of the emperor's subjects
paved the way for the anti-*yankeesme* of Jules Ferry's citizens.

Was all 1860s France pro-South? Certainly not. And still less "pan-Latin."
But, on the other hand, the French were far less enthusiastic about Lincoln
and Grant than rosy postwar reminiscences would make them out to be
when they recalled an overwhelming surge of sympathy for the abolitionist
North. The collective consciousness also has screen memories—very deliberately placed ones. The Third Republic, once it had settled into power,
would tackle the unglamorous job of reestablishing ties between the two
countries. France's marked hostility toward the Union during the war would
be chalked up as part of Napoleon the "Lesser's" now-despised reign and
the "real country" credited with a show of pro-North solidarity that had in
fact been made by only a few militant minorities. In this operation of ideological reconstruction, the Third Republic had Victor Hugo's anthumous and
posthumous clout; his unwavering philo-Unionism was thrown like Noah's
cloak over the cautiousness and ambivalence that had abounded during the
war. But for a less legendary image, Jules Verne is the place to look.

Hugo was the lighthouse, Jules Verne the photographer. One upheld the
legend of France's solidarity with the winners; the other, in two novels written twenty-two years apart, put all of France's ambiguities on display. Jules
Verne does have a few surprises in store for readers who might think that a
belief in progress and science went hand in hand with anti-South sentiment.
Sure, there was *Nord contre Sud,* where Verne comes across as a vehement
supporter of the North. There, the action takes place in Florida. The Burbanks, militant abolitionists from New Jersey and humane plantation owners, become the special target of secessionist agitators led by a disturbing
felon with no family or roots, the cruel Texar. Pillage, murder, kidnapping,
innocents unjustly convicted by a terrified local court: nothing is too horrible
for the two-faced villain. (The secret of Texar's ubiquity and the key to his
impunity is that he has a twin, his lookalike accomplice. . .) All will end well
for the Burbanks and the state of Florida, though, mostly thanks to Zermah,
a big-hearted mulatto woman. The long-awaited Northern reinforcements
get there a little late and hardly have time to take a bow before the curtain
falls on a resounding profession of faith: " 'Yes, Federals, Northerners, abolitionists, Unionists!' the man replied, puffed with pride in voicing these diverse qualifications for the party of the good cause."[72] That is what you call
hammering it home.

But the hammering would be more like a nail in the coffin: the coffin of a South that had long since been beaten to death. For, interestingly—an unimportant detail for its young readers, but not an uninteresting one for the historian—*Nord contre Sud* was not written during the Civil War, as its "militant" tone and snoozy declarations might lead one to believe. Far from it! Jules Verne published it in the *Magasin d'éducation* in 1887, nearly a quarter of a century after the events described. The time lapse gives its proselytizing an old-fashioned taint. How admirable the Union's cause had become under the shining Third Republic! The South had since been taken to task and "reconstructed," the empire was dead, and liberty had been given a new home. Was Jules Verne fighting the "good fight"? A recent preface to *Nord contre Sud* describes it as a "new chance [for Jules Verne] to express himself clearly" on "emancipation and the right of nations to self-determination."[73] It cannot be said that Verne seized the opportunity at a time when the war's outcome was uncertain and the North's few supporters were having trouble making themselves heard.

In fact, *Nord contre Sud* is an act of literary contrition, a tardy touch-up to a very different snapshot Verne took in an undeservedly less well known novel, *Les Forceurs de blocus* (The Blockade Runners). Here, the "subject" of the Civil War is dealt with in the heat of the moment: the novel was serialized in a magazine in October 1865 before being reprinted in book form in 1870.[74] And it told a very different story than the politically correct *Nord contre Sud*. It caught the American war at an oblique angle—one that reflected the collective French scene as much as Manet's canvas had the previous year in the wake of the naval combat at Cherbourg.

In 1865, *Les Forceurs de blocus* was a significant title. Everyone understood that it referred to the blockading of Southern ports by the Union navy. It had not been forgotten that this brutally applied measure had pushed England and France within inches of declaring war on the Union; the best-informed would add that Napoleon III himself, at the time of his famous meeting in Vichy with the Confederate commissioner Slidell on July 16, 1862, had expressed his regret at not having denounced and run the blockade throttling the South. Jules Verne did not shy away from novelizing a war the emperor had not dared to declare. And even more politically, he portrayed the imperial chancellery's most unwavering wish: war against the North, by proxy. Therefore, logically, there is not a single Frenchman in the novel—and few Americans. *Les Forceurs de blocus* is an English novel. The action starts in Liverpool, a port that had long been linked to Southern interests and where, despite the war, the cotton trade was still in going strong, more lucratively than ever. That port was won over to friends of the South;

the *Alabama* had been secretly built there under the code number "290." The blockade to be run is in Charleston. The English captain is motivated by essentially commercial considerations, but he also has a more general anti-North stance on the freedom of the seas and against the Union's unlawful behavior. As the adventure's hero, he draws the reader down an "objectively" pro-South path. But complications arise (and a balance is restored) when a mysterious last-minute passenger turns out to be a young American woman also bent on breaking through to Charleston so she can rescue her father, a Northern officer being held prisoner and threatened with execution. The blockade will be run, the cotton loaded up, and the father saved—and the courageous young woman will marry the valiant captain. The final twist, a dramatic escape from the port of Charleston, has a particularly symbolic importance.

The novelist did not choose to set his story in Charleston arbitrarily. As we have noted, the treatment inflicted on Charleston's magnificent harbor was unanimously condemned in Europe as an act of "barbarism."[75] Indeed, not satisfied with blocking access to the harbor, the Union government had sunk an entire stone fleet there. Sending down ships loaded with rocks had seemed at the time like a true war crime. The French press had been no less vehement than the English papers in denouncing it, with the official *Moniteur* stating its "profound sorrow" and "repulsion."[76] It is clearly not unimportant that Jules Verne chose a "martyred" Confederate city as the backdrop for his adventure. But probably even more symbolic is Captain James Playfair's final exploit. Equipped with his cotton and his father-in-law, he leaves the infernal harbor under fire from both sides: Yankees trying to sink the blockade runner and Confederates informed of his hand in their prisoner's escape.

A fine tour de force, and a nice sleight of hand, this Civil War epic as seen from the deck of a British ship! If Jules Verne's readers caught a glimpse of the Civil War, it was from afar and through a spyglass, like the onlookers in Cherbourg who had witnessed the *Alabama*'s last fight. As another political allegory of the French view of the Civil War, *Les Forceurs de blocus* would have deserved the title *Neither North nor South*—with the epigraph: "Gentlemen of the English guard, fire first!"

☆ ☆ ☆

These were the strange circumstances in which the French rediscovered the United States: by dreaming of its split. After a half-century of indifference barely interrupted by Tocqueville's solitary voice, France took a new interest in the republic across the sea, just as it was starting to look doomed. Never would so much be written about the rights of nations and the prerogatives of federal governments; on the economic developments of the country's two "sections"; on the parties and their leaders; and of course, on all the material and moral aspects of a war that gave America a new face—a martial and conquering one. Faced with a Franco-French debate dominated by the conviction that the United States would soon be wiped off the map of the world, America took on a paradoxical concreteness, which romanticism's fanciful land had lacked.

The disappointed dream of the country's split had aftereffects in France: there is nothing more embarrassing than an unfulfilled malevolent wish. A still unformulated apprehension can be detected in the schism scenarios the press and the government had indulged in: the United States of the Reconstruction would seem all the more daunting because nearly everyone in France had been convinced it would die out. Tribulations like these make or break a nation, and the Americans had not been broken. Before long, the victory they had won against each other would start to look like the precursor to measures turned against others.

The Civil War was thus an important stage in French anti-Americanism's crystallization process. It reactivated flagging interest in the transatlantic republic's destiny and marked the end of "the distance and the remove." But the newfound proximity was more suspicious than cordial. The era of verbal violence had not yet come; the tone was one of a sometimes slightly suspect solicitude in the face of the ravages of a fratricidal struggle. But the essential consequence of the national debate it created in France, with its proliferation of pro and con arguments, was that it formed an arsenal that would be used by the 1880 generation. That was when most of the arguments developed in the heat of the debate would reappear, often misused, sometimes misinterpreted: grievances against the North and admonishments toward the South would, in a sense, be thrown to the masses and recycled into overarching criticism of the United States, which, against all expectations, had been "reconstituted." Faced with the re-formed Union, warnings from the war years about the country's slide into authoritarianism would not be forgotten. The theory, developed in 1861, of a North that could win only at the expense of a serious alteration of its political nature would resurface with the force of a prophecy come true, and the treatment, considered iniquitous, of the conquered South would seem like the first sign of a thirst for domination that the simple suppression of the rebels had not quenched.

—So, you have an aristocracy?
—*An* aristocracy? They have at least two of them!
  Victorien Sardou, *L'Oncle Sam*

 # 3

Lady Liberty and the Iconoclasts

The Civil War was a key period for anti-Americanism's *sedimenta-tion*. In reaction to current events, French observers produced a flood of highly unfavorable analyses. Criticism and disapproval would intertwine for four years running, subtly but profoundly modifying representations of the United States.

It would take some time, however—two decades—for the full extent of the change in images to come to light. No sooner had the fighting between the Unionists and Confederates ended than France's attention shifted, entirely mobilized by events in Europe. In 1866 came the rude awakening of Sadowa and the shock of German unification, along with a controversial French interven-tion against Garibaldi's troops in Italy in favor of the pope. France had turned its back in embarrassment on the dismal Mexican affair. It now had a wary eye on Prussia, where the enemy lurked. The disastrous defeat of 1870, followed by the Paris Commune and its brutal suppression, brought the civil war home to France. The American conflict's recent bloodbaths were easily overshad-owed by France's domestic tragedy. The days of drawing-room speculation and a somewhat voyeuristic curiosity in a distant war had come and gone. Other, more pressing matters than the fate

of the Southern states appealed to French hearts and minds. Memories of the
bombardment of Atlanta or plantations burning down paled in comparison
with the great bonfire of insurgent Paris.

France's mutilation and its uncertain future set the nation's nerves on
edge. Yet if the French no longer had time to take an interest in America's
Reconstruction, they were no less bitter about the symbolic wounds the
United States dealt them when, for example, in 1870 pro-Prussian demonstrations were held in American cities with large German populations, or,
worse, when President Ulysses S. Grant sent a telegram to Wilhelm II con-
gratulating him on the birth of an empire proclaimed in Versailles's Hall
of Mirrors in a downtrodden, occupied, and humiliated France. Whether
Grant's move was a blunder or a low blow, the French would not soon forgive
that sign of indifference to their sufferings.

Twilight of a Model, Rise of an Idol

The paradox of the 1870s was that political circumstances that should have
favored a rediscovery of the American political model led instead to its nearly
universal refusal by the very people in France who had been its most ardent
defenders: the new government's republican instigators, with Gambetta[1] on
the front lines.

Once French soil had been freed from the Prussians' military presence
(at the cost of an exorbitant "indemnity" and the loss of Alsace and Lorraine),
the question of which institutions to set up in France became a pressing one
and brought the United States back to the fore of French political debates.
Throughout the years of the empire, the "country of Washington and Lincoln" had been the republican opposition's major reference point. The republicans were far from a majority in the National Assembly elected in 1871, but
their prestige as opponents of Napoleon III was coupled with the credit they
had acquired as the driving force of national defense. It would have been
only natural for them to make the most of their prestige and credit and forcefully plead in favor of a constitution inspired by the model republic's. Even
conservative representatives would have had a hard time remaining indifferent to the exemplary stability of America's institutions, which were almost
a hundred years old and had proved their mettle by surviving the secession
crisis.

But something very different happened instead, despite the Americanophiles in France, and unforeseen by them. A strange political and theatrical
incident could have opened their eyes, though. Popular "boulevard" theater
was one of the best barometers of Parisian opinion at the time, and on the

stage, the dramatist Victorien Sardou's word was law. Just after the debacle of 1870, he wrote a comedy, *L'Oncle Sam,* that was a violent satire of the United States. The attack was so brutal that Adolphe Thiers, acting as the provisional head of the government, prohibited the play, which "would keenly wound a sister nation," from being staged.[2] It would finally be put on at the Vaudeville on November 6, 1873. Sardou went much further than his predecessors. He went beyond simply presenting a few ridiculous or un-couth American stereotypes. His comedy lashed out at America's daily life and its institutions right and left. It denounced the press's corruption and the business world's disloyalty, unmasked democracy as a fraud, and pointed a finger at the travesty of "religions" invented by charlatans. Ignorance, greed, vulgar cynicism: that was America. "When I think that some animal both-ered to discover it!" This line of dialogue gives an idea of the play's tone. The model country had suddenly become a foil for France. The message was explicitly driven home in the first act: "You must stop that maddening habit of offering us *you* as a model!" the play's French heroine tells the Ameri-cans.[3] It was a premonitory remark: applauded on stage in 1873, it would also be approved two years later on the benches of the Assembly.

However logical and probable it was, the "resurgence of the [American] model" in post-imperial France would be strikingly "ephemeral."[4] In 1875, the offensive launched during a constitutional debate by the moderate repub-licans of the "American school" would prove to be a failure—and a personal failure for its leader, Édouard-René Lefèbvre de Laboulaye. A grandson of one of Louis XVI's secretaries, Laboulaye, born in 1811, was a jurist and his-torian who entered the political arena when it was under the revolution of 1848's sway. He was appointed professor of comparative legislation at the Collège de France in 1849 and was one of the most prominent spokesmen for a liberal-influenced moderate republicanism under the empire. From then on, he became deeply involved in endorsing the American model—as a way of opposing both what he saw as the usurpation of sovereignty by the imperial regime and the post-Sieyès radicalism of France's revolutionary tra-dition. In 1863, he published *L'État et ses limites* and *Le Parti libéral,* his two principal doctrinal writings. In 1865, he came up with the strange idea of offering the Americans a statue of the figure of Liberty for the anniversary of their revolution. The most surprising thing was not that Laboulaye was unable to impose his not unreasonable plan of having France, in its new beginnings after the Battle of Sedan, adopt a republican constitution loosely inspired by the American constitutional model; it was that he succeeded in the much more far-fetched project of bestowing a French-made colossus on America.

Elected to the National Assembly in 1871, Laboulaye immediately launched a campaign in favor of American-style institutions. He appealed to public opinion, publishing *La République constitutionnelle* in May 1871. In this programmatic text, written as a letter to Eugène Yung, the editor of the *Journal de Lyon*, Laboulaye reminded his readers that the Americans were the "great organizers of modern democracy."[5] For him, there was no doubt about it: "The Republic best suited to France is one that looks most like America and Switzerland's governments."[6] But especially America's. In his *Esquisse d'une Constitution républicaine*, published in 1872, the American model is favorably contrasted with the French revolutionary school, though Laboulaye does not tackle the question of presidentialism. In 1873, he chaired the special legislative committee, called the Commission des Trente, responsible for examining constitutional law proposals. He also—with Waddington, who would soon become president of the Conseil—shared the responsibility of making a comparative study of the European and American constitutions. In early 1875, as the time for decision making drew near, Édouard de Laboulaye started paving the way for an outcome compatible with his vision. The proposal he put forth on January 29 was rejected by a vote of 356 to 336. His amendment had been written in these terms: "The government of the Republic will be composed of two houses and a president." The next day, another amendment introduced by representative Henri Wallon won by a narrow majority of votes and founded the republic, with this sentence: "The President of the Republic shall be elected on an absolute majority vote by the Senate and the Chamber of Deputies convening in the National Assembly."

With the Laboulaye amendment, the very hypothesis of American-style presidentialism was rejected by a majority of representatives. Jacques Portes stresses the importance of this refusal: "It is not without interest that the Laboulaye amendment of 29 January 1875, . . . however innocuous and formal it may have sounded, was rejected as too close to the American example with which everyone was bound to associate the name Laboulaye."[7] Gambetta and his followers' hostility to Laboulaye's American inclinations would remain unmitigated over the following weeks and months, as shown by another confrontational exchange on the floor of the Chamber of Deputies. The leader of the republican Left, who had been enthusiastically pro-American under the empire, scored a big hit by mocking the American ex-model:

> Some have made a great deal of to-do about the American senate. They even went so far as to commission from an American (*laughter on the left*), whom I suspect of being from Seine-et-Oise (*general hilarity*), a consultation on the analogies that might exist between the French senate and the American senate. . . . There is no

way to compare America with France, and on this occasion it would have been better to go simply from Paris to Versailles than from Paris to America (*approval and laughter on the left*).[8]

Without making this parliamentary episode out to be more revealing than it is, we can consider the distance taken from the American model as symptomatic, and the boisterous assent shown by the benches on the left revealing. Winning over the scoffers at the United States' and its sycophants' expense—with Noailles and Laboulaye first in line—Gambetta prefigured a much more widespread movement: the republican Left's detachment from the "model republic" it had praised so highly under the empire. Were the French republicans anti-American turncoats? That might be taking things a little too far. Nevertheless, the intellectual and emotional ties were loosening. Refusal of the American "model" was a sign of more radical reversals to come: on the front lines of early anti-Americanism, as of 1883, would be Frédéric Gaillardet, a republican who had recovered from his Americanophilia so completely that he devoted an entire book to burning down the very object of his former affections. In addition to being a rhetorical gesture and tactical maneuver, Gambetta's oration was indicative of a more than incidental sea change, corroborated also by America's disappearance as a reference point in the republican propaganda of the time. That does not mean the United States would thereafter be bereft of friends and supporters on the French political scene. But its supporters would represent only a small aristocratic band of conservative republicans, whose figureheads would disappear one after the next. Laboulaye himself would die in 1883, before he ever saw his colossal dream materialize in the harbor of New York.

Lady Liberty's Tribulations

The great and only triumph of this little Americanophile faction was Bartholdi's[9] famed statue, naturalized as Lady Liberty. It was a colossal success but was also riddled with ambiguities.

The ambiguity began in France. Throughout the French subscription campaign and the celebrations that followed, uncertainty reigned in the official speeches, which were caught between praising the principle of liberty, exalting the republic as a system of government, rekindling a languishing Franco-American alliance, and making a free-exchange apology for trade and industry.[10] The statue clearly had broad shoulders. The idea proposed during a banquet on May 21, 1884, of installing a replica of the statue at the site of the new Panama Canal, if it can be explained by the fact that Laboulaye had been replaced by Ferdinand de Lesseps as head of the Franco-American Union, is also indicative of the project organizers' symbolic fluctuations.

The ambiguity continued and worsened with the standoffish reception America gave the most cumbersome gift ever offered by one nation to another. Raising the statue on American soil became a laborious affair when first Congress, then local New York authorities, refused to shoulder the cost of constructing a pedestal. An American caricature from 1884 shows the statue as a decrepit old woman (bearing a strange resemblance to Pigalle's sculpture of an aged Voltaire) sitting directly on the rocks of Bedloe's Island in a posture of complete discouragement. At her feet, a tiny bricklayer is vaguely busying himself with a block marked "cornerstone." The drawing's caption does not exactly arouse the reader's optimism: "The 'Statue of Liberty' One Thousand Years Later; Waiting."[11]

She would not have to wait that long. Two years later, in 1886, a national subscription and press campaign (in which Pulitzer figured prominently) would give her the chance to set her feet on solid ground. But these embarrassing tribulations, if they stimulated the ingenuity of American caricaturists—who represented the statue as a pauper, a beggar woman, or a bag lady—did not have many people laughing in France. By offering the Americans such a disproportionate token of France's affections, the Americanophile group led by Laboulaye was taking a big risk: the risk of seeing its lucky recipients pale at the offering. There is nothing so devastating in love as an unwanted gift. Lady Liberty had been generated by the frustrations of a French liberal under the empire and offered by a still shaky republic to a distant and indifferent so-called "sister" nation; in this, the statue not only summed up an ideological program (and moreover a muddled one), it also admirably embodied Lacan's definition of love: "Giving what you do not have to someone who does not want it."

The imbroglio over financing the pedestal had not yet been resolved when Bartholdi and the French committee decided to send the statue off, for better or for worse, to New York. The situation seemed about to turn from a bureaucratic farce into a diplomatic drama. And if everything was fixed in extremis, if American subscribers filled in for the authorities' shortcomings, if Grover Cleveland himself—who as governor of the state of New York had vetoed allocating funds for the project—participated in its inauguration in his new role as president of the United States, the call had been a close one. America's official stance was incomprehensible and had been restlessly tolerated in France. It would become, just a few years after the statue's installation in New York, a point of French recrimination against America. Of the whole affair, Edmond Johanet, a correspondent for *Le Figaro*, would only recall Congress's insulting stinginess and "the injury dealt to France by representatives ungrateful to a nation that had so strongly contributed to American independence."[12] Another essayist, Émile Barbier, pushed the disabused disparagement even further, mocking the statue itself, "that enormous art bauble, braced with a utilitarian quality" (because it was also a lighthouse), and waxed ironic about the "subtle thought" that had guided France, which had "correctly guessed America's tastes" in designing the monstrous gadget.[13] The Great Nation's bronze ambassador, the peaceful Trojan horse forged to reestablish France in the heart of the American city, was, for Barbier in 1893, nothing more than a kitschy colossus straight out of some Cincinnati bazaar, one of those ugly and cumbersome things you give a provincial aunt with notoriously bad taste—a political white elephant.

Maybe Bartholdi's statue simply got there too late. It was obviously too late to commemorate 1776, as Laboulaye would have wanted. It was also too late for the belated anniversary the French committee had considered: the treaty of 1783 that had ended the War of Independence. Inaugurated on October 28, 1886, the statue was not part of any commemorative calendar, and the mediocre rituals that accompanied its unveiling (speeches, a parade, a marching band) had trouble filling the void. Also late in coming, from the French side, was an allegory too tempered to really mobilize a left-leaning republican political imagination. Bartholdi was an Alsatian scarred by the 1870 defeat. He had defended Colmar as a soldier in the National Guard and fought alongside Garibaldi after being sent to Italy by the "national defense" government, which had established itself in Tours. He had originally envisioned his statue trampling a broken chain, but Laboulaye preferred to see it holding the tablets of the U.S. Constitution.[14] This Liberty was clearly only a distant relative of the beautiful barricade warrior painted by Delacroix. The young giantess was part of the same age and mood as her instigator Laboulaye—the dream of a conservative republican under the empire. She was also the same age as the august old man who paid her a solemn visit before her departure: the national poet, America's unwavering friend, Victor Hugo.

On November 29, 1884, an enfeebled Hugo, accompanied by his granddaughter Jeanne, entered the Gaget Gauthier company on the Rue de Chazelles. Others before him had already made the visit or pilgrimage: ministers, ambassadors, dignitaries of all stripes, up to and including President Jules Grévy. But it was on this day, as the poet painfully climbed the stairwell inside the statue and stepped out onto the construction's second landing, that the real encounter took place. The feeling was palpable, and someone in the crowd called out: "Behold! Two giants are regarding each other."[15] Bartholdi's allegorical figure was indeed the colossal contemporary of a preeminent peer, the cast-iron sister of the gigantic Entities—Liberty, Justice, the Future—so obedient to the Wise Man of Guernsey[16] that they came at his beck and call and tapped out on his séance table the decrees of destiny recoded as verse. Laboulaye had died the year before. Bartholdi was still alive, but he was in charge of the medium rather than the message; no doubt he was devoted to liberty, and maybe even America, but when all was said and done, his real passion was for colossal statues, and in 1869, he did not hesitate to offer one exactly like Lady Liberty to France's Khedive friend, to light the way into the Suez Canal. . . No, decidedly there was only one man who could generate some added symbolic value and give so much matter a little meaning, and that was the elderly Hugo.

The *vates* knew what to do. He came, he saw, he pontificated. "I said, on seeing the statue: 'The great and restless sea observes the union of two great, becalmed lands.' I have been asked to allow these words to be engraved on the pedestal." That is what he would write the next day in his journal, with a sense of having done his duty.[17]

Hugo died a few months later, also before the New York coronation. The orphan idol of a generation now in its grave would rise up over Manhattan like a fallow sign. Hugo died before learning, of course, that his last effort at writing an inscription would go unheeded and that the words the statue had inspired in him would never be engraved at its base. He died without suspecting that he was not the man of letters—or *woman* of letters, in this case—who would have the honor of writing the statue's inscription, and that the final epigraph, neglectful of France, would usher the statue into a new symbolic career. The poetess Emma Lazarus's verse, engraved on the pedestal, transformed Bartholdi's statue from a pledge of France and America's friendship into the tutelary divinity of the poor of all nations, the Mother Protector of the immigrants who would be corralled a stone's throw away on Ellis Island. "Give me your Tired, your Poor, your Huddled Masses. . . ." In venerating the poor, Emma Lazarus's lines were in fact closer to the spirit of Hugo than old Hugo himself had been in dedicating the statue to the two nations' alliance. These lines, which would soon be memorized by schoolchildren all over America, would nevertheless confirm the separation of a quickly nationalized Lady Liberty from her native land. More semiologically flexible than she appears in her cast-iron corset, Bartholdi's statue would not represent "the fraternal understanding of the two republics" for long. She indulged her new compatriots, letting them decide just what she stood for.

France-America: the Great Illusion

If a promise, as they say, binds only the one making it, a gift binds only the one offering it. The stubborn effort of Laboulaye and his friends was less an attempt to win back American public opinion, which had grown indifferent to France, than it was of reviving, in France, an unsure and already shaky affection for the "sister republic" of yore. Behind the scenes of this monumental gift was the muted apprehension of a Franco-American estrangement.

The great idol had no sooner left its native soil than the first iconoclasts entered the stage, men bent on showing that Franco-American relations were null, inane, and fraudulent. In the early 1880s, as republican France gained in political stability, the United States would come back under essayists' and travelers' pens. One might have thought there would be renewed friendship, praise, or at least understanding and curiosity. But it was quite a different bell that started ringing: a strange anti-American chime with an unexpected pitch, which set the tone for the 1898 alarm.

This watershed moment, in which disenchantment was already breaking through and hostility emerging, was epitomized by two antithetical and complementary figures: Frédéric Gaillardet and the Baron de Mandat-Grancey. A priori, the *boulevardier* and the baron had nothing in common. Nothing, except precisely their early anti-Americanism. Shadowy torchbearers for the coming wave of hostility, Gaillardet and Mandat-Grancey were the first to offer the French reading public, in hundreds of pages (apiece), a caricature of contemporary America, along with a completely negative revision of Franco-American relations. Polemical polar opposites with diametrically opposed pasts and convictions, these two pioneers of the 1880s were exemplary in putting forth a perfect illustration of the convergences between the Left and the Right that would characterize French anti-Americanism.

The vocabulary of lost love might seem excessively sentimental and abusively metaphorical when applied to relations between countries. It was nonetheless insistently used by the United States' first systematic detractors in France—especially Gaillardet, disenchanted by all things American. His *Aristocratie en Amérique* was published in 1883. Its allusion was transparent and its ambition clear: correcting Tocqueville and debunking the too-favorable image Tocqueville had given of America. To be honest, his thick volume was not up to the task, and its digs hardly touched their illustrious victim. *L'Aristocratie en Amérique* would also not have the kind of resounding success Gaillardet had hoped for; his main claim to posterity was (and still is) a play he had co-written with Alexandre Dumas half a century earlier, the lucrative *Tour de Nesle*. His essay is nevertheless worth exhuming for at least three reasons.

The first is that it assembled and systematized, for the first time, a whole set of historical, political, and cultural grievances against America that future

French polemicists would never tire of articulating. *L'Aristocratie en Amérique,* if it was not the antidote to Tocqueville's magnum opus it purported to be, was in fact the first anthology of anti-Americanism. The second reason for its importance is its author's pro-American past. *L'Aristocratie en Amérique* is not the work of one of the essayists who consistently professed disdain for the United States, such as Georges Ohnet, for example, who wrote for *Le Figaro* and was a notorious adversary of all things American.[18] Quite the contrary. Not only did the author spend ten years of his life (from 1837 to 1847) in America, but he also "championed it for forty-five years," as he himself admitted, notably in the *Courrier des États-Unis,* a periodical of which he had long been editor-in-chief. A repentant lover, vexed militant, and apostle turned heretic, Gaillardet embodied a completely new figure in the French intellectual landscape: one who was disappointed by the model republic and disenchanted with the New World. He revisited America, both literally and figuratively, and returned from his trip with an unflattering portrait of the United States, one that in fact expressed (as he preferred warning his readers) "great severity" toward the country he had spent his whole life praising.[19] Since Gaillardet had not disavowed his republican ideals in the least, it had to be America that had faltered.

The third reason his testimony is important has to do with his intellectual personality and political position. Frédéric Gaillardet was a "progressive," a 1848-style republican and antisocialist neo-Jacobin with leanings similar to those of General Cavaignac, who had suppressed the radical insurrection of June 1848 but later failed in his presidential bid against Louis-Napoleon Bonaparte. Hostile to the Commune, Gaillardet was staunchly faithful to the principles of the Revolution—the French Revolution, that is. His closing remarks against the United States had very personal overtones but were also part of a larger wave of repudiation of the transatlantic model by the French republicans of the 1880s.

This was a man from whose eyes the scales had suddenly fallen. Gaillardet had to make amends. He took up his pen to denounce an illusion that had also been his own, one the French had held dear since the reign of Louis XVI: that they were "loved" by the Americans. It was high time the French followed his example and opened their eyes.

American gratitude for the aid France had once given the insurgents? An outdated notion. A French fantasy shared by few on the other side of the ocean. Wasn't the first rule of nations to forget their debts? Hadn't the Americans proved, as early as 1792, while France was confronting the coalition of kings alone, that they had either a short memory or a passive way of being thankful? Tocqueville had excused them for abandoning the French, arguing

that it was a wise decision, one that responded to their vital interests. Gaillardet found the excuse of national egotism a little thin but retained the lesson in realpolitik. If the affection between two nations can be snuffed out at
the slightest hitch, at the tiniest bit of friction between their respective interests, the French should at least stop deluding themselves with a legend of
friendship that was as illusory as it was sentimental.

The "natural" solidarity between revolutionary nations? A dangerous
myth. An error of perspective and judgment. This, because the Americans
were "revolutionaries without a revolution."[20] (Here the anti-Tocquevillian
Gaillardet was stealing from Tocqueville: "There has been no democratic revolution [in America].")[21] And they hated France's. The proof was that the
newborn United States turned its back on France, its benefactor, just as
France was becoming republican. America's very hypothetical "gratitude,"
which remained moreover purely "platonic," "died out in the first years of the
republic founded by our fathers in 1792."[22] The Terror and its abuses were
only a pretext. Republican solidarity was thus a historical legend and a political lie. In fact, by founding a genuine republic, France had forced America
to show its true nature as a masked aristocracy. The Americans (and their
wives, "republican women as proud as duchesses"),[23] felt an instinctive repulsion for the French Revolution's essential legacy: the aspiration toward a
social democracy inherent in the spirit of 1792, and which the Third Republic had put back on the agenda.

Gaillardet was indignant: how stupid the French had been, how stupid *he*
had been! It had taken all the gullibility of yore, all Tocqueville's partiality, all
the obliviousness of Michel Chevalier, Gustave de Beaumont, and Major
Poussin to create an illusion of fraternity and keep the French believing it![24]
Nothing could be more hateful to France's very ideals than the American
republic. No creature could be further from the French republican than the
Homo americanus—unless you counted his female version, which embodied
the fundamental hypocrisy of the North American human. "Those little democratic women, democratic in name only," Gaillardet wrote, "are true aristo-
crats by nature."[25] However anecdotal or biographical it may have been, the
delusion about American women that overcame Gaillardet still had its place
in the semiological table of his anti-Americanism. The discourse of animad-
version is impure, mixed with pockets of personal fixation; the cord of the
argument is stretched tight by various humors, affects, prejudices, and memories. Historical semiology has to become "impure," as well, in order to grasp
the effects of these affects.

Moreover, *L'Aristocratie en Amérique* is a serious work, in its way: better
informed, better documented, historically speaking, than many later essays

that would be hastily sewn together by earnest authors unsullied by any knowledge of their subject matter. It is neither a fashionably scribbled scrapbook nor a simple piece of rhetoric. The author knew what he was talking about. The same could not be said for the dozens of hurried travelers and raging essayists who would offer the French reading public their "impressions" of America between the 1880s and the Great War. If Gaillardet allowed himself a few fits of bad temper, they did not last very long. An extensive personal history filled and fueled his anti-Americanism but did not make it seem self-indulgent. He could have looked back over his past, his forty-five years of good and loyal service in promoting America; instead, he chose to question the past of an illusion the French still clung to: that they were loved by the Americans. And if he occasionally pontificated, he more often reasoned and attempted to provide demonstrations.

"There is no love, only proof of love," Cocteau would write. That was already Frédéric Gaillardet's view of things. And he had sought proof of the Americans' love for the French in vain. In his revisionist rereading of nineteenth-century Franco-American relations, he found, instead, traces of the contrary with every step. What he discovered and what he revealed to his readers was a hidden saga of long-standing animosity, of inexorably worsening antagonism, and of the unstoppable rise of America's aggression against France, after nearly a century of muted hostility. The suspicious machinations and shady patches were nothing new; they sprang from the very years that should have drawn the two republics together in fraternity, the terrible years when the French Revolution was taking its first steps. The history of America's ill-will had to be traced back to the beginning. As early as 1794, Gaillardet reminds his readers, America had secretly betrayed France, colluding with its colonial stepmother by signing a clandestine treaty with England allowing it to capture French ships.[26] It was the first loop of a specious net that French goodwill would often get entangled in. In 1835, President Andrew Jackson threatened to wage war on France over a simple matter of naval indemnities, then forced Louis-Philippe to buy peace at the cost of 25 million francs. In 1838 came the pressure in Mexico and the Veracruz incident. Next was the Crimean War: the Americans, far from supporting the French, backed the Russians. In 1862, back in Mexico, there were hostilities when Maximilian was put on the throne. In 1870, during the great calamity of France's defeat by Prussia, "Americans everywhere applauded the Germans' victories."[27] And just recently, in 1881, at the commemoration of the Battle of Yorktown, America's preference for the ignominious Germany had come to light when seven Germans were invited—and only one Frenchman.[28] In passing, Gaillardet slipped the Civil War under the rug; he had no intention of acknowledging that France's sympathies for the South could explain the Union's unfriendly behavior during the postwar years.

After giving all this evidence, the disabused Americanophile could re-state the question: "Do the Americans love the French?" He did not think so. There was no longer the slightest trace of a smile on the imperious and icy face of the new America, only grimaces and simpering. The Americans, as he had finally come to understand, "have never had for France and the French anything other than *purely* formal sympathies."[29] And formalities were not their strong suit; the Yankees preferred *content,* tangible realities. Empathy was a luxury; Americans only indulged in it when it was free of charge. Whence this bitter conclusion, which is like a distant echo of Figaro's famous speech in the Beaumarchais play: "The Americans only have sympa-thy for us when our interests do not conflict with theirs—or China's, or Mexico's, or with any country's, finally, that they use as an instrument and a marketplace."[30]

"All of Humanity into Its Orbit"

Here we are, then. Where? At the concrete heart of the matter. The hard evi-dence of facts and figures. The reality principle that is newborn America's entire civil religion. French idealists, open your eyes! Face the past in all its stark reality! Contemplate France's *real* relations with the United States dur-ing the nineteenth century! And most important, find the courage to ponder the future in light of a debunked present! The examination would prevent greater misfortunes, because what would appear as clear as day was the man-ifestly conquering destiny of a country that was "but yesterday an obscure satellite of England's power," and which "now aspires to nothing less than drawing all of humanity into its orbit."[31] Today, Mexico; tomorrow, the world. That was the true and only slogan of this mercantile and imperial republic—imperial because it was mercantile, to its former admirer's newly opened eyes.

As for the naive hopes of those who had not stopped fantasizing about the Union's dissolution since the Civil War, Gaillardet replied that the coun-try would not fall apart. The desire for cohesion would win out over cen-trifugal temptations, because it was driven by an unimaginable, irrepress-ible, and irrational "thirst for annexation" that would protect the Americans from their own demons.[32] The Americans in the North, the South, and the West could not care less about fraternal feelings. What kept them much more firmly united, and would make them ever more united, was "the ambi-tion they all nurture of extending their empire well beyond its current limits.

A short time ago, this ambition did not go beyond Mexico, but now it stretches all the way to the Isthmus of Panama,"[33] since Ferdinand de Lesseps had come up with the grandiose project of the canal—a canal that would ferry grist to the anti-American mill both before and after its takeover by Theodore Roosevelt's muscular America. We should, Gaillardet admitted, therefore resign ourselves to the fact that the United States of America would continue to exist, because the cement that held the Union together was not democracy. Or the principles proclaimed by the founding fathers. Or the federal compact based on the free will of the states, which had been trampled on by the North's refusal to let the Southerners secede. The cement was the Monroe Doctrine, hereafter elevated to the status of a "national dogma."[34]

Monroe had never gotten much good press in old Europe. It is hard to see how such a menacing principle—"America for Americans"—could have won him popularity. When it was created in 1824, the French, English, Spanish, and Dutch were still ubiquitous from the Pacific to the Caribbean, in some cases just a few miles away from the new North American power. For a long time it had not attracted much attention beyond a narrow circle of diplomats, most of whom, however, were more prone to conciliation than confrontation. In the absence of a concrete crisis (and the only major crisis, the Mexican expedition, would be both an indirect and distant one), the Monroe Doctrine had no real reason to move the French masses. In that respect, the years between 1880 and 1890 were a turning point, and Gaillardet's analysis prefigured a collective awakening accelerated by the Spanish-American War of 1898. France was now listening closely, and what it heard in the doctrine was not a principled affirmation of sovereignty and autonomy phrased by the United States on behalf of the American continent as a whole, but the ominous rumble of war preparations against Europe—which the North Americans had started calling "with a certain disdain, the *Old World*."[35]

This rereading of the Monroe Doctrine as "national dogma" was a direct consequence of the Civil War and its aftermath of disenchantment. We have noted how the French, compelled by more immediate catastrophes, had lost sight of American events in the years between 1865 and 1875. It was not a time of forgetting, however, but of incubation; afterward, the Civil War would once more become a privileged subject of retrospective analyses and speculations. The demolished and humiliated South would win new and sometimes surprising supporters. It would benefit from the sympathy France gladly bestowed on losers, and all the more so because the abolition of slavery had cleared away an awkward obstacle. Now sympathy for the Southerners as victims of the imperialist North could be expressed without let or hindrance. The French could even identify with them and see their fate as a kind of prefiguration of the Europeans' destiny.

The return to the Civil War after a twenty-year latency period was an inaugural moment for the anti-American discourse, which chose as its star actor its preferred villain, the Yankee. This was because, for the French commentators of the 1880s, the war's most tangible outcome was less the abolition of slavery (they would take pleasure in saying that emancipation had destroyed the South without improving the blacks' situation) than the "Yankee" takeover of the United States' entire territory and wealth. Beyond the ideological differences, the North's victory was retrospectively analyzed as a failure for France. Anti-Americanism was anchored in regrets over a lost opportunity. A distant, "localized" war suddenly took on unexpected proportions. Just recently, General Robert E. Lee's capitulation had been nothing more than the forgettable epilogue to a very foreign war. Now, all of a sudden, doubt was taking hold. What if the whole chessboard of international relations had been knocked over? And what if the face of the world had changed? Those were the questions gnawing at the tardy chroniclers of a war that had been lost not only by the South, but, it would seem, by France as well.

One regret tormented the French: their nonintervention. The republican Gaillardet's 1883 conclusions fell in line a posteriori with Southern propaganda and the official imperial press: France ought to have thrown all its efforts into helping the South win, thereby dividing the Union. Moreover, "strictly speaking, the South was constitutionally in its rights, by the federal pact and the very act of American independence."[36] The former Jacobin did not shrink from the most nitpicky legalism, and his republican regrets look just like the emperor's circuitous wishes. Napoleon III was now accused not of collusion with the South, but of timid weakness toward the North: "Once Napoleon III had come to share England's [anti-North] views, what should the two European powers have done? Not just recognize the Southern Confederacy's independence . . . , but also form a defensive and offensive military alliance with the Confederacy to force the North into peace." Alas! Instead of taking this "straight and courageous path, England and France followed a different one, one that was pusillanimous and convoluted." This was a considerable revision and a spectacular change of perspective. During the war, liberal associations and militant republicans had bitterly reproached the imperial government for its overly favorable stance toward the "slave owners" and overly reserved one toward the North. Now the accusation was reversed: the empire should have intervened on the South's behalf and used all of France and England's military weight to tip the scales! Instead, the two countries' inertia had allowed a fearsome reunion of the divided states to take place, under the North's iron rule.

But it got worse. France and England were not equally responsible for the fiasco. Great Britain was obviously the loser in the situation, insofar as a reunited United States with immense resources would become its industrial competitor, hamper its trade, and before long make claims to being a great naval power. In the long run, though, the negative outcome for England would be offset by a phenomenon Gaillardet considered essential—and one that would become a French obsession in the last decade of the nineteenth century: the American continent's Anglo-Saxonization. The new, post–Civil War United States' imperialist impulse would be combined with the "Anglo-Saxon race's" rise to power within the Union itself. In fact, as Gaillardet saw it, the two trends were one and the same: the Anglo-Saxons in America, by eliminating or marginalizing other ethnicities and cultures, were paving the way for much larger conquests. The new Americans had "set their sights on nothing less than the Anglo-Saxon race's domination over the entire North American continent."[37] Crushing the South was a decisive step in the plan for domination. But it was just one step. As early as 1865, the conquering race had started looking farther afield. It was already eyeing other prey. Was he accusing the Americans based on their intentions? Not in the least, Gaillardet replied. The facts spoke for themselves, and they were eloquent. Yankee buccaneers were now active in Mexico; William Walker had ruled over Nicaragua for two years. Such deceptively wild ventures were the forerunners of the Union's systematic expansion beyond its frontiers. Europe had noticed but considered this the blundering of a feverish young power in the territory immediately surrounding its borders. That would be mistaking the country's real nature, Gaillardet warned his readers. In reality, America's push south was the logical follow-up to the so-called Civil War, which had in fact been the testing ground for a vast Anglo-Saxon conquest.

This reassessment of the Civil War made it out to be the birth of a specifically Yankee imperialism. Consequently, the French bestowed the decisive role of exemplary victim on the conquered Southerner. The loser was now the main character in anti-Americans' reinterpretation of the story. The Indian had long been a solitary figure, a living image of the injustices committed on a continent stained with his blood. The Negro slave, brutally deported and odiously mistreated, had joined him not long after. But by the end of the nineteenth century, these victims had lost much of their woeful prestige: the emancipated black no longer seemed as "interesting," and the Indian, stripped of his romantic aura, seemed helplessly doomed to ignominious extinction. Their misfortunes had come from too far off—colonial

America, or the "medieval" practice of slavery—for an era obsessed with the future. Hadn't their cause seen its heyday, since slavery no longer existed and there were almost no Indians left?

Paradoxically, in the last years of the nineteenth century, championing the Southerner as Yankee imperialism's protomartyr would bring about a renewed interest in the Indians' fate, as well as the blacks'—or, more precisely, a declared "solidarity" with their sufferings. For these declarations, as we will soon see, were singularly lacking in empathy. They lacked the admiration and the sensitivity that had animated the romantics and the abolitionists. They were eminently tactical: their ambition was to form, behind the humiliated Southerner, a longer line of plaintiffs to testify against America's injustices.

The (white) Southerner thus had a major part to play in the creation of twentieth-century anti-Americanism's essential mechanism. His job was to help indict America, in French, in the name of Americanism's American "victims"—the Indian, the black, the white "minority" (from the ostracized Italian American to the un-American Communist of the McCarthy era). In a very structural irony, this showy solidarity with "the other America," the America of the offended and humiliated, would evolve in the 1880s and 1890s from the idealized Southerner, who had been subjugated in his own country by a hostile and dominating race. The Indian would not get his aura back (except, fleetingly, with Gaillardet); the emancipated black would remain unpopular; the worker who rose up against the police would never be a reassuring figure; all of them would nevertheless be shamelessly exhibited by French anti-Americans as witnesses for the prosecution of the United States. During their day in court, they would regain a little of their former shine, like the shifty characters who don a suit and tie to make a good impression on the jury.

A new nation was thus born in the French mindset: the "other America," which would be regularly summoned to testify in the permanent trial against America's crimes. For the whole first half of the twentieth century, men indifferent to the fate of peoples colonized by the European powers would become passionate about the American Indians and treat the blacks with astonishing solicitude—at least the blacks in Alabama or Illinois. This strikingly unequal treatment now looks like flagrant bad faith. And clearly, the rhetoric is full of it, from the days of André Siegfried[38] in the 1920s right up to today's National Front. It would, however, be a mistake to consider it the only element at work. If, over the course of the twentieth century, French anti-Americans, *including racist ones,* would invoke the extermination of the Indians and the exclusion of the blacks as evidence in their case against

America, if they did not blink at becoming the unlikely spokesmen for such victims, it was because the original scenario, the initial script of this pivotal discourse (one of whose first writers was the modest Gaillardet) had created an obligatory, categorical, and incontestable link between external "Yankee" imperialism and internal "Anglo-Saxon" hegemony.

It is therefore worth our while to look more closely at how *L'Aristocratie en Amérique* portrayed the racial "Anglo-Saxon" policy that had spread throughout the entire country after the 1865 victory.

Our Enemies' Enemies

On the front line: "the indigenous race," as Gaillardet put it—the Indians. In France there was a strong tradition of sympathy for the Indians that drew from different sources. It was based on a philosophical and moral condemnation of the wrongs the Indians had suffered, which was an uninterrupted trend from the sixteenth to the eighteenth centuries—from Montaigne to Diderot, Raynal, and Marmontel, along with the writings of numerous missionaries. In the specific case of northern America, it went back to the anti-English alliances of the French and Indian Wars as much as to Chateaubriand's enchanting prose. Even before *Atala* was written, a taste for all things Indian had led the Montagnards to identify with the Iroquois, and in 1794 *Le Mercure* published Indian war songs in order to demonstrate their affinities with the sans-culotte anthem "Ça ira!" But since then, a lot of water had flowed under the bridges of the *Meschacébé*.[39] The savage's stock had been falling since the end of the eighteenth century. The "degenerate" Indian encountered by late-nineteenth-century travelers was nothing but a source of often disgusted commiseration. Gaillardet's first task was therefore to revive the faded colors of a tired old myth. His Indian would be the hero of the days of epic primitivism: part Ossian, part Chactas.[40] For "there is something Homeric and biblical about the Indians, a kind of Oriental and primitive grandeur," he wrote, citing the Abbé Rouquette, a Louisiana missionary he gave the nickname—once Las Casas's—of "the Indians' advocate."[41] His Indian regained the archaic virtues humanitarian philosophers and romantic poets had successively bestowed on him. But this renewed championing of the Indian was purely tactical. The Indian became "biblical" in opposition to his Bible-brandishing executioners, and "Homeric"—noble, free, and poetic—in contrast to Yankee America, that sinister "swarm of men," that "uniform hive whose only poetry is work."[42]

Next, moving on from primitivist myth, Gaillardet turned to historical legend. He resuscitated the old Franco-Indian war camaraderie against the

English, this time to fight the Yankee. Historically, the battle had been lost, but this did not mean that the solidarity was either vain or illusory. The Indians and the French were made to understand each other and get along. Unlike the disdainful Englishman and his successor, the murderous Yankee, Gaillardet's Frenchman was a good neighbor who did not mind sharing a cabin and mixing blood with the Native Americans. The North Americans' plan was to extinguish the Indian race by corralling the Indians into reserves; by way of contrast, Gaillardet recalled the Edenic image of St. Louis, a French beachhead on the Mississippi and a "creole city."[43] ("Creole" had a meaning different from that of the eighteenth century: it now meant "of mixed blood.") Evicting the French, as we can read between the lines of Gaillardet's nostalgic evocation, marked the end of this harmonious era. Here, we can see hints of a persecution fable, a shared martyrdom. The Acadians' Calvary—they had been cast into the sea and often into death by the "Anglo-Saxons"—was now being repeated on the Indians, who were condemned to an "exodus [that] could obviously have only one outcome: death, total demise."[44]

Next up were the blacks. Obligatory extras in the American racial drama as staged by French critics, they were routinely displayed as exemplary victims: no longer of slavery, but of the destruction of the paternalist South. A double hypothesis in Gaillardet's book would dictate future analyses of the blacks' emancipation: abolition was a political lie; far from bettering the blacks' economic fate, it had worsened it. It was therefore not surprising that the freed blacks had voted with their former masters: "The slaves had understood, in their ignorance, that the freedom the North had granted them could be the freedom to do nothing at all."[45] But Gaillardet did not stop with the disturbing observation that emancipation had been pointless. He traced the imposture back to its source and found it in the North. The original lie had been in representing the North as an equitable place for blacks. In fact, their condition there was not an enviable one. They were not really citizens. They were not even allowed to serve in the militia: "At best, liberty, equality, and fraternity allow them to aspire to the dignity of a bassoonist, a sutler, or a beast of burden," Gaillardet bitterly noted.[46] In short, America's blacks had not gained a thing with the South's defeat, and they had nothing to hope for from their liberators in the North. They even had reason for fear. Behind the lie of emancipation was the hidden truth of their coming extinction. "Total extinction" was what the future held for the African Americans. "The Negroes will undergo it in the United States just like the Indians, because, like the latter, they only reproduce amongst themselves."[47] So white America was genocidal twice over.

Was that all? Had Gaillardet covered all of victimized America? No, because he still had not mentioned the most noble victim of "the spirit of conquest and domination" that characterized the new Yankee America. This oppressed "pariah," as Gaillardet put it, was none other than the former master of the South. Heedless of the fact that he was contradicting his earlier analysis about the freed blacks being on the losing side of emancipation, he now wrote that the Northerners had turned "the plantation owners into pariahs and given them their former slaves as masters."[48] In this new setup, which overlapped with the previous one, "a former wrong" had been "replaced by an even greater wrong." So the lie of emancipation was coupled with the injustice of the plantation owners' devastation and "enslavement." The flimsy treatment Gaillardet gives the blacks—they come across without a trace of historical, sociological, or even simply human substance—allows them to be portrayed either as the oppressed or the oppressors, as needed; and thus the North, that is, the new America, could be blamed both for not really having freed the blacks and for giving them the upper hand over their former masters. Using the American black as the joker in making incompatible contentions would also have a future; more than one "humanist" of the 1930s, from André Siegfried to Georges Duhamel,[49] would set down with a profoundly racist pen his commiseration for America's black population.

We should stop a second here and examine this historico-ethnic ruse, which would lastingly fuel French anti-Americanism. One of the secrets of its longevity was that, faced with the American enemy (classified as the Yankee, the "Anglo-Saxon"), it identified American *friends:* the blacks, the Indians, the Southerners. And too bad if the aforementioned friends were hardly friends with each other and only met up in the pages of French books. And all the better if the characters in this French fable were mainly projections: the allegories were only destined for the French, after all. The analogy between the oppressed American minorities and the French, even if a little spurious, did not scare off our decipherers of America—on the contrary. Not only were they unafraid of identifying with these groups, they accepted and promoted this identification. Gaillardet thus compared the policy of eradicating the Indians with America's aggressive harassment of foreign countries: "The Americans' policy with regard to the indigenous race of the country they occupy has been a kind of filibusterism no longer operated externally but internally."[50] The parable suggests the global nature of the hegemonic policy established by the masters of America. If on their own soil the Indians had been subjected to the same filibustering exactions as Nicaragua and Mexico, and soon Cuba, or, perhaps later, the Antilles, how could the French be sure that one day they too would not be slated for the same "extinction" as the Indians? The annihilation or subjugation of the Indians, blacks, and Southerners in writings such as *L'Aristocratie en Amérique* served as a warning.

But most important here was the massive use of racial references, which would become a central paradigm in the anti-Americanism of the late nineteenth century. America faded out as a country or nation and became the perpetually expanding lebensraum of a self-assured and domineering race. Gaillardet's long diatribe, which was still marked by a sense of brokenheartedness, would be amplified and used with a "scientific" argumentative extravagance throughout the following decade as a whole new take on the United States developed. Its breeding ground was not novelistic or theatrical fiction, but rather the newborn sciences, with their aura of slightly sulfurous prestige: political psychology, sociology, ethnography. It was the job of these new specialists, these experts working on the sidelines of the university and scholarly institutions, to scratch at the boil of the Civil War—until it was lanced and drained by the shock of 1898.

What was the new stance for which Gaillardet had simply lighted the way? It started with the idea that the Americans and the French had until then only considered themselves separated when they lost sight of their deep-seated solidarity and common vocation of embodying universal values. But this belief was itself an illusion. The truth was completely different. It had come out of the ruins of Charleston and the carnage at Gettysburg. The new truth said that the Americans and the French were truly estranged, not by diplomatic and economic rivalries, which were always negotiable and could sometimes be remedied, but by their very being, which was determined by racial aptitudes and the social formations they produced. The language of misunderstanding was no longer just the language of figures, assessments, and costs; it was the deep and muted voice of blood, of roots, of collective traits and atavistic dispositions, and the resulting social structures were both their emanation and confirmation. Thirteen years before Edmond Demolins published *Anglo-Saxon Superiority: To What It Is Due,* Frédéric Gaillardet wrote what was a pioneering work showing the French and the Americans to be doubly separated by "racial facts" and "social reality."

Social Tyranny

Despite its title, *L'Aristocratie en Amérique* did not open any kind of dialogue, not even a polemical one, with *Democracy in America.* Alexis de Tocqueville's name, mentioned in *L'Aristocratie*'s preface alongside that of his 1833 travel

companion Gustave de Beaumont, quickly drops out of sight. Gaillardet was
not refuting Tocqueville; he was content with paradoxically inverting Tocqueville's theory on the "equality of conditions" generating American reality.
Tocqueville had postulated that "the Americans' social state is eminently
democratic."[51] Not at all, Gaillardet countered; the Americans' social state
was eminently aristocratic. At a distance of ten years, the former *boulevard*
writer concurred with Victorien Sardou: "So, you have an aristocracy?" asks
a character in *L'Oncle Sam*. "*An* aristocracy? They have at least two of them!"[52]
Gaillardet took it even further: America was nothing *but* aristocracies. There
was a race aristocracy: the entire WASP set.[53] A "wealth" aristocracy: the class
made rich by capitalism. But there was also, above all, an aristocracy of the
masses—masses "no newspaper would dare to insult," plebs who were the
object of a "national courtship,"[54] a ruling rabble against which Gaillardet, a
veteran of 1848, would suddenly lash out. "The United States' political and
social constitution has poeticized power and glorified the rabble . . . ; where
a European would see men in rags, the American sees a political meeting."[55]

Tocqueville had honestly wondered about the residual forms of aristocracy a "democratic social state" like the United States might contain. He
found traces in the Indians, with their "aristocratic politeness."[56] He detected
hints of it in practices like setting bail—inherited from the English—which
a democracy in which the poor were the majority should logically have suppressed. He pinpointed the equivalent of an aristocracy in the social stratification itself, not among the rich, but within the new class of lawyers and law-
makers.[57] Gaillardet's book no longer shows any echo of or interest in
Tocqueville's investigation: he describes the whole of American society as a
bunch of competing aristocracies elbowing each other for room, all of them
trying to impose a very real oppression that was palpable beneath the country's abstract freedoms. The citizens of the United States undeniably enjoyed
political freedom, even "unlimited political freedom," he willingly granted;
but their "social freedom is subject to numerous restrictions." And "social
freedom" was the more important of the two. "One is gained at the other's
expense, but it is the more precious of the two that is sacrificed. Social freedom is a basic necessity, whereas political freedom is needed only in a few
specific cases."[58] For an old-school republican like Gaillardet, this was a cultural revolution. But beyond the specific case of Gaillardet, a conversion of
the left-wing stance on America was taking shape—a "sociological" conversion. In the traditionally pro-American republican camp, the right to pick
America apart had replaced abstract loyalty. Elective democracy, which had
been the goal of the struggles leading up to the fall of the Second Empire, no
longer seemed like an end in and of itself; soon it would not even seem like

a beginning. Unafraid of voicing blasphemies against universal suffrage, Gaillardet affirmed from the start that the right to vote on anything and everything was not the *nec plus ultra* of the expression of freedom. Real democratic life was elsewhere, and "the right to go or not to go to church or the theater, or to drink what you want, is even better!" As the first of a long line of irritated travelers and discouraged observers, the former writer for the *Courrier des États-Unis* threw down on paper a jumble of obstacles to freedom fomented by America's social tyranny: innocent pleasures were prohibited, private life and religious practice monitored; behavior was conformist, work a veritable religion. To these forms of daily oppression could be added the dysfunction of a "society" that was more invasive than effective: lack of public safety so pronounced that Communards exiled in the United States started missing the French *gendarmerie;* an "inferior" legal system; uncertainty about the value of diplomas (especially worrisome in the field of medicine); "government employees' demoralization"; ever-growing betrayal of trust, for which the United States shared the gold medal with Russia, and so on. The length of this catalog shows that Gaillardet's apprehensions went beyond the simple frustrations of a *boulevardier* deprived of entertainment and brandy. To those who might criticize him for putting the right to vote and the right to drink cocktails on the same level, he could easily point to the Chicago Beer Riots, which, in March and April 1855, set a largely German-born population against the despotism of "Anglo-Saxon" representatives who wanted to prohibit beer on Sundays. Real freedom started with the beer mug. The associations that had orchestrated the "ridiculous temperance parade," Gaillardet stressed, "are no less oppressive" than the religious groups that attempted to dictate individual morality in Europe.[59] The "expense" was indeed too great, if shackles on your conduct were the price to pay for putting your slip in the box.

Gaillardet's position was therefore not a political change of heart. It was really—even if the expression is a little weighty for the author of *La Tour de Nesle*—an epistemological conversion. For the left-leaning "progressivists" of the late nineteenth century, the days of giving America a blank check solely on the promise of its institutions were over. The primacy of the social over the political paved the way for new criticism of America based on its "civilization"—a category that would continue to grow in importance among the anti-Americans. If the period leading up to World War I was dominated by attacks on the most brutal forms of the American "peril," if cultural satire had a relatively modest part to play, criticizing America's "way of life" was a path that would soon become a major thoroughfare. Well before the "American way of life" started showing its loathsome wares in the chronicles of the

1930s, the case against America's horrors was being sketched out, this time for more sociological and less aesthetic reasons than in Stendhal and Baudelaire: the horrors of a life given over to labor, "whose only poetry is work"; of a leveling society where "there is no intermediary class; strictly speaking, there are only workers—penniless workers and millionaire workers—who never stop working";[60] the horrors of a "uniform hive," of "the swarm of men," of the "anthill."[61] Gaillardet's successors would remember these claims in their descriptions of America's "society of the masses"—wisely forgetting the label *aristocratic* Gaillardet had tagged it with as a provocation.

A Baron in Cowboy Country

Past acquaintance with the United States had given Frédéric Gaillardet a head start, but his anti-American venture would not be a solo one for long. Ten years later there would be a great editorial rush toward America, the Uncle Sam rush. For the moment, Gaillardet had to make do with the unexpected Edmond de Mandat-Grancey as a traveling companion.

A distant cousin of Tocqueville, whose ideas he boasted of not sharing, the Baron de Mandat-Grancey was an ultraconservative. A serene racist and confirmed antidemocrat (he predicted the rapid demise of New York, an inevitable result of "the spirit of heedlessness which is inherent in democratic governments"), he seemed more interested in the enhancement of the equine race than in the workings of America's social and political institutions. Spry and instructive, he peppered his travel diaries with remarks that gave off a whiff of high society. Thus he disapprovingly noted that in New York one saw "very few private carriages" and that "those one does see are illharnessed, ill-kept, and driven by coachmen with unspeakable mustaches."[62] Elsewhere, he waxed indignant over "the incommensurable culinary ignorance" of Chicago's 600,000 inhabitants, who had never prepared crayfish *à la bordelaise,* despite the fact that "all the streams in the vicinity are literally crawling with the admirable crustaceans."[63] It would take all the irascible baron's aplomb to articulate such serious grievances with solemn gravity and use them to flesh out the docket in his case against the United States. Clearly, he and Gaillardet were not of the same school of thought or on the same political side. But if Mandat-Grancey's works were less destined for posterity than *L'Aristocratie en Amérique,* they remain interesting precisely for their points of convergence with Gaillardet's essay.

Dans les Montagnes Rocheuses (In the Rocky Mountains) was published first in *Le Correspondant,* then by Plon in 1884. In 1885, Mandat-Grancey repeated the offense: *En visite chez l'Oncle Sam: New York et Chicago* lashed out at urban America this time, but with the same acrimony as the earlier book. The target had widened, and the content had become more radical. The tone had shifted easily from mockery to indignation. A capricious author, Mandat-Grancey also had certain fixations. Gaillardet had fantasized about America's democratic duchesses; the baron was obsessed with cowboys. His obsession was clearly not unrelated to the existence of a familial ranch in the Dakotas, baptized Fleur-de-Lys, which a later traveler, Paul de Rousiers, would mention in his *American Life* in 1892 as a kind of patriotic laboratory, where American mares were inseminated by French stallions.[64] Nevertheless, *Dans les Montagnes Rocheuses* paints an unflattering picture of America's cowboys, men "too lazy to work in the mines or on a farm, . . . constantly warring with the Indians" and "the terror of the [white] inhabitants" to boot.[65] "The plague of the West," they even pursued Mandat-Grancey into the cities his second book was devoted to. "The inevitable cowboy" did not come riding in in the flesh, of course. As "the favorite hero of America's modern novelists," he galloped across the literary scene. This unbridled myth—whose glorious future in Hollywood he did not foresee—enraged the baron. That a subproletariat of "poor devils" could pass for a modern form of chivalry, that lasso-twirling grunts working themselves to death "for a meager salary of 41 dollars a month" should be considered valiant knights, was sufficient proof that there was something rotten in the state of America.[66] Mandat-Grancey was all the more disgruntled with the cowboys' literary vogue because he had come up with a radical solution for ridding America of them: replacing them with the Indians. Indeed, the Indian could "advantageously replace the cowboy." And, he added for the sardonic reader, "The idea I am advancing is not a utopia."[67] He probably even believed it.

The admirable proposal of replacing the cowboys with the Indians, which reads like one of Alphonse Allais's tales,[68] closes an analysis of the "Indian question" remarkably similar to Gaillardet's: the French and Indians had fought together on the battlefields of yore; the Yankees' policy of extermination was cause for indignation; the French could identify with the victims. "The Americans' policy toward the Indians in general is abominable," Mandat-Grancey wrote. "Its goal is their extermination. The politicians hardly hide this fact, but excuse themselves by saying that it is the only way to make an end of the Indian question." This excuse was unacceptable to Mandat-Grancey. He proclaimed this justification for genocide "absolutely false" and as proof, mentioned, like Gaillardet had, the example of the French and Indians' harmonious cohabitation in old Canada and abolished Acadia. *Et in Acadia ego. . .*

But try as he might, the baron did not really seem to believe in the future success of Indians transformed into cowboys through France's good works.

"What will be the future," he inquired, "of the race in which we Frenchmen have the duty of taking a very particular interest, because it was our faithful ally for over a century?"[69] It did not look like the baron, or France, knew the answer to this question. Because the faithful Indian, here as for Gaillardet, had no promised land. Ejected from his lost paradise (the idyllic fleur-de-lis-covered America he had once fraternally shared with the French), he was doomed to exodus and death. There is a fine line between Gaillardet's nationalistic melancholy and Mandat-Grancey's nostalgic chauvinism. For France's anti-Americans, a good Indian was the same as General Custer's: a dead Indian, and lamenting the Indians' demise was a good excuse both for glorifying a vanished French America and accusing the Yankees of genocide.

A *community of discourses* would start to build, on the modest scale of a still-hesitant anti-Americanism, for now. These Frenchmen, with different roots and convictions, and with a whole century's worth of contradictory political passions, were suddenly speaking the same language. It was an imaginary reunion, or rather, one that doubtless took place *in* the imagination. But if the ideological consensus on America was a *trompe l'oeil,* the convergence of different pronouncements was in and of itself a "fact" that, in turn, had ideological and political effects. The system of converging extremes that would continue to crop up over the long history of French anti-Americanism could already be found in these early examples: the author who believed in the republic and the one who did not had nothing in common, but they came together in rejecting the United States. This paradoxical convergence is particularly striking in the case of the fate of the Indians and blacks.

Frédéric Gaillardet maintained a simultaneously postromantic and republican stance concerning the Indians, a mix of literary sympathy and automatic attachment to the universality of the rights of man. The Baron de Mandat-Grancey, though, was a "modern" antidemocrat: he believed in the different races, and specifically that there were inferior ones. His portrait of the Indians did not resuscitate the noble savage in any sense of the word. The Indians, wrote their insensitive protector, were "of a repulsive and sinister ugliness." There was something of the hippopotamus or rhinoceros about the way they looked. "With their large, hard, and set features, [they] seem to lack some sort of finishing touch and give the same impression of being incomplete" as these animals.[70] We are worlds away from Chateaubriand's Indians—and also from the sensitive and unsentimental portrait Tocqueville had painted of them in 1835. Mandat-Grancey's Indian is a hybrid, part sepoy before the fact, part endangered species.[71] This "faithful ally" is described as more animal than human. At best, he allows the benevolent baron to "get a

sense of prehistoric man." But none of that disqualifies the Indian from playing the part he is given by Mandat-Grancey as honorably as in Gaillardet—as
a witness for the prosecution against the genocidal Yankee. Mandat-Grancey
perfectly illustrates the aforementioned axiom: in anti-American writings, a
vehement defense of the black and Indian races as oppressed victims of the
Anglo-Saxons was perfectly compatible with the open or embryonic racism
of their "advocates." And the antagonism between Gaillardet's position and
Mandat-Grancey's, based both on their principles and on their stand on
French politics, lost all relief, as though it had been flattened by America's
vasty plains, with their inescapable perspective.

These authors' treatment of the "black question" was both more brutal
and more circuitous. Mandat-Grancey's racism was not paved with a single
good intention. He did not mince words, declaring the black race "absolutely
inferior to the white race."[72] Abolitionism was an abomination to the baron,
who had not forgiven Victor Hugo (and this in 1885, when France gave Hugo
a state funeral) for having "spilled so many tears over the misfortunes of
John Brown and all the Dombrowskis and Crapulskis of the Commune."[73] It
speaks volumes about Mandat-Grancey's intellectual universe that he would
associate Communards with unpronounceable names with the famous abolitionist hanged in 1859 in Charlestown for having roused the blacks to
insurrection. But this fundamental racism, loudly and clearly expressed, did
not stop the very same Mandat-Grancey from placing the entire responsibility for the unworkable and explosive situation created by the "black question"
on the hated Yankee's shoulders. Without the North's hypocritical propaganda, the blacks would have stayed in their place. It was the Yankees who
had opened Pandora's box, and in this sense, they were more hateful than the
former slaves misled by their promises. How could you blame the Southerners for taking a few steps toward self-defense—such as creating the Ku
Klux Klan—in reaction to an unbearable "state of things"? And how could
you avoid fantasizing (aloud) about the Yankees' annihilation by the very
people they had purported to want to free at any price? "If this continues,"
Mandat-Grancey glibly prophesized, "the Yankees, who struggled so hard to
free the blacks, will be conquered by them like the Tartars were by the Chinese, or else they will have to suppress universal suffrage."[74]

After substituting the Indians for the cowboys, why not replace the Yankees with the blacks? At least the choice he was offering America's Anglo-
Saxons had the merit of being clear-cut. They could choose between their
own demise or the destruction of their founding institutions, starting with
the tradition of "one man, one vote." The blacks would practically find favor
(a very temporary one) in Mandat-Grancey's eyes. Immanent justice held

that they should be the ones to inflict punishment on the self-same Yankees who had, in more than one sense of the word, unleashed them. Frédéric Gaillardet had been satisfied with a less apocalyptic historical irony in stressing the fact that the freed blacks had used their right to vote in favor of their former masters. But for both writers there was the same dialectic, in which the Yankees were presented both as the exterminators of the non-Anglo-Saxon races and the sorcerer's apprentices of a false and calamitous emancipation.

Were Gaillardet and Mandat-Grancey fighting the same battle? In France, certainly not. But all they had to do was set foot in America to suddenly start speaking with the same voice. The convergence is troubling, especially since it was not limited to racial issues or solidarity with the Yankees' victims, which would become, as we have noted, a future axis of the anti-American stance. In fact, the proximity of their historical analyses on Franco-American relations was perhaps even more spectacular because they came from two schools of thought that had been locked in a firm, reciprocal hatred since 1789—because Mandat-Grancey fully subscribed to Gaillardet's diagnosis of the Americans' infamous lack of love for France. He too had been struck by the indifference or hostility toward his country in the places and people he had encountered, with the honors going to Chicago: "I have rarely encountered a hostility toward France as characteristic as the one conveyed by the general tone of the Chicago press."[75] In France there was a misunderstanding on the matter that went back to the late eighteenth century, in his opinion—exactly as Gaillardet believed, but for completely different reasons. If Gaillardet had accused the United States of betraying the young French republic as early as 1792, Mandat-Grancey reproached the American War of Independence with destabilizing the monarchy and paving the baleful way for the French Revolution. In Gaillardet's view, the American population had shown terrifying ingratitude, which should put France on its guard for the future; Mandat-Grancey held that the very same American nation, ever since it had made its first steps toward emancipation, had been "fatal" for France.[76] But in taking these rigorously opposite paths, both reached the same conclusion and advocated the same defensive vigilance, founded on history's lessons, toward a falsely friendly and actually hostile nation.

Their views about the Civil War's being a missed opportunity were also identical. Mandat-Grancey's sympathies are less unexpected than Gaillardet's: how could a conservative aristocrat not be on the Confederates' side? Like Gaillardet, then, he reshuffled the diplomatic cards; he recast the dice and replayed France's hand with big swipes of "we should have" and "we would only have had to." For "we would only have had to unequivocally back [the Confederates] to make America permanently split into two rival States, which would have mutually paralyzed each other, and of which one, made up of populations with preponderantly French roots, would have been a precious ally for us."[77] Self-interest and honor worked together here: "Having started the war in Mexico, it was the only way of getting out of it honorably." So it was the same old story? No! France's spinelessness was what had allowed a devouring monster to come to life—"the reconstructed United States." It had now "achieved the economic conquest of Mexico by constructing its network of railroads, and soon it will take over the Isthmus of Panama in order to profit from the millions we are so madly spending there." But Mandat-Grancey was a better prophet in announcing France's misfortunes than in wishing them on the United States. The Panama Canal would be taken over in the end, as he had predicted, but the secession of the American West, which he considered just as inevitable, would not take place.[78] In Mandat-Grancey's opinion, France had played its cards so badly during the 1865 conflict that it would only have been sporting of America to give it a second chance with an encore of the Civil War—but his wish would remain unspoken. . .

The Plague and Phylloxera

Unlike Gaillardet, Mandat-Grancey was not disappointed by his travels. He had not come to America to scrutinize democracy, "that mysterious power, in its largest sanctuary,"[79] but to unmask the fraudulence and shake the foundations of the snake-oil sibyl known as America. For all his contempt and impudence, however, the baron never stopped being afraid. When his satirical verve runs out, we catch a glimpse of a nervous grin. For all its shortcomings—politicians' complete corruption, the mediocre "quality of [recent] immigrants,"[80] the idiocy of the "republican form" that had "diminished the qualities" of the country's inhabitants—America was nonetheless a dangerous reality.

It was, so to speak, physically dangerous, on account of its size, its growing economic weight, its congenital rapaciousness, and the brutal energy that could be found even in the way the Americans spoke the English language. "Their neologisms are so energetic they sometimes give one goose bumps," wrote the baron, who was no chicken.[81] Despite a tone of impatient superiority, these pages betray a certain anxiety. From one line to the next, irony gives way to veritable panic, less articulate but more intense than Gaillardet's rational worry. As soon as Mandat-Grancey turns his focus away from the grotesque details that give him such boisterous amusement, his tone becomes sinister. Out of the blue, America's hostility reminds him of "the story of a comrade captured by the Kanaks, who wanted to eat him."[82] It is a strange association of ideas, and what follows does not shed any light on its meaning, but rather simply seems to suggest that, gripped by America, his mind starts racing. "We are somewhat in the same situation," Mandat-Grancey continues, as the comrade threatened by the Kanak cauldron. "We are aware of what has been done here; we see very clearly what will happen. . . . If we do not set things straight, the future will be our ruin; a general overthrow; the whole of France reduced to 15 million inhabitants." Would there be a French ethnocide?

Set things straight. The expression is strong and smells of gunpowder. How long until the French gunboats reached the Hudson? It is striking to see Mandat-Grancey's somewhat unbridled aggressiveness once more meet up with Gaillardet's more circumspect misgivings on a theme that would inflame Frenchmen's imaginations up to the end of the century: that war with the United States was imminent. Mandat-Grancey seems to long for a preventive war he sees as indispensable to France's survival. Gaillardet had noted soberly but somberly that war had already almost broken out as recently as 1881, with America's interference in the clash between Chile and Peru. "If the cabinet in Washington had persisted in imposing its arbitration on Chile and Peru, it would have meant war with Europe's naval powers."[83] While stressing that "America's new generation . . . thinks itself strong enough to cast the die against Europe as a whole," Gaillardet still wanted to believe that the majority would be more sensible. The anti-Americans of the 1890s would not share his measured optimism: they would be preoccupied with proving, on the contrary, that between the United States and France a logic of war prevailed. For them, the only question was what kind of war it would be. Open war? Covert? Widespread? Until then, they all concluded, like Paul de Rousiers in 1892 (six years before the war in Cuba), that "the only plan to adopt is to be armed for the fight."[84]

It was not necessarily open warfare that America was brewing in Mandat-Grancey's cauldron. As though from Pandora's box, the baron pulled out the ruin of rural France by competition from California wines and beef at 8 sous a pound (as opposed to 20 sous in Le Havre: "this cannot go on")[85] or the subversion of French society by the "school of admirers" of America who were forcing an "adoption" of steadily growing numbers of "American institutions," starting with the deplorable jury system.[86] An insidious Americanization was being fomented in France by saboteurs stretching from late cousin Tocqueville, guilty of having "supplied several generations of doctrinarians with quotations,"[87] to some mysterious pro-American "Communists,"[88] and including Victor Hugo, John Brown's bard.

In this perspective, the risk France was running was less of being invaded than of being contaminated. Mandat-Grancey was probably the first anti-American since De Pauw to designate America as an infectious agent and even (still more ominously) a kind of carrier for political and social ills. "Over there, one finds a host of institutions which are, for the Americans, what phylloxera is to their vineyards. They suffer from them but do not die. Transported to our land, they become mortal."[89] The metaphor was timely. It was in the 1870s, with plant disease spreading throughout the vineyards of southwestern France, that the French became fully aware of the disaster. *Phylloxera vastatrix* and its American cousin *Pemphigus vitifolia,* which was identified in 1854, were a nightmare for a France that was still largely rural, eminently wine producing, and massively enophilic. The metaphor would be heavily used until it was supplanted by the even more dramatic image of an "American cancer," which would be the title of an essay published in 1931. Could phylloxera itself have been a conspiracy? "One of these days," Émile Barbier wrote in 1893, "shiploads of American Bordeaux will reach Pauillac to replace our vintages destroyed by phylloxera."[90]

Precious phylloxera! Synonymous with both invasion and devastation, it was an ideal metaphor for the rampant evil of Americanization. For Americanization was not the simple adoption, imitation, or even imposition of America's institutional, social, or cultural traits. It was a mechanism for contamination and corruption. What was being transmitted from America to Europe and breeding there, in the infectious sense of the word, was always *for the worse.* There was never a productive transfer between "them" and "us," only contaminated exchanges. Gaillardet considered this a kind of natural law: "Europe is being Americanized with every passing day, but the two races are exchanging their defects and not their strengths."[91] In this scenario of contagion, Europe was discovering for the first time how fragile, weakened, and lacking in immune defenses it was: "an old continent which has become their prey," wrote a French traveler in 1893.[92]

☆ ☆ ☆

Though they were the initial sharpshooters of late-nineteenth-century anti-Americanism, Gaillardet and Mandat-Grancey were not spokesmen. Their fears, disappointments, and anger were eminently personal. Yet their testimonies were a preview of the essential contours of the following two decades' most deliberate anti-Americanism.

Indeed, in their writings can be seen the first formation of an anti-American vulgate, made up of shared clichés. Historical topoi: the dis-

enchanted revision of Franco-American relations; lamenting French neutrality during the Civil War; and denouncing the hegemonic goals of the
"reconstituted" United States. Racial topoi: criticizing the fate reserved for
non-Yankees, likened to genocide; glorifying, on the other hand, a "mixed-
race" past characteristic of France's presence in America; and systematic
recourse to the notion of an "Anglo-Saxon race" to designate the new America's dominant element. Lastly, cultural topoi: already too numerous in the
two polemicists' books to recapitulate, but whose nomenclature, while leaving room for personal touches (such as Mandat-Grancey's cowboys), can be
grouped under headings that would have an important future before them:
the cities' ugliness and people's lack of taste; impoverished intellectual
exchanges and inane conversations; women's excessive dominance in the
home and in society; ineffectual, corrupt, and venal government bodies; and,
of course, the religion of the dollar, that golden calf of a democracy Gaillardet
preferred to call an "aristocracy" and that Mandat-Grancey denounced as a
plutocracy.

The planet has its limits. . . . What will become of a
disorganized Europe faced with this realist ogre?

    Jules Huret, *En Amérique* (1905)

The people in possession of this continent will
dominate the world in the twentieth century. There can
be no doubt about that.

    Urbain Gohier, *Le Peuple du XXe siècle aux États-Unis*
    (1903)

 4

From Havana to Manila: An American World?

The 1880s were the age of doubt. Did the much-praised and
highly self-satisfied United States really warrant France's admiration—and its own self-importance, a little too ostentatious for
certain French travelers' tastes? Gaillardet and Mandat-Grancey,
from opposite ends of the ideological spectrum, publicly asked
the question—and both answered it in the negative. Theirs were
solitary voices, as we have noted, but not for long. In the 1890s
they were joined and surpassed. The anti-American crowd was
growing, the buzz spreading, and the tone changing. After the
age of doubt came the era of suspicion. It was no longer enough
to simply lament America's insensitivity or indifference. The
transatlantic republic's active hostility and brutal ambition were
reviled. Its "imperial" transformation became an object of apprehension. In just a few years' time, muted concern turned into a
veritable state of alarm. The "American peril" was no longer hypothetical or projected over the long term. It was impending, and
unavoidable.

    Yet the idea that America was dangerous to France was not
self-evident, however little sympathy France felt for the country.
And it would probably not have spread so quickly if not for an

event that, two years before the end of the century, stamped a still-vague set of misgivings and presumptions as "real." In 1898, alarmists' dire predictions were spectacularly confirmed: the United States declared war on Spain, destroyed its naval fleet, invaded Cuba, and was preparing to land in the Philippines. The Spanish-American war had massive reverberations in France. Paul Valéry would later describe the "unforeseen shock" as a profoundly traumatic event. In any event, the "aggression" was a powerful catalyst for a great wave of French anti-Americanism.

Only twelve years separated the nautical carousel that had peacefully celebrated Lady Liberty's installation in the harbor of New York from the U.S. Navy's bombardment of the port in Havana. But those twelve years upset a world of representations. Afterward, a rowdy, brilliant, and boisterous crowd had joined anti-Americanism's pioneers, or rather, taken over from them—equipped with new grievances and backed by new arguments.

If we were to give French anti-Americanism a baptismal certificate, it would have to be dated 1898. Doing so would not really be compatible with the logic of our investigation, though: a system of representations does not just sprout like a mushroom; it evolves through a slow sedimentation of discourses. Nevertheless, at a precise and identifiable point, *it takes*. Ideas that had been traveling along separate avenues start parading down the main street of public opinion. Or, better put, *it takes shape*. Unattached prejudices, misty grievances, unhappy historical memories: a cluster of matter composed of unarticulated reproaches and drifting resentment forms a deposit and settles. Highlighting the year 1898 is therefore not the same as endorsing the illusion of a "point of departure." On the other hand, we can describe it as a threshold, in that from this moment on, French anti-Americanism was stabilized. This means not that it would no longer change, but that its ulterior varieties (ideological, political, or moral) would only be derivatives of the fin-de-siècle precipitate. The inventiveness of America's denigrators would not dry up, any more than its critics' verve. Each historical occurrence would allow successive generations to enrich existing anti-American arguments. Other "interventions"—crueler wars than 1898's—would reawaken indignation at America's imperially imposed "might makes right" attitude. Multiple economic, geopolitical, symbolic, or moral differences would periodically prime the anti-American pump again. But the canvas had been tacked down in the late nineteenth century.

Crystallization

The 1898 shock was not "unforeseen" for everyone. In any case, not for those who had been crying their worry in the wilderness for over a decade. Spain's

injury gave these Cassandras of France and Europe's collapse the bitter satisfaction reserved for prophets of doom. Events confirmed their warnings
about the United States' rising military power, the red flag they had been
waving over the American "ogre's" out-of-control appetites. But different suspicions with other origins fell into the breach of French trust, as well. Troubling but isolated symptoms were now compiled, correlated, and arranged
into the nosographic table of an American evil that was not limited to imperialist itching. Along with an imperious and imperial America, the new diagnosis revealed an inegalitarian and brutal one. Awakened by the spectacular
workers' crises of the 1870s and 1880s, the French were astonished, and
floored, to discover the violence that lay behind social relations they believed
had been pacified by democratic culture.

The awakening took place little by little, notably through the World's
Fairs and the reports made by French worker or artisan delegates on their
stay in America.[1] At the 1876 Philadelphia Exposition, representatives of
twenty or so trades profited from this exceptional contact with the New
World and pored over the myths and realities of the American worker's condition. Their verdict was unenthusiastic. To them, the workers' paradise
that pre-1870 republicans had dreamed of already seemed like a lost paradise. Workers' organizations across the sea had not kept their promises;
far from it. America was a capitalist country just like the others—perhaps
worse than the others. (The argument, as we will see in a coming chapter,
would fuel European socialism for several decades.) In any event, there
was no doubt for these visiting workers—mechanics, in this case—that
the division was as clear-cut as in Europe between "those who live on the
works of others and those who produce," and that "the latter are, in all
the hideousness of that term, at the mercy of the former."[2] Other delegates
went even further: "Far from being the Promised Land of the worker,
the great American Republic has become just like Europe, a veritable social
hell. The antagonism between labor and capital, which is clearly becoming
more vivid and ardent every day, must dispel the last illusions of those
who like to show the United States as the last refuge of human happiness."
Jacques Portes, who quotes from this tailor's report, notes that it is "not
really exceptional" in its severity.[3] The impressive exposition organized in
Chicago in 1893 would be an opportunity for workers' delegations to confirm
their pessimistic analyses, which had been worsened by growing fears
(shared by business owners) over the growing sophistication and spread of
machinery.

These observations and analyses were made by limited groups. Their distribution could have remained strictly in house, among workers or militant

circles. But the astounding social explosions of 1877 and 1886 gave them considerable resonance, while the Haymarket trial went on to deal the death blow to another illusion: the association, in French republicans' minds, of democratic institutions and legal equality for all.

The Statue of Liberty's inauguration, in this sense, could not have come at a worse time than the terrible year 1886. Less than ten years after the almost insurrectional confrontations of the Great Upheaval[4] in 1877, the whole country was once more shaken by a wave of extremely brutal strikes: nearly 1500 in a single year, affecting 10,000 companies, which estimates say involved nearly half a million people. The Knights of Labor union, established in 1869 by a handful of textile workers, would swell to more than 700,000 members in mid-1886 (compared to 111,000 one year earlier).[5] Mainly opposing salary cuts by employers in all the industries, some of the strikes were victorious, like the Southwestern Railroad System's, which forced Jay Gould, the "Wizard of Wall Street," to concede; but many others fell through because of the systematic use of strike breakers and private militia forces, which did not shy from the use of armed force.

The nationwide push for an eight-hour workday increased the number of confrontations. The city of Chicago, where unionists, anarchists, and Knights of Labor had settled their differences, was the movement's epicenter. That was where an event destined to go down in history—far beyond Illinois and even the United States—would occur. On May 1, 1886, the strike for the eight-hour workday was a success, with more than 30,000 strikers. Victories piled up in industry after industry, leading to additional strikes. Then on May 3, in the thick of the action, the police opened fire on strikers as they started laying into the McCormack factory's scabs, leaving four dead and many wounded.

Protests were planned, along with a meeting in Haymarket Square on the night of the May 4. The gathering was small. Near the end of the rainy evening, it had dwindled to three hundred people. That was when the police intervened to break it up. A bomb was thrown, killing one policeman and wounding several others.

Afterward, the attack was attributed to Chicago's firmly rooted anarchists, unleashing a violent press campaign against the strikers and brutal repression by the police. Massive, arbitrary arrests were made. Seven anarchists were indicted and sentenced to death, despite the absence of witnesses or proof. Four would be hanged.

The impact of these events on French opinion was enormous and not at all limited to workers. Protests by syndicalists and socialists brought the situation to widespread public attention, but the conservative press

would not be outdone: it was too good a chance to vilify the model republic so dear to their political enemies, and to ridicule the liberals' cre-
dulity.

French syndicalism would carry the torch year after year by holding an
illegal and frequently bloody day off on May 1. A "judicial crime" committed
in America was thus placed at the center of the workers' consciousness. The
memory of Haymarket, and especially the legal and police repression
brought to a head by the assault, would remain an integral part of left-wing
anti-Americanism. It also became permanently ingrained partly because it
was revived, at thirty-year intervals, by two other political and legal dramas
perceived as repetitions of the original legal crime: the trials of Sacco and
Vanzetti and of the Rosenbergs.

The American political system had been desecrated by tales of corruption
and rumors of electoral fraud; to this was added a radical disillusionment
with the social model and an immense disappointment in the legal process.
Negative perceptions would get worse and worse—all the more so in that, far
from subsiding, murderous strikes almost like civil wars would continue
unabated (Carnegie in 1892, Pullman in 1894), while workers' wages stagnated until World War I. Images of America brutally plummeted in France.
One year after it was erected over the port of New York, Lady Liberty became,
for many militant workers, "the goddess of assassination."[6]

Monroe: From Doctrine to Dogma

While a new, brutal, and even bloody image of industrial America was becoming firmly established in the public eye, more limited circles—though
they were close to the centers of political decision—were starting to worry
about another kind of violence: the long-term threat to France represented by
America's growing militarization. Technical awareness of the Americans'
(chiefly naval) arms went hand in hand with a new understanding of the
Monroe Doctrine as an expansionist charter or even a new kind of imperialism. Even before the Venezuela crisis of 1895, and a fortiori before the Cuba
crisis of 1898, the image of the great pacifistic republic had started to fade out
and be replaced by one of a power bent on fulfilling its "destiny"—even at the
cost of armed conflict with Europe.

During the Civil War and its mechanical massacres, a few voices had
tried to warn the French that the United States was becoming a formidable
military power. But the Union drastically reduced the number of enlisted
men after its victory, putting a temporary clamp on this alarmist discourse—
which also appeared retroactively suspicious, since it seemed to dovetail a

little too neatly with Second Empire propaganda. Yet the voices started up
again, softly at first, in the early 1890s.

Sober, technical Justin Prosper de Chasseloup-Laubat, Napoleon III's
minister of the navy, was one of the first specialists to describe the United
States' naval armament efforts. His *Voyage en Amérique et principalement à
Chicago*, published in 1893 as an "Abstract from the Records of the Society of
French Civil Engineers," was clearly not aimed at a general readership, nor
was it of a nature to stir up strong emotions. Chasseloup-Laubat was interested in facts, not effects. He transcribed with calm precision the power and
"truly formidable armament"[7] of the warships he had seen: the cruiser
Columbia, sent out on July 26, 1892; the *New York;* and also the *Oregon*, the
Indiana, and the *Massachusetts*, "three identical combat ships" produced in
succession. These were formidable ships, but the French had nothing to fear
from them. Chasseloup-Laubat imagined they were intended for "destroying
English trade, in the unlikely case of a battle between the United States and
Great Britain."[8] On the whole, there was nothing to alarm the benevolent
reader who might have stumbled upon this collection of *mémoires* written for
civil engineers. The Americans' anti-British armaments were more like a
"fortunate event" for France, added the author with cynical candor.[9] But his
serenity was not shared by those who would use his facts without adopting
his hypotheses. Supposing that England was the target, it was certainly not
alone. One thing was clear: "Once America has an imposing and costly fleet,
the positivist mentality of the American people will not accept that the ships
be used for simple pleasure cruises."[10]

Charles Crosnier de Varigny was not among those who erred on the side
of naiveté or optimism. His virulence, along with his varied angles of attack,
made him one of the most striking detractors of the United States of the
century's last decade. Contrary to Chasseloup-Laubat, he was not a man of
technical reports and limited editions; he published at large publishing
houses such as Hachette or Colin, for a wide readership. An eclectic observer,
Varigny started with a study on *Les Grandes fortunes aux États-Unis et en
Angleterre* (1889), then investigated *La Femme aux États-Unis* (1893). But it
was mainly in a collection of articles published in 1891 under the title *Les
États-Unis: Esquisses historiques* (The United States: Historical Sketches) that
he gave his mistrust and hostility free reign.

Varigny's anti-American angle embraced, in part, economic anti-Americanism's party line: criticizing American protectionism was a key element to
his arguments. But his analysis of expansionism was enriched and renewed
by the importance it gave the question's ideological and religious dimensions. Varigny's innovation was in linking the two motifs. Whence his cho-

sen bugbear, an American politician who perfectly embodied the coming-together of tariffs and a "mission": James Blaine, "the American Bismarck,"[11] who since 1881 and the Garfield administration had dreamed of imposing exorbitant customs duties on a weakened Europe; but also, what is more important, Blaine, the apostle of a new nationalist mysticism, bard of the United States' "providential mission." Comparing Blaine to Bismarck had less to do with the men themselves than their doctrines. Varigny was trying to alert the French to the similarity between American and German nationalism, both of which were inspired by a "providential" outlook. The French, in 1891, were haunted by a victorious Germany; they would be wrong, though, to see that country as the only power whose brutal expansionism drew its strength and justification from the myth of divine election. "Prussia is not, in our time, the only power that claims or believes to be invested with a 'providential mission,'" Varigny insisted. "The great American republic also has its providential mission, its *manifest destiny.*"

Manifest destiny: the expression Varigny was commenting on had been in use for over half a century. It was coined in 1845 by the commentator John O'Sullivan, editor of the *Democratic Review,* in the straight and narrow Jacksonian spirit. President Andrew Jackson, in his 1837 farewell address, had invoked providence's plan for entrusting the United States with protecting freedom the world over. He had thus nationalized a deep-rooted and powerful Puritan conviction. It was indeed a founding theme of New England Puritanism to see the colonies as a lighthouse in the night of the world and a haven for persecuted faith. In this view, America had already been granted the vocation of sheltering freedom of thought—not freethinkers' thought, of course, but freedom guided by a conscience defined as "a man's judgment of himself, according to the judgment of God of him."[12]

In the 1840s John O'Sullivan would put his very biblical eloquence to work for this idea and make unremitting efforts to glorify America as "the ark of human hopes."[13] But if the expression "manifest destiny," introduced in 1845, sprang from this tradition, it would go beyond it—like the American people would go beyond their constantly stretching borders. "Our manifest destiny [is] to overspread the continent allotted by Providence for the free development of our yearly multiplying millions": this was the good word propagated by the eloquent O'Sullivan. It was a shift from the traditional conception of a refuge, a patch of land preserved from iniquity, to a much more dynamic vocation. The entire American continent had become a promised land. The force of the verb *overspread*—with its connotations of spreading out, but also overflowing—is intensified by its echoes of the word *overspill,* hinting at a state of overpopulation. From the citadel of the righteous to the masses' vital space, America had decidedly made progress. The continued use of religious vocabulary only partly masked the change of perspective. And the slogan of "manifest destiny," as revisited by the French in the 1890s, only seemed like a way of giving the new imperialism some spiritual meaning, especially since, over the course of the 1850s, its broad success in America had gone hand in hand with a redefinition of the Monroe Doctrine as a "justification for American expansion."[14]

Varigny was very discreet about the process. He refrained from pointing out to his readers that the idea of "manifest destiny"—the key to contemporary America he was offering them—was nearly fifty years old. What he had to say sounded fairly new to his audience, which had just started rediscovering America. Both O'Sullivan's expression and the expansionist reinterpretation of Monroe's doctrine had come onto the scene during the "distance and remove" years, at a time when precious few in France paid any attention to what was happening across the Atlantic. Charles Crosnier de Varigny's book offered a remedial course on America's rise to imperialism; but the emphasis was on the present: a current or imminent threat. The fact that a large part of the American population and political world had adopted the idea of "manifest destiny," Varigny stressed, did not imply that the Monroe Doctrine had been abandoned, but on the contrary, that it had been reinforced and concentrated into a new formula that "summed it up," while investing it with a religious dimension it had lacked in the past. Supplying the Monroe Doctrine with a providential ideology, Varigny concluded, had "raised [it] to the loftiness of a dogma."[15] Dogma: Gaillardet had used the word; Varigny was now explaining what it meant.

Protectionism (in the name of America's superior interests) and "annexationism" (in the name of providence's superior interests): from now on, this was America's double creed. Moreover, such a practical nation did not intend to stop at professions of faith. Varigny was thus particularly attentive to the hegemonic intentions announced by the Pan-American Congress in 1889. Monroe's slogan, "America for Americans," he warned France, had taken on a new meaning and now summed up a double objective: "a federation of the three Americas, grouped under the aegis of the United States," "a continent closed to European products."[16] The next probable prey: Cuba. Was this a case of remarkable prescience? No, it was simply foresight with no risk implied. For over a century already, Cuba's geopolitical inclusion in continental North America had been part of a debate started by Jefferson. Around 1890 more than one American politician had bluntly spoken of annexing it. Blaine had been the first, as Varigny did not hesitate to note, proclaiming that "of all the annexations we can rightfully lay claim to, Cuba's . . . is the most legitimate."[17] Therefore, it is not tolerable, Blaine continued, that yellow fever, which is rampant on that germ-infested island, continue to contaminate our Mississippi valley. In Varigny's view, it was clear that the countdown had started; it was also clear that the force of their destiny would pull the Americans far beyond Cuba.

More credible than Mandat-Grancey and less strictly technical than Chasseloup-Laubat, Varigny came onto the scene a little too early to be heard. Until the 1898 war, scenarios such as his were considered intriguing but unconvincing. Anti-American alarmism was still premature and could easily be dismissed as monarchist spleen or Bonapartist rancor. Criticism and praise were both suspect, Varigny himself noted, stressing how rare impartial historians of America were, since they were all "mainly looking for arguments that were either hostile or favorable to the republican form."[18] Was that why he decided to devote his last American opus to a more lighthearted topic, *La Femme aux États-Unis?*

Varigny's cautionary remark, however, was pertinent. Identifying America with the "republican form" had sharpened several polemical pens in the last years of the century (such as Mandat-Grancey's), but it also cast doubt on an animosity that seemed more aimed at Marianne than Uncle Sam. As for the republicans, if they had largely stopped claiming to be inspired by America, they held their fire against a country that had long given them hope. But the situation Varigny evoked was just about to change: the "republican form," having triumphed in France, was no longer an open question. Likewise, America no longer mainly symbolized a type of government: it now represented a social formation dominated by capitalism and machinism. The symbolic transfer would eliminate the last remnants of self-restraint and give French anti-Americanism new momentum. Until such time, though—for a few more years—the anti-American diatribe was a rather solitary and fairly marginal exercise. The days of an idealized America—the "sugar-coated America" that had been one of the bones Sardou had to pick with Tocqueville—were obviously over. But irony rather than vilification was still the preferred tactic. Apprehensive voices were few and far between, and they were less concerned with America's naval weapons than its advances in developing machine tools.

"America is invading old Europe; it is flooding it and will soon submerge it," Émile Barbier wrote in 1893. But he was talking about a flood of merchandise: locomotives, coal, silk, fruit, cotton, and even "American Bordeaux."[19] Paul de Rousiers, an economist with the Musée social, found himself on common ground when he wrote in *American Life* (1892), "America has ceased to be an object of curiosity in becoming an object of dread."[20] It was a strong word. But once again, it was aimed at America's impressive industrial progress and mechanized agricultural system. Rousiers, like Barbier, was aware that economic competition between the United States and Europe was intensifying. With good reason: a decisive decade for French anti-Americanism, the 1890s were also a time when American production would take a great leap forward and become the world leader, ahead of Great Britain—surpassed in steel in 1887, iron in 1890, and coal in 1899. America, Rousiers explained, "has grown to be a formidable rival to the Old World." Not for a second, however, did he imagine it would use brute force to conquer or conserve its markets. Rousiers did not make the leap from competition to colonization, except in fixating on the infiltration of American products with a symbolically charged anecdote: "The French soldier carries canned meats, prepared in Chicago, in his knapsack."

America was not really all in people's minds yet, but corned beef was already in the lunch bag.

A "Splendid Little War"

In 1898, the electroshock of Cuba brutally changed the meaning of words and the scope of accusations. The anti-American generation that included Varigny, Barbier, and Rousiers had rung a few warning bells; from now on, the alarm would sound. After crystallization came the catalyst. The war declared by the United States against Spain precipitated, in the chemical sense of the word, a suspended anti-Americanism. The event, which was of short duration and concerned France only indirectly, was thus paradoxically a key moment for French anti-Americanism.

We should quickly recall the circumstances of a conflict that has now been practically forgotten by the French. By the end of the nineteenth century, all that was left of the immense empire Spain had carved out for itself in the Americas were the islands of Cuba and Puerto Rico. And its hold on them was anything but comfortable. Cuba, the pearl of the Antilles and the source of so many Spanish riches, was the site of a series of rebellions against both the metropolis and large landowners. A ten-year campaign (1868–78) had been necessary to tamp down a first uprising. Another revolt began in 1895. Cánovas del Castillo's conservative government in Spain intended to crush the adversary once and for all: he handed the task over to General Weyler, who organized a forced "reconcentration" of the villagers and peasants into the towns and cities. This was just like the system of "strategic hamlets" applied years later (and with just as little success) by the Americans during the war in Vietnam. Humanly, politically, and economically, the operation was a disaster. While, in the United States, propaganda in favor of the rebels and a "junta" opposition based in New York was intensifying in all quarters, in Madrid, the liberal Sagasta replaced Cánovas del Castillo, who had been assassinated in the Basque country in 1897. It was a radical political change. "Butcher Weyler," as the North American press called him, was dismissed, and the Spanish minister of the colonies, Moret, announced that Cuba would be given local autonomy as of 1898.

Spain considered the crisis over and, pointing to its goodwill and willingness to admit reform, asked the United States to stop sheltering and providing arms to the now illegitimate "junta" opposition. Calm had not returned to Cuban soil, however. The rebels outdid themselves by executing a Spanish colonel who had come to demonstrate the autonomy plan, while partisans of the colonial status quo took to the streets in violent protests against the "reformists." In early 1898, as the election of a Cuban parliament was being planned for the month of April, the skirmishes multiplied.

Then, on January 25, a powerful North American warship, the *Maine*, invited itself into the port of Havana. At the request of consul general Fitzhugh Lee (nephew of the Confederate general Robert E. Lee), President William McKinley had sent the *Maine* on a mission to protect U.S. citizens in Cuba from hypothetical mistreatment. The Spanish government greeted the initiative with an understandable lack of enthusiasm. Prime Minister Sagasta chose, however, to consider the unexpected visitors guests, and to save face, he sent a brand new cruiser, the *Vizcaya*, to pay a courteous visit to the port of New York. The agitation in Havana remained relative, and the strife that was supposed to have justified his presence did not keep the *Maine*'s commandant, Sigsbee, from attending several bullfights. Everything went along fairly smoothly, then, until the fatal night of February 15.

That night, at 9:40 P.M., a gigantic explosion shook the harbor and the city. The *Maine* had blown up. There were 268 dead, including two officers. While Spain protested its innocence, the Hearst group's popular press unleashed a virulent attack on the "enemy" and its "secret infernal machine." And as of February 18, Joseph Pulitzer's *World* was calling for war. The politicians were not to be outdone, and Bryan, a Democrat who had been McKinley's losing opponent in the 1896 election, openly endorsed an intervention.

In this climate, the inquiry the navy was charged with turned into a criminal investigation. The members of the commission gave little thought to affronting the torrents of public opinion; they were much more interested in exonerating the navy itself from any error or negligence that would explain the explosion. The commission concluded, without giving proof, that a submarine mine had gone off. Working separately (since the United States had denied Spain a joint investigation), the Spanish commission concluded that there had been a fire in a coal bunker and that heat in the forward magazine, which was too close to the bunkers and insufficiently insulated, had caused the explosion. The latter theory, which most historians now consider accurate, was sanctioned in 1976 by Admiral Rickover in an official publication by the Department of the Navy's Naval History Division.[21]

As for the public, it did not wait for the experts' judgments to cry for revenge. Ignited by the press and fueled by the majority of politicians—with a particularly belligerent assistant secretary of the navy named Theodore Roosevelt first in line—"war fever" made the political temperature rise. The United States sent Spain a note that read like an ultimatum, demanding referee status in the process of Cuban autonomy, which should, as America saw it, lead to the island's complete independence, after which, adding insult to interference, the McKinley administration proposed to purchase Cuba from the Spanish government for $300 million. War was now unavoidable. What would be a "splendid little war" for the American jingoists[22] would be, for Spain, a humiliating and disastrous conflict in which not only Cuba, but also Puerto Rico and the Philippines would be lost.

France United against Filibustering America

And what was France up to at the time? Events as distant and hazy as the ones taking place in ever more exotic theaters of war seemed unlikely candidates to attract the attention of a country reputed for its ignorance of geography. Yet they had a considerable resonance.

First, the French press got heated up about the United States' military operation. The explosion of the *Maine,* which had been used to justify opening hostilities, left both diplomats and journalists skeptical. No one believed the Spanish had perpetrated a covert attack; it was easier to believe that it had been a provocation on the part of the reformist "junta" or its North American accomplices. For when all was said and done, who benefited from the crime? The American popular press's bellicose hysteria surprised and shocked the French, and reinforced their suspicions. A venue as level-headed as *Le Temps* did not mince words and, when the United States took Havana, spoke of "international buccaneering."[23] The tone was set, and it was all the more bitter because everything was going in the filibusters' favor. The disaster that hit the Spanish fleet in Manila, news of which reached Madrid on May 1, 1898, plunged the peninsula into unease. But the astonishment was hardly less pronounced in Paris, where the worry was shared. Never had military events as remote—and in which France was not directly affected—provoked such a reaction, which also arose despite a worrisome internal situation, marked by the most violent surge of anti-Semitic activity of the Third Republic.

The conjunction, in the spring of 1898, of what Pierre Birnbaum has called the "anti-Semitic moment" with a violent anti-American reaction was accidental.[24] But it revealed an essential trait of French anti-Americanism: from that moment on, it would be a profoundly unifying force. In the thick of the Dreyfus affair, on the heels of Zola's denunciation, an astonishing unanimity struck one Cuban observer:

> One would say that hatred for the Americans is the least divisive sentiment
> among the French, for never has such unanimity been seen. Republicans are
> defending a retrograde monarchy; freethinkers are clamoring for the triumph of a
> nation of fanatics; and conservatives, those guardians of tradition and the family,
> are calling "pig farmers" the maternal ancestors of the gentlemen who will soon
> bear the most illustrious names in France![25]

It was a strange spectacle, and nicely captured by that sardonic visitor: republican, anticlerical France joining in with the France of manor houses (which marriages to rich Americans helped restore) to boo the United States and cheer on the Spanish monarchy!

The description was not only comical, it was prophetic. At the high point of civil discord in a divided France, anti-Americanism was the only "French passion" that calmed the other passions, curbed antagonisms, and reconciled the staunchest adversaries. This reconciliation at the United States' expense—or, at least, the cease-fire between the different French factions in the face of a supposedly common enemy—would remain a constant of political and intellectual life in France. It is impossible to understand French anti-Americanism and its placid permanence without a sense of its *social and national benefit* in manufacturing consensus. If this is its function (or at least one of its functions), we should not be surprised that it blossomed and took root with the war in 1898, and that it was also a reaction to the violent divisions in France at the turn of the century. It was only logical that anti-Americanism, an antidote to internal quarrels, should spring "from the days when the French did not like one another."[26] At least they now knew whom to hate together.

A second characteristic of the 1898 crisis would also be repeated in the subsequent history of anti-Americanism: the gap between the public's exasperation and elected officials' moderation. The French government's stance was effectively one of restraint. France was, in the end, not one of the belligerents; it had no part in the conflict other than protecting Spanish nationals in

Cuba. It was French *citizens* who showed increasingly violent indignation toward the United States. The atmosphere was tense and the pressure strong enough to have the heads of French diplomacy worried—as Gabriel Hanoteaux would later recount—about being pushed by popular opinion to break with the United States. The immediate feeling was intense; but the Spanish-American War would also provoke a deep and lasting stir. Even more than the immediate commentaries on America's "aggression," a new image of America quickly spread and captured people's attention. Over the months and years to come, the event's shock wave would continue unabated. Editorialists' indignation had barely waned when essayists and writers took over. Suddenly, as if by magic, serialized and popular novels were filled with unsettling Americans. The ridiculous Yankee was replaced by the terrifying Yankee, and Gustave Le Rouge, a budding novelist who would soon become a master of the serialized novel, kept his readers on the edge of their seats with *La Conspiration des milliardaires* (The Billionaires' Conspiracy), a breathless tale of geopolitical fiction published starting in 1899. The plot—a secret committee of Yankee magnates attempts to subjugate Europe using an army of automatons—would have seemed ridiculous ten years earlier. Now, fiction was lagging behind current events, and Le Rouge's heroes only had to imitate, at the height of his glory, the very real Pierre Loti, who rushed to Madrid right at the start of the hostilities to assure the queen regent of the French people's "sympathy" and express the "revulsion" they felt toward the despicable aggression of which Spain was the victim.[27] There was even a rumor in Paris that the author of *Iceland Fisherman* and *Disenchanted* would be given command of a cruiser and take a run at the Yankees. Loti regretfully denied this. It was neither true nor, unfortunately, possible. For lack of a sword, he used the pen. Instead of cannonballs, Loti would fire a sheaf of pages in vengeance: "In Madrid, the First Days of the American Aggression."[28]

Why was everyone in France so stirred up? There were many contributing factors: a long tradition of alliance with Spain; the two countries' parallel situation in having preserved colonies a stone's throw away from the American continent; the recent propaganda in France in favor of Latin solidarity; and above all, perhaps, a constant hostility to the Monroe Doctrine—a hostility Napoleon III's propaganda had awakened back in the days of the Mexican venture, and that anti-American writings of the 1880s had rekindled. But independent of any other consideration, the Cuba affair, followed by the conquest and occupation of the Philippines, was immediately perceived in France in its symbolic dimension. For the first time, the United States had taken the initiative of declaring war on a European country. A threshold had been crossed. A taboo broken. The Cuba aggression was a stinging repudiation inflicted upon the Great Peaceful Republic's credulous admirers. Victor Hugo had died just in time: he did not live to see the model nation turn into a power like any other.

The 1898 war was interpreted all the more dramatically in France because the United States' bellicose conversion foreshadowed a transformation of war itself, hints of which had already been glimpsed in the Civil War. America's wars would be created in the image of Yankee America: unaesthetic and inhuman. Crushing the Spanish in Cuba and the Philippines was not only a low blow to old Europe; it was the exportation of a new kind of war. Of course, cried an indignant Loti, the United States did not invent war. But they had turned it into a hideous death industry; they had made it "ugly, reeking of coal, chemically barbaric."[29] This was the kind of war "the enemies across the sea" excelled at, given that they "have more money, more machines, more gasoline to dip their shells in, more explosives." The cliché of America's vulgarity and poor taste, which had already triumphed in the previous decade, found an unexpected application here: waged by such philistines as the Americans, even war was no longer pretty. And no one but they could consider it "splendid."

Off with the Masks

But that was not the most important thing. The important thing, the essential, was that the mask had fallen. The most arrant optimists, the most incorrigible idealists could no longer hide their faces or turn a deaf ear. The cannonades of brand new U.S. battleships breaking in their howitzers on Havana or Manila were a rude awakening for those who had harbored illusions about the North American Union's essentially peaceful nature. Between the naive sycophants who had raised statues to American democracy and the more lucid minds who had been trying to warn France for the past ten years, it was clear who was right and who was wrong.

Octave Noël was one of the first to draw these conclusions from the event. Writing in *Le Correspondant,* a Catholic review that was turning toward anti-Americanism, from January to June 1899 he published a series of articles that were republished in book form to which he gave the expressive title of his March 25 chronicle: *Le Péril américain.* The time for metaphors was over; the peril had become all too real. Not only had the United States entered a phase of aggression through the use of open force, but the attack that took the Europeans off guard had been premeditated. Even worse: it was written on the great scrolls of America's destiny as they had started to unfurl at the turn of the century. "The brutal aggression the United States committed against Spain, however sudden and hard to justify in right and equity it was, was not an unexpected fact. It was the result of a premeditated plan, and it constitutes a new episode in the political stance inaugurated in 1810 by the transatlantic republic."[30] That had already been Frédéric Gaillardet's theory fifteen years earlier: now it was weighed down with cannonballs. The war with Spain was thus written in the United States of America's geopolitical heritage. This did not make it any less of a decisive stage: it was part of the globalization of North America's ambitions. It had been a long time, of course, since the Monroe Doctrine could reasonably pass for a purely defensive doctrine. However, even converted into an aggressive dogma, it still involved only the New World, to the exclusion of the other continents. Of course, "the formula never had any other part of the world but Europe in its sights,"[31] but a Europe that had to be extricated from America, not attacked from the other side of the planet. A new step had been taken—a small step for Cuba, a giant leap for Manila—toward worldwide interventionism. Now, Noël wrote, "the Yankees are ready and willing to give their former president's doctrine an extension he had perhaps not foreseen."[32] They had just printed the new version—"larger and more suited to their aspirations"—with the Filipinos' blood. It was a new version, Noël added, that could be summed up with a slogan: "The world for Americans."[33]

The conflict with Spain was a Janus-faced war. Its Cuban side was still turned toward the past; according to Noël, this was because the United States had failed in its attempt at a diplomatic takeover of Latin America (with the Pan-American Congress ending fruitlessly on April 19, 1890); it had "adjourned its revenge" and "pounced on a less guarded prey."[34] Since the Latin States of America had refused to fall into place under the Stars and Stripes, the Americans would go plant the flag on Cuban soil without asking permission. The Cuban "reformists'" radio-controlled insurrection was pan-American diplomacy continued by other means: the "insurrection was born in the trusts and clubs of sugar entrepreneurs in New York, and in Florida's cigar factories."[35] When all was said and done, Cuba was a consolation prize. A splendid little prize, all the same: the "key to the Gulf of Mexico and the future transoceanic canal."[36] Sneakily packaged and wrapped up in philanthropic wrapping paper: "In the final scenes, the government intervened and . . . renewed the philanthropic act that had worked so well in 1861."[37] There was nothing like using abolition or the emancipation of the oppressed Cubans to move forward on the path to world domination. "Philanthropy" had always been used by the Yankees like Noah's cloak, to cover their unseemly will to power. . .

In Cuba's wake, then, came the Philippines. This was the new face of Monroe: an America whose ambition was spilling over the borders of a continent it had started seeing as too narrow. The Philippines were also a key: the "key to trade with the Far East, which holds a considerable fascination over the Americans."[38] The mask the Americans had not wanted to lower in 1890 during their pan-American disappointments had now been torn off. Washington had stopped disguising its global ambitions. The Americans had stopped hiding their goals: "They want to expand beyond [their] natural frontiers, which are nonetheless already excessive."[39] Since Monroe, America had been secreting "the most bitter bile against the old continent."[40] The sac of bile had just burst, and a confrontation was inevitable. "At every point on the globe, the United States is now fated to go to war with Europe."[41]

Octave Noël never forgot to point out the economic roots of this imperialist aggressiveness. As an economist himself (he would become a professor at the École des Hautes Études Commerciales on the eve of World War I), he did not neglect to stress that if America was launching attacks, it was because the country had a vital need for "perpetual expansion." Once again, protectionism was the original cause of the unquestionable American will to conquer, since it forced the Americans to "die of starvation with their treasures or extend indefinitely, and at any cost, the circle of their influence and even their commercial domination." It was a vicious circle, in this case, where the need for new markets and the obligation to inexorably conquer came one after the other. "This," Noël added, "led, first of all, to the recent attempts to rejuvenate and interpret the Monroe Doctrine, which remains the epitome of Yankee gospel; then to the spirit of conquest and search for new openings that characterize its current policies."[42] This led to what would henceforth be the fatal clash of two worlds: "The struggle for life, for economic supremacy, between Europe and America, is about to take on a character of as-yet-unheard-of brutality and bitterness."[43]

In August, *Le Correspondant,* attentive to American affairs, published an article entitled "The World for the Americans."[44] The expression would take hold. Its author, Edmond Johanet, was an old hand at reporting on America. In 1889 he had published *Un Français dans la Floride,* an insipid travel narrative whose best passage was a famous line quoted from Labiche: "What a journey! my God, what a journey! as the bourgeois moan in *La Cagnotte.*"[45] Ten years later, the tone had changed, and the founder of Johanetville, Florida, had transmuted his anecdotal insults into a universal incrimination of the United States. Political corruption; lobbyists earning their keep by "mediating between the corrupters and the corrupt";[46] a dictatorship of trusts over all the different industries (which were entirely "entrusted");[47] rich people's egotism; Protestantism's inferiority to Catholicism, with its "more beautiful charity":[48] *Autour du monde millionaire* (Around the Millionaire

World) offered the nearly complete arsenal of Catholic and conservative anti-Americanism with a virulence that had still been latent in 1889 but that the Cuba affair had unleashed. The Florida vacationer volunteering his shallow and tasteless tales had been transformed into a destroyer of the American Babylon and the "All-Plutopolis" that, in Johanet's opinion, governed that so-called democracy. It is striking to see how his tone was radicalized between 1889 and 1898, an indication of anti-American discourse's rapidly rising power.

The War of the Worlds

The war against Spain was thus doubly decisive. On the one hand, France's image of the United States was recentered around the imperialist theme; on the other hand, and at the same time, Europe came into existence for a certain number of people in France, both as a cohesively threatened entity and as the only force capable of holding its own against the "American peril"—if it could silence its own internal divisions.

First, imperialism. The 1898 campaign definitively ended the peaceful image of the United States promoted by France's republicans. It was a stinging negation for those who had faithfully upheld the legend, as well as for those who had lent it credibility, like Paul de Rousiers, who could not believe that the United States had turned bellicose and had insisted that the American army was weak in numbers.[49] "The United States are not absolutely shielded from war," wrote the Musée Social researcher in 1892; he could imagine only a war that would be imposed *on* the United States. Six years later, it was Europe that was no longer shielded from an American war, and in 1904, the journalist Jules Huret took pleasure in correcting the copy of such so-called experts, who had only been interested in the number of men enlisted in the American army, never in its budget. "For a country that does not have an army, or at least, whose army is only fifty thousand strong, America has a military budget of *a billion and a half francs!* Higher than France's," Huret wrote, hammering his point home with more vehemence than accuracy.[50]

Anything could happen, and in any theater of operations. The war, waged in both the Atlantic and the Pacific, had also given the lie to a calm conviction held by observers from the previous decade: that the United States' expansionist yearnings would find a sufficient outlet on the North American continent and did not necessarily imply that there would be a direct conflict with Europe. The most pessimistic observers had foreseen the possibility of friction with Great Britain, which was jealous of the United States' growing influence in Latin America. No one had imagined a deliberate frontal attack against one of the countries of old Europe, or that the conflict would spread over both hemispheres.

The Civil War victors' military imperialism in 1865, which until that point had been presented as a latent yearning, had become a patent reality. Accordingly, the face of "Yankee" America changed, in the eyes of the French. A new American had arrived: the peaceful farmer and the debonair shop-keeper had been replaced by an industrial-age warrior who burned down cities and massacred civilians. In the furious text he launched in literary retaliation against the Yankee aggressor, Loti used bombs dipped in gasoline as the symbol of the dirty war invented by the Americans, with "their cap-tures before war was declared, their bombardments without forewarning, their shells wrapped in gasoline-soaked canvas that set cities on fire."[51] It was slaughterers' warfare. (And yet Loti was writing before the bloody "pacifica-tion" of the Philippines.) Cheaters' warfare, since the invasion of Cuba used the excuse of an attack against the *Maine,* which was completely made up. Bluffers' warfare, too, because the gauntlet thrown down before Europe was a test of its will, of its ability to resist. Pray that Europe understands! Loti exclaimed. That it will learn its lesson and not leave its sword sheathed! That the European nations will strike as one against the common enemy! Loti dreamed of this sacred union at the residence of the German ambassador in Madrid as he regarded an allegorical painting "painted by Emperor Wil-helm": women dressed as Valkyries representing the different European nations. "It would doubtless have been a more fitting allegory," Loti remarked, "with a more immediate message, if the genie with open wings had been pointing out to the assembled warrior women, across the ocean toward the New World, the whole western part of the sky lined with electri-cal wires and blackened with factory smoke."[52] What a striking panorama! Pierre Loti was most likely the first Frenchman to dream of a great anti-American crusade led by a Valkyrized Europe.

Though his zeal took a singular turn, Loti was not the only one stirred up. Among the converging testimonies, Valéry's and Suarès's are the most strik-ing, the former for its sober concision and the latter for a vehemence that would make Loti look like a moderate. (We will also come back to both of them in our chapter on pro-European anti-Americanism. Indeed, their writ-ings would not appear until the period between the two world wars.) Valéry's essay describes the Spanish-American War as a fundamentally traumatic event, which he associates with the Sino-Japanese War of 1895. The two conflicts are decisive for Valéry, not because of their direct consequences, but as warning signs of the European world's irrevocable disruption. His

retrospectively melancholy meditation prolongs in a strangely solemn way
the cry of anger and distress Loti uttered at the time:

> A shock that reaches us from an unforeseen quarter can give us a sudden, novel
> sensation of the existence of our body as an unknown quality.... I do not know
> why the action by Japan against China and that of the United States against Spain,
> which followed the first quite closely, made a great impression on me at the time.
> They were only limited conflicts in which forces of only moderate importance
> were engaged.... And yet I felt these distinct events not as accidents or limited
> phenomena but as symptoms or premises, as significant facts whose meaning far
> exceeded their intrinsic importance and apparent scope.[53]

Europe was born, for Valéry, not from a mythological ravishing, but rather
from a violation just as highly symbolic: old Europe's violation by its children
or disciples—especially ungrateful America. For if the 1895 war gave Europe
good reason to worry, as "the first act of power by an Asiatic nation [Japan]
remodeled and equipped on European lines," the 1898 war, as "the first act of
power by a nation [the United States] derived and, as it were, developed from
Europe against a European nation," left Europe indignant and wounded.

Loti, in the heat of his inaction, dreamed of a flight of the Europeans
against the American enemy. Valéry discovered Europe as one discovers a
flesh wound:

> We had been unaware of some part of what we were, and suddenly this brutal
> sensation makes us realize, by an aftereffect, the unsuspected size and shape of
> the field of our existence. Thus that indirect blow in the Far East and this direct
> blow in the West Indies made me dimly perceive something in myself that could
> be affected and troubled by such events. I found I was "sensitized" to situations
> that affected a kind of virtual idea of Europe which until then I had not known
> I held.[54]

This, a generation before the disastrous period of 1914–18, could truly be the
birth certificate of a defeated Europe—defeated, just as Spain was in the
Cuba affair. Europe, daughter of fear? Europe, the involuntary creation of a
matricidal America?

The French versus the Yankees: The Serial

A writer addressing a completely different audience did not need to wait
a quarter of a century to react to the shock of 1898 or call on Europe to form

a sacred union against the American enemy: the novelist Gustave Le Rouge. Just a few months after the explosion of the *Maine* and the invasion of Cuba, Le Rouge offered his popular readership the first volume of an extraordinary anti-American saga: *La Conspiration des milliardaires,* a sensational serial that exalted the heroic and solitary struggle of a handful of Frenchmen against a Yankee conspiracy bent on subjugating Europe.

La Conspiration des milliardaires ran in eight parts from 1899 to 1900, and it sticks out in the history of anti-American narratives for being both ahead of its time and strikingly radical, and for reaching a large reading audience. This cheap novel (each volume cost four sous) was Gustave Le Rouge's first work, co-written with Gustave Guitton. For a first try, the man who would be nicknamed the "shopgirl's Jules Verne" pulled off a master stroke. At thirty-two, he successfully synthesized the popular Manichean melodrama à la Eugène Sue with a Verne-style tale of technical anticipation. But above all, it was the choice of subject that made *La Conspiration des milliardaires* a first in the world of French fiction. Cleverly capturing the anger and worry created by the Cuba affair, Le Rouge spun his plot around the American peril. Both opportunistic and militant, he depicted the Yankee as the enemy and mobilized an audience that was ready and willing to believe that the United States as it was in 1899, with its pitiless universe and its imperialist frenzy, could pose a real threat of world war. What seems like an inexpiable war is avoided in the end, and the conspiracy foiled. But up to the happy ending, for several hundred pages, a North America more filled with dollars than scruples deploys all its mechanical muscle and psychic energy with the goal of annihilating Europe.

The drama's argument is frequently called to the reader's attention, as in the following passage, with its breathless (and lucrative) paragraph breaks:

> A civilization has risen up to face Europe, hasty and monstrous. In one century's time, the United States has realized the impossible and attained the summit of material activity.
>
> For the rest of us, that is the real peril. Up to now, the Americans were content with being astounding industrialists. That is no longer enough for them.
>
> We can sense them stirring and struggling with economic problems. They seek to impose their commercial tariffs on us; they use all means possible to reach their goals.
>
> Their armaments are already growing and being perfected. . . .
>
> What will be the outcome of this enormous conflict? Can we imagine a widespread war without trembling in fear?

Such are the meditations of the young Olivier Coronal, an engineer and humanist, on "the American peril, the real danger for the Latin races."[55] Like all science fiction, *La Conspiration des milliardaires* forms the simple future using a perfected past mixed with a pinch of the immediate present. Our hero, whose worry comes panting along in serialized stanzas, is not really saying anything Octave Noël had not. Though Le Rouge's story is baroque in its ingenious details (the Yankees have a regiment of hypnotists at their disposal for stealing ideas from the French), there is nothing exaggerated about its basic conceit or about the long and sententious pronouncements of its positive characters. The warning he relentlessly hammers in is the same as the one voiced by the Cassandras of the 1890s: "The transatlantic peril has become a reality."[56]

La Conspiration des milliardaires is therefore doubly relevant. While its success demonstrates that anti-Americanism was being popularized, the stereotypical insistence characteristic of the genre makes Le Rouge's serial a semiotic treasury of the anti-American details that were either accepted or acceptable at the turn of the twentieth century.

The enemy designated by Le Rouge, however, is not the American but rather the Yankee. The term is used systematically and on practically every page—by French characters referring to their adversaries, by the narrator in the course of his anthropological and political reflections, but also by the Yankees themselves: the billionaire Boltyn refers to his own government as a "Yankee government."[57] The nomenclature is a central part of Le Rouge's innovative demonizing of the American enemy. By vigorously imposing the term, with its negative connotations, as the "normal" way of designating the inhabitants of the United States, Gustave Le Rouge turned the page on romantic, epic, and brotherly America. *That* America, whether a haven or a land of adventure, was nothing but a memory; the friendly nation that had occupied it was an outdated myth. Instead of two nations side by side—France and the United States—Le Rouge's serial sets up two continents in a face-off—Europe and the "Yankee country." Two continents and, more specifically, two races. Between the Europeans and the Yankees, "between the two races standing face to face on the shores of the Atlantic," the "difference" was "enormous."[58] So enormous that even the English would start to look like Europeans, in comparison...

The constant use of the designation *Yankee* was therefore not just the simple transcription of a term that was gaining in popularity. Le Rouge's insistence gave America a new face; the nation and its history faded away, to be replaced by race and its eternal qualities. The tale's complete lack of any real Americans (the only popular and sympathetic character our heroes meet turns out not to be American after all) is a logical follow-up to the elided name. Substituting the Yankee for the American was an operation that went well beyond onomastic defamation: the United States (which Le Rouge calls the Union, as if the Civil War were still being fought) is now defined by the dominant "race" that "occupies" the American territory. The villainous circle of bellicose billionaires, that "handful of ambitious Yankees" who have the means to annihilate Europe, are nothing more than a hard core, the condensation and exacerbation of a ruthless and vindictive race.

So there was no longer an American nation. American soil no longer existed, either. The country Le Rouge's heroes travel through is one big abstraction. The fact that Le Rouge had never set foot in America obviously did not help him with the descriptive passages. But, in fact, a flimsy evocation serves his purpose better. The "Yankee country" remains vague and lackluster, given that it is only a negative image of "America"—that lost continent whose vistas and populations had been forevermore relegated to children's books. The adventuresome and colorful prairie novels had been replaced by a dismal topography of disfigured nature and a conquered terrain.

Such is the spectacle that greets the young engineer Olivier Coronal and his faithful servant Léon (from Belleville) when they set out in search of the mysterious and secretive base where the billionaires' automaton armada is being constructed—a terrible phalanx of "steel specters." It makes for a bleak and disappointing vision: "The train sped straight ahead at full steam. The young Frenchman recalled with a smile the adventure novels that had charmed his childhood, Fenimore Cooper and Gustave Aymard. . . . Where had Long-Rifle, Leatherstocking, Hawkeye, and all the wonderful heroes of the prairie gone . . . ?"[59] There is no longer any room for such novelistic characters in the "Yankee country." The United States of 1899 had driven out its adventurers, just as it had massacred or corralled the Indians, "using the excuse that they were giving them a taste of civilization's benefits." This is America as a steamroller of men's dreams, as a normalization factory; the ex-America traversed by Olivier and Léon debases everyone up to and including its victims, whose lives are spared at the price of their own decadence: "The last representatives of the red race, decimated by useless revolts, have started dressing like the Europeans and doing business." The Yankee country was a blank slate, but not a utopian one: it was a standardized desert. Its devastated countryside was covered with "the aluminum houses that have replaced branch huts." Its wandering humanity was a devastating force; replacing the Indians, the "unemployed . . . cross the United States, weapons in hand, pillaging and burning everything, as happened again during the last railroad strike."[60] In a word, it was a human disaster—a civilization that had "erected the theory of 'might makes right' " and that "worried little about those who went under in the struggle."[61]

If America had been capable of conceiving the monstrous plan of invading Europe to turn it into a "vassal," it was because America itself was a land of violence and injustice. "The enslavement of the Old World by the New" was now "a matter of months, perhaps days," Le Rouge's reader discovered with trepidation. In the billionaires' view, invasion was a simple export strategy. Europe would merely be included in the modern enslavement that had already taken over the United States. The goal was to ensure that all the markets would be dominated for good, to globalize the dictatorship of the four hundred. Was this the burning obligation of a robust young country, as admirers of Teddy Roosevelt and the "strenuous life" pretended? The growth spurt of an America brimming over with its own energy? Not at all, Le Rouge replied: this was the global exportation of a plutocratic gerontocracy's grim despotism.

> But who will triumph with America? The four hundred multimillionaires who hold all the capital! More powerful than Caesar and the greatest kings in history, the billionaires will share the world between them; gold will become the universal religion, and factories twenty stories high will be its sanctuaries, just as iron towers and gigantic bridges will be its venerated monuments.[62]

At the top of the Yankee pyramid, reigning over a "civilization that takes no pride in philanthropy," would be, of course, the billionaires; but also their henchmen, with the indispensable mastermind of the robotic conspiracy first in line: the "famous Hattison" from Zingo Park, "the world-renowned electrician."[63] In this shady character, the French reader of 1899 had no trouble recognizing Thomas Edison, of Menlo Park. His trip to France ten years earlier had made the front page of all the newspapers. But the inventor of the phonograph and the incandescent lamp, which were all the rage in Parisian salons, was portrayed as a sorry soul, a "little, quiet man with a perpetually morose physiognomy,"[64] more cunning than inventive, as much a clear-sighted exploiter of other people's ideas as a creator of his own, ready to give all his efforts to furthering the bellicose plans of the capitalists drawn together by the king of canned goods, William Boltyn.

A mechanized and hierarchical world, a pitiless universe, this unnatural America was ruled over by a fiendish pair: the unscrupulous capitalist and the soulless inventor. It was just this team that defined most exactly "the odious Yankee type, the scientist with no high-minded ideas, the industrialist with no humanity."[65] To describe one was to know them all—and unmask the whole species: "It is only now," reflects the valiant Olivier, who has been betrayed and fallen into the Yankee enemy's hands, "that I fully understand it, in all its nuances."

Was this just Manicheanism for shopgirls? Maybe. But the eminent *Figaro* reporter Jules Huret was not reasoning any differently when he opposed true French *savants*, "apostles whose only salary is renown," with the "inverse phenomenon" particular to America—"scientists who consent to cure their peers only on the condition of amassing riches." "An excessive egotism, an exaggerated practical sense": these dominant traits of the Yankee "destroy any noble virtuousness, any sense of duty or human solidarity."[66] Furthermore, "every invention utilized or perfected in America was invented in old Europe."[67] *Corruptio optimi pessima,* repeated France's defenders of humanistic science. The worst corruption was the one that corrupted the heart of humanity: its great men's humanism. Science without a conscience and specialists without scruples marked this infamous America, where greed sullied the noblest vocations. There was no research other than on how to make a profit. Highway robbery where emulation had reigned. The "shameless pillage" of patents, the theft of copyrights had logically become a national industry in a country where "the 'scientists' are as shameless as the profiteers."[68] The picture sketched by the *Figaro*'s field reporter was practically a carbon copy of the serial writer's panorama: the only thing missing was the "regiment of hypnotists" that Gustave Le Rouge imagined pumping Frenchmen's scientific thoughts from strategic garrets in the Latin Quarter.

Out of Hatred for Europe

For Gustave Le Rouge, there was, strictly speaking, no longer an America but rather a Yankee country with a missing population, whose authorities were mere puppet figures. Everything derived from the secret circle that really governed the country. This parallel leadership most likely obeyed the logic of self-interest, but as an aggravating circumstance it was also electrified by a pure hatred for the Europeans.

The taciturn Hattison, the conspiracy's mastermind, is consumed by a constant, uncontrollable rage against Europe:

> The engineer Hattison . . . had indeed only one goal, to which he subordinated all his actions and the incredible energy that he housed in his weak and sickly body. Above all else, he hated the Europeans, their manners, their ideas. . . . He dreamt, with a shudder of pleasure, of the total destruction of the barbaric races across the sea, whose social principles and commercial ineptitude had the gift of exasperating him.[69]

As for the sanguinary Boltyn, the head of an empire of slaughterhouses, his feverish tirades do not help calm him down. He needs an outlet for all his rage: an art gallery where he paces up and down the enormous halls "gashing here and there with jabs of his cane the great works of the European masters."[70] It is a striking representation of American resentment, with its enraged impotence in the face of Europe's artistic superiority. And one that is all the more significant, it would seem, because it is an undisguised knockoff of a famous short story by Maupassant, *Mademoiselle Fifi* (1882), where the part of the vandal is played by a sadistic and effeminate officer in the Prussian occupation, whose daily amusement consists of exploding powder charges amid the *objets d'art* in the castle he is occupying in Normandy.[71]

We have already come across the strange Prussian analogy with Crosnier de Varigny, in the form of a parallel between Blaine and Bismarck. Here it has a different meaning. It decidedly seems as if, for the pacifist Gustave Le Rouge, the enemy is no longer across the Rhine; as if the great menace rising in the west could exonerate France's oppressors from 1870. So Gustave Le Rouge agreed with Captain Loti, calling the Valkyries to the rescue against the enemies across the sea and their dirty warfare. On this point, he also joined Edmond Demolins, whose widely read essay *Anglo-Saxon Superiority: To What It Is Due*, published in 1897, was still fresh in everyone's mind. In *La Conspiration des milliardaires*, it is the wise Monsieur Golbert, Olivier Coronal's mentor, who has the job of discussing the different theories. He does not credit the hypothesis that the Anglo-Saxons possess an absolute and generalized superiority ("their intelligence does not reach beyond the limits of practical realities, indeed it cannot possibly do such a thing"),[72] but he shares with Demolins the idea that the French should not mistake their enemy by continuing to demonize the Germans, who would be infinitely less threatening in the long run than the Yankees.

A secondary but not transitory effect of the growing force of anti-American sentiment was that Germany seemed less hostile in comparison, and certainly less foreign. The idea of a defensive alliance ushered Germany back into a confederacy of nations in the name of a "European" logic sometimes pushed to extremes—so far as to envisage an anti-American coalition under the guidance of Wilhelm II![73] It even seems fairly clear that for some (such as Loti), anti-Americanism authorized choosing Germany as a preferred "civilization." (We will later see how Proust depicts the character of Charlus as harboring an irresistible Germanophilia along with an irrepressible Americanophobia.) Le Rouge, in 1900, was satisfied with inviting "the emperor of Germany with his martial face" to join in the ending of *La Conspiration des milliardaires*—which is not too bad a deal. Because the ending is of course a happy one. Faced with so much hatred backed by so much money, our honest intellectuals' chances seem rather slight. They triumph, however, and humanity with them, using two equally magical weapons: love and a "psychic accumulator." The first changes people's hearts (even Americans'); the second generates benevolence on a wide scale. Hattison's own son, Ted, subjugated by a Frenchwoman and corrupted by too many visits to French museums, betrays his father's ignoble cause. And symmetrically, Boltyn's icy daughter, the arrogant Aurora, will end up yielding to Olivier Coronal's charms and the good life on the banks of the Loire River. . . As for the "psychic accumulator," fittingly directed at the people who are the most resistant to benevolence, it makes them as gentle as lambs: "From several kilometers away, all you had to do was point a few at a city in order to influence and transform its whole population. Political struggles, age-old hatred, and individual and caste rivalries instantly disappeared."[74] The Yankees would really be too beastly if they resisted a machine like that—which moreover had the approval of both Wilhelm II and the czar! So everything ends joyously, after an impressive Peace Parade in the eponymous Château de la Paix, where scientists from all over the world.have come together, while a transfigured Boltyn ends up a Parisian dandy. This time, Europe has been saved. The only problem is that up to the last minute and an "unexpected outcome"—the miraculous psychic fumigation of the aggressive populations—Europe had been no match for the Yankee Goliath.

So to neutralize the American threat, it took the magic of science and a heavy dose of modern miracles. But the real miracle of Le Rouge's serial was *man*—of the European variety. And the real psychic accumulator was the federal superstate, reconciling the divided nations of the old continent. Behind the scientific fable, the ideological program was clear, and very close to Loti's fantasies and Valéry's recollections. It can be summed up in two words: a United Europe—united against the United States. The United States of Europe was an old dream of Hugo's, as the serial writer would remind us. But Le Rouge set to the task of reinterpreting the dream—pretty audaciously—as an anti-American dream. If "the great poet" had longed for a United States of Europe, "was it not in order to oppose the invading flood of the United States of America . . . ?"[75] This subversion of Hugo is disingenuous, a fact of which Le Rouge is well aware. Hugo's logic was one of emulation, with a federalist and peaceful American union showing a monarchic and backward Europe the way. Now it was no longer a question of emulation, but rather one of retaliation and self-defense. If the United States had a part to play in Europe's unification, it was because of the real terror it inspired. "To counter the American peril," cries Olivier Coronal, overcome with a "fever of evocation," "who can say if Europe will not form an immense republic, encompassing all the powers of the old continent that age-old quarrels still divide? After all, it would only be logical."

Le Rouge did not invent this European logic, which will be worth coming back to; but he was probably the first to popularize it in this form.

☆ ☆ ☆

What made the "catalyst" of 1898 important was not only the reaction it provoked in the heat of the moment, which was vivid and often violent and created a strange unanimity of disapproval among the French.[76] It was the mark it left on a whole generation. Case in point: Valéry. Not to mention André Suarès, who in 1898 had the idea of an essay on the "European principle," which would not be published until 1926. The tone varied wildly, as we will see further on: Valéry's lamenting meditation is far from Suarès's xenophobic exasperation. But one cannot help being struck by how parallel their reactions, whether worried or enraged, were toward America's "blow." By giving a striking confirmation of the warnings pronounced up to then by isolated voices, this "limited conflict," had transformed France's expectations of America: the most extreme violence could now occur without seeming unreal.

By setting foot in Cuba, which could have looked like not much more than extending its coasts, the United States seemed to the Europeans to have stepped over the Atlantic; in invading the Philippines, it had signaled that it could intrude wherever it liked. The fact that this imperialism was atypical—in its hesitation to annex and its refusal to govern the territories it had trampled into—did not necessarily make it more reassuring. The United States seemed to want to behave like the great colonial powers without joining their club, which would predictably be a source of other tensions in the future. It wanted to lay its hands on new territories without getting them dirty—a hypocritical and Puritan version, the French thought, of having your cake and eating it too. American expansionism's self-restraint reassured the diplomats but did not save its image in public opinion from the fallout caused by the bombardment of Havana and the dirty war in the Philippines. By 1903, the tumult had started to wane and the atmosphere to clear. But the face of America had been changed: it crossed the century's threshold wearing the Yankee's ugly mug.

The largest part of the continent discovered by
Christopher Columbus has been, for nearly five
centuries, in the hands of a race that conquered it.

    Octave Noël, *Le Péril américain* (1899)

Jonathan is John Bull's cousin-german, but not as
German as you might think.

    Max O'Rell and Jack Allyn, *Jonathan et son continent*
    (1900)

 5

Yankees and Anglo-Saxons

So the new American was here. Brutal, dim-witted, uncultivated,
and devoid of disinterested curiosity. A cool gaze, a quick hand,
carnivorous teeth. Undisguised greed, unscrupulous rapacity—
besides, scruples were against his religion. This was the disturbing individual the French were so frightened of in 1900. Not even
an individual, but rather, as Gustave Le Rouge wrote, a *type:* the
"odious Yankee type" hallucinated by Olivier Coronal in the dark
night of his underground hideout. The typology was new, and radically different from the one that had held sway up to the 1860s,
back when the American had been no more than a summary and
contradictory silhouette—a more vulgar Englishman or "swarthy
foreigner with a riding crop."[1] Now, though, picturesque, ridiculous shapes no longer came striding from a saloon or off the pam-
pas: the days of hog sellers pulling out their checkbooks or Texan
braggarts firing six-shooters were over. If they still strutted across
the French stage, it was because as a general rule, the theater
adheres to a stability of "uses" and drags its heels when it has to
change a "type" audiences easily recognize.

    The only things the new American had in common with these
outdated caricatures were his dollars and his love for them. *La*

Conspiration des milliardaires, a remarkable document of post-1898 stereotypes, perfectly illustrates the transformation. What was the Yankee like in
1900? A "scientist with no high-minded ideas." An "industrialist with no
humanity." An intellect reduced to calculating the profitability of his acquisitions and incapable of "go[ing] beyond the limits of practical realities."
A pathological wheeler and dealer who, once he was too old to do business,
collapsed into "suicide or madness." But that was not all. He was also an
arrogant nationalist whose extreme chauvinism could only be expressed by
an untranslatable term, a barbarous word that had become familiar to the
French: "jingoism."[2] An insatiable predator; a tireless expansionist. In short,
an imperialist. (Once more, a bit of *franglais,* despite appearances: the word
was coined in America;[3] in France, until then, *impérialiste* had meant "partisan of the imperial regime.") And an imperialist who stepped forth cloaked
in candid piousness, dressed in the white linen of his "providential mission."

The Yankee had been fleshed out; he was no longer just a puppet. His
traits had become distinct, you could even say they had hardened—a real
contrast with the fuzzy profiles of yore. He had broken away from the British
stereotype. It was no longer possible to mistake him for an Englishman. But
he had also freed himself from the stereotypes the English had started trading in during the first thirty years of the nineteenth century. The Yankee, in
belle époque France, was no longer indebted to Fanny Trollope or Basil Hall:
he had become an indigenous construction that reflected the rise of a home-
made anti-Americanism. And, as though to emphasize the rift, the French
even produced their own etymology of the word "Yankee"—one that English
speakers had never heard of.

In order to understand the scope of this emancipation, we have to retrace
the succession of words and images.

Yankee and Yankie

The word *Yankee* first appeared at the time of the American Revolution. Its
probable etymological origin was as an epithet by British soldiers for their
adversaries, the rebel colonists. *Yankee* was thus derived from *Yanke,* "little
Jan" in Dutch. The diminutive cropped up among the English troops as a
xenophobic gibe, pushing the insurgents back to their foreign roots and discrediting the true nature of their rebellion. The pejorative term was then
picked up on the rebound by the colonists; in a process of semantic bravado
often seen in situations of revolutionary turbulence, they adopted it to refer
to themselves. Such is the etymological scenario adopted by the majority of
historians, as well as the *Oxford English Dictionary.*

After America's independence, the term continued its pejorative career in Great Britain, designating the Americans of the northeastern part of the country. Fanny Trollope, in *Domestic Manners of the Americans*, defined the Yankee by his geographical habitat, but also by a habitus described in ethnic terms. On the one hand, the Yankees were indeed simply the inhabitants of New England, which Mrs. Trollope calls "the yankee or New England country"; for her, then, there was indeed a "yankee country," and this area was limited to the six states situated east of the Hudson River (Connecticut, Rhode Island, Massachusetts, Vermont, New Hampshire, and Maine). But on the other hand, the Yankee came with a composite and complex ethnopsychological "nature." However easy it was to situate the Yankees on the map, it was quite another story, she explained, to define *a* Yankee: the best one could do was sum up a kind of collective personality by using a triple analogy. So the Yankee "in acuteness, cautiousness, industry, and perseverance . . . resembles the Scotch"; he resembled the Dutch in his frugal neatness; and, finally, "the sons of Abraham" in his "love of lucre." To this she added a fourth trait, in which "he is like nothing on earth but himself": his frank and superlative admiration for all his own peculiarities.[4] The caricature would pervade all of Europe. And furthermore, if we are to believe the British author, it was accepted by the interested parties themselves. For, Mrs. Trollope specified, not only did all the Yankees agree that their compatriots were "sly, grinding, selfish, and tricking," but they "will avow these qualities themselves with a complacent smile"![5]

This English-style Yankee, buoyed by the success of *Domestic Manners of the Americans*, would shape French representations for a long time. It is striking to see its influence stretch even to the most favorable writings on America, such as Philarète Chasles's *Études sur la littérature et les mœurs des Anglo-Américains au XIXe siècle* (1851). Considered in his day an unconditional admirer of the United States, Chasles nevertheless drew up an unflattering psychological and moral portrait of what he called "the Northern Yankie [*sic*]." In an epilogue entitled "The Future of America," the *Yankie* is presented as the "utter figure of the former colonist, with his speculative finesse, his impassive silence, his cunning curiosity, his cold daring, and his formidable wisdom."[6] The same Philarète Chasles who deferred to the authority of Tocqueville and Michel Chevalier in his introduction did not balk at perpetuating Mrs. Trollope's stereotypes in evoking the human "type" found in New England.

But was this really all about New England and its inhabitants? Chasles's expression—"Northern Yankie"—is ambiguous. Without necessarily suggesting the existence of some enigmatic Yankee of the South (about whom

Chasles does not breathe a word), the expression widens the Yankee territory into a "North" no longer circumscribed by what is historically known as New England. Discreetly deterritorializing the Yankee allowed Chasles to sidestep a troublesome contradiction. He was effectively one of the rare Frenchmen who went along with Tocqueville in his praise of the New England Puritans, even if he shifted the emphasis. Tocqueville saw Puritanism as the heart of the democratic American Enlightenment;[7] for Chasles, Puritan "autonomy" was chiefly a manifestation of "energy." According to Tocqueville, Puritanism, through its emphasis on and respect for knowledge, contained the seeds of democracy and the republic; for Chasles, it contained power and glory. The Puritans, he wrote, had "set down the egg of a colossal empire onto the sands of America."[8] And Chasles kept opposing the "moral strength . . . , sincerity, beliefs, perseverance, and courage" of the Puritan background with "our moral weakness, our inability to take action."[9] How could this vibrant apology of the Puritans be reconciled with a denigration of the Yankee, their direct descendant, other than by separating the "Yankie" type from the New England to which British anti-Americanism had confined him? Philarète Chasles, whether he knew it or not, thus pioneered an extended conception of the Yankee that would soon characterize use of the term in France.

Chasles's book, which was published at the halfway mark of the nineteenth century, can also be seen as straddling two semantic eras. Throughout the first half of the nineteenth century, French use of the term *Yankee* was infrequent, scattered, and indecisive. Its absence from the two *Democracies* in 1835 and 1840 may come as a surprise, given that they were contemporary with Fanny Trollope's popularity in Europe. That her popularity seemed inappropriate to Tocqueville, however, can be seen in the biting tone of the chapter "Some Reflections on American Manners," where the viscount mocks the "ruthless critics" from the English middle classes who "make game of American manners" without realizing that "the cap fits them very well too."[10] Mrs. Trollope's taking the Americans to task was a case of the pot calling the kettle black. In any event, it was out of the question for Tocqueville to adopt a terminology with dubious relevance: for him there were only "Anglo-Americans."

In France during this period, *Yankee* was, so to speak, an unregistered trademark, with an uncertain referent and variable connotations. Its pejorative use was already clearly well established, but it did not exclude neutral and even laudatory uses. An anecdote and a quotation will sufficiently illustrate this semantic flexibility.

The anecdote's main character is Baudelaire, and the insult "Yankee," the punch line. Baudelaire's passion for Edgar Allan Poe is well known. In the early 1850s, while he was fruitlessly trying to obtain information about the "mad wretch," Baudelaire learned that an American he thought would be knowledgeable in the matter had arrived in Paris. He rushed to the man's hotel along with his friend Asselineau—who would later describe the scene. Alas! All Baudelaire got from the churlish personage (whom he disturbed trying on pairs of boots) was a few grumblings unflattering to the author of *Eurêka*. He saw red and slammed the door with these words: "He is nothing but a Yankee!"[11] Clearly, Baudelaire's anathema was not aimed at the crafty New England speculator described by Mrs. Trollope, but rather the pan-American philistine, the boor from across the sea, born enemy of the arts. A very French Yankee, as it happens.

The counterexample dates back to 1853. That was the year the noun *yankisme* was first used in French. Patient lexicographers have pinpointed the first occurrence in a book called *Les Hommes et les moeurs en France sous le règne de Louis-Philippe* (Men and Manners in France during the Reign of Louis-Philippe). The use showed no hint of any pejorative connotation and appeared in a completely positive context. "The club or café regular," the essay reads, "is in harmony with the individualism that has entered our manners in the past fifty years. What is more, a little *yankisme* in the habits of our Catholic population would not do the nation's spirit or its business any harm."[12] In its first printed entry into the French language, *yankisme* is not brandished as an accusation, but rather exhibited as a model to follow.

In 1900, that was all over. The coexistence of very differently connoted uses belonged to a forgotten past. Not that there was perfect agreement about the referent; the leeway for personal interpretation remained fairly wide. (Lanson's Yankee, for instance, is synonymous with "nouveau riche"; he is "the billionaire who has not yet cleaned himself up, the *business-man* who, in the struggle for money, starts seeing money as the only goal in life.")[13] But the very possibility of a positive use was ruled out. In fact, the inexorable shift to the pejorative had started in the 1860s. The Civil War had three main effects. Until then, the Yankee had been a geographically hazy figure, found in New England or else the "North" of the United States, or even the entire North American continent; he was now assimilated with the "Northerner," as opposed to the "Southerner." At the same time, pro-South war propaganda definitively gave the word a negative connotation. While Lincoln's America was singing "Yankee Doodle," only the North's enemies used the word *Yankee* in Europe. (Its supporters said "the Union" or "Federals.") Monopolized as it was by hostile pronouncements, the term was definitively taken out of all noncontentious circulation. In the end, the last stage of an evolution spurred on by the Civil War was that the North's victory led the French to retool the word's meaning. The Yankees (Unionists) had become the masters of the whole country, so all of (white) America would be considered "yankee country." We have observed this with the early anti-Americans of the 1880s: *Yankee* designates, with denigrating overtones, the North American in general. The word's prior multiplicity of meanings was consolidated and stabilized: *Yankee* had become the generic pejorative for the *Homo americanus nordicus*, excluding the Indians and the blacks.

Between the middle and the end of the century, then, the definition of the word *Yankee* changed, along with its scope and connotations in French. Its derivative changed, too. The positive use of *yankisme* by the neologous essayist of 1853 was now stamped with obsolescence. When the word reappeared with the spelling *yankeesme* (used by Octave Noël, for example, in 1899), it lent itself only to highly pejorative uses—as in "*yankeesme*'s egotistical ferocity."[14] All the semantic bets were in. From then on, there would no longer be a single neutral use of the word, let alone a positive one. In the negative register, "Trollopian" uses were only holdovers.[15] The English-style Yankee had petered out in France. (For different reasons, it had also fallen out of favor in Great Britain, where the call to Anglo-Saxon unity had replaced cultural sarcasm toward the uncouth cousins across the sea.)

Tardily but decisively, French anti-Americanism had appropriated the Yankee and reshaped him for use as the central figure in a scenario of Franco-American relations in which England's role had completely changed.

Etymological Manipulation

The most curious effect of the French appropriation of the term *Yankee* is that it endorsed an *à la française* etymology for the word. We have seen how a well-established, if not perfectly verifiable, tradition attributes the creation of the word *Yankee* to British soldiers confronting the insurgents. But a completely different explanation of its origins was circulating in France and ended up winning out at the end of the nineteenth century. It made *Yankee* out to be an Indian deformation of the word *English*. The lexicographer Émile Littré weighed in with all his authority in 1877: "Sobriquet by which the English informally, and with a sort of denigration, designate the inhabitants of the United States of North America. It is the word *English* disfigured by the Red-Skins' pronunciation." Littré's first sentence unsurprisingly describes the relationship of "denigration" established (and perpetuated) by the English toward their American cousins. But the second sentence, with its positivist sobriety, is a real shocker. It is not the English, Littré tells us, who named the Yankee: they themselves were called *Yankees* by the Indians. Littré does not cite any sources for an assertion that contradicts the Anglophone tradition and strips the English of any baptismal authority in the affair of the nickname: far from being able to claim he was the initiator, the Englishman was in fact the first object of this denigrating appellation, which he now blindly used against the Americans.

Where did Littré dig up his etymology, and why did he impose it on the French in such a peremptory way, without even mentioning that it did not jibe with the most common hypothesis in the Anglophone community? Despite Littré's silence on the matter, his source is identifiable, and it sheds light on what he meant by the gesture. It was in Philarète Chasles's 1851 *Études*, which we have already mentioned here, that Littré found the etymological solution he adopted and accredited. Indeed, Chasles follows his short typological portrait of the "Yankie" with this curious semantic note: "The word Yankie, currently applied as a sobriquet to the agricultural and commercial populations of the north, is nothing but the word *English* transformed by the defective pronunciation of the natives of Massachusetts, *Yenghis, Yanghis, Yankies.*" He adds: "We gleaned from one of the most learned men of that region this curious etymology, found in no American or English work."[16] And for good reason. This extremely evasive precision—since Chasles does not identify his source, either—is nevertheless precious. By stressing the fact that his information had never appeared in print, Chasles presented himself, if not as the inventor, then in any case as the initiator of the French etymological tradition. Whatever his American "source" may have been, Chasles was in fact the first link of the chain Littré would hook onto. So now we have a better idea of the implications of "Frenchifying" the etymology. "The English," Chasles added, "when they abuse the *Yankies*, are abusing themselves."[17] This is the same logic, and turn of phrase, Tocqueville used to ridicule the "ruthless [English] critics": "they do not notice that they are abusing themselves."[18] All that, one might ask, just to give France's arrogant neighbors a little lesson in humility? Clearly not. But, in fact, in order to ask the more serious question of the connivance between the English and the Yankees—their Siamese-twin solidarity, their Anglo-Saxon identification, which the English etymology of "Yankee" attempted to deny and which the French etymology was bent on pointing out. And it is not surprising that the specter of the Anglo-Saxon, which would haunt the whole end of the century, made one of its first French appearances right in Chasles's *Études* in 1851, and right in the chapter "The Future of America," which revised the origins of the word *Yankee*. Despite his deference for Tocqueville, as we have noted, in no way did Chasles make the principle of democracy the focal point of his analysis of the United States. More precisely,

he constantly postulated that the viability of the democratic principle depended on the vital energy of the population that put it into practice and went
so far as to doubt that the American model could hold any interest at all for
the "decrepit children of our jaded world."[19] "The Future of America" is
something he saw as inscribed in the American race's past: "The old sap
runs through the veins of a society composed of several million Anglo-
Saxons worthy of their forefathers, and who, hammer and ax in hand, labor-
ing on, are chopping out an immense clearing for the future."[20] When he
stopped looking backward (to Fanny Trollope's Yankee), Chasles saw a new
figure of the Yankee, one that was inseparable from the Anglo-Saxon problem that would take over French anti-Americanism at the end of the century.

After several decades of tortuous trekking, the term *Yankee* would be
consecrated in the last quarter of the nineteenth century, somewhere
between Littré's inclusion of it in his dictionary and its popularization by
such novelists as Gustave Le Rouge. It would hold sway over the entire
twentieth century as an inexhaustible nickname for the American enemy.
Boches and *rosbifs* (krauts and limeys) have long been relegated to the French
museum of invective, but *Yankee* is still carrying the torch of its career in
polemics. The same cannot be said for its derivatives, *yankisme* and *yankeesme*, which vegetated without ever taking root.[21] There is more than one
possible explanation for this failure, starting with the word's lack of eu-
phony and a hesitation about its spelling. But we might suspect a more essential reason: *yankisme* and *yankeesme* are too abstract, too intellectual-
ized; their very form implicitly calls up a doctrine, a moral, a social project
(as *américanisme* would attempt to do, in its French version), while the figure of the Yankee belongs to another sphere of representations. Early-
twentieth-century French anti-Americanism's Yankee was not an ideological
or political figure, but an ethnic and a social one. The "-isms" that failed to take
hold in popular speech lacked precisely what made *Yankee* work: it embodied an imagined type.

We should think back to Villiers de L'Isle Adam's *Ève future*, that strange
novel that made Thomas Edison out to be the demiurgic creator of a living
female automaton: the Andréïde, destined to replace Lord Ewald's real and
disappointing beloved. In this mechanical miracle, giving life meant giving
flesh—a miraculous artificial flesh, the inventor's pride and joy, an "Epider-
mis, which is the most important thing."[22] The *Yankee*, too, in order to be
incarnated in the French social imagination, needed artificial flesh. The
semantic skeleton had to be brought to life. The artificial flesh, part historical, part "scientific," was supplied by the racial discourse in the form of an
Anglo-Saxon myth.

It was a decisive encounter. On the eve of the twentieth century, a new anti-American rhetoric was joining forces with a field that would give the mannequin weight and density: ethnography, which defined races and ascribed to them specific, intangible characters. Or to put it more precisely, it was the tardy reelaboration of French-interpreted Anglo-Saxonism that, combined with a surge of post-1898 anti-American fever, fleshed out the Yankee. Now the Yankee had a history that went back to the Dark Ages and a "nature" dominated by Germanic roots. The Yankee, that "shady character," might well pass for a beginner, a young actor in the freshly cast story of the melodrama of nations; but he had roots and even a whole family tree behind him. The "type," as Chasles and Gustave Le Rouge would both say, thus acquired a true physiognomy.

The Original Anglo-Saxons

In the beginning were the Angles, the Saxons—and most likely a few other clans who were less lucky with posterity. Tradition held that these Germanic peoples (the Angles apparently inhabited part of Schleswig) had been called in the eighth century to the isle of Britannia, where they had served as mercenaries, before carving out their own kingdoms at the Celtic kings' expense. At the time of the Norman Conquest, the different Saxon kingdoms, along with the kingdom of the Angles (what is now East Anglia) covered the larger part of modern England. But in 1066, Harold, the last Saxon sovereign, was defeated and killed at the Battle of Hastings. The dispossessed Anglo-Saxons went down in history, only to rise again as legend.

Actually, they first spent some time in purgatory. It was in the sixteenth century, and for reasons related to the religious struggle, that the Anglo-Saxon legend was awakened from its long slumber. In 1530, references to the Saxon Church appeared as justification for the split with Rome and support for Henry VIII's schism. Under the aegis of Archbishop Matthew Parker, studying and interpreting England's Anglo-Saxon past became a systematic scholarly activity, with the aim of further validating the British crown. By 1563, in books such as John Foxe's *Acts and Monuments*, religious erudition and reconstructions of the past were being persuasively mixed with affirmations that the English people had a specific nature whose key could be found in an Anglo-Saxon heritage. A second—and crucial—stage came at the start of the seventeenth century. This time the debate was legal and political. Saxon institutions were glorified in contrast to a system of oppression put in place by the Norman invaders. The return to Britain's origins was synonymous with revitalizing fundamental "Germanic" liberties as

Tacitus described them in his *Germania,* the obligatory source for all Anglo-Saxonists, from Renaissance England's scholars Verstegen and Camden to Enlightenment America's Thomas Jefferson.

A rift developed in this combative historiographical terrain between Whig thinkers who were, roughly speaking, satisfied with the freedoms the Glorious Revolution had reestablished in 1688, and the more radical Whigs, the "Real Whigs," who considered that Saxon (pre-Norman) England's purity could be restored by a new revolutionary push. The rift would become most consequential with the transfer of the narrative to America. So we will just let the "great legend" run its course on English soil, on through to Walter Scott and Rudyard Kipling, and follow the men who exported it across the Atlantic. As is clear, the Americans of the revolutionary generation inherited what was already a well-trodden historiographic myth. They generally adopted the radical, "Real Whig" version of it. Reginald Horsman has shown in detail through just which privileged channels (legal textbooks and English history books) the Anglo-Saxon narrative came to irrigate American thought in the second half of the eighteenth century. The entire body of colonial political literature of the 1760s is suffused with it. Jefferson's case is only a particularly salient example of the American infatuation with the Anglo-Saxons. Up to his death, the master of Monticello would faithfully continue his research on the old Saxons: his "hobby," he said, but it was also an essential body of knowledge he hoped to see taught at the University of Virginia, which he had founded. All his life, he read and reread the indispensable Tacitus—the "first writer in the world, with no exceptions"—along with the indispensable Montesquieu; he meditated on Molesworth[23] and Catherine Macaulay, as well as the Frenchmen Paul de Rapin-Thoyras, author of a *Histoire d'Angleterre* (1727–38) he particularly esteemed; Pelloutier, a specialist on the Celts; and Paul Henri Mallet, author of a *Histoire de Dannemarc.* Jefferson pushed his adherence to the Anglo-Saxon myth and his attempts to revive it in the United States surprisingly far. His vision of emancipated America as a juxtaposition of small agrarian republics was inspired by Saxon territorial organization and aspired to resuscitate that land's virtues. It was self-evident, for Jefferson, that the new American nation should explicitly place itself under the invocation of its Anglo-Saxon ancestors, whence his proposal that one side of the Great Seal of the United States should show Hengist and Horsa, the Saxon chiefs who had landed in England in the eighth century. (The other side was reserved for the children of Israel in the desert, guided by a cloud and a column of fire.)

Anglo-Saxon mythography, for Jefferson, was not just a mine of argumentative material, as was the case in religious disputes and even for many

Real Whigs; it became the overriding fantasy of an active "back to roots" policy. "Is it not better now," Jefferson wrote in August 1776, "that we return at
once into that happy system of our ancestors, the wisest and most perfect
ever yet devised by the wit of man, as it stood before the 8th century?"[24] It
was a striking plan for a regressive construction of the future. Only Mably
could be a point of comparison in France; there was with no equivalent in the
French Revolution itself. It is therefore not surprising that contemporary
French observers failed to see the archaic side of the American revolutionary
discourse.

   During Jefferson's lifetime the debate began to fall under the influence—
which Horsman considers decisive for America—of Indo-European research. Such research had started before the end of the eighteenth century.
It was in 1786 that the founder of *Asiatic Researches,* Sir William Jones, gave
his founding talk on Sanskrit. The Anglo-Saxon myth would thereafter be
used in a much wider perspective: that of linguistic and racial Aryanism.
While Great Britain, anxious to conserve the Saxon's preeminence as three
centuries of laborious erudition had established it, seemed to reject this
broadening of the saga's scope, the United States enthusiastically jumped
into a "scientific" use of Aryan institutions. Very early on, in the wake of English precursors such as Thomas Percy, Anglo-Saxon mythography and Indo-
European research converged in the United States. This convergence generated a whole body of works with scientific pretensions and strong ideological
overtones, affirming the Anglo-Saxon race's intrinsic superiority. Phrenology
hit its peak in scientific prestige and social acknowledgment well before
1840, much earlier than in France. While "before 1815, the term Anglo-
Saxon was not used to characterize the American population in any sense,"[25]
starting in the 1840s the term fed into a comparativist, hierarchical, and
racist discourse. When it joined up with the rhetoric of "manifest destiny"
that emerged, as we have seen, in 1845, the Anglo-Saxon myth was firmly
planted as a pillar of expansionism.

The Anglo-Saxons in French Translation

Contrary to a persistent legend, which is probably a result of the tenacious
flippancy with which they misused the expression,[26] the French did not
invent the Anglo-Saxons. The myth of Germanic roots took shape in England
and was modified in the United States according to religious and political
concerns that were far from France's preoccupations. For a long time, a very
long time, the Anglo-Saxons were, for the French, nothing more than . . .
Angles and Saxons, the protagonists of one part of Europe's distant past.

We have seen how highly Jefferson regarded Paul de Rapin-Thoyras's *Histoire d'Angleterre*, published in French in the early eighteenth century. Indeed, the French had not waited for Walter Scott or Augustin Thierry to take an interest in English history, including the dark ages of Saxon implantation. The adjective *anglo-saxon* was used by French men of letters as early as the late sixteenth century. During the Enlightenment, there would be a surge in the number of works carving out a niche for the Angles and the Saxons in the context of English history or the growing field of Celtic history: they were sometimes still referred to as "Angles-Saxons,"[27] but this copulative form had already been abandoned by most authors, who, like Voltaire, adopted the noun form: "the ancient Anglo-Saxons."[28]

We must be careful, however, not to confuse these acclimated Anglo-Saxons with the ones shaped by two centuries of controversy across the channel. They had neither the same functions nor the same status. Not because France was indifferent to primitivism's charms. That temptation had not spared the philosophes, even the ones who were the least inclined to "walk on all fours," as Voltaire once wrote to Rousseau. Montesquieu and even Voltaire had given in: the former in considering that English freedoms had been born in the forests of Germania, the latter by depicting the Scythes (another "Nordic" tribe that would soon be associated with the Aryan saga)[29] as freedom's heroes and the Americans' moral ancestors. Nor because France had been spared the disputes over historiographic legitimacy that had been all the rage in Europe since the time of the Reformation: in matters of royal prerogatives, fundamental liberties, and feudal or parliamentary usurpations, the struggle had been as dramatic as elsewhere. But it had used Franks, Romans, and Celts as proxy.

It was "to each his primitivism," and France, in this respect, already had one. It had its Germanic ancestors all set: the Comte de Boulainvilliers and Abbé de Mably's Franks. Whatever scenario they were associated with, and whatever sauce (aristocratic or democratic) you served them with, the Franks had an important enough stature to satisfy the demands of historiography. Thus the Franks' "partisans" could not care less about the Anglo-Saxons. The Celt specialists were more welcoming, but on the condition that they blend in. For a Mallet or a Pelloutier, the Anglo-Saxons were "Nordics" like the others; they belonged to the great Celtic family but did not have any particular distinction. While, in England, brandishing the Anglo-Saxon myth—against the Normans, of course, but also against the Celts—was a sign of difference, superiority, or even election, French historiography stopped ignoring the Anglo-Saxons only in order to dilute them in the ocean of Celtitude. Such were the respective positions toward the Anglo-Saxon narrative at the end of the century of Enlightenment. These positions were not overthrown, despite appearances to the contrary, by the romantics' reinterpretation of the myth. The "Nordic" trend was strong in France in the empire years, and not only because of Ossian. In a kind of vague syncretism, it regrouped the Scandinavians, Bretons, and Samoyeds. But these misty epics were not treated as models or warnings: the Great Nation did not feel the need, and, if it took an interest at all in the Dark Ages, imperial France preferred its reverie to include Charlemagne.[30]

So it was not until Augustin Thierry that the Anglo-Saxons would regain their strength and majesty. And even then, it would be in the role of the conquered, since the story Thierry told was the *Histoire de la conquête de l'Angleterre par les Normands* (History of the Conquest of England by the Normans). The phenomenal success of Augustin Thierry's prose and the book's multiple editions (1825, 1826, 1838) brought the mysterious Saxons to a wide audience. The scholarly and stylish color atlas, especially engraved in 1839 to accompany the third edition, even opened with a "Map of Angla-Land or Saxon England" worthy of Baedeker: the Anglo-Saxons were clearly worth the trip, and henceforth the French could meander through the wild kingdoms of the heptarchy in their imagination as though they were preparing an excursion to the châteaux of the Loire Valley.

Augustin Thierry was an impressive literary agent for the historic Anglo-Saxons. But if his undertaking literally put them back "on the map" in the ambient *völkisch,* ethnicizing style, it nevertheless remained impervious to English or American attempts to transform Anglo-Saxon studies into a laboratory of ethnic hierarchies. As a chronicler of the barbarians, Thierry did not join forces with their toadies. Reading Walter Scott had impassioned him in his youth, and, on his own admission, he had adored *Ivanhoe.* But the historian he became remained aloof from the political and social mythologies that were being grafted onto the Saxon saga. Far from conveying to his readers the myth of superiority that had become the heart and soul of English and American Anglo-Saxon legend, he chose to delve into the work of the least "nationalist" and "ethnicist" English specialist of the previous generation, Sharon Turner. In his *History of the Anglo-Saxons,* published between 1799 and 1805, Turner obviously played up all that England's institutions owed to the Saxons' passion for freedom, but he believed in humankind's racial unity and quarreled with racist Anglo-Saxon scholars such as John Pinckerton. The fact that he is the only author cited by Augustin Thierry in his 1838 preface is significant, as is the paradoxical theory of the conquerors and the conquered that he was the first to sketch out. The theory held that the "invaders" had settled in the flatlands and become serfs in the very countries they had conquered. The "most ancient races," the conquered races, those of the handful of natives who had sought refuge in the mountains, were the only ones who had "remained poor, but independent."[31] So much for the conquerors, Saxons or not. Augustin Thierry may have been passionate about *Ivanhoe;* his historical heroes—England's obscure first inhabitants, who had been pushed off into inhospitable heights—resembled Montesquieu's troglodytes more than the feather-capped champions of Anglo-Saxonism.

It took the French a long time to notice the ideological role the Anglo-Saxons had taken on across the channel and across the Atlantic and to start worrying about the rapprochement between Great Britain and the United States that would be fostered by a history of origins rewritten as a racial saga. We have seen Philarète Chasles, in 1851, refer to the "millions of Anglo-Saxons" populating the United States. But while the expression in English was, starting in the early 1830s, used to mean both the English and Americans, Chasles, twenty years later, continued to use it from a genealogical and primitivist perspective. When he designated the North Americans as Anglo-Saxons, he meant to underscore their double heritage as Christians and Teutons;[32] he made no mention of England or the English. In a kind of genealogical short-circuit, Chasles went straight back to the Teutonic and Christian source, to the dark times and the vast forests of Germania. By eliding the English articulation of *Anglo-Saxon,* he eluded the daunting problem of a collusion between America and Britain, which would become an obsession of the following generation.

How much of the French refusal to recognize Anglo-Saxonism's new importance in the United States was pure denial? A lot, judging by how violent the reactions were, once the state of things had become clear. But whether it was a defense mechanism or not, the willful blindness was undeniable. In 1877, Littré still classified as a neologism the use of the expression "les Anglo-Saxons" to mean the English and the Americans conjointly. This confirms that there was a considerable chronological gap—more than forty years—between its Francophone and Anglophone use.[33] The entry "Anglo-Saxon" in his dictionary starts obviously with the historical definition: "Belonging to the mix of Angles and Saxons, Germanic peoples who took over the island of Britannia with the fall of the Roman Empire." Then it moves on to the "Anglo-Saxon language," which, mixed with the Norman language, produced English. Lastly, Littré notes the spread and shift in meaning the term has just undergone: "When speaking of the race to which the English and the Americans of the United States belong, it is often said that they are Anglos-Saxons [*sic*]." He is cautiously recording a recent, vague, and perhaps incorrect use of the term, which, as a scrupulous lexicographer, he indicates without completely sanctioning it ("it is often said"). But he also makes extremely clear ("when speaking of the race") that the expression has shifted from the historiographical sphere to the realm of racial anthropology. Twenty years later, at the dawn of the new century, there would no longer be a single Frenchman who, on seeing the word "Anglo-Saxon," would think of the Angles and the Saxons. . .

How did France shift, in the last quarter of the nineteenth century, from nonchalance to vehemence and from indifference to obsession with the word "Anglo-Saxon" and the Anglo-Saxon "motif"? What made this myth, which had been so harmless for three centuries running, suddenly so threatening that there was an urgent call to arms against it?

The answer is simple. During the seventeenth and eighteenth centuries, the French had distractedly followed the debate, which was considered a purely English concern at the time (the most contentious of the "Anglo-Saxonists" were content with denigrating the Scottish, Welsh, or Irish). During the first half of the nineteenth century, they had been able to ignore pretty much completely its American echoes: the racial exploitation of the myth of origins seemed like nothing more than an "internal" problem intensified by the presence of non-Anglo-American people on U.S. soil. Everything brutally shifted, however, when the French discovered in the 1870s that the Anglo-Saxon myth had changed, not so much in nature as in function: that, after having been "racialized," it had been globalized; that it was no longer a simple excuse for dividing and classing the different ethnic groups within the United States, but laid the groundwork for a planetary redistribution of roles in which the Anglo-American couple would evidently be the star. The Anglo-Saxon myth was not a problem for the French so long as it fed into internal, specific, and clear-cut political agendas in Great Britain and the United States. Everything changed when it started to look like a tie and a common language between Great Britain and the United States—and why not the two powers in Germany next? They could also take an interest in playing up "Teutonic" affinities with the two "Anglo-Saxon" nations. The perspective was disturbing, and it is not hard to understand why, in France's diplomatic isolation following the 1870 defeat, the Anglo-Saxon stopped being a colorful and provincial barbarian and turned into the terrifying specter of a community based on blood, customs, and language, one from which France would be excluded and by which it would soon be victimized.

Was this just French paranoia? Whatever the case may be, France did not have to look very far to find substantial fuel for its worries in pronouncements made by the "Anglo-Saxons" themselves. For on the heels of archaeologists' and historians' benign figure of the Anglo-Saxon came the more threatening Anglo-Saxon of politicians and poets.

That Carlyle, for example, who had once been a fervent admirer of revolutionary France, was now the bard of organic Saxon unity; that in his efforts to eradicate any French component of Britain's past he claimed the "Normans were Saxons who had learned to speak French";[34] that he preached in favor of an "All Saxondom" with the same zeal he had shown in defending the universalism of 1789; that he had even abjured his British pride so far as to accept the transfer of "Saxon" power to Boston or New York, the future capitals of this racial multinational—such things could indeed worry the French. That across the way, on the other side of the Atlantic, the Yankee Ralph Waldo Emerson had taken it upon himself to intone England's grandeur (in *English Traits*); that he did so in the name of some hypothetical common ancestors in the forests of Germania; that he opposed their grandeur to the Latins' abjection; that, without beating around the bush, he bestowed "the scepter of the globe" on the Anglo-Saxons, which scepter they had amply merited by their "commanding sense of right and wrong"; in a word, that the most eminent thinker in modern America had offered up a paean to the "Teutonic tribes" and their "national singleness of heart, which contrasts with the Latin races"[35]—such things could and should alarm the French.

Which Anglo-Saxon's Superiority?

The most resounding cry of alarm to contemporaries' ears was unquestionably the one Edmond Demolins let out in his 1897 essay *À quoi tient la supériorité des Anglo-Saxons? (Anglo-Saxon Superiority: To What It Is Due)*. It was a peremptory title, despite the interrogative form; the superiority in question was considered a given. All the French could do—meager consolation—was unravel the causes. The essential theories are well known; we will not go into detail about them here. More interesting is the tension, at the heart of Demolins's book and its argumentation, between the desire to affirm an Anglo-Saxon unity (an Emerson-style unity of "virtues" is the work's central thesis) and a permanent attempt to dissociate its components (Great Britain and the United States are clearly differentiated, Germany is simply pushed aside, and the rest of the Anglo-Saxon world is reduced to a walk-on part in the show). Demolins's book is doubly significant: for the electroshock it gave French public opinion (the publisher announced a printing of fifteen thousand copies for two editions in the year 1897 alone), but also by the curious strabismus of its author's diverging gaze—as though, in the end, the Anglo-Saxon entity was not easy to home in on.

Offering a wake-up call for the French, not an indictment against the Americans, Demolins aimed at producing a rational explanation, if that was possible, for the workings of a hegemony. Less in order to denounce it, moreover, than to propose that the French take it as a lesson. His objective, pragmatic report was conveyed in a rhetorical style that had nothing alarmist about it. (But it was precisely this seeming objectivity that would worry his contemporaries the most.) On closer inspection, though, Demolins's method is strange. The whole argument, as we have noted, is based on the profound conviction of a homogeneous Anglo-Saxon bloc. But the bloc crumbles away under Demolins's pen.

It starts by losing its base: the Germanic roots from which the whole lineage had sprung and from which all its virtues emanated. These Teutonic ancestors are banished from the adventure to which they have given their name. Indeed, Demolins starts off by putting the modern German out of bounds and out of the question. The Germans were a threat, he noted, because they came "with great battalions and sophisticated weapons." But the real group to fear, the "true peril," was the Anglo-Saxon from across the channel or the Atlantic: an intrepid individualist "who comes alone, with a plow."[36] According to this disciple of the social economists Frédéric Le Play and Henry de Tourville, "social force is one hundred times more powerful than all the armies in the world," and one had to be clear-sighted to discern, behind the apparent enemy (Germany), the real danger (the Anglo-Saxon): "The great peril, the great danger, the great adversary, are not, as we believe, across the Rhine: militarism and socialism are ridding us of that enemy, and it will not take long. The great peril, the great danger, the great adversary are across the channel, across the Atlantic." This warning, pronounced in 1897, would come to seem like a prophecy, even if its author, far from having imagined the Cuba crisis, analyzed the Anglo-Saxon "peril" in terms of "social predominance, the only reality,"[37] rather than military imperialism.

So the German component was eliminated from the new figure of the "Anglo-Saxon." Not for opportunistic reasons, in Demolins's view, but because of a fundamental divergence in what he calls the "social formation of the race": for "the social formation of the Anglo-Saxon race is as deeply individualist as the German race's is deeply communitarian."[38] To put it more simply, the German was gregarious and potentially collectivist, while the Anglo-Saxon's main characteristic was individual energy. One decisive proof of this incompatibility of ethnic temperament was the two groups' differing attitudes toward socialism. While the Germans were inclined to accept it, the Americans remained reticent, to say the least, despite Marx's efforts (transferring the seat of the International to their country only to find that his "hopes were dashed"), along with his prestigious *missi dominici:* "In an attempt to convert the English United States to socialism, several German agitators were sent, including, among others, Mr. Liebknecht and one of the daughters of Karl Marx, the one who married Mr. Aveling. It was all in vain."[39] Socialism's failure in the United States—or, better put, the Anglo-Saxons of America's insurmountable indifference to socialism—became for Demolins decisive proof of the radical difference between the English and the Americans, on the one side, and the Germans, on the other.

Exit Germany, in what amounted to a major redrawing of the Anglo-Saxon landscape. But another shift would more discreetly follow: this time, a shift of focus from Great Britain to the New World. Straight off the bat, Demolins sets down a principle of consanguinity between "the Englishman and his brother the Yankee."[40] But throughout his essay, when giving examples of their dangerousness, he imperceptibly slips from the former to the latter. The preface is significant in this respect. "The Anglo-Saxon has supplanted us in North America," Demolins observes without much originality. But then, on the following page, Anglo-Saxon societies suddenly become "those young societies"—a qualification that does not exactly fit Queen Victoria's Britain. Discreetly and perhaps unconsciously, in the preface as well as in his development, Demolins unhitches the British wagon from the American locomotive. "Those young societies," he adds, in what amounts to an involuntary admission of his fixation on the United States, "are already calling us, with a certain disdain, the *Old World*."[41] The second and third parts of the book confirm these inclinations. Great Britain and its dominions are not completely lost from sight, but it is really the United States that the social observer's admiring and worried gaze is bent on, because "the United States is now at the fore of social progress, just as it is at the fore of mechanical progress."[42] The beating heart of a "race that seems to want to follow the Roman Empire in governing the world"[43] is to be found no longer in England but rather in America; once more, that was where the Anglo-Saxons' "particularist" spirit had truly triumphed, honed and elevated by an "energetically virile environment."[44]

This widely read book had a doubly paradoxical destiny. *Anglo-Saxon Superiority: To What It Is Due*, which contrasted the reality of a "social force" with illusions of military violence, would add grist to the mill of those who, after 1898, no longer believed at all in the United States' "complete repudiation of militarism."[45] As for equating the English and the Americans, which is the book's central tenet, its readers would subscribe to that all the less because it was already coming apart under its author's pen. Demolins wanted to explain "the riddle of the prodigious power of expansion"[46] particular to the Anglo-Saxons and offer the French the key to their shared success. But this "universal" key grew rusty before it was ever used, because in French representations, the United States had already broken away from the British model. And if some of the clichés French travelers brought back from America still showed traces of "a long tradition of French Anglophobia," it cannot be said that at the end of the nineteenth century the United States was only an "extension of England" to them.[47] During the Second Empire, as we have seen, warnings about the Anglo-Saxons made a very clear distinction between Great Britain, an old and sensible country, and the United States, a wild and unpredictable power. The negative cultural images burgeoning in French travel narratives accentuated the contrast. With the help of the Cordial Entente, the "transatlantic Anglo-Saxons" would soon single-handedly amass all the holy terror Edmond Demolins sought to inspire in describing "the hell-bent spirit of initiative, the talent for coming out on top, which we would pay a pretty penny for, and which every penny we so laboriously, so humbly save, only serves to stifle."[48] Addressing a miserly, Malthusian France obsessed with its ideal of the idle *rentier*—"we live like beggars and practice systematic sterility so our children will be free to do nothing at all"— Demolins tries hard to present the Anglo-Saxon "race" as a single entity, yet the monster he is waving before the French is truly a two-headed one—and from here on, the Yankee head is the frightening one.

And of the Yankee Was Born the Anglo-Saxon . . .

The French anti-Americans of 1900 seemed to have followed Carlyle's plans, in their own way: they too transferred to America what could be called the social seat of Anglo-Saxonism, the hub of its intensity—and, therefore, its dangerousness. But the transfer was in fact completely the reverse. It was only after the French had become aware of how dangerous America was, and how in its ingratitude it could very well collude with France's other enemies, that the French image of the Anglo-Saxon thrived. The French version of the Anglo-Saxon figure only *seemed* genealogical. In its original version, the racial heritage implied by the Anglo-Saxon myth allowed the English or the Anglo-Americans to claim their ancestors' feral virtues. But in the French portrayal, the Anglo-Saxon lineage now operated backward: it was founded from its finishing point, not its origins. (Which made it that much easier, as for Demolins, to leave out the Germans completely.)

As latecomers to this serialized mythology, the French had not only missed most of the episodes, they had run the film backward. Out of the Yankee they reinvented the Anglo-Saxon. It was his neobarbarian physiognomy that helped decipher the traits of a fearsome legacy. This was the modern predator that had them quaking in their boots, even as they rhetorically dressed him up in the ruffian's rags of yore. It was the Yankee's power they feared, all the while worrying their fear, as though scratching at a wound, at the thought of ancestral solidarities and dangerous consanguinities. The reader of these French texts waits in vain to catch the archaic silhouette of a superbly brutish Saxon taking shape behind the modern Anglo-Saxon; the barbarian haunting these texts comes from the future, not the past. He is the Yankee barbarian, with his overdeveloped jaws and his overly material hostility, his thirst for conquest and his brutality in quenching it. France's conception of an Anglo-Saxon United States was based on racial characteristics, which allowed it to mask America's historicity by rooting it in European legend. But neither Germanness nor Englishness is invoked to justify French allegations and fantasies about the "Yankee country," hereafter considered the central nervous system of a planetary peril. On rare occasions—Maurras in 1919—the Anglo-Saxon figure would once more expand into a menacing network of "ethnic powers" allied against France; but Maurras is the exception. At the end of the nineteenth century, the *translatio imperii* to the United States was an accepted fact in the French imagination—and with it, the transfer of fear. France's Anglo-Saxon is the product of this transfer; we could also say: the revenant.

Writers could therefore, concurrently but not contradictorily, incriminate the "Anglo-Saxons" and only mean the Americans, as Gustave Le Rouge did in his 1899–1900 serial. (The British character Tom Punch is one of the Frenchmen's allies in their struggle against the Yankees, and the King of England is a "good guy" like Wilhelm; both participate in the final festivities of Europe's triumph.) Le Rouge went even further in his efforts to dissociate the Europeans as a whole (including the British) from the Americans, describing the hostile face-off of "the two races facing one another on the shores of the Atlantic." At first glance, this seems like a distracted or ridiculous sentence, since in "racial" terms, the line should be drawn at the channel and not the Atlantic. But the absurdity is understandable and consistent with an "Anglo-Saxon theory" overwhelmingly propelled by excessive Yankee advances. The Anglo-Saxon race, as Le Rouge explicitly admits here, was henceforth both subsumed by and perfected in the figure of the American, "the odious Yankee type."

At the ends of the earth, I would recognize the American type.

    Jules Huret, *En Amérique* (1904)

Americans may have no identity, but they do have wonderful teeth.

    Jean Baudrillard, *America* (1986)

 6

Portraits of Races

When the Yankee's summary silhouette was crossed with the figure of the Anglo-Saxon, it took on a new consistency. Graced with a physiognomy (and even, as we will see, a *physiognomics*), the American was no longer just a hasty ideogram sketched out in a few key traits—conformism, philistinism, provincialism—as had been the case up to the 1860s. Other traits—greed, brutality, chauvinism, a will to power—were superimposed on the previous ones without effacing them. Not only were the new traits more acute, more worrisome; they came out of a different logic. Until then, the Americans' imputed flaws, such as bad manners or ruthless profit seeking, could seem like the remediable consequences of a provisional social state, an uncivilized country with rough manners and rudimentary appetites. But now, when it came to the Yankee, the French were describing and denouncing innate deficiencies and hereditary defects: the phrase "Yankee race" would now be "part of the common *doxa*."[1]

    All was not quiet on the western front. An enemy race loomed. People said so—repeatedly—so it is no stretch to believe they actually thought it. The Yankee race was radically foreign. Profoundly antagonistic. And doubly menacing. This *hostis novus*,

perched on the edge of the western world, embodied the most modern threat
of all, even as it perpetuated a long line of hereditary hatred in the French
imagination. While the figure of the Yankee was painted in the shape of a
very modern aggressiveness (materialist, industrial, and mechanistic), the
French were still using the stencil of a racial antagonism that went back to
the dawn of time. The new adversary, a calculating capitalist and cold-
blooded worshiper of the "stinking god" of modernity, trod under the secret
weight of a past loaded down with age-old animosity.

The situation was not without irony. Just as great waves of immigration
were beginning to transform the North American population, the French
caught the Yankee in their Anglo-Saxon lens. An almost comic scene, like a
photographer busying himself under the black cloth while a whole mass of
people unexpectedly piles into the room behind him. This eclectic troop,
with its innumerable faces from all over the world, would have to wait a few
more years before it entered the French picture. But then its intrusion, rather
than calming France's obsessions, would only add to the alarm. Superimposed onto the hateful wariness the Yankee had already inspired would be a
kind of worried disgust toward this jumble of people, this human hodge-
podge. "Cosmopolitan dreck" breaking in wave after wave over the "Corinthian bronze" of the "American race"; "the mud of all the races" trying to
form an alloy with Yankee metal—this would not reassure the French anti-
Americans but rather double their hostility.

The *Corinthian bronze* of the *American race; cosmopolitan dreck, mud of all
the races*—the men thinking, writing, and publishing these expressions
around 1900 were not obscure racist pamphleteers but lords and peers of the
French intelligentsia: the eminently talented Paul Bourget, the eminently
serious Octave Noël, the eminently respected Émile Boutmy[2]—psychology,
economy, and political science. Pre-1914 anti-Americanism was already an
elitist and intellectual affair. But it contrasts interestingly with subsequent
anti-Americanism. In this decisive phase, as the anti-American discourse
was being stabilized, "men of letters" were not on the front lines. Instead, the
ranks were filled, for the most part, with economists, sociologists, and political scientists; Paul Bourget, a best-selling novelist, who might appear to be
an exception here, was keen on presenting himself as an expert on racially
induced collective mentalities and eager to remind his readers that he was
not only a literary man, but a scientific "observer" of human psychology and
a theoretician of the "racial question." These were men (very rarely women)
whose authority was drawn from new and daring disciplines. Not all of
them—far from it—ranked as scientists or experts. But it was by invoking
modern science and not timeworn culture, and by using the conquering

vocabulary of the new social sciences rather than the nostalgic idiom of offended erudition, that they took up their pens against the American enemy. Later—starting in the 1920s—would come the days of great writers, humanists and spiritualists, poets and ideologues; for now, it was as though such eminent figures did not yet feel concerned, or threatened, by the "American peril."

These pronouncements, which came from very diverse methodological (and ideological) standpoints, were nonetheless surprisingly homogeneous. It would be going too far to say that French anti-Americanism, in this ascendant phase, spoke with a single voice. But it is striking to see, from text to text, the same arguments repeated, and often articulated with the same inflections. Beneath the variations and embellishments, a *basso continuo* can be heard: the throbbing motif of race. A shared conviction that we might call "ethnographic" fed into and brought together these so-called scientific discourses; it was also what would put them on common ground with the writings of nonspecialists, from Huret-style reporters to serial writers like Le Rouge. They all showed a common propensity, or even passion, for ethnicizing their object: whether they were explaining Theodore Roosevelt's personality or the phenomenon of trusts, the violence of the workers' strikes or American girls' shocking freedom, the last word on the subject always came back to "native dispositions" and the spirit of the race. From harmless observations on the "national character" to the most brutal genealogical assertions, descriptions of America and the Americans were abundantly fueled by references to atavism, acquired characteristics, and hereditary moral and psychological traits. These new descriptions of America painted a "racial portrait" with a varied palette and pushed historical analysis into the background. "Contaminated" history (or compromised historians) would persist well beyond World War I, as the opening chapter of the historian André Siegfried's *America Comes of Age* (1927) illustrates; that stupefying passage of floridly racial (and racist) prose, with its strategic position at the start of a future "classic," shows the kind of priority given, in France, to the ethnic elucidation of the American "mosaic."[3]

Was this a concerted, militant effort? Were all these anti-Americans proponents of the racial theories developed in France and elsewhere over the second half of the nineteenth century? Certainly not. Belle époque anti-Americans hailed from all over the ideological spectrum. Their racism was as run-of-the-mill as could be. Not one of them professed to be a disciple of Gobineau or Chamberlain. A few of them cited Darwin, but none mentioned Vacher de la Pouge. Their zeal or fury about the Yankee took its inflexions not from racist theorists, but from a diffuse set of racial beliefs, probably most effectively conveyed by Renan's works.[4]

It is true that Renan's writings raised the problem of describing civilizations and offered a definition of race ambiguous enough to pave the way for
a third course alongside Tocqueville's approach—historical, sociological, and
culturalist, and in total decline at the time—and exclusively racial theories.
Perched at the crossroads of religious history, philology, and a sort of cultural
philosophy, Renan wildly disseminated a conception of race that combined a
historical dimension, an ethnic component, and a cultural stratification (in
which language played a decisive part). The definition of race he proposed
was far from consistent;[5] but it was precisely its slippage that facilitated its
adoption into both culturalist theories and physiologically based ethnographic constructs. Renan's was ultimately a paradoxical impact. As Maurice
Olender writes, "From the standpoint of cultural anthropology Renan invites
his readers to agree that 'history is the great criterium of races.' Here his historical vision is perfectly static, however."[6] By making race out to be "the
secret of all events in the history of humanity" and "the principal explanation
of the past,"[7] he forced history to yield to the terms of racial ethnography
while sparing "elected" races from this determinism—that is, races that, by
their high degree of civilization, had risen above the atavistic traits that were
nonetheless the source of their grandeur. Such was the privilege of the Europeans: the civilizing process had diluted the "anthropological" component of
their "races" to such an extent that it was negligible. For them, "race was the
combined effect of language, laws, and mores, more than of blood."[8] This
reversal transformed race in Europe (though only in Europe); what had been
the starting point for a predestined evolution became the result of a complex
interplay of various forces. The word "race" suddenly took on a dual meaning in Renan's two-tiered epistemology, now split along the Europe/non-
Europe divide. Because as soon as the borders of Europe were crossed, race
suddenly had the taste of blood. Once more, the ethnographic flaw indelibly
stamped certain peoples. Once more, belonging to a group was equated with
heredity. Aptitudes were measured on the skull.

"No one is entitled," Renan told the Europeans, and particularly France's
cousins in Germany, "to go around the world probing into craniums and
then grabbing people by the throat and telling them, 'You are our blood; you
belong to us.'"[9] The same went for pan-Germanism—and why not Anglo-
Saxonism?

Yet Renan made no attempt to stop the very same European from heading out into the rice paddies and savannas to affirm his superiority. Renan
even incited him to it: this was the European's mission. On the one hand,
then, were the European nations, "peers in a great senate, each of whose
members is inviolable,"[10] which should accordingly sense the injustice and

absurdity of any racial predominance *among them*. On the other hand were the races confined to the determinism of their natural aptitudes, destined for manual labor, doomed to toil under the European's guidance. This wide-reaching master plan would not only inform the Third Republic's colonial ideology, but would also promote the idea of an indispensable European solidarity in the face of non-Europe.

Just as Hegel had once excluded North America from his conception of humanity's development, Renan left the space marked "United States" blank, and the question of its role in the global allotment of tasks hanging. North America could be identified only by a "neither-nor" construction: neither a member of the "European Senate," nor ruled over by Europe's "scepter" and "sword." Anti-Americanism's long-standing stubbornness in denying the United States, despite all evidence to the contrary, a "history" and a "civilization" takes on its full sense here. By refusing the North Americans any claim to historicity ("America is the only country that went from barbarism to decadence without civilization in between," as Oscar Wilde said), Frenchman such as Renan were not just highlighting what they might see as America's dearth of human experience or its cultural impoverishment—as proved by the absence of any châteaux on the banks of the Potomac—they were postulating a radical difference between America and the European nations. Because of its historical and cultural deficiencies, America was implicitly categorized as belonging to a "third world"—a world that could not symbolically fit into late-nineteenth-century colonial Europe's binary universe.

Did the French have the right to go and measure people's skulls? In any case, they had no compunction about sketching America's portrait—a "racial portrait" like the ones Renan advocated. In France, ethno-stereotyping the Yankee was common to serial writers and ambassadors alike.

Monsieur Roosevelt and Miss Betty

May 1900. While Gustave Le Rouge's readers were relishing *La Conspiration des milliardaires*' happy ending, Jules Cambon, the French ambassador to the United States, was attentively following a different serial: Theodore Roosevelt's presidential campaign. The now endangered art of the diplomatic dispatch was in full flower at the time, and its pinnacle was the portraiture of sovereigns or heads of state. It was the ambassador himself (unless he was notoriously incompetent) who had the job of producing physical, psychological, moral, and political portraits for his minister. These confidential identification sheets are precious documents: they now tell us as much about those who exchanged them as about those they depict.

On May 8, then, Ambassador Cambon took out his finest pen to capture the fall elections' Republican candidate, Theodore Roosevelt, the future twenty-ninth president of the United States. "M. Roosevelt," Cambon wrote, "is very ambitious, very intelligent, and totally committed to the imperialist and military policy he has supported in his writing and in his actions. He is an excellent representative of that young Anglo-Saxon race celebrated in the poetry of M. Rudyard Kipling and inspired by the history of M. Seeley."[11]

Four years later, as he was finishing his term, the very same Theodore Roosevelt, the first American president since Lincoln to interest the French, became the object of a hagiographical biography penned by his appointed translator, Albert Savine. The book was entitled *Roosevelt intime,* and it also opened with a portrait of the great man—one that was both extremely close to and very different from Cambon's. "To Holland, Theodore Roosevelt owes his sedate habits and his solid attitude; to Scotland, his subtlety; to Ireland, his combative and generous aspects; to France, his vivacity, his imagination, and his boldness. Such a mixture of blood is bound to produce a virile, original, sincere, and balanced being."[12]

Comparing the two is troubling: the two portraitists were visibly of the same school, but it is as though they were not painting the same model. They worked with the same palette and in the same tones—race and roots—but they did not mix the same colors. The Anglo-Saxon paragon had been replaced by a cosmopolitan European. Cambon's Roosevelt was the archetype of the "young Anglo-Saxon race." Savine's is a cultural mix, an old European crossbreed, a wonderful synthesis: the ideal hybrid for a French market. Dutch was just fine. Scottish, Irish, that was great: he was close to France both in blood and history. And it did not hurt, of course, that he was also French. But that the dosage was perfect is especially clear in the missing ingredient. Not one drop of English blood tainted this Roosevelt for French exportation! The empty "Anglo" slot averted the risk of his being labeled "Anglo-Saxon."

By making Roosevelt out to be a multi-European, Savine was attempting to ward off the specter of the Yankee, that village paranoid prepared to conquer the world without ever getting to know it or deigning to understand it. It was a good, and necessary, thing for his image (in France) that the president had a monopoly of European roots. But the roots still had to be inoffensive and his origins benign: without a trace of Englishness or, of course, Germanness. Clearly, France's herald of the Rooseveltian message had understood two things. First, that his portrait of Roosevelt could not avoid the issue of race. Second, that to appeal to the French (and he would), Roosevelt had to be neither Anglo nor Saxon; he needed friendly roots from which to draw the sap of the same qualities that for Cambon had made him a prototypical "Anglo-Saxon." And this is why the faithful Savine worked hard at copying a purified legend onto the racial palimpsest: he was proposing a kind of improved genealogy of Roosevelt's virtues.

It was apparently impossible, on the eve of the belle époque, to avoid discussing ethnic forebears: all the work went into making the voice of blood speak. Cambon would not have been a scrupulous informer if that had not been the starting point for his portrait of the future president. Savine would have been inept if, to make sure Roosevelt got a good reception by the French, he had not begun by removing the president's Anglo-Saxon background. Cambon, Savine, Le Rouge, each in his "genre," adhered to the same narrative codes, because they shared with their readers, from the minister of foreign affairs to the maid, the conviction that race was an explanatory principle.

Ethnic description's hermeneutic status was explicit for both the ambassador and the biographer. For the serial writer, it was "proved" by the tale itself. The "billionaires' conspiracy" is a result of the Yankees' irrepressible thirst for ethnic domination. The unavoidable antagonism between the Yankees and the Europeans at the heart of the novel is racial in origin. But race also intervenes as the story's internal organizing force, this time in terms of plot twists, since it often "explains" an unhoped-for alliance or a providential rescue the hero benefits from. If it triggers conflicts, it also, at crucial points, helps lock up the villains and makes the righteous prevail.

Why does Ned Hattison, son of his terrible American father, choose the good side? For Lucienne Golbert's pretty eyes, of course. But would he even have noticed her eyes if his mother, the late Mrs. Hattison, had not been Canadian? French Canadian, needless to say. (But it is said.) The fact that Ned joins the good side is therefore also an ethnic act. Humanity's maxims are powerless against the iron law of profit, if they are not aided and abetted by the voice of blood. Another privileged witness to the law of ethnicity is Miss Betty, the only simple "American"—neither a billionaire nor a billionaire's daughter—we are given the chance to meet. When Léon Goupit (from Belleville) meets her in the jungle of America's cities, he hesitates for a second before confiding his weighty secrets. Only a second, though. "Beneath her little straw hat, Miss Betty had a sweet face, lit up by an intelligent and firm gaze. Her lips were not thin and pinched like English women's usually are." And for good reason, because, thank God, she is not English after all. Or American. In fact, she is Irish. "'You are not American!' the Belleville lad exclaimed. 'Ah! Well, I'm glad to hear it. I have to tell you that the Yankees and I have never been on the best of terms. All those ham-eaters seem like nasty, slack-limbed marionettes to me.'"[13] Betty shares his feelings: "Oh! I hate them too, etc." This is probably the first scene of flirtatious anti-American banter in the history of the French novel. . .

In *Journey to the End of the Night*, often described (a little too hastily) as a monument to anti-Americanism, a woman also appears in the hell of the big city to help and care for the antihero Bardamu. Céline, who is less racist in this respect than his liberal predecessor, did not feel the need to make his redemptress a descendant of Norman or Picard or Louisiana stock. But Gustave Le Rouge rushes to specify the ethnic makeup of his different characters. Young Betty, the lone positive figure in all of America, is peremptorily *de-Americanized*, just as Savine had done with Roosevelt. If Miss Betty can be Léon's providential ally in full-blown enemy territory—until the end, when she becomes Madame Léon Goupit—it is thanks to precious "racial affinities" that cannot help but unite a Frenchman and an Irishwoman. Trust runs deep, and complicity is inscribed in the arch of her Celtic-ly plump lips. Full lips never lie. Betty's origins could be read on them, even before she opened her mouth—to Léon's joy: "'You know, Miss Betty,' declared the Belleville lad, 'I intend on seeing you again. The Irish, that's pretty much like the Northern French.'"[14] Non-Anglos of the (European) world, unite! Léon, who is zealous about universal principles—another French passion—is ready to expand the definition of the "good" race in order to better exclude the enemy: "We are all part of the same race, as long as we are not American."

What does this race Léon Goupit banishes from the others look like? To find out, we will open the door of the anthropological warehouse. We will wander through its hall of American "racial portraits." We will see how, from painting to painting, from travel diary to social novel, "the odious Yankee type" evolves.

The American Woman, Future of the Yankee Race

It was generally agreed upon that the *type* was best revealed by the American woman: she was the one who expressed and perfected the spirit of the race better than her masculine partner. Charles Crosnier de Varigny, author in 1893 of *La Femme aux États-Unis*, seems to have been the first to affirm this female preeminence, in terms that echo the Goncourts' diary mixed with Renan's reminiscences: in the United States, as elsewhere, "woman had to appear, at a given point, as the definitive expression, the superior type of the race and environment. Today, she is that."[15] The American woman was the (already present) future of the American man. This theory would quickly attract followers. Several years later, it would be repeated as a truism. So this was how French observers of the belle époque scientifically justified their overwhelming interest in the American woman, to the detriment of the Yankee male, who failed to mobilize their forces. "In Europe, the American woman is as popular as the [American man] is still unpopular,"[16] Crosnier de Varigny willingly acknowledged, reconciling the whims of fashion with the demands of epistemology. . .

The fact was that in less than a generation, the American woman, still discreet in the works of writers like Gaillardet and absent from those of Mandat-Grancey, had taken center stage in French descriptions and analyses. The feminist movement and "suffragism" certainly had a hand in this, at least indirectly. It is hard to confirm; other than militant literature, most French texts written before 1914 do not mention the topic. Le Correspondant, generally attentive to all things American, flippantly evoked "the gynocratic movement," confirming that in America it had "its most important base of operations. That is where its general staff holds its deliberations and where its assault columns against male tyranny receive their orders."[17] But on the whole, the French press did not bring up the topic, not even ironically. Most books about America gave it no space at all. Male chroniclers' probable lack of interest or enthusiasm was coupled with the unshakable conviction that woman was the "real sovereign of the great Republic," as Urbain Gohier would repeat ten years after Crosnier de Varigny.[18]

North America was a gynocracy. This affirmation was dogmatic or at least axiomatic in France as of the 1890s. The American woman's supremacy was thus twofold. The superiority of her "type" also corresponded to the empire she had taken over the opposite sex. The same cliché was tirelessly repeated, somewhere between fascination, fear, and reproach: the American woman ruled over the country just as she governed her home. The American man was her servant, or even her slave. The Yankee husband was not master of the house. He was lucky if he was not treated too badly! What Frédéric Gaillardet had once called the "republican duchess" had moved up from the footstool to the throne. And she occupied it as a despot rather than a sovereign.

The omnipotence the French saw American women wielding did not make them laugh, even at the husbands' expense. This was no time for sly witticisms or colorful pleasantries; this upside-down world did not enchant its explorers. They did try to reassure themselves by repeating that the French woman would never be interested in that kind of domination because, first of all, she had no taste for domination, and second, she was already the dominant one—à la française, without making a show of it. But it was clear that their heart was not in it—that they feared the American woman was setting a bad example, and a contagious one. Crosnier de

Varigny let his worry peek through the banter by presenting the "dame" (in English) as the most pernicious American export: it was not only France's economic scales she was in danger of throwing off balance, but the fragile French harmony between the sexes. The author of *La Femme aux États-Unis* firmly believed that "the 'dame,' not satisfied with having also conquered the New World, is well on the way to Americanizing the old one."[19] One more push and that born dominatrix would substitute the right to flirt for the rights of man and the citizen, because "the freedom to flirt is as sacred and inalienable in the United States as the immortal principles of 1789 are in our country."[20]

Crosnier de Varigny was not the only one worried about American women's power and their potential propensity to come and exercise it on French soil. Jules Huret, traveling through America in 1904 as a reporter for *Le Figaro*, cites a letter from Mrs. Flora Thompson in which the eminent New York upper-crust socialite condemns the Parisians' deplorable taste for female nudes. They should make the most of it while they could, she added menacingly; the day was coming "when our nation will find the time to invade yours and reform you." This somewhat rough banter set off a severely acrimonious response in the normally serene Huret:

> Mrs. Flora Thompson wants to colonize France—and probably Europe, too. Here, she is imprudently betraying the secret wishes of the most notorious of her imperialist compatriots, who not only dream of making the Old World the outlet for their industrial overproduction, but also a vacation spot! The question is whether Europe will comply.[21]

On this point, the French clearly failed to get the joke. That *Le Figaro*'s correspondent could transform a New York socialite into a Valkyrie of *yankeesme* speaks volumes about the place American women held in belle époque France's imagination.

Aside from fortune hunters, French observers' intense interest in the American woman was strictly hermeneutic: she was a fascinating riddle—the riddle of Americanity itself. It was only later, between the two world wars, that her erotic status would gradually be affirmed. For the time being, even when she was beautiful, she was not considered seductive. Young women's free behavior was troubling and disconcerting. Married women's seriousness was discouraging. But they captivated Frenchmen's attention like a well-formulated mathematical problem. Solving the equation would mean entering into an intimate relationship with the "Yankee country," of which the American man was only a rudimentary representative. Stronger and more mysterious, a concentrate of the virtues and vices of her race—autonomy, energy, egotism, the will to dominate—the American woman had all the keys to America. But the Jason or Theseus—in short, the Latin—she would bestow them on had not yet been born.

Female coquettishness itself had a different meaning in the United States. For men, it was not a promise of happiness but a source of serious misunderstandings. For, noted the pitiless Urbain Gohier, "in France, women are coquettish for men; in America, for themselves."[22] In fact, American women were cold, inaccessible, untouchable. Winning them over was impossible; seducing them, unthinkable. The same Jules Huret (briefly) recovered his sense of humor and detachment and described Latins' frustration faced with the "Bastille of indifference" that was the American woman: "The Latins are exasperated by the American woman, her coldness, her unmistakable self-control, her narrow-minded realism, the meditated calculation of her every move. . . . And she has no imagination to trouble, no curiosity to excite!" Poor Latins, poor Jules Huret. The final touch is pitiable: "You give up the struggle with the muted resentment of an unmasked impostor."[23]

A type within a type, the East Coast American woman, the supreme stage of Yankee femininity, was an icy sphinx: "There is a type of East Coast American woman, neither young nor old, with golden spectacles, I will particularly remember, as I met several examples. She has thin lips, an icy gaze, an impassive face."[24] We can easily see in this New England gorgon the Frenchman's classic nightmare: an unpleasant cross between the Americano-Puritan and the prudish Englishwoman "with thin lips." The anti-Miss Betty . . .

Described by the French, these belle époque American women seemed as imposing as America itself, and as inflexible as President Roosevelt's foreign policy. The fascination rapidly changed into irritation, then exasperation. Disappointed investigators joined the "unmasked impostors": the American woman responded to neither the latter's advances nor the former's expectations. Therefore, when all was said and done, she provoked a hostility proportionate to the power she was seen as holding. The rejected Don Juans agreed with the grumbling moralists; disgusted Frenchmen saw as sins the very virtues that made her the exemplary embodiment of her race. Her characteristic traits, seen in a negative light, were doubly harmful, since the female American, as a woman and a Yankee, threatened the observer first as a man and then a second time as a Frenchman. Her energy became brutality; her autonomy was considered egotism and excessive independence; her practical intelligence, nothing but trivial materialism and a calculating mind.

Caricatures of the American woman abounded in the years between 1890 and 1920. Some, like Crosnier de Varigny, considered the topic important enough or "evocative" enough to warrant an entire book. The same year, 1893, in which his *Femme aux États-Unis* was published, he found a rival in the person of Émile Barbier, who published a *Voyage au pays des dollars* (Travels in Dollar Country). Barbier did not spare the American woman, either. He repeated the old saw about males being domesticated: the women led their lives as they pleased and their husbands by the nose. He railed against the intolerable despotism wielded by wives who were as lacking in domestic virtues as they were in matrimonial good intentions.

> And what about woman? We were going to say: *she is.* Let's be prudent and modest, and rectify that: *she appears to us* ignorant and pretentious, incapable of carrying on a conversation, cold enough to freeze us . . . ; silent, bad-tempered and prudish. . . . Does she have any domestic virtues? Not a one. The American woman is laziness incarnate. She does not even have the will to mend her dresses or sew a button onto her husband's underwear.[25]

Barbier continues his "modest" criticism at length, in the same vein, without ever exhausting a subject he ended up coming back to the following year in a companion piece, *Cythère en Amérique.*

We could object that the inveterately lazy American woman described by Barbier contradicts the dominant myth of the aggressive Yankee shrew. But such is not the case. The slovenliness is strategic and the *farniente,* assertive. The housewife was looking out for number one; she was holding a sit-down strike. She did not lack energy; she simply refused to come to her husband's help. Her domestic "laziness" was just one more affirmation of her empire. The one wearing the trousers is not the one who mends them. Émile Barbier uses a curious expression to illustrate the American man's sufferings and the injustice he endures. American women, he says, have made it so that "with his lawful wife, man remains on the same footing as a Frenchman with his mistress"[26]—a situation that, for Barbier, fails to stir up any image of lust. His comparison is not about debauchery but rather structure. Barbier simply means that the man is the loser twice over, since he is forced to "keep" his wife without enjoying in return the minimal amenities a well-kept house might afford. A decidedly unfortunate country, if domestic dragons could claim the prerogatives of France's courtesans!

The shameless exploitation of the American man by the American woman, or rather of the husband by the wife, was a theme the French held dear. Even the most Americanophilic of them could not resist it. Thus André Tardieu, the future bête noire of French anti-Americans in the interwar years, would in 1908 sing the praises of a "charming book" that had "given

[him] very precious information" about the American couple. When he goes into detail, though, we see that the information can be boiled down to this essential equation: "the husband works, the wife spends."[27] Thus André Maurois, perhaps the most pro-American French traveler of the early 1930s, repeated the cliché of the loyal husband as a "checkbook Don Quixote."[28] What would a Georges Duhamel have to add to that? He was satisfied with soberly reminding his readers that the American husband was a subservient being, that he was a *good provider* whose marital function was limited to paying bills and who, sitting in the back seat of the automobile driven by his wife, kept "profoundly silent . . . smoking a cigarette—like the criminal just before his execution."[29] Decidedly, "the American woman lives a sheltered life," as one of André Maurois's American hostesses would admit.[30] Sheltered, the French would comment, by leaving their husbands out in the cold.

Paul de Rousiers, in 1892, reached the same conclusions. The American husband, the Musée Social investigator observed, "is always in some measure his wife's guest. It is she who rules."[31] In the United States, there was something superfluous about the husband. It was as though he was simply passing through his own home, which also meant that he could just as well pass it up. Varigny, whose training as an economist left him with a taste for figures, did not miss the chance to offer one that, in 1893 was tailor-made to impress his readers: 328,716—the number of divorces "in twenty years."[32] In America, an avalanche of injustices broke from women's undeserved prerogatives and tumbled straight to couples' dissolution. The reversal of roles paved the way for the disintegration of the family, until such time as society itself crumbled.

If the inversion of the American couple was particularly flagrant, though, the disorder was obviously more general, as another problematic figure showed: the girl.

Before the Great War, the American girl did not have too bad a reputation in France. Her "little flirtations at the age of twelve" were judged harshly—but in the name of poetry rather than morality. For "what would become of 'love's delicious turmoil,' the 'blushing modesty,' and the 'agitation of the senses' described by Latin literature's age-old metaphors?"[33] Yet it had to be granted that misconduct was rare: girls may have enjoyed extravagant freedom, but they did not seem to abuse it. Or was their incredible chasteness due to the boys' dubious capacities? Jules Huret suspected that the notorious *flirt* was not the modern, diabolical invention his compatriots felt threatened by, but the American transposition, "the memory of the 'Everything but not *that*' of peasant and working-class liberties, permitted by people who are still uncouth and are only shocked by *the rest*."[34] The *flirt*, in sum, was far from being a slippery slope leading to perdition, but rather part of the school for self-control. Young Americans could almost be reproached with being, if not too chaste, then at least too prudish: an Urbain Gohier would make fun of the male and female students at Evanston who had "founded an *Anti-Kissing League* to prohibit kisses, 'which are disgusting and spread diseases.'"[35]

Educators aside, pre-1914 Frenchmen were much less interested in the girl than in the married American woman. High-society debutantes, those costly "rosebuds" described by Edmond Johanet, were part of a world that was cosmopolitan, closed to outsiders, and unreal. That left all the others, whom the French always encountered with the same astonishment, surprised that such encounters, on the street, at work, were acceptable and even commonplace; and even more surprised by the sexual neutrality of such encounters. An admirably earnest Paul de Rousiers thus wondered about the "Western girls" and their virginity. The waitresses in bars and restaurants seemed to him to be "of a separate sex" (the third sex, already?), "neither embarrassed nor provoking, neither graceful nor clumsy, which corresponds to nothing known to us in France." Not little girls, mothers, or whores, "perhaps all of them are not virtuous, but every one has an air of honesty."[36] This was Greek to him. No wonder the "Latin" lover was feeling a little lost.

In any case, it was better to be prudent and stay away from the "separate sex." For if the American girl seemed quite capable of mastering her potential passions, she was also rumored to be an expert in hanging offenses and other traps for single men. Victorien Sardou, in *L'Oncle Sam*, had brought to the stage the sordid maneuvers Yankee maidens were capable of in order to "catch" a husband: a passionate declaration written on a dance card and the naive suitor was done for. The law was on her side, as Paul de Rousiers warned his readers: "Laws against seduction so strongly protect any woman reputed honest that she is a danger the lady-killer lost in America must avoid."[37] Furthermore, the inexperienced or absent-minded would escape the snares of deceit and the rigors of the law only to succumb to open force. Paul de Rousiers had personally received the confidences of a "young Frenchman in the West" forced, "at the muzzle of a revolver, to marry a St. Louis girl who had led him into a trap."[38] A half a century later, Sartre would inform his *Figaro* readers that there was "a school in New York [that] gives a course for girls on how to get their boy-friends to propose to them"[39]—without recourse to firearms.

One girl, however, got off easy: the *college girl* discovered at the turn of the century by the first French professors to answer the call of the campus. Invited as part of an early exchange between the Sorbonne and Columbia and Harvard, Gustave Lanson was clearly not blind to his female students' charms. To this we owe a striking portrait of what Lanson audaciously calls the *"girl* américaine." But—banish the thought!—his interest was in the *girl* as a type. And as a racial "type," of course. Because to Lanson's favorably predisposed eyes, only the "girl" convincingly embodied the American race and preserved a type that had been impaired by the melting pot. In a society that seemed like a mix of "all the races, all the human types"—this is in 1910— only the girl represented the unattainable ideal of an "American type." "It is impossible," Lanson says with astonishment,

> to define a type that would be the American type. From time to time, however, a
> slim, athletic young girl with regular features, a pure profile, blond or brown hair,
> clear blue eyes, a laughing, frank, and firm gaze, lithe and confident gestures,
> nothing of the English stiffness, a mixture of strength and grace, a free, rich, and
> joyful expansion of life: that is what I think of as the American *"girl"* type.[40]

These tremulous lines devoted by Gustave Lanson to his gracious girl students make for a fine subversion of the "racial portrait," with the authority of an ethnographic investigation leading to a *blason* of young Yankee bodies.

But Lanson's emotion was far from common. A good thing, too! Because there was nothing more terrifying than the very same girl, one or two years later, setting out to conquer Paris, if by a stroke of bad luck she happened to be "pretty as the devil." In her novel *De trop* (Too Much), Mademoiselle Zénaïde Fleuriot, a prolific children's author, portrays the melodrama of a well-to-do family whose serenity is suddenly threatened by the father's plans to remarry "a twenty-year-old American girl, pretty as the devil, with a fortune in the savannas, a flimsy religion, ruinously expensive tastes, and who behaves like a madwoman."[41] In this household, with its footmen and butlers, where at times conversation turns to Drumont's *La France juive* and at others, the comparative merits of different carriage horses, wedding plans involving a Miss Arabella Blunt are an act of high treason. But all's well that ends well: the father really does want to remarry, only not the American miss his household suspects, but rather a perfect Frenchwoman with a face like the Virgin Mary's. These were solitary loves, then, that Lanson felt in the green paradise of his New England campuses. Fleeting, too. The modern world would wreak havoc in these very same retreats.

Ten years later, the 1920s would bring along the Fitzgerald era, of emancipated flappers,[42] short hair, and crazy ideas—a little too crazy for the French. The American girl's excessively liberated attitude rekindled blame and censure: she still embodied the "type's perfection," but now she was tyrannical, egotistical, arrogant, and all the more pernicious because she was desirable and cynically deployed her flagrant sexual freedom.

The gracious girl familiar from Henry James's novels and Lanson's memoirs was replaced by young egotistical teases and cynical, rich hussies. A novel from 1928, *Des Américains chez nous,* shows just what dubious water has flowed under the bridge. We will come back to this allegorical story, in which a little patch of Normandy is colonized by Nathaniel Birdcall, an American millionaire; let's simply mention here that his daughter, the spirited Diana, is an interesting counterpoint, a quarter of a century later, to Gustave Le Rouge's Aurora Boltyn—also a millionaire's daughter, imperious and a little willful, but noble at heart and capable of falling in love, Corneille-style, with Daddy's enemy. The American Diana of 1928, "flighty as gossamer," comes from the same mold of anti-American novelistic stereotypes. But the times have changed, and the tone has hardened. Diana seduces the French narrator, physically enslaving him, though she does not deprive herself of other unsavory affairs. The portrait of the heiress as a spoiled child turns into a grating caricature. Diana's whims are so many exercises in dominating others and showing herself off, as in the strange scene where, delighted to have shocked her companion with the story of how one day, on horseback, she "pissed without getting down from the saddle," she "repeated, cried, screamed: 'I will piss. *I will piss.* I WILL PISS' . . . " which goes echoing out across the countryside.

"How could an American girl feel embarrassed about mentioning or doing those little natural things?" The sadistically treated narrator's sweetly backstabbing commentary fools no one. Beneath the feigned "cultural" justification lurks the conviction of an absolute antagonism, a face-off, or rather an inexpiable hand-to-hand struggle. Another paroxysmal scene exhibits this anthropological rupture even more clearly, with a kind of clinical detachment. A run-of-the-mill scene of carousing—the Americans do not know how to throw a party, so they get drunk—is suddenly broken by an obscene and strident streak: "Miss Diana gets up; she lifts her short skirt up to her face. She dances the most Negro steps, in white underpants. The underpants twist and gape. I see tufts, her shady crotch, her genitals. I get a joyless eyeful."[43] This is a strange dive into American femininity's heart of darkness— there is even the indispensable racist touch of "Negro steps" animating the white Diana's pallid body. What is racism but a hatred for the body of the other, projected onto his nationality? In Raoul Gain's novel, the line is unmistakably crossed.

The outcome fits right in with the atmosphere of sadistic cynicism the narrator is drawn into: villainously wounded by his rival, who has rather phallically slashed one of his nostrils, he is left stranded by the disgusted American girl. "I'm through with that boy!" Thus ends a derisory saga in which an Americanized Frenchman loses his honor and his nose. Thus culminates, in the Jazz Age, the misogynistic caricature of an American woman who combines all her species' flaws and all her culture's vulgarities, peppered with a fatal salaciousness. Miss Diana, *ultima Pandora*. . .

This avalanche of negative stereotypes obviously betrays the reaction of men worried by a new and undesirable division of roles and prerogatives between the sexes. The descriptions, moreover, whether indignant or already resigned, are not incompatible with the admission that the feminine condition had been "improved." Jules Huret never fails to acknowledge, albeit half-heartedly, that "this state [the new balance of power between the sexes] has produced a general elevation of the woman."[44] Though they spoke up more infrequently, Frenchwomen such as Marie Dugard picked apart the legend of women's domination in America. They went over and carefully examined the advantages of the feminine condition across the sea, compared to the situation in Europe. But this often led to an ambiguous conclusion: can we really be sure, Marie Dugard asks, that these "advantages" compensate for the drawbacks of the "primitive and inferior form of existence"[45] that is the Americans' laborious and calculating life, in general? In the end, the skeptical clear-sightedness of the cultivated Dugard, who is too well informed to be taken in by the French legend of an American gynocracy, produces the same kind of obsessively calamitous picture as the ones painted by her masculine compatriots, in which America is inclement for men, for husbands, for Latins; Marie Dugard's conclusion, though, is that women do not have enough advantages in America to recommend a stay in that country.

Jaws

The American woman was not safe. Resisting her was not a good idea. Giving in to her was not, either. American husbands knew a thing or two about that. As for lovers, that kind of thing was against the law. In the interwar years, Luc Durtain would relate the tragedy of a chaste and hardworking young Californian, seduced and abandoned by a passing man-hater. Disoriented by their one-night stand, to which he can imagine no other outcome than marriage, and even more distraught by the young woman's disappearance when the weekend is over, the formerly successful young man, now an aimless wreck, seals his absurd fate in a movie theater where, without the least bit of premeditation or desire, he lays his hand on a woman's knee—a hideous woman, to boot. A scandal, near-lynching, trial, prison sentence, and plunge into abject poverty follow. In the closing scene, we catch a glimpse of the reprobate working as a farmhand. The plot, which might seem inspired by the ravages of political correctness as perceived in French nightmares, nonetheless dates back to the 1920s, like the tale of Miss Diana's escapades. Its title, "A Crime in San Francisco," is deliberately ambiguous, but the reader is led to conclude that the real crime is not the furtive caress so fatal to the unstable Californian, but rather the reigning terror of the American sexual order.[46]

So the American man was not having much fun. That was a known fact in France as of the late nineteenth century. His home was a contentious place where he suffered his daily martyrdom with resignation. Fortunately, he was not really wanted there, and his occupations, which kept him working long hours at the office, reduced his sufferings. But was he completely innocent? At the end of the nineteenth century, more than one French traveler suggested that the American man deserved his misfortune, or that at least, because of various shortcomings, he had his part in conserving the status quo that set the wife up as domestic tyrant. Some went so far as to question his desire for women. To the question, "Is the American a good husband?" Jules Huret responded with this tactful parable: "A man says: I love to read, and he reads two or three books a year. Do we really think he loves it? No. However, he believes it, and he is sincere."[47]

For the Frenchmen describing it, the American man's situation did not arouse any notable commiseration or sympathy. Perhaps because the same man—a docile and self-effacing husband, a domestic serf deprived in his own home of all the sexual and/or gastronomic satisfactions that could justify marriage—turned back into a menacing predator once he left the house: *vir americanus horribilis*. Never trust a man wound around his wife's finger. When he unleashed on the outside world the energy he did not use in his private life, the maritally subjugated Yankee became a fearsome overlord. Though self-effacing and shy, unrecognizable in his domestic setting, as soon as he was outside he turned into a wild beast, recognizable at a glance.

"At the ends of the earth, I would recognize the American type."[48] The shrewd physiognomist making this pronouncement is not a character in *La Conspiration des milliardaires* but rather the real Jules Huret, crossing America in 1904. And by what physical sign, what stigmata, would our reporter recognize the "American type"? Simply by his jaws.

It was in a train, or rather a Pullman, that the *Figaro* correspondent had his revelation. Thanks to the forced intimacy of the setting, he was able to catch the type in its raw state and seize, in all its simplicity, the Yankee nature torn from sleep. A good thing to know: early mornings in the corridors of sleeping cars produce craniology's best results; there, half-asleep Yankee males reveal to the vigilant Frenchman the "direct and tenacious will inscribed in their bony heads." Jules Huret's physiognomic illumination transfigures the commonplace scene of a railway awakening into a racial epiphany: "Condensed in the hard eye, the chin, the willful jaws, was the deep-seated expression of the race's characteristic signs." This was when, in its unmasked nudity, the American countenance revealed its secrets. Afterward, it was too late; washing blurred the ruthlessness of the profile, and furthermore, one might suspect the Americans of making so very many ablutions not for hygienic reasons, but as an act of pure concealment. "The cold water ablutions . . . quickly removed the overly prominent signs of their national energy. But that early morning vision stayed with me all day, and since then, I have been haunted by the look of the chins and jaws."[49]

Fearsome jaws, then—the only ones capable of taking on a "true American steak," "the most resistant thing a vertebrate being has ever had the idea of entrusting to his mandibles for mastication."[50] So these were also prodigiously disturbing jaws, and a born serial writer like Le Rouge would not miss the chance to exploit their symbolism. His scene also takes place in a Pullman, and comes directly after a reference to the Indians exterminated from the great prairie. "The former militia colonel neglected the young miss. All he could think about was vigorously attacking the roast beef and potatoes, that inevitable main course of any American meal." But the roast beef would not offer much resistance to the dentition of the colonel and his neighbor, Mistress [sic] Bottmund, whose mouth "suggested a row of Breton menhirs animated in a jackhammer motion"![51] All this gluttony does not stop the Yankees from carrying on, before the stoic Frenchman, a braggartly conversation in which they proclaim, between bites, their firm intention to "become the masters of the world." Whether grandiose or grotesque, American jaws were in any case disproportionate, just like the Americans' appetite for power. They betrayed the race's hubris. They were its seat and organ. Furthermore, the Yankees were aware of this, and took pains to keep their jaws strong through permanent exercise. In a second revelation, on the heels of the first, Jules Huret also manages to solve the riddle of chewing gum, the inexplicable national passion that had travelers so intrigued. Paul de Rousiers had produced his own theory about it: American women had given up chewing tobacco, and as a substitute they masticated a sugary gum. He considered this hygienic measure praiseworthy, since he ascribed American women's sterility to "climatic influences, [and] the abuse of chewing tobacco,"[52] yet he did not hide the aesthetic pitfalls of this civilizing measure: "no pretty girl can stand such defiguring."[53] Huret's interpretation was completely different and had a real future before it. If the American masticated, Huret affirmed, it was "to develop his jaws." Unable to "keep from moving," he had come up with the idea of moving his mandibles "in public places where he is forced to remain inactive."[54] Chewing gum thus satisfied two impulses at the same time: his hatred of idleness and his constant attempts to improve his devouring potential.

A little myth was born. Fifty years later it still worked like a charm, and a sardonic book published in 1953 took it at some point between face value and irony. The traveler Jérôme, an enthusiastic French innocent, admires a magnificent white porcelain skyscraper in Chicago, the Chicklett Building:

> Tcherbek [the American guide] told me it was dedicated to a kind of scented gum the Americans chew to toughen their willpower by fortifying their maxillaries. "Jaws," Tcherbek told me, "are, you know, where powerful decisions are made: when you clench your teeth, you *want* the strongest. Gum played a very important part in our gaining superiority over the other nations."[55]

The superiority of the Anglo-Saxons of America was proved by their dentition: that was something Edmond Demolins had not thought of in 1897! He had sensed that their superiority had its moral base in the teeth—teeth the English knew how to clench like no country's business. Demolins had extended tenacity, the British attribute par excellence, to their American cousins. But the Yankee was not only tenacious, he was voracious. Like the Englishman, he knew how to hold down the fort (as illustrated by the settler and squatter types); but he was also a man whose forte was getting what he wanted. He was always ready for manducation—as a preamble to devouring: such was the Yankee whose maxillaries were pumped up by chewing gum, the secret weapon of the power-hungry. Like Baudelaire's Boredom, this jaw-heavy America could swallow the world—though not with a yawn, but with a vigorous chomp.

Caught in full mastication or at rest, jaws would continue to identify the American in drawings and caricatures and also recall a fundamental ferocity or arrogance. Duhamel, of course, would not forget to collectively endow the "people who jostle you in the streets of New York or of Chicago" with "jaws of beasts of prey on the hunt."[56] Logically, America's presidents—including presidents as non-swashbuckling as Wilson and Franklin Delano Roosevelt—would be ritually bestowed with prominent jawbones by French observers, as the double symbols of their "race" and their duties. Maurois, as we will see, went looking for the "powerful jaws" of the late President Wilson in the leafy shade of the Princeton campus. Even more curious was the portrait Jean-Paul Sartre sketched out of FDR after the interview the president granted French guests in the Office of War Information on March 10, 1945: "something open and communicative that mixes strangely with the somewhat ferocious ruthlessness of the jaws."[57] But the most treacherous and teasing of the bunch was probably Cocteau, who preached to the Americans about changing their dentition, something he did not really believe they could do: "The mind has sturdy teeth," the poet reminded them in his 1949 *Lettre aux Américains;* "Chew things with those sturdy teeth."[58]

What is "Tcherbek's theory"—solemnly exposed to a flabbergasted Frenchman before the splendors of the Chicklett Building—but a comic parody of the French "racial portrait" of the early twentieth century and the racial ideology it derived from? In the rich body of satirical French tales, it is an occurrence uncommon enough to make us take notice: even as he turns his humor on America, the author of *Le Voyage de Jérôme en Amérique* is providing an ironic take on France's own American stereotypes and their inner workings.

Far from the Madding Crowd

Now we have a better view of what was considered the "embodiment of the Yankee" at the turn of the century; we also have a better understanding of why, after having "squatted" in the Anglo-Saxon myth, so to speak, the anti-American discourse took some distance from Demolins's version of it. Demolins's paradox is that he raised what was basically a culturalist theory on an ethnic flag. He was not interested in the *body;* for him, Anglo-Saxonness was an acquired *mental framework* that could be learned. On the other hand, for the anti-Americans, the Yankee body was the site of a profound difference (including in relation to the English). "I would recognize it anywhere," Jules Huret affirmed. Not gestures or clothes or language, but the Yankee mug. "Those are real American mugs!" a character in Raoul Gain's novel would exclaim thirty years later, on seeing the nocturnal ship-wreck victims of an unidentified yacht.[59] The belief that concrete physical identification is possible betrays an obscure politics of the body within the very origins of the anti-American discourse in France.

We noted in the preceding chapter that Demolins's analysis suffered from a certain strabismus. We should stress how much it was hopelessly skewed. It was historically skewed about the main threat: not only was Great Britain becoming France's ally, but it was progressively being surpassed on nearly every economic front by the United States; the British leopard was turning into a domesticated animal, compared with the new, sharp-toothed

America. But above all, Demolins's analysis was epistemologically skewed, since its argument was rooted in the innate, yet it concluded with the notion of education. "We should not put our sons on a German regimen, but an Anglo-Saxon one," Demolins counseled, "if we want to keep them from being crushed like the Indians in the Far West."[60] Aside from the fact that the Indian comparison betrays the American obsession underlying the Anglo-Saxon theme, the use of the "regimen" metaphor to qualify the Anglo-Saxon education French children should be given only underscores the awkward position of a mindset ossified into the racial framework it has shut itself into. "Men must be educated" for the "struggle for life,"[61] Demolins also affirmed. It was "a question of life and death."[62] But could people learn how to be Anglo-Saxon? What "regimen," even if it was carnivorous, could transform the French into great industrial, banking, and business beasts? Or even, more simply, football players? The anti-Americans countered this pedagogical utopia with the notion of natural incompatibilities written on the body itself. Whence the importance of sports in their descriptions.

The interest in sports was a new one. It was probably stimulated by recent debates in France over introducing "physical education" and collective sports into the educational system. It would not be until the 1920s, however, that authors such as Duhamel would take their details from observations of America in order to argue against "this comedy of sport with which the youth of the world is befooled and fascinated."[63] The first travelers who consigned to their notepads the strange rituals going on inside America's stadiums were not of that persuasion; they still thought France was immune to such influences. Far from considering American sports as a model, even a questionable one, for the future of French learning establishments, they described them as a quintessentially American phenomenon, radically and incomprehensibly strange. Everything about these games was obscure to them—starting with the rules. If describing a match became an obligatory part of any travel narrative at the end of the nineteenth century, it hardly instructed the French reader. Every author, without exception, admitted to an utter incomprehension of the "rounds" they were describing. *Base-ball* was completely impenetrable to them. Paul de Rousiers saw in it "some similarities with English cricket."[64] Jules Huret was able to affirm that it was a "ball game," after which his efforts fell short: "It is very complicated and I only understood this: there are two sides and a very hard ball that is thrown in the air with a long stick held in both hands."[65] Therefore it was not their job to explain it. It was even with undisguised satisfaction that Duhamel would show off his virtuous incompetence: "I do not know this game of football, famous though it is throughout the world."[66]

The true object of such evocations was not to familiarize French people with the games, but to exhibit Yankee bodies and crowds in the most savage of their collective demonstrations. If football, far more than baseball, captured French travelers' attention, it was as an illustration of the violence inherent in the Americans' "racial traditions." Well before Duhamel devoted a whole chapter of his *Scenes from the Life of the Future* to it, football was already the star of the show. Not that the French understood its inner workings any more than baseball's, but because it was a cruder example of the expected revelation. "It is an almost ferocious entertainment," Paul Bourget wrote in 1895, a "terrible game." A yardstick for civilization as well as a racial feature, football "alone would be enough to measure the distance separating the Anglo-Saxon world from the Latin world."[67] A Frenchman could not take part in it without crossing the species barrier. Jules Huret went even further: not only could the French not learn or play it, they could not even watch it without radically breaking with their very nature. The French did not have it in them to scream "Kill him," and "Break his neck," like the fine young man who fascinated Huret at a Harvard-Yale game: "He was a young man of nineteen or twenty years old, dark haired, beardless, decent; his eyes shone with a piercing flame beneath his furrowed brows; his teeth were clenched, which made his maxillaries stick out all the more."[68] No, the French certainly did not have the same jaws, or the same passions. And they would not want them for all the money in the world. That was why they would never play football. Not because they were "crotchety scholars who never use their muscles, who are either lazy or timid," Duhamel would insist later in a chapter that spiritedly compiled his predecessors' descriptions, but because American football brought to a state of paroxysm the "comedy of sport" and the human imposture of these "competitions," which "bec[a]me brutal and dangerous" and looked like "assaults rather than recreations."

What did football reveal? The characteristic habitus of a predatory race. (The team, Duhamel would say, was a "pack . . . watching its prey.")[69] What did it threaten? Nothing less than civilization itself. Duhamel once again recoined the phrases his elders had already produced: "a game that leads to such a frenzy of brutal struggle cannot be good for civilization."[70]

In this sense, the alarmed evocation of American football was no more harmless than the constant reappearance of the Chicago slaughterhouses in the writings of diverse travelers, and even of those who did not travel. It became a digest of different cultural resistances: against the brutality of the game itself, the vulgarity of the crowd, the mass hysteria—a "burning fever"[71] Urbain Gohier would qualify as typically American—not to mention the tribalistic fans, the intellectual vapidity of the shouting, music, and dancing, the moral baseness of the cheerleaders' shows—with college girls transformed into Amazons: "With a megaphone in her hand, and with her skirts flying in the wind, she screamed, flounced about, gave play to leg and haunch, and performed a suggestive and furious *danse du ventre,* like the dances of the prostitutes in the Mediterranean ports."[72] The alarming spectacle of these ritualized "brawls" took on all the more weight in anti-American arguments because they involved students of the very best society. French observers' surprise was quintupled by a sense of social unseemliness: "respectable" young men were screaming out their hatred for the adversary, and the cheerleader swaying her hips like a prostitute "bore . . . one of the most honorable names in the country." That such orgies of brutality and vulgarity took place in the ivory towers of culture and knowledge was enough to disqualify any potential American "lesson." "I do not believe, *a priori,* that Europe has anything to learn from America's pedagogues,"[73] declared Jules Huret in the same pages in which he described the absolute strangeness and barbarism of the Harvard-Yale game.

After the symptomatic maxillary, was this proof by football? Yes, because the football that fascinated the French was more than just a sport; it was a paradigm, just as *megalognathism* was a prediction. Jules Huret, when he wanted to give an idea of the "revolting violence" of ordinary behavior (the New York habit of storming the streetcars, for instance), naturally resorted to this image: "It is brutal and short, like football." Beyond all the practical reasons for the French *not to* adopt the Anglo-Saxon school in the literal sense, there was one that could dissuade them in the figurative sense, as well: the Americans had a different type of body; they were not cut from the same cloth. Jules Huret was not talking about the instruction offered in universities—he did not seem to take much interest in the topic—but rather the striking incompatibility he observed between the two peoples' "natures." When Huret, still shaken up by his day at the stadium, hides out in the Boston library, he feels a "sensation of extraordinary unexpectedness: that of Americans not in motion," and he "want[s] to ask them if they are really Americans."[74]

The impossibility of learning is thus both a fatality and a refusal: the two themes are incessantly intertwined in travelers' accounts when describing different examples of disciplined behavior, which are alternately presented as incompatible with the Latin (or Gallic) temperament *and* inadmissible to free spirits proud of their "personality." The infamous American "will" could not be taught. Furthermore, it was more of an instinct than a moral aptitude. This imperious (and soon imperial) restlessness had already struck Philarète Chasles in 1851 as a characteristic trait of the American Anglo-Saxon: his "perpetual *go-aheadism*."[75] This was Teddy Roosevelt's "strenuous life." It ran deep and in America's veins: the country's pioneer past and its first inhabitants' living conditions had only amplified a natural disposition. Either you had it or you didn't: the chorus was nearly unanimous. To this was added the refrain that having that kind of implacable and feral will was as Yankee as could be: "an immoderate love for speculating, hatred for the competition, attempts at global commercial domination,"[76] "ruse and deceit,"[77] etc. An Americanized Frenchman would be a monster, if he were not an imaginary beast. Several travelers started quaking in their boots, though. Jules Huret, who has been in America for all of three pages, is suddenly gripped by panic: "Is this country's power of absorption so great that I am becoming American?"[78] Urbain Gohier, who has arrived in America unsullied by any knowledge of English, surprises himself by dreaming in the language and, after five months, discovers he has been "Americanized."[79] These are passing terrors—Gohier and Huret would turn back into the Frenchmen they always were—that highlight not so much a real risk as a kind of phobia of deformation.

Yankeeism is a bloc, like the French Revolution was for Clemenceau. Take it or leave it. "Taking it"—if that was even possible—would not only mean giving up the joys of existence, as was repeated at every turn by the travelers who were all so happy to get back to their Parisian homes. Olivier Coronal had already wondered whether you had to join them to beat them. Did you have to learn how to "earn money, a lot of it and fast"? Make it "your only goal in life"? To beat the Yankees, did the French have to become "the odious Yankee type, the scientist with no high-minded ideas, the industrialist with no humanity"?[80] That would mean betraying, denying their very essence. Becoming the deformed Frenchman Sartre described at length with undisguised disgust, in one of his 1945 articles, as an "Ovidian metamorphosis."[81] The hideous mutant that "America already half-possessed" and that leaves Sartre pensive—"I speculated curiously as to the powerful forces that had to be brought into play in order to achieve these disintegrations and reintegrations so surely and rapidly"—is still, for the anti-Americans of 1900, just a quickly rejected fantasy. Not everyone was prognathous, and not everyone wanted to play football. Not everyone could be a Yankee.

☆ ☆ ☆

But how could you avoid it, other than remaining permanently on your guard? The Yankee was not the type to leave the French the choice of playing field or ball. And still less to offer to go to bat first. Stay on the lookout, remain limber, keep an open eye: that was what "observers" and essayists

kept repeating in all different tones. The game was about to begin. The bill
had changed since the 1860s. It was no longer the Anglo-Saxons against the
Latins. It was the Yankees against the Europeans in no uncertain terms: "Our
generation has witnessed nothing but the struggle the nations of Europe
have undertaken and are still undertaking to win the upper hand. The generation that comes after us will witness Europe and the United States struggling for preeminence over the globe."[82] That was in 1888; the time was
drawing near.

The fight would surely have several rounds. The economic boxing match
was well under way. As far as world domination went, the French were still
wavering between the theory of the lucky hand and that of the iron fist. And
who knew if the next year, the next day, France would be out cold, like Jules
Huret in his sleeping car, surrounded by American jaws?

The awakening would not really happen until after the Great War: we will
see further on how verbally violent it would be. And sometimes physically, as
well, as a strange incident that took place during the 1924 Olympic Games
in Paris attests. It was a significant breakthrough for the North Americans.
A certain Weissmuller, who was not yet known as the celluloid Tarzan he
would become, won the hundred meters (in fifty-nine seconds) and the four
hundred meters without a hitch. But then it was time for the final rugby
match—the French football. At the time, France dominated European rugby.
To everyone's surprise, it wound up facing the American team, which had
reached the finals. A little casual about it, according to the sportswriters of
the day, the French team was soundly beaten, 18 to 3. Extraordinarily violent
riots then broke out, an unprecedented occurrence in the short history of the
modern Olympics. An uncontrollable Parisian mob descended on the stadium to do the Yankees some harm. The local police had to beat people off
with their nightsticks to stop them from lynching the winning team, which
the furious crowd followed into the streets. As Duhamel would so rightly say
in stigmatizing American-style sports: "When competitions lose their gracious character of pure play, they become poisoned either with considerations of gain or with national hatreds."

From what Tower of Babel flowed this confusion of skin
tones—reds, yellows, whites, and blacks—holding their
rendez-vous on United States soil?

   Duc de Noailles, *Le Correspondant* (1877)

What a contrast they make, when you look closely, with
the fundamental homogeneousness of all Frenchmen!

   André Siegfried, *America Comes of Age* (1927)

 7

"People of Enemy Blood"

Such are the ironies of bad timing: as we have said, the French
fantasy of a confrontation with the "adversary race" of Yankee
America developed right when massive immigration was profoundly transforming the American population.

   Ignored, avoided, or minimized in their wide-reaching reality by French observers up to the early 1890s, the waves of
immigrants—the vast majority of whom were not Anglos, Saxons, or Protestants—were finally accepted as an essential dimension of the new America. In this respect, Bourget's *Outre-
mer*, published in 1895, is a pioneering text. It contains precious
little documentation and even fewer figures, but Bourget's interest in the races and their conflicts directed his gaze to a phenomenon that had largely gone unnoticed in France until then.
From then on, what the French called the "new immigration"
rapidly came to play a central part in analyses of and commentaries on America. In 1927, in the first edition of his *America
Comes of Age*—essential reading for at least two generations—André Siegfried turned "Anglo-Saxon" America's distortion by foreign immigration into the American question par
excellence.

How would the anti-American discourse in France, which had only recently chosen a purely Anglo-Saxon and intrinsically Yankee America as its
target, integrate this new reality? With brio. It would even use it as a new
source of inspiration.

It seems tricky, however, to reconcile two theories: the Yankee's imperious continental (and soon global?) domination, and an America submerged
by heterogeneous immigration. How can Octave Noël, who concluded in
1899 that "the largest part of the continent discovered by Christopher
Columbus has been, for nearly five centuries, in the hands of a race that
conquered it,"[1] be reconciled with Paul Bourget, who in 1895 had already
proclaimed the arrival of "an immense crowd of workers of a foreign race,
animated by foreign ideas," and prophesied a gigantic "ethnic duel," a civil
war of the races that would ravage the United States?[2] In fact, reconciling
them is only superficially tricky. Hostile rhetoric is not discriminating but
rather cumulative; it suspends the principle of noncontradiction in favor of
worsening the charges. Bourget, who, as we have just said, was the early
prophet of an American-style "war of the races," is also the first example of
this argumentative compatibility of two logically exclusive assertions: at
some times, *Outre-mer* describes Anglo-Saxon America as locked in a struggle to survive "excessive immigration," and at others, it portrays the "American race" in all its power, "that Corinthian bronze"[3] unaltered by the tidal
wave of foreigners.

His violent scenario would have few followers: clearly the "war of the
races" would not take place. Not, in any case, as a remake of the Civil War, in
which "foreigners' America" would confront "Americans' America"[4] on the
battlefield. On the other hand, his cumulative rhetoric would be generally
adopted. And as we will see, there would be, in his wake, an outpouring of
texts that combined an anti-Americanism of resistance (against the brutal
and dominating Yankee) with one of repugnance (toward the "new immigrant" and the "gangrene" he represented).[5]

Racist and Multiracial: America's Double Offense

This paradoxical overlap had its rhetoric, which we can describe as "racistly
antiracist": its goal was to denounce the United States as a legally and culturally racist nation while using a discourse that was itself racist toward the
same groups the Yankees were reproached with ostracizing. In this schema,
the United States added crime to weakness: guilty of the racism exerted by
the dominant WASP group, it was *at the same time* racially suspect—an ethnic chaos, a medley of peoples.

The Americans set a doubly bad example: on the one hand, they banished entire ethnic groups from humanity (the Indians and the blacks, of course, but also and in a different way the Asians, the Italians, and the Irish), and on the other, they were allowing their country to become a multiethnic Babel. Reading French commentators, we can clearly see that the apprehension this ethnic mix provoked won out over any discomfort at seeing egalitarian principles trampled on. The testimony of Urbain Gohier, one of the French travelers of the turn of the century with the most "advanced" ideas, is significant in this respect. Concerning the American blacks, this internationalist and militant pacifist was shaken up in his "doctrinary convictions": "It is a point on which a European, a son of the French Revolution, feels most troubled when his doctrinary convictions enter into contact with reality." But it was not long before the iron pot of reality broke the clay pot of the ideal. Gohier, swallowing his convictions, got it off his chest: "The blacks are universally cheats, liars, and lazy. They are still more depraved. They are obsessed with the idea of the white woman, and this obsession frequently leads them to the most craven of crimes."[6] What would Gohier have said if he had not been "a son of the French Revolution"? We should add, for the sake of fairness, that many of his liberal and enlightened contemporaries did not even bother with rhetorical scruples.

The discourse on America's "racial question" was a two-stage rocket that could accommodate many passengers: they were not all headed for the same destination, but they all spent some time on the anti-American flight path. In the first decades of the twentieth century, these views were held (and heard) in the most far-flung sectors of French public opinion. Nearly every single author in the first thirty years of the twentieth century tapped into the anti-American vein, with unequal ingenuousness and varying ingeniousness. Recognized specialists on the United States (from Boutmy to Siegfried) systematically mined the topic. Duhamel carved out a few precious nuggets. Exploitation intensified during the Vichy years: the ambiguous imagery that had once reflected contradictions between France's "sons of the Revolution"—torn between an adherence to the rights of man and an obsession with "cohesion"—would attain its exaggerated climax in the caricature the collaborationist press relentlessly churned out of a North America that was both racist and "crossbred."

When the rhetoric fell into place around 1900, French travelers and observers were not propagandists: they were speaking for themselves, and their moods and reactions reflected individual prejudices and sometimes principles. There is no trace of an organized campaign in these anti-American writings. The hostility is in good faith. The "bad faith" lay in the silences, and particularly in the deafening silence concerning French colonization and the status of the colonized. The parallel was, however, on everyone's mind, and had been for some time.[7] But that was where it would stay. "Don't bring it up!" could be the caption for these analyses of race in America; behind them was the constant implication (unformulated or suppressed) of the French "colonial question." They did manage to bring it up, however, by vituperating against Reconstruction. By making a show of their disgust for the freed black. By repeating the cliché of the Southern whites being the slaves of their former slaves. And especially by getting indignant, or even up in arms, about the freed blacks' right to vote. Between the lines, French commentators of the American racial question and the so-called crisis of the melting pot were obviously describing their own worries: managing a multi-ethnic empire and assimilating "foreign" elements into the national community.

These subtextual preoccupations explain another characteristic of French analyses of the time: they equated human groups that, in America, seemed to be very different in status. As a problem, the "new immigration" was perceived as so profoundly heterogeneous that it was treated by the French in the same pages and almost on the same footing as the two historical "minorities," the Indians and the blacks. The theme of the "unassimilable" or even the "barbarian" grouped the most indigenous Americans and the most "exotic" newcomers into one category. This conflation crops up frequently in writings by turn-of-the-century travelers. An Edmond Johanet, for instance, who is racist toward the blacks "pullulating" in the South,[8] evokes the working masses of the North, composed of recent immigrants, as "barbarian hordes," potential "scourges of God" like Attila the Hun.[9] Marie Dugard, like many of her male compatriots circa 1900, even as she wonders if the American Negro is not doomed to extinction,[10] reserves her most racist observations for the Asians; she likes San Francisco, but "one spectacle spoils this likable city and abruptly gives you the Far West's sense of incompletion: the Chinese, more numerous there than in Portland, and more ruthless . . . ; they are forty thousand strong, teeming like rodents, which they resemble with their rapacious aspect, their sharp teeth, their thin tails [sic!], and even their subterranean habits."[11] In a much more learned and sober vein, André Siegfried began his *America Comes of Age* with two short chapters, "The Origins of the American People" and "The Assimilation Crisis,"[12] which, in fact, are really one and the same: from the black to the Jew, across the whole "medley of peoples" of post-1860 emigration, Siegfried mapped out an impossible assimilation and transmitted to his French readers the ambiguous shudder he got from the "lack of homogeneity" of the modern United States, "for which possibly there is no remedy."[13]

But that the Indians, confined to their reservations, or even the blacks, often kept from voting and held on the outskirts of white life, even in places where there was no legal segregation, and who were long undesirable even in workers' unions—that the Indians and the blacks had a lot in common with the immigrants, even those of the "worst quality," was far from obvious in America itself, except perhaps to the most extremist xenophobes, from the Know-Nothings of 1850 to the Ku Klux Klan, revived in the 1920s. It was in fact the viewpoint of these Anglo-Saxon and Protestant resistance groups— hostile to the blacks, Jews, Catholics, and all other un-American elements lumped together—that French appraisals of the situation consciously or unconsciously adopted.[14] An already well-established tradition of "understanding" Southerners' problems clearly made embracing this viewpoint easier.

In the French imagery, the big losers in America's new state of affairs were the Indians and the blacks. Their presence had been discreet in French narratives of the last two decades of the nineteenth century. When they were once more dragged out onto the argumentative stage—right when it was being invaded by the motley masses of Ellis Island—they were nearly unrecognizable.

Dismal Indians and "Depraved" Blacks

Until the 1860s, the Indians and American blacks had been shrouded in a romantic aura or tendered humanitarian solicitude in France. In the 1840s, there was fiery indignation against the Union's Indian policies: the "treaties" imposed but rarely respected were castigated as barbaric by "all the shades of public opinion."[15] The black question roused just as much emotion. Through the efforts of the Société pour l'Abolition de l'Esclavage, founded in 1834, campaigns were organized to oppose the fate of the African American slaves. There was also a budding awareness of the racial prejudice stigmatizing the free black, an awakening responsible for the success of Gustave de Beaumont's 1835 novel *Marie, ou l'Esclavage aux États-Unis* (Marie, or Slavery in the United States). If slavery's continuation in the French colonies generated partisans for the "peculiar institution" until 1848, if certain liberals' adherence to the American cause led them to justify the unjustifiable and advocate the status quo of slavery, French public opinion, as we have seen, was largely antislavery before and during the Civil War.

The period stretching from Reconstruction to World War I, on the other hand, was a time of backsliding: the Indians and blacks had a much less important role in French debates and descriptions. Their cause did not rouse much interest. A revealing indication of this can be seen in the fact that "the great events of Indian history, such as Little Big Horn or Wounded Knee, found little resonance in the French press," where they were "referred to . . . only in the most indirect manner."[16] Most importantly, the tone had changed. The Indians were no longer *literarily* fashionable. French essayists had trumpeted their extinction for so long that they probably thought it had taken place. "Nowadays, there is no more than a negligible quantity of them," stated the serial writer Gustave Le Rouge; "American civilization found them bothersome."[17] In 1904 and 1905, Jules Huret only devoted a few lines of his two thick tomes to discussing the Indians, whom he judged to number about 200,000. Between the romantic Indian of the early nineteenth century and the late-twentieth-century counterculture's politically symbolic Indian lay a vast desert of signs. Travelers' tales pushed restraint to the point of desiccation and reduced the Indian to an allegorical silhouette, the ghostly *desdichado* of a prairie that had also been tamed. At the expense of this abstraction, the Indian could still glean a few well-intended words in the form of epitaphs. And in any case, he was better off hiding out in this melancholy shade, considering the way he was depicted when he did come to life. Sauvin, in 1893, found his false brethren on stage at the Châtelet more to his taste: "How much better the Redskin looks in a grand spectacle at the Châtelet theater! . . . The type is animal-like and coarse, men and women seem misshapen." The Indian's final indignity was that after having been reproached with it for so long, in the end he is even denied his "race"—"This is not a race," Sauvin esteemed, "but a degradation of the human species."[18] So it was back to De Pauw. Urbain Gohier, in 1903, was peremptory: "They are ugly with a gentle and servile air. They accept slavery on the land where their fathers lived freely: they are unworthy of interest."[19] Jules Huret, the *Figaro* correspondent, was hardly less brutal. He did not approve of evicting or displacing the Indian populations, but the few lines he gives them come off sounding pretty casual. "We ask ourselves in Europe: What are the Americans doing with the indigenous Indians? In fact they are not doing much of anything at all. Every year they push them a little farther toward the deserts in the West. The plots of land they give them are worse each time. As soon as the land gains any value by its position, the Indians are forced off it." This state of affairs does not fill Huret with excessive commiseration. He too seems to find the extras onstage at the Châtelet more gay: "One day they may get angry; for now, they are simply disgruntled." On their own soil (if the expression could still be used), the Indians had "the same disoriented, foreign look they had in Paris when the cowboy Cody brought them here."[20]

The post-emancipation black was no less downtrodden. Now that he was free, he was much less "interesting" to European sensibilities. And what had he made of his freedom? At best, nothing. At worst, he had turned it against his former masters. French travelers voiced a collective outcry against Reconstruction and the oppression into which it had cast the conquered of the white race. In 1875, Louis Simonin, in *À travers les États-Unis* (Across the United States), repeated in his own words Southern prejudices about the blacks' laziness and the risk of anarchy that the United States ran so long as the black race was not extinct.[21] Frédéric Gaillardet also foresaw the blacks' extinction in 1883, without any superfluous regrets. In 1889, the French stereotype of the South having become an "upside-down world" because of the North was well established, and Johanet could make an attempted witticism about it: "Jacksonville is pullulating with Negroes. You would trample them, if only they could be crushed; but, quite the contrary, how many whites they crush!"[22] We have already seen how Gohier's "convictions" did not stop him from painting a picture worthy of Klan literature of the black as a rapist. Jules Huret attempted a timid resistance: segregation "bugs [him] a little," and "for a little while I stayed away from Louisiana." He movingly evokes a black funeral, and he is decidedly indignant that "Cleopatras [who have] immigrated into the brutal New World civilization" are set apart "like lepers."[23] But he practically apologizes for these outbursts: he wants to "understand" the segregationists and promises to make inquiries. And the chapter he finally devotes, in the form of a dialogue, to the "state of the Negro question" gives the Southern whites' arguments pride of place.

These reactions are revealing in their convergence, all the more so because they are corroborated by opinions hostile to blacks' citizenship, which were multiplying at the time in France. These were not travel impressions or mood swings, but learned pronouncements produced by great scholars and intellectuals. The most authoritative voices in France spoke up to condemn the policies of Lincoln's successors and deplore the blacks' accession to citizenship: a brilliant economist such as Leroy-Beaulieu; or the founder of the École des Sciences Politiques, Émile Boutmy. They "all concluded, despite differences of opinion on many points, that the Republicans had made a mistake when they declared the blacks to be citizens."[24]

The unanimity is crushing; the way the accusations are formulated is even more so. Leroy-Beaulieu speaks of "a race placed at the lowest rung of the anthropological scale and moreover morally degraded by four hundred years of slavery."[25] Boutmy, who early on approved the measures taken, state by state, for blocking the black vote, sticks to his guns in his *Éléments d'une psychologie politique du peuple américain* and is glad to see that the Supreme

Court has let the Southern states multiply barriers to the black vote, from requiring a literacy test to imposing a poll tax. In just a few years, André Siegfried, having decreed the "negro *bloc*" ethnically "*inassimilable*," would propose this apologue: "Have you read Wells's *Island of Dr. Moreau*, a fanciful story about animals transformed by a scientist into semihumans, who demand the same rights as man and all end up being killed? That is the Negro question."[26]

The blacks and American Indians, who had had many friends and advocates in France until the 1860s, fell into disgrace. Did that mean that Anglo-America, so often the object of finger pointing for the "barbaric" way it treated them, came out of the nineteenth century exonerated? By no means. The denigration coming from the one side did not cancel out the other side's accusations. Sympathy for the former victims of "Anglo-Saxon" America dwindled (sometimes down to nothing). Unyielding descriptions of their ugliness, failings, and vices increased. Yet they were still instrumentalized; these unpleasant witnesses were called on to confound Yankee iniquity. They were no longer "interesting," as Gohier so neatly put it, neither sentimentally nor intellectually (information about them available in France became extremely sparse)—but they were still useful.

Uprooting America

Indians and blacks, America's internal pariahs, were overtaken by a scene that began to fascinate French observers in 1900: "the inundation," as Siegfried wrote, of a "cosmopolitan" immigration. They were lumped together with this "foreign invasion" (again Siegfried) and qualified as "foreigners" themselves. Indeed, their presence on American soil only heightened what was already beginning to seem like a critical state of heterogeneity. In 1885, fifteen years after they had attained citizenship, Émile Boutmy defined the American blacks as "outlaws"; in 1902, he went for a second offense: "Once, [the black] could pass for a minor member of the nation; his master's supervision was, *à la rigueur,* a tie between him and the white race." (Admirable *à la rigueur*. . .) "He became a *legal* citizen in 1860 [*sic*] only to fall into the *social* condition of a foreigner."[27] Boutmy's analysis reproduces, this time for the blacks, Jules Huret's fantasy about the Indians: both groups clearly had something "foreign" about them. Wasn't it time for these old Americans (because even the blacks, as André Siegfried would remind his readers, were "old Americans")—wasn't it time for them to get off the stage? After the Indians' extinction, why not the American blacks'? From Frédéric Gaillardet to Marie Dugard, the possibility was seriously entertained. André

Siegfried, with his apologue taken from *The Island of Dr. Moreau,* perpetuated that hypothesis—albeit in a "fantastic" vein. But maybe it was simply a matter, as in a fantasia at the Châtelet, of clearing the stage for the next scene . . .

And what a promising scene, what a spectacular episode! A cast of millions, a troupe as "mottled" as you could hope for, as "cosmopolitan" as the devil. It would have been called, in a royal ballet, the Entrance of the Exotics (the word *exotic* crops up four times in Siegfried's introduction alone). They were the ones who would make the great destabilizing push, not the old, ossified minorities. They were the ones who would make the melting pot explode. Welcome, "scourges of God"—and of America! Not that French commentators *admired* the new immigrants for their nefarious potential. On the contrary, there were no words brutal enough to describe them. Johanet qualified them as "barbarians." Varigny, mainly preoccupied with Asian immigration, announced the white race's overthrow in California as "certain."[28] Noailles, who was also worried about the Chinese, predicted that "the pure-bred Anglo-Saxon, already crossed with Germanic and Irish blood, [would] be lost in this promiscuity of inferior races."[29] In 1889, Octave Noël considered the American nation nothing more than a "nation of cosmopolitan dreck." But all that had still been, so to speak, somewhat epidermal.

Now things were more serious, more thoughtful. Now there was Émile Boutmy, a pioneer of "political psychology" and founder of the Institut des Sciences Politiques. He would explain, calmly and learnedly, that it "is fairly exact to say that each generation arriving [in the United States] happened to be morally and intellectually inferior to the previous one."[30] Let's see how he explains this decline. "The contingents posterior [to the Pilgrims] seem to have obeyed less elevated impulses, along with the fact that they were made up of more varied elements." The evil ran deep, and "diversity" had long been a threat. "But vigor and willpower, the spirit of adventure and the love of money still gave them a very precise and very clear common physiognomy." Good-for-nothings, perhaps, but not nebulous ones! On the contrary, they were clearly typed. Next came the inevitable biological metaphor. "Until approximately the mid-nineteenth century, Europe was still handing off to the New World healthy, living tissue that could be grafted onto it; later, notably after 1860, it was more or less damaged or gangrenous cells it cast off." So the new immigrants were "gangrenous"? Of course, since they were illiterate, immoral, and liked to eat rotten fruit, as Boutmy notes. "Political psychology" was an exact science; therefore, Boutmy's demonstration should be cited in its entirety.

The new immigrants are bereft of all technical acquisitions—76 p. cent are pure manual laborers—; illiterates—in Massachusetts, of 122,000 unschooled persons, 108,000 are foreigners, and it is because of them that the coefficient of ignorance is growing from decade to decade in the North-East—; immoral—in Massachusetts, foreigners, who make up 27.1 p. cent of the population, produce 46 p. cent of those charged with crimes—; degraded in their lifestyle—especially the Polish and the Italians, who live piled up in filthy hovels and feed themselves on crusts of bread, rotten fruit, and stale beer.[31]

The America of "energy and faith" was thus replaced by an America "made up of the mud of all the races."[32] Boutmy's "political psychology" had not forgotten the lessons of racial anthropology. Its Yankee was—or rather, *had once been*—a completely Nordic mix: "the Norwegians or the Danes, dispersing from their fjords; the Teutonic knights struggling with the Estonians; the Hanseatic League and its trading posts: there is something of these three types in the Yankees."[33] Onto this base was grafted a "refugee Christianity."[34] Thus, "in a sense, the Yankee made America; religion and the church made the Yankee."[35] But what Boutmy now saw, what he wanted to show the French, was that all that had come apart; the race had been diluted; religion itself had been deformed. Because if America had remained "very decidedly Christian," there "was, in the final analysis, only a kind of residue of Christianity, dregs half-squeezed and drained, which can still make a pungent and comforting wine, but without generosity or bouquet."[36]

Well-rooted America disappeared in a cloud of seafoam, "the foam cast off by European society."[37] A note, a little further on, evokes "the scanty roots of those human plants" that are the new immigrants.[38] It is a striking and symptomatic repetition, in Émile Boutmy's pen, of a very old apothegm: Queen Isabella's comparison between America's untrustworthy inhabitants and its trees, which were "not firmly rooted."[39] Just as the "rootless" indigenous people were becoming extinct, a new group of rootless people appeared, much more modern and cosmopolitan; *heimatlose,* with a "wandering lightness," as Boutmy put it—and for him it was not a Nietzschean compliment. André Siegfried would remember this description in 1927 when he summed up America's "vital problem" as a confrontation between "tradition and cosmopolitanism." And to combat the threat of uprooting, his greatest wish for the country was that it would develop a salutary nationalism: "[America] has already had its Drumont. We can only hope it will give rise to a Barrès."[40] America would be so much closer to France if it were to breed, instead of simpleminded jingoists, a full-fledged *intellectual* novelist able to repopulate the American imagination with truly patriotic characters! Actual Americans being what they were, though, this was of course both a pious wish and an optical illusion: "What a contrast they make," Siegfried

would soon deplore, "when you look closely, with the fundamental homogeneousness of all Frenchmen!"

The "Overworked Melting Pot"

Bourget, Boutmy, Siegfried: from 1895 TO 1927, French representations of
the United States and its new immigrants followed the same intellectual
flight path. There was a good reason for it: this path was guided by the same
preoccupation. The question that obsessed the French was that of "assimilating" foreign elements into a national community.

Paul Bourget, with disarming frankness, admitted the preconceived nature of his American investigation. It had allowed him to verify his "vision . . . of the irreconcilable antagonism between the races"—a vision he
had "brought over" with his luggage.[41] The "very general hypotheses"[42] he
confidently spotted from the first week of his stay were a direct consequence
of the primacy he gave the struggle between the races. America, with its
new immigration—that "second outgrowth of civilization"—obligingly illustrated a law the novelist had already recognized and established: "The class
struggle is only an illusion. At bottom, there is an ethnic duel taking place."
In short, "it is once more a struggle between people of enemy blood"[43] that
the explosive situation in turn-of-the-century America would lead to.
Whence the catastrophic scenario of an East-West war that would set two
racially antagonistic Americas against each other: "The day excessive immigration will truly have created two Americas in America, the struggle
between these two worlds will be as inevitable as that of England with Ireland, of Germany with France, of China with Japan."[44] Watching the United
States periodically replay the Civil War was clearly a long-standing French
dream.

The extreme hypothesis Bourget proposed of a civil and even extracivil
war would have few followers. But that is not his central argument; the
breakdown of assimilation is. "For the past thirty years now," Bourget
affirms, "'Americanization' has no longer been functioning."[45] It was this
real or imagined dysfunction that captivated French observers throughout
the first third of the twentieth century. *Americanization:* the word had clearly
taken on a different meaning since Baudelaire had coined it. It did not refer
to the United States' contaminating influence on old Europe, particularly
France. It referred to the United States' capacity to absorb newcomers, to the
melting pot and its efficiency. To this persistent question—which had a visibly projective dimension, if only in the systematic use of a very French
vocabulary of "assimilation"—the two historians and political scientists who

oriented French analyses of the United States during this period would give two different but fundamentally complementary answers.

First, Boutmy. He did not, as we have seen, make much of the new "Latino-Slav" immigration. For him, the inferiority of the successive waves of immigrants was as clear as day. However, he did not reach the diagnosis that "Americanization" would stall out, as Bourget thought. The machine was not broken. But it was grinding up matter that had become so vile it would perhaps have been a better thing if it did break down, after all. For Boutmy, the melting pot was not the problem; what came out of it was. The mix was made, for better or for worse. But it was *because it was made* that America was degenerating. All these immigrants, in the end, "become American in their feelings, ways, and habits, after an astonishingly brief lapse of time. But Americanism on the whole presents increasingly simple and clear-cut characters, because they are increasingly impoverished and reduced, and less and less harmonious and healthy."[46] Boutmy left the melting pot churning, but only in order to drown Americanness.

Then there was André Siegfried. With him, we have to step over World War I and land squarely in the golden age of anti-Americanism that was the interwar period. But this giant step is justified. First, because the war, as we will see, only took a very thin slice out of the already thick mass of negative representations of America; then, because Siegfried continued the tradition of American investigations for the Musée Social (his book appeared in 1927, published by Armand Colin in its "Bibliothèque du Musée Social" collection) and because, as a professor at the École Libre des Sciences Politiques, he also took over Boutmy's teaching position. Later on, we will return to *America Comes of Age*—that mandatory breviary for American studies up to the 1950s—but the pages he devotes to the "assimilation crisis" are better discussed here, as the culmination of an alarmist literature that had been announcing the ethnic balkanization of America since 1900.

Siegfried transmitted an up-to-date image of the United States (observed in 1925) by using historical lighting like a blinding spotlight, to reveal the reliefs of the present. Faithful to the investigative traditions of the Musée Social, he exposed and treated the country as a problem. Or rather, as a triad of problems, of unequal magnitude. In the second part of his introduction, Siegfried states the three main points of attraction in any examination of the contemporary United States: the "phenomenal material progress" it had achieved; the new global balance in which its position was important; but above all, on the very first line, the "pacific invasions of immigrants that are stealthily transforming the race."[47] The whole first part of his book will thus be devoted to the "American people's ethnic and religious crisis," with a clear-cut angle: "Will it remain Anglo-Saxon and Protestant?" This is the heyday of "national characteristics"; but for Siegfried, national characteristics are strictly tributary to ethnicity; his reflections are always irrigated by "blood." Proof of this comes in the very first sentence of the first part of the book: "The essential characteristic of the post-war period in the United States is the nervous reaction of the original American stock against an insidious subjugation by foreign blood."[48]

With Siegfried, every sentence, each turn of phrase and metaphor, deserves commentary. Because the historian was a stylist. He "wrote well" and sometimes overdid it. If his book, written and intended for pedagogical use, had such a strong impact on interwar anti-Americanism—equaled only by Duhamel's *Scenes from the Life of the Future* and Luc Durtain's American stories—it was first and foremost because of the writerly brio it boasts, Siegfried's way with words and memorable images. Extremely clear, with a plainspoken ease in discussing facts and figures, Siegfried's was a galloping pedagogy: the professor was something like a Paul Morand reined in by Paul Bourget. "Racial portraits" came freely flowing from his pen, each of them in swaths of purple prose. The picture he paints of America's ethnic mosaic, in a fairly twisted narrative procedure, is worth citing in its entirety. Siegfried's reader is invited to imagine he has the most diverse of ancestors "to sympathize with the innermost aspirations of all the races that have been cast into the Melting Pot." An impossible mission, of course, since the American mix stretches far beyond the "hereditary possibilities." It is an elegant way of endorsing not only the scientific pertinence of "national characteristics," but also a troubling epistemological stance in which belonging to a group is the prerequisite for knowing it.

This fantastical family tree whose impossible ramifications were supposed to give an idea of the American mix begins with a "heritage of English non-conformist Protestantism" and fades out into the frontiers of the white race, alongside the "nigger mammy" and Asians in California, "that furthermost boundary of the Occident," with, right in the shrewdly calculated center of the civilized and other worlds, a strange "window on the soul of the Jew and of the Orient": "Surely you can lay claim to some Israelite uncle from London or Frankfurt. He is sure to turn up again in New York. Or even better, can you not unearth some Alsatian Jew, a kike from Breslau, a 'sheeny' from Lemberg or Salonika, or even—and I do not exaggerate—some Hebrew from Asia, with goat eyes and patriarchal beard?"[49] History, according to Siegfried, is a poetics of Babel. For over fifteen lines he gives us a list of all the peoples in American Immigration's census, from the Africans to the Welsh and "West Indians." To heighten the sense of confusion, Siegfried translates them but leaves them in their *English* alphabetical order (*Africans*, etc., up to *Welsh* and *West Indians*); in French, this produces a chaotic list running from *Africains* to *Gallois* and *Originaires des Indes occidentales*. This list of forty-four nations or ethnicities, without any indication of their numbers or percentages, has no informative interest; its only goal is to disorient the reader. The demographic data turns into an onomastic incantation. The fake statistics are unreeled in a Célinian litany. This is clearly the goal of the operation, that the reader should be unable to see the light at the far end of the tunnel: "The statistics, unable to enumerate them all, are forced to add: 'other peoples.'"[50]

From Boutmy to Siegfried, the ethnic kaleidoscope has started turning, the racial rhetoric has grown more heavy-handed, but the conclusion of failure has also become more damning. Like his predecessor, Siegfried stresses the poor quality of recent immigrants. He notes that "from the American point of view, the new immigrants were not the equal of their predecessors."[51] A clever rhetorical ploy. Is he simply reproducing the American viewpoint—and if so, exactly which Americans? Or is he magnanimously taking a lofty view of America's best interests and, himself, Siegfried, passing judgment? No matter; behind these little ruses, he is clearly the one describing those lowest common immigrants, "a bewildered and inarticulate crew" enticed only by "a wage level that seemed high in comparison with the mediocre standard of living of south-eastern Europe."[52] "Standard of living" is in English in the original French: using the phrase to refer to the poorest part of Europe, Professor Siegfried is being playful—and scornful as well.

The heart of the matter: for the so-called assimilation crisis, Siegfried's tour de force is to couple Boutmy's solution with a contradictory one he himself proposes. Siegfried effectively affirms the failure of "Americanization," but he also retains the idea of a general decline through the excessive injection of dubious elements. Theory 1 (Boutmy-style):

> Assimilation, like a steamroller, ruthlessly crushes the finest flowers of the older civilizations, and as a rule only allows primitive, implacably standardized beings to survive. The immigrant arrives old with centuries of inherited experience, but America makes him young, almost childish.[53]

Theory 2:

> The classical conception of America as the Melting Pot of races was widespread, and it was generally believed that the New World could assimilate, more or less slowly but completely, an indefinite number of immigrants. . . . Those were the

days when environment was believed to be more powerful than heredity. About
1910, at the high tide of the Latin-Slav influx, there began to be doubts as to the
efficacy of the Melting Pot. The War brought the matter quickly and decisively to
a head, and the lack of national unity came as a startling revelation to thinking
Americans.[54]

These "thinking Americans" look a lot like a Frenchman by the name of
André Siegfried, who, on August 4, 1914, observed, bewildered, the obviously
contradictory reactions to the war coming from New York's diverse communities—a city with a "fantastic ethnic cosmopolitanism."[55] And despite the
easy out of speaking in their name, it is of course André Siegfried who concludes, for all thinking Americans: "Hundreds of thousands—even millions—of foreigners were still unabsorbed, although the Americans had
been flattering themselves that they had completely assimilated them." And
it is once more Siegfried who pronounces these bitter words: "With such 'citizens'—what derision there is in that word!—the United States became a sort
of ethnic mosaic and ran the risk of being no longer a nation."[56] It is funny
to see André Siegfried, in a fallacious prosopopeia, project on some convenient "thinking Americans" a vision so typically French that we can effortlessly
see in it, three-quarters of a century before the fact, the intellectual revolt of
Jacobin, unicultural France in the face of polyethnic multiculturalism. André
Siegfried, or "French ideology."[57]

What is the point of all this ventriloquism? That the United States is like
"Sinbad's ship in the *Arabian Nights* which sailed so close to a magnetic
mountain that it had all its nails suddenly drawn out of it." *Wishful thinking,*
as the Americans say—with the dream of the federation coming apart replaced by the barely secret hope that the United States would break up into
numerous small ethnic communities.

In holding onto both of the two scenarios developed in France about
America's ethnic future, André Siegfried got his money's worth out of the
anti-American discourse. Or, in any case, he thought one of two things would
happen. Either the many different groups landing in America with their language, religion, customs, and so on would conserve their identity and also
become "blocs inassimilables," in which case, America as a nation would be
done for (Siegfried suggests—and we will come back to this—that such was
already the case with the Jews), or else the same America, which had been
homogeneous up to then—by excluding the blacks and eliminating the Indians—would for better or for worse manage to ingest, integrate, and assimilate millions of foreign bodies; and so, inevitably, this massive absorption of
elements that were both exterior and "inferior" would result in the dilution

of Americanness. In short, America could avoid breaking into pieces only at the cost of its own identity. Whatever happened, the United States would end up losing, or lost.

☆ ☆ ☆

Should we rehabilitate Bourget? His vision of a continental duel between "Americans' America" and "foreigners' America" is simplistic. And moreover, it is hard to see how Bourget, who spent most of his time in Newport, Rhode Island, could have done any better: "Newport is a disastrous place for the unacclimated observer, evidently," deadpanned Mark Twain.[58] But if Bourget did not paint America, he admirably reflected the ambiguous Manicheanism that would thereafter animate French anti-Americanism, organizing a confrontation between Yankee America and a foreign America that was "exotic" and *inassimilable,* whose relentlessly pointed-out defects and inferiority became "interesting" for the dissolving effect they could have on the Yankee "Corinthian bronze." Neither the "new immigration" nor the indigenous pariahs it was conflated with aroused the interest or even the sympathy of the French observers calculating the chances of a race war in America. No, Bourget was not the only one dreaming of inexpiable combat. Martial metaphors describing the "flood tide," the "invasion" of the new barbarians abounded. Some even dreamed, as during the Civil War, of new servile wars breaking out. The new wars would leave the American empire a rubble heap, destroying monuments and profaning tombs: "Will the centuries be kinder to the New World's tombs? How do we know if barbarian hordes, scourges of God, will not one day come down from America's mountains, spring from its mines, demolish dikes and factories, and throw themselves in vengeful torrents upon the monuments of the tyrannical million and the tyrants themselves?"[59] It is an extreme scenario, and one that is rarely put so explicitly as it is here by Edmond Johanet, but that translates the widespread fantasy of a vengeful mission with which the anti-Americans invested "the other America": destroying Babylon—or, at least, dispersing Babel.

8

The Empire of Trusts: Socialism or Feudalism?

There was still one tile missing from the turn-of-the-century discursive mosaic that was forming the image of a nefarious America—and not a small one: the capitalism tile. And a word we have not seen much of in the preceding chapters: socialism.

Identifying the United States with triumphant capitalism seems obvious nowadays. But we should stress that it came onto the scene fairly late in the history of American representations. For most of the nineteenth century, the United States was perceived as an essentially agricultural country dominated by small landowners.[1] This rural America, Washington-Cincinnatus's worthy daughter, was personified by the farmer rather than the plantation owner, the shopkeeper rather than the industrialist. And negative stereotypes were just as out of step with reality. Stendhal imagined America as a vast subprefecture: around 1840 or 1850, to wary Frenchmen's noses it smelled like manure and general stores. But as the century rolled on, the store expanded. The Cincinnati pig breeder took over from the Crèvecoeur-style farmer and, in turn, was replaced by the Kings of Canned Goods. By the end of the century, America had become the country of "King Dollar"; it was a "plutopolis," a "millionaire world."[2] The shopkeeper's greed had blossomed into a *libido dominandi:* Caesar had broken through the Yankee Birotteau.[3]

A decisive boundary was crossed in the last years of the nineteenth century. Up to then, inborn racketeering, aggressive mercantilism, and extreme protectionism had been the points of aversion. The French were obsessed with the "tariff": a tax barrier raised to Himalayan heights for the greater prosperity of the American economy. It was the tariff that had pushed France and the United States to the brink of diplomatic crisis several times; it was what was now pushing the United States to conquer new markets, in South America or Asia, that were not protected by European "retaliatory" barriers. On the eve of the twentieth century, the tariff still preoccupied the French, but it had lost the spotlight to the trust.

For once (and perhaps the first time), there was practically no lapse between an American event and its French echo. The trust system took hold without any attention gap. It caught French notice and mobilized French pens. Its magnitude obliterated the old cliché of Yankee greed. In the French imagination, America definitively ceased to be the farmer's plot of land, the shopkeeper's paradise, the kingdom of seven-year-old penny-pinchers selling their eggs to Mrs. Trollope for a small fortune. Little Jonathan had grown up: he no longer counted in pennies or even in meticulously amassed dollars; his unit of measurement was the million. There were still kids selling their dads candy they had just been given for twenty cents a piece,[4] but these anecdotes of juvenile greed now paled in the light of a "millionaire world." The trust system, moreover, was more than a simple change of scale; it represented a profound mutation, a derailing of the "ordinary channels" of profit. As Edmond Johanet noted, "You do not pile up million upon million through the ordinary channels; small shovelfuls do not suffice"; a new kind of tool was needed, and "this tool is the trust."[5] Yankee "racial qualities" were probably not unrelated to its invention. Its extraordinarily rapid development probably owed a lot to the same "materialist" cupidity that in the past had taken the form of a more rustic stinginess. But in its structure and enormity, this new social formation went well beyond the boundaries of known capitalism and traditional behavior. For the trust was not just a "tool," as Barbier wrote in 1893; it was a "system." The conviction spread quickly and is reflected in the universal adoption of the expression "trust system," considered more appropriate than simply "trust."

To many observers, the trust system represented a qualitative leap that was social in nature. The word *système,* in the French semantic field, was anything but neutral: at the end of the century, it designated a whole web of collusions between politics and business. It was easy to conflate the image of the French political and economic "system," which perennialized the exploitation of the "little man" by "big business," with the American trust system, which appeared to institutionalize a kind of macroexploitation by absorbing and affiliating small businesses. But conflation or not, French commentators' enthusiasm for the expression "trust system" proves that more than the trust as an entity, people were worried about "trustification" (another French neologism of the time). The trust was clearly not just a financial and industrial tool, or even a machine: it was a new social universe. The qualitative leap was also a leap into the unknown. A completely new financial and industrial structure, with serious human implications, had been inexorably put in place, on a national scale; it was already sprouting tentacles prepared to grip the rest of the world. This was a revolution, and the revolution was planetary. By 1900, America, for the French, had become *the empire of trusts:* its circumference was everywhere, its center nowhere. Globalization had begun.

Translating this radical innovation into the existing lexicon was not an easy task. The economist Pierre Leroy-Beaulieu understood that defining the trust was a tricky thing; he himself considered it a "group of establishments that has managed to secure the monopoly of a given industry . . . or at least a sufficiently preponderant part"; his preferred translation was "industrial combination."[6] This was, for the liberal Leroy-Beaulieu, a protective definition: he was affirming, against the grain of popular opinion, that "not every trust aims at monopolizing an industry, and still fewer succeed." That was the most widespread perception in France: the trust was an instrument of monopolization. Paul de Rousiers soberly described it as a "private monopoly,"[7] but Edmond Johanet, the same year, saw it as "a big industry's financial confederation to monopolize all similar midrange industries."[8] Octave Noël took the same approach: "trusts; that is, monopolizing unions."[9] These translations and interpretations put the term "trust" into a long-running historical context: they recalled, by association, the *accapareur* (monopolizer) of ancien régime rumors and thus facilitated the term's acceptance in France. The American "truster" combined the weighty mythological heritage of the *accapareur* of yore with the no less hateful pedigree of the modern speculator, the financial lynx. The image of the trust propagated in France at the time reflects this dichotomy: it was distinctly embodied in the traits of a few "magnates" (Rockefeller, Morgan, Carnegie, et al.), and at the same time, its amorphous and anonymous nature was a source of worry.

It was also, on another level, the object of a double interrogation: the first question was whether it was industrial or financial in nature. The trust *produced.* But its productive calling was often masked, in French descriptions, by the importance of conquering and controlling the means of distribution. Marxists and liberals converged on this point: the trust organized and dominated entire sectors of production for the greater profit of a handful of economic conquistadors who did not have the least involvement in production itself. Thus John D. Rockefeller and his associates, the founders of Standard Oil, had "never extracted a liter of oil and only know gas from having burned it in lamps."[10] The weight of Saint-Simonian tradition led many economists to suspect that this financial takeover and subordination of the producer by the "truster" was a new kind of social parasitism. In his important Marxist study, Paul Lafargue was also inclined to see the trust as a formidable financial machine for controlling industry, rather than as a new type of industrial organization. "The trust system forces its control over trade, which until now had laid down the law for agriculture and industry,"[11] Lafargue wrote. The trust was the start of a new phase in the history of the relationship to production. The trust system was a kind of "super-commerce" that was capitalism's final stage. More powerful and sophisticated than the former system, it was destined to replace it, as an "art of hijacking production." Lafargue insists on this point: "the Rockefeller gang," "trustification's" pioneers, had neither invented nor improved the tools of production; they had simply "proved their superior business skills."[12]

These interpretations, which described the trust system in terms of a global mutation of social relationships, gave it a decisive momentum that over the course of the twentieth century would propel it to the forefront of negative metaphors about North America. Thus was born, in the late 1890s, the most widespread image of Americanness in France, its dominant metaphor. For over a century, the word "trust" captured not only the image of American capitalism, but also the image of capitalism as American. "Standard Oil, more palpably than the Christians' good Lord, is omnipresent," noted Paul Lafargue, describing the first of the trusts. Omnipresent, omnipotent: the trusts' divine attributes would become those of an America that was increasingly feared.

Paul Lafargue wrote *Les Trusts américains* in 1903.[13] But this son-in-law of Karl Marx was beaten to the punch by several economists, sociologists, and essayists who were not the least bit Marxist. There was a general interest in the phenomenon. A very rapid one, as well. Rockefeller's Standard Oil Trust was founded in the early 1880s. By 1894, it had its first American historian (and critic) in the person of H. D. Lloyd.[14] In France, the trust system debate was already in full swing four years later. In the decidedly decisive year of 1898, Paul de Rousiers published an essential description of the trust system in the Bibliothèque du Musée Social collection, *Les Industries monopolisées (trusts) aux États-Unis,* while Edmond Johanet published his *Correspondant* articles in book form as *Autour du monde millionaire.* Less than a year later, again in *Le Correspondant,* Octave Noël came back to the trust system, defining it as the offensive weapon of an "American peril" whose defensive weapon was protectionism.[15] (In contrast, Crosnier de Varigny, whose books *Les Grandes fortunes aux États-Unis* and *Les États-Unis: Esquisses historiques* were published only a short time earlier—in 1889 and 1891, respectively—had been unaware of the trust system.) When Lafargue came onto the scene, there was intense interest in the trust system, and this new object was so familiar to readers that neither Gohier in 1903 nor Huret in 1904 felt the need to define it.[16]

All French observers were aware of the economic threat to Europe the trust system represented, but it was the theoretical problem raised by its development that mainly preoccupied them. Seen from France, the problem was that the trust system contained the seeds of collectivism the way an egg contains an unhatched chicken. The emergence of the American trusts necessitated reformulating the question of collective appropriation of the means of production in terms neither Marxist theorists nor liberal economists were prepared for.

The liberals' dilemma can be summed up as follows: the trust system resulted from free competition but seemed to be in danger of abolishing all competition. Could the concentration of supply and the "agreements" it supposed remain compatible over the long term with a healthy liberal doctrine? The easiest way out was to deny not that the trust system existed, but that it was historically important at all: far from being the inescapable face of future capitalism, the trust system was a mere accident, a growth fever; it was no more than the passing anomaly of an overheated economy. Pierre Leroy-Beaulieu thus explained in 1904 that "far from being essential organs, most of them are instead, in our view, passing outgrowths of America's industrial progress";[17] they were therefore already showing signs of fragility, "stumbling and collapsing on all sides," "like a house of cards," because of the "trustomaniacs' exaggerations."[18] So, for the liberals, it was important to distinguish between concentration and rationalization (proof of effectiveness, low prices and high salaries) and the speculative maneuvers of excessive capitalization that came in their wake. This dissociation obviously was readily accepted by the Marxists. The trust system nevertheless created a certain discomfort in the liberal camp, where reactions ranged from moral disapproval (the trust system disrupted healthy competition; it was "disloyal") to political uneasiness (the trust system as embryonic collectivism, potential socialism).

Unease can also be seen in Paul de Rousiers, who was the first to produce an analysis of the trusts informed by fieldwork. For this anticollectivist reformer, the trust system raised a tough problem. "If evolution," he wrote in his preface, "inevitably leads to monopolies, we must bow to collectivist theories. . . . It is true that the American trusts are private and not public, like the general monopoly that is collectivism's dream; but when the collectivity finds itself face to face with a single capitalist in each industry, it will find it easy to replace him."[19] This was exactly the way a libertarian such as Gohier thought. For him, "the [American] public produces socialism without realizing it, like [Molière's] Monsieur Jourdain produces prose"; he concluded that "the nationalization of the property monopolized by the trusts will only wrong a tiny number of property owners. The way to collectivism is wide open in the United States, unlike in France."[20] Paul de Rousiers was less hasty, and in his conclusion he revised the very assumptions he seemed to have established in his preface. Three hundred pages after positing that a collectivist future would spring from the trusts, Rousiers decided instead that the trust system was an "accident" or a "pathological case,"[21] adding that if by chance it was not, the fault did not lie with the trust system itself but with the American economy's embryonic socialism, which had allowed the trusts to flourish: "If the Trust is paving the way for socialism, it is because socialism, in the form of a wrongful intervention by the government, allowed the Trust to be born."[22] For Paul de Rousiers, the harm had been done; America had been insidiously *socialized* (by ultraprotectionism and "the confusion of private interests and public ones")[23] even before it had been *entrusted*. Later, we will see Bertrand de Jouvenel take a fairly similar approach.

These convolutions in the writings of one of the most serious observers of the American social scene give us an idea of the trust system's resistance to the analytical gaze; we also see how France's debate over the trusts was, above all, a debate over collectivism. We might imagine that here the socialists were more in their element. That was in no way true. They agreed neither on an analysis of the trusts' oligopoly nor on the political lessons that could be drawn from it. In their view, the new economic order created by "trustification" could not be described in the absolute, independently of the power relations between the classes as they existed in the United States in this specific phase of capitalist development. And on that point, opinions were wildly divergent. Perspectives on the trust system were slanted right from the start and were inseparable from a global appraisal of the American situation and its related strategic choices. America had been a bone of contention for the republicans at the start of the Third Republic; it was one here for the revolutionary socialists and the reformists, and the terms of the argument would leave a lasting imprint on leftist anti-Americanism in France.

America: Socialism's Flag—or Shroud?

We have seen the casual tone with which Demolins summed up the North Americans' distaste for socialism: however hard Europe tried—giving them a second chance, sending over Liebknecht and Eleanor Aveling-Marx—all efforts had been useless. There was no way of "converting the American English."[24] American socialism remained a German transplant, rejected by the "Anglo" body politic. For Demolins, this was calmly obvious—and confirmed his theory about the radical difference between the "communitarian" nature of the Germanic race and Anglo-Saxon individualism. This observation of socialism's failure was widely shared in the 1890s, including by a number of theorists and militant socialists. But for them, there was no question of taking it lightly, or of judging an ethnographic explanation satisfactory.

It was unavoidably clear, in any case, by the late nineteenth century, that socialism had an "American problem." In fact, it could be argued that the problem went further back, to repeatedly unsuccessful attempts to implant so-called utopian socialist or Communist communities. Confronting socialist ideas with American reality had indeed begun with the arrival of strange immigrants come to stake their dreams to a reputedly virgin land. A refuge for "model" communities, a haven for Cabet or Fourier's disciples, the United States had welcomed the men but shrugged off the ideas they brought with them. Throughout the nineteenth century, a string of small collectivities formed, expanded, and collapsed. Barely established, these communities seemed to melt in the blazing sun and vanish on the vasty horizons of California or Texas. When Th. Bentzon (the pen name of Thérèse Blanc), an author of numerous books on American literature and society, published *Choses et gens d'Amérique* (American People and Things) in 1898, her first chapter was titled "Communism in America"—but it was about the Shakers, "the only true communists who exist in America"![25] A joke, to be sure, but nonetheless one that did not garner its author any refutations.

Small-community socialism had existed since the 1860s. That the graft had not taken did not surprise scientific socialism's founding fathers, who set their sights on America—not to seek the land and freedom conducive to experimenting with ideal forms, but rather to attentively follow the capitalist machine's development and the progress of workers' organizations. Willingly disdainful of its "utopian" predecessors, their socialism would have its own pitfalls. The socialist movement in general and Marxist groups in particular would remain on consistently bad footing with the United States, with their great expectations and big disappointments, before settling into a resentful resignation. We will simply mention the main points of this tormented history in order to measure its impact on the anti-Americanism of the French Left and Far Left. Doing so is a doubly tricky task. Pre-1914 French socialism, in its disconcerting diversity, hardly had its attention attuned to the American theater, nor was it especially attentive to socialism's "chances" across the Atlantic. As for Marxist positions on the United States— starting with those of the founders and their immediate followers—they fluctuated, drawing from a social tale full of sound and fury, made up of the workers' movement's erratic accelerations and chaotic dips. Hard to pinpoint, they were also hard to interpret, given that they were almost always linked to dogmatic controversies and internal quarrels within the International.

At several historical points between 1861 and the start of the twentieth century, the United States took on a considerable importance for Marx, Engels, and their successors. It is very hard, however, to get a good focus on their image of it: it always seems "blurry," as if America were an unruly child, systematically spoiling the socialist family picture. Was America really already moving too fast for theory to catch up with it? Or was the shaky picture the photographer's fault? The historian Laurence Moore offers an interesting remark: "European Marxists," he writes, "were always looking to American society as if it were on the verge of a great change. . . . The America emerging from their portraits was an abstraction, the model of a society as it was to be after a few more years of capitalist development."[26] If Marx and Engels's United States, like Lenin and Trotsky's later on (Trotsky being the most pro-American of the four), never appeared to be a stable element that was politically, socially, and economically well defined, it was indeed because they looked at it with a perpetually prospective eye. From enthusiasm to discouragement, the Marxist tale of the United States was not only an analysis full of peaks and valleys; taking the future's pulse was always more important than dissecting the present. America had the strange gift of being able to transform historical materialism's supporters into fortune tellers endlessly announcing mutations as imminent as they were inevitable: they did not paint America as it really was, but as it soon should be. European Marxism thus created the spectacle of an America that was never the current country, but rather what it would be soon afterward. Whether writing in 1880 or 1900, the militant observer was interested in America as it would be in five or ten years' time—even if that meant regularly extending the date.

New life had been breathed into the old rhetorical scheme in which America was a young, unformed, not-yet-stabilized world. But the perspective had radically changed. It had even been inverted. Developmental insufficiencies were no longer what was blurring America's image; it was the astounding pace of capitalist growth that kept its traits from being captured. This led, of course, to perpetual projection. Infant America's unformed face had become the mask of a collective future, deformed by the speed it was traveling at, like the elongated heads of racecar drivers the futurists would soon paint. Gone were the not-so-distant days when Hegel had judged it superfluous to include America in the scheme of worldwide evolution. The Civil War, passionately followed by Marx and Engels, had reinscribed the United States into the dialectic of world history. And now the dizzying acceleration of mechanical progress in the years from 1865 to 1890 had placed it in the forefront of history's evolution. At the turn of the century, from sector to sector, the figures attested to America's industrial supremacy. But for the socialists, the fact that the United States was economically "surpassing" England had an eschatological weight. Calculating material power necessarily led to another computation: evaluating the part each country would play in the capitalist drama's last act. Because, for late-nineteenth-century socialists, capitalism's days were numbered. Numbered in years: five, ten, at most; rarely in decades.

Where else would the death blow come from but a country where the forces of self-destruction would be unleashed by the most complete (and brutal) freedom? "The country that is more developed industrially only shows, to the less developed, the image of its own future." This quote from Marx was used by Paul Lafargue in 1903 as an epigraph for his book on the trust system. If the United States had reached the top rung of the ladder of capitalist species, it was clearly urgent to go read Europe's future there. This became an essential theme—not an anti-American one, but one that would feed into anti-Americanism: America as a laboratory for the future, an experimental melting pot for European destinies. For Marx, Engels, and their disciples, the theme was catastrophic (insofar as escalating productivity led to irremediable entropy) and apocalyptic (insofar as America would reveal the capitalist system's inherent nature to itself). Tonic and dynamic when considered as part of a planetary economic upheaval, the theory, as we will see, did not arouse the same enthusiasm among the working classes as it did in their leaders.

Marx, Engels, and Lincoln: Fighting the Same Fight—or Not?

Harry Turtledove is an American writer of "history-fiction" who has written a series of "anti-novels" on North America's potential past.[27] A "plausible" hypothesis kicks off his very unusual American history: the Civil War ends without a winner or a loser. The country is divided and the North becomes a

Union of just a few states. The historian-novelist spices up the situation by imagining a radicalized Lincoln (who obviously has not been assassinated) allying himself with *Sozialdemocratie*. Under his leadership, the United States becomes the world's first socialist republic.

The first part of the scenario would have delighted Napoleon III. The second would not have disappointed Karl Marx. Harry Turtledove's radicalized Lincoln is, after all, the leader Marx and Engels would have dreamed of throughout the war; and his North America, "revolutionarized" by the conflict, is the country they were constantly wishing for, from 1861 to 1865, without much hope of having their wishes granted.

To shed some light on the complex relationship the Marxists had with the United States at the turn of the century, we have to go back to the Civil War, to Marx and Engels's journalistic partisanship in favor of the North. We did not broach the subject earlier in our chapter on the war because their articles, which appeared mostly in German in *Die Presse* and in English in the *New York Daily Tribune*, did not have an impact on the internal French debate. It is their entry into the corpus of Marxist "political writings" that would later confer on them the status of essential reading on America. These publications were nonetheless dictated by pressing events, informed by information that was hard to regulate, and dependent on the two friends' fluctuating moods—especially Engels's, who was often annoyed with the North and discouraged by the tide of the war. Rereading these articles and the correspondence between Marx and Engels strikingly reveals a more complex and contentious relationship with the Union than expected.

The general thrust of the articles was unvarying: they supported the North against the "four millions of 'white trash'" in the South, who were "filibusters by profession."[28] In their public writings, neither Marx nor Engels ever faltered in this choice. As for the war's causes and tensions, far from adopting the "realistic" attitude his disciples would later affect, far from considering the brutal struggle a simple conflict of material interests, Marx unwaveringly insisted on the central importance of the slavery question. More, he devoted one of his first and most important articles to criticizing the bourgeois (and pro-South) press, which denied slavery's importance and attempted to explain the entire situation away as a conflict of interests between a protectionist North and a free-trade South. These arguments, which were so often repeated later on by the Marxist vulgate, were singled out by Marx himself in the British press and denounced as "their arguments": the South's, the adversary's.[29] Marx rejected them not for tactical reasons—such as pulling at his readers' abolitionist heartstrings—but in the name of a broader vision, a historical conviction: nothing "progressive" could work under the flag of slavery. You could say what you liked about the North and judge Lincoln's actions narrow or tightfisted: "this does not alter their historic content."[30] For him, abolition was an important matter and did not simply represent the clarification or modernization of an exploitative relationship.

"The whole movement [of the war] was and is based . . . on the *slave question*,"[31] Marx bluntly stated in an article from October 1861. He was adamant in contradicting the "realists" of the enemy camp who repeated, in Great Britain as in France, that the slavery question was only a pretext. Even if slavery had not been the "aim" of the war, the question of freedom had truly become the crux of the conflict. Doubly so: for the long-range historical importance American abolition would have in and of itself, but also, more immediately, because the unduly delayed freeing of the slaves would become a "revolutionary" measure capable of changing both the face of the conflict and the nature of democracy in the North. This was because slavery was at the same time "the foe's most vulnerable spot" and "the root of the evil," as Marx and Engels wrote with a single pen in late 1861.[32] Here we can see what separated Marx from his historical adversaries and so many of his future disciples: he refused both historical cynicism and fetishizing commodities as history's *ultima ratio*. A Northern victory was more important to humanity and the working class than making the Secessionists toe the line was to Northern capitalism. So it was wrong to chime in with the bourgeois press and repeat its easy cynicism by considering the emancipation question an accessory, secondary, or even indifferent factor in the Union's martial actions.

Especially since there was no lack of more legitimate reproaches to be made against the Yankees, and particularly Lincoln. A second characteristic of Marx and Engels's reading of the war was the severity of their judgment of the Union. This severity comes through loud and clear in the correspondence, but there were also glimpses of it in their publications, as when Marx, in *Die Presse*, reproduced a particularly violent speech by Wendell Phillips, the head of the Boston abolitionists, against Lincoln's dithering.[33] Marx and Engels, like the French pro-Unionists, went through periods of discouragement that turned—especially for Engels—into ravaging judgments of the side they favored. A passionate strategist, Engels analyzed military operations with great acuity. (In March 1862, he opposed the "anaconda" stranglehold plan and advocated a massive breach from Tennessee to Savannah that would cut the Confederacy in two—a plan finally adopted by Grant in 1864.)[34] But to him the Union was a dismal thing, when it came to military matters, and Northerners proved themselves very disappointing, from commanders in the field to men in the street. Its generals were incompetent, if not traitors. A pusillanimous Congress was taking derisory steps that "the honorable Lincoln so qualifies . . . that nothing at all is left of [them]." The North's population hardly fared any better: "This slackness, this collapse like a punctured pig's bladder, under the pressure of defeats that have annihilated one army, the strongest and best, and actually left Washington exposed, this total absence of any elasticity in the whole mass of the people—this proves to me that it is all up."[35] These words date from the summer of 1862. Engels would darken the picture even more that fall: "Despite all the screams of the Yankees, there is still no sign whatever available that the people regard this business as a real question of national existence."[36] Marx took him to task, but Engels did not relent: "I must say I cannot work up any enthusiasm for a people which on such a colossal issue allows itself to be continually beaten by a fourth of its own population and which after eighteen months of war has achieved nothing more than the discovery that all its generals are idiots and all its officials rascals and traitors."[37] The November 1862 elections, in which the Democrats had a few wins, confirmed his suspicions: "The fellows are capable of concluding peace, if the South returns to the Union on condition that the President shall always be a Southerner and the Congress shall always consist of Southerners and Northerners in equal numbers. They are even capable of proclaiming Jeff Davis president of the United States forthwith and to surrender even the whole of the border states, if there is no other way to peace. Then, good-bye America."[38] A year and a half earlier, Engels had mainly attacked the Yankee leaders. His antipathy was now general: "I no longer know what I am to think of the Yankees. That a people placed in a great historical dilemma, which is at the same time a matter of its own existence, can after eighteen months' struggle become reactionary in its mass and vote for climbing down, is a bit beyond my understanding."[39] He made the same judgment in early 1863: "Things look rotten in Yankeeland," Engels wrote. "The signs of moral slackening are increasing daily, and the inability to conquer is daily becoming greater." And he sarcastically added: "It is lucky that a peace is a physical impossibility, otherwise they would have made one long ago, merely to be able to live for the almighty dollar again."[40] This is no longer "critical support" but caustic support! His impatience with the Yankees even led him to sing the Confederates' praises: he had no trouble contrasting the "helplessness" of the Northern population, which seemed worse off "than if it had lingered three thousand years under the Austrian scepter," with the valor of the Southerners, who "fight quite famously."[41] He repeated the offense a month later: "The lads in the South, who at least know what they want, strike me as heroes in comparison with the flabby management of the North."[42]

It was time for Marx to call offsides and remind him that just because the "white trash" had martial skills, that did not make them the heroes of the story. But Engels's anti-Yankee mood would probably have not irritated him so much if he had not felt largely the same way. Marx himself produced severe criticism of the North and of Lincoln throughout the war; it was tempered by remarks on the need for solidarity with the "good side," but was nonetheless every bit as radical as Engels's, if not more so. Because at the root of the military reversals that so enraged his correspondent, Marx insisted, was the North's political inability to wage a "revolutionary"-style war. There was a "moral" to be drawn from the setbacks of the summer of 1862, Marx wrote to Engels, and this moral was "that a war of this kind must be conducted on revolutionary lines, while the Yankees have so far been trying to conduct it constitutionally."[43] Lincoln, for whom Marx had a clear antipathy right up to his assassination, embodied this inability. "All Lincoln's Acts," Marx wrote to Engels in October 1862, "appear like the mean pettifogging conditions which one lawyer puts to his opposing lawyer."[44] Such acerbic remarks were not restricted to private correspondence. He had made them public two months earlier by publishing the violent speech in which Wendell Phillips declared, "It will take years for Lincoln to learn to combine his legal scruples as an attorney with the demands of the Civil War."[45] Marx completely approved. Like the abolitionist leader, he judged Lincoln, who was "legally cautious, constitutionally conciliatory,"[46] with the utmost severity. Marx would never really give Lincoln much credit. But he would soon find a "Brechtian" argument—the Brecht of "Woe to the country that needs a hero!"—that would help him accept Abraham Lincoln's weaknesses. Lincoln was mediocre, "a first-rate second-rate man," as Phillips put it.[47] But that was not really what mattered. "The new world has never achieved a greater triumph than by this demonstration that, given its political and social organization, ordinary people of good will can accomplish feats which only heroes could accomplish in the old world!"[48] Lincoln would become Marx's hero only with his death. In 1865, the address written by Marx in the name of the International contained lines that have the ring of a discreet mea culpa: "Such, indeed, was the modesty of this great and good man, that the world only discovered him a hero after he had fallen a martyr."[49] As for his successor, Andrew Johnson immediately came under the same suspicions of opportunism and compromise the assassinated Lincoln had been absolved of: "In six months," Engels wrote to Marx, "all the old villains of secession will be sitting in Congress at Washington."[50]

It was a strange, primitivist scene of sour solidarity, and one whose criticism and reticence toward the North would be retained by the Marxist tradition.[51] Marxist exegesis would effectively pull these texts in two principal directions. The first was toward affirming the primacy of economic causes in the war, to the detriment of the importance Marx saw in the historical and political weight of emancipation; by thus putting the accent on the war's mechanical nature, Marx's successors deprived the North American Union of the little historical "merit" it could have been granted. The second was toward denouncing bourgeois democracy, all of whose defects and failings the North illustrated. And the Marxists would be faithful to this second point—if not to the letter of Marx's published articles, at least to the spirit that inspired them and which the correspondence reveals. "Of course, like other people, I see the repulsive side of the form the movement takes among the Yankees," Marx replied to an Engels who had his back up over the North's "flabby" population; "but," he added pedagogically, "I find the explanation of it in the nature of 'bourgeois' democracy."[52] That was the key to an ambivalence constantly peeking through the solidarity. Marx and Engels did have the same two objectives for the war: the Southern oligarchy's defeat and a debunking of the North's bourgeois democracy. Engels summed this up in a long "dialectical" declamation that is worth citing in full: "Good as it is from one aspect that even in America the bourgeois republic exposes itself in thoroughgoing fashion, so that in future it can never again be preached on its own merits, but solely as a means and a form of transition to the social revolution, still it is mortifying that a lousy oligarchy with only half the number of inhabitants proves itself just as strong as the unwieldy, great, helpless democracy."[53] It is a strange rhetorical fluctuation that casts the very order of priorities into doubt. The vulgate is right in this: neither of the two confrontational Americas had the founding fathers' sympathies. Their sympathy was reserved for a potential or imaginary America.

Capitalism's Tell-Tale Heart

With the Civil War over, the reunified United States was still a socialist preoccupation. It would once more occupy the place it had been assigned by Marx and Engels twenty years earlier: that of capitalism's "tell-tale heart." Marx and Engels's interest in the United States' emerging economic prowess went back to the 1840s. It was then that Engels had announced a coming reversal of the balance of power between England and its former colony. The time was near, he predicted in 1845, when American competition would shake the British industrial colossus.[54] The Civil War produced the expected confirmation. By destroying the South's old rural economic structure, it accelerated an industrial monopolization that would not spare even agriculture itself, as Lafargue would soon point out, following the founders' hard line.[55]

The acceleration was doubly beneficial to the revolutionary cause, since it asphyxiated the European economy and stifled America's desire for immigrants. That would be the end, Marx and Engels thought, of the American social outlet and attempts at inspired emigration of European proletarians enticed by the free spaces of a chiefly agrarian economy. The less America had to offer, the more its industrial exploitation would look like (a worse version of?) Europe's, and accordingly, the risk of seeing the more enterprising elements of the European proletariat give in to the siren song of departure would be diminished.

The socialists, on this front, perpetuated the Enlightenment's old mistrust, and Marx was no less hostile to emigration in the name of the proletariat than Cornelius De Pauw had been in the king of Prussia's. Eighteenth-century naturalists had threatened the emigrant with degeneration; Marx and Engels lamented his desertion and feared his domestication. The proletarian who emigrated to the United States, like De Pauw's dogs, might stop barking—or biting. In any case, he would become one more militant lost to Europe, and not necessarily gained by the New World. Marx, and then Engels, were thus in the curious position of herding along an American socialist party largely made up of Germans whose emigration they stridently disapproved of.

The Marxist repudiation of emigration—which in France coincided with a strong tradition of cultural repugnance for exile—was a fundamental element in the troubled relationship socialism had with the United States. There was obviously something paradoxical about it, since it was rather "moralistic" to admonish those who were making such a choice—most often under terrible political, economic, religious, or ethnic pressures. For those emigrants, emigration was a grasp at survival; they had hit bottom, and America was what they shoved against trying to reach the surface. But these pressures were not what interested Marx, Engels, and the other socialist theorists contemporary with the triumph of steam. Capitalist society was, for them, a speeding locomotive whose furnace should be pushed to explosion. The emigrant was thus doubly wrong: objectively, he lowered the pressure in Europe, and subjectively, he gave credence to the idea that elsewhere, somewhere in the world, there was a more breathable atmosphere. He believed the lie of fresh air. European socialism, on principle, condemned the individual escape hatch of emigration because it delayed the revolution. More mutedly but more passionately, it detested the air duct known as America.

Of all their contemporaries, it was Nietzsche who most bluntly described the "socialist leaders'" obsessive attempts to rein in their troops. The fragment of *Daybreak* entitled "The Impossible Class"[56] is worth citing in full here; it is a page of striking argumentative lyricism in which Nietzsche opposes his New World symphony to the refrain of "the Socialist pied-pipers" with their "wild hopes" of seizing power. They were the only ones, in Nietzsche's opinion, with a vested interest in turning the proletarians away from the American adventure, that "great swarming out" of "the European beehive," that "free emigration in the grand manner." To counter the captious warnings of leaders fearful of seeing their troops melt away, he proposed the voice of the proletarian nomad: "Better to go abroad, to seek to become *master* in the new and savage regions of the world and above all master over myself; to keep moving from place to place for just as long as any sign of slavery seems to threaten me." Anything, even death, "rather than to go on becoming soured and malicious and conspiratorial!" To the prison devised by socialist leaders in the suffocating arena of old Europe, proletarians should prefer the open seas. They should save themselves, and Europe with them: "Let Europe be relieved of a fourth part of its inhabitants! They and it will be all the better for it!"

Nietzsche formulated this impious wish in 1881. His America of the Great Promise—which was not a promise of ease—was precisely the one all of Marxist literature, at exactly the same time, was attempting to extirpate from militant spirits, by repeating, like Poe's raven, that it was already too late, that America was saturated, that it was as stifling as Europe, that "nevermore" would it be a land of "opportunity."

American Socialism's "Prodigious Zigzags"

There had been, however, in Marx and Engels's opinion—for a few years, in any case—an American promise: a collective one born of struggles, a promise of revolution. The America of the Gilded Age and the Great Upheaval was not only the site of a great economic leap forward that led Marx to affirm in 1879 that Great Britain's growth rate had been surpassed,[57] it was also the country of mass strikes with insurrectional overtones, and brutal repression, symbolized by the death sentences pronounced after the bloody Haymarket Square riot (May 4, 1886). Marx was able to catch a glimpse of this march toward radicalization before his death in 1883. It already seemed to be bearing political fruit. The campaign of Henry George, an independent, "social" New York mayoral candidate running on the United Labor Party ticket, was an unhoped-for success. The writer finished a very honorable second

(Theodore Roosevelt came in third). This glorious defeat enthused Engels, who would almost forget that the author of *Progress and Poverty* was in fact one of the reformist bourgeois he so often frowned on.[58] "History is on the move over there at last," he rejoiced in 1887, before deciding the following year to make the trip to America.[59]

The euphoria would be short-lived; but between the end of the Civil War and the 1880s, when labor emerged as an autonomous force with the same energy, it seemed, as the trusts imposing their empire on the economy, the United States' stock rose wildly on the socialist market. Until then, America had only been an indirect trump card in the game of the global workers' movement. In ceasing to be a postcolonial outlet for European overproduction and a safety valve for the Old World's overflowing work force, the United States was "objectively" sabotaging a system it had up to then helped survive. Not only did the growing efficiency of a production system constructed far from Europe's protectionist barriers now situate it as a competitor to European capitalism—which was suddenly ipso facto weakened—but the brutality of monopolization created a heightened revolutionary consciousness in America itself. By the early 1870s, socialist thinkers were no longer relegating the United States to an adjunct role: hopes raised by America's political progress led them to consider socialists' rise to power as not only possible, but perhaps closer to becoming a reality than in Europe. Moreover, it would only be logical and orthodox that the country in which the powers of production had clearly attained their highest level of development was also the one in which socializing the means of production was the most readily practicable. The contemptible trust system was surely just one of history's tricks: a shortcut to collective appropriation. In short, America, in the course of the revolution, would overtake England (where socialism was dragging its heels) and even Germany (where *Sozialdemocratie*'s electoral successes seemed powerless to shake the government's authority).

Except, of course: on this decidedly unpredictable earth, which the Marxists were always systematically trying to fit into known and universal schemas, nothing seemed to follow a completely steady path. Ups followed downs with disconcerting speed. It would take a shrewd theorist indeed to truly tell which way the wind was blowing. Right after the Great Upheaval, it became clear that the movement was extremely unstable and its experiment precarious. The Socialist Labor Party, after making progress in 1878, lost steam in 1879 and lagged for several years before gathering its forces in 1885.[60] At the height of his American euphoria, Engels himself had sensed socialism's imponderable volatility across the Atlantic. In the same letter in which he rejoiced at seeing America on the move again, he added that in no case would it follow "the classic straight line"—European-style evolution—but would move forward in "prodigious zigzags."[61] Rather than in thunderous jags, though, it was in increasingly disconcerting small dips and rises that the American movement progressed (and mostly regressed). The socialists, in turn, like the democratic republicans they abhorred—though for completely different reasons—would be the ones disappointed with America.

Disappointed first by the violent social movement's drop throughout the 1880s. Then by the painfully slow rise of socialist membership, followed by the Labor candidates' electoral stagnation. Between 1892 and 1898, De Leon's[62] Socialist Labor Party rose from 20,000 to 80,000 votes. It was an impressive growth spurt, but in numbers the tally was still paltry. Under the leadership of the charismatic (but hardly Marxist) Eugene Debs, the Socialist Party of America garnered 400,000 votes in 1904 and more than double that in 1912: a tidy sum, but one that nevertheless only represented 6 percent of the vote. Some twenty years after Engels's trip to the United States, the American socialists only had one representative in the House and only governed one city, Milwaukee, won over in 1910. Even more than these feeble breakthroughs, though, it was American militancy's weakness that provoked the skepticism of European observers. A qualitative weakness: it is a euphemism to say that American Labor was not very well armed, doctrinally speaking; and to consider this, as Engels did, an effect of American culture's disinclination for "abstraction" was a very relative consolation. A quantitative weakness, as well—and above all—since the number of adherents remained extremely low (25,000 in January 1904). After the electoral high-water mark in 1912, a rapid and irrecoverable descent began during World War I because of the party's neutrality, for which it was often perceived as pro-German rather than pacifist. "An implantation with brilliant beginnings would be cut short," Marie-France Toinet writes—a sober assessment of a failure that would continue to echo long afterward in European socialism.[63]

French Socialists' Uncertain Gaze

Synthesizing the letdowns and summing up European uncertainties, a book by Werner Sombart asked the question in 1906: *Warum gibt es in dem Vereinigten Staaten keinen Sozialismus?* Why on earth, after all, *was* there no socialism in the United States? The Tübingen sociologist would not keep his saintly aura among orthodox Marxists for long, but at the time he was still one of the most effective popularizers of Marx's economic thought. His book gave voice to a debate that was already latent in Europe. No country, no strain of socialism would be able to bypass the question. Through the American example, the postulate of a "necessary" correlation between capitalist development and the advent of socialism was called into question.

The impact of Sombart's work was due to neither its originality nor its rigorous analysis. The idea of a deficiency, proclaimed in the title and extensively elaborated on in the body of the work, concludes, pretty bizarrely, with a prophecy announcing the advent of socialism in America *in spite of everything*. But it was perhaps in its very ambiguities that Sombart's book exercised its most lasting influence. By reducing American socialism to its meanest share, he rubbed balm on the wounds of European socialists mortified to see themselves so quickly surpassed by the transatlantic offshoot. By describing the living conditions of the American workers as superior, he offered an explanation (furiously contested by the Marxists, but which interested the "possibilists") for their strange indifference to socialism. But he also described the well-paid American worker as the most brutally exploited worker in the world. He was a lemon to be squeezed and tossed out, and this left the door wide open for future revolt.

Ambiguity decidedly had its dividends. By maintaining both that America, the "land of the future," had a working class that was fundamentally alien to socialism, but that reversing this situation could be the work of a single generation, Sombart may have pleased no one, but he interested everyone. His answers disappointed or irritated the militants. But the evil had been rooted out. The question that had haunted the most confident socialists since the days of Engels's promises had now been spoken aloud. The book, in this sense, had a revelatory importance. Even in the reactions it aroused, it brought to light a disenchantment with American socialism that manifested itself in Europe, starting in 1905, as a lack of contributions on or new theories about the United States.[64] It is true that the 1905 revolution in Russia, as well as tensions and threats of war in Europe, did play a part in turning attention away from America. But there was clearly, aside from dashed hopes, a certain weariness over the American conundrum.

Warum? Sombart's question was better stated than his answers. The detractors of his "possibilism" did not neglect to point this out. Not unjustly, either. For who could boast of having solved the American riddle? Engels himself seemed to have given up at the time of his death. That is suggested in a letter to Sorge in which a desperate Engels seeks refuge in the most worn-out cliché: that of the New World's "youth," rewritten in this paradoxical form: "America is the *youngest*, but also the *oldest* country in the world. Over there you have old-fashioned furniture styles alongside those you have invented all yourselves . . . in the same way you keep all the intellectual old clothes discarded in Europe. Anything that is out of date over here can survive in America for one or two generations."[65] In this dialectical parable, America had shifted from the avant-garde to the rear guard. Ideologically, it was still playing in democratic Europe's old sandbox. Engels's idea, in fact, was itself no longer a toddler. Volney had already mocked, as we have seen, "the extravagant mistake of writers who call a *new* and *virgin people* an assemblage of inhabitants from old Europe."[66] That was in 1803. Which goes to show that permanent intellectual rehashing is not a strictly American phenomenon. It was a meager consolation, for the American friends of an elderly Engels in utter political confusion, to hear the nearly century-old refrain dialectically remobilized once more to calm their militant impatience.

France did not escape a debate that mobilized most of the European followers of the socialist tide: Liebknecht, Bebel, Aveling, Hyndman, not to mention Marx and Engels themselves, along with sympathizers from Sombart to H. G. Wells. Furthermore, how could one keep at arm's length a controversy whose every aspect (from the American worker's "well-being" to the notorious synchronous development of capitalism and revolutionary forces) had weighty doctrinal consequences? There were many differences, however, between the way the "American question" stirred the German and English socialist parties and the way French socialism reacted—which consequently created an "imagined America" particular to the French Far Left, which was internationalist by vocation but Gallocentric by tradition.

These differences can chiefly be explained by French socialism's double remove in this affair: the remove from the Marxist approach to America of an important part of the movement, dominated by the voices of "independent" socialists, Proudhonians, "possibilists," or "anarcho-syndicalists"; and a greater remove from America itself. Most French militants, whatever their ideological family, kept their distance from an unfamiliar country and an American party that, though it was a sister organization, was still seen as mainly an offshoot of German *Sozialdemocratie*. This perception was moreover not particular to the French, and it corresponded to a concrete fact. German immigrants and Americans with German roots would long produce the majority of American socialism's leadership and even its troops. The Socialist Labor Party was truly German-speaking, literally as well as figuratively, since the majority of its press was written in that language—despite Friedrich Engels, who was wary of expatriates he saw as a little too steeped in "traditional struggles" and exasperated by the haughty isolation they seemed to indulge in.[67] *Internationalisme oblige:* while Engels had no problem qualifying his ex-compatriots as sectarian hens, French comrades remained respectfully discreet on the matter. Yet they hardly had any affinities with these often dogmatic socialists who deliberated in German, with just a hint of an English accent. Because if the Socialist Labor Party had tight and practically filial relations with *Sozialdemocratie,* it was also in permanent, close contact with the British socialists, who were glad to have an influence that their mother country often refused them.

The Germans and the English thus had a near-monopoly on relations with the American movement, due to a shared language, culture, and militant tradition. And also the simple fact that men (or women) circulated. As early as 1872, when Marx decided to protect the International from both bourgeois repression and the heterodox ambitions of rival factions, he transported its headquarters to New York—not because it was a land with a mission, but rather as a kind of "Anglo-Saxon" no-hunting zone. It was an ambiguous transfer, in all respects, and one the First International would never really recover from: four years later, in 1876, it would be buried in Philadelphia without flowers or wreaths. But even in the somewhat bleak muddle of transferring the moribund International, Marx and his followers' close ties with America are apparent. Furthermore, far from slowing exchanges, liquidating the First International led to a proliferation of visits from British and German comrades in the following decade.

Clearly, the ties the French socialists had with the United States and the social movement that was forming there were far less solid, a fact that bespeaks an interest in the American situation that was both limited and intermittent. They did not have any particular part to play with the American Socialist Labor Party. They were neither mentors nor privileged interlocutors. Their information, almost always secondhand, had to be drawn from other European socialist sources or worse, from the dubious accounts of non-Marxist or even antisocialist French experts, journalists, or travelers.

A prominent source of information on American labor, in this context of scarcity, was the openly anti-Marxist Musée Social. The Musée Social prolonged the intellectual legacy of Frédéric Le Play and his "social economy," which, "contrary to political economy . . . was based on an inductive methodology of positive observation."[68] In the years from 1880 to 1900, it regrouped or compiled the majority of empirical studies on the United States. It was as part of its ambitious program of international missions that Paul de Rousiers, after having visited England's trade unions, made his trip to America. Lasting contacts were established with the U.S. Department of Labor and the American Institute of Social Service. In 1896, William Willoughby, an expert with the U.S. Department of Labor who would take over as head of the Institute for Government Research in 1916, described the French Musée Social as a true "international bureau of labor."[69] In addition to this, the Musée Social had ties with the École Libre des Sciences Politiques, founded in 1871 by Émile Boutmy, which boasted personalities such as Jules Siegfried (father of the historian who would write *America Comes of Age*) and the liberal economist Leroy-Beaulieu. Even if the Musée Social was more interested in Great Britain than the United States, it was still the most active center for investigation and analysis of American society in France at the turn of the century. Such an intense interest on the part of these "economists," who were endlessly denounced by the Marxists and subject to a violent antisocialist campaign in 1895, could only cast doubt on the country that was the object of their attentions. And it was clearly not this impure source that the socialists would go to for their information on the United States.

America itself did not help further its own cause. While sources of information in France were scarce and unreliable, in America they were nonexistent. There was no large proletariat of French extraction to play the part of collective "correspondent." Limited to the world fairs, militant workers' trips remained a marginal phenomenon. The leaders themselves, who did not have the same problems financing their trips or making the time to travel, were no less disinclined to cross the Atlantic. Indeed, it was not the French leaders who crossed the ocean, met with American militants, and spoke at congresses in Chicago and Milwaukee, but rather the two Liebknechts, Wilhelm and Karl; not Jaurès, but Engels and later Trotsky. It was the founders of the English party, such as H. M. Hyndman, who would go to the United States several times between 1871 and 1880. It was not Marx's French sons-in-law, Paul Lafargue and Jean Longuet—although they had both written on the United States; it was his third son-in-law, the flamboyant Edward Aveling, Eleanor Marx's husband, whose lavish American expenses would lead to serious tensions between the SLP comrades asked to pay them and the British socialists . . . If the French "possibilists" close to Kautsky seemed to be the most interested in the American example, they were nonetheless in no hurry to go verify their theories in person. And while Ramsay MacDonald, the future Labour prime minister, also made the ritual American journey, visiting Pittsburgh's steel mills or the slums of New York did not seem indispensable to his French counterpart, Alexandre Millerand. The same thing went for writers interested in social problems. Zola was not about to set out for the New World; it was the author of *The Time Machine* and *The War of the Worlds*, H. G. Wells, who went there to observe the class struggle and came back with *The Future in America: A Search for Realities* (1906).

Throughout this period, France dispatched only two well-respected writers to the United States—Henri de Régnier and Paul Bourget. Social problems were not their forte. The highlight of Henri de Régnier's journey was fainting in the middle of a visit to the Chicago slaughterhouses. When Jules

Huret, in turn, made the ritual visit, he was "shown the place where Monsieur Henri de Régnier, that delicate poet of melancholy idylls, princesses in hyacinth gowns, thyrsus-bearers, palms and unicorns, was unwell."[70] From unicorns to corned beef—it is not hard to see how that could have been a shock. Much younger and more literarily sanguine, Paul Bourget nonetheless did not have a background as a social observer. He had just made a fine show with *Cosmopolis*, a "novel of manners" set in an extremely chic Italy that was no longer exactly Grand Tour and not yet jet-set. As the East Coast socialites' darling, Bourget was kidnapped by the rich Mrs. Gardner and proceeded to observe the "American soul" from his vantage point in Newport. Over the course of his eight-month stay—a very respectable length of time for a French traveler in America—he would leave the "house of mirth" only to do a little slumming at parties in New York, in the Bowery. Mark Twain was not the only one who made fun of him. He "only saw the New-Port [*sic*] 'four hundred,'" ironically noted Urbain Gohier, one of the rare French visitors interested in the workers' world to make a trip to America in the early twentieth century. Intellectual France's emissaries to America were nothing but "academic freeloaders or mercenary moralists,"[71] Gohier scoffed.

But Gohier, that rare bird of transatlantic exchanges, was an exception that did not prove any rule. How can we classify a man who published a piece entitled "Spartakus" in Péguy's *Cahiers de la quinzaine* and wrote in 1903, the same year as his American study, a scathing attack on the socialist Left, in which he particularly roughed up Waldeck-Rousseau,[72] a man working for "great monks and great Jews,"[73] and Jaurès,[74] "the most verbose, inconsistent, and brazen charlatan the South of France has unleashed on the capital in a long time"?[75] A pacifist and internationalist, anticlerical and hostile to "familial tyranny" but disappointed with socialism and Dreyfusism, Gohier was particularly ambivalent about the American unions, which he described as "threatening the capitalist regime much more seriously than our clubs and little politicians,"[76] even as he refused to call a winner between "capital and work trusts."[77] He would later, from 1919 to 1939, write for the *Bulletin du service mondial,* whose headquarters were in Erfurt, before descending into collaborationism and signing violently anti-Semitic articles, notably in *Au pilori*. In 1903, this unclassifiable libertarian, who rebelled against any and all labels, often trumped Paul Bourget for political incorrectness: when he jeered, for example, at the unionized comrades in Chicago who "demanded that policemen's nightsticks carry a union sticker"![78] Between the populist Gohier, who observed with ambiguous irony America's "fat, well-dressed, well-scrubbed, well-rested workers," who were given the "salary of professors at the Collège de France,"[79] and Bourget, the high-society psychologist who could not imagine a redemptive change for America unless it came "from the worker"[80] (a species he had not frequented much), the ideological to-ing and fro-ing often defied all social standpoints. It was not, in any case, with informers like these that the French socialist movement could get a clear idea of what was happening in the United States.

There were numerous smoke screens, then, blocking America from the French socialists; and American socialism and unionism had an important part in this, with their impenetrable ways. Gohier's ironic remark about unionists who would only accept "being beaten with clubs made by unionized workers"[81] is more than just a joke. It indicates a widespread incomprehension among the French working class toward the mysterious unions, formidable instruments called into service for demands the French judged derisory. For the same Gohier did not fail to recognize "the solid organization, discipline, and resources of American workers' unions."[82] He even took a sly pleasure, as we have seen, in favorably contrasting them to the French proletariat's politicized organizations. But he would have trouble bringing the French militant socialists around to his convictions. Judging by the reports emanating from the workers' delegates who made the trip to America, notably for the world fairs, their viewpoints remained utterly divergent. What was the use of having such a powerful organizing force if the demands were so unrevolutionary, if they did not at least force the "social problem" in its entirety to be dealt with? That was the logic—and would stay the logic for quite some time—of the "worker-delegates . . . thus confronted with the veritable paradox of an admirable organization serving unambitious ends."[83] Were the unions in America absolutely and fatally self-serving? Reformist? Potentially revolutionary? All of the above? There was no way of knowing. Or rather, no one was saying. While Gohier was crossing paths with union men who did not joke around about where the nightsticks came from, the national congress of the American Federation of Labor just barely managed to overrule a motion backed by the socialists inviting American unionists "to organize their economical and political power to secure for labor the full equivalent of its toil."[84] And if the extremely antisocialist head of the American Federation of Labor, Samuel Gompers, had tongues wagging in France over his huge salary ($25,000 a year, as much as a boss!), he was nevertheless invited to speak at CGT[85] headquarters in 1909, with all the honors due to his rank.

Such contrasts or contradictions disconcerted French militants. All these "exotic" traits, from the most benign (the worker dressed like his employer) to the most brutal (the strikers fighting back, bullet for bullet, in gunfights with the Pinkertons) were so many cultural and social riddles, which the militant press attempted to solve while the popular press mined them for its serials and melodramas. It was a hard task and a rarely successful one. Of the different aspects of American life, work relations and conflicts were probably the hardest to translate into French terms and customs, and travelers' accounts seemed impossibly contradictory or simply unbelievable. On the whole, these disoriented witnesses betrayed their confusion when faced with a "working world" so different from their own. The *Figaro* correspondent Jules Huret notes that it is hard to talk about the country. Writing *En Amérique* was a real challenge, he admits, because, over there, "the usual expressions do not apply."[86] In this, bourgeois travelers and militant observers were in the same boat. Welcome to the land of disconcerting truths! People talked profusely and hid nothing. They laid out figures and things. They presented men. No one got in the way of Frenchmen's curiosity, no one was reticent to questioning. This open book was, however, none the less incomprehensible. Urbain Gohier, who scoffed at Bourget for having frequented only the rich and famous, himself gained a sense of intellectual relief from the wealthy, who were soothing in their immutability: "There is however one immutable thing: the extravagance and ineptitude of multi-millionaires who make up the troop of the 'Four Hundred' or Society."[87] The rich were limpid, in contrast with the strange workers, who were "fat, well-dressed" and even "well-scrubbed," and who were perhaps the French workers' brothers, but certainly not their likenesses.

There were information gaps, interpretive difficulties, striking flares of interest—at the time of the Haymarket trial, notably—followed by rapid drops into near-indifference: pre-1914 French socialism maintained relations with the United States that were both distant and intermittent. The absence of direct ties via a proletariat of emigrants with French roots that could facilitate the transfer of political cultures deprived these relations of a human dimension, of any real familiarity. If the French workers or their delegates, on meeting their American counterparts, did not feel any kinship, it was first and foremost because they did not identify with them. They were also unanimously hostile to emigration.[88] Their profound distrust for the myth of an American land of plenty and their attachment to a national identity that was already considered to be inevitably pulverized by "the absorbing force of the American nation"[89] was far more effective in quelling their desire to leave than all the militant exhortations in the world. Too disembodied in militant analyses or too strange to be completely believable, working America failed to "take" in the French movement's imagination. The few traits that won workers' attention were contradictory and disconcerting. How could the extreme violence of the strikes and their repression be reconciled with the comfort the American worker was said to live in? What explanation could be made for the fact that in a political system said to be totally democratic, no party representing the workers had ever emerged? How could the flooding into America of a work force from fifty different nations not be detrimental to the cohesion of the workers' camp? None of these questions had an answer, and then current events brought up a new question: What on earth was the United States—described as pacifist and anticolonialist, though it may have dislodged Cuba from the Spanish monarchy—doing in the Philippines if not exactly the same thing as the Europeans: chasing after empires and footholds?

The Three Anti-Americanisms of the First Wave of French Socialism

In the French socialist camp, before World War I, there were three ways of being anti-American.

The most classic arose from the imperious necessity of fighting and unmasking all those "republicans" and "democrats," who were as harmful on the ideological front as the "economists" were in another sphere. America had always been a model for some of them, starting with the most venerable, the one whose funeral was a national event in 1885: Victor Hugo, an admirer of John Brown, Lincoln, and American unionism. These Second Empire "republican democrats'" idealist speeches relied heavily on the American reference, potentially misleading the French workers into believing that "democracy," sheerly as an institutional form, was the solution to their problems and the right answer to their aspirations. In the thick of the Civil War, as we have seen, Marx and Engels did not forget for a second the shortcomings of the very government they supported. Denouncing the imposture of this false model remained a major preoccupation for the inheritors of the Marxist legacy. Because if the image of a sister republic had been largely decaying in France for several decades, convergence was still a danger; the baton might be passed from a previous generation of republican bourgeois who had snowed the workers to a new generation with swelling numbers of reformist renegades. It was a potentially formidable collusion, especially since it was embodied by such a figurehead as Jaurès: Jaurès, who cloaked the collectivist project in humanist ideals; Jaurès, who did not repudiate Millerand's participation in a "bourgeois" government; that same Jaurès who rarely missed a chance to praise American institutions. The "scientific" Marxists' counteroffensive inevitably included denouncing America as a false model.

Then there was the "sectarian" way, linked to the movement's doctrinal, internal debates. The United States was an excuse to liquidate old quarrels, because revolutionary socialism was caught between a rock and a hard place. It had to keep up its guard to the Left and the Right: reformists who pointed to social progress in the United States to back up their theories, and revolutionary syndicalism, tempted by anarchy, which culled arguments and martyrs from America's social violence.

The reformists, first off. Very early on, following Eduard Bernstein, whose *Socialisme évolutionniste* appeared in 1899, European "revisionists" instrumentalized the American case. They first used it to theoretical advantage, since socialism's meager progress in the United States did not seem to confirm the Marxist theory of a parallel development of capitalism and the forces destined to topple it. Since the superpower of America's capitalist economy had not given rise to an organized workers' movement of equivalent force—far from it—the American case justified doubts about the theory of "insurmountable contradictions," the orthodoxy's cornerstone. With this doubt tossed out, "revisionism" could propose partial and temporary advances, whose model was also American. Was it so wrong, the "possibilists" suggested, to win certain stages now, like the American unions, rather than waiting for dying capitalism to finish its last lap? Especially since these "timely" gains, far from being mere crumbs from the bourgeois banquet, were called, for example, the eight-hour workday? It was easy for "possibilists" and "Broussists"[90] to point out that the International's high-priority demand had already been satisfied in some of America's industries. Some, like Gustave Rouanet, an undisguised admirer of America, pushed the ideological deviation even further, suggesting that socialism could arise only in a context of material abundance and after the intellectual and moral elevation of the proletarians had made them worthy of their historical mission. Without going quite so far, greater and greater numbers of militants began to wonder about a peaceable passage to socialism being facilitated by industry's concentration into trusts. A revisionist like Eugène Fournière went so far as to write an apology of the trusts in *La Petite république:* they were less oppressive to the worker because they guaranteed him the best wages, and by substituting organization for competition, they helped regulate production, thus sparing workers from the ups and downs of industrial crises. "The trusts," Fournière concluded, "have been the agents of this formidable power. Criticizing them would not accomplish anything. I consider, moreover, that the socialists would be wrong indeed to look on these formidable collective enterprises with an evil eye, and still more wrong to applaud the legislative proposals whose object is to break them."[91] The same went for the antitrust laws—which in any case reunited French socialists of every stripe, along with the liberals, in shared incredulity.

The American model of high productivity and high salaries presented a considerable danger of leading the proletariat astray: the America of workers' well-
being and so-called social advancements was in desperate need of debunking.
The goal of Lafargue's *Les Trusts américains* was to denounce Bernstein as a
"prophet of the bourgeoisie" and quell the rising tide of reformist socialism by
reaffirming the fact that capitalist concentration was first, inevitable, and second, harmful to the workers. Because not only was the credibility of Marx's economic analyses at stake; so was the class struggle's strategic centrality. An
attempt would thus be made to relativize, minimize, and finally deny any real
interest in America's socialist victories. The same eight-hour workday for which
European workers were called on to make all possible sacrifices, now that it had
been granted in the United States, suddenly appeared derisory and almost frivolous. It was being applied there, yet it had not diminished capitalist exploitation one bit, since, as Lafargue reminded his readers, "in a capitalist civilization,
nothing works to the workers' advantage, not even the reforms that seem to be
in their favor at the start."[92] Whence the ambiguous reaction, too—a mix of
indignation and "relief"[93]—to the Haymarket events and other "crimes of capitalism": the reaction was heartfelt, but there was also a bitter satisfaction to be
had in seeing a capitalist and policed America drop the mask.

But the orthodoxy also had to keep an eye on the Left: anarchy was competing with socialism within the workers' movement, notably in the CGT.
Among the side effects of the Haymarket affair was a surge of solidarity for the
condemned militant anarchists and, through them, the anarchist movement
in general. No faction of the French Far Left missed the chance to protest
against a verdict that seemed like legal murder. And from the same podium,
Guesde, Longuet, Vaillant, Rochefort, and Louise Michel[94] all proclaimed their
solidarity with the accused. The Haymarket event called attention to the anarchist current's vigorous development in the United States, and the French partisans of "direct action" were not indifferent to its upsurge. The most notorious
of these partisans was Émile Pouget, editor of *Le Père Peinard*. In 1886, Pouget
borrowed from American events and the methods of "propaganda by facts"
endorsed since the London Congress. Appointed editor-in-chief of the CGT's
organ, *La Voix du peuple*, in 1900, Pouget was then able to dispatch to the entire
syndicalist movement a theoretical and tactical vision inspired by the American struggles. The decision made at the Bourges Congress in 1904 to launch a
national action for the eight-hour workday in the form of a general strike that
would start on May 1, 1906, directly acknowledged its roots in the Chicago
International Workers Association's strategy. The anarcho-syndicalist enthusiasm for an American "example" whose "imitation"[95] Pouget urged intensified
Marxist distrust for American-style militantism, while the stinging failure of

the 1906 general strike *à l'américaine* would long dissuade French syndicalists from seeking their inspiration across the sea.

The third way of being socialist and anti-American in France largely overflowed the context of theoretical debates or strategic positionings: it was the workers' way, which was different from that of the movement's thinkers. For the theorists of scientific socialism, as we have mentioned, America in 1900 was the epicenter of the awaited apocalypse, the country of capitalism's "ultimate stage," since "the trust system is working to prepare men and events for [its] 'catastrophic' end."[96] Paul Lafargue, who was announcing the good news here, put the adjective "catastrophic" in quotes. To underline history's irony? Or to spare the sensibilities of his readers, who doubtless had a personal investment in seeing wage earners disappear, but who were also more directly concerned in the cascade of catastrophes that would necessarily precede it? The third socialist anti-Americanism reflected a twofold reaction: a reaction to impressions of America received in the workers' world (bloody strikes, fierce repression, iniquitous trials like the Haymarket one, disqualifying and job-destroying mechanization), but also a reaction to the theoretical enthusiasm of the movement's leaders for the menacing American promise. This anti-Americanism was that of workers who had perfectly understood the analysis Marx and Engels had given in the 1880s; who had heard the tales and remembered the remarks their delegates had made on returning from the United States; who had seen the reports in *L'Illustration* about Mr. Pinkerton's army; who had perhaps been entertained by Gustave Le Rouge's anti-Yankee serial or had read, some evenings, the first translations of a comrade from over there named Jack London. It was these workers, these artisans, these syndicalists who would remember the brutality that cropped up during America's social crises, and who adhered to the Marxist idea that America's extraordinary growth would destabilize Europe's capitalist economy, though they did not exactly draw the same conclusions. Because clearly, the apocalypse would not be joyous. They were told that the steamroller of American competition would clear the way for the revolution by pushing European entrepreneurs into bankruptcy—they admitted this was a good sign, though they did not exactly rejoice. They were told that European capitalism had been backed into a corner of the ring and was about to fall— they wanted to believe it, but also wanted to know what price, what deterioration or destruction of their own lives, would pay for this collapse. Then they were told that of course the immense leap into the future that America was forcing on them would imply, in the short run, staggering unemployment and huge salary cuts—and they ended up wondering, and asking aloud in their reunions and congresses, if there really was cause for cheer. Rather than the International's free-trade-friendly decisions, those workers would not have minded having a little protectionism sweep in to save their bosses and their jobs; they were indignant, like their employers, that American customs duties closed a majority of markets to the Europeans; and if they were willing to rejoice at the living standards of some of their comrades across the Atlantic, it was conditional on not paying for it themselves. Those anti-Americans were, in sum, all the workers in France who (like those in Germany and England) had no problem adhering to the idea of America as a "great social laboratory," in the expression revived by Jean Longuet[97]—as long as they were dispensed from being its long-distance guinea pigs. Behind the theoretical Marxist analysis that made America out to be a golem that would devastate its capitalist demiurges, and beneath the flourishes of a paean to necessity, what dominated workers' and militants' representations and carried a much heavier weight was the obtuse certainty that nothing good could come of this America-Moloch, which, after having absorbed the European proletariat by boatloads, now threatened to swallow up, with the European economy itself, those who had so far escaped it. "If capitalism blows in America, it will blow in Europe," Lafargue promised in 1903. His prophecy would have better pleased the French proletarians to whom it was addressed if it had not been coupled with an evocation of the "victims, which, in all levels of society, will be in the millions."[98]

The trusts' disastrous apotheosis was at the heart of a messianic socialism whose tone grew more and more exalted over the years, as if the good word of the "system's" violent end was trying to compensate for the dismal bulletins coming from the American syndicalist or political front. Lafargue saw perfectly well that the apocalypse would be not only unsmiling but unprofitable to the proletarians, if conscious and organized revolutionary forces did not seize the opportunity. On the penultimate page of *Les Trusts américains*, he slipped in a tardy homage to the "New World comrades," the way you give a weak student a bonus point. A praiseworthy attention, but one that hardly offset the aura of omnipotence left by his description of the trust system. The capitalists, he wrote in summing up, "think that the trusts, well stocked with capital and solidly organized around a national and international base, will resist the economic torment and rise up even more gigantic upon the ruins around them."[99] What reader, after having closed Lafargue's little book, would not share their viewpoint?

Collectivism and Feudalism

At the turn of the twentieth century, North America had become the irritating x in a socialist equation where the trust was a second variable. But the importance the trust had taken, not only in specialist analyses, but also in the collective imagination, reflected a confusion in the face of America's social configuration that did not only involve the socialists. The fascination exercised by the trust system was part and parcel of a twofold obsession: that of America's rising power and that of an aggravation of the "social question." The trust system did not provide these worries with any answers. It *fixed* them, whence its rapid and lasting implantation in the French imagination and vocabulary. From Left to Right, everyone believed in the trust system's omnipotence; it was thought to represent far more than a simple economic tool; it was generally considered to be the new cornerstone of the American social institution. The trust system, that financial and economic ogre, was swallowing up or would also swallow up all social relations. Its iron law would replace the interplay of politics. It alone would be the power and the law, the source of all wealth and authority.

Its success was primarily semiotic. It had no use for descriptive precision or analytical pertinence. On the contrary, it had a capacity for sustaining ambivalence. The trust system was a good "mythological" vector for the passions it aroused, but also and especially for the leeway it left its commentators to freely exploit contradictory conceits. Thus the trust system was presented both as a typically American ill—"all the American industries have been *entrusted*," wrote Johanet[100]—and as a structure with universal authority—"it is spreading over the whole world," wrote Lafargue.[101] Still more strikingly, the trust system described by the French combined absolute innovation with the most radical archaism. It "prefigured" a future with the features of the most distant past. The American trust system was the future of the world, but this future cast humanity back to the Middle Ages.

Probably the strangest and most disconcerting aspect of the growing literature on the trust system in France was that it coupled a fear of modernity ("Americanization," globalization, anonymous structures, "new trade" dominating production) with a fantasy of regression to humanity's brutal preindustrial youth. The Middle Ages was not exactly a positive reference around 1900. The big surprise is that the feudalism metaphor is everywhere in these texts. The trust system, that paragon of modernity, threw humanity back to the Dark Ages. As though by an unconscious return of cyclical thought, the final stage of capitalist development revived the most ancient of times. "Trust system" was thus no longer an essentially economic and social descriptive category, but rather an implicit historiographic category modeled on the (nineteenth-century terms) *monarchic system, imperial system*, and, fittingly, *feudal system*. In this second schema, the leap into the future was a cry of "Onward into the past!" The "go-a-headism" [*sic*] that Chasles made out to be a characteristic feature of the Yankee was hustling everyone into the past. Rockefeller's America was an electrically lighted repeat of the feudal night, an industrial remake of the age of barbarity. In an astounding condensation of contraries, America's present had become both Europe's future and its past: a future as unforgiving as it was inevitable, and all the more terrifying because the Europeans had already lived through it. It was a nightmare scenario: the dreamer is all the more terrified of the imminent catastrophe because he is convinced he has already been through it.

This "barbarous," "medieval," or "feudal" fantasy was the common ground for French commentaries on the trust system. It was not unrelated to the major theme of the 1880s: "American aristocracy." The important thing, in both cases, was to denounce democratic American modernity as a myth. Thus Paul de Rousiers, reproaching Tocqueville for having given credence to the idea of America as a democracy, added that if the "ancient Southern chivalry . . . seem[ed] to be sinking more and more into mediocrity," another had taken its place, that of the Carneggies [sic] and the Morgans. Not only was "the American Republic . . . not a whit more of a union of men absolutely equal among themselves, [but] from one point of view they are more unequal than anywhere else," since there was nothing to check the power of the mighty.[102] The trusts' reign confirmed and aggravated the observation. Little by little, medieval imagery replaced ancien régime analogies. The myth of American equality was now proved false not only by the existence of an unavowed aristocracy, but also by the fact that the poor and the weak were subjugated. The iron law of profit redoubled the iron law of race "to such an extent," Bourget wrote, "that, from time to time, this democracy gives the impression of an aristocracy—I was going to say, of a feudal state."[103]

A superfluous rhetorical precaution; by the end of the century, the paradox of a feudal America had entered the doxa. Edmond Johanet gave another example of this. Like Paul de Rousiers, he showed a marked continuity with the previous generation's skepticism toward the false American democracy (Johanet refers back to the Baron de Mandat-Grancey),[104] but his innovation was the medieval imagery he called on to illustrate democracy's elimination: "The aristocracies of name and fortune have made themselves the masters of America's democratic constitution, and one can say without exaggeration that politics in the United States has in fact turned into public government by a privileged caste's private interests."[105] Johanet devoted some hundred pages to describing a universe of privileges and usurpations, in which Ward Max Allister, the "inventor" of the Four Hundred,[106] rubbed shoulders with the fair maidens of New York society, whose cost of upkeep was estimated at a thousand dollars a year.[107] He took his readers on a lengthy stroll through "millionaires' churches" such as the Presbyterian church on Fifth Avenue. But he was really describing a trip back in time: "lords of high lineage, noble fathers or young squires, suitably accoutered in the latest style, escorting princesses from the golden age."[108] A peaceful domination. The masters of the "house of mirth" were also masters of the world: "Isn't the democratic nation in the power of an aristocracy armed with all a feudal regime's instruments of domination?"[109] And the federal government? It was under supervision. Like Tunisia's "Beylical government" it "lived happy and satisfied under the conquerors' tutelary rule."[110] America's institutions? A "political protectorate."[111] And the protectors, the internal conquerors, the new lords and masters, were obviously the heads of the trusts.

> The Middle Ages had no higher or more powerful barons than these American lords, all decked with gold, who gallop over plains crisscrossed by their railways and then withdraw into the fortresses of their banks and great companies that merge into trusts, those machines of oppression in which all independent competition is crushed, all commercial freedom annihilated, every object of basic human necessity taxed.[112]

In this French version, as we can see, the robber baron was not a highwayman (or railwayman), an outlaw, drunk with his own unbridled force; he was a conqueror in a subjugated land. He made the laws, paid off the politicians, and "protected" the government; he endowed the churches and married his daughters to his Fifth Avenue peers and companions. If the trust system was the world's future, these gracious lords had been given sole possession of the planet. Such was the "aristocratic regime of a completely modern feudalism to which the democratic nation is subject."[113]

From conservatives like Johanet to Musée Social researchers like Paul de Rousiers, the medieval imagery reappears too insistently to be disqualified as a simple rhetorical shorthand. As for considering it an ideological subterfuge for eluding a "materialist" analysis of the trust system, we are better off, before risking such a hypothesis, taking another look at Lafargue and his 1903 *Trusts américains:* here we find the Middle Ages again, no longer as a metaphor or an analogy, but rather as the etymological and historical base in which the trust system is rooted. Of all the *Ivanhoe*-style portraits of the United States, the most striking came from neither the "economists" nor the anticollectivists, but from Marx's French son-in-law. The illumination is all the more disconcerting because *Les Trusts américains* is a more austere piece of writing. Lafargue cultivates neither anecdotes nor typical scenes. His tableaus are completely pedagogical: the companies, their capital, and their profits are organized into neat columns. His "monographs on the trusts" valiantly assumed their status as militant treatises. Billionaires, "captains of industry," and "trustifiers" pass through his tale without embellishment. (Of Rockefeller, we learn simply that his "stomach is so worn down that he can feed himself only with milk products.")[114] But Lafargue does not deny the trust system itself the novelish qualities he refuses the Morgans and the Rockefellers. Exactly at his book's halfway mark, he suddenly stops, breaking off at the magical monosyllable he has repeated page after page. He takes it up, turns it over, draws it out. It is impossible to remain ignorant any longer, Lafargue says; the word *trust* is in no way a neologism. On the contrary, it is a kind of paleologism, a primitive signifier, "a word from a barbarian time." And not just any barbarians: "*Trust* is a word from the old Scandinavian language, which Grimm sees as derived from *trôt* or *traust,* which signifies protection, supervision." Enter the Angles. "*Trôst* is used for protector in the Nibelunge." Enter the Saxons. "Being in a chief's *truste,* being his *antrustion,* meant being in his protection. Free men and serfs who were in the Merovingian kings' *truste* were given a superior *wergeld* (compensation) for any wrong inflicted on them." Is this gratuitous erudition, pedagogical pedantry? No: he is reestablishing a pedigree, adding supplementary information in the case against the trust. Despite appearances, we have not left Detroit or Pittsburgh; we are flipping through the family album of the new overlords. "The word fell out of use in the French language, but is still used in the English language, where it conserved its barbarian meaning." Lafargue takes the opportunity to reestablish *trustee*'s etymological precedence over *trust:* "The heads of Standard Oil, the father of the trust system, were the *trustees,* that is, men the stockholders could rely on. This is probably where the use of the word *trust* to designate industrial corporations came from."[115] Before the trust were the *trustees.* Behind the industrial décor was the primitive Anglo-Saxon stage. Scratch the reader of *Capital* and you would find someone poring over Augustin Thierry. Between Hengist, Horsa, and the Nibelungen, economy was seen through the spy-hole of legend, and scientific Marxism hitched to mythography's chariot. This astonishing passage is not a gratuitous philological digression. It points to the same line of reasoning by which Lafargue thinks fit to begin a treaty on trusts with an exposé on the organization of medieval guilds. He spells it out: the trust system, in its advanced stage—and, he adds, "far from all the trusts, even the best organized and consolidated, reach this stage of evolution"—"applies the overriding principle of precapitalist production seen in the patriarchal, feudal period."[116] What could be more accurate, more fitting, once that had been said, than "to designate its organizations with a word from barbaric times"? Lafargue thus chimes in with the conservative Johanet in a similar attempt to decipher the trust system through a medieval grid and thus understand a system that has gradually spread throughout America's social hierarchy. "The American general," Johanet had written, "is none other than a duke, in the primitive sense of the word; the governor of a state of the Union has the same civil, administrative, military, and legal powers that a count would have had in the olden days; the American railroad magnate can be likened to a baron."[117] But whether they were bourgeois "economists" or Marxists like Lafargue, those who took the medieval metaphor *literally* were not the ones we might have suspected. Armored with an unshakeable seriousness, Lafargue gallops right along with Johanet's heroic fantasies, which had evoked the "high and mighty lords" of Manhattan, or those of Gustave Le Rouge, which portrayed the fearsome William Boltyn in *La Conspiration des milliardaires* speeding full steam ahead in his private train, across a prairie deserted by the trappers, like a "European head of state"—or more simply like a real baron of the new Middle Ages.

☆ ☆ ☆

The French novel of the trust system is *A Connecticut Yankee in King Arthur's Court* told backward: Mark Twain transported his Yankee to Camelot; French Marxists and liberals, equally fascinated by "trustification," projected the Middle Ages onto the United States of 1900.[118] It was decidedly the end, not only of the democratic imagery of the United States naively produced by the idealists of previous generations, but of the idea of progress on American soil. The country could only be modern in reverse. It landed squarely in medieval horrors at the end of its mad dash into the future. Late-nineteenth-century French socialism, through the complex tensions of its own internal divisions, massively confirmed its adversaries' anti-American apprehensions. In the turn-of-the-century coalescence of negative French imagery of the United States, socialism would even go much further than the conservatives irritated by American demagogy or incivility. Throwing the weight of "economic science" and its authoritarian rhetoric into the battle, it denounced the Americans' freedom as a fraud and their political system as the corrupt emanation of a real power held by the trust system. To them, Gilded Age America had given birth to more barbarism than socialism. As for the Great Republic so dear to Hugo, far from aspiring to spread a democratic ideal throughout the world, it was only interested in one thing: imposing on Europe a feudalism reestablished by "the empire of trusts."

PART II

A Preordained Notion

≡ 9

The Other Maginot Line

1917: "The Americans arrive in France. American national anthem and arms." An Épinal image.[1] A real one. It was produced in the famous Pellerin workshops. The Sammies[2] land and are greeted by French soldiers in "horizon blue." The décor has nothing realist about it; it is stagy, with a highly symbolic quality. Another plate showing the transatlantic allies is apparently more documentary: "Around an American ambulance post." This image shows the uniforms and equipment of the medical squads. And though both were "instructive," these vignettes were also heavy with intentions: their aim was to celebrate the heroic gesture of the stretcher-bearers and volunteer nurses who preceded the American soldiers onto the French battlefields.

The long-standing French clichés on this period are very similar to these two Épinal images: both would have us believe that World War I ushered in a new era of fraternal affection between the French and the Americans and revived in one fell swoop a flame that had been guttering for 125 years. Without the charming colors of the mythological template, however, the picture looks pretty different. Not only did this renewal have no future, but rarely had brothers-in-arms left the field more disgruntled with each other. Two or three years after the first Sammies arrived, France and the United States were keeping their distance again; this second honeymoon had abruptly come to a close.

At least for the Americans, entering the war opened the door to Épinal imagery, in which representations of the United States up to then had been minimal bordering on nonexistent. Out of a total production of about fifteen thousand images, mainly generated in the second half of the nineteenth century, only fifty or sixty have do to (and sometimes only slightly) with the New World.[3] An extraordinarily meager figure, and one that needs to be cut down even further, since it includes scenes of Latin America, as well as all the plates that only incidentally evoke the United States—such as, for example, "What time it is around the planet when it is noon in Paris." If we take into consideration only those images that really focus on North America, the number falls to under a dozen. No less significant than this small number of images is the choice of subjects: the discovery of America, the Savages, the Indians, General Tom Thumb, "A Clown among the Red-Skins." Current events and recent history hardly find any place among these drawings, which are devoted to America's legendary origins or to picturesque anecdotes: the uprising of the "last Red-Skins" in their reserves in the West in 1891; the "Statue of Liberty in New York" (a model kit); and, more unexpectedly, the invention of the sewing machine by Elias Howe. Clearly Pellerin cannot be accused of having *Americanized* the little French children.

Did the two images inspired by the United States' entering the war in 1917 signal a turning point—or even a revolution—for the mythological indicator that was the Épinal factory, after decades of indifference? It seems doubtful. The Pellerin company was fulfilling its patriotic contract. Since the start of the war, it had not left out a single French ally. It would have been hard to give the Americans less exposure than the Montenegrins. Like the slim volumes praising the United States that flourished between 1916 and 1918, these two images, which dutifully celebrated, on commission, the cliché of an "age-old friendship," were more the fruit of war propaganda than any real tide of opinion. The colors had barely dried when the symbol of the alliance proposed to French boys and girls had truly become . . . just a picture-book image.

From Fervor to Rancor

The Foreign Office and French diplomacy had ardently appealed for the United States' engagement in World War I. The troops were then joyously celebrated when they finally became a reality in the fall of 1917.

Congress had voted for entering the war against Germany on April 6. In May, the authorities hurried to draw 500,000 recruits from a mass of 10 million potential draftees. Pershing would soon land with a first symbolic division. By the end of 1917, 200,000 American soldiers were already on French soil, with 100,000 more landing each month. In January 1918, the Sammies, who at first had been mixed with existing corps, were regrouped into entirely American units. In July, during Foch's counteroffensive, they alone held thirty-five kilometers of front. Colonel Stanton's inspired line, "Lafayette, we are here!"; the dashing American youths, whose bravura made up for their inexperience; the weight they had thrown onto the right side of the scales at the crucial moment of Russia's defection and the Italian collapse in Caporetto: these elements all joined up to make 1917 not only an hour of grace for Franco-American relations, but also what seemed like the start of a lasting rapprochement.

Yet eighteen months later, relations had plummeted to a rarely attained degree of coldness, while the press of every stripe spouted attacks against the United States and its president. Greeted with extraordinary fervor, Wilsonian America went away dissatisfied and weary, leaving behind it a rancor the following decade would only exacerbate. Far from rekindling Franco-American warmth, the solidarity of 1917–18 had no future. Vanished as quickly as it had appeared, this euphoric moment would soon seem like an illusory aside in a relationship that had once more become distant and acrimonious. Even the memory of it would be spoiled by a widespread feeling of disappointment or even deceit in France, which was echoed on the other side of the Atlantic by the frustration of young veterans who had trouble finding their place in American society. Their great disillusionment would furnish the preferred theme of a literary generation epitomized by F. Scott Fitzgerald.

Stanton's pronouncement at Lafayette's tomb in the Picpus cemetery was a fine stroke of invention.[4] The historical parallel, however, would give him more than he bargained for. Because just as French aid to the insurgents during the Revolutionary War had not stopped bitterness and hostility from setting in between the two nations less than ten years later, Frenchmen's heartfelt applause at the Sammies' first appearance would even more promptly turn into hissing and booing at an America judged as arrogant as it was egotistical. The wreaths woven for the "boys" of the Argonne and Saint-Mihiel had hardly wilted when reproaches and accusations began shooting off in France. Without a transition, brotherhood in the trenches was replaced by a new, uncomprehending transatlantic dialogue; it would last until the next war—and beyond it.

So, we have a paradox: it was just after a war won together that anti-Americanism worsened and *set in* in France. "How is the fine gold changed to basest lead?"[5] By a fatal alchemy mixing the lead of battles with the gold of banks, the burden of debt (real and symbolic) with the weight of representations. And, at the heart of this negative transmutation, a man, first adulated, then reviled: the incomprehensible president of the United States, the impossible Mr. Wilson. He had been "received by all the peoples of Europe as a Savior" in Paris in late 1918 for the Peace Conference. (This is how Freud put it, and since he hated Wilson, we can take his word for it.)[6] He would leave the City of Light amid general hostility, only to confront an America that had also disowned him by handing the two houses of Congress over to his Republican adversaries in November 1918.

Between misunderstandings and misfirings, disagreements and disclaimers, the gap had widened again as of 1919. The socialist Left, back in its pacifist stance or dazzled by the Soviet Union, that "great light shining in the East," denounced Wilson for advocating an intervention against the Red Army: his containment policy infuriated the pro-Soviet internationalists as well as those—even more numerous—who feared it might reignite a global war in Europe. Out of solidarity with "the Soviet motherland" or exasperation with the continuation of the war, rank-and-file militants on the Left and Far Left violently rejected Wilson's interventionism—a rejection they would soon be ready and willing to extend to all things American. The deterioration of the American image on the Left did not come out of the blue. As we have seen, it had deep roots in the globally negative framework that had been in place since 1880 in the socialist camp and among the syndicalists. There was now a pervasive perception that the United States was a brutal land for the workers, and that the American socialist movement was riddled with disappointing setbacks. The country's democratic image had been seriously shaken by the violence of the police and big business during the Great Upheaval and was still crumbling in French militants' minds. In the face of institutions whose operations were often impenetrable, along with incomprehensible "comrades," there was only the concrete truth of repression and injustice. The Sacco and Vanzetti affair, which began in 1920, would refresh the memory of such wrongs for anyone who had forgotten the unfair proceedings at the Haymarket Square trial and the subsequent hangings.

But America did not look any better seen from the other side of the political spectrum. On the Far Right, in 1919, Maurras's powerful voice would cast anathema on the "naive president" of America and draw up the balance of his failings: "What is clear is that Mr. Wilson was unable to leave the Old [World] without realizing that his way of thinking had been completely eclipsed."[7] It was an observation that went well beyond the Action Française, and the nationalist Right would willingly rally to it. Public opinion in general was irritated by Wilson's efforts to moderate the victors' appetites; these efforts were considered detrimental to French interests. Incurious about internal American politics, the French were flummoxed by the United States' refusal—that is, the Republican Congress's—to join the League of Nations, which Wilson was tirelessly preaching in favor of; they were scandalized by the hostile welcome the Senate gave the Treaty of Versailles in 1919; and they were indignant at Congress's reiterated refusals to ratify the treaty, in November 1919 and March 1920. Irate at being refused the essential—an American guarantee of the borders created by the treaty—France once more turned away from the United States. Which paid France back in spades, with a landslide victory for the "Americanism" of the isolationist candidate Warren G. Harding, who was triumphally elected in 1920, and then of his successor in the White House, Calvin Coolidge.

A trial of intent followed on the heels of France's recriminations, and mistrust was retrospectively cast on the motivations and behavior of its ally America during the war. Though it had just barely been turned, the "page of glory" composed together was already being rewritten by the French.

Eleventh-Hour Workers

Wilson's attitude after 1914 was pored over and suspiciously reexamined. Hadn't he done everything he could, for several years running, to keep his country out of the "rightful war" in which France's and England's democracies were in danger of being overtaken by imperial, militaristic regimes? Hadn't he reacted with utter spinelessness to Germany's war crimes and aggressions—including when they torpedoed the *Lusitania* on May 7, 1915—and been satisfied with the vague denial of responsibility presented by the Germans right when American public opinion at last seemed ready to go much further? Hadn't he been reelected in 1916 on an ambiguous platform, promising on the one hand to keep his country "out of war" and affirming on the other: "[we] shall, if necessary, spend the whole force of the nation . . . to fight thus for the ultimate peace of the world and for the liberation of its peoples" (Omaha speech)? Hadn't he, moreover, on the eve of his country's entering the war, proposed the inadmissible objective of a "peace without victory"—which he would later convert into a "just peace" to calm his European partners? In short, if the Germans themselves, all too confident in Wilson's inaction, hadn't pushed their provocations into the realm of the unacceptable by renewing torpedo attacks on ships and urging Mexico to take the *yanquis* unawares, would America have entered the war? It was doubtful, and the doubts were spoken aloud.

And moreover, hadn't America entered the war a little late to play referee to Europe's destiny? The months of fighting side by side were a fine memory but would have been more trenchant if it had been *years* rather than months. As eleventh-hour workers, the Americans could not lay any claim to having made the same sacrifices or suffered the same woes as France, which had been invaded and bled dry. "Your intervention in the War, which you came out of lightly . . . cost you but 56,000 human lives instead of our 1,364,000 killed."[8] Words spoken not by an irresponsible muckraker or some other rabble-rouser, but by the former president of the Council and Secretary of War—Clemenceau himself—who addressed these words to the Americans in 1930; they had arrived late and taken the field even later. This lost time meant spilled blood for France: "It was heartrending to see our men being mown down unceasingly while, under the command of their good leaders, large bodies of American troops remained idle, within earshot of the guns."[9] A strange posthumous polemic with Foch[10] revealed to the French the details of a dispute that, during the conflict itself, had secretly opposed the two men over the use of American reinforcements—which Clemenceau would have preferred to draw on more quickly and massively.

These were acerbic thoughts, and part of a widely shared perception. Disappointed by the transatlantic ally, the only thing the French remembered was that America had been slow and late in coming. Proust, being the inspired entomologist of discourses he was, pinned it down in *Time Regained*. The page was written in the early 1920s and reflects the disenchantment of the time; but Proust, placing the dialogue during the war, reinforces the provocative effect of the bittersweet remarks made by the Baron de Charlus about the tardy American ally:

> "I do not want to speak ill of the Americans, monsieur, . . . it seems they are
> inexhaustibly generous and, since there has been no orchestral conductor in this
> war and each entered the dance considerably after the other and the Americans
> began when we were almost finished, they may have an ardor which four years of
> war has quenched among us."[11]

With smart acuity and multifaceted irony, Proust records the force of an anti-Americanism (here, Germanophile, "inverted," and aesthetically minded) that neither the baron's superficial patriotism nor his fear of "allow[ing] his point of view to be too clearly seen" manages to rein in. Pronounced by a cunning Charlus in the (fictive) context of 1918, when it was still taboo, the grievance of the Americans' delay in "entering the dance" was now on everyone's lips.

Similarly, the real weight of the American intervention would be subject to downscaling as the differences between the allies—which up to then had been cloaked in military secrecy—were progressively brought to the public's knowledge. Clemenceau's book *Grandeur and Misery of Victory* was the climax of this great outpouring. It was a caustic reply to Foch's posthumous attacks in a *Mémorial* that had just brought to light the little war-within-a-war that had opposed the general with the president over the way to use American reinforcements. While Foch put himself in the most flattering light—that of the "patient" leader—and gave himself the credit of having avoided a major Franco-American crisis by his tactful handling of General Pershing, Clemenceau did not back down: "The slow organization of the great American Army"—as opposed to an immediate incorporation of American soldiers into French and English divisions—"was costing us . . . seas of blood."[12] And all because "their fierce super-patriotism . . . wanted nothing less than a heaven-born strategical *coup* that should enable them to begin and to end the War spectacularly with one stroke."[13] Clemenceau hardly sounds any different than Charlus: supposedly "inexhaustibly generous," the Americans had in fact been quite sparing with their efforts and less eager to relieve their suffering allies than they were concerned with coming across as the conflict's dei ex machina. We are clearly worlds away from Épinal images here.

All in all, for the country purporting, through Wilson, to give Europe some pointers, the Great War had been short: "Fifty-two months of war, thirty-two of which the self-appointed adviser spent in a state of neutrality and twelve in military inactivity."[14] This cold summary dates from 1927. It was signed by the French politician who had been most understanding of the United States, the French high commissioner in Washington during the war: André Tardieu. And it was the same André Tardieu who, in order to dispel the "fundamental error" of basing policy on the myth of "friendship," offered, again in 1927, this pitiless account of Franco-American relations:

> Our two countries, bound by such ties of sympathy, have never made a combined effort that was not followed by immediate rupture; indeed in all other circumstances the absence of conflict can only be explained by the lack of contact. May I add that the short periods of political coöperation—less than ten years in all, out of one hundred and forty—were the result not of sentiment, but of interest; and that as soon as interest lapsed, sentiment did not suffice to maintain coöperation.[15]

Americanophiles of this stamp left little grist for the Americanophobes' mill.

Outcry against Woodrow Wilson

"Ah! That strong jaw is still present in the leafy shade of Princeton," proclaimed Maurois in a book published in 1933.[16] This assertive jaw belonged to Woodrow Wilson. The former president of Princeton University, then president of the United States of America, had died nearly ten years earlier, in 1924. But Maurois was not the only Frenchman obsessed with him.

The inscrutable face of Woodrow Wilson was, for the French, central to a new surge of anti-Americanism in the immediate postwar period. Revered and then execrated, the preaching president was the first American public figure to pay the price of embodying anti-Americanism. The rapid and violent reversal of public opinion about him reflects the disaffection for the United States that supplanted, without a transition, enthusiasm for its brave young soldiers. As the very symbol of an incomprehensible America, Wilson would continue, even after his death, to catalyze hatred and recriminations. His shadow haunted not only the groves of Princeton, but all the classics of French anti-Americanism of the 1930s. Three presidents later, Robert Aron and Arnaud Dandieu's *Le Cancer américain* would still go after "that Attila in tortoiseshell glasses" as though he were the scourge of Europe.[17] As for Maurois, his desire to shed some light on the "Wilson case" seemed so pronounced to his Princeton hosts that they obligingly organized two successive dinners, pro and contra, to satisfy his curiosity![18] To many in France, the Wilson riddle seemed like the American riddle itself: mystical yet brutal, religious yet pragmatic, excessively scrupulous yet fiendishly sure of itself. The impenetrable president, wrote Clemenceau, had "mixtures of empiricism and idealism that could never appear singular to an American"[19]—but that left the French flabbergasted.

In 1919, however, the president of the United States triumphantly arriving for the Peace Conference was not yet the incomprehensible Mr. Wilson. He was only the cumbersome ally who kept thinking up ways to put a spoke in the wheels of the victors' diplomatic wagon. In just a few weeks' time, his attempts to rein in French demands dissipated the enormous reserve of confidence he had been granted on his arrival. They were, however, mostly ineffectual. "Wilson talks like Jesus Christ and acts like Lloyd George": this quip made the rounds at the Conference.[20] Just like his ideal League of Nations, Wilson, on a practical level, kept losing ground, literally as well as figuratively. He let Great Britain take over the German colonies and reorganize the

Middle East as it saw fit; he granted Italy the German-speaking Bolzano, in contradiction of the minorities' rights he himself had pronounced. To the French he conceded the important principle of an *unlimited* timeline for Germany's reparations payments; he would even resign himself to the occupation of the Rhineland as a "deposit." In the end, it was the text of a treaty that had little resemblance to the spirit of his "Fourteen Points" of January 1918 that he would vainly attempt to have his compatriots accept. During the American campaign he made to promote its ratification, Wilson collapsed. He had barely reached Washington when a left-side hemiplegia confined him to the White House for the rest of his term.

Was he "a light that failed completely," as was recently suggested by a historian—a Princeton historian, at that?[21] Whatever the case may be, the sense of his failure is not a recent development. Wilson hardly succeeded in leaving his mark on the Treaty of Versailles; he was too obsessed with the League of Nations, which Clemenceau called his "mystical creed."[22] His own country rejected the treaty and the League of Nations. His vague desire to referee the Paris Peace Conference indisposed the victors, and his last and pathetic struggle for Congress's ratification did not win him back any sympathy. He was the one, and not the Republicans (who were in office from 1920 to 1932), that America's desertion continued to be blamed on. Clemenceau wrote in 1930, about Wilson and his "Fourteen Points": "When such responsibilities are once magnificently accepted can they be thrown off in the airy freedom of a 'separate peace'?"[23]—as though Wilson had not, before his death, given a final veto to the separate peace jointly voted for by the two houses of Congress. Clemenceau was most likely reasoning as a Frenchman, with a certain idea of the continuity of government, but at the same time, Woodrow Wilson had truly become a synonym or synecdoche for the United States. Pursuing him all the way into his grave, the French demanded an explanation for what he had done, for what he had not done, and even for what had been done despite him.

Being identified with Wilson dramatically changed the face of America. Very early on, Wilson was presented as mythomaniacal, neurotic, and possibly even insane. Through his "case," America itself was pathologized, no longer in the vein of physical deficiency, as in the eighteenth century, but in the modern tenor of mental illness. At the Peace Conference, the anticlerical Clemenceau was content to mock this strange head of state, with his Christlike ambitions. The nationalist Right, headed by Maurras, worsened the diagnosis and, what is more important, applied it more generally to the American psyche. The imputation of religious neurosis or even mystical mania was thus added to the common base of anti-American representations. It quickly became the object of a disconcerting unanimity whose most spectacular testimony was doubtless

the striking "psychological study" of Wilson co-authored by Sigmund Freud
and the American diplomat William Bullitt.[24] *Thomas Woodrow Wilson: A Psychological Study* is disturbing, not only because of the questionable and contentious nature of the work, but also because there are important echoes
between this analytical Austro-American monograph and the pathologized
"figure" of Wilson proposed in France in a completely different context—a
polemical, political one. In the *Psychological Study* we also find, not surprisingly, unambiguous traces of Clemenceau; he is cited as an informer ("[Wil-
son] thinks he is another Jesus Christ come upon the earth to reform men"),[25]
but also, and even more strangely, the implicit mark of the man who in 1919
had launched the theme of a neuropathic Wilson: Charles Maurras.

It is a striking book, especially in its animosity. Freud shows an unmasked
"antipathy" for Wilson in a preface he personally signs: "I do not know how to
avoid the conclusion that a man who is capable of taking the illusions of religion
so literally and is so sure of a special personal intimacy with the Almighty is
unfitted for relations with ordinary children of men."[26] And the final judgment
is categorical: "The qualities of his defects raised him to power; but the defects
of his qualities made him, in the end, not one of the world's greatest men but a
great fiasco."[27] But beyond this justified animosity—Freud considers Wilson
responsible for Europe's plunge into destitution between the two wars—the
coauthors of the *Psychological Study* shared with French anti-Americans the conviction that Woodrow Wilson's personal pathology was a window onto the
morbid universe of American culture itself. Wilson-madness could only be
American; America was the "pathogenic environment" that explained Wilson.

On these two points, there was complete agreement between Freud-*cum*-
Bullitt's late and finally posthumous text (it was only in 1938 that the two
would agree on the definitive version) and Maurras's essay, *Les Trois aspects
du président Wilson*, published in 1920. Across national borders, years, and
the gulf separating their different thought processes, the Austrian psychoan-
alyst's pitiless verdict corroborates and exacerbates the diagnosis sketched
out by the French nationalist. Their Wilsons are undeniably similar. For the
one, a major paranoid, for the other, a "budding autocrat," and compared by
both to Wilhelm II, Wilson was a virtual lunatic. Freud put it bluntly: "If he
had not been able to make his daily submissions to God, he might indeed
have taken refuge in paranoia and developed a 'persecution mania'; he might
have become not the occupant of the White House but the inmate of an asylum." Better yet, Wilson had escaped the asylum only because he was lucky
enough to have been born in America: "The screen of rationalizations which
allowed him to live all his life without facing his passivity to his father would
have fallen early on the continent of Europe. He was fortunate to have been

born in a nation which was protected from reality during the nineteenth century by inherited devotion to the ideals of Wyclif, Calvin and Wesley."[28] If Wilson had not ended up institutionalized, it was because he was already locked up in the madhouse of Puritan America! America: the country where a common paranoid can become president. . .

Maurras did not go quite so far. But he noted the disturbing solipsism and denial of external reality that (in his view) characterized Wilson in 1918. "After the armistice," Maurras wrote, "Mr. Wilson's eyes, nostrils, ears, and all his other human political senses seemed to have closed up. . . . It seems that, for once and for all, he went back up the mysterious stairwell only he holds the key to, into an inaccessible tower."[29] Freud leaned toward paranoia; Maurras described a kind of autism. The theme had been put forward, in any case, that the American president's "idealism" was religious monomania. How could the "naive president who plays the trumpet" have any doubts about his providential mission, since "with each of his summations, [he] thinks he sees the Dominations and the Thrones and the other European Powers of Evil roiling in the abyss"?[30] Puritan and insane, insane because he was puritan:[31] in France, the idea seemed so clear and distinct that it would have been a shame to limit its application to Wilson. It would indeed outlast him and be unthinkingly transferred to his successors. When a 1931 tract, after mentioning the White House, added in parentheses "nice name for an asylum!" the private joke was not lost on its readers.[32]

This focus on Wilson right after the war went far beyond the resentment aroused by Peace Conference frictions, or by an American defection the conference had been unable to prevent. Using new anti-American imagery, it helped create the figure of a megalomaniacal America, victim not only to a "dizzying power" (as Maurras wrote), but also to the most emblematic religious mania. Andrew Jackson, who coarsely threatened France in 1835, and Ulysses S. Grant, who dealt it a low blow in 1871, were after all nothing but a couple of old warhorses. Teddy Roosevelt had not always been easy on Europe, nor tactful with its Panama Canal; but at least he had not confused his big stick with the staff of Moses. The gentle Woodrow Wilson, living in a permanent duplex with God, irritated the French a whole lot more, just as an America that had gone back up into its "inaccessible tower" worried them; after intoxicating the Europeans with it sermons, it had suddenly stopped taking their calls.

An Autarchic Discourse

The United States' "defection" obviously established the general context of French resentment between the two world wars. However, the anti-American crescendo in the late 1920s did not arise from any given action on America's part, as could have been true in the past, with the tariff wars or the invasion of Cuba. An atmosphere of decline—both announced and repudiated by the French—was what fueled anti-Americanism, rather than any specific incident or clash. Even if it "peaked" with exceptionally emotionally charged events such as the execution of Sacco and Vanzetti in 1927, anti-Americanism no longer needed precise circumstances to emerge: it had now formed a discursive sphere that was largely autonomous from current events. The polemical wave broke in 1927. Which is to say that it coincided with the period's only episode of Franco-American diplomatic convergence, the Kellogg-Briand Pact. Which is also to say that anti-Americanism broke out before the depression and its French consequences, felt mostly after 1931. Anti-Americanism was mobilized against a prosperous and powerful America, not a crisis-stricken one. Its groundswell cannot be seen as the reaction to a global bankruptcy for which the United States was considered responsible: the accusation would only come a posteriori and would reinforce an already largely extant hostility.

Between "facts" and representations, cause and effect often seemed to have been inverted. From 1920 to 1940, there was no irremediable difference of opinion between the two countries, or even a serious point of contention other than war debt. The debt situation would unquestionably intensify anti-Americanism in the public mindset, but as we will see (in the following chapter), it was itself tangled up in a new and powerful anti-American sentiment. The declamatory heights reached by the debate over war debts in 1931 cannot be separated from the anti-Wilson diatribes and caricatures of America that had proliferated in the late 1920s. The anti-American discourse had begun to weigh on reality and distort perceptions. Wrongheaded proceedings, dangerous inertia, and transatlantic snags during the interwar years were often the product of automatic behavior resulting from a very summary image of America. No debate, no military, economic, or financial negotiation came unburdened by a heavy irrational weight.

The first feature, then, of the new anti-Americanism was its *autarchy*, which means, here, not only its increasingly self-referential logic, but also its tendency toward self-sufficiency. The rhetorical treasury amassed over the three or four previous decades, considerably enriched by a new generation of writers and polemicists, had become stabilized into an anti-American "culture" produced by a limited milieu, but widely spread beyond it, given that it was totally consensual.

Consensus does not mean unanimity. Some rebelled against this discursive straightjacket. A handful of intellectuals: André Maurois, who timidly rectified certain caricatures; Élie Faure, the author of luminous pages on New York's architecture, which make for a spectacular contrast with Duhamel's wild imaginings and Claudel's pontificating;[33] even Paul Morand, with his equivocal *New York;* and above all, Céline, the Céline of *Journey to the End of the Night,* whose clever duplicity we will come across later on. To these names, we should add several works in praise of the New Deal on the eve of World War II, and that is about all. Among politicians, the species was even rarer (and endangered): André Tardieu, whom an early and direct knowledge of American affairs had vaccinated against the tide of shared opinion, and the socialist André Philip, perhaps mollified by other contacts (he married an American woman); both of them would wear their reputation for Americanophilia like a ball and chain.

Dissidence from the anti-American consensus was highly dangerous. In France, there was nothing as useful for discrediting a public figure as making him out to be a friend of America. This technique, tested out at Tardieu's expense between the wars, would be repeated on a broad scale after the liberation. Tardieu, who had never been indulgent with America's foreign policy, had been called "the valet from *The Liar*"[34] and "a dealer in our independence."[35] Post-1945 Communist propaganda would systematically use the defamatory labels of "foreign party," "American party," and even America's "fifth column" against its adversaries. In 1948, Georges Soria denounced "what is now called 'the American party' in France, the epithet with which popular good sense designates those French politicians whose attitude consists in agreeing wholeheartedly with American demands concerning the country's political and economic life."[36] A Communist tract from 1950, *La Cinquième Colonne, la voici!* (Here's the Fifth Column!), gives the names of twenty-three Yankee agents— the most notorious being Robert Schuman (a Christian Democrat), Guy Mollet (a Social Democrat with strong Marxist leanings), and . . . Charles de Gaulle.[37] Thirty years later, the arrow was still poisoned, as Michel Rocard would discover when his faction within the Socialist Party was stuck with the label "American Left." Whether it was a political blowpipe or a gun going off in every direction, the weapon's imprecise nature did not make it any less fearsome. Among the intelligentsia as in the political world, it was a formidable ostracism machine. The consensus from which it drew its strength was not generated in the interwar years, though: it had been clear as of 1898, when anti-Americanism was already the least divisive issue in France. The new element here was that the Cuban war was no longer needed to throw the switch, as it were. French anti-Americanism was now self-starting.

As well as being autarchic, the discourse was also unanimous. The surge of anti-Americanism in the late 1920s cannot be said to have "opened a debate" on the United States; it "vituperated against" it, as Flaubert would say. None of the anti-American classics that were appearing at the time, starting with Duhamel's *Scenes from the Life of the Future*, contested or refuted any particular adversary. If real or supposed Americanophiles were informed on, their theories were blacklisted without commentary. And if the polemicist exceptionally happened to give himself interlocutors, like Aron and Dandieu in *Le Cancer américain*, the designated adversary was himself an anti-American—in this case, Georges Duhamel—considered insufficiently or too stupidly anti-American!

Were the French divided over America? Yes, if you like. But only between right-wing anti-Americans, left-wing anti-Americans, and nonconformist anti-Americans—the most virulent—who espoused a "neither Right nor Left" stance. From the nationalist, monarchist, and fascist Right to the revolutionary Left, and including various nonconformists, that made for a lot of people. Among the intellectuals who now took the affair in hand, that meant nearly everyone.

Mobilizing the Intellectuals

The second characteristic feature of the new anti-American era was the driving force of "intellectuals," who were no longer the same as before 1918, as if the production of anti-Americanism had been subjected to a kind of transfer of competence.

Before the war, in the period from 1880 to 1914, American images and analyses had mostly been passed on by travel narratives or specialized monographs, and much more rarely by fiction or essays. There were few celebrities, moreover, among the contributors: Paul Bourget is the only really well-known name in a corpus that is nonetheless substantial. In the 1920s, the equation was inverted. The great French purveyors of American images were now writers or "philosopher/writers" and were the most famous of them. From Morand to Céline, from Claudel to Duhamel, then from Sartre and Simone de Beauvoir to Jean Baudrillard, the United States was covered by a new group within the intelligentsia: novelists, poets, moralists, polemicists, essayists, and philosophers. It was a considerable and irreversible change: the arrival of film and then television images would only widen the playing field and the audience for this fictionalization of America.

The organizers of American imagery were no longer (or not principally, in any case) experts from all disciplines: the economists, political scientists, psychologists, or protosociologists whose views had overwhelmingly directed the late-nineteenth-century French gaze. Not that all those specialists turned

away from the United States. Of course there would still be scholarly investigators making analytical trips: as ever, there would be pedagogues, agrono-
mists, and increasing numbers of economists and hygienists, along with the
first specialists in human relations and industrial organization. They would
all continue to interrogate the "laboratory" of the future. But if some of
their works—those of a Georges Friedmann on the breakdown of work into
individual operations, for instance—were destined for a fine posterity, in
the short run, they did not contribute much to shaping or modifying the
collective image of the United States. By specifying their objects and disci-
plining their processes, the new social sciences lost in influence what they
gained in credibility. It was quite the opposite with historians. Few among
them had previously taken interest in a country "with no history"; belatedly
discovering America as a research field, they grew more influential over the
American representations being fabricated than before. An André Siegfried, who merged the investigative tradition of the Musée Social with remnants of racial anthropology and traces of a Boutmy-style political science,
would become an unavoidable reference, most likely (among other reasons) because he was the ideal intermediary between the "scholarly" prewar
writings and the literary essayism that would take over the United States
afterward.

But a Siegfried himself, or a Bernard Faÿ,[38] came into the picture only as
reinforcement. The triumphant anti-American discourse was no longer in
need of expert authority. Now, all it wanted from the scholarly disciplines and
methodical travelers was confirmation. "What preconceived notion are you
going to verify over there?" Hippolyte Taine asked a disciple who was setting
out for England. The anti-American men of letters who were making the trip
took, along with a whole library of earlier works, their checklist of prejudices
to validate. Maurois noted that no one could slough off the layers of previously read descriptions; no one could make any claims to having a fresh
view of things: "I am no longer sure. . . . Travel memories are spoiled by
reading. Was I the one who saw that country? Or was it Keyserling? Or Siegfried? Or Romier? Or Luc Durtain?"[39] It is a clever way of stressing that
because he was more aware of this cumbersome baggage, he, Maurois, would
be better able to cast it off than most of his contemporaries. Pre-1914 anti-
Americanism had been born of a piercing doubt. What if the sister republic
was not what the French had thought it was? What if the United States was
less friendly, pacifistic, democratic, prosperous, socialist, and so on, than its
French sympathizers had imagined? Those days were over. There was no
more doubt. The case was closed. This was a real "changing of the guard"
among anti-Americanism's intellectual personnel. A huge coalition of men

of letters took on the topic: anti-Americanism had become a nonspecialists'
specialty, the prerogative of an intelligentsia that had appointed itself guard-
ian of threatened values.

A new corpus took over. In the years leading up to the mid-1930s, the
wave would hit all the different genres: essays, novels, journals, theater,
tracts, reporting. The titles highlight a verbal violence, from *Le Cancer américain* to "Procès de l'Amérique"[40] (America on Trial). Testimonies grew caustic and accusations, frontal. An important detail is that the travel narrative,
frequently used before 1914, was no longer the indispensable springboard
for such criticism: the United States could now be weighed and judged without even having been visited. Duhamel, though, was faithful to the tradition
of road notes and on-site sketches; it is therefore all the more interesting to
hear him declare, when his book became a sensation: "I did not need to go
to the United States to say what I said; I could have written most of the chapters of my book without leaving Paris."[41] His young rivals Robert Aron and
Arnaud Dandieu denounced at a distance and argued *in abstracto*. This
abstraction did not undermine their contentions: if it deprived the reader of
satirical vignettes and vitriolic anecdotes, it facilitated the overall rejection,
without nuances or regrets, of a quintessentialized Americanism.

The accumulation of materials happened with surprising speed. In just a
few years, France's American library was enriched by several major works in
every genre, and special issues of journals and *grands reportages* were multiplying. For the *Revue des deux mondes,* André Chaumeix, in June 1930,
counted "no fewer than a dozen works" on America published in the space
of a few weeks.[42] In fact, the peak stretched from 1927 to 1932, with books as
differently remarkable as André Siegfried's *America Comes of Age* (1927);
Lucien Romier's *Qui sera le maître, Europe ou Amérique?* (Who Will Be the
Master, Europe or America? [1927]); Paul Morand's *New York* (1927) and
World Champions (1930); Raoul Gain's curious novel-parable *Des Américains
chez nous* (1928); Luc Durtain's two volumes of stories *Quarantième étage*
(Fortieth Floor [1927]) and *Hollywood dépassé* (Hollywood Overcome [1928]),
to which he added a slim volume of poems and numerous articles;
Duhamel's *Scenes from the Life of the Future* (1930); the special issue of *Réac-
tion* (1930); Aron and Dandieu's *Le Cancer américain* (1931); and Bertrand de
Jouvenel's *La Crise du capitalisme* (1933)—not to mention Céline's *Journey to
the End of the Night* (1932). And to this flourishing French crop we should
add several translations of authors considered in France—for sometimes
enigmatic reasons—to be authorities on the United States: thus the profuse
Keyserling (*Psychanalyse de l'Amérique* [America Set Free] [1930]) and the hazy
Waldo Frank (*Nouvelle découverte de l'Amérique* [*The Re-Discovery of America*]

[1930]). All of this represents a considerable stock of images and ideas. It was the last time there would be such a concentration in numbers and, more important, in originality: in the 1950s, and again during the Vietnam years, the French production of polemic, more narrowly focused on America's alleged warmongering and imperialism, hardly enriched the spectrography of America made between the two world wars.

"By 1931," notes the historian David Strauss, "it was virtually impossible for a French traveler or commentator to think about the United States without reference to one or more of the six authorities who had emerged in the period between 1927 and 1930."[43] In his opinion, these six authorities were Siegfried, Tardieu, Romier, Duhamel, Durtain, and Morand. Of course, Cornelius de Pauw had already traveled by proxy, Chateaubriand recopied his landscapes, and the nineteenth-century sightseers would transport trunkfuls of their predecessors' books. Nevertheless, it is true that in just a few years' time, French anti-Americanism produced a decisive reference base: the intellectual Americanophobia of the 1920s and 1930s remains, even now, the unsurpassed crest of French anti-Americanism.

"We Are Shifting to the Defensive"

The new American library was massively hostile. Favorable voices were so rare that it seems hard to use the word "trend," as Loubet del Bayle does, to qualify the few dissidents, who were well aware that they were going against a torrent of popular opinion.[44] But that was not the novelty; rather, the hostility's new logic was.

Up to then, hostility toward the United States had been diffuse, splintered, scattered into isolated moods and localized worries. Its diverse motivations intersected without intertwining. It was a very visible constellation, but not yet a structured galaxy. From racial anthropology to economic analyses of the trust system, from "political psychology" to sociology or cultural history, fledgling disciplines offered competing frameworks for analyzing the "peril." And if many observers were already calling for ripostes, it was in a dispersed manner, with more vehemence than coherence. Their analytical schemas each appealed to the portion of the population for which they were destined. What was still missing was what French marketing would later call, in a word imported from across the Atlantic, le cross-over: the threshold beyond which a discourse, like a well-launched product, no longer appeals to a specific user group, but to anyone and everyone.

It was the intellectuals' job to realize this operation by dislodging the condemnation of the United States from the particular fields it was operating in.

A universal conviction would henceforth win out over specific incriminations. Those involved in "the re-discovery of America," as Waldo Frank's title
put it, had the shared ambition of describing it as a closed and self-sufficient
system, opposed *in every way* to what the French were or wanted to be. The
anti-American discourse became much more compact, with a much greater
impact.

So was there a general offensive against America? No, but in fact a *general defensive*. This was the third—and essential—feature that deeply and lastingly modified the tenor and tone of French anti-Americanism. The Enlightenment's anti-Americanism had been stamped with commiseration; the
early nineteenth century's, with disdain; in the years from 1880 to 1900, it
had been marked with astonishment, worry, and especially anger. The new
anti-Americanism taking shape in the 1920s (which would dominate the
twentieth century) was both reactive and resigned, a standpoint of the con-
quered-in-advance, the already colonized. Hatred for America fed on violent
self-loathing. Symptomatically, Raoul Gain constructed his novel *Des Américains chez nous* around a collaborator-narrator enslaved to the invaders'
whims: this fable from 1928 set the tone for a new era, but fiction was only
one step ahead of analysis. Robert Aron and Arnaud Dandieu's *Le Cancer
américain*, in 1931, ended similarly and significantly with a portrait of the
French as scroungers for financial and sexual favors, prostitutes to the new
Rome, modern-day "*graeculi*, lap-dogs of all professions, sexes, and stripes,
flocking to Yankee banks or boudoirs."[45] The days were already long gone
(1895) when Maurras could compare New York to some "half-barbarian city
settled near the Tauric Chersonese."[46] The poles of power had been inverted:
for anti-American imagery, the great capital was now across the Atlantic, and
in 1930, the French were the new Greeks of the decadence, begging the victors' favors on the edges of the empire. Submission, humiliation, assimilation: such was the plan for enslavement that the French anti-Americans
would now unflaggingly denounce.

There is no inconsistency, either, between the nonconformist vehemence
of the 1930s and the Communist or Gaullist alarmism of the post-1945
period, which would remobilize the same rhetoric of consensual abjection
and betrayal. The French Communist Party's press tirelessly presented the
"Atlantists" as "men of Munich," or, more simply, as new collaborationists.
But the Gaullist Étiemble, in 1964, no longer had the excuse of the cold war's
logomachic excesses when he described the "Yankee slave-drivers" of Rem-
ington and General Motors as "devastating France"; when he depicted France
itself, page after page, as a "concession," a "dominion," a "feeble colony"[47]
of the American masters; when he did not shrink from comparing the

American occupation to the Nazi occupation—and concluded in favor the Nazis, who at least "took the trouble of writing their appalling honor rolls in real French."[48] Surely the torture victims were touched by this German decency, which Étiemble opposed to the linguistic atrocities of the American occupants. *Parlez-vous franglais?* triumphed in France at the height of renewed prosperity, in the peaceful France of 1964. But its rhetorical violence was like Stalinist bludgeoning and revived prewar nonconformism's imprecating tones. Was it a voluntary homage? Étiemble concluded, in any case, where Aron and Dandieu had started off: with an "American cancer" that, as he wrote it, had become a "*cancer yanqui.*"[49]

The intellectuals' anti-Americanism knew how to stay the course.

☆ ☆ ☆

An autarchic discourse of defensive denunciation monopolized by intellectuals: that is, roughly speaking, how the new French anti-Americanism produced after the Great War presented itself. With the catastrophe of 1914–18, American hegemony had become patent, undeniable. The Europeans themselves, with their internal dissent, had allowed this to happen, and to solidify. French anti-Americanism, which had still recently been sparkling, insolent—lively, in any case, and combative—fell back on a front of gloomy refusal. It cultivated bitterness, took pleasure in showing its impotence and scratching at it like an open sore. From now on, beneath the most extreme rhetoric could be heard a lamentation, often self-indulgent, over Europe's decrepitude. Verbal violence evaporated, along with the implicit or explicit vanity of the resistance it wanted to arouse. The enemy was within, or, at least, he was controlling the gates. The most zealous anti-Americans did not hide it. Duhamel, right from his title, presented the horrendous transatlantic *way of life* as France's "future." Aron and Dandieu's *Le Cancer américain*, probably the most violent tract of the period, was also the most defeatist, the one that stated the most brutally that the American enemy had already won the fight, that the world was already his. A defeatist bile chokes these aggressive texts. Only recently, between two indignant broadsides, writers had poked fun, sometimes with panache, at America, which had none. Now there was still sniggering, but it was the idiotic sniggering Céline lent Bardamu and his companions on reaching Manhattan: "What we suddenly discovered through the fog was so amazing that at first we refused to believe it, but then, when we were face to face with it, galley slaves or not, we couldn't help laughing, seeing it right there in front of us." Céline: casting out the nines—nine times funnier and crueler than the others. Railing against a police-run, fecal America—not a bad idea! But the typical French jeremiad about America is also put through the wringer. *Journey to the End of the Night* is a heroicomic poem to the Old World's shabbiness. With the Infante Combitta's galley slaves, all of crass Europe cracks up over a sight it does not even understand. "We laughed like fools."[50]

Loti and many others had cried: up and at 'em, let's get those Yankees, all hands on deck! Such bravado was out of fashion. Now it was more like: all hands under cover! In defense of France, in defense of Europe, in defense of Man, in defense of the Mind! Such were anti-Americanism's slogans, to which we should add this tacit command: in defense of the (French) intellectual, in defense of the intelligentsia. The anti-American discourse had chosen its line: the Maginot line. "We are shifting to the defensive," Mounier wrote in 1933:[51] this phrase from the founder of *Esprit*—one of the most constant critics of fraudulent American civilization, Pharisee bourgeoisification, and "the man born of the age of comfort"—could be painted on the flag waved by the intellectuals of the two postwar periods.

Lido, Seville, rue de la Paix, Bond Street, the Rotunda
Manet, Cartier, Dostoevsky, Pommery, Larue, Napoleon,
Chabannais, Marcel Proust,
so, do you like
all the new states the Union's annexed
since 1917?
Yes, yes. Ya, yea, yep, yep.
    Luc Durtain, *USA 1927* (1928)

 10

Facing the Decline: Gallic Hideout
or European Buffer Zone?

So it was defense. Defending everything threatened by America. Reacting. Not accepting decline. Turning a deaf ear to the siren song of resignation. Not losing hope—especially not in France. Because wasn't it in France's name and honor that the majority of anti-American vows were taken? Wasn't it "for France" that the intellectuals had been mobilized and gone on the defensive since the late 1920s?

The answer is less simple than we might expect.

Of course uneasiness over France's decline was lurking behind the accumulating maledictions of America. The most virulent anti-American essay of the interwar years, Robert Aron and Arnaud Dandieu's *Le Cancer américain,* forms a diptych with their *Décadence de la nation française,* as Tony Judt has noted.[1] Nonetheless, the tract's closing words are not directed at France, but rather Europe: "Europe, wake up!" And the book is full of invectives against narrow-minded nationalism. In this respect, at least, the two angry young men of the New Order had joined up with the man they called anti-Americanism's Everyman, the outdated Duhamel. The entire end of *Scenes from the Life of the Future*—a quintessentially French book—is an appeal not to France, but to

Europe. It is to the "people of Europe" that Duhamel addresses his send-off. It is in "our European civilization" that he places his ultimate hopes.[2] Several years later, it was still Europe—granted, a very different Europe: that of a neo-European family gathered in the bosom of Germania—that the collaborationists would call on in the struggle against Bolshevism *and* "plutocratic" America. And when, from across the way in England, where he had joined up with De Gaulle, Maurice Druon chose to caution the Americans, whose victory was approaching, against the heady lure of success and the disdain they might feel for a diminished France, he also decided to call his appeal not *Lettres d'un Français,* but in fact *Lettres d'un Européen.*

We could give numerous examples, from all the different camps, that indicate what could be called the French counteroffensives' spontaneous Europeanization. The sickness, without a doubt, was France's downfall. But the recommended cure was almost always, at the time, European. Maurras and his descendants were the exception; their only desire was for a national uprising. Then as now, the few jingoistic anti-Americans buttressed by nationalism alone were the exception: the ones Yann Moulier-Boutang, a contemporary French philosopher involved in the "altermondialiste" movement, describes as trumpeting against globalization with the "crowing of the Gallic cock scratching its feet in the desert."[3] Between the Maurrassians of yore and today's new nationalists, the terrain is pretty bare—Gaullism itself (at least De Gaulle's) was about more than just nationalism and was able to maintain a logic of resistance to American hegemony on a European or (in certain cases) international scale, behind the curtain of an insistent nationalist rhetoric.

French anti-Americanism, in this sense, is not chauvinistic. Neither in 1930 nor in the first years of the new millennium did those who defended France against the American peril *only* count on France to counterattack. As with military operations carried out under the international flag, the anti-American discourse, which is intensely French in its themes and workings, is almost always used in the name of a superior entity. Man, and the Spirit—we will come back to this. But also, for some time at least, Europe.

A Divided Europe Faced with a "Realist Ogre"

It seems incontestable that the rise of French anti-Americanism is tied to the bitter perception of a national decline. Yet one notion of decline can hide another. In the last years of a nineteenth century in which French anti-Americanism had grown and flourished, the unease was directed less at France than at Europe. America's "imperial" ambitions were perceived in the

1880s as a collective threat to which the Old World powers should react together. Even Great Britain, which would have liked to think it was protected by "Anglo-Saxon" affinities, was wrong in believing itself immune to underhanded vassalization. Such was at least the opinion of most French commentators. Some even predicted that the English would be the first ones devoured by their cousins and congenerates. But whether they associated or dissociated the British case from their own, belle époque French anti-Americans were concerned with Europe as a whole. More than any specifically French downfall—as would be the obsession a few decades later—what they feared was that the entire continent would lose its power and influence.

Putting Europe to the fore in calling for anti-American resistance was crucial for Henri de Beaumont, who published the pioneering article "De l'avenir des États-Unis et de leur lutte future avec l'Europe" (On the Future of the United States and Its Coming Struggle with Europe) in the *Journal des économistes* in 1888. Beaumont starts with a very general observation: the economic center of the world was continuously moving from east to west—in keeping with the classic scenario of *translatio imperii*. This shifting supremacy led to the prediction that "the business center will . . . be established in New York or Washington, which will become the capital of the civilized world."[4] Inversely, Beaumont added, "Europe can only describe an arc opposite to the United States' ascension, and everything the European nations possess today—the advantages of geographical position, hereditary aptitudes, an existence based on a long past, accumulated riches—will all disappear in the final decline."[5] Europe and North America were linked by a mechanism of weights and counterweights: if one declined, it would be a purely mechanical effect of the other's rise. In this fatal seesaw, Europe seemed all the more disadvantaged because it was going broke and tearing itself apart. The future was bleak for "our continental nations, which are striking out at each other with our money and armed forces," which would therefore have a hard time "winning a perhaps fleeting supremacy, and which, worn and impoverished, will be an even easier adversary for that young nation."[6] England itself, though less suicidal than France and Germany, was starting to worry about America's rising power—and rightly so, Beaumont opined, taking advantage of the Darwinian theory that a species first attacks its closest "varieties" to back up his argument that the Americans would first take on other Anglo-Saxons.[7]

In any case, Europe would have its fate decided *as one,* and in the very short term. "The United States, when it has become more powerful and rich than any of the European nations and perhaps than any nationality or association of nations joined by common interests, will change its attitude toward Europe." Its irrepressible expansion would provoke a confrontation:

> When the [United] States grows to the maximum population it can contain, it will
> unavoidably overspill. Inevitable competition and the struggle for life will force it
> to expand beyond its borders. The Americans will then spread out everywhere, not
> only into the two Americas, but the whole world, looking to settle down, claiming
> rights and privileges, and perhaps becoming the masters of the Old World
> nations.

The theme of America's madding crowds was launched; in another decade, it would be associated with the Asian "swarms."

There was thus "a future truth in the famous assertion that America is capable of 'whipping the universe.'" The future according to Beaumont? In the short run, an offensive use of the Monroe Doctrine was to be expected: "We can be sure that the day the United States feels strong enough, it will apply the Monroë [sic] Doctrine in all its rigor and start by expulsing the European powers from the American continent and islands." The Cuba affair, ten years later, would begin to fulfill this prophecy. In the meantime, the struggle would hit Europe: "Our generation has only witnessed the struggle for first place in which the European nations have involved themselves and in which they are still involved. The generation that follows ours will see Europe and the United States struggle to win preeminence over the entire globe." An open war? An embryonic conflict? Beaumont was not forthcoming; only the outcome interested him, and that would be identical: "One day, Europe will wake up and realize that the fate of the world is no longer in its hands." Whether it was a military conquest or a "pacific conquest"—that is, an economic and financial one—Europe's fate was sealed, unless there was some immediate and vigorous uprising. For Beaumont, it was clear that there could only be a European solution to the American peril. An isolated France would be condemned to suffer; the counter-attack had to be collective. Here, Beaumont wanted to come across as realistic and set modest goals. France and Germany were not ready to stop the arms race. No Professor Golbert had yet invented the "psychic accumulator" that could pacify whole populations with its positive vibrations.[8] "What can we do? Disarming America is impossible. But at least we can put a stop to the tariff wars in Europe."[9] A federated Europe was the horizon of this self-defense plan, situated in some unforeseeable long term. The important thing, here, is that for the first time, the American peril had been presented both as the best justification and the most powerful stimulus for a European political union. "A common danger is one of the best motivations for unification. Perhaps we will one day be compelled to create a European federation. God willing, it will not be too late."

A certain idea of the United States of Europe crystallizes in Henri de Beaumont's reasoning—no longer in emulation and echo of the United States of America, but as an act of retaliation to the threat presented *by* America. Beaumont's voice would not remain solitary for long. Over the next two decades, French apprehensions about the United States' planetary ambitions would increasingly be expressed in European terms. The priority given even by the most patriotic voices to the European dimension of resistance against *yankeesme* is at root not as paradoxical as it may seem. It was a reaction to an American aggressiveness perceived as generally anti-European. Moreover, it was not a new conviction. Its roots can be traced back to Monroe's 1823 declaration.

Monroe's formal demand had been addressed to any power liable to interfere in American affairs; but behind the general nature of the statement, there was no mistaking that it was Europe the doctrine was aimed at.[10] Unanimously considered the founding charter of a new American hegemony, the "doctrine" created a de facto solidarity among the European nations; at least that was the French conviction when debate over the famous document was revived at the end of the nineteenth century. We have already seen in what terms. Not only had the "doctrine" taken on a new status as gospel, but rather than a defensive declaration, it had become an aggressive manifesto. Beaumont, in 1888, made sure to refer to it—"we are aware of the famous Monroë Doctrine preached by Adams and Jefferson"—though he saw no need to make lengthy remarks about a document whose noxious nature his readers were all perfectly clear on.

The diplomatic lull that followed the Spanish-American War did nothing to change this conviction. The least anti-American observers thought Teddy Roosevelt's "theory of the big stick"[11] extended and aggravated the Monroe Doctrine. Here is the analysis offered in 1908, in *Notes sur les États-Unis*, by a young man with a future, André Tardieu: "Bismarck, twenty years ago, called the Monroe Doctrine an 'international impertinence.' Today, the impertinence would be in mistaking its scope. We should not forget, too, that over the past ten years the United States has amassed a military force that will weigh on its history: because if the purpose creates the organ, the organ develops the purpose."[12] This confirmed Octave Noël's diagnosis, which had warned the French in 1899 that "at every point on the globe, the United States is now fated to go to war with Europe." "We have seen the terrifying industrial war equipment they can arm against us,"[13] Noël added. The potential for aggression in 1899 had become a formidable reality in 1908: you do not pile up ships and howitzers just to let them sit there rusting.

The Yankees hated Europe and everything European, Gustave Le Rouge repeated in each installment of *La Conspiration des milliardaires*. They did not hate it, Tardieu corrected, but you had to admit that they did not like it much and held it in real contempt. A high-ranking American personage he questioned about Europe replied: "Our policy regarding Europe is a policy of indifference, qualified, if you want the honest truth, by a certain amount of disdain." Tardieu commented: "It is hard to better express the state of mind of the politicians across the sea regarding the Old World."[14] The equitably allotted disdain, and the threat collectively suspended over the Old World, were good enough reasons, for the French, to call for a unified counteroffensive. Or to dream about one. Or to lament the obstacles that impeded one. "You know," Huret wrote in 1904,

> that America is getting ready for a great economic struggle which will break out one day between the old and new continents. . . . And America is piling up its arms, building battleships, and will continue building them, endlessly. Indeed, the Yankee is not a man who worries about obstacles. For him, as for the Englishman, only strength has any worth. And so we will witness the most formidable duel the earth has ever seen. Because the planet has limits. . . . San Francisco's position, fifteen days by sea from Yokohama and twenty days from Peking, gives the United States an immense lead on Europe. And when the Atlantic on the one side and the Pacific on the other have become American lakes, crossed by steamers loaded with cheap merchandise and by war ships packed with explosives, what will become of a divided Europe faced with this realist ogre?[15]

Europe, once and evermore. . . The geopolitical and commercial vision presented here, in one of the least polemical books of the period, reflects a perception that was so common among his compatriots that Jules Huret nearly apologizes for the banality of his remarks. The provocative theory defended in 1888 by Henri de Beaumont has already become, fifteen years later, a shopworn cliché.

When he gives a sigh of regret over "a divided Europe," the *Figaro* correspondent is in harmony with the spontaneous Europeanism accenting his contemporaries' anti-Americanism. The time was ripe. Great Britain had become a cordial ally. Many intellectuals had hopes for a peaceful resolution of the German tensions. In France and Germany, the remarkable electoral advances of the socialists, reputedly internationalist and pacifistic, gave weight to these hopes. Anti-American Europeanism had chimed in. As Beaumont noted, and as the pan-European outcome of Gustave Le Rouge's serial illustrates, choosing a common enemy was perhaps the best way to put an end to Europe's lethal antagonisms. Here, America had, against its will, a great historical part to play: it was a foil and thus also a catalyst for European identity. Because if, as the buzz increasingly suggested, America was the perfect antithesis of Europe, it could do the Europeans the inestimable favor of enlightening them as to what they were.

At the start of the twentieth century, it seemed obvious that to counter the strong-jawed Americans, a defense of France should be coupled with a defense of Europe. No one had forgotten Victor Hugo's words: "France is Europe." For the French, Europe would be France's child. Therefore, they had no trouble turning their national awareness of an American "peril" into a European concern. But there were still the stubborn facts evoked by the realistic Beaumont: forgetting the injuries between France and Germany still amounted to a pious wish. At the same time, until 1918, calling for an anti-American Europe was still a propitiatory incantation more than a real rallying cry. It would take the disaster of the Great War to give the rhetorically suggested European recourse a more concrete, deliberate, and militant shape.

Finis Europae

"I wonder if all this—Europe—will not end in dementia or a general softening. 'AT THE SOUND OF THE TONE'—it will be exactly . . . the *end of a World*."[16] This note in Valéry's *Notebooks* dates from 1939, twenty years after "The Crisis of the Mind" was published. But for Valéry, as we know, the European countdown had begun much earlier—even before the great carnage of World War I, at the end of a nineteenth century in which Beaumont had already seen Europe's star waning. Evoking the hour, which was perhaps at hand, when "the old nations, abandoning their rivalries too late, stop fighting over a supremacy that no longer has any value," Beaumont concluded his article in the *Journal des économistes* with a very Valéryian Latin clause: if France failed to react, "the only thing we will leave our descendants is the sorry obligation of murmuring: *Finis Europae*."[17]

The obsession with the end of Europe running through all of Valéry's writings is in keeping with this admonition. Its roots can be found in the melancholy soil of the end of a century haunted by fallen angels: Doubt, Decline, Downfall. In 1919, Europe was in ruins, which confirmed with tragic acuity a presentiment that was now exacerbated by a sense of guilt and the irreparable. Valéry drew a lesson from it in "The Crisis of the Mind": "Nous autres, civilisations, nous savons maintenant que nous sommes mortelles." Or rather: "We civilizations now know that we are mortal"—

because this famous text first appeared in English, an aggravating circumstance that would have seemed even more ominous if the French readers relishing its melancholy lament had been aware of it.[18]

Valéry's lament would go around the world, and in France itself, it would innervate the most varied accusations of deficiency or weakness for years. Valéry was neither the first nor the last to announce Europe's eclipse: but he gave the idea an incomparable form and authority.[19] The entire anti-American discourse between the two world wars was marked by him, whether implicitly or explicitly—starting with André Siegfried's essential *America Comes of Age*, whose conclusion opposed "European civilization and American civilization" to predict, in the end, the former's historical eclipse by the latter. Valéry did not even have to enter the anti-American polemical arena to exercise his influence over it. Nothing could exacerbate repulsion against the Americans' so-called civilization more than the idea that it would outlast the Europeans' own: in this sense, the diatribes against this "false civilization" that proliferated in the 1930s owed much of their bitterness to Valéry's bad news.

The readers of "The Crisis of the Mind" mulling the text over with an eye on America did not yet know, in 1919, how right they were. Only in 1931 did Valéry, as we have said, reveal the secret of its origins: the idea of Europe, of a vulnerable Europe, did not spring up in him on seeing the ruins left by the Great War, but through the "unforeseen shock" of the 1895 and 1898 wars. Before that time, Valéry wrote, "it had never occurred to me that *Europe* really existed. This name was to me no more than a geographical expression."[20] It is a strange echo of Metternich's phrase: "Italy is only a geographical expression." Because if the Austrian chancellor's intent was to deny Italy any national reality, Italy had come together, despite him. Valéry most likely wished Europe would also refute his negative prophecies; he repeated them, though, as though he were unable to believe in this Europe that had been revealed to him like an open wound.

Valéry's Europe is born *defeated*—and defeated by non-Europe. The two smaller-scale wars were ominous forerunners of things to come. Dark portents announced the most morally mortifying aspect of global warfare: the "despairing recourse of both sides to non-Europeans, very much like the recourse to foreigners during civil wars."[21] This was a fatal choice, Duhamel stressed at the same time in a talk published under the title "Entretien sur l'esprit européen" (Considerations on the European Spirit). "The 1914–1918 war grievously weakened Europe's authority," he explained to an audience of schoolteachers, because the "auxiliaries in all the colonies" no longer recognized the "dazzling and terrible demigod."[22] (He meant "the white man.")

Europe had not only left millions of its dead in muddy trenches, it had also left its prestige there. It had lost its empire over the minds of the colonized. The "treasure" of European civilization was in danger. And those who counted on America's support in defending it were strangely deluding themselves: "The evolution of that great nation, far from diminishing the enemy's dangers, adds to them." Not only because its enthusiasm for Europe was still unsubstantiated, but also because "mechanical, industrial civilization [is], through extreme development, especially in North America, heading into a new barbarism."[23] Duhamel was not the only one, in the interwar years, to hint at the theme of a collusion between American "barbarism" and that of the nonwhite races: we will come across it again in an exasperated André Suarès. Three years before his trip to the United States, Duhamel, in Valéry's wake, had already described Europe as succumbing to its errors, threatened on the one side by disingenuous savages and on the other by the new barbarians of the "machine civilization."

When the European "senate," as Renan put it, began tearing itself apart, it handed Europe over to "the foreigners." Foreigners from the west, the east, and elsewhere were "called" by the European powers to the battlefields of 1914–18, thereby countersigning the downfall they had been notified of in 1895 and 1898, when the Japanese and Americans had invited themselves to the banquet of world history. While Duhamel, in the 1930s, gave all his efforts to combating the civilization of "slaves" threatening European culture, Valéry was incessantly prophesying the annihilation of "a *Europe*," the stillborn fruit of a futureless awakening. The necrological lament of "The Crisis of the Mind" is in this sense only the first of a long series of obituaries recorded in the *Notebooks,* in the long-imminent wait for "the sound of the tone." Right up to these lines, dated 1945: "Europe's career is over. Look at the map of the world. 1945 – 1815 = 130."[24] A strange way of marking the Nazis' defeat. On Europe's funeral plaque, Valéry engraved a subtraction in the place of an epitaph.

The Siegfried Line, Suarès's Folly

From 1919 to 1945, Valéry indefatigably tolled the bell for Europe. But the sound many of his readers heard in the 1920s was the shrill ringing of an alarm. Despite himself,[25] Valéry contributed all his prestige to mobilizing his compatriots against an America that would take over the field only when its older sibling had left it. This is what seems to lie between the lines of Valéry's texts, and the idea of a new, American power taking over from the Europeans' exhausted strength became the central theme of a number of essays written in France in the wake of "The Crisis of the Mind." Their goal was also, however, to counteract Valéry's melancholy resignation, which seemed like a capitulation. His epitaph to *Europa moribunda* was in fact the paradoxical epigraph to a whole body of anti-American literature, which took on his historical pessimism without necessarily accepting his demobilizing verdict.

Two texts, published a year apart, in 1926 and 1927, illustrate Valéry's double legacy. The first is a fairly short essay by André Suarès: "Vues d'Europe: Le principe européen" (European Views: The Principle of Europe); the second is André Siegfried's overnight classic *America Comes of Age*. A scathing attack, on the one side, and a pedagogical survey, on the other, the two works do not seem to have much in common—not even their subject. But Suarès's Europe is an anti-America; Siegfried's United States, first presented as a European mosaic, is defined at the end of his analysis as a non-Europe. Both of them enter into a dialogue with "The Crisis of the Mind," and Siegfried and Suarès both draw—albeit in contradictory veins—their American lessons from Valéry's essay.

Siegfried's debt is clear; he would later write, in 1935, a book with an explicitly Valéryan title, *La Crise de l'Europe*. If *America Comes of Age*, in 1927, was mainly presented as a compendium of demographical, economic, and social data, Siegfried nonetheless did not neglect to give his book a "philosophical" conclusion. The work ends with the assertion that there is an irreducible historical antagonism between the two continents, which he files under "civilization"—and this gives Siegfried the historian a chance to vie with the philosopher in him. Entitled "European vs. American Civilization," the final chapter strikes its 1927 reader with a few brutal truths. First and foremost: "The old European civilization did not really cross the Atlantic."[26] This plainspoken sentence is a small revolution. Up to then, America's detractors had been content with affirming (and lamenting) North America's progressive and rapid abandonment of the customs, institutions, and fashions that tied it to the Old World. Paul de Rousiers devoted the introduction of his *American Life* to commenting on this progressive distancing and proposed a chronology of it. "For almost three centuries," he then wrote, "America was looked upon as a European dependency"; the War of Independence was "in a measure . . . the first phase of a disillusioning, which is still far from being complete." "Today," Rousiers concluded in 1892, "we are witnesses of the second phase of this disillusioning. America has not only a separate existence of its own, but it has grown to be a formidable rival to the Old World."[27] André Siegfried broke with this tale of separation: the United States had not relinquished European civilization; it had never received the delivery. He swept away the last illusions of those who, like Valéry (the Valéry of 1898 or of 1931?), were still clinging to the notion that the United States was a "nation derived from Europe." Nothing could be more inaccurate, Siegfried stressed. The American populace had not broken its moorings; it had no ties: it was "now creating on a vast scale an entirely original structure which bears only a superficial resemblance to the European." And it was precisely this "creation" that prefigured Europe's marginalization and historical eclipse. "It may even be a new age, an age in which Europe is to be relegated to a niche in the history of mankind; for Europe is no longer the driving force of the world." Because "Europe and America are diverging in their respective scales of value," and "this contrast was brought to a head by the war."[28] America, in its prosperity (a prosperity about which Siegfried, two years before 1929's Black Thursday, had no doubts), was the polar opposite of Europe, the "land of paupers." But did this Europe that was lagging behind in the race for prosperity really want to pay the same "almost tragic" price as America had: sacrificing the individual on the altar of automatism? It was obviously a completely rhetorical question if, as Siegfried suggested in closing, there existed between Europe and America the "fundamental difference between two epochs in the history of mankind."[29]

The last (and unexpected) word is not the least worrisome for "European civilization": "So the discussion broadens until it becomes a dialogue, as it were, between Ford and Gandhi." It is a strange conclusion, and a good subject for an engraving: "The American Means of Production Conversing with the Asian Means of Production." It is the reader's job to decide if this is an allegory or a historical painting. What could be more striking, in any case—and more pregnant for Frenchmen's worried imagination—than a mute Europe sitting out like a wallflower while above its head the Far East and the Far West learnedly confer?

The historian André Siegfried was disabused about declines. The essayist and critic André Suarès, however, grew virulent over them. It was the *Revue des vivants*, moreover, that published swaths of his anti-American treatise in 1928. Death could wait, and "Le Principe européen" was anything but languishing. There was a wild-eyed prophet in Suarès. Close to Péguy[30] and friends with Maurice Pottecher and Romain Rolland, Suarès liked sturdy souls and clear-cut writing. Strangely labeled "Byzantine" by Benda,[31] his works are full of flashes and flares. Suarès was fond of neither frills nor laments: his text's violence sets it apart, even in a time of systematic inflammatory excess.

In making his prophecies about Europe, André Suarès, like Valéry, wound up poring over the map of the world: "If you look at the map carefully, you discover Europe's history. What is Europe, then—an Asian peninsula, a dash of land cast into the oceans—other than the West's four-pointed star?" It is hard not to think back to the central question of "The Crisis of the Mind": "Will Europe become *what it is in reality*—that is, a little promontory on the continent of Asia?"[32] Once more, we find the promontory, the peninsula the new Europe is destined to shrink to. Once more, Asia crops up, as if it were an indispensable reference when discussing America. But Suarès is also tied to Valéry by other threads. He was a child of the same fin-de-siècle, his obsessions born with the same cannon blasts. He too was a spiritual son of 1895 and 1898, of the yellow peril and the Yankee horror. His essay's violence is a result not only of his personality as a polemical swashbuckler, or the Condottiere character he forged for himself early on (his *Voyage du condottiere* was first published in 1910). It is also the product of two eras, the accumulation of two anti-American angers: those of the end of the century and the 1920s. Anger squared is what makes Suarès explode in the interwar years. His project goes back to the previous century, as his correspondence and a rough copy conserved in the Fonds Doucet[33] show, and his source is exactly the same Valéry's: once, as always, the Cuba "shock." The 1928 text retains numerous traces of this distant origin, starting with an obsession with the Munroë [*sic*] Doctrine that would be more at home in the 1890s than the 1920s, even if Suarès tries to adapt his reference to the new isolationist situation: "America made the Munroë [*sic*] principle play to its needs. Now it is demanding that Europe stay out of its affairs; and it intends to be the only judge of them. It avoids any and all Amphictyony; it declines all authority, any international court." Suarès deduces from this the only line of action open to the Europeans: self-defense by counterattack. Resisting the Yankees is at the heart of the "European principle": in fact, it defines it. "Europe's duty and need to ban American policies and the American spirit from the Old World—that is the European principle's base and its primary use."[34] The "Munroë principle" calls for retaliation: "It is against the Munroë principle and its fatal consequences that I raise the European Principle"; and, once more: "Therefore, the time has come for a contrary principle that will legitimately oppose America's taking part—however small a part it may be—in Europe, Africa, and Asia's affairs."[35] Thus defined, the "Suarès principle" would not be limited to protecting Europe from American interference; it would also bar America's access to other continents—colonial Europe's "no-hunting zones." A big job. And as optimistic as Valéry's meditation might seem pessimistic. . .

Like others before him (Demolins judging Germany less dangerous than the Anglo-Saxons) and after him (Robert Aron and Arnaud Dandieu presenting the Germans as victims of Americanization, too), Suarès advised the

French not to set their sights on the wrong target. The enemy, despite appearances to the contrary, was not the German, but America, that "gray rat." In his writings, he pursues the rat with a breathless hatred that makes his syntax stutter. A note from 1911, written after Suarès had met some Americans in Brittany, throws a pretty stark light on the strange racist alchemy that made his stills bubble and boil:

> Miserable Yankees. . . . Everything, including their nasal accent and the pitch of their laugh, predestines them to join forces with the Chinese to take over the world. . . . With the Chinese, they will make the gray race, the race of tattered money, bundles, deeds; the positive race. . . . A man's name, a work of art, genius, the divine—everything has its price tag. Those miserable Yankees do not understand any of it and condemn it all. . . . Turks, Chinese, even Negroes will enter my house, if I ever have property. But the Yankees will not come in: with lashes of the whip, *get out.*[36]

The Condottiere did not mince words. Anti-Americanism and racist xenophobia work well together, here—we will see in the chapter "Cosmopolis" that Suarès was not the only one combining them.

"L'essai sur le principe européen" can be read as a layering of two ages of French anti-Americanism. In the older layer: a definition of the European spirit as a "classical spirit" (and the American spirit as "the classical spirit's opposite"); a loudly proclaimed certainty that the Americans' pretense "to be the first nation in the world [has] no foundation, not even mechanically"; an overriding belief in the destiny of France, which is at the center of "the four-pointed star of the West" and around which the neighboring nations "are constellated"; in short, an elaborate mythology or cultural dramaturgy still marked by the reassuring certainties of the previous century. These certainties are, however, contradicted, in the very same pages, by a new sense of the fragility of the spirit in the Manichean struggle against material power. Suarès's militancy is suffused with doubts and failings. The tone grows exasperated when his observations darken, turning to antimaterialist warnings, refusing "matter machinated into the industrial order and the moral order, [which] is starting to rule the world," making an insistent call to the "powers of the spirit" that the European "venerates, even when he denies them," and defining America itself as "the machine": all of these traits belong to the interwar period; and Suarès, pursuing America with a long-standing rage, also confirms his status as a precursor to the nonconformists' irate tracts.

From Valéry to Suarès and Siegfried, beyond their differences in projects and approach, theorizing Europe's decline and eclipse is genealogically tied to the irruption of America as a threat. The fundamental scenario is the same: Europe is faced with, and opposed by, new populations imperiously knocking at the doors of history. Valéry, in polished language, correlates their two irruptions in 1895 and 1898. Siegfried closes his reflection with the allegory of a helpless Europe reduced to silence and excluded from the dialogue of civilizations between America and Asia. Suarès does not beat around the bush; he tosses out the word they avoided: what was threatening Europe was a confederacy of "barbarians." "The European principle consists in defending the conscience and reality of Europe against what is not part of the European spirit, sentiment, and order: against the Barbarians, against Asia, against the Blacks and the Yellows, to be sure, but first of all against the North of America." That is putting it pretty clearly. And he adds, for his overly prudish colleagues: "Denying that there are Barbarians is a juvenile game.... North America seems to many like the clear polar opposite to any Barbarism; it is nonetheless the Barbarians' hope and their model."[37] This would also be, almost word for word, Robert Aron and Arnaud Dandieu's opinion.

Suarès was an exaggerated European, a solitary writer, a literary maverick: the rashness of his anti-American rhetoric implicates no one but himself. It is not hard, however, to see in the fanatical accents of his anti-Americanism the same obsession with Europe's demise that a Valéry or a Siegfried would expose in a much more genteel way. And Suarès was not alone, as we will see, in turning his European lament—that interwar leitmotif—into an anathema against barbarism, a convenient concept that could be used to group blacks, yellows, and Yankees in collective detestation. When the humanist Duhamel wrote, "The adult inhabitant of Western Europe who is normal and educated, finds himself more at home among the troglodytes of Matmata than he does in certain streets in Chicago,"[38] he was saying much the same thing as the imprecating Suarès; he was simply saying it in a more devious, roundabout way.

Pan-Europe versus All-America

Europe as a defensive project for protecting civilization had other supporters in the 1920s, though they were less hotheaded and came off as more constructive than Suarès. Their logic was not far from the Condottiere's, however. But rather than vituperation, they preferred organization, negotiation, proposals. Their attempts to give Europe's material and moral crisis a European answer did not display any aggressive anti-Americanism; it was, however, the specter of American hegemony they were trying to ward off by endorsing the United States of Europe.

The most important of these undertakings, for its ambitions as well as the prestigious support it drew, was Coudenhove-Kalergi's Pan-Europa. Pragmatically idealistic, it revived the idea of a federative European riposte to the American challenge. Not long after the European massacre of the Great War, the question Henri de Beaumont had raised in 1888 was publicly repeated, amid the rubble of a bruised Europe; but it was repeated with more tact and diplomacy. What if, faced with the "realist ogre," France's salvation could be found in the idealists' Europe? The federative project was far from a new idea in Europe, but the recent war disasters had breathed new life into it. Its partisans were eager to regroup and take action. Richard de Coudenhove-Kalergi would give them the chance to.

A Czech citizen and cosmopolitan count, Coudenhove-Kalergi published the "Pan-Europa Manifesto" in 1923. In it, he endorsed "the political and economic union of all the European nations, from Poland to Portugal." It was a threefold federative project: joint arbitration and security; a trade and monetary union; and a supranational parliament (which would not replace existing national institutions). Coudenhove-Kalergi was part of "a line of dreamers" stretching from Homer, whom he blithely associated with the pan-European project, to Victor Hugo, who had envisioned a reconciled and reunited Europe.[39] But his dream was well argued, and his project did not go unnoticed.

His plan for Europe did not involve the USSR, whose government he felt excluded it from this virtual community. He also left Great Britain in limbo.[40] It was too "imperial," the manifesto suggested. But between the lines, we can also read: too Anglo-Saxon and close to the United States. In 1924 Europe, the manifesto won the conservatives' sympathies, insofar as it appeared clearly anti-Communist. But it also interested and attracted pacifists mainly identified with the Left, such as Aristide Briand and Édouard Herriot, in France, or the young Konrad Adenauer in Weimar Germany. Intellectually speaking, the project presented itself as both antinationalist and anti-internationalist. Was it anti-American? The text of the manifesto avoided any frontal attack. It even seemed to adopt Hugo's old theme of the American federation as a model: "The crowning of pan-European efforts will be the constitution of a United States of Europe, on the model of the United States of America." Reforging the chain of crushed hopes, Coudenhove-Kalergi took upon himself the prophecy pronounced by Hugo after the Franco-Prussian War, from Hauteville-House at the Lugano Peace Conference: "We will have the *United States of Europe,* which will crown the Old World like the United States of America crowns the New."[41] But if Hugo's ideal resurfaced, it was in a modified version. However many ambiguities the manifesto wound around the American reference, its plan was clearly directed *against* the United States, or, in any case, against American hegemony. On closer inspection, it is not the United States to which Coudenhove-Kalergi compares the "United Europe" he is calling for. The parallel he draws is between Pan-Europe and Pan-America: the continent-wide Pan-America that successive administrations in Washington had been attempting to build since the 1880s. The United States of America was only, in this entity under construction, the "first power," whose job was to initiate the union, just as France, the first European power, could "take the initiative in the unification process." This of course situated the project very clearly not only in a context of emulation, but, more important, in one of continent-to-continent competition.

Implicit in this parallel, the message becomes explicit when the manifesto lists the "advantages" that the Europeans would gain from the federation. The fifth and last of these advantages is the "possibility of withstanding competition from the American and British industries and later, those of the Far East and Russia." The project's anti-American dimension is even more visible in the passage in which Coudenhove-Kalergi analyzes the baleful consequences of European unification's potential failure. "The continuation of Europe's current policies," he writes, would inescapably lead to the "continual politico-military *interference* of *extra-European powers* in Europe's affairs," on the one hand, and "the inability to withstand competition from Anglo-Saxon industry; bankruptcy; and economic enslavement" on the other. An "extra-European" military intervention, economic and financial subservience: you did not have to be a great intellectual to name the only country capable of vassalizing old Europe.

Coudenhove-Kalergi could be even clearer. To the text of the manifesto, which was already pretty evocative, he added a kind of codicil aimed at the French: an "Open Letter to the French Parliament" in June 1924, which banked on their double refusal of the USSR and the Anglo-Americans. Three powers, he stressed, presented a direct threat to Europe and its sovereignty: the Soviet Union, the British empire, and the United States. This approach to presenting the project was an effective way of lobbying the French political class and the press. The idea of a European riposte to American pressures fell on politically fertile ground: the Washington naval conference had embittered the French, and attempts to reclaim debts contracted during the conflict got them heated up. A dynamic was set off on the highest political level, with Édouard Herriot proclaiming before the chamber his adherence to the idea of a United States of Europe. Up to the end of the 1920s, there was a "parallel development of anti-Americanism and the movement for European unity."[42]

Even more than the politicians, French intellectuals sold on Coudenhove-Kalergi's European action illustrated the undertaking's strong anti-American component. While preparations were gathering speed for the 1926 pan-European conference that would give the movement a permanent structure, many important names rallied to the cause. Before it was swept away by the great European catastrophes of the stock market crash and a rash of dictatorships, the Pan-Europa movement had the time to awaken strong interest and impressive adherence among the French intelligentsia. Among those who accepted to participate in the Vienna conference, Paul Valéry was on the front lines. Also involved were Paul Claudel, Georges Duhamel, Jules Romains, Luc Durtain, and Lucien Romier. It is an extraordinarily suggestive list, and one that almost perfectly overlaps the list of French writers and thinkers who, in these same years from 1925 to 1931, were worried or alarmed about America. Led by the master of European decline, Paul Valéry, fewer members of the French delegation at the Vienna congress were crazy about Europe than obsessed with the United States.

Doubtless Claudel cannot be summarily charged with being anti-American, but, in a later chapter, we will see him comment in hardly diplomatic terms on the habits and customs of the country where he was French ambassador. There was also L'Échange (The Exchange), his first great theatrical work, written in Boston; its anti-American theme struck his contemporaries, who were unanimous in considering the character of Thomas Pollock Nageoire, the man for whom "everything is worth so much," an archetypal Yankee.[43] As for Durtain, Romier, and Duhamel, between 1926 and 1930, all three of them were leading contributors to the anti-American library. Only Jules Romains is an exception here: he too was curious about the United States, but he looked more benevolently than his peers on a country in which popular communal life seemed sometimes closer to his unanimistic ideal than European society.[44]

Their presence in Vienna was obviously not a matter of chance or coincidence. These writers had read the manifesto carefully and even between the lines. The interest they showed in Coudenhove-Kalergi's project cannot be separated from the generally suspicious or hostile attention they gave the United States. They themselves explicitly made the connection between their pan-European militantism and the anti-American crusade. The prelude to Duhamel's Scenes from the Life of the Future is a preface in the form of a dialogue with Curtius on the durability of European civilization; and once more,

Europe (a Europe that has not yet "fulfilled its purpose") is where he ends his book—and his descent into modern hell.[45] Adherence to pan-European principles comes across even more directly in Durtain's essays (*Quelques notes d'USA*), but also in his novels, where the stories put "the European man" to the test of American exile.[46]

For several years, a small phalanx of writers and poets united chiefly by a refusal of Europe's announced Americanization would work for this defensive European front. "A common danger is one of the best grounds for coming together," Henri de Beaumont believed. Of course, this was giving fear too many positive qualities. It supposed that fear of America would be strong enough and common enough to allay distrust and resentment—as well as other fears. The manifesto's European citizen, whose ancestor, according to Count Coudenhove-Kalergi, was Odysseus, would not make it through that tumultuous decade with the same success as the Greek hero. Born of a text, the movement culminated and expired in another text: its last will and testament is the memorandum written by Alexis Léger (also known as the poet Saint-John Perse) and read by Aristide Briand in September 1930 before a League of Nations that was itself on its deathbed. The movement had moored itself to a well-intended diplomacy that was leaking all over; the pan-Europe rowboat went under with the League of Nations. The only thing left afloat was the anti-Americanism that had served as ballast and that gave Duhamel the material for some important book sales.

To these intellectuals, European federalism had seemed like the best strategy for warding off France's eclipse and an American stronghold over Europe. The political tally was not great, and the writers who had come to peer into pan-Europe's crib only contributed, in the end, to the painful birth of the Young Plan—the "American bastard"[47] a new generation of anti-Americans would lash out against.

"Europe, Wake Up!"

The notorious and pretty notable writers who rallied around the pan-European project were rapidly replaced, on anti-Americanism's outposts, by more radical groups. These movements, circles, and clusters agreed on a certain number of values: anticapitalism, anticommunism, antiparliamentarianism, the "revolutionary spirit." Not to mention anti-Americanism, which pervades their texts because it was a rallying point and a fixation. Since the United States exemplified, all at once, perfected capitalism, Soviet-style mass collectivism, a caricature of elective democracy, and—as we will soon see in greater detail—the counterrevolutionary country par excellence, the time spent denouncing it was not wasted time. For the young intellectuals who embodied the "spirit of the 1930s," America was the absolute foil. They would make great efforts to give their own tone to a phobia that was already extremely common in France and among intellectuals. Their first concern was to show their difference and profess their rupture from predecessors they refused to feel any indebtedness to, including in the forms their anti-Americanism took. They were therefore not only set on combating the real America and, perhaps even more, a "mental America"; they also had to prove that they alone understood the true nature of the American threat.

The "young reviews" of the 1930s thus presented a particularly wide range of anti-American declarations, whether they appeared in *Esprit, Réaction,* or *Ordre nouveau.* The most violent book of the time, Aron and Dandieu's *Le Cancer américain,* was part of this movement, which Emmanuel Mounier labeled "nonconformist." As leaders of the New Order movement, with its personalist and revolutionary bent, Robert Aron and Arnaud Dandieu combined an extraordinarily vehement anti-Americanism with a no less vigorous idea of Europe—but were, however, violently hostile to both the federalist orientation and the ideal of political dialogue embodied by Briand. Aron and Dandieu were also hostile to nationalism and refused to speak in France's name—especially the France of Monsieur Duhamel, that anti-American Everyman.[48] Their "tract against the Yankee spirit," as they insistently put it, "is not anti-American in the usual sense of the word, that is, in the national sense."[49] As for the Europe they invoked, it was completely different from the "internationalist abstraction" of the Pan-Europa movement. The "young reviews" agreed on this point. *Ordre nouveau,* like *Réaction,* had nothing but "sarcasm for those who 'gargle with echoes of Pan-Europa.' "[50] Aron and Dandieu endorsed a Europe that was yet to be created, and they endorsed it not only in opposition to America, but also in opposition to a "bad" Europe carrying the first seeds of a modern gangrene.

Their argumentation was thus twofold. The first part of their analysis tackled simple things. Europe was the victim of external aggression: "The seat or spread of the evil that is starting to eat away at Europe is situated outside of Europe itself."[51] There had been and still was a conspiracy against Europe. With a single sentence, Aron and Dandieu swept away the mortifications of their predecessors, who had charged themselves, as Europeans, with the sin of World War I's madness. Enough penitence and flagellation: "The cancer of the modern world was born far from the mass graves of the war."[52] They reconstructed the chronology of the disaster in a new light. Europe's fatal date? Not August 1914, as naive people thought. It was "neither Sarajevo," where the assassination of an archduke unleashed the improbable catastrophe, "nor Rethondes," which would lead to the Treaty of Versailles, which would come to no good. The key moments were completely different, and the calendar of Europe's misfortunes was American. It was "1913, the fatal date when the American banks were organized, leading to the hegemony we have been suffering since: the origin of the American cancer." (We should note that Duhamel, from whom they so stridently set themselves apart, had suggested a remarkably similar chronology for the conflict: "The solemn moment in the history of the twentieth century is not the month of August, 1914, or the month of November, 1918. No. Take it from me: it is the moment when the home market became too small for the United States. And then the creature got up on its hind legs.")[53] But Aron and Dandieu had "another fatal date" to propose, one that doubled America's guilt: "1929, when the American organization reached the continent by means of the Young Plan and the cancer spread throughout Europe." Two dates, 1913, 1929: those were the ones schoolchildren should be memorizing. The Great War? A simple clean-up operation. "Between the two, there was the war to sweep the battlefield."[54] The *poilus* had not died for France or the "cannon merchants": in reality, they had died for the Federal Reserve System.[55] And the Americans were ready to reproduce that tidy feat. They were keeping Europe (in 1931) "like a canteen for when they got thirsty." It was all going to start over, and America was already "pacifically preparing its tariff and discount war, leaving the Europeans open to the bloodiest risks of a war in human flesh."[56]

Aron and Dandieu's first Europe was thus a victimized Europe, duped and bled dry, caught in America's snares, misled by its lures, systematically drained by its bankers. But this innocent, blind, manipulated Europe hid another that, mutedly, distantly, was the intellectual root of the evil. It was clear that Europe had not caused the 1914–18 massacre. It had plunged blindly ahead under the American bankers' bemused gaze. But if Europe was not guilty of that, it could not be denied that it was also responsible: responsible for America and its cancer. Whence the curious remark about America: where "the seat *or spread* of the evil . . . is situated." Why the correction, which throws off the polemic? Because America was not the real, first source of the contagion. Because that continent, which had never invented anything, not even epidemics, had received the fatal germ from Europe. Because the "American cancer" was in fact the monstrous proliferation in America of the European rationalist error. "The Yankee spirit is in fact nothing other than the systematic exploration, on a gigantic scale, of the most lamentable error Europe ever committed, the rationalist error."[57] America was Europe's sin, come to punish it; its "permanent nightmare, diurnal and nocturnal"; its dangerous, degenerate descendant.

This is Aron and Dandieu's stroke of originality: in their last appeal, the accusation falls on Europe, which they interchangeably qualify as rationalist, Cartesian, or Hegelian. These dubious Old World products were not enhanced by their trip to America. What Buffon affirmed about the animals had happened to these ideas: transplantation had ended up deforming them. Through the United States, it was European ideas the New Order thinkers were combating. Europe had birthed rationalist error, but the Americanization of European reason had produced monsters: "Modern barbarism is reason in its American form."[58] The struggle against America started at home: in Europe—both for and against it. "Americanism is a sickness," Aron and Dandieu also affirmed—a sickness of which Europe had long been a carrier before falling ill to its metastastic return.

"Europe, wake up!" Aron and Dandieu cried out on the last page of *Le Cancer américain*, without flinching at the weighty reference.[59] The New Order had an explicit penchant for personalist references and was often ambiguous, somewhere between heedlessness and provocation. It set itself apart from the sycophants of Italy's, then Germany's, "experiments"; but the review published a resounding "Letter to Hitler," and Robert Aron wrote in praise of Mussolini's Italy.[60] Editorial overlap and individual crossovers were frequent along the "neos'" poorly demarcated ideological borders. Intellectually, there was no shortage of ties: a revolutionary mystique, an absolute contempt for liberal democracy, a repudiation of capitalism. To which was added—unless it was simply the condensed version of these features—a vehement anti-Americanism, articulated in the name of a new Europe still to be born, quite different from the Europe loaded down with centuries of culture that Duhamel had championed. They were doubtless a little more sophisticated than the "neos," who endorsed a regenerated Europe against the generalized (but particularly American) rot. But the logic was not fundamentally different. The critique of "reason in American form," defining America as "a spiritual aberration," the charge against Kantism and Hegelianism: all link *Le Cancer américain* historically to the Maurrassian Far Right and to the irrationalism of future fascist movements. An essential point in its historical demonstration—American finance's secret responsibility for setting off World War I—would be tirelessly repeated, before and during World War II. In a bit of supplementary slippage (printed by Maurras, but avoided in *Le Cancer américain*), it would soon be the Jewish American banks that were accused not only of having fomented the Great War, but of steering it from month to month in accordance with purely Jewish interests.[61]

Neither Dandieu (who died in 1933) nor Robert Aron (who crossed over to North Africa after the defeat in 1940) can be grouped with the "neos" who fell into the frenzied anti-Americanism of the collaboration. Nonetheless, the Europe they call to the rescue against the American "capitalist plesiosaur" seems closer, when all is said and done, to Doriot than Briand, and it looks a lot less like Valéry's than that of a Drieu La Rochelle—another writer disgusted by Yankee "barbarism." *Le Cancer américain*'s two authors cannot find sarcasm strong enough to denounce old-fashioned anti-Americanism and its "inoffensive saturnalia": criticism of America in France had too long been "a matter for intellectuals or esthetes";[62] it was high time that the revolutionary militants took back the torch; moreover, the French intelligentsia was so contaminated that its criticism of America was, unbeknownst to it, "fundamentally American."[63] This whole radicalized rhetoric, along with all the calls for political activism associating anti-Americanism with anticommunism, could easily be taken as encouragement to build a "New Europe." Aron and Dandieu seem to have foreseen this risk as early as 1931. Otherwise, why would they suddenly recoil, right before reaching their conclusion, as though they had scared themselves off? Why would they torpedo their own ship while protesting that, no, clearly they were not calling for a "holy war"? Why, at the risk of being called, in turn, Everyman, would they end their book by admitting to their readers, in cryptic terms, that "we are Americanized against America even more quickly than for it"?

☆ ☆ ☆

The European reference in French anti-Americanism thus hit its peak between the late 1920s and World War II in three different and successive forms: the pan-European project for economic and cultural unification, centered on Europe's traditional values and against the great empires threatening it; the nonconformists' joint denunciation of rationalist America and an Americanized Europe; and lastly, during the occupation, the defense of a "new Europe" under German hegemony against the alliance of Bolshevism and the American "plutocracy."

With the liberation began a time in the wilderness that has not yet come to an end. Never again would the anti-American crusade be intertwined with a pro-European one. The slogan of "new Europe" reiterated by the German occupancy and the collaboration cast a shadow over the word and suspicions on the idea. Communist propaganda during the cold war, as we will see in greater detail in the next chapter, very effectively extended this shadow to the unsteady Europe of a Franco-German rapprochement. The real, economic, and political Europe whose construction began then was all the less suited to a symbolic anti-American investment because it was denounced daily, by its mostly Communist adversaries, as the United States' creation or even its creature. In a complete reversal of the previous situation and a perfect historical irony, the Europe the French had been clamoring for since Henri de Beaumont, the Europe that would stand up to the American ogre, was brought to the baptismal font with America as its godmother and good fairy. After this sudden shunting, anti-American discourse and the pro-European discourse steamed off down separate paths. When Jean-Baptiste Duroselle dissected the anti-Americanisms of the 1960s, anti-Americanism-by-Europeanism did not fall under his scalpel. It would not nowadays, either. Surfacing from time to time in speeches by the New Right is not much different from being shelved. As for the Left's rhetorical efforts since 1981 to present the European Union as a bulwark against American hegemony, or, more diplomatically, as a critical mass finally attained that can allow the two continents to "speak as equals," they do not seem to have been particularly successful with the anti-European hard core, which is also an anti-American hard core.[64] Neither the coded nostalgia of a museographical New Right nor the cushy anti-Americanism of pro-European strategists seems up to the task of reuniting what history has cast asunder.

A lender is never loved by his debtor. No need to reason
it out; it is a fact.

> J.-L. Chastanet, *L'Oncle Shylock ou l'impérialisme
> américain à la conquête du monde* (1927)

 11

From Debt to Dependency:
The Perrichon Complex

Oscar Wilde liked to tell his American audiences, "We are separated by a common language." Would the wars France and America fought together in the twentieth century have the same effect
on their citizens? "Two wars in thirty years in which we were the
Anglo-Saxons' allies accelerated our enslavement,"[1] Étiemble proclaimed in 1964. For the great destroyer of *franglais*, France's enslavement was not just a metaphor or a linguistic issue.

But on closer inspection, it was the *postwar* periods that were
disastrous—and the twentieth century had been nothing but a
series of postwar periods in France. The first was known as the
"interwar years." The second quickly became the cold war. The
third, as nameless as the wars themselves ("operations for maintaining order" was the preferred terminology), we will call the
post-colonial-war years. These postwar periods played a much
more important part in the strange scenography of Franco-
American relations than the periods of conflict themselves. They
were regularly, repetitively, an occasion for serious tensions. They
left more scars than a common struggle creates bonds.

The three postwar periods did not have much in common,
however. In 1917, the United States was a precious—though

tardy—ally that was later reproached with having done too little. In 1940, France sank from being the foremost military power in the world to the lowest rung of subjection. The liberation ended the disgrace but not the decline. The French sharply felt the humiliation of having become an "assisted" nation, as Mauriac confessed in 1951: "In four years' time, France has gone from the rank of a great nation freely disposing of its own fate to that of an assisted nation: why avoid the word, since such is the case?"[2] But the word was painful, as was "begging," used by Raymond Aron in 1948. To go from debtor to beggar was to slip one more rung down the ladder of decline. Accepting the word meant crossing a new symbolic threshold, going from an ungrateful admission of debt to the furious acknowledgment of dependency. Resentment toward France's overly generous benefactors quickly surfaced. It took the form of a double denial. Their intentions were denied: what they had done had not been done for the French. And their aid itself was denied: they had not helped France all that much anyway. The French wars in Indochina and Algeria did not help the situation, either, since these wars were fought not with the United States' help but under fire from American criticism. This criticism became, for the French, malicious abstention, with suspected diplomatic sabotage—and above all, the fear that America was "reaping the benefits" of stoking animosities.

In a certain sense, everything changed from one period to the next. Starting with the status of France itself and its own self-image. The 1914–18 massacre insinuated into many minds the idea of a nascent decline that the euphoria of victory masked but could not erase. The theme of the end of Europe had emerged at the end of the nineteenth century as a historical hypothesis of a speculative nature rather than as a real emotion. It gained ground now and, as dramatically expressed by Valéry, took on an anguished tone. With the "strange defeat," as the historian Marc Bloch called it, of 1940, this diffuse worry turned into collective consternation. The failures and backsliding of the 1930s had sowed the seeds of doubt; the rout, the German occupation, and the establishment of the Vichy government opened the eyes of even those who had kept them the most firmly shut to signs of decline.

The stage had been transformed, and with it the main characters of the Franco-American confrontation. It was the Right and the Far Right that took an extreme position against the United States in the interwar period, and Maurras who struck the first blows against the statue of Wilson. It was the French Communist Party that, after 1945, was on the brink of war with the American "occupant" and Mr. Marshall's poisoned gifts. And it was Gaullism in the 1960s that would capitalize on the new anti-American resentment tied to the painful process of decolonization. The "pole" of anti-American resistance thus shifted considerably. But it still polarized, each time, various and very different forces. Many people in France who did not sympathize with the Action Française approved of Maurras's vituperation of Wilson and his pathological portrait of America, which would be adopted by both the left and the right. More than a quarter of the French population who voted Communist after the liberation was joined, on anti-American themes, by imposing battalions from elsewhere: leftist Christians, "neutralists," but also and perhaps mainly the Gaullist Rassemblement du Peuple Français. In the 1960s, the current was reversed, and many voters on the Left and Far Left perfectly identified with the general's supposedly "anti-Atlantist" stance: in 1966, "leftist personalities" even signed an appeal in favor of his foreign policy, which shows how much they approved of a withdrawal from NATO's military organization.[3]

Nearly everything shifted, then, but at the same time, nearly everything recurred. The troop was revamped and new actors stepped in. The same dialogue came back, however; the same gibes, the same trip-ups, the same invectives—as though the script were carved in stone. And the script was solidly built around debt: its unbearable weight and its impossible repayment. Since Lafayette, Franco-American accounts had been an inextricable mix of gold and blood.

"Odious" Debt: A Primal Scene

The most tangible of the debts, and the one that has been most explored by historians, was obviously the one France contracted with the United States during World War I and that it balked at honoring afterward. This was the core of the Franco-American unease over the interwar period. It poisoned relations between the two countries and contributed more than any other factor to degrading the image of France in America, as well as to striking up French irritation against the Americans. Saying the spell was broken is an understatement; the myth of fraternity itself had been trampled on, and Clemenceau could write, with bitter sarcasm: "When Colonel Stanton, arriving to join the fight, hastened with all speed to the graveyard of Picpus to utter his gallant and far-echoing salute to Lafayette, it was a sword he brandished in the sunlight, and not a schedule of payments."[4]

André Tardieu, even before the height of the debt-repayment tensions, described its psychological mechanisms with great acuity. The American demand for repayment of loans granted during the conflict, he explained in 1927, was foreseeable and inevitable. If French opinion had reacted so brutally against its former ally, it was because the American demands had suddenly crystallized seven years of frustrations, of which he gives an exhaustive list:

> France lives over again the long series of her deceptions: the futility of the
> sacrifices she and her allies made in 1919 to American ideals; the refusal of the
> American Senate to ratify the Treaty of Solidarity; the separate peace entered
> into with Germany without any attempt at previous adjustment with old war
> associates; the Washington Conference so adverse to France's navy and her
> colonies; the insistence on sharing the financial advantages of a treaty while
> repudiating its obligations; the uncompromising demand for the payment of a
> debt the counterpart of which had been irretrievably jeopardized by America's
> withdrawal in 1920; the unjustifiable refusal to grant the French debtor those
> transfer guarantees accorded to the German debtor.[5]

The cup was full and could only spill over.

All in all, Tardieu was describing an *overinvestment:* behind this concentrated anger there was, he tells us, all the dissatisfaction of a disappointing postwar period. But you had to go further back in time. The debt affair was also part of a much more long-term history. It had come with a backlog of memories from a previous crisis. It had repeated a scene of confrontation between France and the United States that had taken place in the nineteenth century, and it had bluntly raised the old question of American "ingratitude" that had already fed into the arguments of those disappointed by America in the 1880s.

The primal scene took place in 1834–35. Completely forgotten nowadays, it was nonetheless not a slight matter, since it technically pushed France and the United States to the brink of war. Doubly paradoxical, the crisis broke out under the reign of a king—Louis-Philippe, a strong friend to America, which he knew well—and it broke out over a somewhat stale dispute (it went back to the empire) that no one considered very important.[6] Since the First Empire, the United States, applying the Milan Decree (December 17, 1807), had been demanding indemnities for damage to its commercial fleet. According to the decree, reinforced by another decree from 1810, American ships that had been given over to inspections required by the English at the time of the blockade and counterblockade could be considered denationalized and thus free targets for the French navy. American ship owners had lost 558 vessels between 1807 and 1812. Forty million francs: that was the sum the American government had been unwaveringly demanding ever since, in the name of the wronged parties. The French authorities had managed to drag out negotiations throughout the entire Restoration by contesting the figure and introducing, in turn, diverse claims of their own.[7] In 1829, President Andrew Jackson finally accepted the idea of a general negotiation. The 1830 revolution in France, which put an Americanophile prince on the throne, could only speed up the possibility of repayment.

A French commission convened by the new authorities finally recognized the legitimacy of the claim but limited it to some ten million francs. Haggling started up again and ended with the sum of twenty-five million, which was accepted by the ambassador, Rives. It looked like the case was closed. The treaty was signed on July 4, 1831, and ratified by the U.S. Senate in February 1832. The only thing left hanging was French ratification, which was put off from session to session. But when, thirty-two months later, on March 28, 1834, the compensation treaty was brought before the Chamber for a vote that seemed like a pure formality, things went haywire. Boissy d'Anglas, who opened the debate, gave a speech about America's ingratitude. *Le National,* a paper that was normally well disposed toward the United States, spoke of its "excessive ease in forgetting such recent obligations"[8]— an admittedly bizarre way of describing Louis XVI's aid a half century earlier! Lamartine, in turn, intoned a brokenhearted air: "I have always been deeply astonished, when reading about recent history, by the lack of sympathy and gratitude America has shown our country."[9] The rumor awkwardly spread by the officious *Journal des débats* about possible American reprisals if the ratification fell through only stiffened the opposition. In the end, the treaty was rejected by an eight-vote margin.

A confrontation with the United States was inevitable. In December of the same year, President Jackson announced that he would take the payment from French possessions in the United States if the Chamber did not overturn its vote. This produced a considerable stir in France. Paris had no choice but to recall its ambassador, then to try to put an end to a crisis that had gotten out of control. The second parliamentary debate, one of the most animated and longest of the term, took place from April 9 to April 18, 1835. This time, the government closed ranks. The twenty-five million was voted for, paid, and, just as soon, added to the landscape of American infamy, alongside the British-American treaty of 1794. Among the few friends of the transatlantic republic in France's political circles, the wound went deep. Lamartine, seven years later, was still disconsolate: "I voted in favor of the twenty-five million [for America], because it seemed fair to me, though odious—but I voted at the same time for my disaffection with America."[10] He was not alone, as René Rémond points out: "After 1835, there would no longer be the enthusiasm, the spontaneous impulse, the generous intensity of certain sympathies. Friendship was replaced by indifference, or even by resentment. It would not be until 1917 and America's intervention on our shores that the French population's bygone friendship would be restored."[11] A brief reconciliation, nonetheless, and one quickly empoisoned by a new debt situation. René Rémond also judiciously points out the constant and, indeed, only theme of the anti-American campaign of 1834–35: ingratitude. The United States, in light of this diplomatic crisis, seemed to be driven by very different motives than friendship or even equality. "Self-interest," wrote *Le Constitutionnel,* "that is the real motive for the behavior of the government and citizens" of the United States.[12] Speeches in the Chamber by those opposed to the treaty as well as debates in the press show how much the American claims, which were nevertheless in accordance with the law, clashed with public opinion, which still thought France could draw sentimental drafts from America. "What the French were the least willing to forgive the Americans for in the matter was what they took to be ingratitude."[13]

The war debt affair that swelled during the 1920s and culminated in 1932 repeated the primal scene of 1835: only this time it was larger, more complex, and more public—in short, *worse.* Just as under Louis-Philippe, French members of parliament and journalists countered the Americans' idea of their "due" with a kind of historical and sentimental obligation these current creditors had contracted long ago in Yorktown. And like Lamartine a century earlier, the intelligentsia agreed with the man in the street and voted for his "disaffection" with the United States.

America as "the World's Creditor"

The war debt affair had a polemical past. It was also part of an immediate context that aggravated resentments. One of the principal transformations imputed to the 1914–18 war, and one the French had the most trouble accepting, was America's metamorphosis into "the world's creditor." André Siegfried devoted a whole chapter of *America Comes of Age* to this reversal of fortune: "Of one fact we are certain, and that is that in 1914 the Americans were in debt to Europe and now Europe is in debt to them."[14] The assertion was interminably reiterated throughout the 1920s, with bitterness and sometimes suspicion. Before 1914, "America, as a country, was not a *creditor* but a *debtor,*" Raymond Recouly recalled in *L'Amérique pauvre,* in 1933; the change had been so brutal that this had already been practically forgotten. America emerged from the war like "a lucky gambler," Morand would say.[15] "The war was an asset to America before she entered it, while she was in it, and after she withdrew": this was how the Yankee-friendly Tardieu put it in 1927. "Everything that Europe has lost, America has gained," Tardieu added.

"Thanks to the war, America more than doubled her power and laid the foundations of a new empire. Thanks to the war, American prosperity, which in pre-war days was a proud boast, has grown in painful contrast to European distress."[16] *Cui prodest?* Who had benefited from the war, if not America? While the most moderate French voices were satisfied with noting that "rather than a promising lender, [after 1918] the uncle had become a demanding creditor,"[17] the most virulent denounced the lucky winner as Europe's murderer. The "fatal date," Aron and Dandieu affirmed in a page we have already cited from *Le Cancer américain,* was that of "the American banks' organization" under the leadership of the Federal Reserve System: the Great War had immediately followed, to speed up the transfer of gold.[18]

Not all anti-Americans took such a drastic view as to suggest a conspiracy theory in which the United States was not only the main beneficiary but the true instigator of World War I. But everyone repeated the theme of the hemorrhage of French wealth for the sole gain of the ephemeral transatlantic ally. Tardieu said it in 1927 and again in 1934: "Half the gold in existence in the world has found its way into American coffers";[19] "they drained all the gold of the world into their own country."[20] Faced with the scope of the phenomenon and the gravity of its consequences, André Siegfried quickly dropped the austere objectivity of statistics to express the worry this successful monopolization filled him with: "The New York money-lender is now, with respect to the old continent, in the stark and brutal relationship of the creditor watching over his money, the rich man who has helped a poor man and intends to get his advance back—an advance which is a kind of charity, but also, in the most literal sense of the word, a loan. The danger is now that America can do whatever it pleases."[21] So in a double stroke of bad luck, a despoiled France and a "humiliated Europe" also had to get used to the foreseeable brutalities of an America that was, Siegfried added, "gradually and surreptitiously assuming the role of a missionary bailiff."[22]

Was that all? No. Because the new bailiff prepared to seize the planet's possessions for breach of payment was also the usurer to whom the nations were in debt. For the speculating Yankees, amassing all the gold in the world in their coffers was not enough. Right away, they had wanted to multiply their millions by outrageous credit and lending left and right to "the most unreliable borrowers in Europe."[23] There was no way for them to play innocent about it. "It would have been impossible to make greater blunders than they did. It would have been impossible to play the very best cards worse than they did." It was once more Tardieu who made the indictment of America's "lack of balance in its calculations" and "lack of humanity in its decisions."[24] Aron and Dandieu, avoiding an economic discussion in which we can sense they would be on unsure footing, raised the rhetorical stakes against an America that had "speculation in its blood" and embodied "the triumph of credit over gold and the certified check over the nest egg."[25] The supreme irony and ultimate cause for anger: the very same America that was so ruthlessly demanding the money burned up in the inferno of the war had for ten years running been showering a (not unmotivated) manna on the heads of former enemies or perfect strangers who were, moreover, no good at making repayments. A double standard? That was the theory Maurras developed in 1919.

Maurras the Revisionist

Les Trois aspects du Président Wilson: La neutralité, l'intervention, l'armistice, which Maurras published in 1920, was not only the rough draft of a clinical portrait of presidential and American insanity. It was also a way for the nationalist leader to go back in time and rekindle the memory of grievances against America in France. In compiling his pronouncements on the United States since the start of the world war, Maurras was not presenting a simple collection of texts of documentary value: he was proposing a reinterpretation of the brief period of unanimity from 1917 to 1918 in the double light of a troubling "before" and a disappointing "after." The friendly Wilson of the intervention is sandwiched between the haughty Wilson of 1914 and the autistic Wilson of 1919. Which was the real one? Surely not the fleeting one the French had forged and fallen for. Their mistake was understandable; Maurras himself had shared it. But it was high time to dispel it, because President Wilson had become a danger. Or rather, he had always been one.

Pedagogically, in order to dispel the collective illusion, Maurras turned back the clock, retraced the path of the war, and showed Wilson "freezing" the pro-Allied movement with his August 18, 1914, speech, in which he considered the scales balanced between the belligerents, and launching, in 1916, the indefensible slogan "neither victors nor vanquished."[26] Clear-minded thinkers (read: Maurras himself) had judged him "already worrisome" (an admirable "already"). Because his impartiality in 1914, his equanimity in 1916, betrayed his partiality for Germany and his lack of warmth for his future allies. The enthusiasm of a struggle that had become a common one should not have allowed the French to forget Wilsonian America's fundamental characteristics—characteristics Maurras himself had underscored in the articles he was now republishing for his French readership.

The first of these characteristics: philosophical aberration. Wilson's America was Kantian, like the students in *Les Déracinés* misled by a wrongheaded teacher. The theme of "Wilsonian Kantism"[27] hammered in by Maurras was tied in with the whole Barrèsian tradition of demonizing that "republican" philosophy with German origins. Echoes of this can also be heard in the nonconformists—including those who took their distance from the Action Française.

Second characteristic: national arrogance. This was Maurras's chance to make a discreet mea culpa: "We called Mr. Woodrow Wilson an American nationalist. But we never admitted that the president's nationalism could be coupled with a practice of humiliating and belittling an allied nation that his weapons had saved, and without which his country would itself be invaded."[28] (It is hard to say what Maurras meant by this, but it is clear that his rhetorical switch-over was an attempt to restore the symbolic balance of favors.) Maurras seems to have suddenly discovered that nationalisms tend to take reciprocal umbrage with each other. American arrogance was embodied in the person of Wilson, "a magnificent Caesar at our expense." But it went beyond his person. The Americans, whose "dollars and cannons [were] capable of stifling the slightest murmur hostile to their views,"[29] were collectively caught up in a whirlwind of the same "dizzying power" that was reinforced in their president by his religious neurosis. The "philosophical" and Valéryan theme of decline was clearly ceded here to the more brutally concrete one of subjection and dependency. In this, at least, Maurras was a pioneer.

The third characteristic, which seems to be the most important to Maurras himself: the philo-Germanism of the Americans and specifically Wilson, whom Maurras describes as inseparable from his ties to Jewish finance. Announced in the foreword and repeated in the epilogue, the denunciation of an American-German-Jewish conspiracy is manifestly the essential lesson Maurras is attempting to communicate to his readers. The president who wanted to dictate his laws to the world was himself under the thumb of "any given element of high finance which holds a powerful influence over his way of thinking."[30] It was a dependency bordering on addiction: "No energetic willpower or overwhelming reason induced him either to break his prejudicial German ties or to rally to our financial fate his bosses and friends, America's German Jews."[31] Wilsonian America's nationalist arrogance, when all was said and done, was really a Trojan horse with other goals in mind: "the growing global domination of an insurrectional, revolutionary race over productive, conservative, civilizing nations."[32] The thunderbolt of American power did not strike from the Capitol or even the White House: it obeyed the "decisions of the Wilsonian Sinai."[33] A new relationship was created here, in Maurras's text and through the figure of Wilson, between anti-Americanism and anti-Semitism: we will see it rapidly evolve through the interwar years.

Maurras's 1920 exposé went far beyond the context of self-justification in which the nationalist thinker might have skillfully combined a (parsimonious) admission of his pro-American deviation in 1917 and the (insistent) reminder of his constant anti-Wilson vigilance. In fact, much more seriously, he was proclaiming the bankruptcy of the Lafayette myth of everlasting friendship, calling up memories of affronts and malevolence, reactivating prewar anti-Americanism, and abolishing, in the minds of his French readers, any idea of a fraternal, salvageable America; in short, he was wiping out every last trace of France's recent debts by recalling an old liability.

This was why Maurras retrod the floorboards of history, went back over his own texts, and thrust his chronicles of necessary mistrust before the eyes of the French. Among the pages he exhumes, one of the most striking is probably the article from April 7, 1917, in which he comments on the United States' entry into the war, which had been approved the day before in Congress. Maurras portrays this weighty and long-awaited event not as the start of a new era, but as the imperturbable continuation of a power play in which affection has no part. At the center of his painting is the blind chaplain, Congress, charged with pronouncing the prayer that will accompany this solemn decision. It is this same chaplain, Maurras notes, who also officiated when war was declared on Spain, the "1898 war, which marked the American power's first step in Europe's direction." And Maurras continues: "It was not a defensive war, no. Its aim was to 'liberate' beautiful islands, some of them close, like Cuba, and therefore useful and convenient to American life; others far away, like the Philippines, but considered essential to extending the Union empire."[34] What an interesting welcome—reminding the new American allies that in 1898 they had declared war on "Europe"!

If Maurras repeated the offense by republishing this page in 1920, it was so that he could better tie back into a briefly abandoned anti-Americanism that was already a historic artifact. Linking the 1919 predicament to "worrisome" forerunners in 1914 and 1916 and recalling, at the height of the victory celebration, "Europe's" humiliation in 1898, he confirmed the notion of "half-barbaric" America's perennial harmfulness. A ferryman between two ages of anti-Americanism, he handed down to the nationalist right a base of "cultural" criticism on America's noncivilization. But also, taking on the role of witness and workman of both Franco-American ill tidings and the crystallization of anti-Wilsonism, he pushed right-wing anti-Americanism onto a new track: to the model of Anglo-Saxon affinities he added the weighty paradigm of a Judeo-Germano-American conspiracy.

War Debts and "Blood Taxes"

After the shock of America's failure to ratify treaties and its refusal to join the League of Nations, a diplomatic war of attrition began. The French population watched it with unusual attentiveness and growing exasperation, because it struck a nerve: the status of France as a great power, its "victor's rights" and its international "freedom of action." Maurras's indignation toward a foreign president who "thought he could request, right there in the Chamber, that we give up a little of our freedom of action" during the February 3, 1919, session had echoes that went far beyond the Maurrasian family.[35] Old mistrust resurfaced, aggravated by new fears.

Apprehension about an "Anglo-Saxon" conspiracy was reawakened. Hadn't America, during the Peace Conference, outrageously favored Great Britain where colonial and financial compensations were concerned? Hadn't the United States and Great Britain conspired at the Washington Conference (1921–22) to carve up the world for their navies, leaving France the big loser? The explanation by "racial affinities" came back with a vengeance, and between Charles Maurras and André Siegfried there was no divergence as to its validity. "If we may be permitted to state what no one else will say but which many think, or at least feel subconsciously," wrote André Siegfried in 1927—so you had to have the courage to recognize that America was taking over as the "leader of the white race" from a consenting (because it knew how to be realistic) Great Britain. Still, it was important to "understand," Siegfried insisted, that American imperialism "ha[d] nothing to do with land hunger," territorial and political, as it was charged with at the end of the nineteenth century; that its goal was absolutely not a "dissolution of the British Empire"; that it was with the enthusiastic approval of the dominions and the calculated consent of the English that it was becoming, without encountering the slightest opposition, the center of a "new constellation, dominated not by politics but by racial, economic, and social considerations."[36] This racial and geoeconomical reorganization of the world was worrisome for France. The outlook was even bleaker for those who saw "racial affinities" working to Germany's advantage, too. Because how else could you explain the strange solicitude the United States showed for the legitimately punished Germans? Maurras had a ready-made answer: "ethnic and other powers: racial coalitions, cash consortiums."[37] That was the solution to the riddle and the key to Wilson's pro-German politics. Many people in France, though they did not necessarily share the certainties of fervent nationalism, were indignant over America's "understanding" for the German "warmongers."

The debt crisis was therefore not just a matter of big money. The size of the amounts involved was obviously not unrelated to the bitterness of the disagreement, but other factors contributed to making it an inextricable one. From a legal point of view, there were two types of divergence. The French wanted to distinguish, in their debts toward the United States, commercial debts from debts contracted after April 6, 1917 (the date the United States entered the war), which they considered "political" debts. The Americans refused this distinction. A second source of the conflict: the French wanted to link the repayment of their debts to Germany's compliance in honoring its obligation to pay "reparations" for war damages. The Americans, once again, wanted to dissociate the two operations, which they considered unrelated. On one side of the table, talk ran to keeping accounts; the other, the French side, was concerned with stabilizing financial conditions for economic recovery, with the conviction that American help was both necessary and justified. "The famous slogan 'Germany will pay!' did not describe the fundamental economic policy of the French government at the end of the war," writes William R. Keylor. "It would be better described by the phrase 'America will pay.'"[38] But America did not see things this way. French attempts to push the notion of an "interallied economic solidarity" bumped up against a brutal refusal as of the Peace Conference. Worse, Congress rejected the plan, backed by Wilson, of opening a line of credit with the American Treasury to finance France's reconstruction. America refused France its "due"—a precursor to the Marshall Plan. Comparatively, Germany seemed spoiled: it had the largesse of the big American banks, and when it pronounced itself insolvent, it won over the United States' sympathy and diplomatic backing.

Going into the details of the successive negotiations and the restructuring of German reparations would take up too much space here. Between the fall of the mark and Germany's inability to pay, the amounts France expected to receive were dwindling away. Germany was suspected of cheating, but there was more anger directed at those who allowed it to cheat or who were stopping a wronged France from reacting punitively than toward Germany itself. The debt affair created a strong sense of being dispossessed, not only because France considered itself cheated, but also because it had lost control of the process. It was France, after all, that had originally been slated to preside over the Reparations Commission. But in 1920, Poincaré[39] resigned from the commission. The same Poincaré, who was back in the game in 1922 and pressed by the financial crisis, accepted the Anglo-American plan, called the Dawes Plan, which had been launched by President Coolidge and Lord Curzon. In late 1923, the Reparations Commission was removed in favor of the Dawes Commission and a Parker Commission, which was supposed to look into Germany's payment. Nothing was irrevocable yet, but the leading role America's bankers and politicians would have in the double settlement of reparations and debts was laden with nearly inevitable conflicts. The successive plans, each less favorable to France and all of them inoperant, were easy to present to the French as "American bastards."[40]

In 1927 came a period of seeming calm. The Kellogg-Briand Pact, which "outlawed" war, seemed to herald a diplomatic rapprochement. The Mellon-Béranger Agreement for debt consolidation, signed by Poincaré in 1926 but shelved in the hopes of a more advantageous renegotiation, was finally passed by the Chamber, in which Poincaré had asked for a vote of confidence in 1929. That same year, a commission of experts presided over by the American banker Owen Young was named to reorganize the debt calendar; it would also advocate the creation of a Bank for International Settlements to be given important coordination capacities—and which would immediately be denounced in France as an instrument for the complete takeover of European finance by the United States.

Paul Reynaud presented the Young Plan before the Chamber of Deputies on March 28, 1930. André Tardieu spoke on the 29th. Both of them went before the Senate on April 5. The debt affair had changed from a technical debate into a violently emotionally charged public controversy. The press took up the torch. Literary writers did too. Paul Morand, the hurried novelist, transcribed the financial-dispute-turned-culture-clash in *World Champions* that same year, 1930.[41] There was an outpouring of articles and essays denouncing American "greed" and taking as their principal target the Bank for International Settlements. The BIS was contested right from the start in parliamentary debates, notably by Gaston Bergery and Georges Bonnet, who worried about its exaggerated financial power. André Tardieu, before the Senate, tried to wax ironic: "They believed that the 'wall of money' would turn into a citadel (*Smiles*), that the Bank for International Settlements would become some kind of weapon for capitalist domination to be used against governments, against citizens."[42] However Tardieu might pretend to believe that the objections were only coming from a paranoid Left obsessed with the "wall of money" responsible for their governmental failure in 1924, the truth was that the hostility was just as striking on the Right as on the Left, both against the payment of debts and against the BIS's "dictatorship."

The last act would start in 1931. The crisis led President Hoover to establish a one-year moratorium that would suspend both the payment of German reparations to France and the payment of French debts to the United States. Faced with the situation in Germany, the Lausanne conference in July 1932 liquidated reparations: Germany had paid off 11 billion gold francs, or less than a tenth of the sum that had been set in March 1921 at the London conference. André Tardieu, in 1934, evaluated this accounts keeping, which in the eyes of many Frenchmen made France the victim of its former allies and the dupe of its former enemy. In his opinion, between 1919 and 1932, Germany had paid only 6 percent of the sums set by the treaty and 2 percent of the total cost of the war and war damages. He added that, far from strangling Germany, the Young Plan only represented an expenditure of 30 marks per capita per year for the Germans. There, in black and white, was the financial wrong committed against France by "the Anglo-Saxons, in agreement with the Germans."[43] This last little sentence, coming from André Tardieu's pen, is perhaps even more explosive than figures—or than the Action Française's tirades. . .

When the Hoover moratorium expired, Paris (which was no longer receiving anything at all from Germany) was supposed to start paying the Americans back again. Édouard Herriot was in favor of this. He exposed the dangers to France of hurting its international credit and isolating itself diplomatically. He also recalled that the disputed loans had been contributed by some 60 million Americans; if the French stopped paying, the effect would be devastating, not only with regard to America's leaders, but with the man in the street as well. In vain; the Chamber overturned it by 402 votes to 187. On December 15, 1932, France unilaterally declared its payments suspended. In the United States, the newspapers slugged this broken promise: "FRANCE DEFAULTS." Roosevelt's entrance into the White House in early 1933 gave the French a moment of hope of being better understood. On February 20, 1933, the French ambassador, Paul Claudel, had an interview with the new president to set the tone for the visit of a high-level mission to be led by Herriot in April—a mission that was not facilitated by the United States' abandoning the gold standard while Herriot was crossing the Atlantic. This effort would not be enough to untie the Gordian knot of debts, or to loosen France's purse strings. On June 1, 1934, a message to Congress from Roosevelt reformulated the intangible American position: debts and reparations were separate affairs. For the rest of the decade, American indignation was the systematic retort to French disappointment. Each year, Congress would recall, in vain, that France had obligations it was consistently uneager and increasingly less able to pay.

Uncle Sam or Uncle Shylock?

Beyond diverging interpretations of the nature of the debts, beyond disagreement over the ties between France's acquittal of its debts and Germany's payment of reparations, beyond the profound legal differences between the two cultures, the most striking aspect of French reactions was the strong "subjectivation" of the problem and interpretation of the crisis in emotional or symbolic terms. In this France was united. "For once," notes historian Donald Roy Allen, "French opinion was as one person, a person whose feelings were a mixture of hurt pride, righteous indignation, and moral certainty."[44] Even if it was not the first time anti-Americanism had had the magical effect of overriding political divisions among the French, the unanimity was indeed impressive. First, political leaders and editorialists had deserted the legal terrain (where, as they themselves admitted, the ground was not very stable) to try to impose a political or, even better, a "moral" perspective on the dispute. It goes without saying that this moral stance was not shared by the Americans, who considered France's defaulting on normal commercial obligations an act of sheer dishonesty.

The French line of defense drew on another logic, which Tardieu himself defended: whether the Americans admitted it or not, the Young Plan had established an incontrovertible tie between what were supposedly commercial debts and the eminently political issue of reparations owed by Germany. No one in France accepted the American view of the problem, not even those in favor of reimbursement. Raymond Recouly, who thought that the political cost of nonpayment would be more painful than the financial bill, nevertheless opposed the American approach with conviction. He saw the clash between France and the United States as a confrontation between two concepts of the law. "Legally speaking, the United States may be right. Politically, morally, it will never make its European debtors believe that its claim—aside from the fact that it is a *war debt,* which makes it completely distinct from ordinary claims—should not be revised, just as Hoover's intervention forced it to revise its claim on Germany."[45] In one sentence he pointed out the intangible position of the French negotiators (this debt was "special") and denounced the favoritism shown to the Germans under pressure from the same American administration that purported to have no need to intervene in the case of French debts, which were purely "commercial."

On a moral level, the refusal front, which represented the majority of the French press and public opinion during the 1926 parliamentary debate, challenged the American side's technicality and legalism and appealed to other, higher authorities: political responsibility, equity, and fraternity in arms. On a tactical level, the goal was to point out the Americans' bad faith; they were intimately involved in Europe's financial dealings but wanted to exclude French debts from the global negotiations taking place under their leadership. "If the reparations affair does not concern them," said the same Raymond Recouly of the Americans, "then they should not take it upon themselves to deal with it."[46] Sticking your finger into the process—through the Dawes Commission, the Young Plan, and especially the Hoover moratorium—also meant sticking your neck out. As a country. French polemicists thus skillfully repoliticized a course of action the Americans considered purely technical. The reproach of being hypocritical, so often associated with "Puritan" behavior in the past, struck home here. No one could believe for a second the "nonentanglement policy" preached by the Americans, when in fact they had not stopped intervening in Europe with their observers, experts, and political emissaries, stressed Régis Michaud, a contributor to *La Revue universelle* and author of a book on "the American soul."[47] And the dishonesty turned into cynicism when the American press advised France's creditors to abandon France to its fate while American bankers and businessmen colonized and besieged it. There was also no shortage of remarks about the fact that American companies had made enormous profits during the war and the immediate postwar period, generating in turn considerable tax revenues. Basing its argument on figures published by the American Treasury, *La Revue de Paris* concluded that the "advances" given the allies had been "more than compensated for."[48] *Bis repetita...* This line of argument, which the French alone found convincing, was the carbon copy of arguments that had been adopted a century earlier to refuse compensation for Napoleonic captures: American ship merchants, it was argued in France, had reaped such colossal benefits during the blockade that complaining about a few unfortunate captures was just plain bad manners.

Washington's behavior, as analyzed in France by the Left *and* the Right, was conspiring to harm the French by renewing an "Anglo-Saxon understanding," granting Germany favors out of affinity or self-interest (to protect unthinking investments), and creating a supranational authority, the BIS, that threatened France's sovereignty. The Camelots du Roi and the Croix-de-Feu organized street protests in 1932 against America's claims. *L'Action française,* out of all the press, maintained the most hostile stance toward the United States throughout the crisis. The right-wing newspapers and journals were the most mordant. Aron and Dandieu's *Le Cancer américain* railed against the BIS, rebaptized, in best Céline fashion, "International church."[49] But if the impetus came mostly from the Right, opportune anti-American works came pouring from the entire ideological spectrum and shared the same propensity for titles with shock value: J.-L. Chastanet's *L'Oncle Shylock* (1927), Octave Homberg's *L'Impérialisme américain* (1929), Kadmi-Cohen's *L'Abomination américaine* (1930), and Charles Pomaret's *L'Amérique à la conquête de l'Europe* (1931). The first and last of these were works by left-wing elected parliamentarians; the second, by a negotiator in the first war loan of 1915; the third, by an essayist whose admiration was split between André Siegfried and Aristide Briand and who endorsed a Paris-Berlin-Moscow axis as the backbone of a future United States of Europe. The first three were violently anti-American; the fourth was more neutral, giving figures to make the economic and financial case for an American hegemony.

L'Oncle Shylock stands out among the pile more for its title than its content, which is of a fairly ordinary anti-Americanism. Louis Chastanet was a militant syndicalist who had moved into politics. He had been elected deputy of the Isère department in 1924 on the "leftist bloc" ballot and would be reelected in 1928 in La Tour-du-Pin. His *Oncle Shylock* examined the United States' financial policies and developed, without much originality, the theory of an American will to enslave Europe through debt. Being paid was less important to the Americans than the possibility of holding power over their debtors: "What tempts [America] even more is the permanent blackmail the situation allows it to exercise over us."[50] That same year, 1927, a book that no one would have dreamed of calling polemical Siegfried's *America Comes of Age*, made the same assertion in no less dramatic terms: "[America] can do as it likes without consideration for anyone else. It can act as arbitrarily as it pleases. It can strangle whole peoples and governments, or it can assist them on its own terms. It can control them—something it loves above all else— and judge them from its superior moral height, and then impose its verdict."[51] Chastanet chimes in: "One can dominate the world without conquering it. For [America], lending money to others is a way of dominating them. And it has lent money to the entire world."[52] So it was not Chastanet's theory that gave his book its originality, but in fact the grimacing distortion he inflicted on the image of America: "U.S.! These two letters were once the initials of Uncle Sam. You know, the good and generous Uncle Sam. But now he has passed away." And Uncle Shylock had taken over for him. Now, *he* was of another stripe, and his only commandment was: "Thou shalt lend usuriously to many nations and thou shalt dominate them."[53] He was the one who henceforth "was waiting in the wings" of the world; "he is the one who speaks first." But he would not take it with him, so to speak, since "America, by distributing its credit left and right, has only managed to sow hatred. In all probability, it will reap the combined interest of this sentiment." And in one last parable about punishment, Chastanet changes mythologies, evoking Cyrus captured by the Amazons, whose queen forces him to drink a cup of molten gold to his death. But the real trail is clearly indicated from the very first page, by the epigraph from Toussenel, author in 1845 of *Juifs, rois de l'époque* (Jews, the Kings of Our Age).

For many in France at the end of the 1920s, as historian David Strauss notes, "'Uncle Sam' soon became 'Uncle Shylock.'" The sobriquet's success seems indeed indubitable,[54] and revealing in more ways than one. The reference to the most famous usurer in Western tradition condensed the public grievances that had been reawakened by the repayment affair: that America was amassing all the world's riches and making speculative reinvestments with high risks for all of Europe. But the slippage from an America that was "creditor to the world" to an America seen as a planetary usurer was facilitated as well by the rapid spread in the 1920s of new representations of America, in which anti-Americanism was combined with anti-Semitism. We will simply underscore here—before we come back to it in the next chapter— the perfect synchronization between the appearance of the Shylock theme and the fact (thanks to Siegfried, notably) that the notion of a Jewish "influence" over the United States had become commonplace. The theme is insistent in the 1927 edition of *America Comes of Age*. Keeping "more or less apart in spite of themselves," Siegfried explains, the Jews "ferment at the bottom of the Melting Pot, unassimilated to the end."[55] By resisting "Americanization," their specific weight in American society was constantly growing. The Jews kept "apart," but were already (at least some of them) on the summits and among the "great moral and financial forces which control the life of the nation."[56] Uncle Shylock came at the right time to embody the new two-headed America, in which the Jews and the Yankees shared (or fought over) financial power—since, as Aron and Dandieu reminded their readers in 1931, "speculation runs in their blood."

And indeed, a semiotics of blood was central to the new episode of anti-Americanism that was the war debt crisis. Blood, or rather, bloods.

There was first of all the "ethnic" equation, which had grown more complicated since the prewar period, when it had been essentially based on an opposition between the Anglo-Saxons and the Latins. This opposition did not disappear, but the diagram of tensions and affinities became more elaborate. Despite the myth of origins implied by Anglo-Saxonism, the pre-1914 anti-American discourse, as we will recall, dissociated the Germans—cousins who were "not as german as all that"—from the Americans.[57] Now these distant cousins were suddenly reunited, not by Anglo-Saxon roots, but by the presence of important Jewish communities that tied them together across the Atlantic through customs and interests, not to mention what Siegfried called "an obscure community of race."[58]

But there was, at the heart of the anti-American polemic of the 1920s, another blood feud: the rhetorical war of spilled blood, offered blood; blood shed *without keeping track,* as orators and editorialists would repeat; blood that had once been offered up to the insurgents and had flowed onto French soil this time—and this time for the Right of all. Now the French wanted the value of this blood recognized and its price established. They wanted it to *enter into account* in the debt quarrel.

The Shylock allegory did not only explicitly tie in to the image of an usurious America and implicitly to a "Jewified" America; it also alluded to a France that had already paid its "pound of flesh," a France that had already given too much blood for its creditors to dare claim their dues. The mythological success of "Uncle Shylock" mirrored Louis Marin's political triumph before the Chamber in January 1925. In arguing against reimbursing the American debt, Marin's demonstration hinged on the fact that a claim that ignored the human sacrifices France had made was unjust and even iniquitous. "Throughout the entire world," Marin stressed, "no one can forget that there is not simply a debit and credit account involving money, but also an account that involves human lives, suffering and losses of all kinds which should be taken into account."[59] (He also did not neglect to remind his audience, even if it was only a rhetorical gesture, that "the United States entered the war late. I do not mean to imply that they came in as eleventh-hour workers.")

America's loans were simply the form the American war effort had taken. Since it had not (yet) had any men to offer, America had offered its money, while France had paid the blood tax. So the scales were balanced, the accounts already cleared, whatever the Americans thought. The French tithe had even been heavier than American expenditures would ever be: the indebted people were not the ones rumor had it.

The striking success of Marin's speech across all the different parliamentary factions can be seen in the minutes, as well as in the decision to have the text of his address printed and posted in all the communes of France. But the French consensus against Yankee greed was stamped that day with a strange seal. Because who was weighing the bruised flesh and measuring the spilled blood if not the very same people denouncing the American Shylock? Who was presenting the European "bailiff," as Siegfried put it, with the memory of its dead, marked "received"—if not France, through deputy Marin's voice? In a curious and unconscious reversal of the myth, it was the French who professed to be paying, or rather affirmed that they *had already paid* in human flesh, a debt that America, more prosaically, was demanding of them in common currency. The rhetorical scenarios of reimbursement were permeated by a generalized atmosphere of Freudian slips. Witness the famous editorial by Pierre Scize in *Le Canard enchaîné* protesting against the execution of Sacco and Vanzetti: amid a catalog of grievances, Scize denounces an America that "mints coins with its dead soldiers."[60] It is a strange projection on the Americans—who were in fact reproached with having lost so few of their soldiers—to make an accusation that would more appropriately describe the stubborn French attempt to capitalize on its human losses by using them to "pay off" its debts.

One of the most clear-sighted, in this respect, was Georges Duhamel. A curious and rarely cited chapter of *Scenes from the Life of the Future* deals with

America as an "insurance society":[61] a society in which blood could be reimbursed, and paying off accident victims cost less than the necessary measures for avoiding the accident in the first place. But behind the half-humorous discussion on the morality or immorality of the insurance society that the narrator conducts with the inexorable Mr. Stone, the allusion to the Franco-American debate over the price of blood is obvious. Mr. Stone, who has made his fortune by reducing "the kinds of spring mattresses adopted throughout the Union from seventy-eight to four" is also a Procrustes of immaterial values. "Why," the box-spring-reducer asks Duhamel, "do you want to introduce into your calculations sentimental considerations that can't properly be reduced to figures, and that threaten to falsify your arithmetic without helping anyone?"[62] This echoes America's response to the French demand that its dead be taken into account in the war bill. In the Americans' view, these sentimental elements should be "eliminated [like] useless documents," Siegfried comments. "When the question of settling inter-Allied debts was discussed, any mention of the great things accomplished in common on the field of battle was coldly put to one side, as if they were eliminating useless documents in settling up their accounts."[63] It was brutal, but was it unjustified? Inversely, were the French right in demanding the *pretium doloris* for their millions of dead soldiers? Could, and, above all, should there be compensation for what deputy Marin himself called "the imponderable elements"?[64] Duhamel was far from certain. By accepting the financial payoff of the human tithe, he maintained, "I know . . . that I acquiesce in the commercialization of certain moral values; that . . . I depreciate and degrade them, that from the very fact that we are willing to assign commercial value to life and death, pain and pleasure, they lose a part of their human value."[65] I'm insured, however, Duhamel added. And like everyone in France, I "cover these values" with "a certain phrase in Latin."[66]

Thus the author of *Scenes from the Life of the Future*, who never missed the slightest chance to make recriminations against America, remained completely—and eloquently—silent on the war debt issue. He, at least, had understood that moral ground was no better than legal ground.

Marshall Plan and Military Police

From one debt to another? What the French had dreamed of obtaining in 1920—a line of credit opened by the American Treasury for reconstruction—they would receive in 1948 without having "begged" for it, even if the verb regularly cropped up in the press, with the Marshall Plan. Manna fell in the form of over $13 billion allocated to France by the Economic Cooperation Administration charged with apportioning American credit for the period from March 31, 1948, to April 1, 1949. The plan was renewable yearly until 1952. *France-Soir* translated for its readers: "300 billion!" Francs, that is. "An annuity of approximately 7,200 francs for every Frenchman and French-woman."[67] Annuity? An unfortunate choice of words. . . What was the Mar-shall Plan's goal? *France-Soir* also asked. It was an "oxygen mask." France was not only a war convalescent; it had become, economically speaking, Europe's great invalid. Raymond Aron stressed this at length and with great patience in a series of articles published in the summer of 1948: "Of all the countries in Europe, France is the one whose account balance is in the worst shape."[68] And he also used first-aid metaphors. "Oxygen masks and shots of camphor oil have no supporters or opponents."[69] But he knew that was not true. The Marshall Plan had its supporters, who saw it as France's salvation, or at least its short-term resuscitation. It also had its staunch and organized opponents, who considered it a fatal drug. The announcement of such an enormous gift would breathe new life into the dramaturgy of debt. The anti-Americans of 1930 refused to repay; the anti-Americans of 1948 refused to receive. But, as we will see, it was still in the name of a bloody price paid or to pay.

This combat put the Communists on the front line. Their ministers had been expelled from the government in 1947. Furthermore, the USSR, after initial negotiations with Molotov, had refused to be associated with the Euro-pean Recovery Program. Brutally given its freedom, the French Communist Party mobilized all of its forces against the American presence and "Ameri-can party" politicians in France. It was the start of a long and violent cam-paign. The Marshall Plan was presented as a Trojan horse for French eco-nomic vassalization and above all as the first stage of a total war operation against the USSR. American aid was thus attacked from two angles: as a bad business deal, concluded for the sole benefit of a few politicians sold on the United States, which would lead straight to economic (and cultural) enslave-ment; and as an inevitable spiral into war, with dollars being used as a lure to draw France into NATO, exploit its territory for military purposes, and enlist its soldiers for a future American war. Of course the campaign did not stop the Marshall Plan from being applied, but by its wide scope, it did succeed, as Raymond Aron acknowledged from the opposing camp, in "in-timidating the plan's supporters." We should add: and in giving French anti-Americanism a new dimension, a leftist and proletarian one.

A study by the State Department helps measure the success of the anti-American offensive. One year after it was ratified, only a third of the non-Communist French declared themselves in favor of the Marshall Plan.[70] How did such a large percentage of public opinion manage to oppose an offer that was, after all, unhoped for (even if it was not disinterested)? To answer that, we have to look at the huge propaganda effort the Communists agreed to, and on which the major part of the campaigns was based. But these campaigns themselves owed their success to the strategic revival of earlier anti-American themes that could reach a wide and varied audience.

The argumentation was set as of 1948. We find a reliable exposé of it in a book by Georges Soria published in May of that year (with a preface by Frédéric Joliot-Curie): *La France deviendra-t-elle une colonie américaine?* (Will France Become an American Colony?). The book's primary objective is to destroy the myth of a "gift" or a "generous gesture" on the Americans' part. How could the French believe that the Americans, who were hardly known for their altruism, were prepared to tighten their belts in order to assist fifteen distant and needy nations? Obviously, with the Marshall Plan, the United States had a lot to gain, starting with new markets. The Americans were making an investment. What they were "giving" France they counted on getting back, with interest. How? Business as usual: in human flesh, in cannon fodder. It was all, as Soria put it, very "simple and subtle."

So, to sum up the scenario: the Marshall Plan was the result of a conspiracy that had taken shape right when the French Communist ministers were being thanked. But the first act had taken place in Washington in March 1946, when Léon Blum, the Gouin government's extraordinary ambassador, went there to negotiate the famous Blum-Byrnes agreements. The first stage of these agreements stipulated that the French war debts would be annulled. Were the Americans to thank for that? Not on your life! It was a simple "calculation" faced with a financially devastated France, Soria commented—"an intelligent measure for self-protection."[71] It was also a sucker's market: the Americans had used it to get rid of their untransportable surplus goods, all the while compelling the French to buy unusable Liberty ships . . . But the worst part was in the agreements' second stage, which forced France to give up the protectionism that was indispensable to its industries. It was a veritable abandonment of "a part of the nation's sovereignty."[72] Doing so voluntarily, as Blum advocated and aspired to, was resignation pushed to the point of betrayal—the "American party" was using a "philosophy entirely in the spirit of Munich." After dealing with the economic side of things, now it was time for the political and military angle.

Handing over the national economy to the enemy was just one stage in a complete subservience to America's will. The Marshall Plan not was only organizing France's economic colonization; it was paving the way for its military dependency. Diplomatically, the first stage consisted in putting the victors and the vanquished on the same footing: not only would there be no German "reparations," but a Germany that had not been "de-Nazified" would be put back in the saddle. This was a priority for the bellicose Americans in their projected confrontation with the USSR. And the (not so) secret side of the Organization for European Economic Co-operation was that it would lead straight to the European Defense Community and NATO. "All that had a terrible stench, a well-known one: Munich!" Soria, in his functions as a journalist, had met the French negotiators: "These people foresaw the country's economic colonization, just as the people in Munich in 1938 had agreed to give in to Hitler's demands. The ulterior motives were the same."[73] From Hitler to Truman, then, there had simply been a change in coercive tactics: "coercion by starvation (instead of coercion by war)." But in a supplementary Machiavellian stroke, the famine coercion was meant to pull France into the next war. Once again, the pound of flesh—this time in exchange for rations.

In the rhetoric of these anti-American campaigns, which reached a much wider audience than just militants or Communist sympathizers, the struggle against the Marshall Plan was inseparable from a "defense of peace." As Soria wrote, "the Marshall Plan is in the end nothing but a war plan, just like the Truman doctrine."[74] The tirelessly reiterated Munich analogy should be taken with all seriousness. History was repeating itself while wearing different masks. The mechanisms were the same, and some of the actors would never change: the "Anglo-Saxon capitalists." One year later, in 1949, the discussion was getting even more heated. In a "Letter to President Truman" published by the Combattants de la Paix et de la Liberté (a "wide front" organization), Charles Tillon vituperated "the nation's new gravediggers, who have accepted all their American masters' wishes." But also, and much more originally, he lashed out at the United States with accusations the Far Right had charged it with before the war, of having shamefully favored Germany. Which, in Tillon's 1949 version, meant having financed Nazism. France "has not forgotten that Hitler's aggression was made possible by a growth of German industry fostered by an influx of Anglo-Saxon capital."[75] "Truman, Hitler's authentic successor": the expression would no longer surprise anyone. In 1951, during a speech before Communist officials, the Communist leader Georges Cogniot repeated it as automatically as a Homeric epithet.[76] This was not just a verbal escalation; it was physical, too, whether it took place before the Assembly, where brawls were not uncommon, or in the ports, where dockworkers blocked equipment destined for American bases. The Mouvement de la Paix launched spectacular initiatives and contributed to the success of the Stockholm Appeal's signature campaign: 15 million Frenchmen and -women thus requested a ban on nuclear weapons (which the USSR did not yet possess). Convinced, like Georges Cogniot, of the importance of "*ideological* weapons,"[77] the Communists made considerable efforts to denounce a Europe they stamped "made in USA."

An important side effect of these campaigns was that they acclimatized,
on the Left and in the new social strata, an anti-American virulence that had
previously been much more characteristic of the Far Right or elite intellectual
circles. When Maurice Thorez, in *Fils du peuple*, detailed the United States'
evolution from the Monroe Doctrine to the Truman Doctrine and concluded
that "Truman's new phrase is 'the universe belongs to the Americans,'" the
formulation itself was not in the least surprising. It had been heard as early
as the 1890s. What was new was that it was pronounced in popular rallies,
before millions of people, and not only among political scientists or in diplomatic circles. Cold war *oblige:* a grassroots political anti-Americanism cut its
path through thousands of pamphlets and public meetings. To the illustrated
brochures spread by the American services exalting free unionism or vaunt-
ing workers' living standards in the United States, the Communists responded with a flood of texts and documents, from strictly political tracts to
articles debunking the American way of life to the current-events rhymes that
were the Communist Youth's specialty. Even literature was mobilized, and
André Stil was awarded the Stalin Prize in 1952 for a novel, *Le Premier choc*,
that exalted the dockworkers' resistance to the new occupants. Anti-Americanism was booming more than ever among the intellectuals, aside from a
handful of political pro-Americans (who, moreover, were often cultural anti-
Americans);[78] it was making inroads into public opinion, where prewar intellectuals' tirades had fallen on deaf ears, and despite the fact (if the polls are to
be believed) that the French were still as unconcerned as ever about the American "cultural threat." In fact, in 1953, only 4 percent of the French population
polled perceived America as a cultural threat.[79] *Reader's Digest* frightened
them less than strategic bombardiers. Who can blame them?

The Marshall years witnessed the flare-up of anti-Americanism in a France
cornered by debt. Between those who preached the humility the country's situation compelled and those who vilified the invasive benefactor, the choice was
automatic. The interwar anti-Americans had said that America the creditor
foreshadowed America the bailiff. Postwar predictors warned that America,
with its loans, would control France's fate. Worse than a bailiff, it was the MP
that would come knocking at the door: "It comes as no surprise," Pozner wrote
in 1948, "that the Marshall Plan has the same initials as your Military Police."[80]

Not Guilty!

The hard core of the formidable anti-American mobilization of the 1950s
worked at a "defense of the USSR." But anti-Americanism's success was
essentially due to the slogan "Defense of peace," coupled with a successful

demonizing of the United States as a warmongering nation. In decrying America's bellicose nature, Communist propaganda revived prewar pacifists' traditional themes, now dramatized by the existence of the terrifying weapon only America possessed: the atomic bomb. The bomb furnished a new argument, associated with frightening possibilities. With its incommensurable powers of destruction, it helped relegitimate the discredited stance of "total pacifism." At the same time, the bomb made the only country that possessed it suspect: not only because of the abuse America could make of it or already had—and we will see Emmanuel Mounier explain American aggressiveness as Hiroshima guilt—but also by the simple fact of possessing it. An "atomic" society was not like the others. An "atomic" nation could not profess to embody democratic values. On this ground, the Communists were joined or even surpassed by unexpected allies, such as Georges Bernanos, who wrote in 1947: "An atomic democracy—it makes me laugh! Why not hand the atomic bomb to every voter, along with his ballot?"[81]

The risk of an atomic war did not only furnish arguments; it procured allies, as well. The "neutralists" did more to spread and legitimate anti-Americanism in intellectual circles—though sometimes against their will—than Communist and pacifist propaganda put together. Not that the neutralists, for whom *Le Monde* became a rallying point (but who were also a presence at *Esprit*, *Les Temps modernes*, *Franc-Tireur*, and *France-Observateur*), were all anti-Americans—far from it. Maurice Duverger, in *Le Monde*, stated it clearly: "Between a Sovietized Europe and an Atlantic Empire, the second solution is clearly preferable, because in the first case, slavery is a sure thing, whereas in the second, war will only be a probability."[82] Most of the neutralists were anti-Atlantist out of pragmatism: there was a better chance, they thought, of preventing world war by resisting the stronger of the two adversaries, that is, America. They saw neutralism as a counterweight. That was *Le Monde* editor-in-chief Hubert Beuve-Méry's line of reasoning. Nevertheless, argumentative logic and the weight of stereotypes would often lead discourses, if not men, astray. The Gilson affair is a good example of this.

During the winter of 1950, *La Nouvelle Critique* was at the height of its most Stalinist phase. Issue after issue, it denounced turncoats and false friends: Bourdet, Cassou, Mounier . . . No one was spared; not even Prévert, who was subjected to a long exercise in Janovian criticism. This was not an amiable time. Which makes the praise showered on "Mr. Étienne Gilson" in an unsigned article all the more surprising. Not that Mr. Étienne Gilson wasn't perfectly praiseworthy. But after all, he was not part of the same world as *La Nouvelle Critique*'s contributors, who professed a "lucid love" for Stalin. A neo-Thomist philosopher like Maritain, a professor at the Sorbonne and then at the Collège de France, he had of course been anti-Vichy, but as a Mouvement Républicain Populaire sympathizer with connections to the European Movement (launched in The Hague in 1948 and denounced by Cogniot as the creation of "the United States' chief spy, Allen Dulles"),[83] Gilson was nonetheless far from being an acceptable traveling companion. Just what was Étienne Gilson's singular merit? Apparently that he had denounced, in an article published in *Le Monde* on June 12, 1946, the poor quality of the American movies brought to France by force and in force through the Blum-Byrnes agreements. "It will not be with a light heart that we will witness," Gilson wrote, "our own people absorbing almost unlimited doses of that narcotic." *La Nouvelle Critique* was glad to see that "a man as unlikely to be suspected of 'anti-Americanism' as Mr. Étienne Gilson" had had the honesty to denounce "the powerful means for stupefying the population" that were the Hollywood movies massively injected into French circuits.[84] Clearly the invasion of American films preoccupied the Communist Party and its intellectuals. But Gilson's low opinion of the movies was not his only pull on *La Nouvelle Critique*'s sympathies, or, for that matter, the most essential.

In 1948, Étienne Gilson, in the columns of *Le Monde* that Beuve-Méry had given him out of friendship, had advocated a "neither-nor" approach—neither Washington nor Moscow—and he had multiplied increasingly acid chronicles against the Atlantic Pact. What did Gilson say over these months? That the Americans should not count on the French to be "the extreme tip of the front guard" of a future war. That France had already given. That "it is the United States' turn." That the Atlantic Pact was a one-sided treaty that procured the United States menials on the cheap without creating any kind of obligation on the American side. That the United States had only one interest: obtaining "foot soldiers," because "they were becoming a rare commodity." That it was ready, as always, to put a price tag on them, to "buy them with dollars." And with dollars, "it was once more our blood" they could buy.[85] It was at this point of his escalating rhetoric that the whistle was blown. Protests shot off from all directions. Hubert Beuve-Méry was in a tight spot. In the fall of 1949, publishing another series of extremely anti-American articles—by Pierre Emmanuel this time[86]—heightened the pressure. Gilson stopped contributing to *Le Monde* in September 1950. He would soon abandon the Collège de France for Toronto.

The invisible line Gilson had crossed was as symbolic as it was political. The blood auctioned off to the Americans had the made cup of neutralism spill over. But if *La Nouvelle Critique*'s enthusiasm for a persecuted Gilson was partly a tactical position, there were deep affinities in their stances that went beyond the cultural anti-Americanism the philosopher did nothing to hide. Resuscitating Uncle Shylock was not enough for Gilson. He valiantly undertook to rid the French of their guilt. "They" want "to prove to us that we are guilty," Gilson wrote. But we are not guilty. We are not obliged to give any explanations or excuses. To anyone. And especially not the Americans. "We carried the weight of the 1914–1918 war and the United States gets to wear the laurels." And even, "we carried the weight of the new world war practically alone, with Poland." France was not guilty. It was a better idea to look for the guilty parties across the Atlantic. It was a better idea to consider whether, for instance, "the Hoover plan and the refusal to back our action in the Ruhr did or did not pave the way for Nazism." This analysis, which many nationalists adhered to before the war, became the agreed-upon version of America's prewar errors after the liberation. It had too often been said—particularly to Vichy—that France was guilty; why not look over at the country doing the moralizing? Gilson's reinterpretation of the interwar period was thus in synch with the Stalinist one that privileged two main guilty parties: the felonious French bourgeoisie and the arch-enemy, America. Charles Tillon, in his aforementioned "Open Letter to President Truman," pushed the same accusation as a historical truism: "The Dawes and Young Plans for economic recovery were the forerunners of Schacht and Goering's war plans."[87] Emmanuel Mounier gave his own, strange version of the reversal of guilt by presenting Vichy as an American dream and suspecting the United States in 1949 of wanting to recreate it: "Could [American ambassador to Vichy] Mr. Leahy's dream, a Vichy sanctioned and protected by the Americans, be implemented by those who saved us from Vichy?"[88] The theme hammered in by the Communist Party of an "American-made" Hitler and an America that was now standing in for Nazi Germany was adopted, in more subtle forms, by a wide range of anti-American intellectuals keen on "freeing" France from its new, real, and especially symbolic bondage. Accusing America—which for Bernanos went as far as suggesting that the "machine civilization" should be judged at Nuremberg[89]—was a formidable instrument for erasing debt. After all, the French were not going to thank the United States for having contributed (very little) to slaying a monster America had created itself . . .

Within the arguments and analyses, what united these heterogeneous anti-Americans the most was that they all stamped the debt "return to sender." And the two most unanimous slogans, more informally put than in the petitions, would be: "We owe you nothing" and "It won't work with us." You will not get our infantrymen, Gilson wrote. Or our artillery, Mounier added: "America, if you will, is nineteenth-century England. It considers the Atlantic alliance a division of military work. France is specifically called on to be the Atlantic army's infantry and artillery."[90] The song the Communist Youth sang to the tune of "Jingle Bells" was starting to make the rounds:

> President Truman
> Said to old Schuman,
> "You must sign my Pact,
> It's like Hitler's back!"
> It's made to wage war
> With the USSR,
> With the workers' lands,
> To put cash in U.S. hands.

With the reply, in the chorus:

> But the people said to him, "No, not by a hair!
> The Soviets won't find us fighting over there.
> We won't be the flunkeys of some big old billionaires.
> In the end, all you sharks will die before we'd dare."[91]

"The Atlantic pact gives us no serious guarantee, and in the case of aggression does not commit America to any disposition its own self-interest would not have automatically dictated," Mounier summed up in 1949, citing Gilson, moreover.[92] America had no obligations. France had no hope. For the Yankees did not even intend to buy soldiers but cannon fodder. The French would only be "Atlantized" in order to be vaporized. "Modern warfare"? That meant "war itself sending the goal of war up in smoke. There is no war for freedom, because after a totalitarian war, there is no more freedom."[93] Physically annihilated or at least politically nullified: that would be France's fate if it cooperated with America. After all, wasn't liquidating Europe an integral part of *their* plan? Bernanos thought so: "We understand more and more clearly that anti-civilization, mass civilization, could not proceed in its evolution towards universal slavery without first achieving the liquidation of Europe."[94]

From Tillon to Gilson, from Thorez to Mounier, there was a broad intellectual front that countered culpability with inculpation and rebuffed debt and donation. But we should broaden it even more to take into account the scope of an anti-American consensus whose strength was in its ambiguities. On the slope sliding into a reinterpretation of the interwar period as a neo-defeatism of the "Better Red than Dead" stripe, and including a denial of Vichy, which had been turned into an American affair, one man went further than all the others: Marcel Aymé. And the most significant text of the period was not printed in *Le Monde* or *La Nouvelle Critique* or *Esprit*. It could well be the astonishing synopsis (or true fiction) the writer published in the *Gazette des lettres* in 1951—it appeared on January 15, before being reprinted on January 18 in *Combat*.

Roland Dumay, the editor-in-chief of the *Gazette des lettres*, had asked a number of writers to describe the novel they would have liked to write but never would. Marcel Aymé sent him "La Fille du shérif" (The Sheriff's Daughter). The action takes place in "1952 or '53." An atomic war breaks out on "French territory, which our government long ago sold the free use of to the U.S.A. in exchange for a few ministerial comforts." While the French are vaporized by tens of millions, France's "real government" is holed up in a little town in Missouri. It is led by "Messieurs Moque and Choumane"—for Jules Moch and Robert Schuman. After an ultimate American offensive, "France is ransacked, torn apart, pulverized. And the second day of the offensive, the American papers triumphally announce: *Paris Is Destroyed.*" Everyone rejoices. The follow-up is worth quoting *in extenso*.

> After an offensive that lasts for eight days, the Americans discover that their war no longer has any objective, since nine-tenths of the French population has perished. A peace treaty is signed. Once back in France, the members of the real government reconstruct the political parties, execute 100,000 people, imprison 200,000, or a tenth of the population, and get mixed up in a new wine scandal. Disgusted, the U.N. decrees that France will be crossed off the map of the world. The female element will be directed to the U.S.A., where maids are hard to come by, and as for the men, their b[alls] will be cut off, since they were only hanging by a thread anyway.

And what about the sheriff's daughter? Well, in the little town in Missouri, she has fallen in love with the son of France's "real Minister of Registration." She bears his child and wrests a begrudging consent from the more-than-reticent sheriff. The young Frenchman Nénesse comes back to "fix" things, all the while "carefully hiding the fact that he has been subjected to the U.N.'s decree and is now cut off from having a sex life. The novel ends with a delightful study of the castration complex."[95]

A synopsis of this synopsis? Politicians (all of them rotten) have sold France to the Americans (all of them Puritans) who calmly organize a genocide of the French (except for those who are in Missouri, like the ones who had been in London) under the hardly troubled gaze of the people "really governing" France (with Gallicized names, which they needed), who immediately start up their shady dealings again after the liberation (which is really just a purification).

"La Fille du shérif" admirably confirms Raymond Aron's diagnosis of the same year, 1951: the French "like to think" of the global situation as a personal fight the Americans are trying to pick with the Russians and in which the "Europeans are no longer protected but rather victims."[96] Frenchmen would thus be vaporized or castrated, separated from their domestic females, and disappear from the surface of the earth—eradicated by the American friend. A few years earlier, Thierry Maulnier had described, when Sartre's *La Putain respectueuse* came out, his "intolerable discomfort": "If there had been an American soldier in the audience, I would not have dared to look at him."[97] Marcel Aymé, luckier than Sartre, had apparently not scandalized anyone with his anti-American and Vichyesque fable—not even *Combat*, which republished it.

In the Legation Quarter

Denying any debt to the United States thus became, after 1945, an essential anti-American gesture. Right when the Marshall Plan was ensuring France's economic survival, the French were up in arms about its *symbolic* survival.

"They take our dollars and spit on us," Roger Vailland had a hypothetical American officer say. This was not a bad way to sum up the French attempt to restore a psychological balance in 1944, when De Gaulle showed the way by describing Paris as having "freed itself." The intellectuals issuing the non-IOUs were in perfect agreement with a population that had taken the chocolate but decided early on that it owed the Americans nothing—not even being freed from the Nazis. In 1944, to the question raised by the budding Institut Français d'Opinion Publique, "Which country contributed the most to Germany's defeat?" the French responded massively: the USSR (61 percent), with America obtaining only 29 percent of the responses.[98] This perception was most likely linked to the importance of the battles on the Russian front at the darkest moment of the occupation. But far from being qualified or corrected over time, it would be maintained and reinforced, not only by the important propaganda machinery of the French Communist Party (PCF), but by a considerable number of non-Communist intellectuals who would illustrate the legend of a "victory over Nazism" that was all thanks to the USSR.

In 1955, the year he wrote *Nekrassov* and in which he was closest to the PCF, Sartre pronounced an allocution at the Salle Pleyel before an audience assembled by the Association France-URSS, of which he was a member. He offered the crowd a particularly energetic version of his historical vulgate. Not only had the Soviet Union done nearly everything, but the United States had only intervened in Europe when it was forced to. "Our fate was not decided in Normandy or in Belgium," Sartre declared, "but in the U.S.S.R. beside the Volga. It was Stalingrad that made the Normandy landing possible; I'd even say necessary. If the English and Americans wanted to take part in the final victory, they had to, willy nilly, take part in the assault." (Clemenceau had already reproached Pershing for having waited for the final "big push" in 1918.) "So what the repeated requests of the Russian command had failed in the dark hours to obtain was hastily agreed upon after Stalingrad. That's not the first time someone has rushed reinforcements to a victory."[99] And then, before an audience that probably had not dared to hope for as much, Sartre contrasted the "Germans, our age-old enemies," with the Russians, who had "shed their blood to save their future, our future, and the future of the Universe."[100] Toward them, the philosopher concluded, "only one attitude is possible—gratitude and friendship."[101]

Declaring a debt to the USSR implied lightening the *other* debt—the "odious debt." Some ten years later, Étiemble would once more evoke the "distant, involuntary, but decisive" hand the Soviets had had "in the liberation of our capital and our entire country." Despite being a declared anti-Stalinist, he pushed his regrets over the fact that it had been the Americans and not the Russians who had liberated Paris further than any Stalinist. "The Americans would never have landed in Europe if millions of Russian, Turkmeni, and Uzbeki soldiers and civilians—victims of the policies of that ingenious strategist, Stalin—had not died to attack the Nazi army." The Russians had been unjustly "confined to Berlin and Vienna." As liberators and occupants, they were preferred by Étiemble. This was because, "drained by their victory, they could not have provided us with canned milk or gadgets, with all the accompanying vocabulary." With the Russians, at least, there were no debts that would justify a future despoilment, so France and the French language had both been spared "colonization."

The colonial metaphor that triumphed in the 1950s in describing France's situation in relation to the United States is revealing; a final step had been taken toward dependency. The metaphor was not absent from interwar writings (or the public imagination), but the more brutal and less humiliating one of invasion or conquest was still preferred. Those images, though, had clearly been hyperbolic: no one took Aron and Dandieu literally when they evoked the American Attila, nor even Duhamel, who asked no one in particular: "Are we also to be conquered, we people of ordinary lands?"[102] True, many things had changed. The presence of foreign troops, the sometimes tense coexistence of the population with the GIs, the abundance of goods in their "enclaves," which sharply contrasted with continued rationing: this all easily led to translating the situation into colonial terms. Communist polemicists had no problem mixing metaphors and promptly crossed the racist imagery associated with a slave-owning America with the political leit-motif of America as "heir to the Nazis." Referring to De Gaulle, Georges Bidault, and Jules Moch, *La Nouvelle Critique* wrote: "Their ambition is to be-come galley slaves to the modern slave owners that are the sovereigns of the dollar. Their ideal is to become the 'Capos' of the 'new European order,' in a version revised and corrected by Truman-Acheson."[103] Nothing is ever lost; and thus solid discursive habits were created. But the colonial metaphor's success, in its scope and duration, went far beyond the rhetorical matrix of the cold war, of which Georges Soria's book *La France deviendra-t-elle une colonie américaine?* is the paradigm. It took root in very different writings, from the Far Left to the New Right, and was visible even in the titles of books on the United States—such as Jacques Thibau's *La France colonisée* (1980). It became unavoidable for the anti-Americans themselves: Jean-Jacques Servan-Schreiber, in *Le Défi américain* (The American Challenge) in 1967, repeated without blinking—or adding any shades of meaning—the imputation of "neocolonialism" that the United States was now shackled with.[104]

Compared with the earlier imagery, invasion or "colonization" suggests a more intimate coercion, a more complete control, a more accepted enslave-ment. It can be heard as a call to revolt—since colonies are destined to eman-cipate themselves—but in truth, the anti-American works that used and abused the colonial image are more striking for their resigned resentment. A kind of masochistic bitterness toward the United States often blossomed into a projective identification with the "real" colonized and the nonwhite world in general. Bernanos, in 1947, identified with the fate of Japan, raped and sullied well before the war by America's anti-civilization. (Imperial, fas-cist, and racist Japan was for him nothing but an Anglo-Saxon prosthesis imposed on an eternal Japan.) In 1961, Audiberti evoked "the *legation* quar-ter," implicitly comparing France to the China of the opium wars.

Reading Audiberti, Étiemble exulted: "The word has been uttered: the legation quarter; that puts us in our place—in the colonial or semicolonial state that, from a linguistic point of view at any rate, is now ours."[105] The qualification is pure lip service, given that Étiemble has a very loose concep-tion of the "linguistic point of view." *Parlez-vous franglais?* has a reputation as a brilliant Queneau-style formal exercise, a well-calibrated mockery of con-temporary linguistic sticking points. In fact it is a tract that evinces an uncom-

mon violence toward America, which is accused of aspiring to the death of
France's language, culture, and even ("secretly") General De Gaulle—"since
the OAS did not get rid of him"![106] Nowadays, *Parlez-vous franglais?* is still
striking for its verve but also comes across as stupefyingly brutal. Étiemble
tirelessly repeats that France is heading "from decadence to servitude." He
accuses the Institut des Études Politiques of training the "country's leaders"
to serve "first and foremost the 'American way of life' and the State Department's policies."[107] The new format for the French passport sends him off on
a tirade. It is a "colonist's passport" because it is bilingual! For that act of
treachery, the "Fourth Republic deserved the dollars it was begging for."[108]
A tone that strident would not crop up again outside the New Right or other
far-right anti-Americanism. Étiemble is literally jubilant in pointing a finger
at France's real and particularly its supposed debasement; an undeniable
quiver runs through the potshots of his calamitous predictions; and his agitation is palpable when he announces that English is going to "contaminate
and demolish" not only the French vocabulary, but "everything left of food,
wine, love, and free thinking" in France.[109] But this frenzy of resentment is
mixed with a bitterness linked to the role reversal between the colonizers and
the colonized. A hate-filled lament animates the numerous pages that show,
with a strange insistence, France brought down to the "rank" Indochina and
Algeria have just struggled out of: "The Atlantic Pact has helped colonize
us—and right when we were beset by the pangs of 'decolonization.'"[110]
Étiemble puts the word "decolonization" in quotes, as though it were a myth;
he does not do so for "colonize," to clearly indicate that he considers American colonization an absolute reality.

    With the colonial question, a new mental knot was tied into the net
of the anti-American discourse. The historian Paul Sorum has shown how
widespread was the idea among French intellectuals during this period that
decolonization would be nothing more than a transfer of power to the Americans.[111] Tony Judt rightly notes that, consequently, "the shift in intellectuals' attention after 1956, from communism to anticolonialism, entailed no
abandoning of anti-Western and anti-American sentiment."[112] The United
States' reprimands seemed like the height of bad faith to an anticolonialist
like François Mauriac, who wondered "if we are reduced to taking lessons
from that great exterminating nation."[113] The resentment felt toward the
United States as both anticolonial moralizers and decolonization's probable
beneficiaries turned into a masochistic phantasmagoria in which the Frenchman took the place of the freed native—just like the Southern landowners
had become "slaves" under the crushing heel of the Yankee victors.

Étiemble was far from alone in developing this scenario. It is troubling to discover the same schema and the same ambiguous exhilaration in Roger Vailland, when the Communist novelist describes the French population's "wog" transformation. In these pages, written somewhere between political propaganda and obsessional fantasy, the activist and anticolonialist intellectual Vailland makes his text crawl with racist terms to describe the American troops' alleged Francophobia. There is once more a strange joy in this masochistic proffering, pretty artificially imputed to "American officers" given the task of throwing all the hideousness of the French racist imagination in Frenchmen's faces: "A new kind of racism has been evolving since the so-called Atlantic army's troops have been stationed in France. It is not directed at the wog or the yid, but the 'Frenchy.' Frenchy is the injurious diminutive of French, Frenchman. When applied to a woman, it means prostitute." After these pedagogical precisions, Vailland pursues his "reporting" in the very unjournalistic form of a prosopopeia. He transcribes for his *Humanité dimanche* readers "what the American officers are saying": very freely, as we will see, and without any particular effort at documentary plausibility. "Those damned Frenchies are robbing us. . . . They're so dirty there isn't even a washroom in most of their houses. . . . You can't do anything about it unless you take a whip to them. The Frenchies will always be Frenchies," and so on. It is an easily identifiable parody of the French colonial discourse. For those who have not yet gotten it, Vailland adds: "That's why we're turning into America's wogs, yids, wops, and Polacks, somewhere between their niggers and the Chinks that no longer accept being theirs."[114] Then, sententiously: "Racism is a sickness of which one is often the victim after having been the executioner. Everyone is someone's wog."

Both an exorcism and a smokescreen, the French frenzy in identifying France as a United States "colony" is not unrelated to the worry that peeks through in this homily. Another article by Vailland confirms the interpretation—an article in which he describes the funeral of an Algerian worker, Belaïd Hocine, killed during the violent protests against General Matthew Ridgway's visit to France in May 1952. "For the French, there are no more 'wogs.' That is what Belaïd Hocine's death meant when he was killed alongside the partisans of French peace as they all protested together against Ridgway. That is also the meaning of the grandiose homage the population of greater Paris gave him. It was an extremely important event in the struggle for peace and freedom."[115]

It would be easy to wax ironic about the exorbitant cost of "becoming French" according to Vailland. It is probably a better idea to record the new configuration of discourses we can see by putting the two articles side by

side. Because not only is anti-Americanism used here to imaginarily reconcile the two sides of the French colonial relationship through a sacrificial figure of solidarity. (And this shared death foreshadows the fantasized plans of
the last decades of the twentieth century: identifying, also sacrificially, with
the armed struggles of Third World countries against the United States.) But
more subtly or more surreptitiously, the scene is one of exorcism, which
closes the cycle of debt and dependency. Giving one's skin, not *for* Uncle Shylock, in the "so-called Atlantic army," but *against* him, in the streets of France
and Navarre, is perhaps the only way of purging the accounts.

Monsieur Perrichon's 4-Horsepower

In the merry month of May 1948, a "little *café-au-lait*-colored car" from Renault's
factories made its entrance into New York. Not a triumphal entrance, but
still: five years earlier, Billancourt was being bombed by the Allies; as for the
Germans, they had thought the none-too-industrial French would exclusively
devote themselves to cultivating rutabagas. And suddenly France had its
four-horsepower and was going to show it to the American uncle, like a child
showing his big brother a new toy—with the big brother generally not too
interested in it.

The visit, more diplomatic than economic, was the subject of an amusing chronicle in *Le Monde*. Announcing the first sale of the four-horsepower
in America, Gabriel Dheur hoped that it would be "followed by a second
one." At a time when the French were dreaming of big American cars, even
though they were too impoverished to afford even the runt of the litter, the
editorialist was amused in thinking that "the Yankees" had "had it up to here
with all those cumbersome and costly cars, which were nauseatingly boring,"
that were clogging up their highways. Another Renault sales pitch: the Marshall Plan! Because "since the exigencies of aid to Europe will probably constrain the Americans to a certain reduction in their style of living, it seems
that the little *café-au-lait*-colored car could be exactly what they need to get
used to a more Spartan existence." But irony aside, the four-horsepower was
worthy of sincere praise—just as it was. It did not wear itself out "aping luxury cars," like certain Renaults of yore: "This one is sincere and presents
itself exactly for what it is." A car? No, an image: "the image of a little ruined
nation that is nonetheless courageous and honest, which is trying to use the
means it still possesses to preserve a certain tradition of quality." That was
what "our little ambassador" was: a modest emblem of France's artisanal
virtues and its taste for a job well done. "And if it is photographed, with a tri-
color sash, at the foot of the Empire State Building, may it remember

Labiche's well-put phrase: a big Perrichon before a little sea of Ice."[116] Perrichon?

Monsieur Perrichon, in *Le Voyage de Monsieur Perrichon*, embodies many French characteristics, including a propensity for malapropisms and spelling errors. He also tends to think the world revolves around him, and modesty is not his strong suit: he is a curious mix of braggart and bourgeois. But still! Did the *Monde* editorialist mean to suggest that the four-horsepower was a frog—it did look a little like one—that wanted to be as big as a Buick? It has to be said that his final twist does not make for a very lucid allegory. Unless we send Monsieur Perrichon off to other turns, ones that get the play's plot moving again.

The plot is unbelievably simple: Monsieur Perrichon's daughter has two suitors, the perfect Armand and the cunning Daniel. Armand has the good fortune—he thinks—of saving Monsieur Perrichon on the edge of a ravine, into which the father of his beloved is about to plunge. But not long after he is saved from this gruesome fate, Monsieur Perrichon has trouble hiding his acrimony toward his rescuer, to whom he is now indebted. Observing this state of affairs, the young man's rival does not lose a second and falls into another ravine so that Monsieur Perrichon can pull him out of it. Through this ruse, the cunning Daniel becomes indebted to Monsieur Perrichon and is adored by him, while the helpful Armand becomes persona non grata because of his helping hand. *Le Voyage de Monsieur Perrichon* is not a simple fable about bravado; it is a structural parable about ingratitude. Save the day, if you must: but to be loved, it is wiser to let yourself be saved. The main lesson of *Le Voyage de Monsieur Perrichon* is the same as twentieth-century French anti-Americanism's and is the real moral of the *Monde* editorial on the four-horsepower, as its title perhaps involuntarily confirms: "Lafayette, nous voici." Gabriel Dheur's screed is decidedly a forest of symbols.

One of the most precious Gaullist (the real one, De Gaulle's) contributions to the symbolic reconstruction of the country was understanding the Perrichon syndrome very early on. This lucidity helped presidential Gaullism maintain a firm stance between a symbolic challenge to the Americans and concrete solidarity with the American ally in each important crisis (including the Cuban missile crisis). Jean Lacouture has always held that De Gaulle was not anti-American.[117] One would have to be anti-Atlantist, but also and especially very intelligently anti-American, to have the idea of closing the American military bases in France without ever thinking of leaving NATO. The head of France Libre, "assisted" throughout the war by rarely benevolent and never disinterested protectors, had been in good hands. His entourage too, as can be seen in a curious little book by Maurice Druon, dated from Harley-ford Manor, October 18, 1943, and entitled *Lettres d'un Européen*.

One of the letters is addressed "to an American officer" and contains this apologue:

> We are more or less in the following position. I say to you, "My friend, a great misfortune has befallen me. There are many reasons why it happened, but of course, reasons are reasons. Lend me five hundred dollars to save me from pressing need, and extend your goodness so far as to temporarily consider it a gift. I'll start working." Now, you answer me, "Five hundred dollars, you must be kidding! I'll give you ten thousand. And look, your walls are painted green; I'll send you my painter and he'll paint them blue for you. And you normally wear twill jackets. You must go see my tailor, he'll cut you a real one."

To which the questioner gives a premonitory reply, five years before the Marshall Plan, but especially peremptory in the refusal of hateful dependency it expresses:

> "No, for god's sake! Five hundred dollars, wish me good luck, and don't force me to hate your good deeds."[118]

I was born in a land that by its soil, its inhabitants, and
its achievements is diverse, motley, variable, and
ingenious.

   Duhamel, *Scenes from the Life of the Future* (1930)

May America afar crumble with its white buildings.

   Aragon, *La Révolution surréaliste* (1925)

 12

Metropolis, Cosmopolis:
In Defense of Frenchness

In the twentieth century, France was invaded by the United States.
You will not find this sentence in any history book—but there
is another history, intuitive and stubborn, that nations prefer,
in general, to the one schoolchildren learn. In the unofficial an-
nals of France's collective memory, the American invasion is
an obvious fact and, for France, one of the major events of the last
century.

Still, between 1900 and 2000, the French conception of the
invasion changed. It became more complicated. It no longer involved super-battleships or armies of automatons mobilized by
serial writers. The "inevitable shock" did not take place as announced by diplomats and political analysts. The 1917–1918
alliance made scenarios of a confrontation less credible, and the
isolationist retreat of 1920 finally extinguished their plausibility.
Anyway, what was the use? American billionaires were no longer
off conspiring among themselves; they were presiding over commissions for international regulations. Make way for the modern
Yankee, the one holding state secrets and dispensing monetary
manna at his own discretion. Make way for Dawes and Young, the
supreme judges of public debts and reparations between nations.

These modern demigods embodied America far better than its lackluster presidents: Taft, Coolidge, Harding. The new moneyed cosmocrats attracted all different kinds of hatred; they slipped into everyone's dreams and nightmares—or else their alter egos did. Make way, then, for Ogden Webb, a Paul Morand hero who even after his death is still controlling Europe's fate: his wife continues writing and signing dispatches, while the fact that the plenipotentiary is dead is kept a secret. Make way for the international bureaucrats Céline put at the head of the "Church," a caricature of the League of Nations, that Unlimited Unreliability Company. They were the power and the glory. There was no need for a conquering army or a subjugating armada. "When a Yankee lands in Paris," said the journal *Réaction* in 1930, "he sees a conquered land."[1] But a land conquered without a fight and by other weapons than cannons and howitzers. The new America was pacifistic, like a well-fed boa constrictor: its head was dozing in Washington, but its financial loops mercilessly encircled every government and nation in Europe.

This new situation forced French anti-Americans to reinterpret the American peril. It would have been absurd to continue proclaiming that there was a military threat: colonization was not the same thing as war, and the more France plummeted to the rank of a dominion, the more the risk of a conflict diminished. Economically speaking, the time for fear was over; the game was up. France's gold had crossed over the Atlantic, its franc was shaken, its finances were under supervision and its economy on intravenous: another reason for pacification, if not satisfaction.

What was left to defend in France? Frenchness. Not the territory, but the *terroir*; not France's power, but its wisdom; not its vanishing currency, but its consistently high values; not its damaged vitality, but its unparalleled joie de vivre; not the motherland, as in 1792, but its coveted heirlooms, its dismantled cloisters and exported castles. This was a revolution for anti-Americanism: its cultural revolution. France had moved onto the defensive and was defending a quintessentialized idea of itself.

Do You Hear in the Countryside?

The anti-American Maginot line was set up to protect a certain idea of France. Not a France steeped in grandeur and full of serious, De Gaullian conviction, but a more diffuse, worldly, and hedonistic idea in which France looked like a cross between Rabelais's utopian Thélème Abbey and a land of plenty; an epicurean garden, a secular Eden—the whole world's dream. A blessed land. Because it was "temperate," France's soil sheltered a population untouched by excess. Nature was gentle and society mild, a perfect counter-point to America's appalling nature and the horrifying brutality of "Anglo-Saxon" social relations. "For centuries," wrote one of the first analysts of American wealth in 1889, "the Anglo-Saxon race has been in possession of the unenviable privilege of presenting, in stark contrast, the greatest fortunes and the most profound poverty."[2] The idealized France with which anti-Americans countered America's innate injustice was, in contrast, a place of relative equality (sans-culotte style) and organic solidarities (every populist movement's greatest dream). It was a France in which conflict did not imply unqualified rifts. In which contact between social or ethnic groups was not broken like in America, with its slums and ghettos. In which everyone still spoke the same language and talk circulated and created bonds. *That* France was perhaps the most cherished French myth of the twentieth century: from the Unanimists to the Populists, from Giono to Queneau, from Prévert to Pennac, novels (and also movies) never stopped defending and illustrating that charmed land. "The idea of France" that began mobilizing the intellectuals in the 1920s was clearly suffused with political and cultural references, fed on intellectual and spiritual values that could be brandished against America's noncivilization. But it was also, first and foremost, woven around an idealized view of the village or neighborhood; the workshop and the corner store; familial solidarity and camaraderie at school, work, and play; culinary rituals and religious or electoral rites—in short, a whole way of "French living," which was radically opposed to the "American way of life."

From the nonconformists of the 1930s to the Communists of the 1950s and the leftists of the 1970s came the same outcry against the American way of life. Some took offense at an "ideal" so material in nature; others were indignant at what they saw as a trompe-l'oeil expression, a mendacious ellipsis with intimations of illusory prosperity. The two charges were often combined: reproaching America for its dishonorably materialistic ideal of opulence and asserting that it had not even attained it was a way of killing two birds with one stone. The failure of pretensions that were in and of themselves contemptible would be one of the leitmotifs of the Communist campaigns after the liberation. But as early as 1934, and far from Marxist circles, Bertrand de Jouvenel had already vigorously denounced the "legend of high salaries": "So much has been said about American workers' high salaries! All those fabulous figures! Descriptions of the working class riding in cars and wearing dinner jackets! The European bourgeoisie had even started envying the way that ritzy proletariat was 'living large'! And it was only a myth, propaganda, brainwashing."[3] Whether the Americans were rigging their statistics or not was of little importance; wasn't the fact that they were bragging about their "way of life" proof enough that they had nothing else to brag about, particularly not a culture or a civilization?

If satires of America were willingly produced in the name of superior values particular to Europe, it quickly became apparent that a visceral defense of the French way of life was what motivated all of these anti-American discourses, including those that were the most universalist (Duhamel-style humanism), revolutionary (from surrealism to nonconformism), and internationalist (cold war French communism was a permanent paean to the French nation's "traditions"). In America, a "way of life" meant a contemptible ersatz for civilization, but in France, it magically got back its eminent dignity as an "art for living" in harmony with age-old mores. The Americans' way of life versus France's mores: it was all-out war. (Étiemble even nosed out a conspiracy against the French word *moeurs,* which was being threatened by the improbable translation *la manière française de vivre;* but we can legitimately question whether the expression ever really existed anywhere other than in his imagination.)[4] Defending Frenchness and "French life" was the basso continuo of anti-American protestation. Gastronomy had an enviable position here but was not the only salient point. Wine was often glorified, though less from an enological than a eucharistic standpoint: wine was communion, civilization. The habit of drinking it with meals was, "like it or not, a sign of civilization," remarked an author in the 1930s.[5] Similarly, when Duhamel praised France's "little bistros," where "three pals . . . tuck away beef bourgignonne, swap stories, and laugh, for the love of God! laugh and blow on a flute," he was not simply anathematizing the gloomy New York cafeterias with their dentist's chairs; he was creating the miniature utopia of a jovial working-class France, a fraternal nation of the common man.

We have already come across Raoul Gain's novel *Des Américains chez nous* (1928). We should open it back up; it offers a striking anthology of the threatened French lifestyle. This curious realist fable was the first tale portraying France as occupied, sacked, and sullied by the Yankees—not in some imaginary war, but during peacetime and in complete serenity. In the anti-American wave of 1927–1931, Raoul Gain shines with a modest light. The four novels he published before *Des Américains chez nous* did not have a strong impact on their time; neither did his *Poèmes de l'ombrelle* (1923). But Raoul Gain put his modesty in the service of an ingenious project: showing the Americans not in their own country, but *chez nous,* in the most rustic sense of the expression. In France, but not in a château or at Maxim's. Not in diplomatic salons or Parisian high society circles. Smack in the fields of Normandy, among the "primroses," wildflowers the narrator frequently calls on as witnesses. Here, it is no longer the Jockey Club's nomenclature that is jostled by a foreign intrusion, as in *Time Regained,* where Proust introduces an American woman whose genealogical incompetence butts up against centuries-old aristocratic hierarchies.[6] In Querqueville, it is the routines, habits, and small pleasures of a tiny village that are upset—that is, its very existence. Though it starts off as the simple chronicle of "disturbances shaking up our charming and pleasant little villages,"[7] this pastoral in Yankee clothing insidiously turns into a tale of cultural genocide.

Des Américains chez nous tells a story of invasion, corruption, and disfigurement all at once. Ten years after Stanton's "Lafayette, we are here!" the Americans are back, on a foundering yacht. They are saved and given lodgings with their own room and bed. There is a millionaire and his daughter, the less-than-chaste Diana. Their entourage is shady; the shipwreck was in fact phony; bad things start to happen. Convinced there is oil in this part of Brittany, the millionaire, Nathaniel Birdcall, settles down, purchases a castle, buys off the land, and dispossesses the farmers: "Everything is swept away by his dollars."[8] He hires sinister-looking multinational workers who "hunt down the young boys or rape the girls":[9] "Croatians, Ruthenians, Slavonians, Silesians, Moravians, Poles, a few Hungarians arrived in Nacqueville in picturesque little batches."[10] (You would think you were reading André Siegfried describing the "new immigration" in America.) The dollars flow in, bringing corruption and death. A drunkard, the village innkeeper, kills his wife after she refuses to sell Miss Birdcall the family furniture, which the girl has fallen in love with; he later hangs himself, not out of remorse, but because the unpredictable Diana no longer wants anything to do with his antiques. As for Birdcall *père,* he covets the Saint Germain chapel that has been watching over Querqueville since time immemorial: if demolished and "shipped off part and parcel to America," it could be reconstructed "on the grounds of one of his castles." His offer of $200,000, refused by the mayor and the parish priest, tears the village apart, with the "communist minority" pushing them to sell. After the invasion comes the division: "Will this cursed American, after ravaging our land, cause trouble in the community with his vandal's whims?"[11] A purely rhetorical question: this fragile corner of France has already been as morally polluted as it has been physically devastated.

The narrator speaks in the first person. The Americans call him "the boy from Querqueville." He lives in the village, but is half uprooted, since he occasionally travels to Paris on business. He took part in the rescue and helped lodge the Americans, and he becomes Miss Birdcall's lover. As a cultural intermediary between the villagers and the invading clan, he gets mixed up in all the millionaire's negotiations and transactions; he participates in life at the castle and the Yankees' carousing. His physical desire for the American girl gets him in compromising positions and leads him to make compromises, under the reproachful and saddened gaze of his neighbors and friends. He is, before the fact, the model of the collaborator: "I shave myself in the American style. I wear glasses with tortoiseshell rims. I am gradually learning how to create *cock-tails*."[12] It is all in vain: he will not leave with the foreigners. When they take to the sea—disappointed with their oil digs, where the only thing that shot up was mineral water—the Yankees leave him to his fate. This is because, in the meantime, Miss Diana's unlucky suitor has had his nose cut off by a rival, the Austrian engineer Von Tersen: Miss Diana wants nothing to do with an amputee. . .

But the narrator's chopped-off nose is not the only thing with symbolic value here: this strange little novel stockpiles the symbols left and right. The symbol of the Yankee allied with the Austrian swordsman who spends his time shouting: "Long live the emperor!" The symbol of the millionaire entrepreneur who takes over a pipeline installed in 1918 to bring American oil to a war-stricken France: "Now it's the reverse. Oil drawn from French soil will fill American ships," and Birdcall will thus have "re-established a more natural, eminently logical situation."[13] The symbol of Americanization by *things*, shown in the avalanche of goods that comes tumbling down on the Norman countryside: household utensils, domestic appliances, rocking chairs, canned corn, packs of chewing gum, boxes of jelly and ice cream. . . The symbol of a "flood" of immigration with the invasion by foreign workers, rapists and degenerates who "transmit their accustomed maladies to a pure race" and "gnaw away at everything [this] healthy land possesses by way of calm joy and rustic happiness."[14]

When all is said and done, *Des Américains chez nous* repeats, thirty years later, the same theme as *La Conspiration des milliardaires*: France being invaded by the Yankees. But it repeats it as a cold and oppressive fable. When Birdcall, angry over the arrest of one of his employees, starts making threats, the frightened natives think there are "American submarines patrolling the sea" and pray to Saint Barbe to help fight the artillery.[15] More clearheaded and grim, the hero-narrator knows that the attack has already taken place—superficially peaceful, but all the more successful and disastrous as a result. The fact that the enemy ends up taking to the sea because there is no oil is the fate of floating capital. But the damage has already been done. "The gentleman's undertaking did some damage," piteously admits the libido-driven collaborator. Attila-America, as Aron and Dandieu would soon say, left behind it an equally mutilated French countryside and population. As for the compromised narrator, we are left doubting that he will ever regain, in the now Yankeeless Querqueville, his happiness of yore, "a middling Old World happiness."[16]

Raoul Gain's story is a striking portrayal of Yankee "colonization": France's Americanization implies vandalizing a way of life, jointly polluting both the land and its race. In the same breath, the countryside's destruction and the inhabitants' corruption are described:

> The countryside has been mortally afflicted. Oil rigs claw their fingernails into the sky's muslin and soil the nuanced mirror of the waters with their shit. The air, the trees, the birds are being poisoned with debris, combustion, and mineral stench. Polish miners, Italian road workers, Russian specialists, and Chinese coolies are oppressing the region with their vices and the vulgarity of their species.

Industrial globalization's viral contagion leaves neither nature nor culture unharmed: "pleasure in living" changes, with the foreign invasion, "into an abominable stench, into hellish drudgery," and soon the country has nothing left "on [its] rubicund face but pustules, boils, and leprosy!"[17] An invasion of The Hague becomes the prophetic scene of France's degradation by a two-headed Moloch: metropolis-America and cosmopolis-America. The Birdcalls' bucolic name is just one more trap: a decoy. With these millionaires, father and daughter, lucre and stupor, it is the big city, with its brutalities and ugliness, that is invading the French countryside. It is also the world and the world's misery: in the millionaires' wake an insalubrious *lumpen* of degenerate foreigners is sucked in. In this sense as well, *Des Américains chez nous* exemplifies France's new obsessions about America.

In the Jungle of the Cities

In the mid-eighteenth century, America's nature was what inspired fear; it was what Buffon and De Pauw described in detail in order to dissuade people who were considering making the trip. The terror the American metropolis aroused in the 1920s copied this Enlightenment discourse in many ways. But it transposed it from nature to culture, from the deadly wilderness to the deadening megalopolis. Guy Dollian, the illustrator of *Scenes from the Life of the Future*, perfectly captured the ambiguous repulsion the American city inspired in Duhamel—and nearly all of his contemporaries. The volume opens with two woodcuts: the first shows a mineral horde of buildings piled up to the sky; the other amasses faces with exotic features against a backdrop in which the towers of the skyscrapers seem to emerge from a strange flowering of tropical fronds.

Delinquency and crime are not, as we might think, at the heart of the new urban malediction. The gangsterism theme would remain fairly marginal until the 1930s. (On the other hand, it is prominent in the anti-American publications of the occupation.) French anti-Americans took on the American city a full decade before film noir did, and a quarter of a century before that masterpiece of criminal and nocturnal topology, John Huston's *Asphalt Jungle* (1950). Indeed, it would not be until the 1950s that the moralizing climate particular to the liberation would, in France, lead to campaigns against detective and gangster movies, which were considered symptomatic of a decaying American society.[18] In the meantime, in the 1920s, in the writings of a Durtain or a Duhamel, in journalistic treatments and in novels, the city produced horrors that had nothing to do with minor or major fears about safety. The American city had its hoodlums—nothing shocking there. There, as elsewhere, the city's vices were exploited. A little more than elsewhere, perhaps, there were strange understandings between those enforcing the law and those breaking it. But petty crooks had a homey old European air about them. True, they made intemperate use of their tommy guns, but not without injecting into their joyless cities a certain vitality, a paradoxical humanity. In the icy waters of egotistical calculation, at least the "irregulars" had the merit of swimming upstream. The Chicago of the gang wars remained anecdotal. It was the city itself that, in an almost ontological way, embodied and impugned American civilization's inhumanity.

Since the eighteenth century, American nature had had time to be exonerated. Its miasmas had proved to be less lethal than predicted; its snakes, venomous within reason; its manioc, more digestible than one might have thought. To everyone's surprise, the dogs had started barking again—except for Claudel.[19] But there were still irregularities, structural handicaps. There were still excessive spaces, overly vast horizons, the sense of an "empty" or "hollow" continent, to which French writers in the 1930s gave new life. Cities had begun to spread out into the void. They sprawled immeasurably. All the excesses of hostile nature were transmitted into a proliferation of buildings that had none of the features of urbanity. Living there was dizzying, then nightmarish. Duhamel unconsciously joined the chain of timeworn commentaries when he associated, in the same sentence, America's "inhuman cities" and the soil they were raised on, "a soil that never invites moderation."[20] In a land destined for hubris, only arrogant cities could arise. Once, America's inhumanity had been embodied by a corrupt and stubbornly malicious nature. Now there was the city, no less bent on doing man harm. The tentacular city was a continuation of the creeping vegetation. It was no longer manioc that was poisoning people, it was rancid meat or contraband liquor.

It was no longer the watery swamps that killed, it was the factories' noxious vapors. The desperate solitudes of the wilderness had been replaced by urban dereliction. After nature as "wicked stepmother," here was the city as murderess.

"How New York Has Grown!"

The image of the American city went through three successive stages in the space of a century. In the first half of the nineteenth century, the city was pitiable, ugly, and boring, like Mrs. Trollope's Cincinnati. It was banality incarnate, quintessentially parochial, Verrières on the Hudson. This Stendhalian (and Baudelairian) vision faded out toward the end of the century. It was replaced by a horrified fascination with the great industrial complexes, the gigantic factories, the sordid workers' tenements. The horizon was lined with smokestacks; pollution from factories mixed with that of the railroads. The city leached out into the surrounding countryside. Gustave Lanson, in 1912, felt unable to give an opinion of New York, "a city too large, a collection of cities," just like all the cities in America; "amorphous, disparate cities, modern cities that have not yet found their type of beauty."[21] Until that far-off day, expanding industry was devouring the urban landscape. The city's physiognomy was swallowed up by an industrial goiter. The second stage is the least typically American. The depressing uniformity the American building would later be criticized for was already present, but on a mediocre scale: "In order not to waste any space, the floors are multiplied, but each floor is no higher than before: everything appears little and low. The innumerable windows stacked up in uniform rows look like the cells of a honeycomb, or the slots of an enormous vending machine. The facades are flat and boring like those of the factories in our industrial cities."[22] None of which was very different from Europe, on the whole—except that the Americans' apartment buildings looked like Europe's factories. City centers in America were impossible to pinpoint, since they were mired in an urban magma where the European distinction between the city and its outlying *faubourg* no longer had any meaning. But in this sense as well, the American city, with its relentless expansion, was not very different from the industrial conurbations that were beginning to coil themselves around old Europe. The industrial metropolis with imprecise borders was the American version of a general mutation toward the "tentacular city" intoned by Verhaeren in 1893: "The ardent, ossuary octopus / And the solemn carcass."[23] That late-nineteenth-century "tentacular city" could not become a useful vector for anti-American discourse for two distinct reasons: first, it was not characteristic enough of

America; and second, it conveyed associations that were not entirely negative in the fin-de-siècle imagination—if its horrors were not always transformed "into enchantments," as in Baudelaire's poetry, at least the shiver it inspired was not without excitement and even exultation for impartial travelers.

It would not be until after World War I that a third image of the city, this one intrinsically American, would take over the European mindset and become one of French anti-Americanism's favorite topoi. The transfer of malice happened brusquely, as soon as the war was over. In the early twentieth century, the city as such was not yet monstrous. In New York, in 1895, there was nothing for Paul Bourget to report, other than the recently constructed Brooklyn Bridge, which he mentions in passing as an "architectural nightmare drawn by Piranesi"[24]—a curious comparison that hints at a lack of familiarity with Piranesi or, more likely, with the Brooklyn Bridge. The big city did not yet arouse fear, but it already saddened French travelers, as we have just seen with Lanson. Jules Huret describes it in 1904 as an infantile pile of blocks: "agglomerations of domino towers like children make" in which "twenty-story houses . . . are not uncommon." It makes you want to run away: "You tell yourself right away that you would be too sad living there, and you think about the countryside, the peaceful Loire or the lovely Seine."[25] Sorrow would long infuse descriptions of the American city. During an investigation in New York in 1947, the famous fictitious Commissioner Maigret echoes his distant predecessor's accents, and even his fluvial nostalgia. Right after stepping off the quays of the French Line, as he is riding in a taxi "through a grimy neighborhood where the houses [a]re nauseatingly ugly," he thinks back with a pang of nostalgia to his garden in Meung-sur-Loire.[26] Between Huret and Simenon we can insert this vignette by Maurois from 1933: "'For a long time,' this Frenchwoman told me, 'I loved the giant houses, the sharply designed train stations, the white, black, and yellow crowds, the hasty countryside, the feverish pace. . . . Then one day, I said to myself, 'Ah! Give me a canal, poplars, a rowboat, slowness—or I will die. . . ' And so I left."[27] The anti-metropolis, in all these texts, is not Paris; it is France as a whole, a France embodied by the banks of the Loire or the Seine: a mosaic of real countryside and sincere cities, where urbanism is still rustic and nature urbane.

All that changed after the Great War: the scale of things, of course, but also, more subtly, the gaze of observers comparing the extraordinary growth of the great cities across the Atlantic to the real and symbolic razing of a devastated France. This new perception is efficiently played out in Paul Morand's *World Champions*, published in 1930. A bildungsroman set between 1909 and 1929, *World Champions* is the story of the fractured destinies of four young Americans, told by a French narrator (once their professor at Columbia).

The second episode takes place in 1919 and starts with a reunion in New York, whose skyline now stands out against a backdrop of European devastation. "How New York has grown! My eyes are still accustomed to the flat landscapes of Artois, the smashed houses and hacked trees of the front; the trenches have left me with a habit of walking bending down, or bowed as if behind a hearse. Suddenly I see the peak of Manhattan jutting from the sea, with its skyscrapers like piles of mother-of-pearl counters in front of a lucky gambler."[28] Morand had a way with words and was a good hand at using symbols. The America of infantile dominoes was a thing of the past; New York had stacked up the floors of its buildings as the Federal Reserve had done with war-torn Europe's gold ingots. The European now landed there bowed by tribulations and a sense of weakness. America had played and won. "America has broken the bank."[29]

Faced with this insolent prosperity, the French discourse hardened. The big American city was no longer just an inelegant décor. It became—along with the machine and partly for the same reasons—a principal cause of the innate dehumanization of this unanimously decried "civilization." The negation of man, the denial of his real needs and his true joys, was first and foremost rooted there: in the city's rectilinear streets, in its quadrangular buildings, in the "alveoli" of its identical apartments. The mutation of man into insect began when he was transplanted into the hideous anthill of the megalopolis. In "these cities of a new type," which were undergoing "prodigious growth," Aron and Dandieu saw a "terrifying symptom": "There, we put our finger, so to speak, on the cancer in its material form."[30]

Hereafter, the city *stood in* for America; it occupied almost the entire field of vision. At the edge of the United States, in the middle of the desert, it was still the cities that the new travelers saw, hallucinated, and described: temporarily invisible cities, cities in outline, previews of cities, ads for cities. These ghostly cities of the future, projected into the empty space by speculation and advertisements, were now hard for the disoriented traveler to tell apart from cities that had actually been built—but how long would they be standing? Virtual cities and real cities mixed their imprecise outgrowths like the arms of their tentacled civilization. The city had become the continent's only truth: a concentrate of Americanness as well as a teleological figure of America's historical experiment. America's ultimate conquest was nothing other than its own complete urbanization. In the course of a few decades, the cliché of wide-open or "available" space had changed into a stereotype of that space's saturation by the urban throng.

Urbanized Deserts and Simulacrum Cities

Who could forget Tintin the reporter's American misadventure? He falls asleep next to his horse on the prairie, and when he wakes up in the early morning hours, he is in the lobby of a palace built while he slept, right in the middle of a city that has sprung from out of nowhere. When he ventures out, a resentful policeman warns him to respect the crosswalks and, eyeing his cowboy outfit, notifies him that disguises are against the law.[31] Though the Indians have left the picture, pushed off with bayonets, this mushroom of a city already contains all the pitfalls of the American way of life—arrogance, inequality, corruption—and we can sense that it will not be long before the unyielding policeman is respectfully tipping his cap when gangsters pass by, like his colleagues in Chicago. What Hergé is drawing in four vignettes in 1936 is the direct progression from savagery to barbarism, skipping the civilized stage. . .

Another European traveler, a little less famous than Tintin but also very much appreciated by the French, had had a similar experience a few years earlier. When visiting Palm Springs in the southern California desert, Count Hermann von Keyserling, a prolific analyst of the American psyche, had been struck to discover sixty-three real estate agencies for two hundred permanent residents. On the hill overlooking the town, he was overcome with a kind of premonitory vision: "From the summit of it I saw the whole desert already plotted out with street names and the rest. And then I realized with horror that the whole of the Californian Desert may soon grow to be one single town and that this town may even soon merge into the everspreading Chicago."[32] "Inhuman cities"—Duhamel's words—conglomerated into the form of a continental metropolis: this was the new shape the American nightmare had taken.

The nightmare was never better illustrated than by Luc Durtain in the late 1920s. Durtain was the earliest allegorist of the new American city, whether real or virtual, and possibly the greatest, along with Céline, although his works never quite garnered as much fame as Paul Morand's *New York*, not to mention Duhamel's best-selling book. A caustic observer and talented storyteller, in 1927—three years before *Scenes from the Life of the Future* and five years before *Journey to the End of the Night*—he published a collection of three stories entitled *Quarantième étage* (Fortieth Floor). He would attempt to repeat its success in 1928 with a less original novel: *Hollywood dépassé* (Hollywood Overcome). The acidity of Durtain's descriptions; the brio with which he mimes in French, in his dialogues, the syntax and rhythm of the American sentence; his snide tone, enlightened by a real intimacy with the language and the country; all make him an uncommonly striking anti-American. The enthusiastic critical reception of *Quarantième étage* reflects the importance the city had taken on in the French perception of America, because Durtain is both a phenomenologist of the skyscraper and a semiologist of urbanized nature.

Immense America, the most savage west, and the most deserted California are for Luc Durtain, as they were for Keyserling, nothing more than prospective plots, an uninterrupted succession of construction sites. But there are no hallucinations here. Just concrete reality—as its name implies, moreover: *realty*. "Miles and miles of solitude. Vast and sterile stretches, just barely touched, here and there, with a little burnt grass. At intervals, at a crossroads or near some dried-up *rio*, strange white billboards are stuck: the land-sellers' posters . . . *The Best Thing In the World is FOR YOU TO HAVE THIS*. To have this. That, in the desert, is the last echo of the vibrations sounding in men's chests."[33] It hardly mattered if "this" was, literally, nothing. Nothing but an "impudently narrow lot" arbitrarily cut "out of measureless stretches of land."[34] The new America, with its "reality merchants," was a country that had been conquered by an unreal urban reality. This was already the theme of a short story from 1927 in which two jovial drifters discover Longview, "the practical City built by a Vision," the "only one-hundred-percent American city." Longview was essentially perfect because it existed only on the billboards announcing it. Once people had driven through the triumphal arch setting it off, "mediocre vegetation was the only thing in the world visible on the site, aside from the superbly asphalted highway, rectilinear as far as the eye could see."[35] It was an enchanting place, if its inhabitants were to be believed—because there already were some there! But to the French agnostic, America was sold on the power of positive thinking: "The man pointed to the tumbleweeds with assurance. In a country where repeating a certain number of times that you can walk perfectly well cures a broken leg, it is probably good enough, on a patch of wilderness, to indicate where there will be buildings in order to ensure their existence."[36] Longview had "virtual" streets, reduced to the "sidewalks' lines of stones" and unsullied by any buildings—aside from a strange and very temporary fish market with a block calendar displaying "tomorrow's date."[37]

This did not keep Longview from existing. Or from being talked about "all the way up to Portland." Durtain also thought that in America nothing looked more like a virtual city than a real one. There was even, in a sense, more that was unfinished in the cities that had cropped up, hasty and already destined for destruction, than in those that remained a pure "vision" and a joyous speculation. Continuing on the theme of "the city built on a vision" in

Hollywood dépassé, Durtain has his heroes cross through "the future metropolis of the San Fernando Valley": "An iron and concrete trompe-l'oeil behind
which there is nothing: not a roof or a floor or even any human beings."[38]
The virtual city of Gerard has no use for inhabitants; through this circumspect abstention, it realizes a kind of archetypal perfection. Far from contrasting with the "real" cities of New York or Chicago, it pushes the logic of
excluding the human even further. Durtain's invisible cities are the Potemkin
villages of speculative capital: urban holograms planted in the eye of the
mechanized drifter by advertising; empty shells imaginarily filling the immense void that is America.

Clearly, the conception De Pauw had once deployed was still bearing
fruit. America as a whole was a void, a hole, a no man's land and a geological nowhere, an "immense and sterile desert," Cornelius De Pauw had written, circumscribed by "mountainous peaks."[39] A contemporary of Durtain
and not De Pauw, Claudel imagined America, in a striking passage of his
Conversations dans le Loir-et-Cher, as pure energy, an immaterial machine: "a
dynamo inserted between the two Poles and two pieces of continent. What
we are hearing is the tic-tac of the universal machine." But the dynamo was
running in neutral: it was running in the enormous void of a hollow continent. "Empty—that's it. A friend I asked his impression of America, which
he'd flown over from New York to Frisco, said it's empty. The interior is hollow with the lakes and the huge dip of the Mississippi."[40]

This hollow continent was perfectly suited to the virtual city, and its "real"
cities to the hollowed-out carcasses of its skyscrapers—those "cavitied slabs
of granite used by unknown existences like sparrows use a cliff." This is how
the less hostile of Claudel's two interlocutors speaks when discussing America beside a broken-down car on the shores of the Loire.

Fortieth Floor: Totem and Slum

There was, for the French intellectuals of the interwar years, a whole literature of the skyscraper. For emblematic value, it had replaced the Chicago
slaughterhouses. Its admirers were rare: Le Corbusier,[41] Élie Faure, occasionally Morand, impulsively Céline. Its detractors, though, were legion. The
most recent skyscrapers, the ones built "in the crazy years," as essayist
Recouly wrote in describing the Roaring Twenties, "shoot right up toward
the clouds like towers." Towers of Babel, of course: "The men who built them
had obviously lost their minds. They imagined that houses could grow indefinitely, until they got lost in the clouds." The same Recouly, a little further on,
qualifies a new skyscraper near Radio City as a "Babelian tower," "ugly to

behold," and which for lack of just proportions "creates a kind of unease, both physical and moral." He adds this sentence, which practically all of his contemporaries and compatriots could countersign: "As for me, I could not live up in that ethereal construction, lost in the clouds, seemingly tied to this earth by nothing but a thin umbilical cord."[42] Raymond Recouly, an anti-Communist and anti-Hitlerian nationalist, is not among the most caustic toward the United States; his book, published in 1933, even pleaded in favor of a Franco-American rapprochement. But the American city distressed him and its buildings horrified him.

He was not alone. Duhamel, as we will see, was in favor of the sky-scraper's demise. But Claudel, who was mostly inclined to correct him, be-trayed an even deeper allergy. The French ambassador to the United States indeed wanted to save the skyscraper—from itself. A great admirer of the beaux-arts style exported to America, he championed densifying the build-ings by adding "heterogeneous" volumes that would break up their straight lines. He dreamed of "sticking together" the skyscrapers, "to make a stack out of them" so that the eye would be "attracted toward the sky not by the dizzyingly accelerated vertical of a reverse fall, but by a measured ascension, a staircase of associations."[43] In short, Claudel would find the skyscrapers a lot more bearable if they looked a little more like cathedrals.[44] Similarly, the (French) sculptor Duhamel meets in New York is waiting for America's "opu-lence" to finally make the skyscrapers "flower" and "blossom out at the top into statues, *rilievi*, and ornaments."[45] At least he is defending his line of work.

Though it bucked the codes of French-style ornamentation, the sky-scraper could not avoid being allegorized in France. By the 1920s, the anti-American discourse had latched on to it and raised it, so to speak, to the level of an exemplar of Americanness. Which brings us back to Durtain. For if Luc Durtain, in his stories, invented and established the theme of the urban sim-ulacrum, he also set down, for a whole generation of readers, the physiog-nomy of America's cities: the fishbone profile of their buildings and their "warehouses, factories, and docks: cubes or prisms which, with their rectan-gles methodically punctuated by windows and the high cylinders of their chimneys, break up the straight lines of the streets."[46] Durtain did not try to convert the skyscrapers. Or to make them out to be mystical stepladders. He had a cold eye on their nontranscendent pileup: "In sum, rectangles, rectan-gles, rectangles, over a parallel and perpendicular set of streets: that is what American cities look like from above."[47]

The story entitled "Smith Building" succeeds in creating a particular kind of mirror effect. Its supremely American hero, or antihero, an insurance salesman by trade, has gone up to the fortieth floor of a Seattle skyscraper, "the highest edifice in existence west of New York: 1,200 foundation blocks, 500 feet high, 18 miles of electric and telephone wires, 2,314 windows offering the sun 67,736 square feet of crystal." He has gone up to look at the city to which his career has called him. But from this gigantic balcony, it is American life the novelist's gaze dives into. And while Howard the insurance salesman tries to grasp the city's layout and to do the same for his future career, Durtain puts his reader before a forest of symbols: "The insurance salesman does not suspect that the buildings raised and adored in every American city by conquering tribes of Pale Faces, that this very skyscraper from which he is looking out, are, with their layers upon layers of monstrous Companies (civilization's grimacing divinities!), exactly like the totem poles once revered by the natives of the Tongass Islands."[48] A rectangular phantasmagoria, the building proffered, one by one, America's secrets, from hasty greed to Puritan rigidity: "Well now, the little boys have done a good job 'making their pile': case in point, these buildings, with their stiff, Puritan shoulders raised on all sides—these buildings, where people are still as dutifully bored as God commanded three centuries ago."[49] Skyscraper syncretism according to Durtain: fetish, totem, transhistorical object, an absolute synecdoche of America. Durtain summons the city like you summon spirits—America's Great Spirit. And it is not hard to see why this summoning struck his contemporaries, Americans included.

Skyscraper: From Mendacity to the Morgue

One of the authors who used and amplified Durtain's summoning was Waldo Frank, who wrote an ambitious *Introduction to a Philosophy of American Life*. The original appeared in the *New Republic*, and a French translation was published by Grasset in 1930 in a collection edited by Jean Guéhenno. Waldo Frank—who would briefly join the American Communist Party—was inspired by Herbert Croly[50] and Walter Lippmann. He championed "the concept of the democratic nation *formed* by an aristocracy of spirit."[51] His critique of America combined a pretty murky radicalism with an analysis of spiritual alienation similar to the French nonconformists'. Citing Durtain's *Quarantième étage*, he revived the urban theme and exacerbated its political symbolism. For Durtain, skyscrapers clustered like "packing boxes set on end": luggagelike cities—as if each American "had just arrived from Europe"—betraying the immigrant, with his suitcases and his inorganic life.[52] Claudel had said as much: the best skyscrapers "are starting to have some exterior design, but there is no organic, internal unity."[53] But Waldo

Frank was not preaching a futile return to the days of cathedrals: the skyscraper sufficed for American idolatry. "The American gods of power have a temple. It is the best we can show as formal articulation of what we are and what we love. We call it the Skyscraper. . . . We are a mass rigidly compressed into a simple structure; our rank is equalitarian, our aim is eminence, our dynamics is addition, our clearest value is the power of the bulk of ourselves." An emblem of pseudo-democratic hubris, the skyscraper, according to Waldo Frank, also revealed the fallacious character of American democracy. "When the skyscraper aspires beyond these real traits, it becomes a hypocrite. . . . The skyscraper is a simple frame in which stones are laid like stuffing; as befits a false democracy the individual stones lack structural importance." We can see why Waldo Frank found more readers in France than his own country, where his literary debut in 1919 had been, as he himself admitted, a resounding flop.

The same year *Introduction to a Philosophy of American Life* was published in French, *Scenes from the Life of the Future* rounded out the caricature of the American city. Dollian's somber woodcuts suffused the text with a heavy atmosphere of urban oppression. We have already mentioned the first of them, the frontispiece, which is saturated with skyscrapers whose vertical rectangles are piled up in a tilted high-angle shot, bare of any ornamentation. The ground is invisible, the sky reduced to a few interstices between these concrete colossi. In the foreground, a lower edifice is crowned with a gigantic clock. "Time is money"? *Tempus irreparabile?* Most likely both. But the symbolic meaning is expressed by another central, and strange, element: above the most boxy of the buildings, we can see the raised torch of the Statue of Liberty, whose forearm is sticking out from behind the other structures. Above the torch is a crane. Are they trying to extract Lady Liberty from this cage of skyscrapers, in which she no longer has any place? Or is it her Bedloe's Island refuge that has been submerged by development fever and swamped with skyscrapers? Liberty was being smothered, in any case, like the spectator faced with this suffocating vignette.

As for Duhamel, he summarily dismissed the skyscraper. For him, the skyscraper is a rushed piece of work. "It . . . grows, and keeps growing," but not with the slow rise of sap and contemplation. "It cannot wait for the inspiration of some, or for the leisurely experimenting of others. Too many allied interests demand that it be finished." Neither maturity nor momentum: the skyscraper was a surge of (speculative) fever, a morbid proliferation. The polar opposite of perennial beauty, "the building lives the life of mortal things. It is built for thirty years, perhaps for less. The very men who built it will demolish it tomorrow, and put into its place something else, bigger, more complex, and more expensive." Thus, this "sole interpreter of the genius of America, architecture," seemed to Duhamel "debased in its designs, in its methods, and in its achievements."[54] The New World's artistic hollowness was betrayed by its own architects: that was the skyscraper's aesthetic lesson.

But what a page like that betrays is the violent death drive that overcame Duhamel the humanist in the face of the American city. A skyscraper housed "the population of a French prefecture." Men, then. Women. Humanity. Right? Maybe not. Whether they were insects or mutants, the skyscrapers' inhabitants were, for Duhamel, a bloc of *inhumanity*, a collective "it": "And the whole of it speaks, eats, works, makes money, speculates in the stock market, smokes, drinks alcohol in secret, has dreams, and makes love."[55] This new humanity was no more human than the skyscraper was really a living thing. The building was blameworthy, it "live[d] the life of mortal things" instead of aiming at immortality; "all the ideas that animate it smell of fashion and death." And not only its ideas—the skyscraper itself stank of and oozed death. On the penultimate page of his book, Duhamel comes back one more time to the skyscraper's lethal nature: "Under my feet the building trembled throughout its height, a tuning-fork of steel, brick, and cement. The chimneys disguised by the ornaments of the spire exhaled a mortal incense, the poisonous gas that, eight hundred feet below, the machinery of the sub-cellar was distilling."[56] How could its dehumanized inhabitants be completely innocent? "The whole of it" could go ahead and perish with this perishable carcass. Of course, Duhamel could not have thought that. Most likely he did not. But he wrote it: "The building lives! In the evening it is lighted up like a mortuary chapel."[57]

A good building was a morgue. Even humanists have an unconscious. But can we still refer to it as an unconscious when the last wish formed by Duhamel, full of "the unspeakable bitterness of being unable to love what I saw," was that America should finally get what it was "missing": "great misfortunes, doubtless, and great trials."[58]

"The Austere Architecture of Distant Zionist Colonies"

Duhamel wished "terrible adventures" on the Americans, which would make them "a really great people."[59] This amicable wish would be granted a dozen years later at Pearl Harbor. Duhamel would not rejoice. But other people in France would see it as a veritable cause for celebration. "England, like Carthage, must be destroyed," was the collaborationist radio chronicler Jean Hérold-Paquis's daily pitch during the occupation. Contrary to Duhamel, the collaborationists who applauded Japanese aviation's sneak attack did not make any claim to having good intentions. The American power's humiliation delighted them; the possibility of its downfall sent them into raptures. For the pundit Henri Nevers, it was a heavenly surprise: "Hostilities break out and, O wonders! with lightning speed, the Japanese squadrons manage to sink the American navy's most magnificent units in just a few days." Here was "Washington's intransigence and ill will" rightfully punished and America brought down a notch: "Washington's bluff paled before the heroism of the little Nippon soldiers." Because "the Japanese nation has great qualities: it is an incorruptible nation, respects its ancestral traditions, its religion, its honor, and its race."[60] A mirror version of America's shortcomings.

When the United States entered the war, anti-Americanism was unleashed among the journalists and caricaturists, after having been held in check, at least in the southern zone, by the Vichy government, which had made a concerted effort not to burn any bridges with Washington. The caricaturists had a field day. They pilloried Roosevelt along with Churchill and Stalin. Roosevelt's part in the trio was increasingly meaty. While Churchill gradually lost his prestige (soon he would have no more than a foldaway seat in the "interallied metro," and his two acolytes would jostle him at the doors),[61] the figure of Roosevelt rose in power and malignancy. Faced with a Mongolized Stalin, frozen in his role as a thick-headed brute, the collaborationist caricature presented an increasingly sulfurous Roosevelt. When in 1941, depicted as a cunning clergyman, he celebrates the union of a blushing Churchill and a moribund Stalin (this is of course *before* Stalingrad),[62] he still embodies nothing more than the Puritan's eternal hypocrisy. But hypocrisy changes into the most obsequious abjection when, as a whorehouse madam, Roosevelt offers an arrogant Jewish client the choice between De Gaulle and his fellow general and political competitor Giraud.[63] Still later, just a few days before the landing in Normandy, in *La Gerbe*, he reappears as a Luciferian Superman: he has stopped playing the pimp and swoops down on France brandishing a menorah that he waves like a torch.[64] Clergyman, brothel keeper, "prince of this world": the promotion is incontestable.

Behind this clawed, horned Roosevelt, it is America itself that has come back into the picture. The demonic president's (cloven) right foot is still planted over there, behind the horizon, on the distant continent the viewer can sense is covered with an immeasurable megalopolis, while his incendiary arm is already raised above a French city clustered around a very visible cathedral—the cathedral in Rouen, perhaps, damaged by Anglo-American bombardments. The living city will perish, annihilated by a monster sprung from the Judaic metropolis. The caricaturist Mara thus drew what anti-American

propaganda brochures had been endlessly repeating throughout the collaboration: solidarity with "English Jewry" was the key to America's aggression
against France and "New Europe."

An archetype of its genre, the pamphlet, signed Henri Nevers and entitled *Pourquoi l'Amérique est-elle en guerre?* (Why Is America at War?), does not
seem, at first glance, like a very complex piece of writing. Its twenty-three
pages, though of a fairly sober stamp, are adorned with several significant
icons: bags of gold marked with the star of David across from a Browning set
down near some contraband bottles; a wild Negro dance; and a traffic-
jammed New York intersection. The last pages present the traditional Jewish
and Masonic symbols (an open Talmud, a menorah, a triangle with an eye),
while the last vignette shows an American cruiser attacked by Japanese
planes, with, in the background, a rising sun resembling the Japanese emblem. With its pseudo-didactic airs, this little work attempts to "explain the
real cause of the new conflict" that has just broken out between Japan and
America. "Surely no one will be surprised to learn"—one of the author's favorite phrases—that the cause is the secret takeover of the American government by "Judeo-Masonic interventionists."[65]

Pourquoi l'Amérique est-elle en guerre? purports to be an authentic testimony substantiated by several quotes inserted "with the sole purpose of confirming" the author's observations. It is in fact an enormous piece of plagia-
rism. The author has done a lot of copying and borrowing—faithfully,
moreover, and without pushing what he borrows too far. In order to understand World War II, a "cultural, political, and social" study on America is
needed, he affirms with compunction right from the start. The declaration,
made comic by the work's slapdash nature, nonetheless clearly announces
the propagandist's strategy: if it just denounced the Judeo-Masonic conspiracy, his tract would only appeal to a small militant minority. But by weaving
his conspiracy theory into the rich tapestry of cultural anti-Americanism,
Nevers could hope to attract interest beyond a partisan circle. Whence the
paradox of an "extremist" text that is mainly an anthology of the "ordinary"
anti-American texts of the 1930s. Whence, also, the unreal effect of an anti-
Semitic, pro-Nazi work in which, to rally his reader to the Reich, the author
takes him for an utterly clichéd ramble through New York, mentioning the
noise, the traffic jams, and the "poorly kept" public gardens, and stressing
the lack of cafés "like the ones that are so beautiful in Europe, especially in
Vienna and Berlin."[66] Off-key? No, ventriloquism.

Nevers's tract is revealing in that it is a mix of two voices: militant anti-
Semitism's and that of ordinary anti-Americanism. The first takes on the task
of giving a "history" of the Jewish presence and the Masonic influence in the

United States. Thus the reader will be "not surprised to learn" that "from 1789 to 1922 [*sic;* 1932], out of twenty-nine United States presidents, twenty were freemasons,"[67] and that as soon as Roosevelt came to power, "the leadership of the different governmental departments was exclusively given to the Jews."[68] The second voice simply repeats "anthropological" details that were already common knowledge for the French public: descriptions of America's cities, people, way of life. The Jews' and Freemasons' shady dealings were thus painted on a familiar cultural backdrop. All the more familiar in that the descriptive part is culled from earlier works that had a wide readership—first and foremost Duhamel's. The Americanophobic collage substantiates the anti-Semitic argument running parallel to it. As a means of revenge, moreover. For America's Jewification "explains," in return, most of the country's specific (and repulsive) characteristics: from the love of money, "the prerogative of the current generation in the United States," all the way to jazz, which shows "the Negroid character inherent in the Jewish race."[69] All the propagandist's effort goes into linking anti-American stereotypes and anti-Semitic stereotypes. And the shortest distance from one discourse to another obviously runs through the city—through New York in particular, a city whose very physical appearance reveals the Jewish conspiracy: "Those monstrous slabs rising up to dizzying heights, enclosing narrow streets between them. The whole thing suggests, on a huge scale, the austere architecture of distant Zionist colonies."[70]

As for the texts cited or plagiarized, they are not the ones we might ideologically suspect. It is not Céline, the collaboration's companion, who gives Henri Nevers his urban décor or his "anthropological" notations; it is the humanist Duhamel's *Scenes from the Life of the Future.* It is not the articles of the prewar Far Right press, or even the nonconformists' anticapitalist indictments that are recycled to depict America's social dysfunction; it is Raymond Recouly's *L'Amérique pauvre,* an essay on the 1929 crisis that its author, a nationalist commentator and biographer of Foch and Napoleon, but also an admirer of Dos Passos and Hemingway, considered full of "vital, ardent sympathy for the great [American] people."[71] (Recouly's book also contains several anti-Semitic notations, but they are more discreet than those of Siegfried or Duhamel.)

Recycling "banal" interwar material unchanged is revealing. The collaborationist pamphlets, by integrating *ne varietur* an anti-American classic such as *Scenes from the Life of the Future,* retrospectively shed light—a stark one—on one of the previous decade's major innovations: a connection between the anti-Semitic and anti-American discourses.

The intersection of these discourses and their partial reciprocal contamination is a characteristic development of the interwar period. Before 1914, anti-Americanism and anti-Semitism did not have much overlap. The themes of the money-kingdom, dollar-god, and "All-Plutopolis" did not lead to the associations that would become commonplace in the 1920s. There was probably more than one reason for this. The first would be the very strong identification of the United States as an Anglo-Saxon ethnocracy. The second is due to the time lapse with which French observers recognized what they would call the "new immigration" from central and eastern Europe, with its important Jewish component. One of the first observers struck by these immigrants' massive arrival into the port of New York was Abbé Félix Klein, the figurehead of the liberal Catholic movement baptized "Americanism": "Israel sent half of this crowd. The city already holds 800,000 of them. And they are starting to take up a lot of room."[72] But Abbé Klein wrote these lines fairly late, in 1910, and as a great admirer of the United States and Teddy Roosevelt, he was not at all representative of anti-Americanism. A third explanation can be found in the inherent logic of pre-1914 anti-American texts. Demonizing the Yankee, they gave him negative qualities very close to those imputed to the Jews: commercial greed, a sharp sense of material interests combined with solid religious convictions. In this stereotype, the Jews and the Yankees were neck and neck, and the latter's Anglo-Saxon tenacity left the former little leeway. That was Demolins's reasoning: "the Jew . . . , a plant that only thrives in favorable soil, . . . does not thrive in England, the Scandinavian countries, the United States, or Australia"—anywhere, that is, where the Anglo-Saxon was in power.[73] Even more explicitly, Varigny observed, also in the 1890s, that the Americans' "energy in conquering fortunes" was "such that in their land, the Jews could not get a foothold and will never prosper."[74] All that would change in the 1920s: America's Jews had become visible. And if the discriminatory measures they suffered were mentioned in passing, what was first and foremost emphasized was their massive presence and their considerable "influence" through the banks, the press, and the movies. We have already cited the pages André Siegfried devoted to the different "types" of American Jews in 1927. The sudden surge of "Jews from Russia or Poland" had transformed the urban landscape: they "formed solid indigestible blocks in the lower quarters of the big cities."[75] By accentuating the artificial and fallacious nature of their "Americanization," Siegfried very officially opened the way for a discourse on America's takeover by the Jews, which would expand over the course of the following decade. "New York is the greatest Jewish city in the world," Siegfried wrote, "with a million and a half Jews."[76] (He added that it was probably also the largest Catholic city.) It is an "immense Jewish city," Recouly repeated in 1933: Jews comprised a third of the population, and "their importance, their influence, from an economic, intellectual standpoint is even greater than their numerical proportion."[77]

From Siegfried to Recouly, along with Duhamel himself—who saw, in a chic club, "a Jewess, still beautiful, though with a beauty that I can only describe as profaned, . . . trying to sell her daughter to a certain decrepit old man"[78]—the ordinary anti-Americanism of the 1930s was a gold mine for the anti-American anti-Semitism that burgeoned under the occupation. And the most embarrassingly florid passages were not always in the most militant texts. Such as this page on New York, which voices doubts about whether it is still "an occidental city": "When the offices down town close at night, and one is crammed into the subway along with countless stenographers with swarthy complexions, hook noses, and a flavor of the ghetto, or when from the narrow streets of the East Side pours out a hurried mass of brown Levantines and bearded Semites, the impression is distinctly oriental,"[79] and "the flowing crowds, unfurling in endless waves, remind one of the human tides of the Asian capitals."[80] The description is not by Recouly or Paul Morand, and still less by collaborationist writers. It was written by the distinguished scholar André Siegfried.

It is not hard to see how, faced with the wealth of material produced in the interwar period by the most honorable names, the lazy plagiarists of the collaboration gave in to temptation.

New York, Open City: A Nauseated Sartre

"It is hard to pass from people who embrace each other to people who eat each other," Voltaire remarks at the start of the article "Anthropophages" in the *Philosophical Dictionary*.[81] It is hard to go from Henri Nevers to Jean-Paul Sartre. Linear time has its non sequiturs just as alphabetical order does. It was through Sartre, in effect, that liberated France rediscovered America.

Nothing predisposed Sartre to becoming the anti-American discourse's ferryman over the swamps of the occupation. He was the one, however, who put the topos of the unlivable American city back into circulation after the liberation: it was all the more successfully relaunched because he breathed a new and very personal "existential" life into the cliché. As well as a central figure of left-wing anti-Americanism, Sartre was also an inspired rewriter of the French unease with the metropolis. World War II had not yet ended when he began publishing articles on America with incontestable brio. Mostly written for *Le Figaro* and *Combat,* before being (in part) reprinted in *Situations III,* these pages on America played a vital part in continuing the anti-American discourse on the city by conferring on old phobias the prestige of original nauseas.

Sartre went to the United States when the War Office Information invited several French journalists in late 1944: the goal was to give these journalists a grand tour so they could observe the American war effort in vivo. The United States was unfamiliar to Sartre, and he had taken no real interest in it before the war. A Germanist and Italophile, what he knew best about America was its movies, which, like Simone de Beauvoir, he preferred to the French cinema; and a few writers, of course, such as Faulkner or Dos Passos, whom he helped find a wider readership in France. But he also knew his classics. Like Simone de Beauvoir three years later, he set out with bookish baggage handed down from the prewar period.

There are echoes of Durtain, if not Keyserling, in his description of American cities as "camp[s] in the desert," as skeletons of cities where the streets are set "like vertebrae" around the "spinal column" of a main thoroughfare.[82] And Durtain (or Waldo Frank) crops back up in his definition of buildings as "votive offerings to success."[83] There is something of Duhamel in his evocation of the premeditated precariousness of an architecture designed not to last, since the "house," contrary to French *demeures,* is a simple "carcass" that "is abandoned on the slightest pretext."[84] Céline is not far off, either. But only to contradict Bardamu's famous description: "Just imagine, that city was standing absolutely erect. New York was an upright city."[85] Not at all, Sartre replies. The European who lands in New York has the impression that "he has been taken in. He has heard only about skyscrapers; New York and Chicago have been described to him as 'upright cities.' Now his first feeling is, on the contrary, that the average height of an American city is noticeably smaller than that of a French one."[86] Bardamu is brushed aside, and in tones that betray a certain irritation, as if Sartre were fed up with bumping into *Journey to the End of the Night* with every step, with every page. Indeed, even his main theme, the metropolis invaded by nature, can already be found in Céline: "High up, far above the uppermost stories, there was still a bit of daylight, with sea gulls and patches of sky. We moved in the lower light, a sick sort of jungle light, so gray that the street seemed to be full of grimy cotton waste."[87] Hence probably the urge to refute the city's verticality; but making New York out to be horizontal is not enough to erase certain literary debts. Fifteen years later, Roland Barthes would discreetly moderate the debate: neither upright nor flat, New York seemed to him simply "seated," and even "superbly *seated,* the way the most fabulous cities are."[88]

There is, however, no denying the originality of Sartre's descriptions. While the collaborationists were just plagiarizing the texts of the 1930s,

Sartre reworked the material: he *composed* America with prewar texts, conserving certain features, but he scraped them out of the mud of a banal and predictable discourse (speed, noise, lack of humanity, etc.) and reorganized them in his way, around a few philosophical and existential themes he insistently hammered home. The first was precariousness. American cities, even when they were not "born temporary," like Detroit, Minneapolis, or Knoxville, were essentially ephemeral and fragile. "The striking thing is the lightness, the fragility of these buildings," Sartre wrote of Fontana, Tennessee.[89] Admittedly, Fontana was a city of prefabricated houses, devised for the needs of the Tennessee Valley Authority. But Sartre talks about New York in the same way; there, the traveler "is struck by the lightness of the materials used."[90] There is no stone in the United States: only metal, concrete, brick, and wood. The houses in the biggest cities are also "jerry-built"; they look like "Fontana's 'prefabricated houses'"; they were not built to last, but to fly away: "In this rocky desert [Manhattan] that will tolerate no vegetation, they have built thousands of houses out of brick, wood, or reinforced cement that all seem about to take flight."[91] It is a striking image, and one that illustrates the ambivalence of Sartre's descriptions. Because on the one hand, this lightness is a proof of freedom: the city does not hold its people down—they can always "flee" somewhere else—but on the other hand, it does not protect them, either. It leaves them open to all the dangers in the world.

The obsession dictating these pages is fear. Not that the American city is especially dangerous—the theme is practically absent from French travel narratives up to the 1960s—but because it does not fulfill its immemorial (European) duty. It is not, for man, the carapace, the "shell" he needs. America's cities are "open cities," Sartre writes, "onto the world," "onto the future." But open cities, too, in the sense of cities with no protection from the enemy. And the enemy, in America more than elsewhere, is nature. Sartre's interpretation thus separates the American city from the European city even more radically than his predecessors' did. It is a separation inscribed in history and myth: "We Europeans subsist on that myth of the great city which we created during the nineteenth century. American myths are not ours, and American cities are not our cities: they have neither the same nature nor the same functions." The reference to the nineteenth century does not have the modernity that, with Baudelaire and Benjamin's help, we might imagine: this nineteenth century is the end of a very long history rather than the dawn of modern times. The first of the "functions" Sartre considers inseparable from the European myth of the city (and the one that is radically missing from the American city) comes from the dawn of time: the rampart. "In Spain, Italy, Germany, and France we find round cities, originally encircled by ramparts which were designed not only to protect the inhabitants from enemy attack, but also to disguise from them the inexorable presence of nature." But if in the United States, human enemies have been driven so far off as to cancel out their threat, nature is, on the other hand, ubiquitous. "Am I lost in a city or in nature itself? New York offers no protection against the violence of nature. It is a city open to the sky. Storms flood its streets, which are so wide and take so long to cross when it rains. Hurricanes shake the brick-built houses and make the skyscrapers sway. The radio announces their arrival with as much solemnity as a declaration of war."

Sartre's expression, "a city open to the sky," beneath the superficial tautology, contains a strong evocative force: it calls up, by contrast, the gallery cities, portico cities, the shuttered and quiet cities of Europe with its ancient parapets. The American city, according to Sartre, is the opposite of all that. It leaves its inhabitants defenseless to "all the hostility and all the cruelty of Nature."[92] It is thus inhuman by virtue of its shortcomings as much as its excesses. It brutalizes men with its inorganic growth without calming their anxiety toward a proliferating, insatiable nature: "all the hostility and all the cruelty of Nature are present here"; "in the furthest depths of my apartment, I suffer the assaults of this hostile, indifferent, mysterious Nature."[93] The American city is no longer the antechamber to freedom, square one of all kinds of possibilities, with each street opening out onto the continent's infinity; it confesses to being a horrible bivouac in which man is perpetually on his guard and affronting insects and elevators: "I feel as though I am camping in the midst of a jungle swarming with insects. There is the moaning of the wind; there are the static electricity shocks that I get every time I touch a door handle or shake hands with a friend; there are the cockroaches running around my kitchen, the lifts that make me feel sick and the inextinguishable thirst burning in my throat from morning to night." It is a shrewd literary composite, in which Sartre fuses together the scourges of an excessively natural world and the wounds of an excessively mechanized civilization, which he sums up in an interesting image: "A wild sky above great parallel rails: that is New York, chiefly. In the heart of the city, you are at the heart of nature."[94]

Loving New York takes work; it is a hard apprenticeship. "I have learned to love it," "I have grown accustomed to it," "I had to get used to it," "once you have learned how to look" are the expressions that punctuate Sartre's descriptions. How successful can a Frenchman be in his painstaking efforts to love "the harshest city in the world"? We might have our doubts, since "to soften the edges a little," Sartre, like the prewar humanists, is forced to take recourse in the poetry of ruins or fantasies of destruction. The days are over, he writes, in which "great buildings dominated the city"; the age has come to a close in which "the skyscrapers were alive": "already, they are being slightly neglected: perhaps tomorrow they will be pulled down. In any event, building them required a faith that we no longer possess." So Sartre tardily, laboriously, adjusts his perspective, gets used to these vain buildings, since they have been vanquished: "In the distance I can see the Empire State Building, and the Chrysler Building, pointing vainly towards the heavens, and suddenly it occurs to me that New York is about to acquire a History, and that it already has its ruins."[95]

So there has been some progress. In "American Cities," Sartre saw the American city as decidedly devoid of a past: nothing in it was a monument. "This is due to the fact that these cities that move at a rapid rate are not constructed in order to grow old, but move forward like modern armies, encircling the islands of resistance they are unable to destroy; the past does not manifest itself in them as it does in Europe, through public monuments, but through survivals."[96] In Chicago, the Michigan Avenue Bridge, the "old" bridge stretching over the canal before the *Chicago Tribune* building or the El, were "a kind of indication of work to be done"; they "are there simply because no one has taken the time to tear them down." At the end of the article "New York: Colonial City," the old "survivals" have acquired the dignity of young ruins.

Where Have All the Concierges Gone?

It is hard not to be struck by the fact that the same wish for annihilation runs through all of these texts. Duhamel's skyscraper is doomed to being a mortuary chapel. Sartre's naturalist reverie takes a more subtle form: it makes the American city out to be a polyp or an earthworm, a lower life form. Try as you might, the city is impossible to kill. "Many of them have the rudimentary structure of a polypary. Los Angeles, in particular, is rather like a big earthworm that might be chopped into twenty pieces without being killed."[97] The infantile impulse of chopping up the earthworm city reappears one page later in the more adult, but just as violent, form of a memory of bombardment: "Suddenly it seems as if a bomb had fallen on three or four houses, reducing them to powder, and as if they had just been swept out: this is a 'parking lot.'"[98]

These musings about fires or buildings crumbling cannot be separated from a fantasy that authorizes their violence: the human void of these nonplaces. Since they were uninhabitable, American cities did not really have inhabitants. Their inhumanity seeped into the crowds that flocked there but who did not really live there and which had "to spend an hour in an Elevated train in order to reach their lodgings—I dare not say their homes."[99] In Chicago, Duhamel was prepared to take "these pink forms in line in front of [him]" for a different species of pigs. The slaughterhouse was not far off; it was lying in wait for them. "Crowds," "masses," "creeping multitude," "jumbled herd," "grim, bustling crowd that was noisy and taciturn at the same time," "poor creatures stupefied by work and anxiety":[100] these are the kind terms the French humanist applies to the American cities' barely human aggregates. Sartre does not share his vulgarity. But if the city is a worm, what does that make the humans crawling through it?

Precarious cities and thronging crowds were the x-and y-axes of the American urban geometry. The former's immateriality is met by the latter's nonhumanity. Livestock: for Duhamel, the cohorts of bodies rattled along by the subway are porcine; for Céline, the American couples Bardamu glimpses from his hotel room are "fat, docile animals, used to being bored."[101] Even more often, there is a beehive or anthill-like swarm, sometimes even vermin: insects of all kinds, and all of them slaves to an instinctive febrility. The city's inhumanity and the humans' low level of humanity produce and reinforce each other. This dialectic of the worst-case scenario is true of the skyscrapers, where worker insects buzz around, but also the streets, which are never really streets but "pieces of highways,"[102] as Sartre puts it. Since the American city has no end or limits, its streets are all "major thoroughfares." You can be run over, which is the only encounter possible. The lack of passers-by, on top of the city's oversized nature, makes the American street something radically different than the European street, which is "half-way between the path of communication and the sheltered 'public place.'" The European street lives, Sartre explains; that is, it "changes its aspect more than a hundred times a day," because "the crowd that throngs the European street changes, and men are its primary element."[103]

The American street is not only a joyless street; it is a humanless street. Barthes recognized this French mythology in the paintings of Bernard Buffet, who exhibited a New York series at David and Garnier in 1959: "Buffet's New York will not disturb many prejudices; it is a tall city, geometrical and petrified, a gridded desert, a hell of greenish abstraction under a flat sky, a real metropolis from which man is absent because he is crammed in everywhere; this new Greuze's implicit moral is that life is clearly happier in Belleville than in Manhattan." It is a self-indulgent handling in which "the Frenchman is confirmed in the excellence of his habitat." Buffet's stance is nothing but an "aggression" against a city he wants to "get rid" of and to which "he gives the death blow . . . by emptying the streets of humanity." But "it is not upward, into the sky, that New York should be looked at, but down below, among the men and the merchandise." With a flick of the pen, Barthes straightens the city out: "Skyscrapers make up blocks, blocks make up streets, streets are there for man. Buffet takes it in reverse: he empties the streets, rises along the building fronts, he runs away, irresistibly skirts the surfaces, he rarefies: his New York is an anti-city."[104] This "anti-city" is the entire polyphobic intelligentsia's as well. And if Buffet, as Barthes believes, painted New York wrong, he nevertheless perfectly rendered this tradition.

But above all, what was dead in the American metropolis was the idea of the city itself. From Céline to Sartre, from Durtain to Baudrillard, this death was expounded on in all different tones. Including the regret—less surprising in Céline than in Simone de Beauvoir—that there aren't any concierges there. "In movies, I have often seen these buildings without any concierge,"[105] wrote in 1948 Simone de Beauvoir, who had not always had a spotless relationship with her own. But she had probably also *read* about them, too—these buildings without concierges—in *Journey to the End of the Night*. Their absence is Bardamu's undoing when he goes looking for Lola: "But there was no concierge in her house. There were no concierges in the whole city. A city without concierges has no history, no savor, it's as insipid as a soup without pepper and salt, nondescript soup." The concierge was the truth, the "undeniable details"; the concierge was hatred, that "vital spice"; that "luscious, tasty hellfire"; in short, the concierge was life and the city: a city worthy of the name in which life was worth living. All that was "cruelly lacking" in New York.[106] The opposite of warming hatred was icy solitude. Like Bardamu's at the Laugh Calvin Hotel: "The loneliness in Africa had been pretty rough, but my isolation in this American anthill was even more crushing."[107] Sartre said it differently, but he was saying the same thing when in 1945 he contrasted the European city and the American city: the former was, unlike the latter, naturally "unanimist." Closed to the outside (the "ramparts"), it was internally divided "into districts, and these are also round and enclosed. . . . Streets break into others streets: closed at both ends, they do not seem to lead towards the outskirts of the town; one just goes around in circles. . . . It is such streets that inspired Jules Romains' 'unanimism': they are alive with a collective spirit that varies with each hour of the day."[108] In France, the streets ran into other streets. In America, they ran across the continent—or straight into the water. Vladimir Pozner, in his highly anti-American *Les États-Désunis*, published in 1948 (and praised by Sartre), prefigured Baudrillard's intuitions on the World Trade Center's "suicide."[109] For lack of the WTC, which had not yet been built, he has Wall Street kill itself: "This street springs from a cemetery and throws itself into the river! A street as short as its name: Wall Street." And the vision continues—a vision that has since become a familiar one: "The cemetery is old, and all the spots are filled. Around the black temple of the Trinity, the dead are crushed together like the courtiers of the Stock Exchange on a day of panic. All around, the skyscrapers hold watch."[110]

If the city has such an important place in anti-American arguments, it is not only as a microcosm of an anti-France or "anti-garden of France." It is also because the teeming city is the negation, the hindrance of the civilized city. Its indifferent promiscuity is the perfect foil for the ideal of civility that is the underlying myth of these disgusted descriptions. Not only is there a superior way of life, but a certain communal life, a French-style conviviality and citizenship. Because in the metropolis, the common man is as absent as the nonexistent concierges. There are only the troubling species of any cosmopolis: "aggregates," "alluvial deposits," tribes, "ghettoes." The reference to the American ghetto, the metaphor of ghettoization in the French discourse, prolongs and perpetuates, at the start of the third millennium, the repulsive fantasies that the mixed-breed metropolis had been setting off among French intellectuals for three-quarters of a century.[111] Contrary to the Parisian *quartier,* conceived as a village, the American neighborhood is always suspected of being part of an ethnic, social, or even religious partition. The *quartier* is "unanimist" without being exclusive, and the European city, in the end, a federation of *quartiers.* The American neighborhood, on the other hand, was conceived as an enclosed space, with the "ghetto" being its logical outcome. The megalopolis thus escaped its nature as a "roofless city" only to break down into divided destinies. The ethnic cacophony, poured into the separate blocks of the urban topography, hardened into an irremediable impermanence.

> Last skyscrapers
> whose architects piled up floors like misers money
> Streets, canyons strangled by the darkness
> Empty streetcars compressed at the terminal
> Saxon mugs, Irish ears, Latin eyes,
> Jewish noses,
> Negro mouths
> Chinese skin,
> not to mention the Nyam-Nyam, Magyars, Bosnians, Romanians, Lithuanians,
>   Neapolitans
> and other swarthy brachycephalics judged harshly by Gobineau, Lapouge and
>   Houston Chamberlain[112]

The final ironic touch is not enough to free this poem by Luc Durtain, "Match de boxe," from being a stereotyped vision of America's aberrant mix, nor to absolve a city whose tribes only come together around a boxing ring and where "all the different nations elbowing each other," as Duhamel put it, would never form the Michelet-style "people" the French were always looking for but never found anywhere in America.

The American metropolis is both saturated with men and void of humanity. But its ultimate deficiency is the lack of a people as a collective figure to guarantee the city's authenticity. This deficiency shocks, troubles, and discomfits French visitors as of the early twentieth century. Paul Bourget is probably the first to comment on it, in *Outre-mer:* "It is a strange thing—this country where everything is made by the people and for the people has none of the characteristics we habitually consider the mark of the population's soul."[113] The farmers and workers looked nothing like the ones in France. And even harder to find were those who gave the French street its physiognomy: artisans, merchants—and concierges. Whether expressed as astonishment, sadness, or indignation, French accounts throughout the century would dwell on this mystery and scandal: the absence of cafés, bistros, real restaurants, walkways, and esplanades, not to mention covered malls and public squares. Cities without "public places," as Sartre put it: how could this be? This disapproval, which we might be tempted to see as a few nostalgic travelers' pained frustration, is worth taking seriously. It reflects a deep unease in the face of an incomprehensible society. At the same time, it betrays the French intelligentsia's attachment to an imaginary urban ethos, a dream of conviviality, and above all, the regulating figure of the people—homogeneous in its differences, diverse but not "communitarian." All commentators, both left and right wing, lamented and invoked the *people* in criticizing America. To the most conservative and old-fashioned, like Jules Huret or Paul Bourget, there was no distinction between individuals and groups; what was missing was the variety of trades displayed by different work clothes, and with it, the subtlety of possible exchanges created by hierarchies in which distance and familiarity were expressed with imperceptible nuances—which Huret contrasted with the disconcerting democratic roughness he experienced in the streets of America and even in the Pullmans. Traditionalists lamented the picturesque, artisanal people; they did not recognize the French countryman, a shrewd and prudent man whose roots went deep, in the American farmer. As for the liberals, they sought an organic civic unity in the streets of the metropolis in vain: the neighborhood—as a commune, a microcosm of direct democracy, a space that worked on the human scale of solidarities, a hub for exchanges between social groups that were not (yet?) living in mutual ignorance or hatred—was what they were looking for. It was not Bourget's "naive and timid" people that they lamented, but the generous, sharing, and jovial people that would make anarchy or even a proletarian dictatorship fun: populism's people, poetic realism's people, Queneau's people, Kanapa's, Pennac's. And, as we have seen, Duhamel's: "Will you disappear one day, our little bistros, with your low-ceilinged, warm, smoky little rooms, where three pals, sitting shoulder to shoulder around a tiny iron table, tuck away beef bourgignonne, swap stories, and laugh, for the love of God! laugh and blow on a flute?"[114] "Shoulder to shoulder" is the euphoric, French version of separated communities' competitive "elbow to elbow."

If in the face of the infinite city, with its houses stacked up like emigrants' suitcases, nearly all French observers became Barrèsian, the headless megalopolis in which peoples "are crowds that do not linger" pushed them back to the "unanimist" dream, as Sartre noted, but also and more fundamentally led them to embrace the myth of fraternity, which, as André Malraux suggested and Mona Ozouf showed, "is the key to the French Revolution."[115]

☆ ☆ ☆

Whether Babel or Babylon, Carthage or Plutopolis, earthworm or anthill, by the 1920s, the American city had concentrated all the hatred the French intelligentsia felt for America. And all those dreams of eradication and wishes for annihilation can be found intact, trembling and alive, in what Baudrillard called the "jubilation" of September 11, 2001. Jean Baudrillard uttered the word: "the prodigious jubilation in seeing this global superpower destroyed."[116] *His* jubilation? He knows better! *Our* jubilation: "Ultimately, they were the ones who did it, but we were the ones who wanted it." But whom did Baudrillard use his jubilometer on? Or was he trying to intimidate us—"Come on, admit it, you know you were jubilant"—like the teacher in Gombrowicz's *Ferdydurke* who orders his students to be enthusiastic? In the end, it is more reasonable to believe that Baudrillard was aware of the long and rich tradition he had inherited and wanted to pay homage to Luc Durtain, whose California desert looks a lot like the one in *America*; or Waldo Frank, who in 1930 theorized America as a "simulacrum"; and even, why not, Georges Duhamel, whose New York fixations would have made the jubilometer explode! It is more reasonable to believe that Baudrillard simply meant: *us*, intellectuals of France, Érostrate & Co., Inc., keepers of the flame of anti-Americanism, since we cannot be its torchbearers. If we believe that, we do not need to note the other echoes his fascination for the "eighteen kamikazes" and their "absolute weapon of death" calls up.

In October 2001, when a petition against the American-led intervention in Afghanistan (in which France took part) appeared in the French press, signed by 113 intellectuals, artists, academic and political activists, under the title "This War Is Not Ours," Liliane Kandel's was one of the few voices to express uneasiness and dismay. Just a few weeks had elapsed since Al-Qaeda's attacks on American soil, she noted, and yet in the so-called 113 petition, the event had already disappeared as such—as if, her title stressed, "All in all, nothing [had] happened on September 11 in New York."[117] With the corollary of conjuring away the victims. The same victims are, in Baudrillard's piece "L'esprit du terrorisme," brushed off in a parenthesis: "(which does not deny their suffering and death)." A nice epitaph, as laconic as the "unambiguous condemnation" of an "event" carefully left out of sight in the 113 manifesto. The war that broke out against the Taliban regime was a "repetitive pseudo-event we have seen before," Baudrillard concluded at the end of a repetitive pseudo-analysis we had read before. Anti-Americanism is also the necropolitics of intellectuals.

Heidegger says that "the world appears on the horizon of broken machinery," and here the machinery never breaks down.

Simone de Beauvoir, *America Day by Day* (1948)

They affirm that they are first and foremost engineers, which in the United States is much more respectable and serious than being a philosopher.

Raoul de Roussy de Sales, *La Revue de Paris* (1933)

 13

Defense of Man:
Anti-Americanism Is a Humanism

André Maurois recounts how he was about to accept an invitation from Princeton University in 1931 when he was admonished by "an old friend who professes violent and precise ideas about America." All the more precise, Maurois adds, because he had never crossed the Atlantic. "My dear young man," the friend told him, "don't go there! You won't come back alive. You do not know what America is. It is a country so frantic you'll never have a minute of leisure time; a country where the noise is so constant you won't be able to sleep or even rest; a country where the men die of overwork at the age of forty and the women leave their houses in the morning in order to join the collective scuttle. Intelligence and the mind have no worth over there. Free thought does not exist. Human beings have no soul. The only talk you will hear is of money. From your youth, you have lived a gentle life in a spiritual civilization; over there, you will find a civilization of bathrooms, central heating, refrigerators."[1] Still, André Maurois went, and at Princeton discovered an "unexpected America"[2] populated by squirrels and people who read Cocteau, where only the deep nocturnal silence would sometimes trouble his sleep.

The old friend's homily makes for an amusing "little mythology" of anti-American repulsions. What is more, it ends with a wink at the most hackneyed of horrific stereotypes: "My friend, have you read the description of the Chicago slaughterhouses? It is a monstrous, apocalyptic vision, I assure you." There is nothing political in the friend's tirade. No recrimination against Wilson or isolationism. No allusion to war debts or the Hoover moratorium. The little slice of anti-Americanism Maurois uses as a sly epigraph for a perfectly civilized stay in America deals entirely with American culture, described as a kind of existential violation. The old friend does not lambaste a hostile nation, but rather an unbearable country in which the European who has "lived a gentle life in a spiritual civilization" can only suffer—body and soul.

Maurois was right on target in describing the anti-American discourse as a bric-a-brac of grievances, an all-you-can-eat of the ambient *doxa*. He was even more on target when he showed the discourse mixing registers, confusing the temporal and the spiritual, prepared to use the existence of bathrooms as an argument for the lack of freedom of thought. He was mocking the strategy of the French intellectual discourse itself, which consisted in mobilizing humanism against Americanism. He was exposing the confusion between man (kept from sleeping by noisy America) and Man (supposedly wronged by the civilization of refrigerators on a more metaphysical level). He was discreetly pointing out strange complicities.

"Defense of man!" was one of the anti-American cultural front's most unifying rallying cries. From Duhamel to Bernanos, from Mounier to Garaudy, the cause seemed clear: anti-Americanism was a humanism. Not all anti-Americans purported to be humanists (the Far Right sometimes did not bother), but no humanist neglected to flare up against the United States. From the nonconformists of the 1930s to the Stalinists of the 1950s, not one detractor of the American way of life failed to pose as an advocate of downtrodden humanity. "American civilization"—that oxymoron—was thus presented for half a century as the absolute negation of the values humanity was founded on. It was "the worst degradation a 'civilization' has imposed on man," wrote Daniel-Rops and Denis de Rougemont in 1933.[3] Georges Bernanos did one better in 1947: "The kind of civilization people still call by that name—though no barbarism has been more barbaric or gone farther in destruction—threatens not only the works of man but man himself." This abominable "civilization," explained the Catholic polemicist, was "machine civilization—which one might well call 'Anglo-American' without offending anyone."[4] On the following page, Bernanos would compare the "monstrous alliance of speculation and machines" to the "invasions of Genghis Khan or Tamburlaine." Still with no offense meant.

As for the Communist press, it bared its fists and struck hard, lashing out at "Wall Street's cultural antihumanism" in the name of "the socialist humanism of the great Soviet people."[5] But here, we would have to cite the entire corpus of Communist or Communist-sympathizing literature of the cold war years, given how often the certainty that "global domination by the gangsters of American imperialism w[ould] be the end of civilization"[6] was hammered home. Nothing American escaped this enormous wave of anger. And when the long list of Yankee crimes against humanity had been completely covered, Roger Vailland still found time to settle the score with Jayne Mansfield, "the dream of some drunk Puritan at the tail end of an electoral banquet in the Midwest."[7] The Communist (and libertine) novelist was no less unfriendly toward the Frigidaire, upon which he heaped the same scorn as André Maurois's "old friend": "In a country like France where, aside from two months out of the year and not every year, it is always cold enough to put a cooler out on the windowsill and keep until Monday, Tuesday, or Wednesday the leftovers from Sunday's leg of lamb," the ostentatious refrigerator, essentially destined to provide ice cubes for Yankee beverages, was nothing but a "symbol" or rather a "ploy," and the artificially aroused need for it aggravated the worker's alienation.[8] Men in general and specifically Communist men should be wary of the "barbarity of comfort."[9]

The intellectuals' anti-Americanism was as insistent a humanism as it was versatile. After all, when you compare man according to Georges Duhamel or Georges Bernanos and man according to Roger Vailland or Roger Garaudy, it seems as though there must have been a mistake somewhere. Personalist man, steeped in God—Maritain's and Mounier's man— reviled secular humanism's man, with his individualism and agnosticism. And the new, regenerated man, real socialism's "fully man" man, cast the earlier two back to their archaic shadows. The massive references to man by the different French anti-Americanisms raise two questions. How, with what representations, based on what reasoning, had America, in the eyes of the majority of the French intelligentsia of the interwar years, come to embody the worst possible threat to man? And second, how did hostile discourses pronounced in the name of contradictory and even antagonistic figures of humanity manage to converge and fuse into a single accusation, one pronounced in unison by intellectuals who were seemingly as different as could be?

Of Robots and Men

"History will most likely show anticapitalism to be the most fortunate trend of the 1930s," Mounier wrote in 1936.[10] But another trend (and a related one) could steal its thunder: antimachinism. Even more clearly than anticapitalism—which operated mostly on the extremes of the political spectrum and in the "young reviews" Mounier had in mind—technophobia was the most widely shared French passion of the day. The entire intelligentsia was awash with it. Dismayed by objects "made by soulless machines for a crowd whose own soul seems to be disappearing,"[11] Duhamel-style humanists were technophobic. Technophobic, too, were Christians like Bernanos, who brandished Christ on the cross against fetid modern felicities, or Paul Claudel, who railed against the "idols made not only of stone and wood, but also iron and electricity, which have ears and do not hear (the telephone)."[12] Technophobic were the partisans of the Action Française, but also the young neo-Maurrassians, who, even when they went against the party line, were still quick to denounce the idolatry of "mechanical conquests" they called America's (false) "miracles."[13] Technophobic were the nonconformists of the New Order, starting with Robert Aron and Arnaud Dandieu, who defined their contentious 1931 Le Cancer américain as a "discourse against technology."[14] Technophobic, too, though selective, were Marxists such as Georges Friedmann, whose analysis of "work in pieces" distinguished between good machines (those that were part of a collective economy) and all the others. Technophobic, finally, were the French Heideggerians who, after the war, took over from the tired humanists to philosophically articulate a distrust both of machinism and of the country that embodied machinist civilization. Simone de Beauvoir had a very precise memory of the day in December 1939 when Sartre, on a stone bench in Sisteron, explained to her how for Heidegger, "the world appears on the horizon of broken machinery";[15] ten years later, the phrase that had struck her found its use in America Day by Day: "Heidegger says that 'the world appears on the horizon of broken machinery,' and here the machinery never breaks down."[16] What was true of the Americans' world was also true of its people. From Bernanos, whose La France contre les robots prolonged the antimodernism of the 1930s into the postwar years, to Simone de Beauvoir and all those who found a new antitechnological inspiration in Heidegger, the changing of the guard was assured.

Identifying America with machinism did not start with Frederick Taylor[17] or Henry Ford. It went back to Baudelaire. His inaugural sentence is hard to forget: "So far will machinery have Americanized us . . . " In hardly less apocalyptic tones, a note in the Goncourts' Journal confirms the association forged in the nineteenth century by French men of letters between America, technology, and the "end of everything": "A friend comes back from America and announces a piece of news we find hard to believe, and which would be the end of everything. *The wash basins are fastened to the walls.*" Running water as the end of civilization: not even Baudelaire could have come up with that one! But even more astonishing than the Goncourts' revulsion is Cocteau's approval of it in the mid-twentieth century: "When you first read it, a remark like that makes you laugh. Then you think about it and start to wonder if that isn't the reason for some of our problems."[18]

The Americanizing prophecy of *Fusées* took a while to come true, but in the end, most French people got over their horror of the sink. The half century leading up to World War I raised high hopes for machines. It was the machines that would be slow to keep their promise: reducing human labor and effort. As for their potential to multiply useful goods, it was often eclipsed in Europe by their horrifying destructive efficiency in the form of tanks, machine guns, and H-bombs. Machinism's disastrous performances on the battlefields of 1914–18 paved the way for the antimechanization turnaround of the 1920s.

The most spectacular symbol of modern machinism, the assembly line, was at first observed with interest in France. Then, "suddenly in 1927, hostility to the assembly line became the central feature of the literature"[19] on Americanization. The historian making this comment advances a hypothesis: there was a close interconnection, at the end of World War I, between the diplomatic circles associated with the American alliance (Jules Jusserand, André Tardieu) and the business circles sold on American methods of productivity (Charles Cestre, Émile Schreiber—the head of *Les Échos* and father of Jean-Jacques Servan-Schreiber—Victor Cambon, Jean Gontard). The anger aroused in France by U.S. foreign policy at the end of the war spilled over onto the industrial innovations endorsed by a group that was seen as too closely identified with American interests.[20] But did the Frenchmen of the 1920s, and particularly the intellectuals, need that in order to swear off machinism? It is doubtful, considering how familiar they were with the proud, deceptively humble stance Cocteau was still adopting in 1949 toward his American hosts: "I'm just a man of the old French barnyard, an artisan who makes his object with his hands and carries it to your city under his arm."[21] The self-portrait is all the more amusing in that it appears as part of a *Lettre aux Américains* written in an airplane above the Atlantic and technologically dated "Paris–New York (Air France), January 12–13, 1949."

The antimachine reaction dominating the interwar period was both part of a general anxiety—illustrated in Germany by Fritz Lang's *Metropolis* (1926) or, in America itself, by Chaplin's *Modern Times* (1936)—and the technophobia specific to French intellectuals as a group. In this area, the intellectuals had no trouble personifying a national nostalgia. Cocteau's coquetry, in his self-portrait as an artisan, reflects an ideal of the entire French nation. "The ambition of every Frenchman," Siegfried noted in 1927, was still "artisanship, now out of date, [but part of] certain conceptions of mankind which we in Europe consider the very basis of civilization."[22] And this ideal, which was "incompatible with mass production," was slated for rapid extinction by unbridled Americanization.

In the French case against machinism, *Scenes from the Life of the Future* appeared as a general, and generally applauded, denunciation; it was, however, neither the most enlightened nor the most solidly argued. Maurice Blanchot, in 1932, ironically noted its limitations: "As a personal enemy of the machine, [Duhamel] bestows it with all the most terrifying characteristics"; in his opinion, "there is no mechanical contraption—a motor, a bolt— that is not found a little guilty"; but so much hatred "gives the idol extraordinary power."[23] In conclusion, Blanchot reproaches the declared humanist for having written a book against America in which "man hardly comes into the picture." We might add that machinism hardly comes into the picture: Duhamel is scarcely interested in the new organization of labor. The machine is, for him, an abstract malediction. Moreover, it is consumption machines and not production machines he describes: the automobile, the elevator, the cinema—totems to laziness and enslavement. His criticism of standardization betrays, more than anything else, the frustration of a hedonist threatened by a qualitative impoverishment of the world, worried for the "fifty different varieties of plum" and, of course, the "more than a hundred kinds of cheese" which made France what it is.[24] To each his "stinking God" . . . Loti, at the end of the nineteenth century, was already denouncing the Americans': the machine spitting coal and sweating oil. Duhamel inveighed, in his wake, against the now ubiquitous machines spreading clamor and ugliness throughout America. From Loti to Duhamel, the repulsion was the same, and the analysis of mechanization had hardly progressed. Only the perspective had changed: what interested Duhamel was showing the invasion of daily life by innumerable useless mechanisms. If he innovated at all, it was by slipping into the skin of the unwitting consumer, the honest man hustled in the street by an ill-mannered civilization.

But the refusal, both visceral and moralizing, he banked to what surrounded him blinded him to the system's recent advances. Though a reader of André Siegfried, he had hardly learned his lesson. Siegfried had nonetheless explained in 1927 that the new industrial revolution taking place in the United States was not only, or even chiefly, a matter of multiplying and perfecting machines; there was actually a new "philosophy of production." This innovation was lost on Duhamel. When he condemned the machine, he did not go beyond what Georges Friedmann called, at around the same time, "the sentimental anathemas of the intellectuals who have come back from America"[25] in a state of culture shock. His reprobation was still fundamentally moralizing, and his moral code was one of "effort": "Man always finds himself at a point where some terrible and mortal effort demands a man and nothing else."[26] There would always be sweat, toil, and even blood, Duhamel indignantly opined; machinism would be of no help there, and those who said differently were charlatans. If it could, machinism would become even more "inhuman." Yet effort was measured by manpower and could not be abolished without harming humanity: "As if effort were not the very measure of life!"[27] Duhamel did not seem to realize that he was thereby weakening his own principal theory: the machine's omnipotence. (Elsewhere and contradictorily, he reproached Siegfried for believing that mechanization had its limits, and that "there are no signs yet of a machine to pick strawberries":[28] "A machine for picking strawberries? Don't set the Americans that task, or, heavens, they will probably go and invent one!")[29] An indecisive Cassandra, he sometimes lost track of whether he should be declaring the end of man, supplanted by machines, or man's loss of humanity, abolished along with his effort.

We cannot help but be uncomfortable in reading his praise for the worker's "mortal" effort. But his traditionalism, the grumbling negativity that reinforced his antimachinistic brio, far from hampering his success, only added to it. The anti-Americanism of the 1930s got stuck in a rut of outraged lamentation: how could *they* do this to us, to us and to Man? The philistinism oozing from his apology of men's toil was, moreover, not specific to Duhamel. In the face of an America full of degrading comfort and dishonorably material pleasures, Duhamel proffered the "humanist" version of a penitent discourse that, from their respective sides, the Christians and the Communists were also voicing. Between those who believed that "man's misfortune is the marvel of the world," those for whom the road to a radiant future was paved with "sacrificed generations," and the author who made dull tasks out to be "the very measure of life," the affinities were deeper than the interested parties themselves realized; and it was not the first time that America had been the catalyst in making troubling complicities emerge. If Duhamel can be set apart, it is mainly for his extraordinarily good intentions. They tell us the machine will ease the most tiresome efforts, he mistrustfully notes; but in fact, "what is it that we call tiresome labor?" His answer is ready-made. It is the final effort of the "exhausted journalist" for whom "the pen between his fingers is heavier than the heaviest of pickaxes." Ditto for the sleepy doctor on call, whose "overcoat seems as heavy . . . as a whole cask of oil." Georges Duhamel was of course a doctor before becoming a man of letters.

Duhamel, Cocteau: heroic workmen, martyrs to cerebral labor. At least Cocteau sketched out his vignette with a refreshing immorality when he shamelessly lamented "the innumerable, gracious help" that once eased the writer's daily concerns: "In the past, water, light, and food were brought to us; we did not have to get up. We were free not to leave our armchair and our book."[30] His deliberate "impropriety" advisedly reminds us that behind many of the French intelligentsia's antimachinistic diatribes was also an often explicit nostalgia for a lost paradise of domesticity—a golden age in which sinks, free to move about, were brought to you by serviceable hands. "The help has disappeared," Cocteau observed. "Mechanisms have replaced them." To the figures of Man threatened, according to France's intellectuals, by the Americanization of modern life should be added in all honesty the butler and the chambermaid. . .

"The Philosophy of American Production"

But in this, Duhamel was the tree hiding the forest. For, between the pre–and post–World War I years there was really a profound transformation in the French view of America as the empire of technology. The vocabulary itself attests to this. In the 1920s, the case against the machine was coupled with a wider indictment aimed at a technical, social, and cultural complex for which the United States was the laboratory and the prototype. Now the expressions "American method" and "American system," or even (in André Siegfried) "philosophy of American production,"[31] were used. The American machine was no longer a simple idol with machinism its isolated cult. The idolatry had turned into a religion: a social religion and even a national religion. The United States now seemed to French observers to have a body of doctrines—scientific beliefs and social practices that formed a unified whole around the twin poles of technology and capitalism.

On the one hand, the French now held the conviction that the United States and capitalism were one and the same thing. As banal as it may seem, this was a new connection: it only took hold in the 1920s, when no one believed that a revolutionary transformation of the United States was still possible. The trusts had not paved the way for socialism. Yankee capitalism seemed stronger than ever. Or even more, as Jouvenel stressed in 1933— never in the history of men had there been a more perfect symbiosis between an institution and a society: "No institution has ever been as inherent to a society as the capitalist institution to the American society, and, as a corollary, no society has ever been as shaped by an institution."[32] This was a big change from the prewar situation, in which there had been serious discussion of the system's potential socialist conversion. It was a decisive change for the future of American representations.

On the other hand, machinism was at the same time no longer only perceived as a material evolution created by the imperatives of competition. It now seemed like just one of the cogs in a greater social machine organized around it. In this "system," everything was interconnected. Ideological and moral preconceptions; production techniques; work, hygiene, and lifestyles; human relations; consumption habits: the "American way of life" was all this and could only be expressed by this tautological phrase.

The chapter André Siegfried devoted to industrial production in *America Comes of Age* established this new vision of the United States for a wide audience. The portrait he drew with a sober pen is no less striking for its broad influence. Six years before Bertrand de Jouvenel's *La Crise du capitalisme américain*, with its more caustic overtones, Siegfried calmly produced the portrait of a society in the stranglehold of an all-encompassing logic. The United States' insolently increasing wealth could not mask a more fundamental phenomenon: the formation of a system that inseparably merged the "organization of production" with "standardization," shaping consumption through advertising, "the methodical selection of personnel" (Taylorism), aptitude tests, permanent recourse to statistical predictions, and government collaboration with the empires of production (in unifying norms, for example); all of this capped off by a "service" ideology. Such was, in the order in which Siegfried demonstrated it, the nexus of the new America. In such a society, there was no longer a gap between the industrial, the political, and the social. As for the distinction between the individual and the collective, if the Americans still believed in it, it was because they were fooled by their own social ideal. "Though an American always pictures himself as being as free and unbridled as a prairie pony, in reality he is the most docile of men," Siegfried explained.[33] He was "molded as easily as clay" and obligingly lent himself to his own "education," that is, the manipulation of his tastes and home life. "Astonishingly alike" by their nature and culture, 100 million Americans let themselves be sanded down to the desired form by the high priests of merchandising: "scientists, economists, and psychologists" in the service of consumption.

The manipulation of people's needs and the transformation of individuals into consumers were central to French commentaries. Duhamel, who was not very attentive to the development of human engineering, was nonetheless struck by the "pack" of advertisers he felt represented an attack on his dignity, a permanent "insult" to man by "those brazen traders who seek to force our assent." An insult to man, sure! But not just man, the "poor folks" they ruined. Man treated by advertising like "the most stupid of inferior animals"; man who was harassed, robbed, and, even more important, brought down to the level of a "sedentary mollusk"; man deprived of his rights every day by America and who nonetheless "as Unamuno said," was "nothing less than a man and a whole man."[34] (Miguel de Unamuno, the antipragmatist par excellence, but also the antirationalist of *The Tragic Sense of Life*, makes for a revealing choice of ally by the anti-American humanist.)

With completely different preoccupations than Duhamel, Bertrand de Jouvenel also treated the manipulation of basic needs as a decisive innovation. He noted that it had modified the Americans' vocabulary: "[Industrial] leaders have made the greatest efforts to provoke such needs. This preoccupation has been so constant that it has even enriched the language with new words: the *cigarette-habit*, the *movie-habit*, the *automobile-habit*, the *radio-habit*, the *refrigerator-habit;* the goal is to give the consumer a whole series of habits in order to ensure an ever-growing market for modern products."[35] A few years earlier, Duhamel was still putting the tweezers of disgusted quotes around the neologism "consumer"; Jouvenel no longer felt the need to. Clearly, the machine was imposing its furious rhythm on semantic acquisitions themselves.

The second grievance, and another attack on man's personality: standardization, to which several French authors attracted the public's attention.[36] The standardization of *things*, a result of economic rationales, would directly lead to the standardization of people. "In countries, like the United States, where the uniform type, the *standard*, holds sway, resistance no longer finds refuge even in individual tastes," Lucien Romier wrote in 1927 in *Qui sera le maître, Europe ou Amérique?*[37] A generally moderate socialist observer such as François Drujon noted an "indoctrination" of human life by standardization far greater than what was thought Soviet collectivism would bring: "For many of us, the land of conformism, monotony, and indoctrination can only be the one collectivist doctrines claim, that is, the Soviet Union. And on the contrary, a politically democratic country like the United States should naturally offer the agreeable semblance of variety. Nothing could be more false! The eating factories, standardized stores, standardized meals, standardized frozen meat, standardized bars, and standardized bartenders are not in the USSR but the USA." And from this he produced a law of historical development: "Standardized life is a by-product of the ultimate stage of capitalism and not socialism."[38] For Drujon, all the towns in America seemed "like so many branches of a parent company. They are as disappointing as the innumerable branches of the Woolworth stores teeming throughout the American land."[39] How could men escape a similar standardization? In this regard, as Siegfried suggested, the "philosophy of American production" inexorably shaped a certain "philosophy" of existence, the one Sinclair Lewis described: "The boy in Arkansas displays just such a flamboyant ready-made suit as is found on just such a boy in Delaware, both of them iterate the same slang phrases from the same sporting-pages, and if one of them is in college and the other is a barber, no one may surmise which is which." Siegfried's interest in these lines from *Main Street* is characteristic of the French rejection of social sameness, equated (frowningly) with standardized products. "For a French woman back home the supreme luxury," Duhamel indignantly wrote, "is to wear a hat that is the only one of its model in all Paris."[40] But the French discomfort with the homogeny of American clothing went well beyond this kind of attachment to personal "distinction." It also betrayed an unease with the fact that the exterior signs by which a person's trade or condition could easily be gauged were disappearing. Through Lewis, Siegfried was prolonging Urban Gohier's turn-of-the-century distress at seeing American workers dressed like the middle class. In this area, too, over the course of a half century, bourgeois nostalgia for a visibly stratified world would concur with the proletarian desire to preserve workers' identity, even in their clothing, by defending corduroy against the jeans invasion, as the Communists did at the liberation. The sameness of appearance that in America was held to be a manifestation and an instrument of democratic equality would long be considered undesirable or even suspect by French conservatives and liberals combined.

The hint of uniformity that "American civilization" seemed to generate, in any case, fed into an anti-Americanism of "difference," championed for individuals as well as social groups. Those opposed to "betrayal" and those averse to "mixing" agreed on refusing the American model. André Siegfried admitted it with feigned remorse: the Frenchman was not "interchangeable"; his burden was his personality. "From the economic point of view, this development of personalities is a handicap, and it would be preferable to pass every one through the same mill." But was it up to the economy, that *ultima ratio americana*, to dictate its law to the French? Siegfried clearly believed this no more than Duhamel, Jouvenel, or any of their contemporaries did—including economists. The Frenchman, "that civilized man," Siegfried added, tells himself "sadly that in Europe mass production and civilization do not go together." But for all his sadness, he would not give up his civilization—that is, *civilization* itself—for a plate of beans, and still less a plate of corned beef.

The New Man versus the Man in Pieces

In the great trial of machinism that took place in France during the interwar years, the Left and particularly the Marxist Left might conceivably have taken the defense of the liberating machine. In the USSR's New Economic Policy period, the future readily took on American tones. Agitprop posters proclaimed this dialectical synthesis: "Let's take the torrent of the Russian revolution/Add the effectiveness of American technology/And construct socialism." But Soviet Russia quickly shifted from emulation to material—and especially ideological—competition. The image of American machinism grew more somber: it was now shown to be indifferent to man; its productions were frivolous or fatal. The war industry had a starring role in this respect. Speed itself, once prized by the futurists and constructivists, had a different meaning in America, where it pulled the masses into the "infernal round" of capitalism. The silent cinema's deadly automobile races, punishing endurance contests, and wild chases reflected industry's enforced progress and disciplined the American masses into an ever more frenzied pace.

French communism was largely untouched by the brief idyll between Leninism and Fordism (Ford tried to offer the USSR machines and engineers to civilize it with the automobile) and hardly needed external encouragement to detest American capitalism. But French Communists would not even consider falling in line with intellectual bourgeois' "philistine" antimachinism. Exonerating machinism while denouncing its American form was the general line taken by Georges Friedmann in the books he began publishing in the 1930s: *Problèmes du machinisme en URSS et dans les pays capitalistes* (1934) and *La Crise du progrès: Esquisse d'une histoire des idées* (1936).

Friedmann's first concern was setting himself apart from the "Jeremiah of the 'soulless world'": all those who considered "Technology" a "universal, metaphysical problem." This included everyone from Duhamel to Bergson, along with the "editors" of journals like *Esprit* and *Ordre nouveau* which, in his opinion, were "paving the way for a theory of French Nazism." "The malediction so many ideologues cast on the 'Machine' is only the sign of their impotence and confusion," Friedmann held, considering Ford more interesting than they were. The machine was not a metaphysical entity. It was not the embodiment of Evil, either. "The assembly line is not in itself a barbaric form of production." Was he rehabilitating machinism? Not so fast. Machinism in just one country—the one in which "what is called technical progress" took on a *"different meaning"*; the only country where one could "sense" that machines "are not contrary" to workers. That is, machinism in the USSR. As for the rest of the world, it was a pretty familiar picture for Friedmann: "Increasingly perfected machines are throwing workers out into the street and derailing the whole economic system through the overproduction of objects the masses cannot afford"; they "compromise workers' health and sometimes their lives"; they upset the bourgeoisie itself, "uncomfortable amid this technical profusion that is crushing them."[41] In a Europe that had been hit full-on by a global crisis originating in the United States, Friedmann was preaching to the converted.

Thus machinism should not be seen as a entity cut off from social realities. There was, as the Soviets were now saying, a liberating machinism (one used in the context of collective production) and a predatorial and depredating machinism (capitalism and cutthroat competition's). For now there was chaos. Soon there would be war and fascism, which Friedmann, in a striking shortcut, presented as bourgeois intellectuals' response to Bergson's desire for a spiritual component that could be breathed into all these techniques.[42]

The first result of the Manichean operation by which Friedmann divided the world in two was that, in describing the capitalist world, it kept intact the right-wing antimachinist expressions he purported to set himself apart from. Concerning debased American machinism, Friedmann repeated without blinking the vocabulary of the very people he was denouncing. He spoke, like the nonconformists, of "blind rationalization" and, like Duhamel, described the men of a nonsocialist techno-society as victims to the "psychosis of everything technology projects on them."[43] But Friedmann's other major effect, which interests us more directly here, was that he reinforced the United States' "guilt." If the Soviet machine could be considered innocent, America and not the machine was therefore the guilty party. While conservatives and nonconformists lumped the United States and machinism together in execration, Friedmann, in the name of historical materialism, dissociated them and lay all the blame on America, which clung to private ownership of the means of production.

In these conditions, the sketchy praise of Ford could only turn into a condemnation. Not that Friedmann attacked the personage himself or the eccentricities of the neurotic and bucolic self-made man who had envisaged, in 1917, chartering a ship of Peace to convince the Europeans to stop the war; who had long aspired to become president of the United States; and who had just launched an anti-Semitic crusade against Wall Street—all without slowing the incessant flood of millions of inexpensive automobiles throughout America. Against Ford, Georges Friedmann did not repeat Robert Aron or Duhamel's imprecations. On this point, as well, he made a distinction. There was, he explained, a realist entrepreneur Ford and a reactionary moralist

Ford; an engineer Ford and an ideological Ford. The former was bold and had flair. The latter was weak-minded, limited, and prejudiced. Ford believed "in high salaries, prohibition, automatic machines, birds and flowers, 'freedom,' industry, short work days, the automobile, and Progress. He d[id] not believe in credit, bankers, poverty, old age, wine, the government, egotism, charity, the Jews, and overproduction."[44] Such was the "Fordist creed" reconstructed by Friedmann. A composite sketch of the man, of course, but even more so of the "civilization" he perfectly represented. With this portrait of Ford, Friedmann was retracing a familiar cartography, that of a naïve yet crafty America, progressive and philistine, Puritan and xenophobic. Not far off was the hypocritical "Service" ideology ridiculed by Morand, mocked by Siegfried, and attacked by the nonconformists,[45] which Friedmann criticized in turn as the fig leaf covering the naked reality of the philanthropic entrepreneur's manipulation of human "needs."

But the other Ford, the great organizer of production—was he really any better than his ideological doppelgänger? The assembly line was not a bad thing in and of itself, most likely, but in Ford's system of production it was an alienating structure. Man did not live on bread alone, or on vacation time: he lived on meaning. And meaning did not come with "work in pieces." Friedmann starkly contrasted the effectiveness and the potential benefits of human-scale mechanization with the frustrating "daily life" of the assembly-line worker. Reducing the number of gestures, while a good way to economize on effort, had a negative impact insofar as it restricted the field of consciousness and left the worker ignorant of the end goal of his work. Specialization, however effective it was, disqualified the "partitioned" worker, who was deprived of any overall view of the process. Friedmann thus came very close to echoing the "humanist" discourse he jeered at. Ford's doctrine would never be anything but an "engineer's doctrine"; and it had all the limitations that entailed. The same reproach went for Taylorism, the systematic and mechanical application of precepts unsuited to the complexity of social and human relations as they were created and ramified in the context of production. Taylorism, a substitute for Scientism, Friedmann explained, was even more unacceptable than Fordism, because it was more ideological in its presupposed conception of man.

Friedmann's analysis is important in and of itself, as well as for the way it reoriented left-wing anti-Americanism. Its convergence with Gramsci's would only reinforce its resonance after the war.[46] It absolves the machine, but not American-style machinism. It preserves the idea of progress (the good machine's) but rejects the forms of it America purported to have found. Friedmann did not propose to separate practical, realist innovations on the one side and a dubious or frankly nefarious ideology on the other. He showed that there was a pocket of air and ideas at the core of the "American system." Between the engineer's innovations and his impoverished creed, though: nothing. And this void was where men's place should have been; once more, America had shuffled them away. The concern for man displayed in America by Ford and his proponents was nothing but smoke and mirrors: ersatz humanism, chipped ideological merchandise. Though it took a completely different path, Marxism met back up here with the chorus of accusations that had been voiced by the right wing in the name of man. Even more so because Friedmann's verdict about Ford, Taylor, and their "engineers' doctrines" extended and amplified a whole anti-American tradition in which the European *savant*, for whom nothing human was foreign, was opposed to the American technician or engineer's narrow-mindedness, as Gustave Le Rouge's caricature of Edison/Hattison demonstrates. The tradition was still thriving, as can be seen in a passage from *Le Cancer américain* where Robert Aron and Arnaud Dandieu define American civilization as a "civilization of technicians, where the specialist is only a tool like any other, or at best a machine tool."[47] As we can see, in taking a stance against the American machine, the ideologists of the New Order were able *in spite of everything* to come to an understanding with Marxist sociology.

"Technocracy" and Voting Machines

In the meantime, what name could there be for this new configuration? What word could be chosen or invented to designate such a system, in which Technology held sway over social issues in their entirety? It was a real problem. Which explains in part the proliferation of metaphors—all of them morbid. Aron and Dandieu used and abused the cancer metaphor. Duhamel, a man of the trade, continually brought infections and bacteria to the rescue. As for Bernanos, who came onto the already well-stocked infectious scene after the Liberation, he would strangely opt for diabetes. Arguing that American civilization "does not even deserve the name of anticivilization," that it "is a result of the functional sickness of human civilization" (which was already Robert Aron and Arnaud Dandieu's theory), Bernanos continued: "On the other hand, to deny it the name of civilization might perhaps be foolish. A doctor does not deny the name of liver, although the diabetic may well die of his liver."[48] And "I cannot help it," Bernanos concluded at the end of a heavy-handed analogy between America and a "functional sickness"; no, he could not help it "if people claim for this mechanical diabetes the name of civilization, that is to say the name of that very thing which it is in the process of destroying."

One attempt, in 1933, to get past this semantic stumbling block is enlightening by its very failure: Raoul de Roussy de Sales presenting the word *technocracy* to the French public.[49] For though the neologism was a success, its promoter's efforts to attach it to the "American system" fell through. Borrowed from the interested parties themselves, too sedate for the feverish French discourses on America, the term seemed above all too limited, too "technical" in fact, to cover all the aspects of an American ill on which French commentators had piled up the most cataclysmic hyperboles. Roussy de Sales's fruitless proposition bumped up against a vision of the American "system" that was already too all-encompassing not to feel hemmed in by this definition. The other point of interest in his article, published in *La Revue de Paris* ("Un mouvement nouveau venu des Etats-Unis: La technocratie" [A New Movement from the United States: Technocracy]) is that, in the face of "technocracy," understood as a machinist ideology in a liberal context, it called for a reaffirmation of the primacy of the political.

Roussy de Sales, the dean of the foreign correspondents in the United States, added that the Americans were far from agreeing on a single definition of technocracy. He, too, suggested two genealogies: on the one hand, engineer William H. Smyth's technical utopia, which he defined as "a system of philosophy and government according to which the nation's industrial resources should be organized and controlled by technicians for the good of the community"; on the other, the methodical gathering of numerical data and economic statistics that had been taking place since 1920 at Columbia University under the leadership of another engineer, Howard Scott. This assessment, which was particularly concerned with how much energy was available at different times and places, showed that in thirty years, a tremendous gap had opened between a traditional society's available energy and an industrialized country's. A single modern turbine, with a force of 300,000 horsepower, running twenty-four hours a day, was "worth" nine million times the power that could be produced by the "human motor. . . . Consequently, four such turbines would be enough to produce as much power as the entire worker population of the Untied States." But this dizzying boom of energetic means, which would probably have dazzled the previous generation, became, in 1933, as the global crisis reached its widest, a source of worry and not of triumph. If we believed the technocrats' figures to be correct, Roussy de Sales commented, their social meaning was catastrophic. These calculations notified men of their definitive uselessness: "We will no longer need them," aside from a "small, ever-dwindling minority of engineers and specialized workers." Luc Durtain, in "Smith Building," had portrayed the rarefaction of men in the "American system": "Under the surveillance of a few sparse workers—such is the American system—there toils a band of machines, steel Negroes."[50] And so, Roussy de Sales continued, "how can we stop the 14 million currently unemployed from becoming 20 million next year?"

As we can see, this presentation of the technocratic doctrine was far from being an apology. The triumph of technology was presented as a Pyrrhic victory. It had ushered in an "absurd" universe in which man would stubbornly and "blindly try to compete, using his muscles, with the formidable machines he has created precisely to economize his strength and serve him."[51] Here we once again find the Marxist theme of industrial capitalism as a "sorcerer's apprentice"—a recurrent theme in the 1930s, seen in Friedmann as well as the nonconformists. Is a system like that viable? It was clearly intolerable for men. Whence the alternative: "abolishing the machines" or reacting to the consequences of human work's utter devaluation by promulgating a "right" to a "security minimum" for obtaining essential goods and services. Roussy de Sales imagined a "new Declaration of the Rights of Man," which would set down individuals' elementary rights: food, lodging, heat, light, transportation. In a system in which man, economically speaking, was no longer "worth" anything, it was essential to reaffirm man's needs.

The reference to the first Declaration and the French Revolution is significant. Why, after all, make a new Declaration other than to put a stop to usurpation and abuse, as in 1789? Thus "technocracy," even before it took on the more governmental, top-business-school meaning we now give it, was seen not only as a production organization that was oppressive for both producers and consumers, but also as a takeover of democracy. The club of America's victims was growing. The man French polemicists were defending was not only the worker shackled to the machine like the serf had been to his patch of land or the consumer riveted to the needs that had been instilled in him or the common man shaped by standardization. They were defending the man tracked by inspections, profiled by psychologists, catalogued by experts in "human resources," weighed and judged on the scales of aptitude tests. (André Siegfried, who did not have a leftist bone in his body, had no problem comparing intelligence tests to a "police record" that "follows you" and "that can never be effaced.")[52] In the end, they were defending the dispossessed citizen—for how could his sovereignty, trumpeted just before elections and forgotten right afterward, conceivably withstand the absolute degradation, the *annulment* that would be his own in the very near future?

How could anyone honestly pretend that man would still be living in a democracy when he was living in a *technocracy?*

The new technophobia thus revived the old theme of illusory democracy which had been a constant of the anti-American discourse since the end of the nineteenth century. The generation of 1880 had countered the illusion with the reality of a profoundly "aristocratic" society. In 1900, it was the crushing weight of a plutocratic oligarchy that gave it the lie. Now, laying the blame on "technocracy" was a third variation on the same theme. Not that this replaced accusations of corruption, dishonest electoral practices, or the permanent repression of the syndicalist movement: these accusations continued apace, especially since there was no shortage of fodder for them. Jouvenel exclaimed in 1933 (just as people had in 1903): "Oh! Those American elections, where the same 'citizens'—who barely speak the language—stumble from voting booth to voting booth, and vote ten times, fifteen times for the candidates they have been told to vote for, and in their spare time, thrash people who attempt to vote for other candidates than theirs!"[53] He could also, like Dos Passos and Dreiser, denounce episodes of murderous repression that recalled the Great Upheaval's darkest hours, as in Harlan Country in 1931, or the Dearborn Massacre (March 7, 1932): "The bosses severely punish any attempt to spoil their docile herd of immigrants. At the least strike, employers hire 'gangsters' decorated 'deputy sheriffs.'"[54] Police brutality and fixed elections were still being denounced, but the heart of the matter was elsewhere: in a general takeover of democracy, which pushed such "unfortunate mistakes" into the background. The very people stigmatizing the exactions of the powerful were even more worried about a coming time when the social machine would no longer seize up, when the underhanded dictatorship would drone on without a hitch.

The metaphors themselves, which entered the American political vocabulary early on—"electoral machine," "democratic machine"—were taken as so many admissions that the "machine civilization" had completely invaded the political sphere. In the United States, the man in the street could not conceive of the political parties other than as "machines," noted historian Bernard Faÿ: any more "ideological" or social definition, European-style, met with blank incomprehension. A party's worth was not judged by its doctrines or even its leader's exceptional qualities, even if he was a "superman." The important thing was that "each of its cogs works harmoniously." It was "the mechanical connection that must be established and maintained between the different elements and workings of the party."[55] In fact, the mechanization of politics in America was so nonmetaphorical that it led, fittingly, to the voting machine, the "symbol" and "center," according to Bernard Faÿ, of any democratic organization.

A full-length portrait of the deity. "You have to have seen this imposing instrument in America at election time—bristling with levers, garnished with arrows and inscriptions, as majestic as a safe and as mysterious as Pandora's box, as alluring as a dentist's apparatus and as appetizing as a diving bell; gigantic, in any case, and noisy—to get an idea of the machine's prestige and place in American life." The industrial machine had been satisfied with devouring its servants, like Charlie Chaplin swallowed up by the cogwheels in *Modern Times*. The voting machine did one better: it forced itself on the voter as an incorruptible guarantee of rational choices and irreproachable tallies. Democracy was too important to be left to ordinary citizens: the voting machine was needed to supervise their human weakness. "It alone seems worthy of tending to the highest workings of human activity," Faÿ commented. "It alone seems to guarantee the exactitude, loyalty, and dignity appropriate to the sovereign citizen. Standing face to face with the machine, the voter gets a sense of his responsibility and royalty."[56] A safe, a dentist's chair, Pandora's box, a diving bell: the images Faÿ piles up are evocative enough to dispense us with commentary about the feelings this button-pushing democracy inspired in the French. America had substituted an *agora* community with the solitary and somewhat shady pleasure of these mechanical titillations—perhaps the political counterpart to the "visual masturbation" that, according to Duhamel, was inculcated in the American citizen overwhelmed by glowing, moving, talking machines.[57] And so the voting machine, a symbol of democracy's technological derision, took its place in anti-Americanism's semiological arsenal. At the height of the cold war, in the crypto-Communist journal *Défense de la paix,* an article on America's electoral mechanisms opened with the photograph of a voting machine, and the caption read: "A gigantic off-track betting machine."[58]

In the year 2000, the Florida machines would confirm the French conviction that American presidential elections were won or lost if not by scratching a card, at least as much by punched ones as by voter turnout. The United States had no monopoly on close elections, and George W. Bush's could also have reminded the French that the corollary of "one man, one vote" was that each man and each vote could swing the tide of an election. But such was not—to put it euphemistically—the dominant reaction of the French media and population. A first wave of incredulous hilarity—the uncontrollable laughter Bergson describes as overcoming us on seeing a musclehead miss a stair—was followed by a long phase of calmer jubilation at the unhoped-for but not unexpected imbroglio, since by putting hundreds of millions of citizens at the mercy of a handful of confetti more or less well detached from a perforated card, it had validated all those in France who, for over a century had held that in this "technocratic" democracy, it was never a far leap from machinism to machinations.

Police America, Totalitarian America

An edifice of imputations was thus built up around the mechanistic Moloch, transforming the French political perception of the United States. The suspicions of injustice generated particularly by the left during the great repressions of the nineteenth century, whose memory was revived by the violent social clashes of the early 1920s, were followed by a certainty that the United States, behind a democratic mask and whitewashed with constitutional principles, had turned into a totalitarian society.

A totalitarian destiny, which Bernanos would soon declare inherent to the "machine civilization," was the true outcome of the American way of life. The "American system" was a bloc. Machinism was not a simple material structure within it, but "a form of life." For Georges Duhamel, mechanization was invading (and corrupting) the pleasures and days: canned music, packaged images, automotive outings where people drove just to drive, automated amusement parks. "The machine has entered all the different forms of American activity," remarked historian Bernard Faÿ a few years later. "It is of course the driving force of industry, but also of commerce, education, opinion, and intellectual life."[59] Machinism did not only alter the gestures, reflexes, and biological rhythms of those who were exposed to it at work; it shaped the mentality of an entire population to suit its own ends. The word *standard*, discovered by the French in the 1920s, was quickly extended by them from objects to humans. Historians, sociologists, philosophers, and journalists all stressed the fact that in America, man was subjected to processes that were supposed to be subordinate to him. Siegfried and Duhamel moralized in unison: "To standardize the individual in order to standardize the things it is intended that he should buy is to lose sight of the fact that goods were made for man and not man for goods"; "The beings who today people the American ant-hills . . . want to own at the earliest possible moment all the articles . . . which are so wonderfully convenient, and of which, by an odd reversal of things, they immediately become the anxious slaves."[60] The same inversion of values was tirelessly denounced by the nonconformists: "Does man dominate the world? No, things lead man into slavery."[61]

Were these metaphors? Not in the least—or in any case, less and less. Not only was *homo americanus* a servant to the Machine; not only was he socially enslaved by the needs that had been inculcated in him; but he was also, bluntly speaking, a prisoner living in an extreme police state of a society.

From the brutal repression of syndicalism, which we have seen Jouvenel denounce, to Siegfried's description of tests as "police records," no aspect of American life seemed to escape the strictest control and, if need be, the most pitiless repression. We have seen how a social-democrat like Drujon made standardization out to be capitalism's ultimate stage. Standardization and democracy seemed contradictory and even incompatible to him; and since everything was incontestably standardized there, could America still be democratic? "America is a democracy. That is all fine. But slow down before you say it's fine. You need to know just how democratic Washington is. Look closely and you will easily discover that it is run by feudal states. But slow down before you conclude that it is not democratic at all. It is, *compared to other dictatorships.*"[62] The worst form of dictatorship except for all the others: that was how Roosevelt's America appeared to this well-intended socialist in 1938, in a Europe that was a patchwork of minor, great, and middling dictators. But why, in fact, should he hesitate to use the word *dictatorship,* which we even find coming from the pen of an André Philip, who was regularly attacked for supposed America-worship? A left-wing scapegoat in this sense, like Tardieu was for the right, André Philip still had a few surprises waiting for readers brave enough to tackle the 552 pages of his big 1927 book *Le Problème ouvrier aux États-Unis* (The Worker Problem in the United States), prefaced by the inevitable André Siegfried. The whole first chapter, which details the pressures, exactions, and murders committed by industry bosses or their henchmen, closes with this unambiguous paragraph: "Therefore we can say without exaggerating that, despite the pseudo-democratic nature of the American Constitution and the Statue of Liberty's presence in the port of New York, the United States currently represents the most perfect example of a *capitalist dictatorship.*" A note on the Statue of Liberty adds this sarcastic remark: "Indeed, the Americans have adopted the French habit of raising monuments to their illustrious dead."[63]

Whence the central importance Prohibition took in accounts about America. Of course banning alcoholic beverages, including munificent wine, was enough to raise doubts about the United States' mental health. Of course, the Volstead Act gratified the French, who could scratch at the Yankee surface to reveal the Puritan beneath. Of course, disregard for the law by the rich, the powerful, and the outlaws let the French dub America hypocritical. But if Prohibition took on such great importance to the anti-Americans, it was also and especially as proof of the "land of liberty's" mutation into an authoritarian and government-ruled land. The blue laws were mocked, at the turn of the twentieth century, for their "almost implausible hair-splitting";[64] the placid Lanson himself was irritated by the "vexing rules" that America was continually dreaming up.[65] But Prohibition was another story; it went "to the very center of the American soul"; it exposed, so to speak, the bottom of the barrel; and it confirmed the foreseen totalitarization of a country in which the "Government substitut[es] itself for God."[66] Duhamel was the one drawing these drastic conclusions; but it was Jules Romains, one of the most lenient toward America in the 1930s, who wrote: "The idea of America as 'the land of the free' was weighted down [during Prohibition] with too much derision. It is impossible for a civilization's dignity to withstand a derision so marked, which turns on principles themselves."[67]

How could you classify an America of trampled freedoms, murderous policemen, and manipulated behavior? What kind of government was there in a land of voting machines, packed speakeasies, and calculated cinematic kisses, since the Hayes Code had set the length of voluptuousness at seven feet of film and not an inch more? During the interwar years in France, the majority response to Hoover's America or, interchangeably, Roosevelt's, was the preceding descriptions' logical conclusion: America is not like us. It is like the USSR, it is like a fascist state.

The USSR first and perhaps foremost. The old nineteenth-century cliché about America and Russia being parallel might conceivably have been snuffed out by the sudden polarized distance between the two governments after 1917. But the exact opposite happened. It was a tic for Duhamel. The sinks (once again!) that travelers shared in the Pullmans were Soviet. Also Soviet were the New York clubs, which resembled a Muscovite House of Writers or House of Architects: "bourgeois communism," Duhamel explained to his American host, who naively thought he was carrying on a British tradition by spending the evening at his club. Up to and including Hollywood which, seen from France, seemed like a Gosplan bureau! A poem by Luc Durtain informed "all those who do not know/that a studio is what most closely resembles/a Soviet ministry."[68] Far from the realm of poetry, Robert Aron equated the two countries unequivocally: "USSR, USA . . . both over-tooled and over-nationalized."[69] So they were associated not only because of their mechanization, but much more significantly, for the French views of the time, because of their all-pervading governments. As for Céline (but who was the butt of his joke—the Americans or America-bashers?), he confirmed the analogy in a gloriously fecal scene in *Journey to the End of the Night*, where the "joyous communism of crap" is presented as an essential feature of American conviviality.[70] The nonconformists, too, harped on the U.S.-USSR equivalence without, in their case, the slightest hint of humor. In 1931 in *La Revue française*, Jean-Pierre Maxence defended the soul, man, and Europe against "Moscow's materialism and New York's racketeering."[71]

Daniel-Rops, then a young and agile ideological swashbuckler, was given the task in 1933 of proposing a synthetic view of the positions shared by the *Esprit, Réaction,* and *Ordre Nouveau* "youth movements." In this piece, he came back several times to the USA and USSR's deep-seated similarities: "Stalinism, far from true Marxism, . . . seems both as vain and as malevolent as American Fordism."[72] He would expand the duo into a trio a few months later in *Ordre Nouveau,* denouncing "the masses, whether they are fascist, American, or Soviet."[73] In 1935, Robert Aron denounced the "false prophets of today who purport to be guides to our era: Ford, Taylor, or Hitler."[74] Nazi Germany had replaced the USSR. But if communism and fascism could be transposed according to the author's ideological convictions, America remained the bolted-down pivot of these transitory constructions.

The literature of the 1930s was full of such "parallels." The general public was already convinced that American "egotism" would give nothing if there was a European crisis, and believed moreover that the United States was fundamentally no different than a totalitarian state; that it obeyed the same collective, if not collectivist, logic; that it was even more totally totalitarian than its "rivals" in Europe. (The non-Communist Left's desperate attempt to look to Roosevelt for some hope against Hitlerism on the eve of the world war came too late and was paid too little in return to modify this image.)[75] Nowadays we are astonished to see Robert Aron speak of Ford and Taylor in the same terms as Hitler. But the dominant feeling, and not only among the nonconformists, was that the "American system" was even more constraining and secured its control over men even more tightly than Stalinism and fascism combined. That is what Duhamel explains to Mr. Pitkin in the chapter "A Short Dialogue on the Sentiment of Liberty" in *Scenes from the Life of the Future.* The passage is worth citing at some length: "Political dictatorship is assuredly odious, and, of course, would appear intolerable to me; but, strange as it may seem to you, I admit that it does not hold any great place among my fears. . . . The Soviet and the Fascist dictator—to cite only those two—call forth, not only in their own country, but in the whole world, a too ardent protest for any philosopher to feel greatly discouraged on account of them." Chin up, then! Count on "the spirit of political rebellion" which "is not extinct in the heart of man," and good luck with your dictators. Still, Duhamel's confidence is not unlimited. What if men should falter in the face of "another kind of dictatorship, that of counterfeit civilization," the one that makes men "slaves of America" and their own slaves? "That is what makes [him] anxious."[76] Julien Benda, writing his famous screed *The Betrayal of the Intellectuals,* had failed to foresee that particular form of betrayal: French intellectuals blinding their readers' judgment, in a time of crisis, by declaring American democracy a worse kind of totalitarianism than Stalin's or Mussolini's or Hitler's.

From one observer to the next, from right to left, from "a democracy too formal to be real" to a "technocracy" too capitalist to be humanist, the "American system" was pushed into the last possible corner. It was a totality that had everything covered, so wasn't it a perfected form of *totalitarianism?* Wasn't this enormity of means used to "coerce man while leaving him the appearance and the illusion of his free will" the ultimate dictatorship? Robert Aron asked the question in his 1935 book *Dictature de la liberté*. His answer—all the more striking because it was aimed at Roosevelt's New Deal America—was that the individual was ineluctably crushed and freedom obliterated; in a word, that there was an invisible and therefore all the more real dictatorship: "All the powers of suggestion, such as the press, advertising—all the indirect pressures, such as distributing rewards and bonuses, or living comforts accorded to individuals roped into selected right-thinking and conformist philanthropic charities for mutual care—all that makes a visible dictatorship's use of open violence nearly superfluous."[77] His use of *nearly* reveals a whole rhetorical strategy that left-wing anti-Americanism would not forget.

The theme also had a real future. What could be more pernicious than an "invisible dictatorship"? And what could be more irrefutable than an accusation whose whole argument lay in the fact that nothing observable confirmed it? Once more, the nonconformist polemicists' strange casuistics became a textual model for generations of leftist or left-leaning Communist intellectuals. The logic of suspicion that took hold in the interwar years would long govern the collective French discourse on America: a sham democracy and insidious totalitarian state. The devil's last trick, as we know, is making people think he does not exist; the same was true for the American "dictatorship." But the French intellectuals were not taken in. Right when fascism was on the rise and Stalinism was being consolidated, it was America they denounced as the great totalitarian Satan. Among the rubble of cold war Europe, half subjected to the Soviet "liberators," it was still in the United States that they uncovered, beneath the patina of formal democracy, the texture of a "true fascism." It was clear, of course, for the Communists, who announced it ex officio. But many others without the same reasons or obligations concurred. Who would rail against young Americans' apathy in the face of "the birth of a fascism" in 1948 but Simone de Beauvoir?[78] Who would speak of a "capitalistic civilization predestined from its birth to become totalitarian" in 1947 but the Catholic writer Georges Bernanos?[79]

Identifying the United States with totalitarianism, or making it out to be the perfect totalitarian state, would not only have the immediate effect of a political and diplomatic blindness. In the longer term, it allowed the cold war–era French Communist party to hammer in the analogy between the United States and Nazi Germany, not always convincingly, but nevertheless plausibly. It also incited prewar nonconformism's spiritual heirs to repeat the barely modified refrain after the war. Echoing ever more fascistic left-wing accusations and in hardly less radical terms, Albert Béguin described America in 1951 as "a dictatorship without a dictator":[80] and in 1959, Jean-Marie Domenach, in keeping with earlier nonconformist imputations, explained that "the American government is liberal but its society is totalitarian: it is perhaps the most totalitarian society in the world."[81]

When, one by one, the European fascist states had been beaten (or died of natural causes); when the Communist regimes had fallen like a house of cards; when the historical totalitarian states had disappeared, then—that is, now—if there was only one left, it would be "Amerikkka."

Dictatorship and Abstraction

Even before the mid-twentieth century, the case against machinism as a system thus produced two major themes: that of "totalitarian" (then "fascist" or "fascistic") America and that of "abstract" America. Just as the mechanization of human life and the manipulation of human beings made the United States the paragon of totalitarianism (whose more expressionistic dictatorships were at root nothing but awkward rehearsals), the mechanization of people's minds, shaped into "schematism" by the domination of figures, calculations, and statistics, made mental America into the kingdom of abstraction. Close ties were thus established in the intellectuals' anti-American discourse between machinism, (formal) democracy, and abstraction.

Denouncing "abstraction" as a structuring form of American alienation became a rhetorical commonplace of both left-and right-wing anti-Americanism in the 1930s. This is both surprising and apparently contradictory. America had traditionally been described in France as the land of practical intelligence. On the other hand, it was said not to be very gifted in intellectual speculation and rarely interested in general ideas. Simone de Beauvoir, in 1948, was conscious of the paradox: "In this country that's so ardently oriented toward concrete signs of civilization, the word 'abstraction' is always on my lips." For it had to be said, abstraction was everywhere. White people's jazz was abstract. Young American literature was abstract. The paintings she discovered in art galleries were abstract. By which she did not mean "abstract painting," but effectively "emptied of their contents": "Cubism and surrealism have also been emptied of their contents, with only the abstract scheme preserved. These formulas, which were living languages in Europe . . . are encountered here, intact but embalmed." Like the Cloisters, bought for millions of dollars? Worse than cloisters bought for millions of dollars: because these works, cut-and-pasted from Europe, were "reproduced and reproduced mechanically, and no one realizes that they are not saying anything anymore."[82] Abstract expressionism according to Beauvoir: mechanics tacked on to uprootedness.

If the theme of America's abstraction was well received on the Left, it nonetheless had a clearly right-wing pedigree. As an abstract federation born of paper declarations, a human conglomerate without any organic unity, the United States had long been beset by traditionalist attacks. The climate of the 1930s rekindled this old hostility. Aron and Dandieu tirelessly pilloried the "prestige of the abstract"—unworthy of a "first-year polytechnic student"—the Yankee nation was so intoxicated with.[83] They waxed ironic about an America steeped in "degraded, Taylorized Cartesianism" and "dishonored Hegelianism."[84] Nonconformism once more led the way. And as for Simone de Beauvoir, she was saying much the same thing as the authors of *Le Cancer américain* in *America Day by Day*. America's equation, she explained, was the double negation of the subject and the spirit: "In Hegelian terms, one can say that the negation of the subject leads to the triumph of understanding over Spirit—that is, the triumph of abstraction."[85] Even better (or worse), for Beauvoir as for the spiritualist anti-Americanism of the prewar years, America idolized money because that "entirely abstract symbol" responded to its passion for abstractions: "Other values [than money] are too difficult to appreciate."[86] And the Americans were all the more easily satisfied with it because they "have no inner flame."

She was sliding down the same slope as Bernanos in "Why Freedom?" and "Revolution and Liberty." For Bernanos not only intended to denounce "Anglo-American machine civilization" loud and clear; he went so far as to proclaim its destiny to be inescapably "totalitarian." He set forth a genealogy of the usury-machine couple that gives the reader an uneasy feeling of déjà vu. There have always been profiteers, Bernanos reminds us, even before the Anglo-Americans, the proof being that they are already mentioned in the Gospel. "Perhaps these people always thought that they would one day become the masters of the world; but they used to be distrusted, suspected." And how right we were! "Remember what the Middle Ages thought of usury and the usurer." How nice it would have been if Bernanos, just two years after the end of the war, had also remembered the historically tragic impli-

cations of such relentless accusations against the "usurer" in Christian tradition. No, he continues with untroubled conscience: "Finally, expected or
not, their hour came. The invention of machines suddenly gave them, at one
fell swoop, the tool they had lacked." Bernanos adds that "machines certainly
have no personal responsibility in this." And, joking around, he adds that he
would not want to "send machines to Nuremberg; the cost of the trial would
be too high." Good thinking. But why not their lords and masters? Why not
the "Anglo-Americans" (no offense meant) and all those mysterious usurers
just waiting to get theirs since the Middle Ages? "In our old monarchy,
almost all the great Ministers of Finance, from Jacques Coeur to Fouquet,
came to a bad end." We catch a whiff of regret. To Nuremberg or Montfau-
con with the "ministers of finance" and the "Anglo-Americans"! This is what
Bernanos calls "help[ing] you revise a number of conventional ideas."[87]

In fact, the imputation of abstraction was made in several registers. On a
basic level, the "abstract" America forged by anti-American discourse countered those who vaunted America's "vitality." It was obviously a cliché to contrast the mechanical with the living.[88] Bergson's name appeared often, in this
context, in anti-American writings. His last work, *Two Sources of Morality and
Religion* (1932), directly attacks the problem of machinism in developed societies. The harmful effects of machinism, Bergson posits, "can all be corrected. . . . But then, humanity must set about simplifying its existence with
as much frenzy as it devoted to complicating it. The initiative can come from
humanity alone, for it is humanity and not the alleged force of circumstances, still less a fatality inherent to the machine, that has started the spirit
of invention along a certain track."[89] We can see where Roussy de Sales, the
following year, found the idea (which he politely dismisses) of "abolishing
the machines": an incredulous economist's discreet homage to the old
philosopher. As for Georges Friedmann, he would openly argue against the
"mysticism" this "philosophy of history" seemed to be tarnished with.[90] But
even before *Two Sources* appeared, a diffuse Bergsonism lent criticism of the
machine a philosophical authority—in Duhamel, for example, who cited
Bergson in one of his developments on the incommensurability of the inert
compared to the living.[91]

From this Bergsonian atmosphere, there was a shift (sometimes in the
very same pages) to a very differently inspired ambience, in which "vitalism"
was more the by-product of a kind of hazy neo-Darwinism. The point here,
as in Bernanos, was to denounce the modern error (or the American myth)
in which the proliferation of machines was presented as a sign of dynamism.
Nothing could be more false, Bernanos replied in 1947: "Twenty years ago,
the Yankees tried to make us believe that mechanization was the symptom of

an excessive burst of vitality! If this had been so, the crisis of the world would already have been resolved, instead of which it does not cease to spread, to grow worse, to take on a more and more abnormal character." No, Bernanos insisted: machinism had no "excessive vitality." And this was even more true of "mechanized man"; he was a "neuropath, passing in turn from excitement to depression, under the double threat of madness and impotence."[92] "Machinery," Bernanos added, was a way of avoiding, of getting around life; in this, machinism was not only an error, but "also a vice of man, comparable with that of heroin or morphine." The truth was that "modern man asks machines—without daring to say as much or perhaps even to admit it to himself—not to aid him in conquering life but to help him evade it, to dodge it, the way one dodges some obstacle that is too rough."[93] The machine—that ultimate drug in an Americanized world—was a "perverse form of evasion," far from reality, outside of life.

The theme of American abstraction thus evolved in strict connection with that of the mechanization of human life and the artificial nature of democracy. "Freedom is not there," Robert Aron wrote. "It is neither in mechanisms nor abstractions."[94] Freedom of thought was not there either, as the historian Bernard Faÿ suggested, stigmatizing the "solidly forged instruction" (the adjective is ambiguous) of the American universities, which privileged abstract formulations as opposed to living language: "Words give way to signs, language to figures, ideas to formulas."[95] Spiritualists and Marxists would all voice this complaint. The former reproached America for its "degraded rationalism," the latter, for its deliberate denial of concrete social realities. By its very generality, the imputation of abstraction mobilized an entire mindset against America—one that was vital, carnal, and organic, but also social and even onomastic. America rang hollow, Claudel said, dumbfounded that it should be so empty. As hollow as the word "citizen" applied to an American, Siegfried added; you only had to listen to hear it. Émile Boutmy, the founder of the Institut des Études Politiques, had already proposed a scientific experiment: "Listen to this resounding name: France. Then pronounce that of the United States. The first stirs deep reverberations, like an echoing voice coming out of an earthy den. The second gives a short, clipped sound, an outdoor sound, like two pieces of flint struck together a few steps away."[96] An excellent tactic for catching America's big secret unawares. Robert Aron proposed another, in his style: he took the United States to the letter and caught it red-handed in its inexistence. *USA*: what was that supposed to be? Not a real country, in any case. A real country was called, for example: "Italy"; and too bad if some unhappy people found it a little changed under Il Duce. "Between Italy, that cradle of the European spirit, and the colonial dependencies with initials for names, USSR or USA, there can never be, from a methodical and cultural point of view, true competition."[97] Then he starts praising Mussolini.

Edmund Burke was already indignant in 1790 that the Revolution had arbitrarily created and named little countries without the least human reality, which he predicted would rapidly vanish: he meant the French *départements*. "Countries with initials for names" is a nice invention, rejuvenating the old accusation of artificiality even as it suggests such countries' constitutive analogy with companies, trusts, or conglomerates—empires with initials. Robert Aron describes as a democratic trompe l'oeil an America in which the "forces of collective oppression are hidden . . . under the names of certain companies or industrial or banking groups."[98] Against this vast conspiracy, eternal vigilance was in order! Fouquet, Jacques Coeur, and their successors were hidden beneath these acronyms. The crafty insignificance of these initials and signs had to be thwarted. It should be explained that the USA was just a figurehead for material power. With the occupation, it would soon be shown that the dollar's abstraction was covering up a Judeo-Masonic conspiracy, as the anti-Jewish exhibition in Paris in 1941 attempted to do, decoding each graphic element of the green bill as a secret signal from the synagogues or the lodges. Under that almighty sign "the USA [had] allied its initials to the USSR's,"[99] as Pierre-Antoine Cousteau reminded his readers in *L'Amérique juive* in 1942.

The false banality of these icons had to be forced to speak the truth, and Duhamel, looking at the two sides of a nickel, was able to find the traces of the Indians' genocide and the extermination of the buffalo.[100] Somewhere between semiology and wild interpretation, a whole faction of suspicious anti-Americanism lay in wait, chalk in hand, for the planetary assassin, ready to mark its back with the infamous sign—not the "M" for murder but rather U\$: a\$\$a\$\$in.

The Third Man

Void, abstraction, simulacrum: the intellectuals' discourse on America represented little of America's reality, or rather it represented a stubborn effort to *unrealize* America. The forms were sometimes crude: opposing America to real countries, organic nations, and concrete dialectical entities. Other times they were more subtle: Robert Aron and Arnaud Dandieu delocalizing "Yankee country" (it was everywhere); Luc Durtain conflating signs and things ("Realty": selling reality, selling nothing); Baudrillard vaporizing America (it is nowhere). Emptying out America, starting in the 1920s, was a way of evoking different figures of Man as missing.[101]

The first man, the oldest man, was God's creature, and God's antagonism with the machine civilization found many exegetes in France. In his most influential book, *Freedom in the Modern World,* Maritain defined the modern era, as exemplified by the United States, as operating a "progressive retirement of man before the forces of matter." He denounced the American "heirs of rationalism" who "seek to impose on us today . . . an anti-ascetic system that is exclusively technological." He appealed for resistance: "If machinery and technical processes are not controlled and firmly subjugated to the well-being of the person, that is to say, fully and vigorously subordinated to his true ends and made the instruments of moral asceticism, mankind is irretrievably and literally lost."[102] Though Maritain later took pains to affirm America's "spiritual" nature, his prewar writings would long irrigate Catholic antimodernism and antimachinism, for which Georges Bernanos became the impetuous spokesman. The texts collected in *The Last Essays* (1953) are among the most violently anti-American of the postwar years; they open with a kind of invocation of man, the man "created in God's image" in whose name Bernanos sets out on his crusade: "But what if man really was created in the image of God? . . . What if man can only fulfill himself in God? What if the delicate operation of amputating his divine part—or at least of systematically making this part atrophy until it falls off, dried up, like an organ in which the blood no longer circulates—should turn him into a ferocious beast? Or worse, perhaps, a beast forever domesticated, a domestic animal? Or, even worse, something abnormal, deranged?"[103] It is an urgent matter: "the world of tomorrow will be either Cartesian or Hegelian,"[104] Bernanos warns, like Maritain and the nonconformists—that is, American. Unless. . .

The second man was not on very good terms with the first one. This was the autonomous, rational individual in a secularized world. (The one Claudel railed against in a letter to Agnès Meyer: "'Individual liberty'! There is no 'individual liberty.' There is only the liberty of God's children.")[105] America flattered itself in thinking it respected this individual and even encouraged his legitimate "pursuits." But watch out for counterfeits! This individualism was not the same thing as French individualism; it was even, as Tardieu explained, its opposite: "In the first place, individualism, on which both countries pride themselves, follows opposite laws in each. American individualism is much more social than French individualism. In the United States the individual seeks company. In France the individual seeks isolation."[106] The individual was under threat and had to be defended from "mass civilization." America, despite its own myths, was not the individual's paradise or individualism's promised land. On this point, there was a clear break between the French discourse that took hold in the 1930s and the "Anglo-Saxon" interpretation that, from Philarète Chasles up through the early twentieth century, had proposed a whole typology—using the squatter, the settler, the frontiersman—of individual American energy. Starting in the 1920s and for the rest of the twentieth century, anti-American discourse worked to eliminate this Yankee mythology and present American society as crushing any individuality. The stakes were high: the truth of imputations of "totalitarianism" hung in the balance; but it was also a means of undermining belief in the self-made man, open society, and readily attainable success. Two myths with one stone. . .

For André Siegfried, America's lack of true individualism was an ethnic and cultural reality tied, first of all, to the absence of French immigration. Pointing to the lack of "Gallic individualism" in the American melting pot, Siegfried concluded that there was an absolute contrast between France and America in this respect: "France, a civilization of individuals, is at the opposite pole from the gregarious nation that is contemporary America."[107] The Frenchman, according to Siegfried, was too "obstinate," too "antisocial," to accept a society that worked to "reduce the originality of the individual."[108] Duhamel said much the same thing. His anti-Americanism was essentially a protest against "the effacement of the individual—his abnegation and his annihilation."[109] Omnipresent in Siegfried and Duhamel, the defense of man-as-individual was not the object of a conservative monopoly. Because defending the individual also implied, in an extension of Baudelaire's protests, championing the rights of the artist, the writer, and the creator, which were in danger of being stifled; and here, intellectual solidarity overrode ideological borders. It was most likely, though not exclusively, the status of the intellectual Simone de Beauvoir was thinking of in 1948 when she wrote: "In America, the individual is nothing. He is made into an abstract object of worship."[110]

Not exclusively—because there was a third man whom, for better or for worse, those writing on America had in mind. The third man was the agent of a paradoxical association between Catholics and unbelievers, fascist and Communist sympathizers, nonconformists and *contestataires;* he was the essential character of the French intellectual dramaturgy of the twentieth century, where he came forth sometimes masked and other times bare-faced. This figure, important in and of itself and cardinal in the anti-American discourse, was that of the *revolutionary man.*

In the twentieth-century French intellectual discourse, the revolutionary man was not a marginal hero or an extreme character. He haunted all the anti-American texts like a benign ghost.[111] So, which infuriated leftist and spurned activist lamented that there was "no revolution in the American ant-heap," even as, in the corner of his soul, he clung to a remnant of hope, "for in the case of man, you never know"?[112] This dangerous troublemaker was Georges Duhamel—someone people never suspected had such passions. Which pro–Third World pyromaniacs, perhaps the theologians of freedom, reproached the United States with having as its "profound goal . . . an avoidance of the psychological revolutionary explosion"[113] that would save the world? The New Order's austere duo, Robert Aron and Arnaud Dandieu, in 1931. We could reel off the crossovers and crossed signals. The Man of the Revolution runs like a fox through the whole anti-American discourse: he is its obligatory protagonist.

Faced with the United States, the intellectuals' discourse was unanimously revolutionary. It had the magic effect, in the most antirepublican polemical writings of the 1930s, of rehabilitating (at least temporarily) an old, disdained thing: the French Revolution. As soon as the words "United States" were mentioned, few writers failed to pull out their "Declaration of the Rights of Man." Robert Aron, who had just proclaimed himself "methodically hostile" to the Revolution, got a new surge of affection for it simply by comparing the two declarations: "French thought was able to make a veritable human dogma out of what, across the Atlantic, was more like a volume on local procedure."[114] We have already seen Roussy de Sales call for a new "Declaration of the Rights of Man" to remedy the consequences of "technocracy." Bernanos himself, in the middle of a particularly violent diatribe against the "machine civilization," suddenly invokes "the last message the world has received from [France], the Declaration of Rights, which was a cry of faith in man, in the brotherhood of man"—but which "might also well have been a loud curse upon a civilization which was going to attempt to make men the slaves of things," Bernanos adds, for the benefit of an audience we imagine stricken; a "loud curse," then, against the civilization he has just called "Anglo-American."[115]

The 1789 declaration as an anathema against the country of the Declaration of Independence: Bernanos's audacity is food for thought. In the works of historians, and particularly American historians troubled by the virulence of French anti-Americanism, we often find the idea that this antagonism was born of a competitiveness between the two great democratic revolutions: the French directed their hostility at the only nation that could contest their democratic primogeniture and that could also boast of having given its institutions more stable and less bloody foundations. The hypothesis is appealing, but analysis of the anti-American discourse does not bear it out. The purported rivalry between the two revolutions did not cross Frenchmen's minds for a second; they never had any doubts about the French Revolution's exemplary superiority—not to mention its epic grandeur and poetic force. The American reference never fed into anything but republican "rivulets" in France— the "thin streams of fidelity" René Rémond describes[116]—precisely because the French Revolution seemed like the only *true* revolution. Frédéric Gaillardet's early self-criticism in the 1880s was anchored in this revelation, which later became the most unquestionable truth: the American nation had never been revolutionary. This is what France—and even the most bourgeois France—constantly reproached it with. French anti-Americanism of the twentieth century would never stop repeating and reformulating this grievance, whether in the name of a real revolutionary conviction or, much more often, in the name of a revolutionary phraseology completely detached from any concrete plan, which was perpetuated up to the third millennium as an integral part of the "French exception."

☆ ☆ ☆

"Europe sketched out its first answer to the fascination of Americanism."[117] This sentence from Jean-Marie Domenach is a curious summary of May 1968. Because if in the preceding months, protest against the war in Vietnam had played a mobilizing part in the student movement, the United States was not the first item on the protesters' or strikers' agenda (which did not even exist) during the "May events." Ten years later, Régis Debray made the exact opposite of Domenach's on-the-spot reaction. He interpreted May 1968 as a scenario of Americanization: "The French path to America passed through May '68."[118] From Domenach's insurrection of the French spirit against "Americanism," May 1968 became for Debray the little theater (or Grand Guignol) of France's submission to conformity: thanks to May 1968, the French could now "become wholly American." Far from having been a detox from Americanism, "the Events" had injected the U.S. morphine of desertion into the French. "One more push, my countrymen, and your last dreams will be gone: the People (workers, artisans, and students), the bloc or alliance of the classes (force of culture + forces of work), the collective reappropriation by the workers of their living and work conditions, protection of the national community, and solidarity with the oppressed of the world."[119] This interpretive gap illustrates to the point of caricature the contradictory investments "America" was subject to. Admiration for May 1968 led to a celebration of the spirit's triumph over the "materialism" and consumerism characteristic of the American way of life. Contempt for May 1968 saw it as the liquidation, both spectacular and underhanded, of a French-style revolutionary sensibility in favor of rampant Americanization. Régis Debray and

Jean-Marie Domenach agreed neither about May 1968 nor, probably, about what constituted "Americanness"—their only common point was making America the negative pole of their diverging analyses.

The post-May discourse dealt in enough contradictory elements to make drawing unequivocal lessons from it a hazardous undertaking. The first step to take should be distinguishing the attraction the United States was starting to hold for part of France's youth culture through its music, films, and sexuality, from the historical and ideological references that formed the core of the 1968 militants' political culture. While they were undoubtedly indebted to the most recent developments of American popular culture, their politics had little to do with America and reveled in "archaism": antimachinism and hatred of technology; the critique of alienation as an inauthentic desire for "things"; the cult of the "speech act"; and, of course, incantatory references to the Revolution. In that regard, Domenach was not wrong in describing May 1968 as a revival of the nonconformist brand of anti-Americanism—an awakening and a protest of the spirit against the material world—just as a bewildered and uneasy Left was not wrong in recognizing revolutionary accents that had been raised, like the barricades themselves, from its own distant past. "Life's insurrection" for some, an upsetting return to nineteenth-century-style revolutions for others, May 1968 indubitably—for a generation, at least—gave a new momentum to the discourses in defense of Man that had all helped build up anti-Americanism since the 1930s. As for importing elements from the American counterculture, the trend was incontestable: still, we should emphasize the "counter" in counterculture and also note that it hardly modified a political script rooted in the best traditions of French leftist internationalism, with constant references to the Spanish Civil War, the Resistance, the Stalinist workerism and activism of the 1950s, and the fight against colonial wars. *Pace* Debray, violently celebrating the Paris Commune, as was done on a large scale in 1971, was not exactly an idea born and bred in Hollywood, or even in Woodstock. . .

The "ideas of May" associated with a passionate opposition to imperialism rekindled the possibility of a globally negative discourse on the United States. Even antiproductivism, which seemed to short-term observers like a decisive paradigm shift, reactivated a strong, long-standing tradition. The machine was the inversion of life: this theme, common to Duhamel-style humanists as well as personalists and spiritualists, reappeared in 1968. It became the substratum of the utopian and libertarian antimodernism characteristic of the "May Movement." Leftism's fusional (and sometimes confusional) energy thus helped converge critiques that had up to then been running parallel: the anticollectivists' principle-based antimachinism and the

Marxist tradition's "selective" antimachinism, which reserved its hostility for machines working within a "capitalist regime." A rocket with a slow-burning fuse that had been lit in the 1930s finally blasted off.

At the heart of this discourse was the Revolution. Between incantation and incarnation, the script written nearly half a century earlier by surrealism was played out on a wide scale. Of all the intellectual and moral "climates" added to the mix in the May 1968 atmosphere, this one was the most clearly present, though often unbeknownst to the protagonists themselves or traveling incognito under the situationist cloak. If any discourse had mutually sustained and justified fetishism for the Revolution and hatred toward America, it was of course the surrealist movement. Surrealism was a decisive intellectual and artistic lightning rod for attracting a clear-cut—or thundering—anti-Americanism, which used a Revolutionary language that was all the more irrefutable because it was fairly careless about real facts and situations. And its influence was all the more powerful and lasting because never once did the extraordinary brutality of its vocabulary, the vehemence of its calls to murder, its general rhetoric of fire and brimstone, of execution and eradication arouse the slightest reservation, doubt, or suspicion in France. "One cannot help thinking," Jean Clair recently observed, "that, unlike other avant-gardes, the surrealists still enjoy a strange leniency."[120] Yet "the surrealist manifestos are not so different, if you take the time to read them with detachment, from the extremist statements pronounced by the rabble-rousers of the day, on both the Left and the Right." Was Jean Clair, in turn, pushing his incriminations too far? In any case, we can only agree with his remarks on surrealism's paradoxical attachment to the past—which May 1968 inherited. Indeed, "the modern world is not its concern," and it is astonishingly indifferent to "the machine, speed, and energy" adored by the futurists and constructivists. In the face of modernity, surrealism was a touchy, stubborn oppositional front. It is therefore not surprising that the surrealists ended up shoulder to shoulder with the hated "humanists" as soon as it was time to attack America. "Destroy," they said. "May America afar crumble with its white buildings amid absurd prohibitions," Aragon proclaimed in 1925.[121] And it would be an offense to the surrealists—for whom metaphors had a logical force, and images, the weight of actions—to invoke "poetic" harmlessness. As Jean Clair also reminds us, the map of the world published in *Variétés* in 1929, where the size of each country corresponded to the importance the surrealists gave it, left North America with Canada and Mexico, border to border: the United States had been eradicated. And it was not Breton's dismal stay, starting in 1939, in the country crossed off the surrealist map ten years earlier, that would improve things.

On April 30, 1949, back at home, Breton was to speak at a political rally held by David Rousset's RDR. This "International Day of Resistance to Dictatorship and War" was an attempted retort to the Stalinist takeover of the pacifist movements. Even more directly, it was a retort to the April 23, 24, and 25 Communist-led Congress of the World Partisans of Peace, from which all divergents had been excluded. The RDR's rally was distinctly less well oiled. In the audience, Trotskyists and libertarians rubbed elbows with critical Marxists and stand-alone pacifists. A speech by an American scientist (imposed on the congress by its secret sponsors: American unions and the CIA) in favor of nuclear dissuasion led to a riot that broke things up before Breton could take the stage.

We have his surprising text, however. In it, Breton starts out by taking his distance from Stalinism. Then suddenly, halfway through, he changes tack, veers westward, and launches into a diatribe against the United States that is far more heated than his "unambiguous" condemnation of the USSR: "Everyone who knows me is aware that I have the most serious grievances against the USA, less personal than extrapersonal, to the point where in five years over there, I did not strike up a single friendship." (A curious proof of America's worthlessness.) Then comes a classic piece of rhetoric: "I hate as much as anyone, and as much as they themselves must, the way the USA treats my friends the blacks, and even more, if such a thing is possible, the way they treated my friends the Indians. I abhor the USA's prevailing sexual hypocrisy, and the shameful laxity it leads to." We will regretfully skip over a passage on American funeral proceedings. "Nothing is more contrary to my way of thinking than America's bargain-basement pragmatism; nothing nauseates me intellectually like their great invention, the *Digest;* nothing revolts me as much as their superiority complex." And it was then the custom in France to jump directly from *Reader's Digest* to imperialism. Breton had no intention of missing out on that one: "I abominate their takeover of Central America, of South America. Considering their actual circumstances, and forced to admit that they are extending their imperialist plans to the Old Continent, I frenetically deny that the stupidity of Coca-Cola, its executives and bankers, could get the better of Europe."[122]

So, it really was worth it to call an anti-Stalinist counter-meeting to rival Jacques Duclos, who had spoken of "the insolent dictatorship the Americans want to see weighing on our country, a dictatorship of illiterate, contemptuous potentates suffused with the dollar's superiority."[123] *Phobia:* it is Breton himself who uttered the word. "I feel some phobia about a language that is like a flaccid version of the English language, and in which the word *angoisse,* for example, can no longer be translated." We know Breton did not speak much English, but not to the point of being unaware that there are in fact at least two words that can be used to translate *angoisse:* "anguish" and "anxiety." So that is not what he was talking about, but rather of a less semantic deficiency or, if you prefer, a more ineffable one, the one Albert Béguin evoked in citing Bernanos: "What American today would accept these words from Bernanos: 'Man's misfortune is the marvel of the universe'?"[124] It was really worth the trouble to badmouth religion and faith—the "place called La Grenouillère"[125]—only to sail on to the brave new world in spiritualism's anti-American flotilla. . . Hating America was clearly, among the French, a miracle of love, if it could make the pope of surrealism speak the same way as the intellectual chaplains of Catholicism.

But how many, like Breton, would not have hated the United States so much if not for love for the Revolution—or rather, its endlessly conjured ghost?

14

Insurrection of the Mind, Struggle for Culture, Defense of the Intelligentsia

We have just seen how the revolutionary postulate, presented as inherent to authentic humanity, gave apparently incompatible anti-Americanisms real ties throughout the twentieth century. Now we have to show how cultural hostility, a permanent and most often dominant part of the anti-American discourse, drew its singular force in France not only from the specific weight the intellectuals hold there—which is clear—but also and more subtly from the confluence of two great traditions, spiritualist and secular, usually disinclined to joining ranks, but exceptionally allied against a philistine *and* pharisaical America. By calling them *allied,* we do not mean concrete alliances—like the symbolically important ones that took place between the Communists and left-wing Christians during the cold war—so much as an *alloy* of two discourses. In this sense, as well, America proved a good melting pot—at its own expense: in the second half of the twentieth century, spiritualist attitudes and cultural protests emanating from what were traditionally hostile camps were gradually melted together. As French society was increasingly secularized, discrediting America's "material" civilization in the name of spiritual and religious values found its echo—its continuation, its carryover, or even its "legacy"—in attacks on the United States coming from completely secular cultural values, which were nonetheless covertly invested with a secularized transcendence. At the crossroads of these two positions was the word *spirit*, whose multiple meanings facilitated the passing of the baton from spiritual revolt to cultural resistance.

Spiritualist criticism of America took on its full force in the 1920s and 1930s. Its objective was to mobilize men's spirits in the name of the Spirit itself. With or without the capital "S," the word lent itself to a wide latitude of interpretation. It was also useful for convergences. Its religious resonance allowed it to unite the wide front of Catholic resistance to Americanization stretching from Claudel to Bernanos and from Maurras to Mounier. But the "primacy of the spiritual" affirmed by Jacques Maritain in an influential book from 1927 was not only a requirement dictated by faith. It was also the motto of many nonreligious "nonconformists." Beyond the circle of believers, in the hazy regions where personalism cast off its Catholic moorings, the spiritual was set up as a combat value to be used against (materialist or rationalist) reductionism, without necessarily presupposing religious transcendence or implying clerical obedience. The defense of the spirit thus presented itself as essentially a call to order for real values that had been forgotten or degraded by America. "What dominates is spiritual and moral factors," Robert Aron postulated in 1935.[1] A few years earlier, *Le Cancer américain* had offered a trenchant definition of America as an "aberration of the spiritual."[2] Of the many incisive expressions forged during the interwar years, this one is particularly revealing. Probably not about America—and Maritain, often invoked in the debate, would feel the tardy need (1958) to withdraw his support, defining the American people as "the least materialist among the modern peoples which have attained the industrial stage."[3] But it is revealing of an anti-Americanism aimed at making America out to be a monster in the eyes of the Spirit.

The transition between a prewar spiritualist rhetoric with cultural corollaries and a postwar cultural rhetoric with spiritualist reminiscences went smoothly. After 1945, eminent "defenders of the spirit" would commune in anti-Americanism with the most strident backers of historical and dialectical materialism. The latter especially were able to shoulder the legacy of a "defense of values" handed down by their ideological adversaries and take over a good part of the symbolic capital stockpiled before the war by spiritualism's flock. Faced with an America accused of "conspiring against intelligence" and wallowing in consumerist madness, they would set an efficient operating line between an apology of intellectual work (devalorized or degraded by American capitalism) and a critique of the vulgar materialism known as the American way of life. Now Stalinist Communists and continuing proponents of Catholic personalism were sailing side by side, united in a virulent anti-Americanism that was pacifistic on the surface, steeped in culture, and fueled by ethical pretensions.

Religious Free-for-All and Spiritual Bankruptcy

Opposition to America in the name of the spiritual was rooted in a confessional tradition it did not always acknowledge, but to which it owed a good part of its inspiration. "The country where the cross is only the plus sign":[4] Paul Morand, on the last page of *World Champions*, threw out this symbol like a murderous flower on the tomb of the young Yankee characters he has just sent, one after another, to their deaths. Behind the crusade that positioned nearly all of his generation against materialist America, it is impossible not to recognize French Catholicism's long-standing repugnance toward Protestantism in general and particularly its American forms. In France, two stereotypes of America's religious or irreligious nature coexisted. Though contradictory, they had both been in place for over a century. The first made America out to be a country steeped in religion, despite its founding fathers' declarations of principle and a secularism legally inscribed in the Constitution: religion "is everywhere in the American republic," scoffed Urbain Gohier at the turn of the twentieth century.[5] The second stereotype, on the other hand, portrayed America as a country that had lost any notion of religion: "belief" was reduced, at best, to some vague social morals; at worst, to a hypocritical pose, a generalized pharisaicalness covering opulent rackets. There was a division of the accusatory labor: clericals were indignant over unsavory American religion, while anticlericals denounced the myth of a republic that purported to be secular but where everything was done with one hand on the Bible or with the Bible in hand. The United States was too religious for nonbelievers and too unbelieving for the religious-minded.

Both sides therefore agreed that America's *false religion* should be stigmatized—either as false, or as a religion. Better yet, the antipathy it inspired drew the two viewpoints closer. Zealous anticlericals put a clamp on their dominant passion. Wandering under the American heavens, they acknowledged a certain charm and virtue in the Catholic heaven. Already, as we have seen, the 1848-ist Gaillardet had turned tail: in his view, there was nothing like spending time with American Protestants for understanding that "there is more blue" in Catholicism.[6] The journey to New York or Chicago practically turned into the road to Damascus. Urbain Gohier, a robust anticlerical, was tempted to convert. "That Sunday, I had the urge to become a Catholic," he admits after a sermon blathered by a "married boy" that left him revolted.[7] Hardened unbelievers and fervent Catholics communed in disgust—a disgust Paul Claudel, during his term as the French ambassador in Washington, confided to his diary in hardly diplomatic terms. A victim of the duties of his post, he attended the Episcopal mass spoken at the National Cathedral in Washington after Franklin Delano Roosevelt was sworn in. "Forced once more, to my profound disgust, to take part in Episcopal foolishness for the inauguration of the new president. Nauseating humbug and hypocrisy . . . ; to explain the emptiness, dryness, pride, and intellectual paucity of the Protestant character and spirit, one must take part in one of these services, which open a window onto the spiritual life of all these poor souls."[8] Too bad this conversion expert did not cross paths with Urbain Gohier the first time he was in America.

The contradictory stereotypes produced in France on the religious state of the Union can in fact be summed up by a single proposition: the Americans are the falsely religious citizens of a falsely secular nation. In the logic of hostile discourses, the two propositions do not cancel each other out; they trace concurrent argumentative lines with combinatory effects. The cumulative effect can be observed as of the late eighteenth century and throughout the nineteenth century. Faced with the Abbé Raynal, who, in the *Histoire des deux Indes,* put New England's Puritanism on trial, from its "revolting intolerance" and its "dizzying nature" to its "bloody forms,"[9] Joseph de Maistre would launch a more complementary than converse case against a completely wayward country that was drifting ever further into Protestant error. Whether a son of the Enlightenment or a child of the church, no one in France seemed to recognize himself in this splintered religious system, with its incomprehensible austerity and unfathomable dogmatic framework. Confirming Talleyrand's quip about the United States—"Thirty-two religions and only one dish to eat"—Fanny Trollope's sarcastic tales of hysterical revivals did not improve the image of religious America in the eyes of the French public. Things had hardly changed by the end of the nineteenth century, when the leitmotifs of imposture and "the soul trade"[10] prevailed. America offered Émile Barbier the spectacle of a "religious free-for-all," a "carnavalesque variety of churches and chapels, in which the most unutterable elite of frauds and hotheads throngs. Laughable priests with mysterious pasts; crooks trading in illicit divinities; puppet reverends spouting pitches and sales talk to attract loiterers into their holy shacks."[11] Ten years later, Gohier said much the same thing: "Business is the American religion, and American religion is a business."[12] But French hostility was not reserved for sects—the disturbing Mormons were enjoying an important literary vogue at the time—or for the strange preachers peppering the back country; it was also poured out over the most well-established and upscale churches. Another belle époque traveler, Edmond Johanet, jeered at the "millionaires' churches" on Fifth Avenue—not in the name of socialism or dyed-in-the-wool radical socialism, but in the name of Catholicism, which was "superior to Protestantism," even, he specified without going into details, "in the conduct of worldly affairs."[13]

While in France the tension between clericals and anticlericals was at its peak, there was a new unanimity of attitude toward the spectacle of the innumerable American religions with their dubious underpinnings. The convergence was not compromised by the French polemic on the separation of church and state or by the debate on Americanism that shook up Catholic circles for several years: aside from the fact that this liberal-leaning and conservative quarrel within the church was only anecdotally American, it remained too limited to small Catholic circles to make an impact on French representations of America.[14]

The only original note at the turn of the twentieth century was the hypothesis Émile Boutmy formulated in his *Éléments d'une psychologie politique du peuple américain*. We have already evoked the sinuous relations Boutmy had with Tocqueville's work. His presentation of the American religious situation is inseparable from the partial, ambiguous rehabilitation he proposed of the author of *Democracy*. Tocqueville's praise for New England Puritanism as a school for freedom did not escape Boutmy, as it had his contemporaries. But it was with great embarrassment that he alluded to the theory, whose importance he was aware of, only to end up circumventing it. Yes, the Yankee was defined by his religious faith. Yes, this faith was a "refugee Christianity." Yes, "religion and the church made the Yankee what he is" and in turn he "made America what it is." Yes, "America has remained unanimously Christian." But in the end, this Christianity was nothing but pulpless dregs, residue "without generosity or bouquet."[15] So far, nothing original there. Boutmy accepted Puritanism's historical importance without seeing it as a vital source for the present. But how could you explain the fact that religious belief, even if watered down, was still so powerfully unanimous among the Americans? Boutmy felt the need to come back to the religion question in the last chapter of his book, where he proposed an explanation: America's indubitable religious belief was a consequence of its hostility to the life of the mind. In America, "no credit is given, as in Europe, to the superior mind that creates original ideas and tries to make them prevail; prevention is against him." Boutmy invented a name for the phenomenon: "the *misonovism or rather phobonovism* (fear of the unknown) of these half-enlightened men." An apparently paradoxical theme: wasn't America—to excess, to dizzying extremes—the land of permanent (and exhausting) innovation? The theme was nonetheless well received among the French anti-Americans of the twentieth century. Among its numerous reappearances, Simone de Beauvoir's is not the least surprising. She outdid Émile Boutmy a half century on: the Americans, she explained in *America Day by Day*, did not "allow themselves to invent anything new"; their existential conformism was total, and "one always has the impression that thousands of invisible bonds paralyze them."[16] The same neophobia could be found in their intellectual life: the Americans were most of all concerned with not being disturbed by new ideas. They had found an infallible method for this, which was to avoid all contact with reading; and here, Beauvoir cited a testimony by Elsa Maxwell, "a famous journalist who writes well-informed columns for the reactionary press," who told her, "In America . . . no one needs to read because no one thinks."[17]

Émile Boutmy was careful not to go that far. He did, however, open a precious line of interpretation for future anti-American arguments, since it established a direct link, in America, between the empty form of religion as a ubiquitous presence and mistrust of the creative spirit. The Americans had become, if not pious, then at least Christian in order to hide their fear of the mind. This killed two birds with one stone, discrediting their religious sentiment while reaffirming, in the tradition of Stendhal and Baudelaire, the Americans' distaste for thought and its audacity. Boutmy concluded with a terrible (or comical) quip: for them, "only Christianity was available."[18] So Boutmy's Americans were assuredly very Christian—even more than Tocqueville's—but it was by default. And even doubly so: both to assuage their intellectual deficiency and because they had not come up with a better solution.

The religious phenomenon in the United States used up a lot of ink in France. This was, however, the first time it had been presented both as a social stopgap and an intellectual cover-up. It was not surprising, then, that this ersatz religion amid an absent intellectual life lacked "bouquet." Spiritual defectiveness *and* an intellectual deficit were henceforth linked in French representations of American "civilization." It was a discreet link but an important one, and as of the turn of the century, it established convenient bridges between Catholic-derived spiritualist criticism and secular criticism pronounced in the name of culture and intelligence. We will see all the use late-twentieth-century anti-Americanism was able to make of this alliance.

From Philanthropy to "Service"

Though colorless and odorless, American-style Christianity, considered a substitute for intellectualism, was nonetheless, in the eyes of French observers, a real and active force. Its force was not very spiritual, though; it was completely *social*. American Protestantism, André Siegfried stressed in 1935, had decidedly veered toward *"social action,"* resulting in "a religion practically deprived of any religious nature and whose congregations look like political conventions."[19] So there was nothing heady or intoxicating about it. But its blandness was authoritarian, and this irreligious religion was just as constricting, socially speaking, as Catholicism. Much *more* constricting, in fact, many Catholics replied, including Claudel: having erased the line between the sacred and the social, Protestantism insidiously infiltrated daily behavior and civil axioms; Catholic "spiritual advisors" were nothing compared to this permanent manipulation. Here, as well, Catholic theories, revived by Péguy, would be in sync with those of a secularized Left traditionally worried about the religious manipulation of social life.

The historical juncture was particularly favorable for drawing French positions together, with the United States serving as a foil. The battle for separation of church and state had been won. Catholic intellectuals had made their *aggiornamento* about it: many even saw it as a chance for a new spiritual thrust. Right when militant Catholicism was being revitalized and a combative spiritualism being spread, the old polemic against the Reformation was adapted to modern times. But instead of inadequate and outdated theological anathema, these intellectuals preferred a polemic centered on the "quality" of faith. The Americans' faith seemed singularly grim to them, lacking both impetus and mystery: it was both prosaic and literal. No point in getting caught up in dogmatic niggling; the spectacle of their tepid virtues was sufficiently edifying. America believed it had faith but had never felt its tremor. It was too suffused with its own certainties and successes to need hope. As for charity, long threatened by philanthropy, it was nothing but a museum piece now that it had been supplanted by "service"—the new civil religion around which French mistrust crystallized.

Thus went the French spiritualists' reasoning, and many important thinkers fell in step with them. The intellectuals of the interwar years no longer had the same worried admiration for Anglo-Saxon Protestantism as their elders of the preceding generation. In their evaluations, they increasingly dissociated the American case from the English model. Even to agnostics and anticlericals, American religious belief seemed rudimentary on an intellectual level. Judged by its deeds (intellectual and artistic), American Protestantism came off as literally uncultivated, enough to make you lament the treasures of knowledge and beauty accumulated throughout the centuries by a European Christianity to which Latin Catholicism was the self-proclaimed heir. A pro-intelligence front took shape in France, uniting believers and nonbelievers, set on opposing a religious stance reputedly lacking in fervor as well as creative drive. Even as it adhered to this assertion of America's intellectual deficiency, a Catholic generation raised on Barrès, Péguy, or even Léon Bloy heightened it by denouncing American religion as dry, "bourgeois," and calculated. Unable to rise to the intellectual heights of age-old Catholicism, American Protestantism was even more unqualified to gather up the spirit of simple people's hearts—the "simple people" in whom, Claudel repeated, "true spirituality was conserved"[20] in Europe. But such judgments, far from being made solely by militant Catholics in France, were part of a very wide consensus that transcended ideological divisions—and disciplinary divisions, as well. A historian like Bernard Faÿ could thus write in 1935: "Everyone powerfully felt the emptiness and coldness of this religion."[21] Who was speaking for *everyone* here: the specialist on the United States or the French intellectual carried away by the flood tide of anti-American *doxa*?

In the 1920s and 1930s, these traditional reasons for disdain took a turn, and with it, an entirely new tone, in response to the surge of social forms in the United States that seemed to directly subsume religion to economic objectives. Religion in America seemed compromised by utterly worldly enterprises: profit seeking, social control, maintaining inequality. Compromised and even prostituted. As Donald Roy Allen writes, to French observers of the 1930s, "American Protestantism had prostituted its dogmatic, mystical, and intellectual elements for the comfortable 'social' dogma it now professed."[22] A new polemic theme perfectly reflected this state of mind: biting criticism of service universally pervaded French writings. The "Calvinist beehive"[23] described by Philarète Chasles in the nineteenth century seemed to have secreted the ideology behind the practice of service.

The exasperation this notion aroused in French observers is hard to understand if we do not place it in the more general context of a hostility for the idea that the social and the religious could intertwine. The word, which the French wrote with a capital letter or put in quotes to indicate its exoticism, designated the civic and religious morals by which the individual put himself "in the service" of the community. Put himself or pretended to. Because, in the unanimous view of the French, if the captains and barons of industry cloaked themselves in the syrupy rhetoric of service, it was both to sanctify their profits by presenting them as the reward for eminent services to the community, and to lock their workers into an ideology that obligated them to work without complaint, conscientiously and devotedly. The French interpretation of the situation thus widely expanded the notion by making service out to be the new American ethic, a mix of manipulation and mystique, of well-intended coercion and ideological tyranny.

Service repelled the French as an adulterated mix of piety and utilitarianism, and it revived the least forgotten of Tocqueville's lessons—the one that depicted the majority's conformism as "enclos[ing] thought within a formidable fence."[24] Here once again, Morand proved to be a brilliant interpreter of France's disgust. But as a skillful crafter of novels, he delegated its formulation to the character of a young American at odds with his own country: "Utility! Service! That's the only word they can say! It's Kundry's answer to Parsifal, the loyal cry of the old humbug who refuses to leave his master! I loathe these words in capitals! And heaven knows this country goes in for them!"[25] It is a burlesque speech for a very serious antipathy. In 1927, right from the beginning of the wave of anti-American writings, Lucien Romier's *Qui sera le maître, Europe ou Amérique?* showed how important service was in the new social state that was the America of the Roaring Twenties: "the American masses receive an education inspired by the two powerful notions of 'service' and 'gain'"—and it was precisely this monstrous but effective pairing that secured the United States' superiority over the Latin nations.[26]

André Siegfried, that same year, devoted four pages of lasting influence to the "doctrine of 'service.'" Indeed, *America Comes of Age* singles out service as the ultimate social mythology of a "prosperous and self-satisfied America" that "likes to tell you . . . that 'service' is an essential condition of profits, and that the great manufacturing and distributing companies are not there only to make a fortune, but mainly to serve the community." Service, as Siegfried describes it, is a delusion or, in the best possible case, a self-delusion ("for the American deceives himself very easily"), a rhetorical artifact of America's good conscience and optimism, a slogan for chamber of commerce spokesmen, "the indispensable password of those who wish to justify their profits." Service was all that, but it was also much more than that. For behind this "hackneyed refrain" (the expression is Siegfried's) of the Roaring Twenties, was a whole new socioeconomic structure, which had shaped representations with fearsome effectiveness. If André Siegfried dwelled on service in his chapter on industrial production, it was because he clearly did not consider it a simple semantic gadget, but rather saw in it a new "doctrine," the cornerstone of a "reform in industrial methods" presided over by the government and more specifically Hoover, in his role as secretary of commerce.[27] The "doctrine of 'service'" seemed in this larger context like "a practical substitute for social morals": the secular-religious ideology that was best suited to the new phase of America's economic development. And it proved to be all the more successful because it was rooted in a cultural base of WASP identity. It was made up of the "civic virtue of the Protestant, the materialism of Bentham, and devotion to progress." Indeed, service was "not a Catholic conception . . . it [did] not flourish in Latin Europe." Siegfried's reason for this is interesting, since it goes back once more to the idea of America's nonintellectuality: "It is not attractive to the intellectual or the artist, who are accustomed to work individually, but it is very pleasing to the merchant, with his sense of credit." In just a few pages, Siegfried makes service out to be a central ideological cogwheel in the new America: the logical outcome of a long social and religious evolution, but also an accurate reflection of the American population in the twentieth century. It was the "doctrine of an optimistic Pharisee trying to reconcile success with justice." A population that wanted to be world champions, as Morand would say, without losing its soul. Behind the verbal tic his young Brodsky poked fun at—"Utility! Service!"—was a master plan for control and domination. "We might be tempted to smile," Siegfried warned, but we should resist temptation! Service should worry us. This new "doctrine"—a word that crops up with insistence in Siegfried's book, unavoidably echoing Monroe's—was an effective weapon in the economic war, since it fused together the government, industry leaders, workers, and consumers, along with "public opinion itself, in impressive harmony,"[28] something France, in contrast, seemed totally incapable of.

The remark was not aimed at reconciling the French with service or with American Protestantism, which—not to offend Edmond Johanet—seemed more comfortable than ever "conducting worldly matters." As degenerated religion's last avatar, service struck them as a degrading secularization of faith, or social manipulation made up to look like civic morals. Like Brodsky in World Champions, the French kept their "nostrils sniffing the horrible odor that rises, they say, from a good conscience."[29] It was this odor they sniffed out in service, the last avatar of a great philanthropic myth.

American philanthropy had never gotten good press in France. It was most often portrayed as a right-thinking charade, a crude ploy on the part of the "haves." Starting in the late nineteenth century, French travelers regularly grew indignant over the ostentatious "foundations" created by billionaires, which they contrasted with the shameful absence of public services in America. Rockefeller, Jules Huret had already explained in 1904, "is the absolute master of gasoline"; and "if one morning he wakes up with the urge to give the gift of a few million to his friend Harper, the president of the University of Chicago, he only has to raise today's rate by one cent, with a stroke of the pen."[30] Now there was a well-organized charity: it only cost *others* anything. And then, alongside such generosity, a city like Boston had "lamentable roads";[31] in Brooksville, Florida, "road maintenance" was in the hands of vultures;[32] as for New York, "town councilors . . . annually pocket eight to nine hundred million dollars and then cynically and almost completely neglect road maintenance."[33] Descriptions remained the same between the two wars: prosperity had changed nothing. Once you left Fifth Avenue, "fifty yards away, you come across actual hovels, half-gutted sidewalks, badly paved streets."[34] Frenchmen's extreme sensitivity to the undeniable potholes pockmarking New York's asphalt made for a deep, unanimous rebuke to a system that, because it privileged private initiatives, neglected the most elementary duties of any civilized collective. Philanthropy versus good government, service versus public services: the quarrel had nothing anecdotal about it. On the contrary, it reflected a strong, lasting cultural and political opposition between France and the United States.

All the component parts of this quarrel can be found in the feverish pages of *Le Cancer américain*. Aron and Dandieu's demonstrative style— deliberately "anti-Cartesian," very uncensored, often on the verge of free association—makes their tract an excellent conduit for mythologies. In it, we find the nineteenth-century mistrust of philanthropy intact, and Robert Aron and Arnaud Dandieu do not hesitate (a little disdainfully) to mobilize Tocqueville against it: "In good old Tocqueville's expression, the Yankees were *philanthropically* eliminating the redskins."[35] But it was the present that interested Aron and Dandieu: a present in which philanthropy was not only the hypocritical fig leaf over a pitiless realpolitik, but one of the economic motors of the country and the master weapon of its symbolic arsenal. Thus, according to Aron and Dandieu, the American philanthropy of the twentieth century was no longer just a legitimizing discourse among others. It had become a pillar of the capitalist economy: in "eighth place among the nation's industries."[36] And above all, it was the new cornerstone of the American psychic edifice: "Insurance and philanthropy: ersatz of psychic happiness."[37] Producing both riches and moral "comfort," philanthropy was at the heart of the civilization described (and denounced) by Aron and Dandieu. In their description, service, the ultimate treasure of a pacifying totalitarianism, had not been forgotten. A complementary structure and mythological additive for the system, according to Siegfried or Morand, service, for Aron and Dandieu, was also a school for forgetting: a formidable instrument for eradicating old values in favor of an American reconfiguration of people's minds. "Social service" was a "school for docility" and, in this sense, it gave conformist fetters their final turn of the screw. But this modern docility was the result of forced amnesia: service's great triumph was "making people forget the individual principles of charity or fraternity."[38] Orwellian before its time, American-style service not only forced people into subjection, it destroyed any memory of the past.

Charity and freedom: the two values doomed to annihilation by service were not chosen accidentally. Fundamental values for the individual, they were also Christian Europe and Revolutionary France's founding historical values. Aron and Dandieu belonged to no political party and claimed to draw their influence both from personalism and 1789, and were thus entitled to ecumenically defend charity, whose heart was on the right, and fraternity, its left-wing younger sibling, against America. In this way, their book was all the more emblematic of the common points between right-and left-wing discourses established with the help of anti-Americanism.

Pharisees and Philistines: "Rah! Rah! Sis Boom Bah!"

Vladimir Pozner, whose book *Les États-Désunis* was published in 1948 (but was written in 1938 and described the Roosevelt era), inserted a kind of logbook drawn from press clippings into his account. On April 8, 1936, he noted that "918 inhabitants of Los Angeles became pastors by correspondence. They only had to write to a certain address and enclose some money with the letter. For ten dollars, they could be ordained priests; a doctorate in divinity cost fifteen dollars; for double that sum, you could be made a bishop."[39] The Marxist Pozner was indignant rather than amused, forgetting that Lenin considered bad priests less dangerous than good ones.

What drew spiritualist and secular intellectuals together the most decisively, what solidified their common front, was the certainty that religion and culture were in the same boat in America: the dollar's. Becoming a priest was a matter of money. Making ends meet as a writer, barring a miracle, required giving in to the laws of the journalistic marketplace.[40] Living by one's art meant satisfying the trite, prudish, and megalomaniacal commissions of an uncultivated plutocracy.

Without going back to Baudelaire's anathema on America for leaving Poe destitute, we should nonetheless stress how far back went French (and European: witness Charles Dickens) complaints about the slight regard given the arts and letters in America. The American was indifferent to the life of the mind as well as to art. If it so happened that his social ascension led him to take an interest in it and acquire some, his bad taste broke out in absurd whims and lavish spending. At Stanford, Jules Huret saw a "triumphal arch with a Mrs. Stanford *on horseback* on the gloriously beautiful frieze, and an immense pedestal crowned with the entire Stanford family, Mr., Mrs., and Baby, in bronze—supremely naive, ignorant, and tasteless."[41] When Paul de Rousiers heard people brag, "You see, we have been in business since the days of the Indians!" he replied under his breath, "Most likely, but your artistic tastes are even more Indian than they were!"[42] Private buildings and public edifices were built with the same criteria: they should be enormous and costly. When entering a bank, "you go up marble staircases with golden-bronze balustrades; the ceilings and walls are decorated with countless gild-ings; the elevators, the screens, everything is gilded and everything looks hideous."[43] This luxury did not appeal to Duhamel either, forty years later, in the movie theater where his soul was nearly pulled out "like a tooth": "the lux-ury of some big, bourgeois brothel."[44] The same thing occurred on a citywide scale, since "beauty is a minor concern in creating public monuments. . . . What the Americans like are big things, extraordinary things, signs of power."[45] The White House was cited as an example of the ambient ugli-ness.[46] As for Huret, he explained that "purely pretty things, that is, things that are pretty in and of themselves, pretty without being useful or trying to be, are the rarest thing in America."[47] Everything was judged by its weight and price. Rousiers quoted the description next to a portrait of Pauline Bona-parte shown in Cincinnati: "It appears from this portrait that [she] weighed 150 pounds, or a little more." Now that spoke volumes about the transatlantic art lover and his habitual occupations: "How obvious the ranchman's experi-enced eye is here!" But "a still safer criterion for the ordinary American is the price of a work of art."[48] In 1893, Barbier noted that "Millet's *Angelus* . . . will owe its value in their eyes to the fact that it was taken from our museums by the force of auctions."[49] Marie Dugard, who was not the most ill-intentioned of the bunch, also denounced the Americans, who, "like the victorious Romans arrogantly removing the Greeks' statues to their own villas, use the might of their dollars to take our Hobbemas and our Rembrandts, our Meis-soniers and Corots to decorate galleries into which they never go."[50] Echoing these reiterated accusations, the taunting Gohier ribbed the French men of letters who did not carry their weight in America: they were too skinny, Gohier affirmed! In a country where everything, including art, was judged quantitatively, France would have to "make its men of letters fatten up a lit-tle"; skinny ninnies had no chance. So we see that the portrait of the Ameri-can as a rich ignoramus is not a recent development. When Lincoln Center was inaugurated in 1966, the French press published "scandalous" photos: the guests had set (empty) champagne glasses on the pedestal of a Maillol sculpture. Three-quarters of a century earlier, Barbier had been indignant to discover, marooned in America, "Monsieur Bouguereau's *Nymphs*," which had become the "principal attraction of an expensive bar in New York."[51]

But beyond the numerous imputations of Americans' lack of culture and pandemic bad taste, more specific grievances were soon articulated, particu-larly concerning the fact that in America, authors' rights were not respected.

Dickens had stubbornly made this the leitmotif of his American lectures—
which unleashed hostile press campaigns against him. Around 1900, the
reproach was ubiquitous among the French. "In a country governed by pro-
tectionists," the authors of *Jonathan et son continent* ironically noted, "it seems
strange that *all* national products are protected except the products of the
mind."[52] It would be superfluous to add that the rights of non-Americans'
intellectual products were even less so. The *Figaro* correspondent Jules Huret
chimed in with Gustave Le Rouge in denouncing systematic copyright theft.[53]
Was it because "the trusts of the intellect have not yet been formed"[54] that the
intellectual was so poorly defended in America? Whatever the case may be, the
writer or artist's fate—including his material one—seemed unenviable to his
French counterparts. It was prostitution, and not very lucrative at that, when
the authentic creator exercised his talent in a country where "what is called
Art, for lack of another, more fitting and more revealing appellation, is the vast
realm of exhibition in all its forms, where the symbolic Barnum reigns and tri-
umphs." The aesthetic sense across the Atlantic, Barbier asserted, was "Rah!
Rah! Sis boom bah!"[55] The onomatopoeia summed up all the American arts.
Including music, which a laconic Gohier summarily dismissed: "There is no
point talking about it. It is completely primitive."[56] The same Urbain Gohier
entitled a chapter: "The press. Literature. Art. Theater. Courts of law." With the
subtitle: "This chapter will unavoidably be very short."

Exhibition and censorship, ostentatious flaunting of artistic booty and
instinctive distrust of "values" that could not be set by quotations: those were
the poles between which America's cultural desire hovered. Covetousness
did not imply any real connoisseurship, and the joy of owning did not cancel
out the secret desire to destroy. We have seen this in Gustave Le Rouge's
millionaire, who strides up and down his private gallery only to slash the can-
vases of the European masters. "A book, a work of art, is an inoculation—perhaps dangerous, from an American standpoint—of superior needs, disinterested pleasures," Barbier commented. "Rather than seeing the salt pork trade
slacken, they prefer that the Book should perish."[57]

A generation later, Barbier's successors discovered with horror that the
Americans had found an even more reliable way of protecting the salt pork
trade: making art and thought into a "new market" analogous in every way
to salt pork.

The Great Marketplace of the Taylorized Spirit

The cultural denigration did not diminish in the interwar years. Its targets
changed, though. The respect of literary property was better secured after the

Bern conference and with new American legislation on authors' rights. Moreover, it became difficult to maintain that America, with its easy money, left its creators poorly compensated. On the contrary: the large circulations of books, journals, and magazines allowed authors to be paid high prices. In the artistic field, experts on America such as Recouly noted, those who succeeded earned much more money than their French counterparts.

Furthermore, it was clear that the United States was no longer prepared to play the part of consumer and client for European works. Even before 1914, it had to be admitted that there was a vibrant and varied national literature, with writers like Mark Twain, Edith Wharton, Henry James, and Theodore Dreiser; and with F. Scott Fitzgerald and Sinclair Lewis, a new generation was set to carry on the tradition. Why, then, should the Americans limit themselves to literature? "We should make fun of them while we can," Gohier had predicted in 1903; "they will have their own art fifty years from now."[58] If American artists up to then had only "copied, copied, copied, and collected, collected," that era could very well come to an end even before the date set by Gohier. Cultural anti-Americanism accordingly changed tack. The absence of indigenous productions was no longer pointed out, but rather the large-scale fabrication and marketing of cultural "products" that undermined the very notion of culture. It was no longer the tyranny of blinkered commandeers, but an even more serious danger that literature and art were coming up against: they were asked to satisfy the demands of the uncultivated masses.

A change of tone was apparent between the pre-and post-1914 periods, even if fears of Europe's losing its cultural hegemony were not yet widespread. Because "from the American side, intellectually, spiritually, and morally, there is nothing, there is no one," affirmed an essayist in 1930.[59] The idea that America could become a real rival in these areas continued to arouse incredulousness and protest. A Frenchman in 1909 summed up the general feeling: "They can try all they like to throw around huge checks and found universities, academies, and museums, it will not do any good; they will have to bow to our intellectual supremacy."[60] The author of *L'Abomination américaine*, in 1930, still firmly believed in "our intellectual supremacy," even if he was worried about the growing disproportion of material forces: "If America had attempted to enslave Europe with its 'thinkers,' it would at most have aroused a feeling of passing curiosity"; unfortunately, Kadmi-Cohen added, it also had the Bank for International Settlements . . . America, a titan of the material world, was still Lilliputian in matters of the mind: "It does not dare attempt the encounter: the American pygmy confronting the Old World colossus."[61] Octave Homberg did not imagine that the United States would risk trying to intellectually govern the planet, either, for fear of a general revolt: "If the American nation, which makes up only 7 percent of the planet's population, decided to dominate where its domination would not be justified—that is, to impose the law of the dollar over moral forces and ideas—it could not help but provoke a revolt that would not be that of the barbarians, but of civilization against a new brutal invasion."[62]

Even if America admittedly remained in a position of patent intellectual inferiority in relation to Europe (which is what Duhamel's entire book, published that same year, attempted to show), its huge material power was in and of itself a threat to Old World culture. Even the French essayists who were the most confident about their superiority did not hide the danger.

The most brutal form the threat took, and the most visible, was artistic pillage. For America's millionaires and benefactors never tired of "collecting, collecting." Their activity, increased by the power of the dollar, became a source of public animosity in the 1920s. Charlus's underhanded praise echoes this: "Even before the war, they loved . . . our masterpieces, of which they have many now";[63] so does the less memorable narrator in Raoul Gain's novel, when the Yankee millionaire Birdcall and his daughter try to acquire the church in Querqueville—"She tells me she loves our old villages."[64] The same theme crops up again at the end of the 1930s in Morand's L'Homme pressé, which recounts semiclandestine attempts to export a monastery from the south of France. This was the era when cloisters and castles were being shipped off in carefully numbered boxes to live a second, "uprooted" life in America—as Charlus says, citing "Monsieur Barrès." The unease aroused by these sales was patent in the 1930s, when initiatives for alerting the public and forcing the government to react proliferated. The plunder of the nation's heritage, ripped from French soil "with lashes of the dollar" often portrayed by fiction writers, was nonetheless practically absent from the writings of French essayists. Perhaps the most pessimistic of them were cheered, like Valéry just before World War II, by the idea that a little bit of European civilization would be saved, thanks to American museums, from the expected disaster? More likely, intellectual creators were just more worried about the fate of their own productions than that of the national heritage. In any case, their worry was invested in other areas: in the fear that the very forms of culture would be subverted under the double influence of a money-making imperative and submission to the taste of the masses.

America, "a quantity-based civilization," as Lucien Romier called it (quoting Paul Valéry), had created a marketplace for creative expression like the ones that existed for all the other products. Culture was becoming a good, a commodity, and it was put at buyers' disposal. In the absence of an elite powerful and organized enough to guide aesthetic choices, the cultural demand would thus be the simple reflection of the masses' "vulgar" appetites or the result of manipulations aimed at "educating" their tastes in the direction desired by the leisure industry. The foundations were set for a lasting quarrel between two conceptions of culture: one that clearly dissociated high culture from popular culture, which aimed at being nothing but entertainment; the other for which culture could not be divided up or negotiated over but was an immaterial "common property" protected by the intellectuals—"what remains when everything has been forgotten," as Herriot's famous maxim put it. This second logic forced even the most liberal French intellectuals to take an elitist stance, while cultivating the exonerating mythology of a symbiosis between the elite's cultivated choices and the "real aspirations of the people." By denouncing mass cultural products, the intelligentsia thought it was fulfilling its duty to the masses—protecting them from themselves; because if the masses were naturally "healthy," as they were in Raoul Gain's Normandy, they were spiritually fragile; and the Hollywood movies, "whose productions come to Europe to corrupt and degrade the soul of the people,"[65] were worse than an opiate: a veritable moral and intellectual toxin.

The principal source of the poison was Hollywood, which the French dwelt on more and more often in descriptions from the 1930s. Not to convey the saga of the studios, but to reveal the true nature of this aberrant outgrowth of productivism. Here once again, Duhamel was not very representative with his overblown passage against the cinema as a "pastime for slaves" and "amusement for the illiterate." In the "brothel"-style theater Mr. Pitkin drags him to, he sees gold leaf, naked thighs, acrobats, disdainful valets, and poor hypnotized souls. But no movies. Only the auditory dreadfulness of the musical accompaniment—a pitiless series of tortured classical highlights—strikes his anesthetized senses as a rough ordeal. The chapter is called "Cinematographic Interlude"; it was long considered an ingenious satire of the seventh art. Rereading it is surprising: there is no cinema in it.

Not all of his peers shared his willful blindness. Published the same year as Scenes from the Life of the Future, L'Abomination américaine was also stirred up over the risk of an intellectual leveling inherent in mass production, but refused to condemn the cinema as a whole, concentrating its attacks on Hollywood, seen as a laboratory of standardization applied to intellectual work. Raymond Recouly was most struck by the tyrannical constraints imposed on creators: "The intellectual workers are kept in a state of strict dependency; . . . their ideas, their conceptions are constantly reined in, if not rained on." The interwar Hollywood that would later become cinephiles' golden age was perceived at the time as a cocktail of Taylorism and contempt for the mind. "Never has everything touching on literary production been held in such perfect contempt. Authors are considered mercenaries, 'ghostwriters,'" Recouly wrote.[66] The brilliant *Hollywood, ville mirage* Joseph Kessel published in 1937 went along with this idea. A subjective piece of reporting—not bitter but not enthusiastic either—Kessel's book describes a world more "absurdist" than wondrous, more laborious than ludic, more industrious than ingenious: a "gilded labor camp, monstrous and deceptive," the labor camp of monomania and specialization, the Alcatraz of Taylorized creativity. "Hollywood is an open city," Kessel wrote, that "fabricates talking images like Ford's automobiles." But here, it was writers and artists working the assembly line, forced to punch in, consigned to their work post. "All the writers, all the composers, even if they are illustrious, even if they are paid between 20,000 and 50,000 francs a week, *must* produce in their numbered offices. Their presence is required at nine A.M. as strictly as if they were clocking in. Their tools are waiting there: typewriter, library, piano, organ, or violin." Beneath the glitter was the grind. The fantasy factory was a penal colony for the mind: "Everything is organized, stratified, standardized. Including thought, including inspiration."[67] The tempo imposed on inventiveness to produce nine hundred films a year was more infernal than Detroit's assembly lines. The cinema "is no longer an art. It is an industrial mechanism." Luc Durtain had said of American factories in general, "Everything runs perfectly. And any time a mechanical activity runs perfectly, it gives off an immense sadness: the impression, beyond words, of a kind of defeat of the soul."[68] "Rush, output, precision, correction: those are the essential characteristics of a Hollywood existence," Kessel noted; "everything is icy, all the cogs turn automatically," and this "game with no warmth . . . gives Hollywood the monotony and vanity of an insubstantial dream."[69]

But neither the "mirage factories" Kessel describes nor the other forms of mass cultural production were solely responsible for the degrading of the American mind. And if God was served by "married boys" and charlatan preachers, intelligence was going down the tubes for lack of its own ministry, intellectuals.

In France, no one really understood, and people became more and more annoyed about the impotence or passivity of those who should have been leading the struggle on their home ground: the writers, artists, and scholars in the United States. Not without ambiguity, they were given approval to come and look in Europe and France for the favorable soil they did not have across the Atlantic; but they were disapproved of if they deserted the American cultural battlefield. The French intellectuals reproached them for not having stood their ground, for not having been able to build themselves up as an intellectual power. Jules Huret, right at the turn of the century, was surprised to note that the elite had "zero influence" in the United States; whence his jibe, which we have already cited: "Up to now, the Americans have only centralized their industrial and financial powers; the trusts of the intellect have not yet been formed."[70] They still had not, twenty or fifty years later. In their place, publishing, film, press, and television conglomerates had been created, and writers and artists were only the cogs in their immense wheels. But even if a few powerful voices—from Jack London and Theodore Dreiser to Dos Passos and Steinbeck—were able to make their criticism of the "system" heard, disappointment with American intellectuals' failure to establish their counter-power prevailed in France. That they were powerless to influence the life of the nation was considered their own failing as much as that of America itself, which once again seemed like an anti-France, forbidding its intellectual elite from playing any part in the social state. Worse: their place was usurped by narrow-minded specialists, self-proclaimed "technocrats," secret experts in the "brain trust." This reproach was formulated in the most unexpected texts, like the very anti-American collaborationist pamphlet that signaled the existence, in America, of a "very distinguished, open-minded, and cultivated intellectual elite. Unfortunately, since there are no salons or urbane life, this elite remains scattered and has no influence over other milieus."[71] It was obviously not the same "influence" Simone de Beauvoir had in mind in 1948, but she too lamented the "clear-cut divorce between the university world and the living intellectual world" in the United States and the "general defeatism" that kept American intellectuals from social involvement: "For many reasons, a tradition of intellectual defeatism has been established in this world, so new and yet already so old."[72] Writers did not exist in the United States, except as entertainers: "writers are not popular, or if they are, it is only as entertainers," Beauvoir also noted; "the writer is unable to have any meaningful effect on public opinion."[73] This perfectly summed up, *a contrario*, the dream of "serious popularity" and civic influence so many French writers clung to.

Whether they were complete victims or partially guilty, the intellectuals' defection was disastrous: it left the field wide open for capitalism and cultural imperialism's maneuvers, as Kadmi-Cohen stressed: "American imperialism has been happy to contemplate the high realm of thought the same way an industrialist contemplates a market open to conquest." In 1930 he still believed, along with many French intellectuals, that "imperialism" was so intimidated by the European elites that it could not directly lay into them. Mass cultural production (with movies first in line) was the Trojan horse of a two-part operation: Europe's population would be won over and "spoiled," and little by little, its intellectual and spiritual mentors would be deserted and end up asphyxiated, like fish out of water; it would then be easy to throw them out and replace them with hordes of "scoundrels of creativity."[74] This was the early draft of the "conspiracy against the mind" scenarios as they would proliferate in the anti-Americanism of the cold war years.

Until then, disturbing symptoms were multiplying. For in the absence of any intellectual power or counter-power, the marketplace was king, and culture, a common product doomed to vulgarity. The "real" creators, the great writers who became scriptwriters (such as Faulkner), were increasingly subjected to very detailed commissions, obligatory collective work, and the indignity of rewrites. But also, more importantly, the marketplace king invented its own cultural forms—literary or artistic UFOs that had started to arouse concern and consternation among French intellectuals. Before 1945, comic books were hardly mentioned, and the digest was only starting to come up. But there was worry about the state of the book itself, which was treated like a piece of merchandise among others. Duhamel evoked American "literature merchants," and the historian Bernard Faÿ could only be uneasy about the proliferating magazines sold in the same stores and sometimes the same aisles as shaving cream. The overly close symbiosis between books, magazines, and newspapers provoked a worried reaction as to the literary quality of such works, with the American press regularly subjected to very negative judgments.[75] But the economic synergies even the universities failed to escape also created worries about freedom of thought. Robert Aron and Arnaud Dandieu tackled the subject in their customarily radical way—an approach that would have many inheritors in the second half of the twentieth century. Anyone worried about the fate of books—that emblem of European-style culture—had not understood a thing about the "American cancer," they said. Whether books were replaced by digests or not was unimportant. The book was already "not the same on Yankee soil as in free countries." In the land of generalized slavery, where "from birth onward, intellectual life is enslaved," where students were "defenseless" and the schoolmaster a "tolerated parasite," the most beautiful libraries were nothing but desultory illusions. When a book was stamped *Free Library*, it should be understood that "in this free library, everything and everyone is free; only the mind is not."

It was not easy for America to break out of this situation. If it produced digests, it was accused of vandalism. But if it opened libraries, it was considered worse than the barbarians, because, as Aron and Dandieu concluded, "it is better to burn down libraries than to make them into bank annexes."[76]

The "Conspiracy against Intelligence"

By the interwar years, all the ingredients of 1950s anti-Americanism's cultural potion were available: apprehension about creative works sinking to the level of merchandise; the symbolic downgrading of intellectuals and creators; the enslavement of thought in general and particularly of the university, confined to specialized tasks; the creation of a mass cultural market completely beyond the intellectuals' control. In the diminished, impoverished France of 1945, these scattered and imprecise fears crystallized into a violent sense of dispossession. In a political landscape in which the fighting Right was temporarily out of the picture and the moderate Left, in office, had no choice but to be "Atlantist" out of necessity, the Communist Party—the rallying pole for a great many intellectuals, scholars, and artists, succeeded in capturing a prize that was essential to its prestige and "ideological battle": becoming the head of the French cultural resistance.

There was a "conspiracy against intelligence," as *La Nouvelle Critique* wrote in 1951. The Communist Party, which was now presented as the nation's only true representative, was also set on coming across as the true defender of France's cultural treasures. "France, the land of Rabelais, Montaigne, Voltaire, Diderot, Hugo, Rimbaud, Anatole France, and the bards of Resistance to the invaders, is being submerged by an imported literature that glorifies what is most vile in man, and by certain American magazines whose stupidity is an affront to the human intellect."[77] The Communist press railed tirelessly against this sabotage by intellectual dumbing-down. On the one hand, its goal was to offset the tentative regrouping of a certain number of anti-Stalinist intellectuals and artists; but most of all, its goal was to exploit an eminently profitable ideological mine and give diverse intellectuals rallied to the French Communist Party the uniting objective of defending their land against a cultural invasion. The impact of these campaigns, as measured by the polls, might seem modest,[78] but their target was less the general public than the "intellectual strata," which had to be won over to the cause and which responded favorably to the message of resistance. Overvaluing culture and its representatives, as Duhamel had done before the war, was wholly embraced, but also politicized through and through: from individual repugnance, it was time to move on to collective mobilization. Defending the "works of the mind" was a matter of public salvation when, "in the attempt to break a nation's spine and suppress its defense mechanisms, its spirit is set into."[79]

The plan for "moral enslavement," which seemed hubristic before the war, was now being seriously put into action by an all-powerful America. The almost colonial status of occupied France lent this scenario a tragic plausibility. In any case, that was what the Communist press kept repeating. In its special issue in June 1951, *La Nouvelle Critique* explained that "perversion" of the culture went hand in hand with political enslavement: "A vast undertaking to pervert science and art and degrade culture is taking place in our country, in imitation of what is happening in the USA. . . . The French do not want to become robots, nor intellectuals the trusts' mercenaries." Pushing the idea of a total junction between cultural struggle and political combat even further, the editorialist concluded: "A vote for governmental party and RPF candidates is a vote for Hollywood and the Ku Klux Klan, for obscurantism and censorship, moral perversion and police in the laboratories, sergeants recruiting in schools, students' destitution, painters' transformation into manual workers, and the death of literature."[80] Imperialism and its henchmen really had their work cut out for them. . .

The Communist use of the cultural self-defense discourse recycled, on the Left, an argumentative arsenal that had been stockpiled mostly on the Right before the war: cultural anti-Americanism became a patriotic duty. The danger was no longer only inherent in the form of so-called mass culture; it was part of a plan for the deliberate destruction of the national cultures obstructing the ideological globalization America desired. American leaders were working to make France "lose consciousness," affirmed the Communist Party's intellectual review, which in late 1951 launched an investigation on the "conspiracy against intelligence": "What the stifling of our economy and the preparation of our foot-soldiers [to be used by NATO] entails is that we all lose our consciousness and find it again, in a derisory form, in theirs." Less Hegelianly put, "By imposing [their culture] on us, they think they will hypnotize us with the myth of a 'community' of ideas, feelings, and history."[81]

Rather than the scorn, sarcasm, and contempt that characterized prewar attacks, alarmism prevailed, couched in conspiracy-theory rhetoric. A corollary to the Marshall Plan was a "Marshall Plan for ideas," whose existence Roger Garaudy revealed in March 1951: "Following the directives given by Truman on April 20, 1950, and Dean Acheson on April 22 concerning 'total propaganda,' which corresponds to 'total diplomacy,' the American State Department created a Cold War Commission." Honorable French newspapers like Le Figaro were now publishing flattering, "outlandish" articles on American culture, directly dictated by the "American Bureau of Psychological Strategy," which was Truman's new Propagandastaffel. The proof was that now you could "read the so-called French press two days before it came out . . . by flipping through the pages of USA and France-Amérique." But the ramifications of the conspiracy went well beyond these crude manipulations by "the Marshall press's pen servants"[82] and they operated along two axes already pointed out by the prewar anti-Americans.

The first axis: the university. The American university system had been the object of very contradictory analyses since the end of the nineteenth century. Scholars and pedagogues, from Gustave Lanson to Jean-Marie Dome-nach—"We will have their crimes. If only we could have their universities, too"[83]—saw real charms and advantages in it. But most French observers found American universities too dependent on big business; they stressed university professors' intellectual isolation; and they criticized the overly abstract and specialized education offered in them. The last two reproaches did not seem contradictory: schooled in the humanities, they considered excessive specialization a form of abstraction, which they saw as the contrary of humanist synthesis—the goal of any education. But up to 1945, no one believed the American university system was contagious any more than they really believed there was an American "cultural" offensive in Europe.

Now the threat was brandished that French universities would be con-sensually or forcibly brought in line with American universities—bran-dished by Maurice Thorez himself: "French education will be forced to fall in line with American war policy." The Americans intended to use its scientific resources, but most of all, they wanted to make it a conduit for ideological transmission. That France was complying was already apparent in the sanc-tions against teachers, seen as the warning sign of a larval McCarthyism,[84] but even more by the deformation of the very content of what was being taught. Oriented toward mind-boggling specialization, empty of substance, American learning offered intellectual resistance neither a weapon nor a foothold. The education to which imperialism doomed France was the "doughnut-making classes" *La Nouvelle Critique* had discovered in the course offerings at the University of Vancouver. Whence the rallying cry, one of the most unusual in a period that was nonetheless full of them: "We say: NO! We will have no doughnut-making classes, and our universities will not be Americanized! We will not allow the shameful degradation of culture that Washington is propagating throughout the world."[85] Despite its prankish overtones, the slogan ties in to earlier worries: Jouvenel, in 1933, was already up in arms against the hotel management courses or marketing training offered in American universities.[86] But it was premonitory as well: exorcising the doughnut as a school subject was a very early synthesis of the French opposition to junk food and to "lite high school" at the end of the twentieth century.

The second axis of American infiltration was one the intellectuals of the interwar years had already feared: French popular culture being taken over by American-made mass culture. Once again, Communist campaigns pro-duced a paroxysmic synthesis of intellectuals' opposition and that of a large part of the general population. Cartoons had been booming in America since the 1920s. In 1933, Procter and Gamble dreamed up and launched the *comic book,* originally as a free "gadget"; starting the following year they were then sold for money, and in ten years rose to 18 million copies a month in the United States. But it was their massive appearance in movie theaters and newspaper stands after 1945 that aroused the hostility of a country in which the children's press had always been part of the "good press."[87] Denouncing these violent and vulgar cartoons and comic books drew the Communist press, the confessional press, and the secular pedagogical press together. When they inveighed against the "cartoons that draw laughs from the tortures inflicted on Donald the Duck or Pluto the Dog"; when they denounced the "particularly scandalous invasion" of the juvenile press by "volumes that are crude copies of cartoons from across the Atlantic," saturated with an "unbelievable mix of pornography, sadism, and everything that calls up the baser human emotions"; when they grew indignant at seeing "skirts half-covering bottoms, and battling breasts," *La Nouvelle Critique*'s contributors were espousing the preoccupations of a whole section of Catholic opinion or those simply attached to a tradition of "educational" children's literature. The Communist press was working on two levels here. It was heavy-handedly appealing to "fathers worried about the bad example preached by the movie screens,"[88] but it also printed Louis Daquin's denunciation of complicity between the Vatican's Index and the Hayes Code—which set the norms for prudery on film—"written in 1929 by a Jesuit."[89] A blow against the "Puritan" censorship of film along with a blow against cartoons' "pornographic" abandon made for two slaps with a ruler on the back of America's hand.

The July 16, 1949, law for the protection of children in France, a true "war tool against American productions,"[90] would repay protesters' efforts. Article 2 stipulated that no publication for children could favorably portray banditry, theft, laziness, weakness, hate, debauchery, or any act liable to demoralize children and youths. On its instigators' own admission, "the designated goal is openly that American comics and *Tarzan* stop being printed by October 1953."[91] As for literature for adults, (chiefly) made up of American-style detective novels, it also aroused massive repulsion. Among its unexpected detractors was Raymond Queneau, who in 1945 curiously associated the detective-novel ambiance with the Marquis de Sade's universe and the world of the Gestapo and the concentration camps.[92] Forcing detective novels or gangster movies on the public meant training the masses for violence and preparing them for war, *La Nouvelle Critique* thought. Pozner went even further: if the gangster was the object of all of America's "artistic" attentions, it was because gangsterism had become "the crime industry of the monopoly age, and its most important branch, racketeering, is nothing other than the continuation of capitalist competition by other means."[93] The only people more despicable than gangsters and their American apologists were the "French writers [who] stoop to passing their creations off as translations from the American"—a probable allusion to *I Spit on Your Graves,* published by Boris Vian under the pseudonym Vernon Sullivan.[94]

But another product encapsulated, so to speak, all the horror of American culture: the digest. Novels shrunk "to thirty pages" aroused general indignation. *Témoignage chrétien* talked of literature compressed into a tablet of aspirin. Vladimir Pozner explained that the digest resulted from the same logic of control as quiz shows and Fordian specialization.[95] Only "time is money" America could have come up with such an infamy. (In fact, abridged, expurgated versions of novels had been very popular in eighteenth-century France; the long novels of the previous century were perfect for that.)[96] The none-too-appetizing word *digest* itself reinforced the disgust inspired by this pre-digested spiritual fodder. As far as cultural material went, France only got to root through America's garbage cans: discolored scrapings, tired old reels of films that had come out fifteen years earlier, not to mention the pure and simple "garbage" (*dixit* Étiemble) known as Coca-Cola. "I recognize it," Pozner wrote in 1948, alluding to his stay in the United States in 1938 and during the war; "the arsenal has already been used; they have not even bothered white-washing it: the movies, the bestsellers, the magazines, the digests, the picture books, the color photos of pin-up girls."[97] Those were the rags these "bungling idiots" (again, Étiemble) were foisting on France and which they were making good money from, as they did from selling their military surplus.

From Mirages to Myths

Of all these battles, the battle of the movies was the most savage. There were numerous reasons for this, starting with the size of the audience reached. Moreover, the professional circles of French filmmaking had a strong left-wing tradition, a good conductor for political and professional mobilization. Another politically determining circumstance came in 1946 with the Blum-Byrnes agreements, which implemented a massive introduction of American movies by establishing *minimum* quotas for their screening in France. Denouncing these agreements as a cultural "capitulation" allowed Communists to bring to light socialist politicians' collusion with "imperialism" and to endorse the portrait of Blum as "the American party's French ideologist."[98] The 1946 quotas were thus tenaciously presented as a betrayal. "Mr. Blum," Georges Soria wrote, "will go down in history as the man who unleashed a flood tide of U.S.-made crime onto the screens of France, and who condemned French film to a slow but certain death."

Propagandists like Soria had a (deliberately) short memory. Because the fear of being submerged by the American industry in fact went back to the 1920s. The French film industry had been very active before 1914 but had suffered from the interruption of the Great War. The investments needed to reconstruct the country had concurrently reduced its financial resources. In 1924, 85 percent of feature films shown in France were American; afterward, the proportion fell, but it was still at 63 percent in 1927. The situation was then judged worrisome enough for Herriot to appoint a Commission du Cinéma, essentially composed of producers. It concluded that there should be *restrictive* quotas: four American films would be authorized for every French film exported. The quotas were applied in 1928 and immediately led the Motion Picture Producers and Distributors to boycott French movies. Before the year was out, the French position was "readjusted": now seven movies could be imported for every movie produced in France. This looked a lot like a capitulation. But resistance was difficult, since three-quarters of the movie theaters in large cities already belonged to the Americans. The very idea of establishing a regulated proportion between American films shown in France and French films shown in the United States seemed, from then on, wishful thinking or pure demagogy, considering the real balance of power. In 1929, only nineteen French movies were shown in the United States.[99] This figure gives an idea of the scale of a problem that had already existed well before the Blum-Byrnes agreements opened the floodgates.

The Communist press's campaign in defense of the French film industry, which was launched in 1947 and went full force in the early 1950s, was a dense mixture of cultural, economic, and ideological arguments. "In the United States, movies have become the most powerful means of subduing the people," noted in 1950 the author of an article that emphasized the troubling number of war movies produced by the United States in a six-month period, and by the ever-growing number of detective movies in which "semi-sadistic violence (comparable to crime novels') is the star feature."[100] The frequently anti-Soviet nature of Hollywood productions was not overlooked: it confirmed the theory of the Americans' cynically propagandistic use of film. *The Iron Curtain, The Red Danube,* and *I Married a Communist* showed how "Wall Street's war" was trying to "corrupt the instruments of culture"; these were the transatlantic equivalents of Sartre's play *Les Mains sales,* which provoked more than a little indignation in the French Communist circles of the 1950s. "Ideological deadening, anti-Sovietism, an apology of the '(capitalist) American way of life'":[101] this was the weekly line-up of the theaters under Hollywood's control.

The film-related anti-American outcry went well beyond the circles already won over to the Communists' campaigns. Part of the trauma was due to the fact that the quota weapon, awkwardly brandished by France in 1927, had been turned against France and its ailing 1946 economy. But the violent tone, which is striking in directors' and many actors' pronouncements, also masked a permanently unspoken notion: the respite the French film industry had obtained when it was protected from "Anglo-Saxon" competition under Vichy. As in the sensitive field of children's publications and comics, the occupation retrospectively seemed like an oasis for French productions. There was a brutal shift from an incontestable (with good reason) preponderance of French productions to the massive importing of often mediocre American works. From January to June 1946, only 36 American movies were shown in France. In 1947, the number rose to 388. Over the course of the decade, American movies, which played on half of the screens, procured about 43 percent of filmgoers.[102] What the people protesting against the American quotas lamented was obviously not Vichy, but there was a strong desire, in the industry and among its friends, for a "cultural salvation" protectionism, which a "strong nation" should have been able to put in place.[103] France was in a state of self-defense: it had to face the invasion head on, or retaliate through sabotage. In order to get around the Blum-Byrnes agreements, the filmmaker Jacques Becker proposed not banning American movies, but dubbing them into French: by this simple measure "we will decontaminate the marketplace of 95 percent of American productions."[104] Decontaminate: the verb Becker chose is telling. Yankee cinema was a poison or a drug—like Coca-Cola, which Communists and wine lobbies combined were trying to have banned for public health reasons.[105]

This, too, was a watershed moment: the anti-Hollywood campaigns of the cold war years were founded on arguments from the 1930s even as they prefigured the most contemporary of image wars. By the 1920s, economic considerations and symbolic overtones had been inextricably merged. Édouard Herriot, writing as a critic and not a politician, had already asked what is now a central question in debates about America's cultural hegemony: nations' right to produce their own images—images of the world and of themselves. Is it a harmless thing, Herriot asked, if Joan of Arc is henceforth embodied with the features of a California girl, and Napoleon with those of an actor from Illinois?[106] Was this not an insidious way of sucking the blood out of France's cultural heritage? Shouldn't filmic images, filmmakers' style and language, celebrate their roots in the culture, in a national and almost ethnographical sense? Such questions began cropping up before the war, mostly from the Left. Jean Renoir proffered (in 1938) a curious mea culpa: "I was naively, laboriously struggling to imitate my American masters; I had not understood that a Frenchman living in France, drinking red wine and eating brie before the *grisaille* of Parisian perspectives, could produce quality works only by founding them on the traditions of people who lived like him."[107] Even lifeless celluloid brought back the carnal difference of voices, bodies, and humors between "them" and "us." A poll taken thirty years later asked the French to name the other nationalities they felt had the closest resemblance to theirs: the Americans came in last, well behind the English, Italians, and Germans. How do you accept being "represented"? And by people you least want to resemble?

"Film is not only merchandise": this key phrase of French reasoning in negotiating the GATT's "cultural wing" in 1993 (and since then, the WTO's) was pronounced back at the time of the liberation by the director Louis Daquin, who had just made *Patrie* (1945).[108] The "cultural exception" discourse would directly inherit this aspiration to protect economically fragile and symbolically sensitive sectors. Today we find the same insistence on the (collective) right to difference, with the production of "indigenous" images conceived as a way of redressing the imbalance in the face of a foreign takeover of the national imagination. The people using this argumentation in France are aware of its ambiguity: whence their references to the "diversity" and "plurality" that images of the world should have. But it is well and truly the defense of national culture that is at the heart of the unease and protest, just as it was at the time of the liberation; it is well and truly an indigenous mythography that is seen as needing protection from being trampled by myths from other lands.

"Your myths are already breaking over France in waves," Vladimir Pozner shot out in 1948. American movies were no longer (only) accused of being creatively impoverished, but of interfering as well. Kessel, before the war, spoke of *mirages*. The word *myth*, much more politically charged, points to a change of perspective. On the left, myth was now strongly associated with historical fascisms, their "irrational" domination of public opinion and their massive use of motion picture images. In a text in *Situations I* (1947), Sartre called attention to the suspicious origins of myth—"very much in fashion since Sorel."[109] Pozner offered his chronicle in *Les États-Désunis* as a "weapon in the hands of the myth slayers"—and of the most pernicious myth, the "democracy myth" in America.[110] Less violent, but still very pugnacious, the mythologist Barthes of the 1950s made sure not to leave out American movies: from Chaplin's *Modern Times* to Kazan's *On the Waterfront*, Hollywood gave him the chance to write a few of his most caustic "little mythologies." We even find the same question Herriot had pondered in 1930, this time regarding Mankiewicz's *Julius Caesar:* could you produce ancient Rome using "the Yankee mugs of Hollywood extras"? Barthes, who was usually distrustful of "naturality," thought only Marlon Brando wore a convincing bowl cut, thanks to his "naturally Latin forehead," while Julius Caesar was "unbelievable, with that Anglo-Saxon lawyer face of his."[111] Confronted with these "Yankee mugs," the subtle stereotype hunter was not safe from typecasting, as we can see in an aside on the sweat beading up on all those pseudo-Roman faces: "To sweat is to think—which evidently rests on the postulate, appropriate to a nation of businessmen, that thought is a violent, cataclysmic operation."[112] The "nation of businessmen," as we are starting to suspect, does not refer to the Romans, and Barthes appends further proof, involuntarily this time, that it is never much of a leap from body types to cultural stereotyping.

If the American film industry attracted the majority of French cultural counterattacks of the period, it is therefore *also* because it was perceived as the "mythological" arm of a totalitarian conquest of the mind. We might smile at the calm conviction with which the monthly *Études soviétiques* denounced, in 1951, "the American capitalists' urge to exterminate two-thirds of the population of any given country in order to force the remaining third to watch only American movies."[113] Cold war talk. . . Like the umpteenth comparison of Hollywood to the *Propagandastaffel:* "In the United States, you hear studio or network heads openly affirm that soon the only images seen around the world will be American. Goebbels said the same thing about German images, in his day." Except that this remark was printed, not in 1951, but in 1991. And we are not reading *Études soviétiques,* but a movie review in *Le Monde.*[114]

The dust of the cold war's polemic blockbuster would take a long time to settle, leaving the question: what is to be done? If America was now capable of importing into and imposing on France a "culture" shrunken like a digest, degraded like a "semi-sadistic" crime novel, or mythifying like James Mason's bowl cut, where should the Maginot Line of the mind be drawn?

"Unequal Exchange" and Counterculture

The second half of the twentieth century had two answers to the question. The first was universally rejecting American culture, theorized by Sartre as a refusal of "unequal exchange"; the second, a corollary of the first, was adopting the American "counterculture" on principle: the enemy of my enemy is my friend.

The period starting in 1945 was marked by the painful awareness of a disproportion in strength: how could a country from which all the means of power and even independence had been removed conserve the cultural

hegemony the French had still believed in before 1940? Thinkers such as
Bernanos resisted the idea that France's intellectual "influence" would necessarily decline along with its position in the world. But they were few and
far between, and the new intellectual generation had no illusions: influence
was also a power issue. And Raymond Aron's appeals to embrace this situation with reasonable humility, until better days came along, distressed Saint-
Germain-des-Prés even more than Billancourt.[115]

Sartre did not come up with a solution to the problem, but he embodied,
for a whole generation, resistance to the "asphyxiation" threatening French
culture. Faced with the advancing American tide, between the patience recommended by Raymond Aron and the Communist Party's paranoid invectives, his was the only voice offering the intellectuals a combat ethic: a kind
of aggressive stoicism. His anti-Americanism sprang from the affirmation of
a now irremediable inequality between France and the United States. France
no longer held its own, and the only retaliation possible was retreat and
abstention. It was this calculation, this weighing of destinies, that made
Sartre a *systematic* anti-American, rather than an emotional one, and even
more than he was a political one. Sartre's obsession was thereafter with cutting ties to America, refusing contact, fleeing the Yankee as Diderot had
advised the Hottentot savage to flee the whites—or kill them. This was the
conclusion of his editorial "Rabid Animals," written after the Rosenbergs'
execution: "Break all the ties that bind us to [America]."[116] It was also the
spirit and the letter of the harsh interview he gave the *Nouvel observateur* in
1972 on the bombarding of North Vietnam: "Dialogue is not possible anymore." He then canceled a trip to Cornell, the nerve center of antiwar
protest.[117] Dialogue was not possible, even with those against the war? astonished Americans asked him. An exasperated Sartre responded that he owed
them no answer. One sentence crops up twice in the *Nouvel observateur* interview: "America is not the center of the universe." It had, however, been the
center of Sartre's preoccupations since the end of the war. And his quaran-
tine measures in fact reiterated, in an eminently political context, a conviction that had already been expressed much more calmly in 1949 in a cultural
context.

The piece is less famous than the ones we have just seen, but it is decisive. It is called "Defending French Culture by Defending European Culture." In it, Sartre invites France to abstain from all cultural relations with a
country that has potential "superior" to its own: namely, America. The cornerstone of his argument is the concept of "exchange without reciprocity." "A
country's political, economic, demographic, and military hegemony imposes
nonreciprocal cultural exchanges," Sartre states.[118] They should be avoided,

and only exchanges with countries of equal potential accepted—a little bit like the way a city has to find a foreign city of the same size to be its "sister city." The concept of exchange without reciprocity is a little surprising coming from the Sartre of 1949. Its vocabulary is more like something out of Mauss or Bataille than existentialism. Here, Sartre was rubbing elbows with the analyses of the gift familiar to readers of *Critique*. And in fact these analyses had just been invoked the previous year in the most inventive book about the Marshall Plan, the one Jean Piel published at Éditions de Minuit, in the short-lived collection "L'usage des richesses," edited by his brother-in-law Georges Bataille. *La Fortune américaine et son destin* is the book of an economist comparing the American propositions of 1948 with the real state of the world and their underlying economic models; but the picture it paints leads to a very Bataillian proposal. Coming back to the March 11, 1941, lend-lease law that had authorized the United States government to provide war equipment and all goods in general to anti-Nazi belligerents without necessarily requiring future repayment for such goods (repayment could be "any other direct or indirect benefit which the President deems satisfactory"), Jean Piel stresses the utterly pioneering nature of such an arrangement. At the hour of victory, the enormous disparity between America and Europe's financial means had only gotten worse: this was the heart of the world's "fundamental imbalance." Balanced exchanges would not even be possible for much longer; there needed to be some compensatory action to right an imbalance that was unbearable for all parties concerned. The "compensation," Jean Piel wrote, "can only lastingly happen by a continued outpouring of capital, probably a growing one and *without reciprocity*, from America to the rest of the world, as well as by establishing a new kind of relationship between the country that will be the only source of this outpouring and those who will benefit from it, exclusive of the legal statutes that have governed debtor/creditor relations up to now, and for which we could, if need be, find an image—a distant one, moreover—in certain forms of the *gift* observed in primitive societies." In short, Jean Piel stressed in conclusion, "*the gift henceforth becomes the best and only form of external credit.*" Could the United States and Europe live up to this fiction, and thus effectively give "American fortune" a real "destiny"? Piel is not so sure, and he soberly notes that "the 'Marshall Plan's' original conception seemed to imply a partial awareness of this necessity."[119] This is what Sartre vigorously contested.

If he adopted the idea of "exchange without reciprocity," Sartre did not for a second imagine that Franco-American relations could be made to fit the logic of the gift. Starting from the same premises, he reached the conclusion that any real intellectual *commerce* with the United States was an impossibility.

This was why Sartre would refuse to go there and give a lecture on any literary or philosophical topic at all. This was why he would remain stubbornly mute when the professors at Cornell demanded an explanation. This was why he would always react to America *unequally*. This was why he would react to ideas with indignation or acceptance based on whether they were American or not. This was why he would unblinkingly consent to the vigorous Soviet cleaning up of *La Putain respectueuse* and *Nekrassov*[120] but take Nagel, his American publisher, to court in the United States for having allowed what was a much less reworked adaptation of *Les Mains sales* to be staged. Sartre would uphold a double standard with America, because he saw the balance of power as warped. In this way, he handed down to future French anti-Americans a durable ideological kit that was a mix of deliberate bias and justification for this bias, founded on the idea of an imbalance of power. The damaging argument of the lack of reciprocity would quietly forge ahead until it was dictating France's cultural policies. At the start of François Mitterand's first term, a very combative Jack Lang would explain in *L'Express* that there was the American dream—the movies he grew up with—but also "the underside of the dream: one industry's hegemony and everyone's duty to invent his way of living and exchange his products *based on reciprocity*."[121]

Sartre's attitude often wavered between denying America's "centrality" and obstinately laying into America (showing "the truth about American society.")[122] But in the end, Sartre's radicalism lay less in the stubbornness with which he accused America than in the a priori repudiation of any and all exchange with it. This Sartrian *abstine* theorized the same gesture made—each in his own way—by Roger Vailland when he broke with a former comrade in arms who had become a "bastard";[123] Pozner taking leave from an "American friend" in his preface to *Les États-Désunis;* not to mention Breton, for whom it was a point of honor not to have made a single friend during his stay in the United States. All of these fictive ruptures illustrate the intellectuals' need to draw on the great fiction of rupture.

So there were no friends in the United States? Well, in fact, there were. Those Breton had called "my friends the blacks" and "my friends the Indians" in 1949. For Pozner, the people in Harlem. In Sartre's plays, the lynched black man and the Salem witch. (Another adaptation story: Sartre violently protested Marcel Aymé's movie version of his play, accusing him of de-Americanizing "what was a specifically American phenomenon.")[124] Sartre's strategic model—rejecting mainstream America and naturalizing an "other America"—would guide, consciously or not, cultural anti-Americanism's tactics up to the end of the century. The only thing declared acceptable in America was non-America, or even better, a McCarthyist neologism that was wildly successful in France: *un-American* America. "My book," Pozner proudly wrote, "is, of course, un-American [*non-américain*], which is patently obvious, since it is a French book."[125] From Jean Genet going over to support the Black Panthers to the provincial teenager struggling to understand Bob Dylan's nasal intonations (his message was much easier to decipher in Hughes Aufray's French version), enthusiasm for what was henceforth called the counterculture was inseparably linked to charges against majority, white, conservative America. "I am not an American," Malcolm X wrote in his auto-biography. That was enough to spark French people's interest. It could even be the motto of the French counterculture of the 1960s, which, far from can-celing out anti-Americanism, worked hand in hand with it. It is utterly para-doxical to present, as has often been done, the French taste for jazz,[126] rock 'n' roll, westerns, Jerry Lewis movies, protest songs, or rap as symptoms of "Americanization": because if the proposition is literally true—all those things "come from America"—it is ideologically false. Validating these forms in France is inseparably linked to the fact that they appear (or appeared in their day) dissident or subversive within American culture. There is no con-tradiction, tension, or non sequitur between the adoption of these forms and their admirers' perpetuation of the anti-American discourse. The taste for the American counterculture is anti-Americanism carried on by other means.

☆ ☆ ☆

In the second *Democracy*, Tocqueville refused the widespread cliché of his time according to which a democratic nation was considered the most detri-mental "to the sciences, literature, and the arts." America, in his opinion, could not be used as proof of this incompatibility: the Americans' situation was too exceptional, since they had Europe as a kind of silo of immaterial goods. "The people of the United States are that portion of the English peo-ple whose fate it is to explore the forests of the New World," Tocqueville wrote. While they were doing this, "the learned and literary men of Europe were undertaking the search for the basic principles of truth, and at the same time improving everything that can minister to the pleasures." Because of this division of labor between the continents, Tocqueville's America could devote itself entirely to industrial and commercial activities; "the accessibil-ity of Europe" allowed it to do so "without relapsing into barbarism."[127]

A century and a half later, the model of shared labor had fallen to pieces. Not only because the United States had long since diversified its woodcutting vocation, but also and more seriously because the nature of the creative operations supposed to be Europe's specialty was no longer clear. Well into the twentieth century, the coalition of intellectuals united by a common self-interest, if not by a plan against America, was able to maintain—at least in its own opinion—the legitimizing fiction of Europe as a cultural pole in the face of America's material pole. All the efforts of French anti-Americans of the interwar years went into affirming the spiritual and cultural precedence of Europe—and preferably a French or French-oriented Europe—over America. They went so far as to consider the whole zone of American influence an irrecoverable cultural and intellectual wasteland: "America is multiplying its anthills, in which Western values run the risk of dying out," wrote Emmanuel Berl in 1929.[128] The disaster renewed by World War II and the fall of colonial empires undermined Europe's ability to assume this ambition just as mass culture was opening a "second marketplace" for creative productions—and a frightening breach in the European monopoly.

From cultural defensive to withdrawal, the preserve was shrinking to the dimensions of Astérix's village, in a French collective imagination that was now as riddled with decadence as it had once been puffed up with its own self-importance. The postwar focus on uneven exchange logically led to the Sartrian plan for an embargo against American culture, an embargo from which only the counterculture, in a pinch, could be exempted. The cultural campaigns of the late twentieth century prolonged the embargo logic in the vein of "positive discrimination": we want to be open to all the cultures of the world, *thus* not America's, since it takes up too much room. The *cultural exception*[129]—whatever the legitimacy of the concerns inspiring it—is not a dynamic slogan, and the ecological mindset surrounding it comes straight out of a half century of Maginot strategy in dealing with the United States.

This Maginot defense already seems to have been circumvented. Not by the American enemy, but by the defenders themselves. The cultural exception's combats cannot hide the fact that most of the cultural battles of the last fifteen years have in fact taken place on the adversary's ground. The crusade against Eurodisney's Mickeys was probably the first trip-up: not only because the Francophone protests against the English names of some of the rides took on a completely unreal quality in the face of machinery that was both mentally and technologically so quintessentially American that it is hard to see how transforming "Pirates of the Caribbean" into "Pirates des Caraïbes" could have helped bulwark France against the American "tidal wave of myths"; but above all, because the Disney-style amusement park itself is the archetype of the American mass cultural production a half century of intellectuals had opposed. It would have startled Bernanos or Malraux if they had been asked to sign a petition in favor of the Parc Astérix... Spelling Caribbean in French or slipping a leaf of lettuce into a McDonald's hamburger[130] to satisfy the supposed demands of *la différence française* is nothing more than crumbs; the bun still tastes the same. The mobilization against junk food clearly perpetuates the tradition of French rebellion against the supposed indigence of American gastronomy; but it has increasingly been staged using "American" criteria: dietetic and hygienic ones as much as or more than gustative or convivial ones. Contemporary arguments against ready-to-eat foods are more the result of a Ralph Nader–style enlightened consumerism than a Duhamel shouting his mouth (and taste buds) off, mixing up French nature and nurture in the process. The fact that McDonald's French franchise was able to respond to the hostile campaigns with an advertising countercampaign that played entirely on the anti-Americanism of its readers should be cause for reflection on the tactical error of a cultural defense strategy that has wandered into the wrong blockhouse. The most clearsighted, like José Bové, have said and repeated that their combat is not anti-American, joining Toni Negri, who told globalization's adversaries, "It is totally idiotic to be anti-American."[131] Anti-Americanism can feed into campaigns against junk food and globalization, but will it dissolve into them as inevitably as "McDonald's into a duck breast"—to cite a particularly indigestible title from *Libération*?[132]

Le culturel can also be dissolved into *the cultural*. Cultural anti-Americans who have stormed the little Mickeys and big hamburgers in the name of Astérix and the croque-monsieur look like Charlie Chaplin playing a soldier in the first scene of *The Great Dictator*, where he marches into battle through a thick fog. When the fog clears, Chaplin discovers he's elbow to elbow with the enemy.

Conclusion

"I've lived long enough to see that *difference breeds hatred*," proclaims Julien Sorel in *The Red and the Black*.[1] Stendhal, who is never far off, shows how wrong he is. Things are in fact a little more complicated than that. Difference can breed hatred, but it can also arouse interest, admiration, respect, desire. The qualitative distances separating love, hate, and indifference are what we could learn from a science of degrees, a "bathmology"[2] like the one Barthes dreamed of for the gradations of language. What Fourierist anthropologist will give us a Lavoisier-style table of the favorable combinations and risks of combustion? What sardonic historian or moralist will continue in the vein of André Maurois's remark, "The marriage of a Frenchman to an American woman is that of two spoiled children: an unstable compound,"[3] and propose a cultural computation of incompatibilities of temperament?

Until such a telemetry of cultures exists, we should ask a simple question: how far are the Americans from the French? Both too close and too far. Too close to arouse awed curiosity, as in the fabled days of savage America; and all the charitable souls, from Valéry to Malraux, who insisted on the cultural continuity between Europe and America only made things worse: why take an

interest in a pale copy when you are the glorious original? But also too far to
suggest any emotional or intellectual community. This is what comes out of
the mass of hostile or simply ill-intentioned texts on America written over
the past hundred years and more. This is what is confirmed by the survey of
public opinion opportunely done in the year 1968 when, according to our
anti-Americans, the floodgates of Americanization had been (once more)
reopened. A simple question: "What nation least resembles the French?"
Massively cited: the Americans (43 percent). An honest second—neatly out-
run, though: the English (22 percent). Inexhaustible Anglo-Saxons. . . As for
the Italians and the Germans, the French adopted them; they were part of the
family (8 percent and 7 percent, respectively).[4] Not even similar national
institutions, political and moral values, and material lifestyles can undermine the muted French conviction that the Americans are not "like us." They
represent the greatest imaginable distance short of desirable difference. This
strange certainty has grown stronger with time, through the accumulation of
an ethnic and cultural discourse of prohibitive antagonism.

Refusing Americans the possibility of being "our likeness" was not the
result of any personal experience or memory the subjects might have had: it
was purely the product of the anti-American discourse. One recent episode
confirmed that the discourse is alive and well—the outcry roused by the editor of *Le Monde* at his little sentence, "We are all Americans," after the September 11, 2001, attacks. Jean-Marie Colombani was explicitly alluding to
John F. Kennedy's words to the people of Berlin: "Ich bin ein Berliner."
Through the interplay of the quote and reference, he was clearly placing his
pronouncement in a historical and not essentialist context, choosing solidarity rather than declaring a common background. A wasted effort! The message of solidarity was received in France as an affirmation of shared identity.
Beyond the fact that they were misinterpreting the phrase, French people's
furious reactions testified to their deep horror at the very idea that you could
call yourself "American" and thus annul, even if only at a time of exceptional
crisis, the long work of differentiation between *them* and *us* that had mobilized a good part of France's intellectual energy for over a century.

☆ ☆ ☆

Genealogies can be traced back but not summed up. Now that it is time for
conclusions, we should not turn this into a digest.

French anti-Americanism exists. In France, we have all seen it and sometimes practiced it. No one is free from the national discourse. If, from Baudelaire to Breton, from Maurras to Bernanos, or from Durtain to Baudrillard,
I have dwelled on certain figures, my intent was not to make this into a

gallery of singular passions. In its repetition and perpetuation, French anti-Americanism must be analyzed as a *tradition*. It is a chain thrown across history: through it we are shackled, unbeknownst to ourselves, to a whole past of repugnance and repulsions.

It is the sunken links of this chain we have brought to the surface, here—from the link of the naturalist discourse to the political link of an America judged less democratic than fascist states and more totalitarian than the Soviet regime, passing through the powerful ring of racial typology riveting French anti-Americanism to the ethnicized figure of the Yankee. All the building blocks of this rhetoric were put into place between the end of the nineteenth century and the 1930s. The anti-American discourse then lived largely on its savings and its momentum, redistributing already available sequences (ingratitude, debt), adapting them to fit the circumstances (after 1945, the end of isolationism revived the imperialist America of the 1900s), adjusting them to their targets' changing demands (the defense of the Spirit was secularized into a battle for Culture). All these "folds" of the discourse were made before 1950, and the anti-Americanism of the second half of the twentieth century was not much more than the fall of a partisan curtain.

Throughout our journey, we have seen the *realia*—the competitions, conflicts, and collisions of interest—running alongside the discourses. There is no unequivocal causal link between the reality of facts and the reality of discourses. Between these two spheres is a whole system of uneven echoes. As the anti-American discourse gained increasing semiotic consistency, it began to free itself from its ties to specific events or—which amounts to the same thing—use them as a mere excuse. So we should not look for an artificial correlation between the history of Franco-American relations and the genealogy of the anti-American discourse. The "rule" of equivalency between the change of a political regime in France and the change of public opinion about the United States formulated by certain historians seems difficult to corroborate.[5] The anti-American discourse cannot be decoded without the companion book of a history of Franco-American relations, but it does not mechanically follow the fluctuations of that history.

Intellectuals' part in constituting and transmitting the discourse is eminent but not exclusive. Like all traditions, this one needed to be carried on and upheld by a specialized corps: the sacerdotal corps Nietzsche described as Fiction's agents and whose role we have seen the intelligentsia assume. The regular flow of anti-American books testifies to their assiduous work: what was true in the 1930s was still the case on the eve of the third millennium.

But the intellectuals' greatest success was the wide spread of their discourse. The French public gradually adopted the polemical argumentation

and the negative stereotyping produced by the intelligentsia. That they would
be roped in was not a given. Even now, anti-Americanism remains less
secure in the country's popular strata than with intellectuals. It is the execu-
tive class and the well educated who show the highest rate of anti-American
reactions. But the essential lesson of recent statistical studies is the increasingly clear homogenization of these reactions: age, milieu, and profession
are now only marginal issues. Only the left-wing political stance continues to
generate anti-American scores consistently superior to those of the Right,
though not by a wide margin.[6] Less virulent in its formulations (but this
slackening off is not specific to it: polemics have grown a lot less strident in
France since the beginning of the twentieth century), the anti-American discourse is more widespread and commonly shared than ever. The homogenization of its presence throughout French society crowns the intellectuals'
unified effort to foist it onto the whole of the domestic symbolic marketplace.

We have already said in the introduction that nothing seemed to point to a
drop or a decline in French anti-Americanism. Comparative polls taken during George W. Bush's European trip in May 2002, even before the French-
American diplomatic crisis began, confirmed that France was still on the top
step of the hostility podium. Another poll, conducted by the Pew Research
Center for the People and the Press in Washington in the fall of 2002, when
the Bush administration's intent to go to war with Iraq had become clear, is
even more enlightening: this particular poll, a worldwide survey of the United
States' image, showed a dramatic deterioration of that image in all countries
(except Russia); the decline in support and sympathy was especially spectacular in those European countries that had been America's closest allies and
friends since 1945, such as Great Britain and Germany; the most significant
figure, though, was France's: despite the French-American face-off at the
United Nations and massive French opposition to a preemptive war in Iraq,
negative perception of the United States had not increased in France: it remained excactly at the same (high) level as before the crisis. (Indeed, it even
dropped from 63 to 62 percent, but a variation of one percentage point is considered insignificant in such polls.) The aforementioned Pew Research Center survey was made public two months after the present book appeared in its
French version: I could hardly have dreamed of a better confirmation for this
book's central point, namely, that in the course of its long history French anti-
Americanism had acquired a wide margin of autonomy; that it was largely
self-sustaining and self-sufficient; that, in any case, it did not depend on particular events, damaging as they may be for Franco-American relations, to

seriously widen the gap—just as, conversely, it would take much more than the French government's good political intentions or a new president of the United States to significantly reduce it.

Is French Anti-Americanism eternal, then, or should we believe those who have been foretelling its demise? Before closing our long inquiry, we should look at the two different scenarios proposing the view that the end of French anti-Americanism is imminent or underway.

The first scenario of French anti-Americanism's extinction is sociological in nature. The days are over, we are told, when there were glaring disparities between the two countries in terms of standard of living, comfort, and income: all the acrimony of the 1950s linked to the envy aroused by the American way of life is through, and anti-Americanism has thus lost indispensable fodder. Furthermore, the massive adoption of American clothes, food, and culture by young people can only lead to the recession of hostility for a country whose products are consumed and whose culture is adopted, at least in part. The first mistake here is that the importance of material envy in creating the anti-American discourse is being overestimated: France's resentment and sense of rivalry have always operated at a deeper, more symbolic level, though they were sometimes fueled (in the post–World War II period, for instance) by more material frustrations. The second mistake is thinking that there is a correlation between consumer choices and cultural acceptance. On the contrary, all signs point to the fact that people can adopt a certain number of reputedly American products and tastes without changing their attitude toward America. A *Libération*-CSA poll from 1999 leaves little doubt in this respect. For 55 percent of those polled in the age group of eighteen to twenty-four years—the age group with the highest consumption of American products, especially cultural ones—America's cultural influence was seen as "too pronounced." Their parents, appropriately, were even more critical (67 percent of those thirty-five to forty-nine years old), but "the gap is not that wide, and since we cannot believe that this generation is sold on strictly domestic cultural consumerism, it is most likely something else that is being expressed through this resistance."[7] We could have suspected it, and this study confirms it: consumption is not adhesion. This was more harshly formulated by an on-site observer: "Wearing Nikes doesn't stop you from wanting to screw America."[8]

The second "exit scenario" gladly put forward by anti-Americans themselves essentially consists in saying: Of course we use the word "America"; of course we still talk about the United States and say a lot of bad things about it. But in fact, we know—and you, reader, do too—that those words have a different meaning nowadays. They no longer denote a territory or a people, but rather a certain "being-in-the-world" that has become planetary. Régis Debray, who willingly calls himself an "anti-American" in quotes, also puts quotes around his America, which he calls "America for export": "The Americanism I am opposed to, and which is not America any more than totalitarianism was Russia, I would define as a simplification of our time—which explains its force." So, Debray adds, we can call *Homo americanus* the man targeted by the mass media, "as long as we are aware that this bogeyman sleeps within each of us."[9] Why not, after all? The French reader will lend himself all the more readily to these mental acrobatics because he has been being trained for them since the 1930s by a whole anti-American tradition. "America—it should be called the Yankee country instead, to clearly show that on the map its borders could not be found," Robert Aron and Dandieu had already written; for them, as for Debray, America was "a way of life, or of saying 'no' to life," a "spiritual illness" spread over the entire world.[10] And when, two generations later, Debray adds, addressing the Americans, "since the spirit of empire is nowhere more fierce than in the colonies, I even believe that we are much more Americanized than you are,"[11] the echo of Georges Duhamel can be heard: "I have seen the strangest 'Americanisms' in Germany," in Frankfurt, in Berlin, in the heart of the Old Europe, which "the American spirit [is] coloniz[ing]" and engulfing in its "new empire."[12] It has been almost fourscore years that French anti-Americanism has been painting America Magritte-style, with the caption: *Ceci n'est pas l'Amérique.* But if the merchandise does not correspond to the label, wouldn't it be easier to change the label, rather than multiplying the explanatory notes?

We can still foresee happy days for French anti-Americanism. Under Napoleon III there was the story of a naval officer who, when he was told that there was a shortage of combustibles for his ship's furnaces, superbly replied: "Heat them with the soldiers' enthusiasm!" French anti-Americanism is the furnace this idealist was dreaming of: no need to feed it with the fires of history; the intellectuals' enthusiasm is enough to keep the pressure up. They have shown no signs of slackening. Wouldn't it be dangerous, even, if they suddenly left the hold and let the furnace go to hell in a handbasket?

If, vaporized with benevolence by Professor Golbert's "psychic accumulator," the intellectuals of France suddenly folded up the banner of their crusade, French anti-Americanism would get a change of personality, not intensity. The horrifying success of Thierry Meyssan's book *L'Effroyable imposture: Aucun avion ne s'est écrasé sur le Pentagone* (The Horrifying Imposture: No Plane Crashed into the Pentagon), whose title sums up its absurdity, gives an indication of what French anti-Americanism would become if it were deprived of its historical "guides."[13] And perhaps, after having pilloried them for their role in creating the anti-American Golem, we should beg the intellectuals of France not to leave their irritable watch on the outposts of the west. Because the most worrisome development, perhaps, would be if—tired, weary, repentant, or simply feeling frivolous—they left the Fiction without a pilot.

As for the discourse itself, we should have no fears for its continued health. Its propensity to self-procreate immunizes it against jolts of reality: the post–September 11 period gave a striking and rather depressing demonstration of this. But it could also be that this type of discourse is particularly well suited to our day and age. In the introduction to this book, we proposed a conservative definition of anti-Americanism as a *discourse*. Can we fine-tune that modest proposal at the end of our journey?

Anti-Americanism shares several features with modernity's "great legends," notably its unifying force and its allegorical capacities—since by talking about America it never stopped talking about France.[14] With, however, one considerable difference: the metadiscourses of legitimization are organized around purely positive nodes—emancipating the citizen, fulfilling the spirit, a classless society, and so on. The "great legends" are dead, outdated by postmodernity's inherent "incredulousness."[15] As for anti-Americanism, it has spread and prospered: a convex "great legend," it remains operational while the metadiscourses of good have lost all their effectiveness, all their powers of coalescence in the social imagination. Which is all the more reason for taking it seriously: this anti-legend, beyond its particular history, perhaps captures the profile of the negative syntheses now at work throughout Europe, which has become the charnel house of universalist legends.

☆ ☆ ☆

"The nation which indulges toward another an habitual hatred or an habitual fondness is in some degree a slave. It is a slave to its animosity or to its affection." This aphorism, drawn from Washington's 1796 farewell address, which we put at the head of this book, offers the same logical structure as a famous pronouncement by Marx: "A nation that oppresses another cannot be free." And what if anti-Americanism were now nothing but a mental enslavement inflicted by the French on themselves—a masochistic laziness, a routine of resentment, a passionless Pavlovianism? Then there would be reason for hope. There are few vices, even intellectual ones, that can withstand for very long the boredom they elicit.

I am not so bold as to think these pages might hasten its demise; but if it should last, this genealogy will not have been useless: after all, even anti-Americanism should be enlightened.

Notes

Introduction

1. Michel Winock, interview with Marion Van Renterghem, *Le Monde*, November 25–26, 2001.

2. These examples are taken from a collective work edited at the time by Denis Lacorne, Jacques Rupnik and Marie-France Toinet, *The Rise and Fall of Anti-Americanism: A Century of French Perception*, trans. Gerry Turner (New York: St. Martin's Press, 1990) (*L'Amérique dans les têtes: Un siècle de fascinations et d'aversions* [Paris: Hachette, 1986]), which remains a solid work on the topic. See, respectively, the introduction by Lacorne and Rupnik, "France Bewitched by America" (1–27), and Diana Pinto's contribution, "The French Intelligentsia Rediscovers America" (97–107) ["La conversion de l'intelligentsia" in the original 1986 version].

3. The word is used by André Kaspi, whose text concludes *The Rise and Fall*, and who noted in 1999 that the presumed death of anti-Americanism as described at the time by several participants was premature (*Mal connus, mal aimés, mal compris: Les États-Unis aujourd'hui* [Paris: Plon, 1999], 31).

4. *Libération*, April 10 and 11, 1999.

5. Jean-Paul Sartre, "A Letter from M. Sartre" [November 18, 1946], *New York Herald Tribune* (November 20, 1946): 2, quoted in *The Writings of Jean-Paul Sartre*, ed. Michel Contat and Michel Rybalka, trans. Richard C. McCleary, 2 vols. (Evanston, Ill.: Northwestern University Press, 1974), 1:139. Sartre is responding to critics who accused him of presenting an unflattering image of (white) America in *The Respectful Prostitute*.

6. Serge Halimi, "Un mot de trop" and "Les 'philo-américains' saisis par la rage" (Rabid "Philo-Americans"), *Le Monde diplomatique* (May 2000): 10; the first title can be translated "A Superfluous Word," but also conveys the notion that the word should be gotten rid of; the second title is an allusion to Sartre's notorious article protesting against the Rosenberg executions, "Rabid Animals." The rabid philo-Americans in question are, in order, Michel Wieviorka, Alain Richard (then secretary of defense), François Furet (posthumously), Bernard-Henri Lévy, Pascal Bruckner, Jean-François Revel, and Guy Sorman.

7. Toinet, "Does Anti-Americanism Exist?" in *The Rise and Fall*, 219.

8. David Strauss, *Menace in the West: The Rise of Anti-Americanism in Modern Times* (Westport, Conn.: Greenwood Press, 1978), 6. My italics. Strauss defines "Americanism" as "a set of values, practices, and institutions which had their origin in the United States and were far more permanent than official policies." American anti-Americans, furthermore, have consistently used the American tradition itself to support their arguments against Americanism and to attack its official versions.

9. Sartre was the only person to truly make an effort to give "Americanism" a non-projective meaning. He saw it as the key to the socialization of the American psyche, and the chief mechanism by which the collectivity coerces the individual in the United States. "Am I American enough?" is the question America (op)presses each American with, the "neighbor's gaze" being the normalizing agent in a society obsessed with conformity. For Sartre, *Americanism* is thus a strictly American affair—as well as a typically Sartrian phenomenon.

10. At the same time, in the Communist press, *Americanism* became a vague term of reproach. An extreme example, from *La Nouvelle Critique* 3 (February 1949): 15: "French writers [who] stoop to passing their creations off as translations from the American" are accused of parroting "Americanism at its most vile."

11. "An ideal polygon with multiple sides: endless, unregulated consumerism; universal merchandise and a belief in the neutrality of technology; citizens transformed into consumers; a deaf ear to tragedy; a confusion of the public and the private; the cult of success and money; the forced reduction of human life to a set of principal activities, etc., etc." Régis Debray, *Contretemps: Eloges des idéaux perdus* (Paris: Gallimard, 1992), 103. Debray's innovation is his perfect awareness of the stereotypical nature of the anti-Americanism he espouses.

12. In an article in *Esprit* lambasting "a new anti-Americanism that has shown itself, in its arguments as much as in its vocabulary, worthy of that of '42–'44": Chris Marker, *Esprit* 7 (July 1948), quoted in Pierre Enckell, *Datations et documents lexicographiques*, 2nd ser., no. 20 (1982). Even *La Nouvelle Critique*, the intellectual monthly of the French Communist Party, uses it—true, in quotes: "a man so blameless of 'anti-Americanism' as Mr. Étienne Gilson." *La Nouvelle Critique* 12 (January 1950).

13. Reinhart Koselleck, *Futures Past: On the Semantics of Historical Time*, trans. Keith Tribe (Cambridge, Mass.: MIT Press, 1985), 88.

14. Toinet suggests in the previously cited article (n. 8) that the word "anti-Americanism" has been "in use since the 19th century"; unfortunately, she doesn't provide any specific references. I personally have not come across it in any work written between 1860 and 1900, which, considering the thousands of anti-American pages I have read, would point at the very least to its extreme rarity.

15. Paul Claudel, *Journal*, January 18, 1933, Bibliothèque de la Pléiade, 2 vols. (Paris: Gallimard, 1969), 2:5.

16. Alexander Hamilton, *Federalist* no. 11, November 23, 1787, ed. E. M. Earle (New York, 1941), 69. The footnote indicates: "Recherches philosophiques sur les Américains."

17. Jean Baechler, *Qu'est-ce que l'idéologie?* (Paris: Idées-Gallimard, 1976), 60.

18. A topic well explored by Raymonde Carroll in her book *Cultural Misunderstandings: The French-American Experience*, trans. Carol Volk (Chicago: University of Chicago Press, 1988) (*Evidences invisibles: Américains et Français au quotidien* [Paris: Seuil, 1987]).

19. See Jean-Noël Jeanneney, ed., *Une Idée fausse est un fait vrai: Les stéréotypes nationaux en Europe* (Paris: Odile Jacob, 2000).

20. Roland Barthes, *Leçon* (Paris: Seuil, 1978), 33; *Oeuvres complètes*, ed. Eric Marty (Paris: Seuil, 1994), 3:809.

Prologue

1. Antonello Gerbi, *The Dispute of the New World: The History of a Polemic, 1750–1900*, trans. Jeremy Moyle (Pittsburgh: University of Pittsburgh Press, 1973) (*La Disputa del Nuovo Mondo: Storia di una polemica, 1750–1900* [Milan: Riccardo Ricciardi, 1955]). A historian of ideas and disciple of Croce, Gerbi left Fascist Italy for Latin America and used successive editions (Spanish, English, and Italian) of his work to compile a considerable body of material on the "dispute." It has never been published in France, however. Recently, James W. Ceaser interestingly prolonged the history of this "dispute of the New World," showing how a nineteenth-century "naturalist" legacy that grew into the "racial sciences" diverged from the tradition of political science *stricto sensu*. See his *Reconstructing America: The Symbol of America in Modern Thought* (New Haven: Yale University Press, 1997).

2. Jean-Baptiste Delisle de Sales, *De la philosophie de la nature*, 6 vols. (1770–74; London, 1777), 4:247.

3. Voltaire, *Essai sur les moeurs* (Paris: Classiques Garnier-Bordas, 1990), 2:340.

4. Cornelius De Pauw, *Recherches philosophiques sur les Américains ou mémoires intéressans pour servir à l'histoire de l'espèce humaine*, 2 vols. (1768; Paris: Jean-Michel Place, 1990 [a facsimile of the 1774 Berlin edition]), 2:191. A short, much-abridged version of De Pauw's work (including his writings on China and Egypt) was published in English in 1806 as *A General History of the Americans, of their Customs, Manners, and Colours: An History of the Patagonians, of the Blafards and White Negroes; History of Peru; An History of the Manners, Customs, &c. of the Chinese and Egyptions, Selected from M. Pauw*, by Daniel Webb (Rochdale: T. Wood, 1806).

5. De Pauw, *Recherches*, 2:137.

6. Durand Echeverria, *Mirage in the West: A History of the French Image of American Society to 1815* (Princeton, N.J.: Princeton University Press, 1957), 15.

7. De Pauw, *Recherches*, 1:v.

8. Guillaume Thomas Raynal, *Histoire philosophique et politique des établissements et du commerce des Européens dans les deux Indes*, 10 vols. (Geneva, 1781), 9:133.

9. An argument found, for example, in Samuel Engel, *Essai sur cette question: Quand et comment l'Amérique a-t-elle été peuplée d'hommes et d'animaux?* (Essay on This Question: When and How Was America Peopled with Men and Animals?) (Amsterdam, 1767).

10. De Pauw, *Recherches*, 2:303.

11. The first Spanish and Portuguese accounts introduced the topos of ubiquitous water. From then on, America's climatic anomalies were interpreted as deleterious to the men who lived there. A quote attributed to Queen Isabella would become almost mythic

over the centuries: "This land, where the trees are not firmly rooted, must produce men of little truthfulness and less constancy." Quoted in Gerbi, 40.

12. Georges Louis Leclerc, Comte de Buffon, *Variétés dans l'espèce humaine* [1749], in *Oeuvres complètes* (Paris: Imprimerie et Librairie Générale de France, 1859), 5:441.

13. De Pauw, *Recherches*, 1:3.

14. Ibid., 1:2.

15. Voltaire, *Essai sur les moeurs*, 2:340.

16. Thomas Jefferson, *Notes on the State of Virginia*, ed. Frank Shuffleton (London: Penguin Classics, 1999), 68.

17. Jefferson to the Marquis de Chastellux, June 7, 1785, in *Notes*, 267.

18. Ibid., 308, n. 111.

19. Buffon, *Dégénération des animaux* [1766], in *Oeuvres complètes*, 8:240.

20. Ibid., *Dégénération*, 8:241.

21. Buffon, *Variétés*, 5:451.

22. Buffon, *Dégénération*, 8:219.

23. They supposed right from square one that there was already an established analogical relationship between the two sets of fauna, one that allowed the naturalist to move on to particular comparisons in light of the place occupied on each table by whatever animal fit in ("the first in size," etc.). The specific comparisons (the llama to the sheep) are disappointing, given that they are analogical only in certain points of detail. Their goal was not to open the door to new discoveries about these animals, but rather to legitimize the first operation: matching up the two tables.

24. Buffon, *Variétés*, 5:241.

25. Buffon, *Dégénération*, 8:217.

26. Ibid., 8:218.

27. Ibid., 8:219.

28. Ibid., 8:217.

29. De Pauw, *Défense des "Recherches philosophiques sur les Américains," par Mr. de P**** [1770], in *Recherches*, 2:205.

30. De Pauw, *Recherches*, 1:188.

31. De Pauw, *Défense*, 2:320.

32. The first Indian-themed play staged at the Comédie française seems to have been *La Jeune Indienne* in 1764. It was also Chamfort's first success, at the age of twenty-four.

33. De Pauw, *Recherches*, 1:3.

34. Ibid., 1:4.

35. Ibid., 1:4.

36. Ibid., 1:19.

37. Ibid., 1:31.

38. Ibid., 1:20.

39. Ibid., 1:4–5.

40. The anti-Americans contradicted Fathers Lafitau—author of *Moeurs des Sauvages Américains comparées aux moeurs des Premiers Temps* (1724) (*Customs of the American Indians Compared with the Customs of Primitive Times*, trans. and ed. William N. Fenton and

Elizabeth L. Moore [Toronto: Champlain Society, 1974–77])—Buffier, and Charlevoix, who compared the Indians to the patriarchs in his *Journal historique:* "I then recalled those ancient Patriarchs, who had no dwellings and lived under tents." *Histoire et description générale de la Nouvelle France: Avec le Journal historique d'un Voyage fait par ordre du roi dans l'Amérique septentrionale* (Paris: Vve Ganeau, 1744–46), 6:254.

41. De Pauw, *Défense*, 2:108.

42. Ibid., 2:109.

43. Ibid., 2:160. De Pauw was sketching a portrait of the natives of California here but added that it was "consistent with the one we have given of all the Americans."

44. See Michel Delon, "Du goût antiphysique des Américains" (On the Americans' Anti-Physical Tastes), *Annales de Bretagne* 2 (1977): 317–28.

45. De Pauw, *Défense*, 2:145.

46. De Pauw, *Recherches*, 1:51.

47. Ibid., 1:354, 1:352.

48. De Pauw, *Défense*, 2:53.

49. Peter Kalm's *Travels into North America* was published in Swedish between 1753 and 1761 (*En resa til Norra America: På Kongl. swenska wetenskaps academiens befallning, och publici kostnad, förrättad af Pehr Kalm* [Stockholm: Tryckt på L. Salvii kostnad, 1753–61]); it was partially translated into French in 1761 and "adapted" under the pen name Rousselot de Surgy and the title *Histoire naturelle & politique de la Pensilvanie* (Paris, 1768); cited in De Pauw, *Défense*, 2:136.

50. De Pauw, *Défense*, 2:206, 2:145.

51. Ibid., 2:118.

52. Raynal, *Histoire philosophique*, 6:376.

53. William Robertson, *History of America*, 2 vols. (London: W. Strahan, 1777), 1:398.

54. De Pauw, *Recherches*, 1:20, 1:91.

55. Raynal, "De quelles espèces d'hommes se sont peuplées les provinces de l'Amérique septentrionale" (On What Species of Men Peopled the Provinces of Northern America), chap. 32 in *Histoire philosophique*, 4:353.

56. De Pauw, *Défense*, 2:250.

57. Raynal, *Histoire philosophique*, 4:459. Same text in the Geneva in 12° edition of 1781.

58. John Adams to Mazzei, December 15, 1785, quoted in Echeverria, *Mirage*, 123.

59. The third American "genius," according to Jefferson, was David Rittenhouse (1732–1796), an astronomer and mathematician who invented and built numerous measuring devices. He held different government positions and was the first head of the American mint. He succeeded his friend Franklin as the head of the American Philosophical Society.

60. Jefferson, 51; the answer to the sixth query ("Query VI") includes a refutation of Buffon.

61. "Living nature is much less active, much less strong." Buffon, from the Paris edition of 1764 (18:122), quoted in Jefferson (48).

Chapter One

1. Gérard de Nerval, *Promenades et souvenirs* (Rambles and Recollections) in *Oeuvres*, 2 vols., Bibliothèque de la Pléiade (Paris: Gallimard, 1974), 1:136.

2. See René Rémond, *Les États-Unis devant l'opinion française, 1815–1852* (Paris: Armand Colin, 1962). "La Distance et l'éloignement" is the title of the first chapter.

3. [Named after their founder, Claude-Henri, comte de Saint-Simon (1760–1825), the Saint-Simonians believed in a state-run rationalized economy combining industrial efficiency with a welfare-style sharing of wealth.]

4. See, on the topic, Rémond, 60, as well as A. S. Tillet, "Some Saint-Simonian Criticism of the United States before 1835," *Romanic Review* 52 (February 1, 1961): 3–16.

5. Stendhal, *The Charterhouse of Parma*, trans. Richard Howard (New York: Modern Library, 1999), 426.

6. Quoted in Georges Lacour-Gayet, *Talleyrand* (Paris, 1928), 1:199.

7. The crisis concerned indemnities for damage to the American merchant navy under the empire; see chapter 10 of the present work.

8. Constantin-François Chasseboeuf, Comte de Volney, *Tableau du climat et du sol des États-Unis* [1803], in *Oeuvres* (Paris: Fayard, 1989), 2:37. Volney had become a celebrity with his meditative travel book *Les Ruines* (1791).

9. [Henri] G[iraud], *Beautés de l'histoire d'Amérique d'après les plus célèbres voyageurs* (Beauties of America's History According to the Most Famous Travelers) (Paris, 1816), 186, quoted in Rémond, 1:258.

10. Ibid.

11. On the negative image of Jackson in France, see Rémond, 1:359–60. With the crisis of 1834–36, he became "synonymous with the demagogue, dictator, or rabble-rouser" and personified "the Yankee's juvenile self-importance, greed, and brutality."

12. François La Rochefoucauld-Liancourt, *Journal de voyage en Amérique et d'un séjour à Philadelphie* (Paris: Droz, 1940), 62. The entry is dated November 27, 1794; La Rochefoucauld-Liancourt had arrived the previous month.

13. Jacques-Pierre Brissot de Warville, *Nouveau voyage dans les États-Unis de l'Amérique septentrionale fait en 1788* (Paris: Buisson, 1791), 1:139.

14. [The first legislative body of the French Revolution.]

15. Echeverria, 190.

16. La Rochefoucauld-Liancourt, 68.

17. Ibid., 73.

18. Talleyrand to Lord Lansdowne, Februrary 1, 1795, in *Correspondance diplomatique: La mission de Talleyrand à Londres; ses Lettres d'Amérique à Lord Lansdowne* (Paris: Plon, 1889), 424. This long letter introduces the argument Talleyrand would expand on in a paper read before the Institute in 1799.

19. Talleyrand, "Mémoire sur les relations commerciales des États-Unis avec l'Angleterre," *Recueil des mémoires de l'Institut, classe des sciences morales et politiques* 2 (Year VII).

20. The myth of the Quaker started showing some cracks at the end of the century. In 1793, *Allons ça va, ou le Quaker en France*, by Beffroi de Reigny—a very popular author during the Revolution, under the pen name Cousin Jacques—portrayed an American Quaker who, disgruntled with the growing corruption of his homeland, joins in the French Revolution.

21. Volney, 23.

22. Ibid.

23. Raynal, 4:451.

24. Volney, 22.

25. Ibid., 29.

26. Ibid., 25.

27. Ibid., 27.

28. Ibid., 28–29.

29. See Gerbi, 417–41, and, on Hegel's "error to the second degree," 438.

30. Volney, 2:31.

31. Joseph de Maistre, *Considerations on France*, trans. and ed. Richard A. Lebrun (Cambridge: Cambridge University Press, 1994), 32–33.

32. Ibid., 61.

33. Ibid., 61.

34. De Maistre, *St. Petersburg Dialogues, or Conversations on the Temporal Government of Providence*, trans. and ed. Richard A. Lebrun (Montreal: McGill–Queen's University Press, 1993), 34.

35. E. M. Cioran, *Essai sur la pensée réctionnaire: À propos de Joseph de Maistre* (Montpellier: Fata Morgana, 1977), 33.

36. "The savages of America are not completely *men* precisely because they are *savages;* moreover, they are visibly degraded beings, physically and morally. On this point, at least, I do not see that anyone has answered the ingenious author of the *Recherches philosophiques sur les Américains.*" De Maistre, *On the Sovereignty of the People*, in *Against Rousseau*, trans. Richard A. Lebrun (Montreal: McGill–Queen's University Press, 1996), 135–36.

37. De Maistre, *St. Petersburg Dialogues*, 45. [Translation modified.]

38. Ibid.

39. Ibid., 46. [Translation modified.]

40. François-Auguste-René de Chateaubriand, *Atala*, in *Atala, René*, trans. Irving Putter (Berkeley and Los Angeles: University of California Press, 1980), 18.

41. Chateaubriand, author's preface to *The Natchez: An Indian Tale* (London: Henry Colburn, 1827), 15.

42. Thomas Hamilton, *Men and Manners in America*, 2:169, quoted in Gerbi, 472–73, n. 111.

43. Quoted in Gerbi, ibid. Harriet Martineau was the author of, among other works, *Society in America* (1837) and *Retrospect of Western Travel* (1838). She spent two years in the United States between 1834 and 1836. A reformer and abolitionist, she criticized Frances Trollope's work for its excessive hostility.

44. Frances Trollope, *Domestic Manners of the Americans*, ed. Pamela Neville-Sington (New York: Penguin Books, 1997), 314.

45. Ibid., 138.

46. Ibid., 37.

47. Ibid., 40.

48. Ibid., 241. Mrs. Trollope gives the quote in its original French; the editor, Pamela Neville-Sington, offers the translation, "Sire, those are downright swine and proud with it." 241 n.

49. On Stendhal's annotations, see René Louis Doyon, "Stendhal. Notes sur l'Angleterre et l'Amérique," *Table ronde* 72 (December 1953): 25.

50. Stendhal, *The Red and the Black,* trans. Catherine Slater (Oxford: Oxford University Press, 1991), 3, 6.

51. Stendhal, *Charterhouse,* 116–17.

52. Stendhal, *Lucien Leuwen,* trans. H. L. R. Edwards, ed. Robin Buss (London: Penguin Books, 1991), 79–80.

53. André Maurois, *En Amérique* (Paris: Flammarion, 1933), 93–94.

54. The passage concludes: "—There!—I write the words with reluctance, disappointment and sorrow; but I believe it from the bottom of my soul." Letter to John Forster, February 24, 1842, in *The Letters of Charles Dickens,* ed. M. House, G. Storey, and K. Tillotson (Oxford: Clarendon Press, 1974), 3:81–82.

55. Alexis de Tocqueville, *Democracy in America,* trans. George Lawrence, 2 vols. (London: Collins, 1966), 1:315.

56. "In the long list of the *rights of man* which the wisdom of the 19th century keeps increasing so often and so complacently, two rather important ones have been forgotten, the right to contradict oneself and the right to *take one's leave.*" Charles Baudelaire, *On Poe: Critical Papers,* trans. and ed. Lois and Francis E. Hyslop, Jr. (State College, Pa.: Bald Eagle Press, 1952), 103. Baudelaire is commenting on Poe's suicidal drinking.

57. Victorien Sardou, *L'Oncle Sam,* a comedy staged at the Théâtre du Vaudeville; premiered on November 6, 1873. Act 2, scene 3. We will come back to *L'Oncle Sam* in chapter 3.

58. Tocqueville, 2:557.

59. Tocqueville, 1:459. "I therefore think it certain that if some part of the Union wished to separate from the rest, not only would it be able to do so, but there would be no one to prevent this"; after which, several pages expand on the notion that "therefore the Americans have an immense interest in remaining united" (1:460) and that there is no conflict of interest serious enough to create a split: "I can see plainly enough that the different parts of the Union have different interests, but I cannot discover any interests in which they are opposed to one another" (1:461). Only excessive territorial expansion could create centrifugal risks in the long run, he wrote.

60. Frédéric Gaillardet, *L'Aristocratie en Amérique* (Paris: Dentu, 1883), 7.

61. Tocqueville, 1:316, n. 2.

62. Philarète Chasles, *Etudes sur la littérature et les moeurs des Anglo-Américains au XIXe siècle* (Studies on the Literature and Manners of the Anglo-Americans in the Nineteenth Century) (Paris: Amyot, 1851), 1.

63. Ibid., 507.

64. Paul de Rousiers, *American Life,* trans. A. J. Herbertson (New York: Firmin-Didot, 1892), 335.

65. Françoise Mélonio, introductions, in Tocqueville, *De la démocratie en Amérique,* ed. Jean-Claude Lamberti and Françoise Mélonio, Collection Bouquins (Paris: Robert Laffont, 1986) 9, 397.

66. Ibid., 9.

67. Rousiers, *American Life,* 335.

68. Paul Bourget, *Outre-mer: Notes sur l'Amérique* (Paris: Alphonse Lemerre, 1895), ii.

69. James Bryce, a law professor at Oxford, had published *The American Commonwealth* to great success in 1888 (London: Macmillan); the book was reprinted in 1890 and

1903; the French translation, *La République américaine,* was published in 1900 and 1902 (Paris: Giard et Brière, 4 vols.).

70. Emile Boutmy, *Eléments d'une psychologie politique du peuple américain* (1902; Paris: Armand Colin, 1911), 3, 5, 7.

71. Ibid., 289. The exact quote does not appear in Tocqueville's work; presumably Boutmy was transcribing in his own words a famous passage from chapter 7 of the first *Democracy:* "Princes made violence a physical thing, but our contemporary democratic republics have turned it into something as intellectual as the human will it is intended to constrain." Tocqueville, 1:315.

72. Tocqueville, 1:17.

73. Ibid., respectively: 1:307, 1:255, 1:270–71, 1:246, 1:272, 1:372, 1:316–17, 1:299, 2:795, 2:692.

74. Ibid., 1:292 and 1:316.

75. Ibid., 1:315.

76. The expression Baudelaire would borrow and apply to America was used by Joseph de Maistre against Locke, who for him embodied the false philosophy of the Enlightenment. De Maistre attacked the vulgarity of his tone: "I hope, Locke said, that the reader who buys my book will not wish for his money back. What a commercial smell!" (*St. Petersburg Dialogues,* 165. [Translation modified.]) De Maistre was paraphrasing Locke, who had written in his *Essay Concerning Human Understanding* ("Epistle to the Reader"), "Thou wilt as little think thy money, as I do my pains, ill bestowed." De Maistre had read the edition published by Becroft, Straham, London, 1755.

77. Baudelaire to Edouard Dentu, February 18, 1866, quoted in *Fusées; Mon coeur mis à nu; La Belgique déshabillée,* ed. André Guyaux (Paris: Gallimard, 1986), 629, n. 5. (Baudelaire's emphasis.)

78. Baudelaire, *La Belgique déshabillée,* frag. 352, in ibid., 293.

79. Baudelaire, "Hygiène, conduite, méthode, morale," frag. 93, in ibid., 128.

80. Baudelaire, "Poe, His Life and Works: 1852," in *Baudelaire on Poe,* 67.

81. Baudelaire, "Original Dedication to Mrs. Clemm," in *On Poe,* 163.

82. Baudelaire, "Poe, His Life and Works: 1856," in ibid., 93.

83. Baudelaire, "Poe, His Life and Works: 1852," 38–39.

84. Ibid., 63.

85. Ibid., 66.

86. Ibid., 53.

87. Ibid., 61.

88. Baudelaire, "Poe, His Life and Works: 1856," 102. Baudelaire's allusion is aimed at an article by Veuillot.

89. Baudelaire, "New Notes on Edgar Poe: 1857," in ibid., 123.

90. Baudelaire, "Poe, His Life and Works: 1852," 40. (Baudelaire's emphasis.)

91. Baudelaire, *Intimate Journals,* trans. Christopher Isherwood (New York: Random House, 1930), 51–55.

92. See André Guyaux, preface, in *Fusées,* 15, n. 18.

93. Baudelaire, "Philosophic Art," in *The Painter of Modern Life and Other Essays,* trans. and ed. Jonathan Mayne (London: Phaidon Press, 1964), 209.

94. Guyaux, preface, *Fusées,* 16.

95. Friedrich Nietzsche to Peter Gast, February 26, 1888, in *Selected Letters*, trans. A. N. Ludovici, ed. O. Levy (London: Soho Books, 1985), 221.

96. Baudelaire, "The Exposition Universelle, 1855," in *The Mirror of Art: Critical Studies*, trans. and ed. Jonathan Mayne (London: Phaidon Press, 1955), 196.

Chapter Two

1. Charles Grayson Summersell, *CSS Alabama: Builder, Captain and Plans* (Montgomery: University of Alabama Press, n.d.).

2. Edouard Manet, *The Battle of the Kearsarge and the Alabama* [1864], oil on canvas, 53 in. × 50 in. (Philadelphia: John G. Johnson Collection).

3. See, in *Manet* (Paris and New York: Editions de la RMN, 1983 [catalog of the Grand Palais exhibition]), Françoise Cachin's text, 218–21.

4. Jules Barbey d'Aurevilly, "Un ignorant au Salon" (An Ignorant at the Salon), *Le Gaulois*, July 3, 1872, quoted in Cachin, 219.

5. Cham, "Le Salon pour rire" (Laughing at the Salon), *Le Charivari*, 1872, quoted in Cachin, 219.

6. Stop, *Le Journal amusant*, May 23, 1872, quoted in Cachin, 219.

7. Manet apparently installed *The Battle of the Kearsarge and the Alabama* in the window of Giroux's department store, alongside "knickknacks, paintings, and fans"—right where *Nana* would be displayed thirteen years later after being refused by the Salon. On this topic, see Oskar Batschmann, "Transformations dans la peinture religieuse," in *Mort de Dieu, fin de l'art*, ed. Daniel Payot (Paris: Cerf, CERIT, 1991), 61, n. 7; as well as Anne Coffin Hanson, *Manet and the Modern Tradition* (New Haven: Yale University Press, 1977), 111. The painting was shown again at the Salon of 1872 before being sold in New York in 1888.

8. Warren Reed West, *Contemporary French Opinion on the Civil War* (Baltimore: Johns Hopkins University Press, 1924), 9.

9. [At the Battle of Sadowa in Bohemia, the Prussian army defeated the Austrians, paving the way for German unification under Prussian leadership.]

10. [The unforeseen defeat of Napoleon III's armies at the hands of the Prussians.]

11. Sainte-Beuve, quoted in André Billy, *Sainte-Beuve: Sa vie et son temps*, 2 vols. (Paris: Flammarion, 1952), 2:63–64.

12. Editorial, *Le Constitutionnel*, December 26, 1860. Founded by Edouard Alletz on January 1, 1849, and edited by Alphonse de Lamartine in 1850, *Le Constitutionnel* then moved into the government's camp.

13. Editorial, *Le Pays*, November 22, 1860.

14. Editorial, *Le Pays*, December 29, 1860.

15. Editorial, *Le Pays*, December 21, 1860.

16. Confidential note from Napoleon III to General Forey, quoted in Paul Gaulot, *La Vérité sur l'expédition du Mexique*, 2 vols. (Paris: Ollendorff, 1889), 1:92.

17. On November 10, France transmitted an official proposal to the Foreign Office for a three-country movement, with Russia, to obtain a six-month cease-fire from the belligerents.

18. John Bigelow, *Retrospections of an Active Life* (New York: Baker & Taylor, 1909), 1:385.

19. Ibid., 252.

20. Eugène Chatard, *La Presse*, June 24, 1863.

21. See West, chapter 8, "From Gettysburg to the Close of the War," especially 130–31.

22. E. Forcade, *Revue des deux mondes* 35 (September 1, 1861): 243–44.

23. Camille de la Boulée, *Le Pays*, January 31, 1861.

24. Chatard, *La Presse*, June 8, 1863.

25. Weed to Bigelow, June 27, 1863, in Bigelow, 23.

26. Editorial, *Journal des débats*, September 28, 1861.

27. François Camus, *Journal des débats*, August 15, 1861.

28. We will come back to this debate in chapter 8.

29. Oscar de Watteville, *La Patrie*, March 25, 1861.

30. John Slidell to Judah Philip Benjamin, no. 24, January 21, 1863, quoted in West, 108.

31. On December 13, 1861, *Le Constitutionnel*, still reluctant to give up its Americanophilia, prepared its realignment with the party line by drawing up an inventory of "racial affinities" and "deep-rooted traditions that can be found even in the names of different provinces of the South"—affinities that deserved to be "listened to" when "the need to take sides [would] have clearly arisen."

32. Edwin De Leon to Benjamin, June 19, 1863, quoted in Bigelow, *Retrospections*, 2:20.

33. Henry Hotze to Benjamin, no. 38, March 12, 1864, quoted in West, 111.

34. Editorial, *Le Constitutionnel*, May 7, 1861.

35. West, 65.

36. Editorial, *Le Constitutionnel*, May 22, 1862.

37. J.-E. Horn, *La Revue contemporaine*, July 31, 1862, 425–26.

38. Editorial, *La Presse*, October 8, 1862.

39. Editorial, *Le Constitutionnel*, October 8, 1862.

40. De Leon, *La Vérité sur les États Confédérés d'Amérique* (Paris: E. Dentu, 1862), 25.

41. Ibid., 29.

42. Ibid., 30.

43. Ibid., 27.

44. Editorial, *Le Pays*, December 20, 1861.

45. De Leon, *La Vérité*, 31.

46. Ibid., 13.

47. Ibid., 32.

48. Ibid., 5–6.

49. De Leon to Benjamin, June 19, 1863, quoted in Bigelow, 2:20; the bon mot "bête noire" was of course in French.

50. De Leon, *La Vérité*, 30; Butler, the fortress commander after the capture of New Orleans, was accused of brutality toward the population.

51. Ibid., 15.

52. Ibid., 30–31.

53. Ibid., 30.

54. Editorial, *Le Constitutionnel*, December 13, 1861.

55. Editorial, *La Patrie*, January 12, 1864, 1.

56. Alfred Mercier, *Du Panlatinisme* (Paris: Librairie Centrale, [1863]).

57. Ibid., 5.

58. Ibid., 7.

59. Ibid., 9–10.

60. With 249 million inhabitants in 1990, the reality went far beyond this ostensibly alarmist forecast.

61. Ibid., 12.

62. De Leon, *La Vérité*, 31.

63. Mercier, 19.

64. Ibid.

65. Ibid., 28.

66. Ibid., 30.

67. Ibid., 28.

68. Bigelow, 281.

69. Mercier, 17.

70. Ibid., 28.

71. Ibid., 20.

72. Jules Verne, *Nord contre Sud* (1887; Paris: Hachette, 1966), 403.

73. Charles-Noël Martin, preface to Verne, *Nord contre Sud*, vii. Verne's so-called clear expression is somewhat spoiled by persistent racist underpinnings. The idiotically vindictive Negro and the racist but "decent" overseer, Mr. Perry, do not quite make the book a bible of emancipation.

74. It was published in the same volume as *Une île flottante*, which stole the spotlight.

75. The adjective "barbaric" was used in the January 12, 1862, issue of *Le Constitutionnel*.

76. "A feeling of profound sorrow and repulsion has greeted, in England as well as in France, the act mentioned by dispatches from New York" (*Le Moniteur universel*, January 11, 1862).

Chapter Three

1. [The leading political figure of the French Republican Party in the 1870s.]

2. Quoted in Simon Jeune, *Les Types américains dans le roman et le théâtre français, 1861–1917* (Paris: Didier, 1963), 168. Sardou's ferocity made for a sharp contrast with the pre-1870 theatrical tradition of the American in the "broad comic" style (162).

3. Sardou, *L'Oncle Sam*, act 1, scene 3.

4. The expression is used by Jacques Portes, *Fascination and Misgivings: The United States in French Opinion, 1870–1914*, trans. Elborg Forster (Cambridge: Cambridge University Press, 2000), 167.

5. Édouard-René Lefèbvre de Laboulaye, *La République constitutionnelle* (Paris: Charpentier, 1871), 16.

6. Ibid., 9.

7. Portes, *Fascination*, 168.

8. Léon Gambetta, Session of the Chambre des Députés, December 28, 1876, *Journal Officiel* (December 29, 1876): 9829; quoted in Portes, *Fascination*, 168–69, who points out that the "allusion to Laboulaye," whose "Letter from an American" had appeared the

day before in the *Journal des débats,* was "transparent" and that the success of Gambetta's "ironic remarks about Laboulaye's projects clearly shows that the Left repudiated any kinship, except its ceremonial side, with the regime of Washington and Lincoln" (169).

9. [Frédéric Auguste Bartholdi (1823–1905), sculptor best known for *Liberty Enlightening the World.*]

10. See Catherine Hodeir, "The French Campaign," in *Liberty: The French-American Statue in Art and History* (New York: Harper & Row, 1986), 120–39.

11. *Frank Leslie's Illustrated Newspaper,* August 30, 1884, reproduced in *Liberty,* 159, ill. 371.

12. Edmond Johanet, *Autour du monde millionnaire* (Paris: Calmann-Lévy, 1898), 56.

13. It is interesting to note that the etymology of the word *gadget* undoubtedly stems from the name Gaget, who had the idea of selling miniature replicas of the statue in his store.

14. On the evolution of the statue's plans, see Pierre Provoyeur, "Artistic Problems," in *Liberty,* 106–19, which also notes that the trampled chain ran the risk of being hard to see or identify.

15. *Evening Star,* January 7, 1885, quoted in Hodeir, 153.

16. [Hugo, like many of his contemporaries, was interested in spiritism, and devoted many evenings during his exile in Guernsey to evoking hundreds of spirits, whose declarations, often in verse, were duly consigned; they now form a volume of Hugo's *Complete Works.*]

17. Victor Hugo, *Oeuvres complètes,* ed. Jules Massin, vol. 15–16, book 2 (Paris: Club Français du Livre, 1970), 915.

18. He is presented as such in the Marquis de Chasseloup-Laubat's *Voyage en Amérique et principalement à Chicago* (Paris: Extraits des Mémoires de la Société des Ingénieurs Civils de France, 1893), 49–50.

19. Gaillardet, 6.

20. Ibid., 5.

21. Tocqueville, 2:553.

22. Gaillardet, 123.

23. Ibid., 157.

24. Ibid., 7. Gustave de Beaumont had traveled with Tocqueville; along with Chevalier and Poussin, he was regarded as an overly optimistic propagandist for American institutions.

25. Ibid., 157.

26. This was the treaty negotiated by Jay; Gaillardet's information came from an article by Peyrat published in *La Presse* on October 28, 1860.

27. Gaillardet, 144.

28. There would be another disaster the folowing year: a planned La Salle commemoration had to be postponed because of flooding along the Mississippi. Gaillardet did not, however, blame the United States for this.

29. Gaillardet, 123.

30. Ibid., 146.

31. Ibid., 3.

32. Ibid., 358.

33. Ibid., 348.

34. Ibid., 349.

35. Edmond Demolins, *Anglo-Saxon Superiority: To What It Is Due,* trans. Louis Bert. Lavigne (London, 1898), xx. Demolins's remark is more symptomatic than exact: the expression "the Old World" had been used as early as 1837 in the United States to designate Europe. And the "disdain" was nothing new in 1897, either . . .

36. Gaillardet, 341.

37. Ibid., 238.

38. [See chapters 7 and 10–12 of the present work.]

39. [Chateaubriand's spelling of "Mississippi."]

40. [Hero in Chateaubriand's tales.]

41. Ibid., 264.

42. Ibid., 5.

43. Ibid., 254.

44. Ibid., 250.

45. Ibid., 66.

46. Ibid., 233.

47. Ibid., 267.

48. Ibid., 343.

49. [See chapters 7 and 10–12 of the present work.]

50. Ibid., 249.

51. Ibid., 75.

52. Sardou, act 1, scene 3.

53. Gaillardet, 66.

54. Ibid., 211.

55. Ibid., 236.

56. Ibid., 58.

57. "If you ask me where the American aristocracy is found, I have no hesitation in answering that it is not among the rich, who have no comon link uniting them. It is at the bar or the bench that the American aristocracy is found." Tocqueville, 1:331.

58. Gaillardet, 155.

59. Ibid., 235.

60. Ibid., 221.

61. Ibid., 371.

62. Edmond de Mandat-Grancey, *En visite chez l'Oncle Sam: New York et Chicago* (Paris: Plon, 1885), 47.

63. Mandat-Grancey, *Dans les Montagnes Rocheuses* (Paris: Plon, 1884), 178.

64. "At the Fleur-de-lys Ranche [sic], for example, in Dacotat [sic], five or six young Frenchmen have joined with the Baron de Grancey in breeding horses. They patriotically mix the blood of Perche stallions with that of American mares too light for draught purposes." Rousiers, *American Life,* 48. (Rousiers's errors.)

65. Mandat-Grancey, *Montagnes Rocheuses,* 13.

66. Mandat-Grancey, *En visite*, 51–52.

67. Mandat-Grancey, *Montagnes Rocheuses*, 32.

68. [Alphonse Allais (1854–1905), author of short comic pieces, can be likened to a French Mark Twain.]

69. Ibid., 31.

70. Ibid., 19.

71. Of Sitting Bull, Mandat-Grancey would write that he "would have made a marvelous cavalry general"—meaning the French cavalry, of course. (*Montagnes Rocheuses*, 236.)

72. Mandat-Grancey, *En visite*, 203.

73. Ibid., 198.

74. Ibid., 202.

75. Ibid., 255.

76. Ibid., 268.

77. Ibid., 269.

78. Mandat-Grancey, *Montagnes Rocheuses*, 164.

79. Gaillardet, 3.

80. Since the *Mayflower*, notes Mandat-Grancey, who sailed on *La Provence*, "the quality of the immigrants has not improved" (*En visite*, 11). This theme would have a future, too.

81. Ibid., 81.

82. Ibid., 266.

83. Gaillardet, 357.

84. Rousiers, *American Life*, 436.

85. Mandat-Grancey, *Montagnes Rocheuses*, 302.

86. Mandat-Grancey, *En visite*, 273.

87. Ibid., 59.

88. Ibid., 270.

89. Ibid., 68.

90. Émile Barbier, *Voyage au pays des dollars* (Paris: Marpon et Flammarion, 1893), 337.

91. Gaillardet, 367.

92. Ibid., 339.

Chapter Four

1. See Portes, *Fascination*, 310–13.

2. *Rapport de la délégation ouvrière libre, Mécaniciens* (Paris: Sandoz, Fischbacher et Vve Morel, 1877), 119, quoted in Portes, *Fascination*, 310.

3. *Rapport d'ensemble de la délégation ouvrière libre à Philadelphie, Tailleurs d'habit* (Paris: Imprimerie nouvelle, 1879), 124, quoted in Portes, *Fascination*, 311.

4. [Violent labor disputes involving miners, railroad workers, and others that occurred in several parts of the United States in 1876 and 1887.]

5. Jeremy Brecher, *Strike!* (San Francisco: Straight Arrow Books, 1972), 28.

6. In the anarchist newspaper *La Révolte*, November 27, 1887, quoted in Michel Cordillot, "Les réactions européens aux événements de Haymarket," in *In the Shadow of*

the Statue of Liberty: Immigrants, Workers, and Citizens in the American Republic, 1880–1920, ed. Marianne Debouzy (Saint-Denis: Presses Universitaires de Vincennes, 1988), 185.

7. Chasseloup-Laubat, 53.

8. Ibid., 48.

9. Ibid., 73.

10. Jules Huret, *En Amérique, I: De New York à la Nouvelle-Orléans* (Paris: Fasquelle, 1904), 51. The second volume, *En Amérique, II: De San Francisco au Canada*, was published in 1905.

11. Charles Crosnier de Varigny, *Les États-Unis: Esquisses historiques* (Paris: Kolb, 1891), 233.

12. The expression comes from William Ames, *Conscience with the Power and Cases Thereof* (London, 1643), chap. 1. The first (Latin) edition dates from 1632.

13. John O'Sullivan, "The Progress of Society," *United States Magazine and Democratic Review* 8 (July 1840): 87, quoted in Claude Fohlen, "La tradition expansionniste des États-Unis au XIXe siècle," in *L'Expansionnisme et le débat sur l'impérialisme aux États-Unis, 1885–1909*, ed. Robert Rougé (Paris: Presses de l'Université de Paris-Sorbonne, 1988), 15.

14. Ibid.

15. Crosnier de Varigny, *Les États-Unis*, 114.

16. Ibid., 257.

17. Ibid., 277; he drew his information from an interview with Blaine published in the *New York Herald* on Feburary 12, 1889.

18. Ibid., 119.

19. Barbier, 336–37.

20. Rousiers, *American Life*, 10.

21. H. G. Rickover, *How the Battleship Maine Was Destroyed* (Washington, D.C.: Naval History Division, Department of the Navy, 1976).

22. "It has been a splendid little war; begun with the highest motives, carried on with magnificent intelligence and spirit, favored by that fortune which loves the brave." John Hay (ambassador in London at the time) to Theodore Roosevelt, July 27, 1898, quoted in W. R. Thayer, *The Life and Letters of John Hay* (Boston, 1915), 2:337.

23. Editorial, *Le Temps*, April 11, 1898, quoted in Portes, *Fascination*, 394.

24. Pierre Birnbaum, *Le Moment antisémite: Un tour de la France en 1898* (Paris: Fayard, 1998).

25. Alberto Ruz, *La Question cubaine: Les Etats-Unis, l'Espagne et la presse française* (Paris: P. Dupont, 1898), 46.

26. This is how Maurras describes the pre-1914 period in a text we will come back to further on (chap. 10).

27. Pierre Loti, "À Madrid, les premiers jours de l'agression américaine," in *Reflets sur la sombre route* (Paris: Calmann-Lévy, 1899), 104.

28. Ibid., 84.

29. Ibid., 152.

30. Octave Noël, *Le Péril américain* (Paris: De Soye et Fils, 1899), 1.

31. Ibid., 32.

32. Ibid., 40.

33. Ibid., 41.

34. Ibid., 38.

35. Ibid.

36. Ibid., 39.

37. Ibid.

38. Ibid., 41.

39. Ibid., 32.

40. Ibid.

41. Ibid., 49.

42. Ibid., 2.

43. Ibid., 42.

44. Edmond Johannet, *Le Correspondant*, August 10, 1898, 498, quoted in Portes, *Fascination*, 399.

45. Johanet, *Un Français dans la Floride* (Paris: Mame, 1889), 75. In Labiche's play *La Cagnotte*, gullible provincials making a pleasure trip to the capital are mocked, humiliated, overcharged, and robbed by Parisians of all kinds. As for Johanet's plaintive travel log, it has few surprises aside from its heavy-handed racism, with our Catholic author reveling in jokes such as the following: "As music theory teaches us, one white is always worth two blacks" (43).

46. Johanet, *Autour du monde millionnaire*, 84.

47. Ibid., 78.

48. Ibid., 355.

49. Rousiers, *American Life*, 382–83. Stressing the extraordinarily low number of enlisted men—25,000—Rousiers nevertheless noted that the soldier's individual qualities and the general atmosphere of patriotism would make the Americans "formidable" if there was a war.

50. Huret, 1:50. America's military spending for 1904 was officially $165 million for a total of 70,387 enlisted men in the Army and 115,937 in the National Guard. Though it had doubled in seven years, the budget was still much lower than the figure Huret gave in francs.

51. Loti, 156.

52. Ibid., 121.

53. Paul Valéry, *History and Politics*, trans. Denise Folliot and Jackson Mathews, Bollingen Series 45, no. 10 (New York: Pantheon Books, 1962), 4.

54. Ibid.

55. Gustave Le Rouge and Gustave Guitton, *La Conspiration des milliardaires*, 3 vols. (1899–1900; Paris: U.G.E., 1977), 1:201. In the interest of concision, we will hereafter refer to Le Rouge when discussing this work he co-authored with Guitton.

56. Ibid., 3:194.

57. Ibid., 3:259.

58. Ibid., 2:171.

59. Ibid., 2:98.

60. Ibid., 2:100.

61. Ibid., 1:314.

62. Ibid., 3:277.

63. Ibid., 1:225.

64. Ibid., 1:60.

65. Ibid., 2:169–70.

66. Huret, 1:267.

67. Ibid., 1:393.

68. Ibid., 2:298.

69. Le Rouge and Guitton, 1:225.

70. Ibid., 1:315.

71. This diversion, which the Prussian officer calls "laying a mine," leaves "the enormous drawing-room . . . littered with the debris of art treasures and look[ing] as if Nero had been allowed a free run of it with a machine gun." Guy de Maupassant, *Mademoiselle Fifi and Other Stories*, trans. and ed. David Coward (Oxford: Oxford University Press, 1993), 12–13.

72. Le Rouge and Guitton, 2:171.

73. Ernest Reyer, "L'Américanisation de l'Europe," *Revue bleue, politique et littéraire* (April 19, 1902): 487, quoted in Portes, "Un impérialisme circonscrit," in *L'Expansionnisme*, 46, n. 26.

74. Le Rouge and Guitton, 3:362–63.

75. Ibid., 2:89.

76. It was among the socialists that the United States was the least criticized, at least at the start of the conflict; but the military occupation and the bloody "pacification" of the Philippines, revealed in all its brutality by the press in 1902, would lead the socialists and syndicalists to harden their position.

Chapter Five

1. Jeune, 162.

2. The word "jingoism" was derived from the exclamation "By jingo!" and used as early as 1878 to designate aggressive chauvinism.

3. During the Venezuela crisis in 1896.

4. Trollope, 287.

5. Ibid., 235.

6. Chasles, 491–92.

7. What Chasles calls "energetic American life" (iv) could be seen in an "en-avant perpétuel (*go-a-headism* [*sic*])" characteristic of American culture (483). Tocqueville expanded on his theory in chapter 2 of the first *Democracy*, "Concerning Their Point of Departure and Its Importance for the Future of the Anglo-Americans."

8. Chasles, 4.

9. Ibid., 4, iv.

10. Tocqueville, 2:785.

11. Quoted in Baudelaire, *Oeuvres complètes*, 2:1202.

12. Hippolyte de Castille, *Les Hommes et les moeurs en France sous le règne de Louis-Philippe* (Paris: Henneton, 1853), 354, quoted in Pierre Enckell, *Datations et documents lexicographiques* 42 (Paris: CNRS-Klincksieck, 1994).

13. Gustave Lanson, *Trois mois d'enseignement aux États-Unis* (Paris: Hachette, 1912),

66; there are also several authors who consider it inexact to extend the term to the entire white population of the United States, given that it "only applies to the inhabitants of New England" (Max O'Rell and Jack Allyn, *Jonathan et son continent: La Société américaine* (Paris: Calmann-Lévy, 1900), 13, n. 1).

14. Noël, 33.

15. In Edmond Johanet's *Un Français dans la Floride*, the Yankee still closely resembles Fanny Trollope's. A Frenchman must make preventive use of "ruse and perfidy" and never let his guard down; if the Yankee smiles, "it is a bad sign . . . he has chosen you as his dupe."

16. Chasles, 491, n. 1.

17. Ibid.

18. Tocqueville, 2:785.

19. "Are the decrepit children of our jaded world right in imitating now, despite their past, an American autonomy they do not even have the seeds of? Will they succeed in the attempt? It seems doubtful." Chasles, 507.

20. Ibid., 455.

21. "Yankeesme" would crop up again with Edgar Morin in 1964; it was not a neologism, since Octave Noël had used it in 1899, but the term did not take in 1964 any better than it had in 1899.

22. Villiers de l'Isle Adam, *Eve of the Future Eden*, trans. Marilyn Gaddis Rose (Lawrence, Kans.: Coronado Press, 1981), 171. [Translation modified.]

23. [Robert Molesworth (1656–1725), author of *An Account of Denmark*.]

24. Quoted in Reginald Horsman, *Race and Manifest Destiny: The Origins of American Racial Anglo-Saxonism* (Cambridge, Mass.: Harvard University Press, 1981), 22.

25. Ibid., 94.

26. See Jacques Portes, "En finir avec une norme: les Anglo-Saxons," in *La Norme,* ed. Yann Janeur, Association des Lauréats de la Chancellerie des Universités de Paris (Paris: Chancellerie des Universités, forthcoming). The article offers an anthology of edifying contemporary uses of the term *Anglo-Saxon*.

27. Thus in 1751, the *Nouvel abrégé chronologique de l'histoire d'Angleterre*, translated from the English by M. Salmon and published by Rollin et Jombert, gives the year 596 as the conversion date of the monk Austin, one of the "Angles-Saxons."

28. Voltaire, *Essai sur les moeurs*, 1:465.

29. In 1787, John Pinckerton would associate them with the Goths and the Persians against the Celts, whom he judged inferior; see Horsman, 31 and 47.

30. See Robert Morrissey, *L'Empereur à la barbe fleurie: Charlemagne dans la mythologie et l'histoire de France* (Paris: Gallimard, 1997).

31. Augustin Thierry, *Histoire de la conquête de l'Angleterre par les Normands* (Paris: J. Tessier, 1838), 7.

32. "The Americans have never dreamt they could break the Teutonic and Christian traditions of their Anglo-Saxon race" (Chasles, 457); elsewhere (431), Chasles speaks of "fraternal Christianity" and "antique Teutonism," still without any reference to England.

33. Which dated back to 1832, according to the *Oxford English Dictionary*.

34. Quoted in Horsman, 64.

35. Quoted in Michael Lind, *The Next American Nation: The New Nationalism and the*

Fourth Revolution (New York: Free Press, 1995), 29; especially interesting is Lind's analysis of the "first American Republic," which he dubs "Anglo-America."

36. Demolins, 112.

37. Ibid., 320.

38. Ibid., 272.

39. Ibid., 269–70.

40. Ibid., 100.

41. Ibid., iii.

42. Ibid., 343.

43. Ibid., ii.

44. Ibid., 272, 339.

45. Ibid., 309.

46. Ibid., iv.

47. David Strauss claims: "Whether Anglophobe or Anglophile, however, travelers regarded the United States as an extension of England"; elsewhere, he judges Demolins's book representative of a change for the better in Anglo-Saxon representations ("this change naturally improved attitudes towards Anglo-Saxons"); the facts do not seem to corroborate either of these two affirmations. *Menace in the West: The Rise of French Anti-Americanism in Modern Times* (Westport, Conn.: Greenwood Press, 1978), 50.

48. Demolins, 110.

Chapter Six

1. An astonished Madeleine Rebérioux notes, "'French race,' 'English race,' even—O surprise!—'Yankee race': these couples, as Marc Angenot has shown for the year 1889, were part of the common *doxa*" ("Le mot *race* au tournant du siècle," *Mots* 33 [December 1992]: 56).

2. Bourget, 12; Noël, 43; Boutmy, 61.

3. [See chapter 7 of the present volume.]

4. [Ernest Renan (1823–1892), a philologist and historian, author of the *Origins of Christianity* and many other essays, was one of the most influential French thinkers of the late nineteenth century.]

5. Furthermore, Renan willingly acknowledged its contradictions. On the subject, see Maurice Olender, *The Languages of Paradise: Race, Religion, and Philology in the Nineteenth Century*, trans. Arthur Goldhammer (Cambridge, Mass.: Harvard University Press, 1992), 51–81.

6. Ibid., 59.

7. Ernest Renan, "Nouvelles considérations sur le caractère général des peuples sémitiques, et en particulier sur leur tendance au monothéisme," *Journal asiatique* (February–March and April–May 1859), quoted in Olender, 58–59. [Translation modified.]

8. Renan, *Histoire du peuple d'Israël*, in *Oeuvres complètes* (Paris: Calmann-Lévy, 1947–61), 6:32, quoted in Olender, 84.

9. Renan, "Qu'est-ce qu'une Nation" [1882], in *Oeuvres complètes*, 1:898, quoted in Olender, 60. [Translation modified.]

10. Renan, *La Réforme intellectuelle et morale* [1871], in *Oeuvres complètes*, 1:455, quoted in Olender, 62.

11. Jules Cambon to Théophile Delcassé, May 8, 1900, quoted in Portes, *Fascination*, 215. Less famous today than Kipling, John Robert Seeley (1834–1895), a historian and essayist, had published to great success *The Expansion of England* (1883), which recounted the history of England's rivalry with France since 1688. He was one of the intellectual leaders of the Imperial Federation League.

12. Albert Savine, *Roosevelt intime* (Paris: Juven, 1904), 2, quoted in Portes, *Fascination*, 218.

13. Le Rouge and Guitton, 2:222.

14. Ibid., 2:224.

15. Crosnier de Varigny, *La Femme aux États-Unis* (Paris: Colin, 1893), 302.

16. Ibid., 303.

17. Henri Destrel, "Le suffrage des femmes aux États-Unis," *Le Correspondant* (February 1887): 5, quoted in Portes, *Fascination*, 276.

18. Urbain Gohier, *Le Peuple du XXe siècle aux États-Unis* (Paris: Fasquelle, 1903), 33.

19. Crosnier de Varigny, *La Femme*, 3.

20. Ibid., 95

21. Huret, 2:340.

22. Gohier, *Le Peuple*, 9.

23. Huret, 2:378.

24. Ibid., 2:384.

25. Barbier, 126–28.

26. Ibid., 128.

27. André Tardieu, *Notes sur les États-Unis: La société, la politique, la diplomatie* (Paris: Calmann-Lévy, 1908), 56. Tardieu gleaned his "precious information" from Eliot Gregory, whose *Worldly Ways and Byways* had had a certain success in 1898.

28. Maurois, 13.

29. Georges Duhamel, *America the Menace: Scenes from the Life of the Future*, trans. Charles Miner Thompson (Boston: Houghton Mifflin, 1931), 67.

30. Maurois, 13.

31. Rousiers, *American Life*, 278.

32. Crosnier de Varigny, *La Femme*, 198.

33. Huret, 1:325.

34. Huret, 2:385.

35. Gohier, *Le Peuple*, 36

36. Rousiers, *American Life*, 124.

37. Ibid., 331. [Translation modified.]

38. Ibid, 286.

39. Jean-Paul Sartre, "Individualism and Conformism in the United States" [*Le Figaro*, February 1945], in *Literary and Philosophical Essays*, trans. Annette Michelson (New York: Collier, 1955), 107–8.

40. Lanson, 55–56.

41. Zénaïde Fleuriot, *De trop* (1888; Paris: Hachette, 1907), 21.

42. F. Scott Fitzgerald's *Flappers and Philosophers* was published in 1920.

43. Raoul Gain, *Des Américains chez nous* (Paris: Editions Montaigne, 1928), 100.

44. Huret, 2:380.

45. Marie Dugard, *La Société américaine: Moeurs et caractère; la famille: rôle de la femme; écoles et universités* (Paris: Hachette, 1896), 311.

46. Luc Durtain, "Crime à San Francisco," in *Quarantième étage* (Paris: Gallimard, 1927).

47. Huret, 2:387. The same theme ends a poem by Luc Durtain, "El Paso," on the locomotives of the Southern Pacific: "gloved mechanics / caress them. / Machines are the only women / the Americans know how to please." *USA 1927* (Paris: Plaisir de bibliophile, 1928), n.p.

48. Huret, 1:318.

49. Ibid.

50. Johanet, *Un Français dans la Floride*, 37.

51. Le Rouge and Guitton, 2:99.

52. Rousiers, *American Life*, 283; American women's "sterility" greatly interested social observers. In 1894, a contributor to *La Réforme sociale*, R. G. Lévy, proposed another explanation for it: there was a direct correlation between women's sterility and their admission into institutions of higher learning ("La vraie Amérique" [Paris, 1894], 15; see Portes, *Fascination*, 251).

53. Rousiers, *American Life*, 332.

54. Huret, 1:304.

55. Maurice Bedel, *Voyage de Jérôme aux États-Unis d'Amérique* (Paris: Gallimard, 1953), 139.

56. Duhamel, *Scenes*, 202–3.

57. Sartre, *Le Figaro*, March 11–12, 1945.

58. Cocteau, *Lettre aux Américains* (Paris: Grasset, 1949), 32.

59. Gain, 25.

60. Demolins, 50.

61. Ibid., 1.

62. Ibid., iv.

63. Duhamel, *Scenes*, 158.

64. Rousiers, *American Life*, 324.

65. Huret, 1:135.

66. Duhamel, *Scenes*, 156.

67. Bourget, 144.

68. Huret, 1:43.

69. Duhamel, *Scenes*, 157, 160, 154.

70. Ibid. [Absent from translation.]

71. Gohier, *Le Peuple*, 13; Gohier, who was not averse to going against the grain of stereotypes, denounced the "energy" cliché (associated with Teddy Roosevelt) as "a legend."

72. Duhamel, *Scenes*, 156.

73. Huret, 1:133.

74. Ibid., 58.

75. Chasles, 483.

76. Noël, 39.

77. Johanet, *Un Français dans la Floride*, 53.

78. Huret, 1:3.

79. Gohier, *Le Peuple*, 251 and 3.

80. Le Rouge and Guitton, 2:170.

81. Sartre, "Individualism," 105.

82. Henri de Beaumont, "De l'avenir des États-Unis et de leur lutte future avec l'Europe," *Journal des économistes* (July 1888): 77.

Chapter Seven

1. Noël, 50.

2. Bourget, 1:295, 297.

3. Ibid., 1:12.

4. Ibid., 1:310.

5. The word comes from Boutmy, 64.

6. Gohier, *Le Peuple*, 244, 251.

7. Here is an example formulated in the 1830s, though written in "private" correspondence: "The American has no pity for the Indians, and it is by treating them thus that he makes philanthropical sallies on the way we are waging war in Algeria." Adolphe Fourier de Bacourt, *Souvenirs d'un diplomate. Lettres intimes sur l'Amérique*, published by the Comtesse de Mirabeau (Paris, 1882), 299, quoted in Rémond, 741 n. 62.

8. Johanet, *Un Français dans la Floride*, 42.

9. Johanet, *Autour du monde millionnaire*, 374.

10. Dugard, 162.

11. Ibid., 93.

12. The book's 1927 American translators retitled the second chapter simply "The Melting Pot."

13. André Siegfried, *America Comes of Age: A French Analysis*, trans. H. H. Hemming and Doris Hemming (New York: Harcourt, Brace, 1927), 6, 7–8.

14. "White" resistance met with understanding from the conservatives, but also, and more unexpectedly, from the Musée Social's researcher, Paul de Rousiers (*American Life*, 366).

15. Rémond, 732.

16. Portes, *Fascination*, 90.

17. Le Rouge and Guitton, 2:98.

18. Georges Sauvin, *Autour de Chicago* (Paris: Plon, 1893), 203, quoted in Portes, *Fascination*, 95.

19. Gohier, *Le Peuple*, 299.

20. Huret, 2:179–80.

21. Louis Simonin, *À travers les États-Unis* (Paris: Charpentier, 1875), 34, quoted in Portes, *Fascination*, 109.

22. Johanet, *Un Français dans la Floride*, 42.

23. Huret, 1:332, 1:398.

24. Portes, *Fascination*, 111.

25. Pierre Leroy-Beaulieu, "Blancs et Noirs dans l'Amérique du Nord," *Le Correspondant* (25 October 1886), quoted in Portes, *Fascination*, 112.

26. Siegfried, *Les États-Unis d'aujourd'hui* (Paris: Armand Colin, 1927), 89. This passage is suppressed in the American translation.

27. Boutmy, 73.

28. "The white race's defeat is certain [in California]. On this pacific ground, it cannot fight on equal terms." Crosnier de Varigny, *Les États-Unis*, 71.

29. Alexis de Noailles, "Les publicistes américains et la constitution des États-Unis," *Le Correspondant* (25 February 1877), quoted in Portes, *Fascination*, 349.

30. Boutmy, 271.

31. Ibid., 64.

32. Ibid., 25, 61.

33. Ibid., 41.

34. Ibid., 89.

35. Ibid., 90.

36. Ibid., 94.

37. Ibid., 26.

38. Ibid., 46 n.

39. See Prologue, n. 12.

40. Siegfried, *Les États-Unis*, 17. Passage suppressed in the American translation. [Édouard Drumont (1841–1917), a journalist and politician, was a key figure in the anti-Semitic movement that became a political force in France in the 1890s. Maurice Barrès (1862–1923), a major figure of the nationalist Right, was also one of the most celebrated novelists of his time.]

41. Bourget, 324. In 1895, Mark Twain wrote a hilarious review of Bourget's book under the title "What Paul Bourget Thinks of Us," in *Collected Tales, Sketches, Speeches, and Essays, 1891–1910* (New York: Library of America, 1992), 164–79. I would like to thank Robert Maniquis for bringing this inspired piece to my attention.

42. Bourget, 26.

43. Ibid., 297.

44. Ibid., 111.

45. Ibid., 295.

46. Boutmy, 68.

47. Siegfried, *Les États-Unis*, 1. Absent from the American translation.

48. Siegfried, *America*, 3.

49. Ibid., 20.

50. Siegfried, *Les États-Unis*, 6–7.

51. Siegfried, *America*, 7.

52. Ibid.

53. Ibid., 18. [Translation modified.]

54. Ibid., 9, 11.

55. Ibid., 17.

56. Ibid., 12.

57. In Bernard-Henri Lévy's sense of the term in *L'Idéologie française* (Paris: Grasset, 1981). His pages on anti-Americanism (281–91) are still utterly timely.

58. Twain, 167.

59. Johanet, *Autour du monde millionnaire*, 374.

Chapter Eight

1. Up to the "July Monarchy, the image of America had not yet completely broken off from the agrarian myth," writes René Rémond, 777–78.

2. As in the titles of Émile Barbier, *Voyage au pays des dollars*, and Edmond Johanet, *Autour du monde millionaire*, whose first chapter refers to America as an "all-plutopolis."

3. [César Birotteau, the eponymous main character of Balzac's novel, is a comic and pathetic figure who adapts himself to suit any situation.]

4. Barbier, 135.

5. Johanet, *Autour du monde millionnaire*, 70.

6. Leroy-Beaulieu, *Les États-Unis au XXe siècle* (Paris: Armand Colin, 1904), 233, 232.

7. Rousiers, *Les Industries monopolisées (trusts) aux États-Unis*, Bibliothèque du Musée Social (Paris: Armand Colin, 1898), vi.

8. Johanet, *Autour du monde millionaire*, 71.

9. Noël, 34.

10. Paul Lafargue, *Les Trusts américains* (Paris: V. Giard et E. Brière, 1903), 41.

11. Ibid., 124.

12. Ibid., 41.

13. He gave an early version to the Guesdist review *Le Socialiste* (January 18–25, 1903) before it came out in book form.

14. H. D. Lloyd, *Wealth against Commonwealth* (New York: Gay & B., 1896).

15. "[The tariff] is in their view a weapon against Europe and they will keep it sharpened until such time as they feel strong enough to crush the world industrially." Noël, 30.

16. Urbain Gohier compared the "capital and work trusts": "two schools of sharks." *Le Peuple*, 93.

17. Leroy-Beaulieu, *Les États-Unis*, xvii.

18. Ibid., 238, 244; for Leroy-Beaulieu, this observation was in no way reassuring, since internal stagnation would drive the American economy outward toward external markets.

19. Rousiers, *Les Industries*, vi.

20. Gohier, *Le Peuple*, 89.

21. Rousiers, *Les Industries*, 326.

22. Ibid., 320.

23. Ibid., 322.

24. Demolins, 270.

25. Th. Bentzon, *Choses et gens d'Amérique* (Paris: Calmann-Lévy, 1898), 2.

26. Laurence R. Moore, *European Socialists and the American Promised Land* (New York: Oxford University Press, 1970), 192.

27. Harry Turtledove, *How Few Remain* (New York: Ballantine, 1997); *The Great War: Walk in Hell* (New York: Ballantine, 1999); *The Great War: Breakthroughs* (New York: Ballantine, 2000). I would like to thank John Mason for calling them to my attention.

28. Karl Marx to Frederick Engels, September 10, 1862, in Marx and Engels, *The Civil War in the United States*, ed. Richard Enmale (New York: International Publishers, 1937), 255.

29. Marx, "The North American Civil War" [*Die Presse*, October 25, 1861], in *The Civil War*, 57–71.

30. Marx to Engels, October 29, 1862, in *The Civil War*, 258.

31. Marx, "The North American Civil War," 71.

32. Engels and Marx, "The Civil War in the United States" [*Die Presse*, November 26, 1861], in *The Civil War*, 82.

33. Marx, "Abolitionist Demonstrations in America" [*Die Presse*, August 30, 1862], in *The Civil War*, 201–6. Marx introduces Phillips' scathing diatribe with these words: "In the present state of affairs Wendell Phillips' speech is of greater importance than a battle bulletin" (202–3).

34. Engels and Marx, "The American Civil War (II)" [*Die Presse*, March 27, 1862], in *The Civil War*, 174.

35. Engels to Marx, July 30, 1862, in *The Civil War*, 251.

36. Engels to Marx, November 5, 1862, in *The Civil War*, 258.

37. Ibid., 259.

38. Engels to Marx, November 15, 1862, in *The Civil War*, 260. The border states (Delaware, Maryland, Virginia, Kentucky and Missouri) were populated in part by slave-owning Southerners, but their historical and institutional ties with the North were strong; they all chose to side with the Union, with the exception of Virginia (at the cost of a split, with West Virginia joining the North in 1863).

39. Ibid., 259.

40. Engels to Marx, February 17, 1863, in *The Civil War*, 265.

41. Engels to Marx, July 30, 1862, 251.

42. Engels to Marx, September 9, 1862, in *The Civil War*, 254.

43. Marx to Engels, August 7, 1862, in *The Civil War*, 253.

44. Marx to Engels, October 29, 1862, 258.

45. Marx, "Abolitionist Demonstrations," 204.

46. Ibid., 201.

47. Ibid., 205.

48. Engels and Marx, "Comments on the North American Events" [*Die Presse*, October 12, 1862], in *Marx and Engels on the United States*, trans. Salo Ryazanskaya (Moscow: Progress Publishers, 1979), 156.

49. Marx, "Address from the Working Men's International Association to President Johnson," in *Marx and Engels on the United States*, 170.

50. Engels to Marx, July 15, 1865, in *The Civil War*, 277.

51. In a bit of unintentional humor, Roger Dangeville, the French editor of these texts on the American Civil War, pays Lincoln a posthumous tribute: "It would obviously be excessive to extend Marx's praise to all the United States presidents" (*La Guerre civile aux États-Unis*, trans. and ed. Roger Dangeville (Paris: UGE, 10–18, 1970), 239 n.). It would even be excessive to extend it to Lincoln himself, during his lifetime.

52. Marx to Engels, October 29, 1862, 258.

53. Engels to Marx, November 15, 1862, 259.

54. Engels, *The Condition of the Working Class in England*, quoted in Moore, 6.

55. "Agriculture, which has progressed phenomenally since the Civil War, has taken on a character of great capitalist production in the United States." Lafargue, *Les Trusts américains*, 88.

56. Friedrich Nietzsche, *Daybreak: Thoughts on the Prejudices of Morality,* trans. R. J. Hollingdale (Cambridge: Cambridge University Press, 1997), 125–27.

57. Marx to N. F. Danielson, 10 April 1879, in *Letters to Americans, 1848–1895,* ed. Alexander Trachtenberg (New York, 1953), quoted in Moore, 9.

58. Paul de Rousiers commented: "It is sufficiently curious to see what socialism has become in the hands of Henry George; it is no longer 'socialism of the tribal state,' as he calls it, but American socialism, still exaggerating the characters that we have noticed in American society—an enforced amelioration, an enforced success, or death." *American Life,* 409.

59. Engels to Friedrich Sorge, August 8, 1887, in *Letters to Americans,* quoted in Moore, 15.

60. See, on the topic, Hubert Perrier, "Le Parti Ouvrier Socialiste d'Amérique du Nord jusqu'en 1886," in Debouzy, 169.

61. Engels to Sorge, August 8, 1887, quoted in Moore, 15.

62. [Daniel De Leon (1852–1914), American socialist leader.]

63. Marie-France Toinet, "La participation politique des ouvriers américains à la fin du XIXe siècle," in Debouzy, 291.

64. Moore stresses that in the Marxist press, "after 1905 little that was said about America was new, and much was drawn directly from old copy and reprinted unaltered." 130.

65. Engels to Sorge, January 16, 1895, in *Letters to Americans,* quoted in Moore, 19.

66. Volney, 23.

67. The Newark Congress (1877) brought together seventeen militants of German extraction, seven Englishmen, three Czechs, and one Frenchman. Hubert Perrier (169) has suggested that the picture should be nuanced and signaled SLP leaders' efforts to distribute as many copies of their resolutions in English as in German, or explicitly request that as many English-speaking delegates as possible be designated. These resolutions also show that the bar was very low . . . Attempts to maintain a central newspaper in English were ultimately unsuccessful.

68. See Janet R. Horne's rich study, *A Social Laboratory for Modern France: The Musée Social and the Rise of the Welfare State* (Durham, N.C.: Duke University Press, 2002), 29.

69. Quoted in Horne, 157.

70. Huret, 2:284.

71. Gohier, *Le Peuple,* 1.

72. [René Waldeck-Rousseau (1846–1904), a left-wing Republican leader and prominent statesman of the Third Republic.]

73. Gohier, *Histoire d'une tradition, 1899–1903* (Paris: SPE, 1903), 9.

74. [Jean Jaurès (1859–1914), a leader of the prewar French socialist movement, was a member of Parliament, an impressive orator, and the founder of the daily newspaper *L'Humanité;* his assassination on the eve of World War I made him a martyr of both socialism and pacifism.]

75. Ibid., 29.

76. Gohier, *Le Peuple,* 88.

77. Ibid., 77.

78. Ibid., 78.

79. Ibid., 16.

80. Bourget, 219.

81. Gohier, *Le Peuple*, 78.

82. Ibid., 88.

83. Portes, *Fascination*, 328.

84. Philip Sheldon Foner, *History of the Labor Movement in the United States*, vol. 3, *The Policies and Practices of the American Federation of Labor, 1900–1909* (1964; New York: International Publishers, 1981), 383. This was the Congress of 1902.

85. [Confédération Général du Travail.]

86. Huret, 1:8.

87. Gohier, *Le Peuple*, 162.

88. This refusal can be read in the reports of workers' delegations on their return from Philadelphia, like that of the roofers, plumbers, and zinc workers: "Emigration has created the material wealth of America, but also its moral poverty" (*Rapport d'ensemble de la délégation ouvrière à Philadelphie: Couvreurs-plombiers-zingueurs* (Paris: Imp. Nat., 1879), 122, quoted in Portes, *Fascination*, 348). Jacques Portes notes that "such warnings" against the temptation of emigrating "were sounded in 1876 as well as in 1898, for instance, by Emile Levasseur," who ominously wrote: "Woe to the insufficiently armed, who will end up vegetating in that country, where the throng of the jobless is too big as it is." Emile Levasseur, *L'Ouvrier américain* (Paris: Larose, 1898), 475–76, quoted in Portes, 348.

89. Huret, 2:246.

90. Brousse would be the only socialist leader not to speak up during the Haymarket trial.

91. Eugène Fournière, *La Petite république* (December 1, 1902): 1.

92. Lafargue, *Les Trusts américains*, 131; see also his article "Les réformes et le parti socialiste," *L'Humanité* (September 24, 1908).

93. The expression is borrowed from Cordillot, 185.

94. [Jules Guesde (1845–1922), one of Karl Marx's sons-in-law, was the leader of a highly doctrinal splinter group, the Guesdistes, in the pre–World War I French socialist movement. Jean Longuet (1876–1930), Marx's other French son-in-law, advocated a Marxist line within the French socialist movement. Edouard Vaillant (1840–1915) was a reformist French socialist leader. Henri de Rochefort-Luçay (1830–1913), a well-known political writer and agitator, was famous for his rebellious temper and his lifelong fight for the freedom of the press. Louise Michel (1830–1905), a militant social organizer and feminist, took part in the Paris Commune of 1871; convicted as a "Communarde," she was deported and spent several years in New Caledonia.]

95. "Let us imitate the Americans, follow their example. . . . Let us set a date and proclaim that from that day forward, in no way will we consent to put in more than eight hours." Émile Pouget, *La Voix du peuple* 23 (May 1, 1901), quoted in Cordillot, 188.

96. Lafargue, *Les Trusts américains*, 124.

97. Jean Longuet, "Aux États-Unis," *La Petite république* (November 5, 1902), quoted in Moore, 90. The metaphor of the "laboratory" applied to the United States had already been used in 1851 by Philarète Chasles, in one of the numerous passages of his *Études* that give the lie to his reputation as a diehard Americanophile: "It is truly and exclusively a workshop, a furnace, *a laboratory for the future fabrication of an unknown civilization,*" he writes of the United States, "and it is so very little a fully-formed, complete nation

encompassing all the results of definitive societies, that after having made one's fortune there, one hurries to come and enjoy it in Europe."

98. Lafargue, *Les Trusts américains*, 138, 137.

99. Ibid., 137.

100. Johanet, *Autour du monde millionnaire*, 78. The neologism is probably calqued on *enjuivé* and points to an epidemiological obsession we will see again in metaphors on the "American cancer."

101. Lafargue, *Les Trusts américains*, 10.

102. Rousiers, *American Life*, 338, 334.

103. Bourget, 12, 318.

104. Johanet, *Autour du monde millionaire*, 212.

105. Ibid., 215.

106. Ibid., 203; he had just died in 1895.

107. Not including college tuition. Therefore, about the equivalent of $22,000 in 2005.

108. Johanet, *Autour du monde millionnaire*, 111.

109. Ibid., 206.

110. Ibid., 209.

111. Ibid., 210.

112. Ibid., 207.

113. Ibid., 211.

114. Lafargue, *Les Trusts américains*, 122.

115. Ibid., 84.

116. Lafargue, *Les Trusts américains*, 84.

117. Johanet, *Autour du monde millionaire*, 224.

118. We should note in passing that Mark Twain's famous novel, published in 1889, was translated as *Un Américain à la cour du roi Arthur*. The word *Yankee* was eradicated— it was already too pejorative in French.

Chapter Nine

1. [The images produced by the Pellerin workshop in Épinal, a small town in eastern France, were naive, colorful depictions of all kinds of activities and persons; for three centuries, they were sold all over the country to peasants and working-class families, who hung them in their homes as decorations.]

2. [One of the nicknames given to the American soldiers, from "Sam."]

3. These figures can be found in the exhibition catalogue *Images d'Épinal: les Amériques*, ed. Brigitte Maury (Venice, 1992), texts by Henri George. See also Véronique Alemany-Dessaint, "La représentation des Américains dans la Première Guerre mondiale," in *Les Américains et la France*, 1917–1947: *engagements et représentations*, ed. Françoise Cochet, M.-Cl. Genet-Delacroix, and Hélène Trocmé (Paris: Maisonneuve et Larose, 1999).

4. The phrase "Lafayette, we are here!" has often been attributed to General Pershing [John J. Pershing (1860–1948), commander in chief of the American Expeditionary Force in World War I], but Pershing himself contradicted this and indicated his aide Colonel Stanton as its author.

5. Jean Racine, *Athalia*, in *Iphigenia, Phaedra, Athalia*, trans. John Cairncross (London: Penguin, 1970), 288.

6. Sigmund Freud and William C. Bullitt, *Thomas Woodrow Wilson: A Psychological Study* (Boston: Houghton Mifflin, 1967), 206. Freud speaks of his "antipathy" for Wilson in a preface he personally signs.

7. Charles Maurras, *Les Trois aspects du Président Wilson: la neutralité, l'intervention, l'armistice* (Paris: Nouvelle Librairie Nationale, 1920), 186.

8. Georges Clemenceau, *Grandeur and Misery of Victory* (London: George G. Harrap, 1930), 165.

9. Ibid., 58.

10. [Marshal Ferdinand Foch (1851–1929) was appointed chief of French General staff in 1917 and assumed unified command of the British, French, and American armies in April 1918.]

11. Marcel Proust, *Time Regained*, trans. Stephen Hudson (London: Chatto & Windus, 1951), 118. The virtuosity of Proust's irony lies in his archaic use of the helping verb "were," which gives "when we were almost finished" a double meaning: the Germanophilic Charlus is saying either "when we *had* almost finished," or "when we were practically done for."

12. Clemenceau, *Grandeur*, 70.

13. Ibid.

14. Tardieu, *France and America: Some Experiences in Coöperation* (Boston: Houghton Mifflin, 1927), 294.

15. Ibid., 6.

16. Maurois, 37.

17. Robert Aron and Arnaud Dandieu, *Le Cancer américain* (Paris: Rioder, 1931), 105.

18. Maurois, 35. Maurois admits to being even more confused after the two dinners than before.

19. Clemenceau, *Grandeur*, 157.

20. Freud repeats it in *Thomas Woodrow Wilson*, 274; Colonel House had recorded it in his diary on May 30, 1919.

21. The title of a review by Jeff Shesol of two works on Wilson, *New York Times Book Review* (October 14, 2001).

22. Clemenceau, *Grandeur*, 162.

23. Ibid., 157.

24. William Bullitt had stepped down from the American delegation at the Peace Conference to mark his disagreement with concessions made to the Allies.

25. Clemenceau, quoted in Freud and Bullitt, 243.

26. Ibid., xi.

27. Ibid., 131.

28. Ibid., 71. John Wyclif or Wycliffe (d. 1384), a theologian at Oxford, translator of the Bible and religious reformer, drew on Scripture to oppose the church's abuses. He proposed a vision of the Gospel that was both ethical and practical. John Wesley (1703–1791), an evangelist and, for many years, an itinerant priest, founded the Methodist church.

29. Maurras, *Les Trois aspects*, 184.

30. Ibid., 165.

31. Metaphorically speaking; Wilson was of course a Presbyterian.

32. Robert Aron and Dandieu, 16.

33. Élie Faure, *Mon Périple* (1932; Paris: Seghers-Michel Archimbaud, 1987), 42–45.

34. [An allusion to Corneille's comedy, in which Cliton, Clitandre's valet, tries to find young women for his master; pro-American Frenchmen prostituting France to their American masters is a favorite theme in Aron and Dandieu's book.]

35. Robert Aron and Dandieu, 92.

36. Georges Soria, *La France deviendra-t-elle une colonie américaine?* (Will France Become an American Colony?) (Paris: Ed. du Pavillon, 1948), 48.

37. *La Cinquième Colonne, la voici!* (Paris: SEDIC, [1950]).

38. [A noted French historian, specialist on the United States.]

39. Maurois, *En Amérique*, 69.

40. The title of a special issue of the journal *Réaction* in 1930.

41. André Rousseaux, "Un quart d'heure avec M. G. Duhamel," *Candide* (June 19, 1930): 4, quoted in Anne-Marie Duranton-Crabol, "De l'anti-américanisme en France vers 1930," *Revue d'histoire moderne et contemporaine* 48, no. 1 (2001): 122.

42. Quoted in Jean-Louis Loubet del Bayle, *Les Non-conformistes des années 30: Une tentative de renouvellement de la pensée politique française* (Paris: Seuil, 1969), 254.

43. Strauss, *Menace in the West*, 69.

44. Loubet del Bayle, 254; in any case, it is an understatement to describe the "trend" as "rather a minority affair."

45. Robert Aron and Dandieu, 240.

46. Maurras, "La France et l'Amérique" [1926], in *Quand les Français ne s'aimaient pas: Chronique d'une renaissance, 1895–1905* (Paris: Nouvelle Librairie Nationale, 1916), 323.

47. Étiemble, 332, 33, 52, 435, respectively. Étiemble took the word "concession" from an anti-American diatribe by Audiberti.

48. Ibid., 244. Through this florid turn of phrase, Étiemble is referring to posters announcing the executions of Resistance fighters and hostages.

49. Ibid., 333. Étiemble's italics, which suggest a deliberate allusion.

50. Louis-Ferdinand Céline, *Journey to the End of the Night*, trans. Ralph Manheim (New York: New Directions, 1983), 159.

51. Édouard Mounier, "Confession pour nous autres chrétiens," *Esprit* 6 (March 1933): 896, quoted in Loubet del Bayle, 243.

Chapter Ten

1. Tony Judt, *Past Imperfect: French Intellectuals, 1944–1956* (Berkeley and Los Angeles: University of California Press, 1992), 191. *Décadence* was published the same year as *Le Cancer américain*.

2. Duhamel, *Scenes*, 215, 217.

3. Quoted in Jean Birnbaum, "Enquête sur une détestation française," *Le Monde*, November 25–26, 2001; here, the editor of the review *Multitudes* is denouncing the sterile anti-American stereotypes of a part of the antiglobalization movement.

4. Henri de Beaumont, "De l'avenir des États-Unis et de leur lutte future avec l'Europe," *Journal des économistes* (July 1888): 76.

5. Ibid., 77.

6. Ibid.

7. This application of Darwinism to international relations would not reassure an Octave Noël, who believed that "the union of the Anglo-Saxon races protects English possessions." Noël, 45.

8. See the discussion of *La Conspiration des milliardaires* in chapter 4.

9. Beaumont, 84.

10. On French reactions to Monroe's declaration, see Rémond, 606–16.

11. In an almost immediately famous speech delivered at the Minnesota State Fair on September 2, 1901, Theodore Roosevelt had cited this "homely old adage": "Speak softly and carry a big stick, you will go far." It was Tardieu who made it out to be a "theory" in *Notes sur les États-Unis*, 262.

12. Ibid., 270.

13. Noël, 49.

14. Tardieu, *Notes sur les États-Unis*, 360–61.

15. Huret, 2:86.

16. Valéry, *Cahiers*, ed. J. Robinson, Bibliothèque de la Pléiade, 2 vols. (Paris: Gallimard, 1974), 2:1498.

17. Beaumont, 83.

18. It was first published in the British journal *Athenaeum* (April–May 1919), then in *La Nouvelle revue française* (August 1919).

19. Only Spengler, with *The Decline of the West* (published in 1918 but conceived in 1912 in the aftermath of the Agadir crisis), can make claims to having had as wide an influence. Musil's excellent *Das hilflose Europa*, 1922, had a much more limited audience.

20. Valéry, *History and Politics*, 4.

21. Ibid., 19.

22. Duhamel, "Entretien sur l'esprit européen," *Cahiers libres* (1928): 29.

23. Ibid., 50.

24. Valéry, *Cahiers*, 2:1552.

25. Valéry considered the joint triumph of machinism and democracy a fait accompli and did not take an active stand against "American civilization."

26. Siegfried, *America*, 347.

27. Rousiers, *American Life*, 10.

28. Siegfried, *America*, 347.

29. Ibid., 353.

30. [Charles Péguy (1873–1914), a political thinker, essayist, and poet, evolved from pacifism and socialism toward mystical Chrisitanity and nationalism.]

31. [Julien Benda (1867–1956), a brilliant writer and polemicist, close to Péguy in his youth, took part in the campaign against the unfair condemnation of Dreyfus at the end of the nineteenth century and against the rise of fascism in the 1930s; paradoxically, though, his most famous work, published in 1927, *La Trahison des clercs (Betrayal of the Intellectuals)*, denounces French intellectuals for jeopardizing their intellectual integrity and talent through excessive politicization.]

32. Valéry, "The Crisis of the Mind," in *History and Politics*, 31.

33. See, on the topic, Jacques Alain Favre, *André Suarès et la grandeur* (Paris: Klinck-sieck, 1977), 118–20 and passim.

34. André Suarès, "Le Principe européen" [1926], in *Europes: De l'antiquité au XXe siècle*, ed. Yves Hersant and Fabienne Durand-Bogaert (Paris: Robert Laffont, 2000), 170.

35. Ibid., 171–72.

36. Quoted in Marcel Dietschy, *Le Cas André Suarès* (Neuchâtel: À La Baconnière, 1967), 70.

37. Suarès, 170.

38. Duhamel, *Scenes*, xiii.

39. See Hersant and Durand-Bogaert, 160–61.

40. England "could be accepted into the pan-European arbitration treaty," but not into the "security treaty." The reason Coudenhove-Kalergi gives for this is Great Britain's excessive and dangerous ties with Asia and the Pacific.

41. Hugo, "Aux membres du Congrès de la Paix, à Lugano," [September 20, 1872], *Oeuvres complètes*, vol. 15–16, bk. 1, 1339.

42. Strauss, *Menace in the West*, 215. See also Jean-Baptiste Duroselle, *L'Idée d'Europe dans l'histoire* (Paris: Denoël, 1965), 274.

43. *L'Échange* was written in Boston in 1893–94, published in *L'Ermitage* in 1900, and staged by Copeau in 1914. In *Scenes from the Life of the Future*, a quarter of a century later, Georges Duhamel would refer to Claudel's precocious insight: "Modern genius does not despair of reducing the incommensurable world of the soul to definite material values. 'Everything is worth so much,' according to Thomas Pollock Nageoire, that American whom a great French writer has invented" (168–69).

44. In *Visite aux Américains* (Paris: Flammarion, 1936), Jules Romains pays a tribute to Times Square and its crowds—"vulgar," perhaps, but without "pettiness": "All those people crowding Times Square are ordinary men; all that joy, profoundly democratic" (45). Further on (chap. 11), we will see how uncommon this vision was.

45. "And even if I believed that our European civilization had fulfilled its purpose, that it had exhausted its ambitions, and completed the sum of its achievements . . . But that, I do not believe." (Duhamel, *Scenes*, 217.) This is the last word.

46. This is notably the case in *Hollywood dépassé*, which is centered on two emi-grants, one Italian and the other French. The theory in *Quelques notes d'USA* (1928), according to which the days of national confrontations are over while those of interconti-nental confrontations have begun, falls in line with the definition given in Coudenhove-Kalergi's Manifesto of Europe as a "united entity in the face of the other continents."

47. Robert Aron and Dandieu, 68.

48. Ibid., 21.

49. Ibid., 236.

50. Loubet del Bayle, 193; he is quoting Jean de Fabrègues, *Réaction* 5 (February 1931): 25.

51. Robert Aron and Dandieu, 17.

52. Ibid., 15.

53. Duhamel, *Scenes*, 186.

54. Robert Aron and Dandieu, 47.

55. Ibid., 46.

56. Ibid., 106.

57. Ibid., 82.

58. Ibid., 144.

59. Ibid., 245. The slogan *"Deutschland Erwache!"* was so closely identified with the National Socialist German Workers Party that *Le Canard enchaîné* would make it the theme of a still famous caricature illustrating the Nazis' 1933 electoral breakthrough: a mechanical Hitler pops out of a Tyrolean cuckoo clock and cries "Wake up!" to a Germany turning a deaf ear. (Pol Ferjac, *Le Canard enchaîné* [May 10, 1933].)

60. The "Letter to Hitler" appeared in November 1933 in no. 5 of *Ordre nouveau* (see Loubet del Bayle, 308–10); Robert Aron defends Mussolini's Italy notably in DICTATURE DE LA LIBERTÉ (Paris: Grasset, 1935), in a passage directed at "America's friends" (108–10).

61. Collaborationist literature is rich in historical revelations of this kind; in it we find the history of the United States completely rewritten, from its origins on, as a Jewish conspiracy—for example, in Henri-Robert Petit, *Rothschild, roi d'Israël et les Américains* (Paris: Nouvelles Études Françaises, 1941), 34–42.

62. Robert Aron and Dandieu, 86.

63. Ibid., 21. Once again, the remark is aimed at Duhamel.

64. On the convergence of anti-Americanism and anti-Europeanism, see Michel Wieviorka, "L'antiaméricanisme contemporain: Les intellectuels en France, la nation et l'Europe," in *Les Antiaméricanismes*, ed. Tom Bishop, Yves Hersant, and Philippe Roger, Florence Gould Lectures at New York University, special volume (Spring 2001): 56–60.

Chapter Eleven

1. Étiemble, 231.

2. François Mauriac, *Le Figaro*, February 24, 1951.

3. *Le Monde*, May 11, 1966. Among those who signed were Jean-Marie Domenach, Pierre Emmanuel, André Philip, and David Rousset.

4. Clemenceau, *Grandeur*, 285.

5. Tardieu, *France and America*, 285–86.

6. Rémond describes the crisis, 779–814.

7. Mainly the compensation of French citizens (including Beaumarchais) wronged by the American government, along with the same government's infringement against the treaty of 1803 (Article 8 stipulated that French ships would be permanently treated as most favored nation in Louisiana; Great Britain had received a complete dispensation of duties in 1815 and France was demanding the same by reason of the treaty).

8. Editorial, *Le National* (March 29, 1834), quoted in Rémond, 788.

9. Alphonse de Lamartine, debate (April 1, 1834), quoted in Rémond, 793.

10. Lamartine, debate (May 20, 1842), quoted in Rémond, 817.

11. Rémond, 817.

12. Editorial, *Le Constitutionnel* (April 19, 1835), quoted in Rémond, 816.

13. Rémond, 816.

14. Siegfried, *America*, 215. The French title of the chapter is "L'Amérique créancier du monde" (America: Creditor to the World).

15. Morand, *World Champions*, trans. Hamish Miles (New York: Harcourt, Brace, 1931), 39.

16. Tardieu, *France and America*, 278.

17. Lucien Romier, preface to André Lafond, *New York 1928. Impressions d'Amérique* (Rouen: Ed. du Journal de Rouen, 1929), xiii.

18. Robert Aron and Dandieu, 47.

19. Tardieu, *France and America*, 278–79.

20. Tardieu, *France in Danger! A Great Statesman's Warning*, trans. Gerald Griffin (London: Denis Archer, 1935), 27.

21. Siegfried, *America*, 227. [Translation modified.]

22. Ibid.

23. Tardieu, *France in Danger!*, 28.

24. Ibid., 27.

25. Robert Aron and Dandieu, 124, 117.

26. Maurras, *Les Trois aspects*, xv. Wilson had spoken of "peace without victory."

27. Ibid., 28.

28. Ibid., 152 [original date: January 24, 1919].

29. Ibid., 200.

30. Ibid., 190.

31. Ibid., 193.

32. Ibid., 195.

33. Ibid., xv.

34. Ibid., 35 [original date: April 7, 1917].

35. Ibid., 158.

36. Siegfried, *America*, 340–42. In French, chapter 26 is entitled "Les États-Unis, leaders de la race blanche?" (The United States: Leaders of the White Race?).

37. Maurras, *Les Trois aspects*, xv.

38. William R. Keylor, "L'image de la France en Amérique à la fin de la Grande Guerre," in *Les Américains et la France*, 161.

39. [Raymond Poincaré (1860–1934), president of France (1913–20), then prime minister and minister of foreign affairs after 1922.]

40. Robert Aron and Dandieu, 68.

41. We will come back to the novel; the name of the character Ogden Webb recalls Ogden Mills, American secretary of the treasury between Mellon and Young.

42. Tardieu, speech pronounced in the Senate, April 5, 1930. In the Chamber on March 29, he had used the same tactic and tried to rehabilitate Wilson: "One man has, in turn, garnered unlimited, excessive popularity, especially with the left, and then excessive injustice: President Wilson."

43. Tardieu, *France in Danger!*, 20. [Translation modified.]

44. Donald Roy Allen, *French Views of America in the 1930s* (New York: Garland Publishing, 1979), 280.

45. Raymond Recouly, *L'Amérique pauvre* (Paris: Les Editions de France, 1933), 325.

46. Ibid., 339.

47. Régis Michaud, *Ce qu'il faut connaître de l'âme américaine* (What Should Be Known about the American Soul) (Paris: Boivin, 1929).

48. See Victor de Marcé, "Autour du problème des dettes," *Revue de Paris* 2 (1933) and the commentary by Allen, 262, n. 5.

49. Robert Aron and Dandieu, 120.

50. J.-L. Chastanet, *L'Oncle Shylock ou l'impérialisme américain à la conquête du monde* (Paris: Flammarion, 1927), 78.

51. Siegfried, *America*, 227. [Translation modified.]

52. Chastanet, 159.

53. Ibid., 9–10.

54. See, for example, Saint-Brice's "Le réveil de Shylock" (Shylock Awakes), *Revue universelle* (December 15, 1932); Hoover is presented as devoid of courage and "open-mindedness"; Roosevelt is hardly more promising: "What we know about the administration of the future is that its only interest is internal demagogy, attempting to subcontract debts through purely fleeting economic arrangements." Generally speaking, America "has shown us that it is incapable of assuming a commitment." 731–32.

55. Siegfried, *America*, 26.

56. Ibid., 17.

57. Max O'Rell [Paul Blouët] and Jack Allyn, *Jonathan et son continent: La société américaine* (Paris: Calmann-Lévy, 1900), 112.

58. Siegfried, *America*, 26. [Translation modified.]

59. Louis Marin, Annales de la Chambre des députés, first session, January 21, 1925.

60. Pierre Scize, "Sacco, Vanzetti et le goût du sport," *Le Canard enchaîné* (August 10, 1927).

61. Among the most curious grievances of the interwar years was the Americans' perceived obsession with "safety." The slogan "Safety First" used in factories and on the roads aroused an astonishing indignation in Morand: "The 'safety first' of the Yanks murders the soul" (Morand, 147). The same vehemence can be found in Luc Durtain's poem "Battery": "*No, sir, not:* Safety first! / *Safety afterward, / long afterward, / like in Europe*" (*USA 1927*, n.p.).

62. Duhamel, *Scenes*, 164–65.

63. Siegfried, *America*, 321.

64. Marin.

65. Duhamel, *Scenes*, 169.

66. [*Pretium doloris,* the expert evaluation of pain suffered, expressed on a scale of 1 to 7.]

67. Jacques Gascuel, *France-Soir* (September 14, 1948).

68. Raymond Aron, "Sommes-nous voués à la mendicité?," *Le Figaro*, August 1–2, 1948.

69. Raymond Aron, "Du plan Marshall à l'Europe unie," *Le Figaro*, July 2, 1948.

70. State Department, *French Attitudes on Selected Issues*, 43, quoted in Richard F. Kuisel, *Seducing the French: The Dilemma of Americanization* (Berkeley/Los Angeles: University of California Press, 1993), 32.

71. Soria, 30, 31.

72. Ibid., 38. Soria also speaks of "customs sovereignty."

73. Ibid., 75.

74. Ibid., 22.

75. Charles Tillon et al., "La Lettre au président Truman," Combattants de la paix et de la liberté, Conseil National (Paris: Imprimerie Aulard, 1949), n.p.

76. Georges Cogniot, "L' 'Union Européenne,' le 'Gouvernement Mondial,' camouflages de l'impérialisme," Speech given before the members of the French Communist Party's Section Committees and the secretaries of the Rhône Federation's business cells in Lyon, March 9, 1951, Les Conférences Éducatives du Parti Communiste Français, 1st ser., no. 9, n.d., 11.

77. Ibid., 3. Cogniot's italics.

78. Thus the journal *Preuves* was pro-Atlantist but explicitly hostile to America's cultural influence. See Jean-Philippe Mathy, Extrême-Occident: *French Intellectuals and America* (Chicago: University of Chicago Press, 1993), 139–40. *Preuves's* intellectual fidelity to anti-Americanism is all the more piquant and commendable in that the journal was subsidized by the CIA.

79. *Sondages*, 1953, 40, quoted in Kuisel, *Seducing the French*, 33. Useful information on French public opinion during the Cold War can also be found in Philippe Roger [no relation to the author], *Rêves et cauchemars américains: les États-Unis au miroir de l'opinion publique française, 1945–1953* (Lille: Presses Universitaires du Septentrion, 1996).

80. Vladimir Pozner, *Les États-Désunis* (Paris: Bibliothèque française, 1948), 18.

81. Georges Bernanos, "France before the World of Tomorrow," in *The Last Essays of Bernanos*, trans. Joan and Barry Ulanov (Chicago: Henry Regnery, 1955), 43–44.

82. Maurice Duverger, *Le Monde*, September 1 and 15, 1948, quoted in Laurent Greilsamer, *Hubert Beuve-Méry, 1902–1989* (Paris: Fayard, 1990), 339; see also, on this period at the paper, Jean-Noël Jeanneney and Jacques Julliard, *Le Monde de Beuve-Méry ou le métier d'Alceste* (Paris: Seuil, 1979), and Jacques Thibau, LE MONDE: HISTOIRE D'UN JOURNAL, UN JOURNAL DANS L'HISTOIRE (Paris: J. C. Smoën, 1978).

83. G. Cogniot, "L' 'Union Européenne,' " 13.

84. "Thèmes et buts du film américain," *La Nouvelle Critique* 12 (January 1950): 114.

85. Étienne Gilson, *Le Monde*, March 2, 1949, and August 24, 1950. An analysis of Gilson's career was made by Anne-Marie Duranton-Crabol in an as yet unpublished talk presented in my seminar at the École des Hautes Études en Sciences Sociales.

86. Pierre Emmanuel, "L'Amérique impériale," *Le Monde*, October 25–26–28, 1949.

87. Tillon, n.p.

88. Mounier, "Le Pacte Atlantique," in *Oeuvres*, vol. 4 (Paris: Seuil, 1961), 221.

89. See chapter 13.

90. Mounier, "Le Pacte Atlantique," 220.

91. Patrice Gauthier and André Senik, eds., *Chants staliniens de France par quelques-uns qui les chantaient dans les années 50* (Paris: Label Expression spontanée, n.d.). I would like to thank Nicole Fouché for calling these audio documents to my attention.

92. Mounier, "Le Pacte Atlantique," 220.

93. Ibid., 223.

94. Bernanos, "Why Freedom?," in *The Last Essays*, 113.

95. Marcel Aymé, "La Fille du shérif," in *La Fille du shérif* (Paris: Gallimard, 1987), 15–17.

96. Raymond Aron, *Les Guerres en chaîne* (Paris, 1951), 423, quoted in Michel Winock, "Les attitudes des Français face à la présence américaine (1951–1967)," *Historical reflections/Réflexions historiques* 23, no. 2 (1997): 253.

97. Thierry Maulnier, *Spectateur* (November 19, 1946), quoted in Michel Contat and Michel Rybalka, eds., *Les Écrits de Sartre* (Paris: Gallimard, 1970), 136.

98. *Bulletin d'Informations de l'IFOP* 1 (October 1, 1944).

99. Sartre, *The Writings of Jean-Paul Sartre*, eds. Michel Contat and Michel Rybalka, trans. Richard C. McCleary, 2 vols. (Evanston, Ill.: Northwestern University Press, 1974), 1:313.

100. Ibid., 314. [Translation modified.]

101. Ibid.

102. Duhamel, *Scenes*, 214.

103. Victor Joannes, "Notre fierté nationale ou le Congrès du Parti de la France," *La Nouvelle Critique* 16 (May 1950): 9.

104. Jean-Jacques Servan-Schreiber, *Le Défi américain* (Paris: Denoël, 1967); the term appears on 52.

105. Étiemble, 36.

106. Ibid., 238.

107. Ibid., 52.

108. Ibid., 241.

109. Ibid., 327.

110. Ibid., 237.

111. See Paul Sorum, *Intellectuals and Decolonization in France* (Chapel Hill: University of North Carolina Press, 1977).

112. Judt, 198.

113. Mauriac, *Bloc-Notes, 1952–1957,* October 12, 1956 (Paris: Flammarion, 1958).

114. Roger Vailland, *L'Humanité dimanche* [February 1955], in *Chroniques II: d'Hiroshima à Goldfinger* (Paris: Messidor-Éditions Sociales, 1984), 200.

115. Ibid., 230.

116. Gabriel Dheur, "La Fayette, nous voici," *Le Monde*, May 29, 1948.

117. De Gaulle's frequent opposition to United States policy does not make him an "anti-American" as we understand it in the present book. De Gaulle did not *maintain a discourse* against America. Qualifying him as anti-American "insofar as he tried to subvert the international order the United States believed was in its best interests" would void the term "anti-Americanism" of any meaning. See Kuisel, "Was De Gaulle Anti-American?," *Tocqueville Review* 13, no. 1 (1992): 21–32; quoted from 27. On this debate, see also Michael M. Harrison, "French Anti-Americanism Under the Fourth Republic and the Gaullist Solution," which introduces a humorous note: "De Gaulle had mixed opinions about Americans like any sensible person–he once said, 'The Americans are strong, courageous, and stupid' (but after all, he made worse statements about his own people, the French)." *The Rise and Fall of Anti-Americanism: A Century of French Perception,* ed. Denis Lacorne, Jacques Rupnik, and Marie-France Toinet, trans. Gerry Turner (New York: St. Martin's Press, 1990), 176. [Translation modified.]

118. Maurice Druon, *Lettres d'un Européen* (Paris: Charlot, n.d.), 112–13.

Chapter Twelve

1. Editorial, *Réaction* 3 (July 1930): 77.

2. Crosnier de Varigny, *Les Grandes fortunes aux États-Unis et en Angleterre* (Paris: Hachette, 1889), 7.

3. Bertrand de Jouvenel, "La crise du capitalisme américain," in *Itinéraire, 1928–1976* (Paris: Plon, 1993), 141.

4. Étiemble, 75.

5. Recouly, 46.

6. "For this American woman, dinner-parties and social functions were a sort of Berlitz school. She repeated names she heard without any knowledge of their significance." Proust, 329. This is Monsieur de Farcy's American wife.

7. Gain, 72.

8. Ibid., 75.

9. Ibid., 73.

10. Ibid., 83.

11. Ibid., 105, 106.

12. Ibid., 71.

13. Ibid., 99.

14. Ibid., 73.

15. Ibid., 157.

16. Ibid., 63.

17. Ibid., 73.

18. Vladimir Pozner's book *Les États-Désunis* carves out a fairly large space for gangsterism. Its author presents the book as having been written before the war.

19. See the introduction.

20. Duhamel, *Scenes*, 89.

21. Lanson, 31.

22. Ibid., 32–33. By 1918, New York had definitively supplanted its rivals as the archetypal American city. François Weil has recently written an excellent history of the city, *History of New York*, trans. Jody Gladding (New York: Columbia University Press, 2004); for its mythical aspect, the reader may refer to Crystel Pinçonnait's *New York: Mythe littéraire français* (Paris: PUF, 2001).

23. Émile Verhaeren, *Les Campagnes hallucinées* (Paris: Mercure de France, 1893).

24. Bourget, 41.

25. Huret, 9.

26. Georges Simenon, *Maigret à New York* (Paris: Presses de la Cité, 1947), 14.

27. Maurois, 69.

28. Morand, 39.

29. Ibid.

30. Robert Aron and Dandieu, 104.

31. Hergé, *Tintin en Amérique* (1931). Tintin's creator admitted "having been influenced by Georges Duhamel," but he mostly relied on articles from the right-wing press, especially *Le Crapouillot*. Hergé gleaned most of his material from an article by Claude Blanchard entitled "L'Amérique et les Américains" (October 1930), as is demonstrated in the comparative analysis of journalistic reporting and the Tintin comics by Jean-Marie Apostolidès, *Les Métamorphoses de Tintin* (Paris: Seghers, 1984), 30–33. As Apostolidès slyly remarks, "After the war, since the trend in French-speaking intellectual circles was toward anti-Americanism, on this point at least, Hergé's works underwent little alteration," and little French children would continue to discover America with the *Crapouillot*'s blinders.

32. Hermann von Keyserling, *America Set Free* (New York: Harper & Brothers, 1929), 41. He is enthusiastically quoted by Claudel, August 28, 1929, in *Claudel et l'Amérique II:*

Lettres de Paul Claudel à Agnès Meyer, 1928–1929; Note-Book d'Agnès Meyer, 1929 (Ottawa: University of Ottawa Press, 1969), 130. Keyserling's success comes as a shock to the modern reader, but it is reassuring to note that Maurois already found it surprising.

33. Durtain, *Hollywood dépassé* (Paris: Gallimard, 1928), 138, 139.

34. Ibid., 141.

35. Durtain, "La cité que bâtit la vision," in *Quarantième étage* (Paris: Gallimard, 1927), 129.

36. Ibid., 131.

37. Ibid., 145, 149.

38. Durtain, *Hollywood dépassé*, 140.

39. De Pauw, 1:2.

40. Claudel, *Conversations dans le Loir-et-Cher*, in *Oeuvres en prose*, Bibliothèque de la Pléiade (Paris: Gallimard, 1965), 790. If American society seems "materialistic" to him, America itself has a tendency to become immaterial for Claudel: "It is essentially a median." ("Projet d'une église souterraine à Chicago," in *Positions et propositions*, 2:230.)

41. Le Corbusier made a splash by declaring to the American press, as soon as he had arrived, that New York's skyscrapers were too small. See his account in *When the Cathedrals Were White: A Journey to the Country of Timid People*, trans. Francis E. Hyslop, Jr. (New York: Reynal & Hitchcock, 1947).

42. Recouly, 12–13, 16.

43. Claudel, *Conversations*, 738.

44. Ibid., 741. He had some hope for Pittsburgh's future Cathedral of Learning.

45. Duhamel, *Scenes*, 86–87.

46. Durtain, "Smith Building," in *Quarantième étage*, 192.

47. Ibid., 206.

48. Ibid., 193.

49. Ibid., 231.

50. Herbert Croly's *The Promise of American Life* (New York: Macmillan, 1909) had also been a success when translated into French in 1913 and published by Alcan.

51. Waldo Frank, *The Re-Discovery of America: An Introduction to a Philosophy of American Life* (New York: Scribner, 1929), 314. [Frank's emphasis.]

52. Ibid., 90, n. 2. Frank remarks that skyscrapers have already been transformed, in just a few years, by "terracing" and adding penthouses: the skyscraper no longer symbolizes its original "chaos," but rather an established deceit.

53. Claudel, *Conversations*, 739.

54. Duhamel, *Scenes*, 87–88.

55. Ibid., 88. [Translation modified.]

56. Ibid., 216.

57. Ibid., 88. [Translation modified.]

58. Ibid., 216.

59. Ibid.

60. Henri Nevers, *Pourquoi l'Amérique est-elle en guerre?* (Paris: Nouvelles éditions françaises, n.d.), 21, 22.

61. Bogislas, "Métro interallié," *Au Pilori* (August 2, 1944); this drawing and the following ones are reproduced in Christian Delporte's interesting *Les Crayons de la*

propagande: Dessinateurs et dessin politique sous l'occupation (Paris: CNRS Editions, 1993), 102.

62. Soupault, "In articulo mortis," *Je suis partout* (July 21, 1941), reproduced in Delporte, 95.

63. Soupault, "Maison de 'rencontres,'" in *Ils sont partout* (1944), reproduced in Delporte, 144.

64. Mara, "La Liberté . . . enfin! éclaire le monde!," *La Gerbe* (25 May 1944), reproduced in Delporte, 94.

65. Nevers, 20.

66. Ibid., 8. Even this praise for the Viennese and Berlin cafés is recopied: it appears word for word in Raymond Recouly's *L'Amérique pauvre* (79).

67. Ibid., 17.

68. Ibid., 19.

69. Ibid., 7, 8.

70. Ibid., 4.

71. Ibid., 7.

72. Félix Klein, *L'Amérique de demain* (Paris: Plon, 1910), 6.

73. Demolins, 149.

74. Crosnier de Varigny, *La Femme*, 220. We can see a late echo of this theme in Duhamel when he hears a strange conversation between two Frenchmen in a hotel lobby: ". . . No, he's not a Levantine, I assure you. He's not a Jew. We have to be fair. I work with Jews here, people who are perfectly acceptable. He's a 'hundred-percenter.' Imagine—Smith!" Only it turns out that this Smith is an even bigger swindler than all the Levantines put together. "Well—there you are. The East is bigger than you think. It begins in the suburbs of Warsaw, swings around the globe, and does not stop till the middle of the Atlantic." Duhamel, *Scenes*, 185–86. [Translation modified.]

75. Siegfried, *America*, 7.

76. Ibid., 16.

77. Recouly, 8.

78. Duhamel, *Scenes*, 125.

79. Siegfried, *America*, 16.

80. Siegfried, *America*. [Absent from translation.]

81. Voltaire, *Philosophical Dictionary*, trans. Theodore Besterman (London: Penguin, 1972), 38.

82. Sartre, "American Cities" [*Le Figaro*, 1945] in *Literary and Philosophical Essays*, 114.

83. Sartre, "Individualism," 111.

84. Sartre, "American Cities," 116. Dominique Jullien finds further echoes of Duhamel in Sartre, noting Sartre's "very real anguish" about the melting pot as a "de-individualizing machine." Dominique Jullien, *Récits du Nouveau Monde: Les voyageurs français en Amérique de Chateaubriand à nos jours* (Paris: Nathan, 1992), 178–79.

85. Céline, 159. [Translation modified.] Unless Sartre, killing two birds with one stone, was also aiming at Le Corbusier: "New York is an upright city, under the sign of the new times. It is a catastrophe with which a too hasty destiny has overwhelmed courageous and confident people, though a beautiful and worthy catastrophe." Le Corbusier, 36. [Translation modified.]

86. Sartre, "American Cities," 119.

87. Céline, 166.

88. Barthes, "New York, Buffet et la hauteur," *Arts* (11–17 February 1959); *Oeuvres complètes* (Paris: Seuil, 1994), 1:781. [Barthes's emphasis.]

89. Sartre, "American Cities," 115–16.

90. Ibid., 119.

91. Sartre, "New York: Colonial City," in *Modern Times: Selected Non-Fiction*, trans. Robin Buss, ed. Geoffrey Wall (New York: Penguin, 2000), 7.

92. Ibid.

93. Ibid.

94. Ibid., 8.

95. Ibid., 9.

96. Sartre, "American Cities," 121.

97. Ibid., 120.

98. Ibid., 121.

99. Duhamel, *Scenes*, 111.

100. Ibid., 110–11, 175, 34.

101. Céline, 172.

102. Sartre, "American Cities," 123.

103. Ibid., 122–23.

104. Barthes, "New York, Buffet et la hauteur," 781–82.

105. Simone de Beauvoir, *America Day by Day*, trans. Carol Cosman (Berkeley and Los Angeles: University of California Press, 1999), 12.

106. Céline, 182.

107. Ibid., 175.

108. Sartre, "New York," 4. [Translation modified.]

109. See Jean Baudrillard, "L'esprit du terrorisme," *Le Monde*, November 3, 2001; "When the two towers fell, you had the impression they were responding to the suicide planes with their own suicides."

110. Pozner, 167.

111. In her paper at the eleventh Festival International du Film d'Histoire, on the theme of "American power" (Pessac, November 22–27, 2000), Sophie Body-Gendrot demonstrated how the word "ghetto" had been metaphorized and misappropriated in France to polemically describe *cités* (housing projects), though the two realities do not have much in common.

112. Durtain, "Match de boxe," *USA 1927*, n.p.

113. Bourget, 2:136.

114. Duhamel, *Scenes*, 182. [Translation modified.]

115. "You know that bellyaching motto the French put up on all their buildings, *Liberté, Égalité, Fraternité*. Well, those chaps weren't such fools as you'd think. Seeing that's just what 'fraternity' means: the opposite of being badgered." André Malraux, *Man's Hope*, trans. Stuart Gilbert and Alastair Macdonald (New York: Random House, 1938), 95; Mona Ozouf, "Fraternité," in *Dictionnaire critique de la Révolution française*, ed. François Furet and Mona Ozouf (Paris: Flammarion, 1988), 731–40.

116. Baudrillard, "L'esprit du terrorisme."

117. Liliane Kandel, "Il ne s'est rien passé le 11 septembre?," *Libération*, November 5, 2001.

Chapter Thirteen

1. Maurois, 70–71.

2. Maurois's American notebooks were first published separately under the titles *Contacts* (Paris: A. M. M. Stols, 1928) and *L'Amérique inattendue* (Paris: A. et G. Mornay, 1931), before being published together in 1953 as *En Amérique*.

3. Daniel-Rops and Denis de Rougemont, *Ordre nouveau* 3 (July 1933), quoted in Loubet del Bayle, 260.

4. Bernanos, "Revolution and Liberty," in *The Last Essays*, 127–28, 129, 130.

5. V. I. Jérôme, "Aux sources américaines de la culture 'occidentale,'" *La Nouvelle Critique* 27 (June 1951): 29, 34.

6. E. Tarlé, "De Wilson à Truman: l'acharnement antisoviétique des impérialistes américains," *Études soviétiques* 35 (March 1951): 11.

7. Vailland, *Arts, lettres, spectacle* [October 9, 1957], in *Chroniques II*, 425.

8. Vailland, "Le ménage n'est pas un art de salon," *La Tribune des nations* (March 14, 1952).

9. This is the title of Michela Nacci's rich study *La barbarie del comfort: Il modello di vita americano nella cultura francese del '900* (Naples: Istituto Italiano per gli Studi Filosofici, 1992).

10. Mounier, "Manifeste au service du personnalisme," *Esprit* (October 1936), 129, quoted in Loubet del Bayle, 217.

11. Duhamel, *Scenes*, 25.

12. Claudel to Agnès Meyer, August 30, 1929, in *Claudel et l'Amérique II*, 132.

13. Roger Magniez, special issue of *Réaction* entitled "Procès de l'Amérique" 3 (July 1930): 83.

14. Robert Aron and Dandieu, 236.

15. Beauvoir, *La Force de l'âge* (Paris: Gallimard, 1960), 363.

16. Beauvoir, *America*, 312. [Translation modified.]

17. [Author of *The Principles of Scientific Management* (1911).]

18. Jean Cocteau, *Lettre aux Américains* (Paris: Bernard Grasset, 1949), 85. Cocteau took liberties with the Goncourts' text, which gives the oculist Landolt's description of "those two famous faucets of cold water and hot water in a marble basin in a corner of the room, which one has no possibility of moving and which are a great inconvenience in washing oneself; and the gas light placed in the middle of the room, which does not allow one to read in bed, next to which there is neither a candlestick nor matches; and the services of the domestic help, who never brush one's clothes." Edmond and Jules de Goncourt, *Journal*, July 17, 1895 (Paris: Fasquelle-Flammarion 1956), 4:820.

19. Strauss, *Menace in the West*, 175.

20. "Their linkage helps to explain the extreme reaction against both," writes Strauss, ibid., 30.

21. Cocteau, 34.

22. Siegfried, *America*, 349.

23. Maurice Blanchot, *Réaction* 11 (April 1932): 14, quoted in Loubet del Bayle, 254.

24. Duhamel, *Scenes*, 201.

25. Georges Friedmann, *Problèmes du machinisme en U.R.S.S. et dans les pays capitalistes* (Paris: Editions Sociales Internationales, 1934), 108.

26. Duhamel, *Scenes*, 208–209.

27. Ibid., 209.

28. Siegfried, *America*, 180.

29. Duhamel, *Scenes*, 192. This is all he seems to have remembered from the chapter on "industrial production," which we will discuss further on.

30. Cocteau, 86.

31. Siegfried, *America*, 166. The word "philosophy" reappears several times in this chapter.

32. Jouvenel, 9. Jouvenel, after having been pro-Roosevelt, switched over to Doriot's PPF but broke with it in 1938 out of anti-Hitlerism.

33. Siegfried, *America*, 168.

34. Duhamel, *Scenes*, 131, 133.

35. Jouvenel, 146.

36. Notably Hyacinthe Dubreuil, *Standards: Le travail américain vu par un ouvrier français* (Paris: Grasset, 1929) and *Nouveaux standards: Les sources de la productivité et de la joie* (Paris: Grasset, 1931).

37. Romier, *Qui sera le maître, Europe ou Amérique?* (Paris: Hachette, 1927), 85.

38. François Drujon, *L'Amérique et son avenir* (Paris: Corrêa, 1938), 158–159.

39. Ibid., 112–113.

40. Duhamel, *Scenes*, 201. [Translation modified.]

41. Friedmann, 80, 79, 81, 80, 78.

42. Ibid., 79.

43. Ibid., 102.

44. Ibid., 104.

45. See the following chapter.

46. It can be seen in *Prison Notebooks*, in which Gramsci advances the notion that Europe can assimilate Fordism coupled with democratic control but not Taylorism, which is an American ideology to reject.

47. Robert Aron and Dandieu, 83.

48. Bernanos, "France before the World of Tomorrow," 44.

49. Raoul de Roussy de Sales, "Un mouvement nouveau venu des États-Unis: La technocratie," *La Revue de Paris* 2 (1933). The word "technocrat" spread rapidly; it is not, wrote Raymond Recouly that same year, "the people we call 'technocrats' [who] will resolve the current crisis." Recouly, 5.

50. Durtain, "Smith Building," 223.

51. Roussy de Sales.

52. Siegfried, *America*, 174. He also notes the test's French origins (Binet and Simon)—another stolen patent. . .

53. Jouvenel, 147.

54. Ibid., 145.

55. Bernard Faÿ, *Civilisation américaine* (Paris: Sagittaire, 1939), 84–85.

56. Ibid., 85.

57. Duhamel, *Scenes*, 81.

58. Gérald Cazaubon, "Élections aux USA," *Défense de la paix* 13 (June 1952): 85–94. The aggressive iconography (we also see a woman's legs painted with the slogan "I Like Ike") contrasts with the factual, nonpolemical information contained in the article.

59. Faÿ, 82–83.

60. Siegfried, *America*, 169; Duhamel, *Scenes*, 202.

61. Fabrègues, *Réaction* 8 (February 1932), 24, quoted in Loubet del Bayle, 260–261.

62. Drujon, 21–22.

63. André Philip, *Le Problème ouvrier aux États-Unis* (Paris: Félix Alcan, 1927), 38. On the copy acquired by Georges Friedmann in 1930 that he donated to the library of the Maison des Sciences de l'Homme, the whole end of the chapter is marked with an approving line in blue pencil.

64. Huret, 2:172.

65. Lanson, 82.

66. Duhamel, *Scenes*, 61.

67. Romains, 31.

68. Durtain, "Hollywood," in *USA 1927*, n.p.

69. Robert Aron, *Dictature de la liberté* (Paris: Grasset, 1935), 173.

70. Céline, 169. [Translation modified.]

71. Jean-Pierre Maxence, "L'Europe en danger," *La Revue française* (March 22, 1931): 266, quoted in Loubet del Bayle, 56.

72. Daniel-Rops, "Positions générales," *La Revue française* (April 1933), quoted in Loubet del Bayle, 455, 454.

73. Daniel-Rops, *Ordre nouveau* 3 (July 1933): 3, quoted in Loubet del Bayle, 85.

74. Robert Aron, *Dictature*, 28.

75. See Allen, part 3, "The Impact of Franklin Delano Roosevelt and the Emergence from Isolationism," 245–321.

76. Duhamel, *Scenes*, 44–45.

77. Robert Aron, *Dictature*, 111.

78. Beauvoir, *America*, 94. [Translation modified.]

79. Bernanos, "Revolution and Liberty," 130.

80. Albert Béguin, "Réflexions sur l'Amérique, l'Europe, la neutralité," *Esprit* (June 1951). Bernanos's *La France contre les robots* is cited in the article.

81. Jean-Marie Domenach, "Le Diplodocus et les fourmis," *Esprit* (March 1959).

82. Beauvoir, *America*, 267. [Translation modified.]

83. And even a first-year polytechnic student "after a few drinks"; Robert Aron and Dandieu, 87.

84. Ibid., 74.

85. Beauvoir, *America*, 384.

86. Ibid., 318.

87. Bernanos, "Revolution and Liberty," 131–33. We should note that Emmanuel Mounier, who before the war had denounced "the inhuman optimism of Ford-Stalin

humanism," quarreled with Bernanos in 1949 (he "never goes beyond the din of eloquence") and more generally with "affective and emotional anti-machinism." *La Petite peur du XXe siècle* (Neufchâtel, 1949); *Oeuvres*, vol. 3 (Paris: Seuil), 364, 367. [On Mounier and *Esprit*'s anti-American stance, see the excellent analysis by Seth D. Armus, "The Eternal Enemy: Emmanuel Mounier's *Esprit* and French Anti-Americanism," *French Historical Studies* 24, no. 2 (Spring 2001): 271–304.]

88. Which would not stop authors (quite the contrary) from imagining transgressions between one kingdom and the other, like Villiers de l'Isle Adam in *Eve of the Future Eden*, or from pretending, like Jules Huret faced with American machines, that they "look like they are thinking." (Huret, 295.)

89. Henri Bergson, *The Two Sources of Morality and Religion*, trans. R. Ashley Audra and Cloudesley Breteron, with W. Horsfall Carter (1935; Westport, Conn.: Greenwood Press, 1974), 296.

90. Friedmann, 99, particularly n. 4.

91. Duhamel, *Scenes*, 167.

92. Bernanos, "Revolution and Liberty," 127.

93. Ibid., 126, 127.

94. Robert Aron, *Dictature*, 22.

95. Faÿ, 83.

96. Boutmy, 77.

97. Robert Aron, *Dictature*, 108.

98. Ibid., 110.

99. Pierre-Antoine Cousteau, *L'Amérique juive* (Paris: Editions de France, 1942), 71.

100. "I have in my pocket several of your small coins on which is stamped the word 'liberty.' And what do you see immediately under that word? The figure of a buffalo or an Indian. Oh, irony! They represent two free and spirited races that you have destroyed in less than three centuries." Duhamel, *Scenes*, 48. The collaborationist author of *Pourquoi l'Amérique est-elle en guerre?* evidently took his cue from Duhamel when he wrote: "'Liberty' is also the inscription engraved on the nickel coin next to—O irony—an Indian head in relief." Nevers, 11.

101. Baudrillard himself finally found his man: the September 11 kamikaze, whose "terrorist act . . . resuscitates both the image and the event." (Baudrillard, "L'esprit du terrorisme.")

102. Jacques Maritain, *Freedom in the Modern World*, in *Integral Humanism, Freedom in the Modern World, and A Letter on Independence*, ed. Otto Bird, trans. Otto Bird, Joseph Evans, and Richard O'Sullivan (Notre Dame, Ind.: University of Notre Dame Press, 1996), 51–52. The last two quotes are repeated from his *Songe de Descartes*.

103. Bernanos, "Revolution and Liberty," 126.

104. Bernanos, "France before the World of Tomorrow," 49.

105. Claudel to Agnès Meyer, July 23, 1929, in *Claudel et l'Amérique II*, 99.

106. Tardieu, *France and America*, 52.

107. Siegfried, *America*, 20.

108. Ibid., 24.

109. Duhamel, *Scenes*, 48. There are seemingly endless passages in Duhamel and his contemporaries in which metaphors of animal gregariousness are used to define American society: hive, nest of termites, anthill, etc. In the interwar imagination,

American society was both "inorganic" and animal—with inferior animal collectivities only prolonging mechanistic imagery.

110. Beauvoir, *America*, 94.

111. Revolution, as Pierre Nora notes in an article on anti-Americanism, is at the ideological heart of the Left, which is itself at the heart of French national culture. (Pierre Nora, "America and the French Intellectuals," *Daedalus* 107 ([Winter 1978]: 334.)

112. Duhamel, *Scenes*, 214.

113. Robert Aron and Dandieu, 162.

114. Robert Aron, *Dictature*, 123.

115. Bernanos, "Revolution and Liberty," 130.

116. Rémond, 826.

117. Domenach, *Esprit* (June–July 1968).

118. Régis Debray, *Modeste contribution aux discours et cérémonies officielles du dixième anniversaire* (Paris: Maspéro, 1978), 39.

119. Ibid., 51–52.

120. Jean Clair, "Le surréalisme et la démoralisation de l'Occident," *Le Monde*, November 22, 2001.

121. Louis Aragon, "Fragments d'une conférence," *La Révolution surréaliste* 4 (1925): 25.

122. André Breton, "Allocution au meeting du 30 avril 1949," in *Oeuvres complètes*, Bibliothèque de la Pléiade (Paris: Gallimard, 1999), 3:1107–13.

123. Jacques Duclos, quoted in *La Nouvelle Critique* 30 (November 1951): 125. The speech was made in September of that year.

124. Béguin, 886.

125. "I have never lived in the place called La Grenouillère." Breton, "Full Margin," in *Selections*, ed. and trans. Mark Polizzotti (Berkeley and Los Angeles: University of California Press, 2003), 106.

Chapter Fourteen

1. Robert Aron, *Dictature*, 26, 28.

2. Robert Aron and Dandieu, 16.

3. Maritain, *Reflections on America* (New York: Scribner, 1958), 29. The book, drawn from a series of talks given at the University of Chicago on the Committee on Social Thought's invitation, shows a clear desire to break away from the anti-American use made of his prewar texts. Maritain is determined to show that he has already defended the possibility of spirituality on American soil—in a lecture given in 1938 and published in New York in 1940, "Action and Contemplation," in *Scholasticism and Politics* (New York: Macmillan, 1940); but neither the place of publication, the language, nor the date would seem to have helped it reach a wide audience in France.

4. Morand, 289.

5. Gohier, *Le Peuple*, chapter 5, "La question cléricale."

6. Gaillardet, 152.

7. Gohier, 115.

8. Claudel, *Journal II, 1933–1955*, March 5, 1933, ed. F. Varillon and J. Petit, Bibliothèque de la Pléiade (Paris: Gallimard, 1969), 10–11.

9. Raynal, chapter 18, 233, 229, 237.

10. Barbier, 167.

11. Ibid.

12. Gohier, *Le Peuple*, 119.

13. Johanet, *Autour du monde millionnaire*, 111, 351.

14. The name "Americanism" was given to a Catholic, liberal, democratic social movement at the end of the nineteenth century (with the Abbé Klein as figurehead) condemned by Leo XIII in 1899.

15. Boutmy, 89, 90, 94.

16. Beauvoir, *America*, 316.

17. Ibid., 171.

18. Boutmy, 288, 289.

19. Siegfried, *États-Unis, Canada, Mexique: Lettres de voyage écrites au Petit Havre, juin–décembre 1935* (Le Havre: Imprimerie du Petit Havre, 1935), 89.

20. Claudel to Agnès Meyer, September 17, 1929, in *Claudel et l'Amérique II*, 137: "Dewey's principal error is his contempt for the European common man. For a long time, it was in the hearts of poor and simple souls that true spirituality was conserved."

21. Faÿ, 282, 271.

22. Allen, 206.

23. Chasles, 456.

24. Tocqueville, 1:315.

25. Morand, 20.

26. Romier, 16.

27. Siegfried, *America*, 177–79.

28. Siegfried, *America*, 177.

29. Morand, 20. Just as the anti-Semitic Morand was writing *World Champions* with Brodsky as the only positive hero—the spokesman for a "mystical" and visceral revolt against America—the former diplomat Octave Homberg was attributing America's inability to "distinguish the spiritual from the temporal" to a joint domination by "Protestant and Israelite" elites. (Octave Homberg, *L'Impérialisme américain* [Paris: Plon, 1929], 5.)

30. Huret, 2:23.

31. Ibid., 1:56.

32. Johanet, *Un Français dans la Floride*, 76.

33. Barbier, 33.

34. Recouly, 15.

35. Tocqueville, 1:421.

36. Robert Aron and Dandieu, 211.

37. Ibid., 200.

38. Ibid., 96.

39. Pozner, 163.

40. "America's writers can only write, for the most part, in their spare time; very few actually live by their pen." O'Rell and Allyn, 29.

41. Huret, 2:68.

42. Rousiers, *American Life*. [Absent from translation.]

43. Ibid., 78.

44. Duhamel, *Scenes*, 24–25.

45. Rousiers, *American Life*. [Absent from translation.]

46. Ibid., 380.

47. Huret, 1:177.

48. Rousiers, *American Life*, 413.

49. Barbier, 293.

50. Dugard, 310.

51. Barbier, 96.

52. O'Rell and Allyn, 30, 29.

53. Huret, 2:298.

54. Ibid., 2:243.

55. Barbier, 288–89.

56. Gohier, *Le Peuple*, 203.

57. Barbier, 89.

58. Gohier, *Le Peuple*, 203.

59. Kadmi-Cohen, *L'Abomination américaine* (Paris: Flammarion, 1930), 106.

60. A. Saint-André de Lignereux, *L'Amérique au XXe siècle* (Paris: Taillandier, 1909), 148, quoted in Portes, *Fascination*, 430.

61. Kadmi-Cohen, 106.

62. Homberg, 82.

63. Proust, 118.

64. Gain, 60.

65. Kadmi-Cohen, 116.

66. Recouly, 246, 252.

67. Joseph Kessel, *Hollywood, ville mirage* (1937; Paris, Ramsay, Poche-Cinéma, 1989), 93, 19–20, 23, 43.

68. Durtain, "La cité que bâtit la vision," 159–60.

69. Kessel, 59, 13–14.

70. Huret, 2:243.

71. Nevers, 7.

72. Beauvoir, *America*, 307–8.

73. Ibid., 340.

74. Kadmi-Cohen, 106.

75. At the turn of the century, Gustave Lanson lamented that American journalists were only "middlingly cultivated" (Lanson, 89). Most French travelers' lack of familiarity with the English language gives their judgment of the press a very relative authority.

76. Robert Aron and Dandieu, 217, 216, 221, 223.

77. Soria, 128.

78. See the detailed analyses made by Roger in *Rêves et cauchemars américains*, notably "Une culture de masse fascinante," 211–23.

79. Soria, 186.

80. Editorial, *La Nouvelle Critique* 27 (June 1951): 3–4.

81. Editorial, *La Nouvelle Critique* 30 (November 1951): 124.

82. Joannes, 9.

83. Domenach, editorial, *Esprit* 354 (November 1969): 625.

84. Guy Besse, "Notre université ne sera pas atlantique," *La Nouvelle Critique* 14 (March 1950).

85. Editorial, *La Nouvelle Critique* 27 (June 1951). "Home economics" was shocking to the French.

86. Jouvenel, 167.

87. See Cochet, "La bande dessinée en France et aux États-Unis dans l'entre-deux-guerres: Deux modèles culturels en action," in *Les Américains et la France*, 200.

88. Soria, 134.

89. Louis Daquin, "Le cinéma," *La Nouvelle Critique* 25 (April 1951).

90. Cochet, "La bande dessinée," 201.

91. Ibid. A member of the regulating commission, René Finkelstein, commented: "Our children will thus be protected from 'comics' aimed at adults, where images coupled with a few onomatopoeias glorify violence, passion, and the superman."

92. Raymond Queneau, *Front national* (November 3, 1945); *Bâtons, chiffres et lettres* (Paris: Gallimard, 1950), 152.

93. Pozner, 161.

94. Edmond Cary, "Défense de la France, défense de la langue française," *La Nouvelle Critique* 3 (February 1949). *I Spit on Your Graves* was published in 1946.

95. Pozner, 14.

96. See Muriel Brot, "Réécritures des lumières," *Critique* 663–64 (August–September 2002).

97. Pozner, 18.

98. Soria, 110.

99. See Carlton J. H. Hayes, *France: A Nation of Patriots* (New York: Columbia, 1930), 186–95; Strauss, "The Rise of Anti-Americanism in France: French Intellectuals and the American Film Industry, 1927–1932," *Journal of Popular Culture* 10, no. 4 (Spring 1977): 752–59; Portes, "L'internationalisation du cinéma—années 1920," in Portes, *L'Amérique comme modèle, l'Amérique sans modèle* (Lille: Presses Universitaires de Lille, 1993).

100. Editorial, *La Nouvelle Critique* 12 (January 1950): 108.

101. Ibid., 115.

102. Figures provided by Patricia Hubert-Lacombe, "L'accueil des films américains en France pendant la guerre froide (1946–1953)," *Revue d'histoire moderne et contemporaine* 33 (1986): 301–14.

103. Soria, 135.

104. Jacques Becker, quoted in ibid., 136.

105. Kuisel gives a detailed analysis of this economic and political skirmish in *Seducing the French*, 37–69. See also, published during the fleeting 1999 "rebound," Jeanneney's article "Coca-Cola: le sens d'un écho," *Le Monde*, June 29, 1999.

106. Édouard Herriot, *Europe* (Paris: Rieder, 1930). Declaring that already "our European folklore is being translated, as is, furthermore, the history of our Continent, by the

honorable citizens of Los Angeles," Herriot pleaded in favor of a "European consolidation, . . . the only means left to us for preserving the correct interpretation of our continental culture." 212–13.

107. Jean Renoir, quoted in Georges Sadoul, *Dictionnaire des cinéastes* (Paris: Seuil, 1965), 190.

108. Quoted in Soria, 137.

109. Sartre, "Denis de Rougemont: 'L'amour et l'Occident,'" in *Situations I* (Paris: Gallimard, 1947), 58.

110. Pozner, 19.

111. Barthes, "The Romans in Films," in *Mythologies,* trans. Annette Lavers (London: Jonathan Cape, 1972), 27. [Translation modified.]

112. Ibid., 27–28.

113. Nicolas Virta, "Une super-Gestapo: Le FBI," *Etudes soviétiques* 36 (April 1951): 32.

114. Jean-Michel Frodon, "Chevauchée fantastique dans la pellicule," *Le Monde,* April 18, 1991.

115. ["To plunge Billancourt [that is, the working class] into despair": a famous line in Sartre's play *Nekrassov* (1955). Billancourt was the site of a major automobile factory and a symbol of organized labor; Saint-Germain-des-Prés had become a gathering place for intellectuals after World War II and a symbol of leftist politics and existentialist attitudes.]

116. Sartre, *The Writings,* 2:211. [Translation modified.]

117. Sartre, "Il n'y a plus de dialogue possible," *Le Nouvel Observateur* (April 1, 1965); *Situations VIII* (Paris: Gallimard, 1972), 9–19.

118. Sartre, *The Writings,* 226.

119. Jean Piel, *La Fortune américaine et son destin* (Paris: Editions de Minuit, 1948), 49, 119, 8–9, 207 (Piel's italics), and 9, respectively.

120. Elena Galtsova, "La Putain respectueuse et Nekrassov en URSS: fox-trot avec Jean-Paul Sartre," in *Sartre: Une écriture en acte,* ed. Geneviève Idt (Paris: Ritm-Université de Paris X, 2001), 221–51. *Les Mains sales* was adapted by Richard Taradash in 1949 as *Red Gloves.*

121. Jack Lang, *L'Express* (September 1982), quoted in Winock, "US Go Home," *L'Histoire* 50 (November 1982) (my italics).

122. Sartre, "Sartre répond" (to Professor Grossvogel), *Le Nouvel Observateur* (April 8, 1965); *Situations VIII,* 25.

123. Vailland, "Lettre au capitaine Jimmy F.B.," *L'Humanité dimanche* (February 1954); *Chroniques II,* 230–31.

124. Sartre, *Théâtre populaire* 15 (September–October 1955).

125. Pozner, 16.

126. See Ludovic Tournès, "La réinterprétation du jazz: Un phénomène de contre-américanisation," in *L'Antiaméricanisme,* ed. Sylvie Mathé (Aix-en-Provence: Publications de l'Université de Provence, 2000).

127. Tocqueville, 2:584–85.

128. Emmanuel Berl, *Mort de la pensée bourgeoise* (1929; Paris: Robert Laffont, 1970), 76–77.

129. The cultural exception France has been invoking in trade and other negotia-
tions since 1993 has three fairly different meanings, which does not help in clarifying the debate. First, it is the affirmation that "works of culture are not merchandise like any

other," a proposition that wavers between being a tautology and a value judgment, and which should not dispense from saying *how* they are not "like any other" and exactly where the line is drawn between them and the "others"; second, the cultural exception connotes a political attempt at cultural protectionism whose objectives can be considered perfectly legitimate; third, the cultural exception flag, raised against the United States alone, has logically rallied the whole cultural anti-American discourse around it.

130. A McDonald's advertising counterattack in November 1999 deliberately played on the anti-Americanism of the French. A full-page photo that ran notably in *Libération* showed an obese, bearded American in overalls and military jacket, saying "Salad at McDonald's? I don't see the point," to which the voice of McDonald's, suddenly the voice of France, told him, "Yes! But in France, people like salad," and went on to condescendingly reel off a number of gustatory and dietetic considerations for the poor *Amerloque*'s education.

131. Toni Negri, *Le Monde*, January 27–28, 2002.

132. Jean-François Perigot, "Le McDo est-il soluble dans le magret?," *Libération*, September 18–19, 1999.

Conclusion

1. Stendhal, *The Red and the Black*, 196.

2. Barthes, *Roland Barthes par Roland Barthes* (Paris: Seuil, 1975), 71.

3. Maurois, 124.

4. Quoted in Kuisel, *Le Miroir américain: 50 ans de regard français sur l'Amérique* (Paris: J.-C. Lattès, 1993), 34. This information is not included in the original English version of Kuisel's book.

5. See Echeverria, "L'Amérique devant l'opinion française," *Revue d'histoire moderne et contemporaine* (January–March 1962): 59. Portes refers to it in *Fascination*, 16. Even for the nineteenth century, to which Echeverria applies it, the "rule" seems to be contradicted by too many exceptions.

6. See the CSA Opinion/*Libération* poll of a representative national sample of one thousand individuals over eighteen years of age registered to vote. *Libération* (April 10–11, 1999).

7. Ibid.; the commentary is by Jean-Michel Helvig.

8. In French, *niquer*—slang for *forniquer*—is pronounced just like "Nike."

9. Debray, *Contretemps* (Paris: Gallimard-Folio, 1992), 104, 105.

10. Robert Aron and Dandieu, 80.

11. Debray, *Contretemps*, 109.

12. Duhamel, *Scenes*, 214–15.

13. On what *Libération* calls "the horrifying imposture," see in that newspaper Pierre Lagrange's interview with Béatrice Vallaeys. "The same rhetoric as negationism" props up Meyssan's book, remarks the sociologist, who is a specialist of "conspiracy buffs." The book's successful sales (the figure of 100,000 books in a week was given) shows the extraordinary attraction over the French public of any scenario depriving the Americans of their status as victims and reinstalling them in the position of suspects or even guilty parties.

14. See Jean-François Lyotard, *The Postmodern Condition: A Report on Knowledge*, trans. Geoff Bennington and Brian Massumi (Minneapolis: University of Minnesota Press, 1984).

15. Ibid., 7.

Index